I0794873

The Laws of Cooking and Warming Food on Shabbat

ספר בישול בשבת

Michael Scharf
Publication Trust
Yeshiva University Press
RIETS

מגיד
MAGGID

Rabbi Mordechai Willig

THE LAWS OF COOKING AND WARMING FOOD ON SHABBAT

•

ספר בישול בשבת

The Michael Scharf Publication Trust of
Yeshiva University Press
Rabbi Isaac Elchanan Theological Seminary

The RIETS Halakhah Series
Rabbi Daniel Z. Feldman, Series Editor

Maggid Books

The Laws of Cooking and Warming Food on Shabbat

First Edition, 2013

The Michael Scharf Publication Trust
of Yeshiva University Press

Maggid Books
An imprint of Koren Publishers Jerusalem Ltd.

POB 8531, New Milford, CT 06776-8531, USA
& POB 2455, London, W1A 5WY, England
& POB 4044, Jerusalem 91040, Israel
www.korenpub.com

© Rabbi Mordechai Willig 2013

Cover Design: Tani Bayer

The right of Mordechai Willig to be identified as the author of this work has been asserted by him in accordance with the Copyright, Designs & Patents Act 1988.

All rights reserved. No part of this publication may be reproduced, stored in a retrieval system or transmitted in any form or by any means, electronic, mechanical, photocopying or otherwise, without the prior permission of the publisher, except in the case of brief quotations embedded in critical articles or reviews.

ISBN 978-1-59264-373-8, *hardcover*

A CIP catalogue record for this title is available from the British Library

Contents

SECTION II: WARMING

פרקים מתוך ספר "עם מרדכי"

Foreword

We are excited to present this second volume of the English-language *halakhah lema'aseh* series of the Rabbi Isaac Elchanan Theological Seminary (RIETS) division of the Michael Scharf Publication Trust of Yeshiva University Press (the "RIETS Press"). It is particularly appropriate that Rabbi Mordechai Willig, who occupies the Rabbi Dr. Sol Roth Chair in Talmud and Contemporary Halakhah at RIETS, and serves as our Rosh Kollel for the Bella and Harry Wexner Kollel Elyon, as well as our Segan Rosh Kollel for the Rabbi Norman Lamm Kollel L'Horaah, has contributed the present volume about the laws of cooking (*bishul*) relating to *Shabbat.*

For the past twenty-five years, Rabbi Willig has taught a special unit of instruction at RIETS to fourth-year *semikhah* students on the subject of this volume, educating them about the intricacies and conceptual framework behind the laws of hot food preparation for *Shabbat.* Rabbi Willig combines classical erudition, masterful analysis and pragmatic sensibility in his presentation and elucidation of the Talmudic and halakhic sources.

Together with legions of other students, I count myself among those who are fortunate to be students of Rabbi Willig, and to have developed under his tutelage a practical understanding of the complex laws relating to cooking and reheating food for *Shabbat* in the modern era. In this volume, Rabbi Willig shares his explanations of age-old Talmudic categories such as *shehiyah* and *hachzarah,* and considerations such as *shema yechateh* (lest one stoke the coals) and *mechzeh kemevashel* (the appearance of cooking), while demonstrating how all of these concepts apply to modern day appliances and situations.

It is noteworthy that a major emphasis of the study of the laws of *bishul,* which is included among the thirty-nine prohibited categories of activity (*melakhot*) on *Shabbat,* is to ensure that hot and delicious food be available in permissible fashion for the observance of *oneg Shabbat* – the pleasurable celebration of the *Shabbat* day.

Over a thousand years ago, the sect known as the Karaites ordained that no hot food should be eaten on *Shabbat* altogether based on their interpretation of the scriptural verse in *Shemot* (35:3) לא תבערו אש בכל משבתיכם ביום השבת – "You shall not kindle a fire in all of your dwellings on the *Shabbat* day." One of their most effective detractors, Rabbi Saadia Gaon (882-942), demonstrated that while cooking is prohibited on *Shabbat,* enjoying hot food is an integral component of *Shabbat* observance (see also the similar comments of the *Ba'al HaMa'or, Shabbat,* chapter 3, at the conclusion of the long paragraph "*ve'im tish'al*"). According to legendary tradition, Rabbi Saadia Gaon's writings inspired the dish known as *chulent* as an antidote to the position of the Karaites. The publication of this volume is a testament to the Torah traditions championed by Rabbi Saadia Gaon, and to the everlasting warmth of *Shabbat* that is appropriately kindled through the study and application of authentic Torah scholarship.

We thank Rabbi Daniel Feldman, who in his capacity as the executive editor of the RIETS Press, has worked painstakingly to ensure the editorial excellence of this volume, and has continued the practice instituted in the first volume of this series of including supplementary comments from other *rashei yeshiva* at RIETS.

Additionally, we express our deep gratitude to the *Nasi HaYeshivah,* President Richard M. Joel, the *Rosh HaYeshivah* Rabbi Dr. Norman Lamm, and our Dean Emeritus Rabbi Zevulun Charlop, for ensuring that the Torah scholarship learned and taught within the walls of our Yeshiva are spread throughout the larger Jewish community. Our namesake,

Rabbi Isaac Elchanan Spektor (1817-1896), was renowned not only for his Torah scholarship, but for his ability to issue practical halakhic rulings that transformed people's lives. We are proud to follow in Rabbi Spektor's footsteps with the publication of this important volume in the RIETS Practical Halakhah Series.

Rabbi Yona Reiss
Max and Marion Grill Dean of RIETS

Editor's Preface

With gratitude tendered to the *Ribbono Shel Olam,* we present before the learning public the second volume of the RIETS Practical Halakhah Series.

It is a particular honor that this volume, on the laws and concepts of cooking and heating food on *Shabbat,* is authored by one of our esteemed *rashei yeshiva,* Rav Mordechai Willig. Rav Willig brings a distinguished perspective to this series, having served for decades as a *rosh yeshiva* and community *rav,* as well as playing a prominent role in the training of generations of rabbinic leaders as the Rosh Kollel of the Bella and Harry Wexner Kollel Elyon and the Segan Rosh Kollel of the Rabbi Norman Lamm Kollel L'Horaah. As a renowned yet accessible *posek,* he provides guidance to countless students, rabbis, laymen and organizations around the world.

In this volume, Rav Willig shares the *posek*'s perspective with the reader, analyzing the relevant Talmudic passages in depth, and navigating the interpretive path through the writings of the *Rishonim* and the *Acharonim* up to and including the most recent contemporary halakhic literature, to conclusively interpret the "*shma'ata aliba dehilkhata,*" to bring the conceptual analysis to its practical application. As such, this is a unique work; rather than focusing exclusively on guidelines for practice, it is a rare English-language glimpse into the halakhic process in all its complexity. Thus, the careful and experienced reader is rewarded with a deep and thorough experience. In addition, summaries at the end of each chapter provide a more succinct and practically directed application of the material.

This series is one of many initiatives currently being undertaken at Rabbi Isaac Elchanan Theological Seminary (RIETS), an affiliate of Yeshiva University, as a new stage in our Yeshiva's efforts to extend the teaching of Torah on a level that is both deep and wide: advanced and uncompromised in its content and substance, and broad in its accessibility and availability. In recent years, we have seen the release of a growing number of volumes under this initiative, both works written in the classic Hebrew style of the *beit hamidrash* and in the modern English idiom that allows for an expanded range of communication.

The RIETS Practical Halakhah Series endeavors to publish volumes, authored by the *rashei yeshiva* of RIETS, which will present the fundamentals of Jewish law together with their conceptual underpinnings. The goal is to convey the halakhic rulings together with an exploration of the process that brought about the conclusions, and to convey the experience of *Talmud Torah* in the sense of textual study, conceptual analysis, and practical application.

It is also our ideal that the volumes of this series, in addition to presenting the views of the individual author, will provide a perspective on the opinions of the broader RIETS faculty. To that end, we have invited commentary from additional RIETS *rebbeim* who are extensivly involved in teaching the subject matter of this *sefer*, and we are pleased to be able to present notes and rulings from Rav Herschel Schachter and Rav Yaakov Neuburger.

We are profoundly grateful to the administration of RIETS for their stalwart guidance of our Yeshiva, and for their dedication in making Yeshivat Rabbenu Yitzchak Elchanan the magnificent center of Torah study and rabbinic training that it is. We are the fortunate beneficiaries of the tireless efforts of President Richard Joel; *Rosh HaYeshiva* and Chancellor Rav Norman Lamm; RIETS Dean Rav Yona Reiss; Dean Emeritus Rav Zevulun Charlop; Associate Dean of Operations

Rabbi Marc Penner; and Administrator Rav Chaim Bronstein. This volume is being published through the generosity of the Michael Scharf Publication Trust of Yeshiva University Press, and we express gratitude to Michael and Fiona Scharf for all of their work in bringing Torah literature to print under the auspices of Yeshiva University. In order to aid the reader in studying the sources cited in the original, we have appended to the back of this volume a section containing many of the primary sources that are cited in the text. This section does not include every reference, and for considerations of space generally does not repeat sources that are brought earlier in the text. Nonetheless, it is hoped that is will prove a helpful supplement that will bring the reader closer to the direct experience of personally studying and analyzing the discussed topics. Thanks are extended to Rabbi Nosson Rich for his work in compiling this section, and to the Bar Ilan Responsa Project for allowing their materials to be utilized in its composition. In addition, we have provided here Hebrew essays by Rav Willig, as published in his *sefer Am Mordechai* and the RIETS journal *Beit Yitzchak*, that address the topics covered in this work.

Further, we are deeply indebted to Shifra Schapiro for wise and insightful copyediting; to Rabbi David Weiss for his careful review of the manuscript and his helpful comments; to Joel Markin for his work in preparing the glossary and the bibliography; and to Rachael Schultz for preparing the index. Finally, a tremendous thank you to Matthew Miller, Rabbi Reuven Ziegler, Tomi Mager, and the wonderful staff at Maggid Books for all of their work in ensuring that the volume is brought to print in the most beautiful way possible.

It is our fervent wish that this volume and those that follow it will add to the realization of our Yeshiva's mission, to study, teach, clarify and spread *HaKadosh Barukh Hu*'s holy Torah, *lehagdilah uleha'adirah.*

Daniel Z. Feldman
Tammuz, 5773

Author's Preface

> Whoever has not learned [*hilkhot Shabbat*] can easily violate them, since there are, in each one [of the categories of prohibited labor] many details of *halakhah* which involve Torah prohibitions.
>
> Especially regarding matters of cooking, leaving [a pot on a fire before *Shabbat*] and covering (*hatmanah*), it is a very complex [area of] *halakhah*, with many specific, practical laws.
>
> R. Yonatan Eibschutz warned that it is realistically impossible to be saved from [violating] the prohibition of Shabbos if one does not learn all the laws clearly, very, very well.

This excerpt from the introduction to the *Mishnah Berurah Hilkhot Shabbat* explains the importance of knowing how one may heat food on *Shabbat* without violating a Torah or rabbinic prohibition, but also highlights the complexity of these laws in particular.

I have been privileged to learn and teach these *halakhot* in our Yeshiva, Yeshivat Rabbenu Yitzchak Elchanan. The Yeshiva learned *Shabbat* twice during the 1980's. Many of the insights in this sefer originated in those *shi'urim* and were printed in the *yeshivah*'s Torah journal, *Beit Yitzchak*.

When Rabbi Zevulun Charlop, *shlit"a*, established a practical *halakhah* series for senior *semichah* students at RIETS, he asked me to teach the *halakhot* of cooking and heating food on *Shabbat*. These shiurim comprise the first eleven chapters of *Am Mordechai on Shabbat*, which was printed in 2005. Additional material, based on shiurim given in 5770 (2009-2010), was printed in that year's *Beit Yitzchak*.

My esteemed colleague, Rav Daniel Feldman, asked me to translate these *shi'urim* for publication as part of the RIETS *halakhah* series. My draft was edited by Rav Feldman and Mrs. Shifra Schapiro. Rabbi David Feinberg typed and enhanced the manuscript.

Notwithstanding the difficulty in capturing the complexity of these laws and the nuances of rabbinic Hebrew in translation, I hope this volume will assist in understanding the sources for these laws and their development from the Talmud until today.

There are many fine works on these topics. Recent *sefarim*, quoted extensively in this *sefer*, include *Shemirat Shabbat KeHilkhatah* and *Orchot Shabbat*. English works include *Hilchos Shabbos* and *The Shabbos Kitchen*.

The present volume delves a bit more deeply into the sources in the Talmud and the *Rishonim*. It traces the *halachot* to the *Beit Yosef* and the *Shulchan Arukh*, with the Rama's emendations.

As such, this is a *sefer* to be studied in depth, not a book to be perused for quick answers. To assist in this endeavor, the original Hebrew sources are included, although the English section is meant to be learned and understood independently.

Many thanks to the RIETS administration: President Richard Joel, *Rosh HaYeshiva* Rabbi Norman Lamm and Dean Rabbi Yona Reiss. To my *rebbeim*, colleagues and *talmidim*, thank you for being my teachers (*Ta'anit* 7a). This includes the members of my shul, Young Israel of Riverdale.

My wife, Faygie, joins me in expressing our heartfelt and abiding gratitude to *Hashem* for blessing us with a wonderful family. To our children and their spouses, we wish continued good health, happiness and success in learning, teaching and raising their families based on the beauty of Torah. May we see our grandchildren develop a strong and lasting commitment to *Hashem* and His Torah, in the spirit of the *Navi*:

ואני זאת בריתי אותם אמר ה׳ רוחי אשר עליך ודברי אשר שמתי בפיך לא ימושו מפיך ומפי זרעך ומפי זרע זרעך אמר ה׳ מעתה ועד עולם. (ישעיה נט כא)

And (as for) Me, this is My covenant with them, says *Hashem,* My spirit that is upon you, and My words that I placed in your mouth will not leave your mouth, nor the mouths of your offspring, nor the mouths of your offspring's offspring, says *Hashem,* from now and for eternity. (Isaiah 59:21)

Section I: Cooking

1

The Definition of Cooking

A. ACTIONS THAT CONSTITUTE THE *MELAKHAH* OF COOKING

Bishul, cooking, is one of the thirty-nine prohibited *melakhot* of *Shabbat.* The Rambam[1] codifies this *melakhah* as being manifested in one of three forms: one violates this *melakhah* if he bakes bread, cooks food or dye, or heats water.

The differentiation between cooking and baking has a textual basis. The Talmud[2] notes that the *mishnah*[3] which lists the thirty-nine *melakhot* omits cooking. The construction of the *Mishkan,* which is the source of the thirty-nine *melakhot,* involved the cooking of dyes. Instead of listing cooking as a *melakhah,* the *mishnah* lists baking in its place, as baking is the culmination of the "order of [making] bread." The sequence of steps for making bread comprises the first eleven *melakhot.* Apparently, cooking and baking are distinct actions, and yet both are equally valid examples of this *melakhah.* Thus, the Rambam's separate mention

---

1. *Mishneh Torah, Hilkhot Shabbat* 9:1.
2. *Shabbat* 74b.
3. *Shabbat* 73a.

of both baking and cooking is unsurprising, as it reflects the distinction found in the Talmud.

B. THE DISTINCTION BETWEEN HEATING WATER AND COOKING FOOD

However, the Rambam's reference to heating water as a separate category requires explanation; is heating water not merely an instance of cooking food? It may be that heating water is singled out because the volume required to be culpable in that case is different than that of cooking and baking. The amount, or *shi'ur,* for which one is culpable for baking is the equivalent of a *grogeret,* a dried fig. This *shi'ur* is found[4] regarding the *melakhot* of reaping (*kotzer*) and grinding (*tochen*), and apparently applies to other food-related prohibitions, including, presumably, cooking food.[5] Cooking dye and heating water, however, each have different *shi'urim.*[6]

A different, more fundamental reason for the separate mention of heating water is based on a continuation of the Talmud's discussion of *bishul.*[7] One who throws a wet peg into the fire violates *bishul,* as the peg softens first before it later hardens. Similarly, one who melts tar violates *bishul,* even though tar re-hardens after it has softened.

Apparently, as can be seen from this Talmudic statement, the definition of cooking includes softening through exposure to heat. The Rambam[8] adds hardening to the definition of cooking as well. In any event, since heating water neither softens nor hardens it, heating water must constitute a separate category of *bishul.*

The distinction between heating water and cooking food may be relevant in interpreting one of the Rambam's rulings:[9] "One who cooks something that does not require cooking is exempt (*patur*)." *Patur* means that no Torah violation exists, but the action is a rabbinic violation

4. *Shabbat* 70b.
5. See Rambam and *Maggid Mishnah, Hilkhot Shabbat* 8:3, 7, 11, 15, 16 and 9:11.
6. Ibid., 9:1.
7. *Shabbat* 74b.
8. *Hilkhot Shabbat* 9:6; see *Lechem Mishneh.*
9. *Hilkhot Shabbat* 9:3

of the *melakhah* of cooking,[10] as is indicated by the Talmud[11] and as R. Akiva Eiger[12] notes.

There is some debate as to the scope of this ruling. According to the *Mirkevet HaMishneh,*[13] any food which can be eaten raw does not require cooking, and one who cooks it is exempt. He equates, for this purpose, *Shabbat* to the prohibition of *bishul akum* (the prohibition of eating food cooked by a non-Jew), which likewise does not apply to food which can be eaten raw.[14]

The *Sha'ar HaTziyun*[15] quotes others who disagree with the *Mirkevet HaMishneh*. The dissenters limit the Rambam's exemption to something that is not improved at all by the cooking. By this standard, fruits, which do improve when cooked, are subject to a Torah violation of *bishul* even though they can be eaten raw. As proof for his position, the *Sha'ar HaTziyun* cites the ruling of the Talmud[16] that one who cooks water is culpable, even though water can be drunk without cooking. This proof that one is biblically culpable even for cooking foods which can be eaten raw, which the author of the *Sha'ar HaTziyun* repeats in his *Mishnah Berurah,*[17] assumes that water is fundamentally similar to other foods.

The *Peri Megadim,*[18] by contrast, distinguishes between water and other foods. Water can be consumed raw, but for water, cooking is defined by heating. He thus implicitly rejects the *Sha'ar HaTziyun*'s proof from water to other foods that can be consumed raw by redefining cooking in relation to various types of food. In regards to fruit and other solids, cooking means softening the food and readying it for consumption. Hence, if the item can be eaten raw, one who cooks it is exempt. For water and other liquids, however, cooking means heating, and the prohibition applies even though they can be consumed raw.

---

10. See ibid., 1:3.
11. *Shabbat* 3a.
12. Commenting on *Magen Avraham, Orach Chaim* 254:14.
13. *Hilkhot Shabbat* 9:3.
14. *Avodah Zarah* 38a.
15. *Orach Chaim* 318:114.
16. *Shabbat* 40b.
17. *Orach Chaim* 318:1.
18. *Eishel Avraham* 254:1.

C. SUMMARY

The *melakhah* of cooking is defined by the Rambam as baking bread, cooking food or dye, or heating water. The *Peri Megadim* defines cooking differently for water (heating the water) and for food (improving the food). Therefore, if a food is edible when it is raw, there may be no Torah prohibition of cooking it, as the *Mirkevet HaMishneh* rules, since the food was previously fit for consumption. According to the *Sha'ar HaTziyun*, however, heating water is analogous to cooking food, and one commits a Torah violation even by cooking foods that, like water, can be consumed raw.

2

Cooking after Cooking

A. BACKGROUND

The *mishnah*[1] states that any food which was placed in water on Friday may be soaked in water on *Shabbat*. The Mordechai,[2] quoting R. Eliezar of Metz, comments: "From here [we learn] that *ein bishul achar bishul* (there is no [prohibited act of] cooking after cooking). Therefore, any fully cooked food may be placed near the fire or in a pot which was on the fire in order to be reheated." This rule is implicit in the *Shulchan Arukh*,[3] explicit in the *Mishnah Berurah*[4] and is universally accepted in practice today. In fact, the *Tosafot HaRosh*[5] considers the principle of *ein bishul achar bishul* to be self-evident, and asks why a *mishnah* is needed to state it. Accordingly, he explains the novelty of the *mishnah* to be a different point: the permissibility of soaking the cooked food to the point that it becomes dissolved (as Rashi in fact interprets the *mishnah*).

---

1. *Shabbat* 145b.
2. *Shabbat* #302.
3. *Orach Chaim* 318:4.
4. 318:32.
5. *Shabbat* 145b.

B. THE RAMBAM'S POSITION ON *EIN BISHUL ACHAR BISHUL*

However, the Rambam's formulation seems to contradict the otherwise unanimous view that *bishul achar bishul* is permitted. He writes: "One who cooks on the fire something that is fully cooked or something that does not need cooking at all is exempt (*patur*)."[6] The language of "exempt" (from punishment, rather than "permitted") indicates that a rabbinic prohibition exists.

The *Eglei Tal*[7] suggests that the rabbinic prohibition involved is not that of cooking, but rather a separate prohibition of returning a pot onto an uncovered fire. (He thereby rejects R. Akiva Eiger's inference that cooking food which can be eaten raw is a rabbinic prohibition of cooking; see above at note 11.) The *Eglei Tal*'s interpretation that the rabbinic prohibition that the Rambam means is not one of "cooking," but rather one of "returning" is unlikely for two reasons: The rules of "returning" are found elsewhere in the Rambam's code,[8] and do not belong in the ninth chapter, where the *halakhah* that one is *patur* for *bishul achar bishul* is found. Moreover, there is no indication that the fire in this case is uncovered.

The assumption that the Rambam prohibits *bishul achar bishul* requires reinterpretation of the *mishnah* which states that any food which was placed in hot water on Friday may be soaked in hot water on *Shabbat* (above, section A). Indeed, the *Beit Yosef*[9] infers from the Rambam[10] an entirely new understanding of the *mishnah*: it permits only soaking, and not *bishul achar bishul*. The Rambam, in codifying the rule of the *mishnah*, states: "Something that is cooked before *Shabbat*, or soaked in hot water before *Shabbat*, even though it is now cold, may be soaked in hot water on *Shabbat*."[11] The requirement cited above in the Rambam's formulation of cooking after cooking ("One who cooks on the fire something that is fully cooked or something that does not need cooking at

6. *Hilkhot Shabbat* 9:3.
7. *Ofeh* 19:8-9.
8. *Hilkhot Shabbat* 3:10.
9. *Orach Chaim* 318:4.
10. Ibid., 22:8.
11. *Hilkhot Shabbat* 22:8.

all is exempt [*patur*]"), that the food be fully cooked before *Shabbat* in order for one not to be biblically culpable for reheating, is omitted in the context of the permissibility of soaking. As long as the food was soaked in hot water before *Shabbat,* even if it wasn't even half cooked (*ma'achal ben derusa'i,* the minimal standard for halakhic cooking, as defined by the Rambam in *Hilkhot Shabbat* 9:5), it is considered cooked so that a subsequent soaking in hot water is not considered cooking.[12]

The *Even HaAzel*[13] notes that the Rambam places this *halakhah* amongst rabbinic prohibitions, and does not permit a second cooking on *Shabbat.* Only soaking, which is a rabbinic prohibition of improving food in a manner which resembles cooking,[14] is permitted after a previous cooking or soaking, because the food was already improved.

R. Uriel Eisenthal, in *Megillat Sefer,*[15] points out that according to the *Beit Yosef*'s understanding of the Rambam, the *mishnah* does not state that *bishul achar bishul,* which only applies after the food has been actually cooked, is permissible even on the rabbinic level. Only soaking is permitted on the rabbinic level. Nonetheless, *bishul achar bishul* must be permissible, as the Vilna Gaon[16] attempts to prove from the *halakhah* that one may return a pot onto a covered fire. However, the Vilna Gaon's proof is unconvincing. The permissibility of returning a pot onto a covered fire could be limited to a pot whose contents are still hot. If the food is cold, it may be prohibited to reheat, against the Vilna Gaon's assumption that returning a pot to a covered fire is permissible even then.

Indeed, the Rambam[17] rules that one may not place cold food on a hot vessel, because he is heating the food on *Shabbat.* The *Megillat Sefer*[18] assumes that placing cold food on a hot vessel is a separate prohibition not due to *bishul,* and asks how it can be reconciled[19] with the

12. See *Machatzit HaShekel* 318:14.
13. *Hilkhot Shabbat* 22:8.
14. *Hilkhot Shabbat* 22:10
15. 3:23:4.
16. *Be'ur HaGra* 253:39.
17. *Hilkhot Shabbat* 4:6.
18. Ibid., #3.
19. *Shabbat* 145b, cited above (chapter 2, section A).

mishnah that allows reheating, and the statement of the Talmud[20] which allows placing cold water into a cup of hot water.

If our analysis of the Rambam's position is correct, placing cold food on a hot vessel is not a separate prohibition but a rabbinic violation of *bishul achar bishul.* As such, the rabbinic prohibition does not apply in the case of the *mishnah,* which does not allow reheating after all; it allows only soaking. Nor does the rabbinic prohibition apply in the case of the Talmud (42a), since the cup of hot water is a *keli sheni,* a vessel which was never on the fire, which does not cook its contents.[21]

C. SUMMARY

Almost all *Rishonim* and *Acharonim* derive from the *mishnah* (*Shabbat* 145b) which permits re-soaking previously soaked food, that *re-cooking* previously *cooked* food is also permissible (=*ein bishul achar bishul*). The Rambam, however, believes that re-cooking previously cooked food is rabbinically prohibited, and that the *mishnah* on *Shabbat* 145b permits only re-soaking.

20. *Shabbat* 42a.

21. *Shabbat* 40b, and see below, chapter 11.

3

Liquids

A. DISTINCTION BETWEEN REHEATING LIQUIDS AND REHEATING SOLIDS

The Rosh[1] quotes a dispute regarding the reheating of liquids. According to the strict view, attributed to Rashi, the *mishnah*[2] allows reheating only for solids, such as chicken, which is mentioned in the Talmud.[3]

The *Beit Yosef*[4] notes that the Rambam, the Rashba and the Ran do not distinguish between solids and liquids, and presumably permit reheating liquids as well as solids. However, if our analysis of the Rambam's position on *bishul achar bishul*[5] is correct, the Rambam's opinion is actually the opposite, and he prohibits reheating both solids and liquids.

B. DEFINITION OF "REHEATING" FOR LIQUIDS

The *Shulchan Arukh*[6] rules strictly in terms of the positions cited in the Rosh, forbidding "cooking" liquids that have cooled off. The *Mishnah*

1. *Shabbat* 3:10, 11.
2. 145b; cited above, chapter 2, section A.
3. Ibid.
4. *O.C.* 318:4.
5. Above, chapter 2, section B.
6. *O.C.* 318:4.

Berurah,[7] citing the *Beit Yosef,* defines cooled off as being no longer *yad soledet bo*. If one's hand does not recoil from the heat, that heat is not considered hot enough to cook[8] or to cause absorption of taste.[9] Since it is not halakhically considered hot, an item at a temperature lower than *yad soledet bo* is viewed as cooled off, and may not be reheated.

C. DEFINITION OF COOKING APPLIED TO REHEATING LIQUIDS VS. SOLIDS

The possibility of a difference between solids and liquids in the permissibility of reheating may depend upon whether there is a distinction between solids and liquids in the definition of cooking. If liquids are basically the same as solids[10] the leniency of *ein bishul achar bishul* should apply to liquids as well. However, if the definition of cooking for liquids is heating, as the *Peri Megadim*[11] suggests, then, if the liquid cools off, the "cooking" has disappeared and a subsequent cooking is prohibited, presumably by Torah law.

In this vein, the *Eglei Tal*[12] compares liquids to metals. The Rambam[13] rules that one who melts metal violates *bishul,* even though the metal was previously melted. We do not apply the rule *ein bishul achar bishul* in the case of metals, because the definition of *bishul* for metal is melting. Once metal hardens, the *bishul* has disappeared, and a subsequent *bishul* is a Torah violation. Similarly, if the definition of *bishul* for liquids is heating, then the *bishul* is cancelled when the liquids cool off, and a subsequent heating is a Torah violation. The Rambam's separate mention of heating water[14] may imply this conclusion.

Interestingly, both the *Peri Megadim* and *Eglei Tal* suggest a distinction between water and other liquids. Water reverts completely to its original state when cooled; by contrast, cold soup is different than

7. *O.C.* 318:24.
8. *O.C.* 318:14.
9. *Yoreh De'ah* 105:2.
10. See *Sha'ar HaTziyun,* above, chapter 1, section B.
11. See above, chapter 1, section B.
12. *Ofeh* 11:6.
13. *Hilkhot Shabbat* 9:6.
14. See chapter 1, section A.

what it was originally before the cooking took place, and thus its cooking has not disappeared.[15]

D. *YAD SOLEDET BO*

The Talmud[16] prohibits heating liquids to the level of heat that the hand recoils from, *yad soledet bo*. The Talmud asks how we can determine what this level of heat is? Rashi explains the Talmud's question: some recoil from a low level of heat and others do not recoil. The Talmud provides an objective equivalent: heat from which the stomach of an infant is scalded. Since we are not sure how to define "scalded," the precise definition of *yad soledet bo* is unclear.

The *Shemirat Shabbat KeHilkhatah,*[17] citing Rav Shlomo Zalman Auerbach,[18] states that *yad soledet bo* is not less than 45 degrees Celsius, which is 113°F, while some allow up to 110°F or 120°F. Rav Eider[19] states that the *poskim* (Rav Moshe Feinstein and Rav Aharon Kotler, respectively) reached their decisions about the 110°F and 120°F levels by checking the temperature at which one's hand recoils.

The *Mishnah Berurah,*[20] citing Rashi,[21] requires the objective definition of the Talmud, that an infant's stomach is scalded. How, then, do the aforementioned *poskim* rule based on the temperature of the hand recoiling? Presumably, they experimented for that standard with many individuals, and found 110°F or 120°F to be the average level at which one's hand recoils, which is comparable to the temperature regarding the infant's stomach, and thus it is that temperature above which one may not heat liquids.

However, *yad soledet bo* may be much higher. *Iggerot Moshe*[22] requires 160°F to be certain that *yad soledet bo* was reached in order to

15. For further discussion of this possibility, see chapter 4, section C and chapter 5, below.
16. *Shabbat* 40b.
17. 1:1.
18. Fn. 3.
19. *Hilchos Shabbos,* fn. 19.
20. *O.C.* 318:89.
21. See *Sha'ar HaTziyyun,* #113.
22. Cited in *Hilchos Shabbos,* fn. 19

permit a subsequent reheating. Elsewhere,[23] he requires 180°F, as does the *Or LeTziyon*.[24] The *Or LeTziyon* also prohibits heating liquids above 104°F, claiming that an infant's stomach is scalded at that temperature. The *Piskei Teshuvot*[25] defines scalding as leaving a mark, which happens only at 113°F. Others consider 122°F (50°C) to be certainly *yad soledet bo*.[26]

The Rashba[27] states that a person does not drink or bathe in "*yad soledet bo*" water. The *Kaf HaChaim*[28] adds that if a person does drink a cup of water, it is not considered *yad soledet bo*. On this basis, the *Or LeTziyon* requires liquid to have previously reached 180°F in order to permit a subsequent reheating, since tea can be sipped until that temperature.

However, the *Piskei Teshuvot*[29] states that the Rashba's criterion that people "do not drink" *yad soledet bo* liquids refers to drinking uninterruptedly, as opposed to sipping tea or soup which is, in fact, done at *yad soledet bo* levels of heat. It is unclear how hot the average person would drink a liquid, such as tea or coffee, which cooled somewhat.

Some, however, have digital temperature adjustments on their showers. The average person can tolerate (based upon experimentaion) about 113°F, confirming the view of the *Shemirat Shabbat KeHilkhatah*, based on the Rashba and the *Kaf HaChaim*.

NYC code requires landlords to maintain hot water at 115-120°F. Higher than that can cause scalding, whereas lower than that is not hot enough for some people to shower or wash dishes. Since most of us add some cold water to cool the shower temperature somewhat, the 113°F temperature of the *Shemirat Shabbat KeHilkhatah* is a good approximation of *yad soledet bo*.

The *Shulchan Arukh*[30] prohibits one from placing a liquid even momentarily near a fire, if the liquid would eventually reach *yad soledet*

23. *Yoreh Deah* II:52.
24. Vol II, ch. 30, fn. 12.
25. P. 253, fn. 5.
26. *Az Nidberu* IX,14; see chapter. 7 Sec C.
27. *Shabbat* 42a.
28. *O.C.* 318:143.
29. P. 253 fn. 5.
30. *O.C.* 318:14.

bo in that place, since, as the *Mishnah Berurah*[31] explains, it may be forgotten there and cooked.

E. OPENING A HOT WATER FAUCET

The *Shemirat Shabbat KeHilkhatah* (1:39) prohibits opening a hot water faucet. When hot water comes out, cold water enters the boiler and is cooked immediately. This is a *pesik reishei deneicha lei,* an inevitable consequence that is beneficial, as more hot water is now available.

Rabbi Dovid Ribiat, in his work *The 39 Melachos,*[32] describes an apartment building system as follows: "The entry pipe into the boiler can only contain an amount of water equivalent to the amount that enters the boiler through a single, open faucet." [Note: Other expert plumbers deny this fact. They state that the amount of water in the tank is always the same. For every drop that goes out, a drop of cold water comes in. If so, the water is heated to 120°F immediately, which is a Torah violation of cooking.] Since it is possible that a non-Jew has opened his hot water faucet, there is a doubt as to whether the Jew cooks water immediately when he opens the hot water faucet. Since some authorities permit a doubtful *pesik reishei*[33] (i.e., if a fact is in doubt, it is comparable to a case where the outcome is in doubt, which is thus not a *pesik reishei*), it may be permissible to open the hot water faucet in an apartment building.

Assuming that ultimately the boiler will be refilled, this leniency must be based on the *Shiltei HaGibborim,*[34] who allows a *pesik reishei* when the inevitable consequence happens only later on. However, in this case, there is one long process of refilling the boiler, which has already begun when the Jew opens the hot water faucet. Moreover, the water which enters immediately can be attributed to the Jew's faucet as well as the non-Jew's. Thus, it is not comparable to the *Shiltei HaGibborim*'s case where the fire does not increase at all until a later time. Therefore, even if there is no immediate increase in the amount of water entering the boiler, it is prohibited to open the hot water faucet.

---

31. *O.C.* 318:90.
32. P. 640 and fn. 264.
33. *Taz* 316:3.
34. *Shabbat* 45a, #2.

F. SUMMARY

The permissibility of reheating liquids is a matter of dispute. The *Shulchan Arukh* rules that liquids may not be reheated, because once a cooked liquid cools to a temperature below *yad soledet bo,* it is as if the liquid has never been cooked at all. This is consistent with the *Peri Megadim*'s contention that the definition of "cooking" for liquids is heating them, and is thus of a different nature than the cooking of solids. However, according to those who equate the definition of cooking for both liquids and solids, it could be permissible to reheat liquids as well. Current practice is to prohibit reheating liquids (see below chapter 5, section B).

The temperature at which liquids are considered cooked is called *yad soledet bo,* which is defined as 113°F. It is thus prohibited to place a liquid near a fire if it will reach 113°F. It is also prohibited to turn on a hot water faucet on *Shabbat,* even in an apartment building, since the new water entering the boiler will reach the temperature of *yad soledet bo.*

4

Partially Cooked

A. THE VIEWS OF THE RAMBAM AND THE RASHBA CONCERNING WHEN *EIN BISHUL ACHAR BISHUL* CAN BE APPLIED

The Rambam maintains that a person is exempt in the case of *bishul achar bishul* only if the food had been fully cooked before *Shabbat*; since it is already fully cooked, the subsequent reheating does not improve the food and thus is only rabbinically prohibited. In the same sentence, the Rambam states an exemption in the case of cooking food which does not need cooking, for the same reason, namely, that there is no improvement: "One who cooks on the fire something that is fully cooked or something that does not need cooking at all is exempt (*patur*)."[1]

The Rashba[2] applies the principle of *ein bishul achar bishul* to food that had been partially cooked. We have seen[3] that the *melakhah* of cooking is defined as cooking food to the level of *kema'achal ben derusa'i*. Ben Derusa'i was a bandit who ate his food only partially cooked: half

1. *Hilkhot Shabbat* 9:3.
2. *Shabbat* 18b.
3. See above, chapter 2, section B at note 12.

cooked according to the Rambam[4] and one third cooked according to Rashi.[5] Since, when the food reaches *kema'achal ben derusa'i*, the food is halakhically cooked, one who performs a subsequent cooking is exempt according to the Rashba, even though the food is improved by that act, and the action is therefore permissible. Thus, while the Rambam only applies *ein bishul achar bishul* to food that is fully cooked and can no longer be physically improved through cooking, the Rashba applies *ein bishul achar bishul* even when the cooking still enhances the food.

B. COOKING: A HALAKHIC CHANGE OR A PHYSICAL CHANGE?

The Radvaz[6] writes that according to the Rashba, one who cooks food which is eaten raw is exempt. After all, if food which only a bandit eats is exempt from the prohibition of cooking, how much more so food which anyone can eat raw. This proof, however, is flawed. In contrast to the Rambam, who focuses on physical changes to the food, the Rashba understands *ein bishul achar bishul* in a halakhic sense, not in a physical one. In his view, food that has undergone a halakhic definition of cooking cannot be cooked again. However, if the food had not been cooked, one might indeed violate *bishul* even if it can be eaten raw. Nevertheless, the point may still be true that the Rashba requires a need for physical improvement as well, and thus exempts food which is eaten raw. The *Peri Megadim*[7] questions whether the principle of *ein bishul achar bishul* applies to food which had been cooked in the sun, a process which is not considered cooking halakhically,[8] despite its physical effect on the food. In theory, this distinction may make cooking in the sun a test case for the difference between the views of the Rashba and the Rambam. According to the Rambam, one should be exempt for a second act of cooking if cooking in the sun is physically equivalent to cooking on the fire, since there is no subsequent improvement with that second cooking.

4. *Hilkhot Shabbat* 9:5.
5. *Shabbat* 20a, s.v. *Ben Derusa'i.*
6. *Responsa* 1:213.
7. *Mishbetzot Zahav, O.C.* 318:6.
8. *Shabbat* 39a.

According to the Rashba, however, one might indeed violate *bishul* for re-cooking food that was cooked in the sun, since there was no previous halakhic cooking. However, if the Rashba requires that there be room in the definition of cooking for physical improvement as well, then one would be exempt from subsequent cooking. This is the conclusion of the *Peri Megadim*.

This issue is relevant to food cooked in a microwave oven, which has no fire and may be like cooking with the sun.[9] According to the view of the Rambam, one who takes food cooked in a microwave and subsequently reheats it on *Shabbat* would be exempt, while the Rashba's position is unclear. One might indeed violate *bishul* for re-cooking food that was cooked in a microwave, since there was no previous halakhic cooking. However, if the Rashba requires that the definition of cooking includes physical improvement as well, then one would be exempt from subsequent cooking of food cooked in a microwave.

Despite his focus on the halakhic status rather than the physical status of the food, the Rashba must concede that if the actual effect of the first halakhic cooking disappears, a second cooking would be in violation of *bishul*. This is evident from the law of melting metal.[10]

C. RAN AND RASHBA: COOKING IS A HALAKHIC CHANGE

The Ran[11] cites a stringency in the name of Rabbenu Yonah: One may not pour water from a kettle into a stew to prevent the stew from drying up. If the water is hot, i.e., *yad soledet bo*, and the soup in the stew is not, or vice versa, the hot liquid has cooked the one that has cooled. Rabbenu Yonah's position proves that *bishul achar bishul* applies to soup as well as water, in contrast to view of the *Peri Megadim* mentioned above.[12]

Rabbenu Yonah posits further: Even if both liquids are hot, once the water leaves the kettle and is being poured into the stew, the water may lose its halakhic status of food in a *keli rishon*, a pot that was in the fire.

---

9. See chapter. 9.
10. Cited above, chapter 3, section C.
11. *Shabbat* 22a in pages of Rif, s.v. *VeHaRav*.
12. See chapter 3, section C.

Thus, when it enters the pot of stew, the water is subject to being cooked, and *bishul* is violated. This change in status is purely halakhic; the water is physically the same when it is inside the kettle and when it is outside of it. Like the Rashba, apparently, Rabbenu Yonah views the principle of *ein bishul achar bishul* from a halakhic perspective, not a physical one.

The requirement of *yad soledet bo* for soup to be considered cooked is instructive. After all, soup is unlike water which is "cooked" when merely heated; soup changes materially during the procedure. It could thus have been thought that even when the soup cools off, it maintains its status of "cooked" and should not be subject to further prohibitions of *bishul.*[13] According to Rabbenu Yonah, however, from a halakhic perspective, soup is apparently cooked in two senses: it is both physically changed and heated. If it loses its status of "hot" (halakhically, when the soup is no longer at the temperature of *yad soledet bo* or no longer in a *keli rishon*), it is prohibited to reheat it even though the physical changes remain, since reheating cooled soup is also considered an act of cooking.

D. SUMMARY

When the principle of *bishul achar bishul* may be applied is a subject of dispute between the Rambam, who applies it only to fully cooked food, and the Rashba, who applies it even to food cooked *kema'achal ben derusa'i.* This dispute may stem from the distinction between cooking as a physical change (Rambam) and cooking as a halakhic change (Rashba and Ran). The distinction may determine whether one has violated *bishul* when reheating food previously cooked in a microwave (since only a physical change, not a halakhic change, occurred in the microwaving of the food), and whether one has violated *bishul* by pouring hot water into hot stew (where only a halakhic change in the water, but not a physical change, has taken place). Even the Rashba, however, may understand cooking as a halakhic change *in addition* to a physical change, not *instead* of a physical change. In line with the positions of the *Shulchan Arukh* and Rama, the stringencies of both views should be followed.

13. As the *Peri Megadim* indeed suggests; see chapter 3, section C.

5

The Rama's Compromise

A. REHEATING SOUP

As we have seen, there is some question as to the permissibility of reheating soup. The Rama[1] quotes the two opinions about *bishul achar bishul* with regard to soup. The first requires the soup to be hot, i.e., above the temperature of *yad soledet bo,* for reheating to be allowed. The second permits reheating cold soup. The Rama concludes with a compromise: "It is customary to be lenient if it did not cool off completely." How do we understand this position? Does the Rama start with the premise that reheating any cooled liquid is forbidden, and add a leniency that soup that is still somewhat warm may be reheated? Or does the Rama start with the premise that reheating any cooled liquid is permitted, and add a stringency that the liquid must still be somewhat warm?

B. THE *MAGEN AVRAHAM'S* UNDERSTANDING OF THE RAMA

The *Magen Avraham*[2] assumes that if the soup cooled down completely, it is prohibited by Torah law to reheat it. This is the simple reading of the

1. *O.C.* 318:15.
2. *O.C.* 253:37.

Terumat HaDeshen[3] who considers reheating completely cooled soup an *av melakhah,* an act prohibited by Torah law. If, however, the soup is fit to be eaten without reheating, comparable to *ma'achal ben derusa'i,* no violation of *bishul* occurs. The *Terumat HaDeshen* quotes this ruling from the Mordechai,[4] *Hagahot Maymaniot*[5] and the *Semag.*

At first glance, this stance is based on the Rashba, who permits cooking food which had reached the point of *ma'achal ben derusa'i.*[6] However, the *Semag* rules like the Rambam, that *ein bishul achar bishul* applies only if the food had been fully cooked. Nevertheless, the *Semag* allows reheating soup which had been hot, but has partially cooled off, and is now comparable to *ma'achal ben derusa'i.*

The question of how the *Semag* can simultaneously hold that *ein bishul achar bishul* applies only to fully cooked food, but yet permit the reheating of partially cooled soup, can be resolved based on our earlier analysis.[7] Those who prohibit *bishul achar bishul* for liquids view the original heating as having disappeared. They rule that the original cooking has disappeared as soon as the liquid is no longer halakhically hot, i.e., *yad soledet bo.* The *Semag* maintains that as long as the soup is still fit to be served as hot food, even if it is cooler than *yad soledet bo,* the original heat has not disappeared. The soup is still considered fully cooked, and, therefore, may be reheated.

This is the Rama's compromise as understood by the *Magen Avraham,* namely, that partially cooled soup is still considered cooked and may be reheated. The Rama[8] allows the reheating of cholent which had cooled, since its temperature is presumably close to *yad soledet bo.* Adding heat is permissible, since it is not considered cooking, presumably because of the principle of *ein bishul achar bishul.* Thus, the Rama's expression of "not cooled down completely" should not be understood literally, i.e., above room temperature. "Not cooled down completely" is not strictly a measure of temperature, but rather it means that the

---

3. *Responsa,* 66.
4. *Shabbat* 456.
5. *Hilkhot Shabbat* 3:2.
6. See chapter 4, section A.
7. See chapter 3.
8. *Darkei Moshe O.C.* 253:7., citing the *Or Zaru'a* 81.

food is still fit to be eaten because of its heat.[9] According to the *Magen Avraham,* the Rama starts with the premise that reheating any cooled liquid is forbidden, but adds a leniency that soup that is somewhat warm may be reheated.

C. THE *EGLEI TAL*'S UNDERSTANDING OF THE RAMA

The *Eglei Tal* understands the Rama's compromise differently. He assumes[10] that even the Rambam, who applies *ein bishul achar bishul* only if the food had been fully cooked, agrees that if it had reached *ma'achal ben derusa'i* there is no Torah prohibition involved, only a rabbinic prohibition. (This assumption is inconsistent with our earlier analysis,[11] that according to the Rambam even fully cooked food is rabbinically prohibited to be re-cooked. If that is true, partially cooked food, by contrast, must be prohibited by Torah law.) Regarding the rabbinic prohibition of cooking food that has reached *ma'achal ben derusa'i,* the *Eglei Tal* understands the Rama to say, we can rely on the view that *ein bishul achar bishul* applies to liquids, and thus reheating partially cooled soup is permitted. However, the *Eglei Tal*'s interpretation is contradicted by the *Semag,* who rules categorically that *ein bishul achar bishul* does not apply to liquids, yet allows reheating liquids that have cooled somewhat but are still fit to be eaten because of their heat.

D. THE *MINCHAT KOHEN*'S UNDERSTANDING OF THE RAMA

The *Minchat Kohen*[12] suggests yet another understanding of the Rama's compromise. He writes that the Rama actually does apply the principle of *ein bishul achar bishul* to liquids. Accordingly, the compromise is a mere stringency. Although this view is against that of the *Magen Avraham* and the early decisors (*Rishonim*) quoted by the Rama, it has been

9. See *Shulchan Arukh HaRav* 318:9.
10. *Ofeh* 10:15.
11. Chapter 2, section B.
12. 2:2.

accepted by recent authorities: the *Mishnah Berurah*[13] *Chazon Ish*[14] and *Iggerot Moshe*[15] all interpret the Rama this way.

The *Iggerot Moshe*[16] thus allows pouring hot tea on cold droplets of a previous cup of tea. This is understandable within the view that the Rama's prohibition is a stringency, and thus it does not apply to a few mere droplets. According to the *Magen Avraham*, however, this ruling is questionable.

The *Chazon Ish* claims that, strictly speaking, there is no halakhic difference between fully cooled and partially cooled liquids. Hence, the Rama's compromise must be a mere stringency. The *Chazon Ish*'s opinion is based on his view that those who prohibit *bishul achar bishul* of liquids view them as fundamentally different from solids. For solids, softening is cooking.[17] This process is never undone. For liquids, which do not soften, heating is cooking. This process is undone when they cool off. If so, the only possible cutoff point is the halakhic definition of heat, namely *yad soledet bo*. Once a liquid's temperature is below *yad soledet bo*, there is no difference between fully cooled and partially cooled liquids. Thus the Rama must apply *ein bishul achar bishul* even to fully cooled liquids, but he imposes a stringency that soup cannot be reheated when fully cooled.

E. *MAGEN AVRAHAM*'S REASONING FOR PERMITTING REHEATING OF COLD SOLIDS AND PROHIBITING REHEATING OF COLD LIQUIDS

According to the *Rishonim* and the *Magen Avraham*, there is no fundamental difference between solids and liquids. Rather, the halakhic difference between them regarding whether a cold item can be reheated is based on a practical difference. Practically, all cooked solids can be eaten in a cold state, equivalent to *ma'achal ben derusa'i*. (*Ein bishul achar bishul* applies to *ma'achal ben derusa'i* food according to almost all

13. *O.C.* 318:99.
14. *O.C.* 37:13.
15. *O.C.* IV,:74, *bishul* 2.
16. *O.C.* IV,:74, *bishul* 19.
17. See chapter I, section B.

authorities except the Rambam.) This is not true of cold soup, which is inedible even by the *ma'achal ben derusa'i* standard, and *ein bishul achar bishul* does not apply.

The *Magen Avraham* rejects the approach later advanced by the *Chazon Ish,* as he holds that one who reheats cold soup violates a Torah prohibition. According to the *Magen Avraham, bishul achar bishul* applies only to a liquid that is fully cooled. Although the *Peri Megadim* suggests a distinction between water and soup,[18] he concludes that the *poskim* reject that distinction.

Interestingly, R. Yitzchak Drazi, in his *Shevut Yitzchak,*[19] quoting R. Yosef Shalom Elyashiv, writes that even if *bishul achar bishul* is a Torah prohibition with respect to water, it is only a rabbinic one concerning soup. However, as noted,[20] the *Magen Avraham*[21] contradicts this distinction, and considers reheating any cold liquid in a pot to be a Torah prohibition.

The *Shevut Yitzchak*[22] quotes the Ritva,[23] who makes a significant distinction between solids and liquids, including soup. He cites a ruling in a situation in which edible food was improperly reheated, and the food was declared permissible after the fact. However, this permission was applied only to the solid foods, and not to the soup. As the Ritva explains, the meat was edible cold, while the soup was not. The *Shevut Yitzchak* adds that if this is the rule, then as long as the soup is edible, reheating it to the degree of *yad soledet bo* should be permitted. This is precisely our analysis of the view of the Rama, as understood by the *Magen Avraham.*

The *Shevut Yitzchak*[24] proves from the words of the *Tur* that the *Tur*'s position is that *bishul achar bishul* of soup is prohibited by Torah law. The *Shevut Yitzchak* suggests that this is true only because one is cooking the water within the soup; it would not apply to gravy and liquid

18. See chapter 3, section C.
19. IX, p. 339.
20. Section B of this chapter.
21. *O.C.* 253:37.
22. P. 342 in fn. 21.
23. *Shabbat,* end of 39a.
24. P. 341.

fat. However, this suggestion is difficult: the water in soup has changed, and no longer reverts to its original state of cold water; it is more akin to gravy. Rather, the position of the *Tur* indicates, consistent with the *Magen Avraham*[25] but as opposed to the view of R. Elyashiv, that the prohibition of *bishul achar bishul* applies to all liquids by Torah law.

F. SUMMARY

The Rama states that it is permissible to reheat soup "that has not cooled down completely." According to the *Magen Avraham*, the Rama means that as long as the soup is fit to be eaten as hot food, it is still considered fully cooked even if the temperature has fallen below *yad soledet bo*. According to the *Eglei Tal*, however, the Rama means that the principle of *ein bishul achar bishul* can be applied to liquids that are partially cooked (*ma'achal ben derusa'i*), such as soup that is partially cooled off. According to the *Minchat Kohen*, the Rama applies *ein bishul achar bishul* to all liquids, but imposes a stringency: soup may be reheated only if it still retains some warmth. The *Mishnah Berurah*, *Chazon Ish* and *Iggerot Moshe* all adopt the *Minchat Kohen*'s approach, and thus *Iggerot Moshe* permits pouring hot tea on a few drops of cold tea. According to the *Tur* and *Magen Avraham*'s understanding of the Rama, however, it is prohibited by Torah law to heat up any cold liquid, because *ein bishul achar bishul* does not apply to liquids unless they are fully cooked (which is defined by the Rama not as "*yad soledet bo*," but as "edible due to their heat"). In light of our analysis of the primary sources, the stringent position of the *Magen Avraham* should be followed.

25. *O.C.* 253:37.

6

The Definition of Liquids

A. PRACTICAL CASES OF REHEATING LIQUIDS

R. Shalom Yosef Gelber and R. Yitzchak Mordechai Rubin, in their *Orchot Shabbat,*[1] accept the practical distinction between solids and liquids (attributed to the *Magen Avraham,* above, chapter 5, section E). Solids which are cooked and cooled are usually edible. Cold liquids such as chicken soup are not fit for consumption.

This definition is relevant in certain ambiguous cases. For example, the *Iggerot Moshe*[2] writes that since ketchup pours and requires a vessel to contain it, it is treated like liquid, and may not be placed in a *keli rishon* or its equivalent. However, *Orchot Shabbat* states that since it is fit for use when it is cold, it should be considered a solid, as R. Elyashiv and R. S.Z. Auerbach rule.

The *Magen Avraham*[3] permits reheating congealed gravy, even though it liquefies when it is heated. This is because at the point when it is placed near the fire it has a status of solid food. By contrast, the

1. P. 14.
2. *Orach Chaim* IV,:74:5.
3. *O.C.* 318:40.

Orchot Shabbat[4] prohibits reheating congealed or frozen chicken soup, considering it *bishul achar bishul* of a liquid, since in its congealed or frozen state it is totally inedible.

In explanation of the view of the *Magen Avraham,* it can be noted that while it seems that congealed gravy is also inedible, nonetheless, if one leaves it at room temperature, it will liquefy and become edible, at least by the *ma'achal ben derusa'i* criterion. This applies to frozen cooked meat as well. Although it is totally inedible, it can become edible by thawing at room temperature. Therefore, it may be reheated.

By contrast, frozen or congealed chicken soup is not edible unless it is reheated. It is the equivalent of a liquid, which is no longer edible when it cools off, and may not be reheated.

The *Orchot Shabbat* permits reheating meat with a significant amount of liquid on top of it, if the liquid is only a small minority of the total food being reheated. Here, too, the meat and the liquid are edible at room temperature. Even the more lenient view, that of the *Minchat Kohen,*[5] that as long as the liquid is a minority, even 49 percent, one may reheat it along with the majority of solid, can be explained this way.

The Rama[6] suggests that if the liquid stew deteriorates when it loses moisture, it may be reheated. Since the prohibition is the improvement of food which was unfit for consumption, the act could be permitted if it is not a complete improvement, such as where it includes deterioration as well.

B. REHEATING SOLIDS AND LIQUIDS BY POURING HOT WATER ON THEM

The *Magen Avraham*[7] discusses pouring hot water on greasy dishes. He does not prohibit it as a form of cooking. R. Akiva Eiger,[8] however, is of the position that pouring hot water on greasy dishes is worse than placing congealed gravy near a fire. When one puts gravy near a fire, he

4. P. 15.
5. 2:2; see *Peri Megadim, M.Z.* 253:13.
6. *O.C.* 318:4.
7. *O.C.* 253:41.
8. *O.C.* ibid.

is passive when the gravy liquefies. However, when one pours hot water onto greasy dishes, after the initial hot water liquefies the grease, he pours still more water onto the liquid. This may be a violation of cooking, as *bishul achar bishul* is prohibited for liquids. Despite the fact that it is not his intention (*eino mitkaven*) to cook the gravy, it is inevitable (*pesik reishei*).

The *Magen Avraham*'s position can be explained as follows. He maintains that *bishul achar bishul* for liquids is premised on the act being considered an improvement, making inedible food edible. The liquefied grease on dishes remains inedible and is discarded. This is not an improvement and is, therefore, permitted. This is not merely a situation of an inevitable but unwanted improvement (*pesik reishei delo neicha lei*);[9] in our case there is no improvement whatsoever.

The *Sha'arei Teshuvah*[10] permits pouring hot tea onto liquefied sugar, as the sugar has the status of a solid. Since it was fit to sweeten the food or drink even when it was cold, heating it is not considered a significant improvement.

The *Arukh HaShulchan*[11] prohibits pouring hot water onto tea or coffee, even if the leaves or grinds were cooked before *Shabbat*, because pouring the hot water is the cooking that makes it fit for consumption. Although it was fit when it was in a liquid state, and now it is a solid, we do not apply the principle of *ein bishul achar bishul*. Since in its current state it is inedible unless it is combined with hot water, there is *bishul achar bishul*, as with frozen soup.[12]

This stringency is not applied by the *poskim* to instant tea and coffee, since they are fit to flavor cold water. Instant tea is actually called ice tea, and many use instant coffee to make ice coffee. Therefore, it is comparable to sugar and is treated like other solids for which *ein bishul achar bishul* applies.

---

9. An inevitable prohibited result of a permissible action (*pesik reishei*) may prohibit the otherwise permissible action even if the result is unwanted (*lo neicha lei* [see O.C. 320:18]).
10. O.C. 318:9.
11. O.C. 318:28.
12. See above, section A.

C. SUMMARY

The *Orchot Shabbat* defines a solid as "something that is edible when cooled after cooking" and a liquid as "something not edible when cooled after cooking." Thus ketchup is a solid, and may be reheated, while chicken soup (even congealed) is a liquid and may not be reheated. Liquefied sugar, instant coffee and instant tea, all of which have been cooked and are fit for consumption even after being cooled even without adding hot water, may be heated by having hot water poured on them. However, coffee grounds and tea leaves, which are not fit for consumption without adding hot water, are not considered edible after being cooked and cooled, and may not be heated by pouring hot water over them.

7

Bringing Hot Water to a Boil

A. AT WHAT POINT IS WATER CONSIDERED "FULLY COOKED"?

The *Shevitat HaShabbat*[1] cites the *Beit Yosef*,[2] who allows the boiling of water which was hot (i.e., *yad soledet bo*), but not boiled before *Shabbat*. This is difficult to understand, as boiling completes the cooking process. Since the *Shulchan Arukh*,[3] authored by the *Beit Yosef*, follows the Rambam in allowing *bishul achar bishul* only if the food had been completely cooked, how can the same author allow the boiling of water which was only hot, i.e., *yad soledet bo*, but not boiled, before *Shabbat*?

We can answer the question based on the *Peri Megadim*, who suggests, as we have seen,[4] that water is fundamentally different from other foods. Heating water is its cooking. As such, once water reaches

---

1. *Petichah* to *Bishul*, 18.
2. *O.C.* 318: 4.
3. *O.C.* 318:4.
4. Chapter 1, section B.

yad soledet bo and is halakhically hot, it is considered fully "cooked," even though it has not yet boiled.

B. REQUIREMENT FOR WATER TO BE PREVIOUSLY BOILED

However, there may be another requirement. The *Shevitat HaShabbat* suggests that one may boil *yad soledet bo* water only if the water had been previously boiled. This is the apparent position of the *Magen Avraham,*[5] as elucidated by the *Machatzit HaShekel.*

To explain this view, we must assume that there are two issues to contend with concerning water. Heating, as mentioned, is defined by *yad soledet bo*. Cooking, however, is defined by what is considered fully cooked in any given time and place. Nowadays, as water is commonly boiled, it is not considered fully cooked until it reaches the boiling point.

Hence, if one boiled water which had only reached *yad soledet bo,* he is guilty of cooking. However, if the water had been boiled and then cooled to the point of *yad soledet bo,* we apply the principle of *ein bishul achar bishul.* Only if it is no longer hot is the water subject to "heating after heating" which is prohibited.

The *Iggerot Moshe*[6] rejects the view that only after boiling is liquid considered cooked. After all, the *Shulchan Arukh* prohibits *bishul achar bishul* for liquids, meaning that the definition of cooking for liquids is heating (as explained above in chapter 5, section D). Thus, water which had been boiled and cooled to *yad soledet bo* is identical to water which reached *yad soledet bo* only, and in either case it is permitted to boil it.

According to our analysis, this view, attributed to the *Magen Avraham,* can be defended as follows. The prohibition of *bishul achar bishul* for liquids is a misnomer. What is prohibited is heating after heating, as defined by *yad soledet bo*. Boiling *yad soledet bo* water for the first time is not *bishul achar bishul* at all. When water has reached *yad soledet bo,* it is still not yet cooked. Boiling such water is first time *bishul* to the point of completion which is prohibited, as the *Magen Avraham* rules.

---

5. *O.C.* 318:12.
6. *O.C.* VI,:74:1.

Nonetheless, the *Beit Yosef*[7] is lenient in this matter.[8] He repeats this leniency elsewhere,[9] as *Shevitat HaShabbat* (3) notes. Apparently, the sole definition of cooking water is heating according to the *Beit Yosef,* and *yad soledet bo* is the sole determinant.

C. KETTLES AND URNS

However, as we have seen,[10] the Rama allows reheating liquids which have cooled below the point of *yad soledet bo.* If so, liquids are not fundamentally different from solids. When it reaches the temperature of *yad soledet bo,* the liquid is only partially cooked. Boiling *yad soledet bo* liquid may be subject to a prohibition of completing cooking by boiling, as the *Magen Avraham* rules. Only if the liquid had been fully cooked, i.e., boiled, and maintains heat equivalent to *ma'achal ben derusa'i,* may it be reheated.

This is relevant to a kettle whose water has reached the point of *yad soledet bo* but had not reached a boiling point before *Shabbat.* According to the *Magen Avraham,* one may not raise it to a higher temperature on *Shabbat.* This may apply to urns, if the water in the tube which indicates how much water is in the urn is not as hot as the water in the urn itself. When water is taken out on *Shabbat,* a small amount of water from the tube enters the urn and is raised to a higher temperature. This may be prohibited according to the *Magen Avraham.*[11]

Interestingly, the *Responsa Az Nidberu*[12] permits the use of an urn, since the water in the tube reaches 50°C (122°F), which is *yad soledet bo. Iggerot Moshe,*[13] however, requires the water to be 160°F in order to be certain that *yad soledet bo* is reached. If so, an urn may not be used if, in fact, the water in the tube is only 122°F and gets hotter when it enters the urn on *Shabbat.*[14]

7. *O.C.* 318:4.
8. See section A of this chapter.
9. *O.C.* 258
10. Chapter 5, section A.
11. See chapter 5, section C.
12. IX, 14; see chapter 2, section D.
13. IV, 74, *bishul* 3
14. See *The 39 Melachos of Shabbos,* p. 665 and fn 380.

D. STIRRING

The *Mishnah Berurah*[15] cites the *Maggid Mishnah*[16] who rules that stirring food hastens the cooking process only until the food is fully cooked. The *Kol Bo* disagrees and states that stirring food directly on the fire is a Torah prohibition of cooking even if the food was fully cooked. The *Sha'ar HaTziyun* (#148) asks: How is stirring more strict than cooking proper, which does not apply to fully cooked foods?

Nonetheless, the *Mishnah Berurah* accepts the position of the *Kol Bo,* and extends it to scooping fully cooked food out of a pot which is on the fire. Therefore, the pot should be removed from the fire before the food is taken out.

If that pot is too heavy or if it is prohibited to return the pot onto the fire after it is removed (see chapter 17), the *Chazon Ish* (37:14) allows the food to be removed from the pot on the fire.

The *Shemirat Shabbat KeHilkhatah*[17] permits pouring boiling water slowly from a kettle onto a pot to prevent its contents from burning. Pouring slowly on a covered fire is not considered stirring.[18]

The *Shemirat Shabbat KeHilkhatah*[19] permits transferring water from an urn (which cannot be moved to be near the pot of food) to a cup, and then pouring it into a pot of food on a covered fire. This appears to be an unresolved question in the Talmud.[20] The *Magen Avraham*[21] rules strictly, whereas the *Sha'ar HaTziyun*[22] rules leniently. *The Shabbos Kitchen*[23] notes that urns do not boil the water. If boiling water which was previously *yad soledet bo* is prohibited,[24] it may not be placed in a pot where it might become boiled.

---

15. *O.C.* 318:118.
16. *Shabbat* 3:11.
17. 1:16.
18. Fn. 42.
19. Fn. 44.
20. *Shabbat* 38b.
21. *O.C.* 253:20.
22. Ibid., 47.
23. P. 68.
24. See above, section B.

E. SUMMARY

According to the *Iggerot Moshe,* it is permitted to boil water that has reached *yad soledet bo* before *Shabbat* because water is considered halakhically cooked when it reaches *yad soledet bo* even though boiling improves it further. This fits with the view of the *Shulchan Arukh,* which defines cooking a liquid as heating it. According to the *Shevitat HaShabbat,* however, it is permitted to boil water that has reached *yad soledet bo* before *Shabbat* only if the water had been previously boiled and then cooled to *yad soledet bo*. This fits with the *Rama*'s view that liquids are similar to solids and thus must be fully cooked (for water: boiled) before *Shabbat.* The *Magen Avraham* similarly prohibits boiling water that had only reached *yad soledet bo* prior to *Shabbat,* since by boiling one is completing the cooking of the liquid. Therefore, according to the *Magen Avraham,* one may not raise the temperature of a kettle which had not boiled before *Shabbat,* and it is similarly problematic to remove water from an urn, because the some of the water in the indicator tube will enter the urn and its temperature will rise. *Responsa Az Nidberu,* however, permits using an urn if the water in the indicator tube is *yad soledet bo* (whose threshold is defined as 122°F, as opposed to 160°F according to the *Iggerot Moshe*). However, according to the Rama, as understood by the *Magen Avraham* and *Shulchan Arukh HaRav,* this leniency is questionable.

Stirring or scooping out food while the pot is on the fire is considered cooking, even if the food is fully cooked, and thus the pot should be taken off the fire before food is stirred or scooped out. Boiling water may be poured from a kettle into a pot on the fire to keep the food from burning. The permissibility of pouring water from an urn into a cup and then into a pot of the fire is debated between the *Shemirat Shabbat KeHilkhatah,* who permits it, and those who prohibit based on the position that boiling water which had previously only reached *yad soledet bo* is prohibited.

8

Cooking after Baking

A. BACKGROUND: WHY IS IT PROHIBITED?

The Mordechai[1] cites the *Sefer Yere'im* who prohibits cooking after baking or roasting. He notes that this is evident from other areas of *halakhah,* in which an act of cooking is considered significant, even though the item had been previously baked or roasted: Cooking a *korban pesach,* even after it has been roasted, subjects it to the prohibition of eating a cooked *korban pesach.* Cooking a *matzah* cancels its status of baked *pat.*[2] So, too, cooking takes effect after baking or roasting with respect to *Shabbat.*

The Ra'avyah objects to the proof from cooked *matzah,* based on a statement of the Talmud.[3] Cooked *matzah* is disqualified, apparently, because of the need for the product to maintain the taste of *matzah.* Otherwise, it would be fit for use; indicating that, to the contrary, the baked status still exists.

To defend the *Yere'im,* the *Eglei Tal,*[4] citing *Tosafot* and the Rosh, reinterprets the requirement for the taste of *matzah.* In his

1. *Shabbat* 302.
2. *Pesachim* 41a.
3. *Berakhot* 38a.
4. *Ofeh* 15:2.

understanding, the rule means that cooking does cancel the previous baking and the new product is labeled *matzah ashirah,* thus unfit for the *mitzvah* of *matzah.* In other words, the disqualification is a technical one that indeed does stem from the second halakhic status overriding the first one, rather than a mere matter of taste.

The *Taz*[5] offers a different defense. The very fact that cooked *matzah* has a different taste makes cooking *matzah,* or bread, prohibited on *Shabbat.* The Torah prohibits specifically *melekhet machashevet,* an act of significant improvement, on *Shabbat.* Since cooking the bread is considered a significant improvement, it thus becomes a *Shabbat* violation.

B. CHANGING A FOOD'S HALAKHIC STATUS

A practical difference between the two approaches of the *Eglei Tal* and the *Taz* is toasting bread. According to the *Taz,* this act would be prohibited on *Shabbat,* since a new and improved taste takes effect. But the *Eglei Tal* prohibits only when there is a new and improved halakhic status, and toasting does not confer a new halakhic status on bread. Cooking, as a halakhic category, supersedes roasting, because it cooks the entire food, whereas roasting, on fire without liquid, only impacts on a finger's depth from the surface.[6] Because cooked food is submerged in a liquid, it exceeds baking as well. However, roasting in no way exceeds baking. Hence toasting bread, which is a form of roasting, is permissible.

The *Shiltei HaGibborim*[7] prohibits cooking after roasting, and permits roasting after cooking. This can be explained only according to the *Eglei Tal,* who focuses on halakhic categories, and not new and improved taste, which exists in both directions. Halakhically, cooking impacts more thoroughly than roasting, and is a more advanced category. Roasting, a lower category, is thus permissible after cooking. Baking, even though it does not involve submerging in liquid, is a more advanced halakhic category than cooking, since it creates the special halakhic state of bread.

5. *O.C.* 318:6.
6. *Yoreh De'ah* 105:4.
7. *Shabbat* 61b.

As such, *Eglei Tal*[8] prohibits baking after cooking even according to the view that cooking after baking is permissible.

The *Shulchan Arukh*[9] permits placing cooked dry food near a fire. The *Be'ur Halakhah* asks why this roasting after cooking isn't similar to cooking after baking, which the *Shulchan Arukh* prohibits.

Following the principle of the *Taz*, we can answer that no change in taste occurs when dry cooked food is reheated near a fire. It does not taste roasted. According to the view of the *Eglei Tal*, the *Shulchan Arukh* can be understood based on the *Shiltei HaGibborim* who permits roasting after cooking but not the reverse, since roasting is a lower category than cooking.

C. THREE STAGES: COOKING AFTER ROASTING AFTER COOKING

The *Be'ur Halakhah*[10] quotes the *Peri Megadim* who permits cooking after roasting after cooking. The *Be'ur Halakhah* cites the statement of the Talmud,[11] that one who eats a *korban pesach* that was cooked and then roasted is guilty of eating a cooked *korban pesach*. This proves that the first process is halakhically extant after a second, different one, at first glance supporting the *Peri Megadim*'s view. However, concludes the *Be'ur Halakhah*, since the second process, roasting, is certainly extant, it is still prohibited to do cooking after roasting.

The *Be'ur Halakhah*'s conclusion, that the existence of the food's roasted status prohibits it from being cooked, can be disputed. Since the first status, cooking, still exists, no new halakhic status takes effect, and according to the *Eglei Tal*, it should be permissible. However, according to the *Taz*, who prohibits any new and improved taste, it is prohibited when the taste changes from roasted taste to the original cooked taste, as the *Be'ur Halakhah* rules.

The *Be'ur Halakhah*[12] does not accept the leniency of the *Taz* that

8. *Ofeh* 15:15.
9. O.C. 318:15.
10. O.C. 318:5.
11. *Pesachim* 41a.
12. O.C. 318:15; see chapter 7, section B.

reheating a cooked item is permitted since the taste does not change. In explanation of his position, it is possible to suggest that the *Be'ur Halakhah* accepts the stringencies of both views, prohibiting reheating cooked food based on the *Eglei Tal*, and prohibiting cooking after roasting after cooking based on the *Taz*.

The *Orchot Shabbat*[13] discusses powders which were cooked and subsequently dried. Perhaps one should assume that the drying is like roasting, and thus the powders may not be placed in hot water, if cooking after roasting after cooking is prohibited, as the *Be'ur Halakhah* believes based on the *Taz*. Alternatively, it is possible that drying does not confer upon the powder a status of "roasted," and thus the original status of "cooked" remains.

According to our analysis, it is permissible to place these powders into hot water. The *Taz*'s prohibition does not apply, since drying, unlike roasting, does not change the taste. The *Eglei Tal*'s reasoning also does not apply. Since the original status of cooking remains, it is permissible to cook it again even after it was halakhically roasted in the interim.

D. SUMMARY

There is a dispute between the *Taz* and *Eglei Tal* as to why it is prohibited to cook after baking. According to the *Taz* cooking after baking is prohibited because it confers a new taste on the food. According to the *Eglei Tal* cooking after baking is prohibited because it confers a new halakhic status on the food. Toasting after baking, which confers a new taste but not a new halakhic status, would be permitted according to the *Taz* but prohibited according to the *Eglei Tal*. Reheating dry cooked food next to a fire ("roasting") would be permissible, as the *Shulchan Arukh* rules, both according to the *Taz*, because the taste does not change, and the *Eglei Tal*, because the food's halakhic status is not raised. The *Be'ur Halakhah* questions this ruling, apparently holding that any change in halakhic status is prohibited. Cooking after roasting after cooking is permitted (as the *Peri Megadim* holds), according to the *Eglei Tal*, since the food's original halakhic status is extant and no new halakhic status is conferred. However, cooking after roasting after cooking is forbidden

13. Ch. 1, fn. 65.

(as the *Be'ur Halakhah* holds), according to the *Taz,* since the taste of the food changes. The *Be'ur Halakhah,* however, also prohibits reheating dry cooked food. It is permitted to place powders that were cooked and then dried into hot water, since the drying does not change the original cooked taste (as the *Taz* prohibits) nor does the drying eliminate the powder's first halakhic status as "cooked" (as the *Eglei Tal* prohibits).

9

Cooking with Solar Heat

A. *IGGEROT MOSHE*: DEFINING THE "NORMAL WAY TO COOK"

The Talmud[1] permits cooking with solar heat on *Shabbat.* Rashi explains why this is permitted by noting that solar heat is not the normal way of cooking. This implies that if cooking with solar heat were to become the normal way of cooking, such cooking would be a Torah prohibition on *Shabbat.* The *Iggerot Moshe* applies this idea to a microwave oven, which contains no fire. He writes,[2] in a responsum written in 1971, that microwaves can cook as well as regular ovens, that those who own them cook in them more than in ovens which have a fire, and that when microwaves become more widespread everyone will cook with them, since microwaves cook better than regular ovens. When this happens, he writes, cooking in microwave ovens on *Shabbat* will be a Torah violation (as a *toladah*). These facts and predictions are questionable, but the principle – when a method of cooking becomes normalized, that method becomes prohibited by Torah law – is clear.

1. *Shabbat* 39a.
2. *Orach Chaim* III,52.

B. DEFINING "USE OF A HALAKHIC FIRE": QUESTION ON THE *IGGEROT MOSHE*

While cooking by solar heat is permitted by the Talmud, cooking with a derivative of solar heat is a topic of debate. The Talmud prohibits cooking by the heat of hot springs, such as there are in Teverya. *Rabbanan* maintain that the prohibition of cooking by hot springs indicates that cooking by the heat of water which is heated by the sun, or by any derivative (*toladah*) of solar heat, is prohibited. R. Yosi, who permits cooking by derivatives of solar heat, rebuts the proof by denying that the springs are heated by the sun, asserting instead that hot springs are heated by passing near "the entrance of *gehinom*," which presumably is a reference to geothermic heat from the earth's core.

Most likely, this debate does not revolve around the factual question of the origin of the springs' heat. We generally assume that our *chakhamim* did not argue about realia which can be readily determined. Rather, they more likely debate the halakhic status of geothermic heat: R. Yosi deems it fire, like any other fire on earth. *Rabbanan* compare it to the sun, since geothermic heat is not a man-made fire but part of nature itself, like the sun which is itself a great ball of fire.

The Talmudic debate over the origins of the springs' heat indicates that there is an objective definition of fire. If the question of whether cooking in hot springs is permissible is merely a matter of what is the normal manner of cooking, it should be irrelevant whether the hot springs are heated by halakhic fire. Rather, the question would only be: is cooking in hot springs the normal way of cooking? If so, cooking in hot springs is *bishul*; and if not, cooking in hot springs is not *bishul*. Indeed, the *Iggerot Moshe* initially suggests, based on the debate between R. Yosi and *Rabbanan,* that to be in violation of cooking, one must cook with a halakhic fire, even it is normal to cook without a fire. Since in the *Mishkan* they cooked with fire, if one cooks without a fire it is not a *melakhah,* even if everyone cooks that way, such as cooking in a microwave.

C. DEFINING THE "NORMAL WAY TO COOK": DEFENSE OF *IGGEROT MOSHE*

How, then, can the view that cooking in a microwave on *Shabbat* is a Torah prohibition be justified? We can suggest that the debate between

R. Yosi and *Rabbanan* be understood as follows: Cooking in the water of hot springs is not the normal way of cooking. Nonetheless, it is prohibited on a rabbinic level. This rabbinic prohibition can be understood in one of two ways.

As a general rule, a *melakhah* done in an abnormal way is rabbinically prohibited. According to R. Yosi, who considers cooking with hot springs to be cooking on fire, it is the abnormal nature of the cooking that downgrades cooking on hot springs to a rabbinic prohibition. (This is not necessarily consistent with the understanding of the *Iggerot Moshe.*)

According to *Rabbanan,* the rabbinic prohibition is for a different reason. They prohibit cooking with a derivative of solar heat, as a safeguard, lest one cook with a derivative of the heat of a fire. Were it not for this concern, cooking with a derivative of solar heat would be permissible, because solar heat is a separate category. In most cases, it cannot achieve the minimal level of cooking (*ma'achal ben derusa'i* or *yad soledet bo*). Therefore, the *halakhah* declares a general permissive ruling, since in the worst case scenario, when cooking transpires, it would only be a rabbinic prohibition. (This reasoning may be relevant for a *keli sheni,* a vessel which was never on the fire, as we shall see.)[3]

Based on this understanding, it emerges that the entire discussion in the Talmud concerning the hot springs deals with an abnormal case. The halakhic dispute is whether a rabbinic prohibition exists, as with abnormal usage of fire (as R. Yosi maintains), or not, as with solar heat (as *Rabbanan* maintain). There is no source from the Talmud addressing a normal case of cooking without fire. Therefore, it is possible to maintain, as *Iggerot Moshe* concludes, that a Torah violation exists even in the absence of fire.

D. *MINCHAT SHELOMOH*: COOKING DEFINED AS USE OF HALAKHIC FIRE

The *Minchat Shelomoh*[4] attempts to prove that cooking in the sun is an independent exemption, and is not based on its being abnormal. If dough is processed in the sun, there is no obligation to take *challah* from it, and

3. Chap. 12, section A.
4. *Responsa* I,12.

dough processed in the sun does not qualify for *matzah*.[5] This is unrelated to whether it is the normal way of baking. However, this proof can be refuted. Perhaps bread specifically requires an oven, as Rashi explains based on the verse, "your bread in one oven."[6] Even a pan, which uses fire, may be excluded for the purposes of *challah* and *matzah*, since it is not an oven. If so, there is no proof from this Talmudic passage that cooking requires a fire, only that baking bread does.

The *Minchat Shelomoh* further attempts to prove that cooking in the sun is an independent exemption, and is not based on its being abnormal, from *korban pesach*. Roasting in the sun disqualifies the *korban pesach*.[7] This, too, cannot be attributed to its being abnormal. However, this proof is also not conclusive. The Torah states explicitly[8] that the *korban pesach* must be roasted in fire. Accordingly, it may be a unique exception; perhaps in other areas cooking in the sun is considered cooking.

The best source for the exclusion of cooking without a fire from the prohibition of cooking is the full phrase in the very *pasuk* brought by the *Minchat Shelomoh* which reads "[don't eat it] cooked in water, but only roasted in fire."[9] This implies that cooking in water refers to water heated by fire, and that the only difference between roasting and cooking is the water. Both, indeed, require fire.

E. SUMMARY

Cooking without fire, such as by solar heat, is permitted by the Talmud. If a method of cooking which does not utilize fire, such as a microwave, becomes a normal method of cooking, it becomes prohibited by Torah law according to the *Iggerot Moshe*, since the *Iggerot Moshe* defines the *melakhah* of cooking as "cooking in the normal way." It is possible, however, that the *melakhah* of cooking is defined by "use of a halakhic fire" as the debate between *Rabbanan* and R. Yosi about cooking in hot springs seems to suggest. Nevertheless, the debate can be explained as

5. *Pesachim* 37a.
6. *Vayikra* 26:26.
7. *Pesachim* 41a.
8. *Shemot* 12:9.
9. *Shemot* 12:9.

a discussion of an abnormal case, and thus has no bearing on the issue of normal cooking without fire. The *Minchat Shelomoh,* disagreeing with the *Iggerot Moshe,* attempts to prove that that the *melakhah* of cooking is defined by "use of a halakhic fire." The *Minchat Shelomoh*'s proofs are not conclusive, but *Shemot* 12:9 seems to indicate that, indeed, there is no halakhic cooking without a fire.

10

Solids in a *Keli Sheni*

A. DEFINITIONS OF *KELI RISHON* AND *KELI SHENI*

The Talmud[1] states unequivocally that a *keli sheni* (lit., a second vessel) does not cook. Rashi refers to the *mishnah*[2] that prohibits placing spices in a pot, even after the pot is removed from the fire, as the pot is still considered a *keli rishon* (lit., a first vessel), a vessel which is or was on the fire. However, spices may be placed in a bowl into which the contents of a *keli rishon* were placed, but which was never itself on the fire. This bowl is called a *keli sheni*. The permissibility of putting spices into a *keli sheni* proves that a *keli sheni* does not cook.

B. POURING FROM A *KELI SHENI* VS. PLACING FOOD INTO A *KELI SHENI*

Tosafot[3] cites a dispute regarding the status of a liquid poured from a *keli rishon* into a *keli sheni* that already contains some food. The prevailing view, as quoted in *Shulchan Arukh*,[4] is that pouring from a *keli rishon*

1. *Shabbat* 40b.
2. *Shabbat* 42a-42b.
3. *Shabbat* 42b, s.v. *aval notein hu.*
4. *O.C.* 318:10.

achieves at least partial cooking of the food onto which it is poured and is thus prohibited.

The *mishnah*[5] permits pouring hot water onto uncooked food. This seems to contradict the aforementioned view of *Tosafot*[6] which disallows such pouring. *Tosafot*[7] suggests that the *mishnah* permits pouring only from a *keli sheni*. This implies that the *mishnah* means that only *pouring* from a *keli sheni* is permitted, and that one may not actually place food into a *keli sheni*. Although placing food in a *keli sheni* does not cook, it has an appearance of cooking. Placing food into a *keli sheni* is permitted only for spices[8] which flavor the food in the pot, and which does not appear like cooking. The *Or Zaru'a*[9] explains that putting spices into a *keli sheni* does not appear like cooking because spices are placed in cold liquids as well. Therefore, placing them in a hot *keli sheni* looks like flavoring, not cooking. For other foods, although a *keli sheni* does not cook and no Torah violation occurs, it is prohibited rabbinically, because it appears like cooking.

The *Tosafot* offer a second suggestion. The *mishnah* permitting pouring hot water onto uncooked food nevertheless prohibits pouring hot water on certain fish products. Since the fish products are thin and soft,[10] even pouring from a *keli sheni* achieves cooking. The *mishnah* permits pouring onto other foods from a *keli sheni* to teach that even pouring from a *keli sheni* is prohibited for thin and soft foods that are easily cooked. The *mishnah* thus does not contrast pouring from a *keli sheni* with placing food into a *keli sheni*. It is not concerned with the appearance of cooking. Rather, the *mishnah* contrasts pouring from a *keli sheni* onto easily cooked foods (prohibited) and pouring from a *keli sheni* onto foods not easily cooked (permitted). Nothing can be inferred from the *mishnah* regarding placing foods in a *keli sheni*, and in reality, even placing other foods into a *keli sheni* is permissible since a *keli sheni* does not cook.

---

5. *Shabbat* 145b.
6. *Shabbat* 42b.
7. *Shabbat* 39a s.v. *kli sheba.*
8. *Shabbat* 42a-42b.
9. *Hilkhot Erev Shabbat* 8.
10. Rambam, *Hilkhot Shabbat* 9:2.

C. PLACING BREAD, SALT AND GROUND SPICES INTO A *KELI SHENI*

The Mordechai[11] cites a Talmudic opinion[12] that salt differs from other spices. Salt can be cooked in a *keli sheni,* and thus may not be placed in one. On this basis, the Mordechai prohibits placing bread into hot liquids, even into a *keli sheni,* since baking after cooking is prohibited.[13] The example of salt shows that some things can be cooked in a *keli sheni,* and bread is analogous to salt. The Mordechai's prohibition of placing bread in a *keli sheni* is a controversial position.[14]

Remarkably, the *Shulchan Arukh*[15] prohibits *keli sheni* only regarding bread, even though some permit placing bread even in a *keli rishon* . The *Magen Avraham,*[16] however, sharply limits the placing of food into a *keli sheni,* since some items can be cooked in a *keli sheni,* such as salt,[17] and we are not expert enough to know what else can be cooked in a *keli sheni.* We must therefore be strict for other foods as well.

Despite this statement that it is necessary to be strict for other foods in a *keli sheni,* the *Magen Avraham*[18] notes that the *Shulchan Arukh* disagrees and permits placing all foods into a *keli sheni* except for bread. The *Shulchan Arukh* adopts the second answer of *Tosafot,* which denies the concept of the appearance of cooking in a *keli sheni.* In addition, the *Shulchan Arukh* limits the concern that other foods can be cooked in a *keli sheni* to bread, which is soft.[19]

As mentioned, the *Magen Avraham* and the Mordechai compare bread to salt. Perhaps the Talmud's excepting of salt from other spices and prohibiting salt in a *keli sheni* refers to ground salt, in contrast to "other spices" which refer to large pieces and are permitted in a *keli sheni.* Fish, onto which even pouring from a *keli sheni* is prohibited, is both thin

11. *Shabbat* 302; see above chapter 8, section A.
12. *Shabbat* 42b.
13. See chapter 8.
14. See chapter 8, section A.
15. *O.C.* 318:5.
16. *O.C.* 318:18.
17. Rama, *O.C.* 318:9.
18. *O.C.* 318:19.
19. See *Machatzit HaShekel.*

and soft, so it is easily cooked. Salt, which is thin and hard, is a matter of dispute because it possesses only one of the characteristics of soft, thin fish. Bread, which is soft and large, also possesses only one of the two characteristics of soft, thin fish. Therefore, like salt, bread should not be placed into a *keli sheni.*

In sum, the *Shulchan Arukh* permits placing foods into a *keli sheni.* He does not prohibit an appearance of cooking. He limits the concern that foods, other than thin and soft fish, be cooked in a *keli sheni* to soft bread. The Rama is stringent for salt, presumably because it is thin.

In contemporary times, many spices are granulated. R. S.Z. Auerbach prohibits placing them into a *keli sheni.*[20] Others object, since even in Talmudic times spices were ground thin, and yet the Talmud seems to permit placing all spices into a *keli sheni.*[21] It is possible that R. S.Z. Auerbach views salt as a paradigm for all ground spices.

The *Magen Avraham* disagrees with the *Shulchan Arukh* and prohibits *keli sheni* for all foods, since it appears like cooking, as the first answer of *Tosafot* maintains. In addition, the *Mishnah Berurah*[22] understands the *Magen Avraham* as prohibiting *keli sheni* for all foods, since "we are not expert" and we are concerned that all foods can be cooked in a *keli sheni.* The only exceptions are water and oil.[23]

D. SUMMARY

The Talmud states that a *keli sheni* does not cook. Nevertheless, according to *Tosafot*'s first interpretation of the *mishnah* on *Shabbat* 145b, it is rabbinically forbidden to place any food except spices into a *keli sheni,* since placing food in a *keli sheni* appears like cooking. According to *Tosafot*'s second interpretation of the *mishnah,* however, spices are an example, not an exception, and any food may be placed in a *keli sheni.* The *Shulchan Arukh* accepts the *Tosafot*'s second interpretation, and prohibits only bread from being placed in a *keli sheni.* The Rama prohibits salt in a *keli sheni,* and R. S.Z. Auerbach prohibits all ground spices, though

20. *Shemirat Shabbat KeHilkhatah* 1 fn. 152.
21. See *Orchot Shabbat,* I:93
22. *O.C.* 318:42.
23. See *Sha'ar HaTziyun* 67,68.

others dispute the prohibition. The *Magen Avraham,* however, prohibits all foods in a *keli sheni,* both because placing food in a *keli sheni* appears like cooking (*Magen Avraham* accepts the *Tosafot*'s first interpretation), as well as because "we are not expert" about which foods can be cooked in a *keli sheni,* and this is the Ashkenazic practice.

11

Liquids in a *Keli Sheni*

A. UNCOOKED LIQUIDS

The *Mishnah Berurah*[1] permits placing liquids which were hot and cooled off into a *keli sheni.* Presumably, since the reheating of liquids and the prohibition of *keli sheni* are both mere stringencies, we are not required to combine them. (According to our analysis that, contrary to *Mishnah Berurah,*[2] reheating liquids may be a Torah violation,[3] this leniency is somewhat questionable.) *Shemirat Shabbat KeHilkhatah*[4] infers from the *Mishnah Berurah*'s permitting cooled off liquids in a *keli sheni* that uncooked liquids may not be placed in a *keli sheni.* The only exceptions are water and oil, which are explicitly permitted by the Talmud.

The *Shulchan Arukh HaRav*[5] equates other liquids to water and oil, and thus permits their placement in a *keli sheni.* The *Shemirat Shabbat KeHilkhatah* proves the validity of the *Shulchan Arukh HaRav*'s view

1. *O.C.* 318:23,39.
2. *O.C.* 318:99
3. See chapter 5.
4. Ch. 1 fn. 151.
5. *O.C.* 318:12.

from the ruling of the *Shulchan Arukh*[6] that permits placing a bottle of water or other liquids into a *keli sheni* filled with hot water.

This proof, however, is questionable. The *Mishnah Berurah* and *Shulchan Arukh HaRav* both accept the stringent view of the *Magen Avraham* that no foods may be placed in a *keli sheni*; they argue as to whether the exception of water and oil extends to other liquids. (According to the *Shulchan Arukh HaRav* it does; according to the *Mishnah Berurah* it does not.) However, the *Shulchan Arukh* rejects the stringencies adopted by the *Magen Avraham*, and allows *keli sheni* for everything but bread. Obviously, the *Shulkhan Arukh* allows other liquids. *The Shulkhan Arukh*'s permitting a bottle of other liquids in a *keli sheni* proves nothing about the *Magen Avraham*'s view in this matter and thus cannot be brought as a proof for the position of the *Shulkhan Arukh HaRav*, who follows the *Magen Avraham*.

B. LIQUIDS IN A JUG

The *Shemirat Shabbat KeHilkhatah*[7] notes that the source that oil may be placed in a *keli sheni* is the statement in the Talmud which deals with oil in a jug.[8] Perhaps it is prohibited to place the oil directly into hot water in a *keli sheni*, which may call for a more stringent approach than placing it in a jug.

In fact, the Maharsha[9] permits placing oil in a *keli sheni* only in a jug. Placing liquids directly into a *keli sheni*, by contrast, looks like cooking. The *Shemirat Shabbat KeHilkhatah* cites the *Sha'ar HaTziyun*[10] who permits placing water and oil directly into a *keli sheni*. Since in the Talmudic prooftext[11] regarding oil the oil was placed in a jug, and the *Sha'ar HaTziyun* does not require a jug, he must equate direct placing with placing in a jug.

6. *O.C.* 318:13.
7. Ibid., fn. 151.
8. *Shabbat* 40b.
9. *Shabbat* 39a.
10. *O.C.* 318:68.
11. *Shabbat* 40b.

However, the *Mishnah Berurah* prohibits placing uncooked liquids into a *keli sheni,*[12] but does not dispute the *Shulchan Arukh*[13] that permits the placing of other liquids in a jug into a *keli sheni.* Apparently, in contrast to the *Shemirat Shabbat KeHilkhatah,* he accepts the Maharsha's distinction between placing liquids in a jug and placing liquid directly. The *Orchot Shabbat*[14] explains that cooking in a *keli rishon* generally takes place without any container holding the item being cooked, and thus only such a placement into a *keli sheni* looks like cooking.

The *Mishnah Berurah*[15] rules that water may be placed directly into a *keli sheni,* as the *Shulchan Arukh*[16] states. Earlier,[17] he permits placing water and oil into a *keli sheni,* "as mentioned later in *siman* 318." While water is found in that source, oil is not mentioned.[18]

Apparently, oil is the source for 318:13, which allows other liquids in a jug in a *keli sheni,* but does not allow other liquids directly, as the *Mishnah Berurah* rules.[19] The brief statement in the *Sha'ar HaTziyun,* allowing water and oil in a *keli sheni,* must be parsed. Water may be placed directly into a *keli sheni,* based on the Talmud's statement.[20] Oil, and other liquids, may be placed only in a jug in a *keli sheni,* as the Talmud[21] and the Maharsha state. This understanding, in contrast to the *Shemirat Shabbat KeHilkhatah,*[22] is found in R. Simcha Bunim Cohen's *The Shabbos Kitchen.*[23]

The view of the *Shulchan Arukh HaRav,* that all liquids may be placed in a *keli sheni,* can be explained based on the *Peri Megadim.*[24]

---

12. See Section A of this chapter.
13. *O.C.* 318:13.
14. Ch. 1 fn. 130.
15. *O.C.* 318:86.
16. *O.C.* 318:12.
17. *Sha'ar HaTziyun,* ibid., 68.
18. The *Oz VeHadar* edition understands this as a self-reference to *Be'ur Halakhah* (318:10, s.v. *asur*). This seems unlikely.
19. *O.C.* 318:23,39;see section A of this chapter.
20. *Shabbat* 42a.
21. *Shabbat* 40b.
22. Ibid., fn. 151.
23. Chapter 2 fn. 21.
24. *Eishel Avraham* 318:32.

Water may be poured into a hot *keli sheni*. This does not look like cooking, since the poured water does not stand by itself, but rather mixes with the water in the *keli sheni*. This logic clearly applies to all liquids.

C. COFFEE, TEA AND MILK IN A *KELI SHENI*

The *Iggerot Moshe*[25] views coffee and tea as spices, which may be placed into a *keli sheni*. By contrast, the *Mishnah Berurah*[26] prohibits tea in a *keli sheni*. R. Shimon Eider, in his *Hilchos Shabbos*[27] explains the *Mishnah Berurah*'s position as follows:

Coffee is prohibited in a *keli sheni* because it is the main ingredient in the cup. Apparently, the *Mishnah Berurah* understands that *Tosafot*,[28] who permit spices which flavor the contents, perceives spices as different from the primary ingredient. The primary ingredient is what appears to be cooking. Spices, which are secondary ingredients, are not as noticeable. Therefore, spices may be placed in a *keli sheni* in which other foods are warmed, but not into a *keli sheni* which only has water, as in making coffee and tea.

However, it is possible to view tea and coffee as spices. As mentioned,[29] the *Or Zaru'a* explains that since spices often flavor cold liquids, placing them into a hot *keli sheni* does not look like cooking. One does not intend to cook the spice, but rather to flavor the liquid. The best proof that in preparing coffee or tea one intends to flavor the liquid, rather than cook the coffee or tea, is from the tea bag, which is thrown out. This explanation supports the view of the *Iggerot Moshe* that coffee and tea are spices and thus permitted in a *keli sheni*.[30]

The *Mishnah Berurah* may hold that since, after all, one who places coffee or tea into water intends to have the coffee or tea heated, the act looks like cooking. Perhaps the *Mishnah Berurah* would concede that one may place cold milk into a *keli sheni* containing hot coffee, as by

25. *Orach Chaim* IV, 74:18.
26. *O.C.* 318:39.
27. Fn. 55.
28. 39a; see chapter 10, section B.
29. Chapter 10, section B.
30. See chapter 12, section B, below, for further discussion about the permissibility of making tea on *Shabbat*.

placing milk one wishes to cool down the coffee rather than heat up the milk. The milk may be treated as a spice which flavors the coffee, as well.

D. SUMMARY

The *Shulchan Arukh HaRav* allows all liquids (but, like the *Magen Avraham,* no foods) to be placed in a *keli sheni* directly, since, like water, all liquids mix with the original liquid in the *keli sheni* and there is no appearance of cooking. The *Mishnah Berurah,* however, accepts the opinion of the Maharsha that only water may be placed directly into a *keli sheni.* Other liquids may only be placed only in a jug, since otherwise it looks like cooking. The *Iggerot Moshe* permits coffee and tea in a *keli sheni,* since they are spices. The *Mishnah Berurah* prohibits coffee and tea in a *keli sheni* because they are the main ingredient in the cup, which gives the appearance of cooking. The *Mishnah Berurah,* however, may permit placing milk in a cup of hot coffee, since one does not intend to cook the milk, but rather to cool off or flavor the coffee.

12

Water in a *Keli Sheni*

A. HEATING WATER TO *YAD SOLEDET BO* IN A *KELI SHENI*

Until now, we have discussed the rabbinic question of the appearance of cooking for water and liquids in a *keli sheni*. A much more fundamental question concerns cooking proper. If, as was discussed earlier,[1] the definition of cooking water is heating to the point of *yad soledet bo*, why may water be placed in a *keli sheni* even if the water will reach *yad soledet bo*, as the Talmud implies and the *Mishnah Berurah*[2] states?

The *Tosafot*[3] answer that since the *keli sheni* was never on the fire, the walls of the *keli sheni* are not hot, and the heat dissipates. Nonetheless, if the water poured into the *keli sheni* reaches *yad soledet bo*, which is the halakhic cooking point for water, why should it matter if the walls of the *keli sheni* are not hot and the heat dissipates?

The Rashba[4] answers that the combined waters are *yad soledet bo* not because the cold water reached *yad soledet bo*, but rather because

---

1. Chapter 3, sections B and C.
2. *O.C.* 318:81.
3. *Shabbat* 40b, s.v. *u'shma minah*.
4. *Shabbat* 42a.

the original water did not cool off. This statement is very perplexing. Since liquids become fully mixed, the cold water clearly does reach *yad soledet bo* and thus becomes cooked. Further, the *Shevitat HaShabbat*[5] cites the *Shulchan Arukh,*[6] which permits placing a jug of water into a hot *keli sheni.* Here the waters do not mingle, and the cold water in the jug still reaches *yad soledet bo.*[7] Why is putting cold water into a *keli sheni,* where the cold water will reach *yad soledet bo,* not considered cooking?

Hilchos Shabbos[8] answers that since the walls of a *keli sheni* cool off, so that usually the *keli sheni* cannot cook, even when the *keli sheni* does cook, it is not "the way of cooking." Thus, there is no possibility of a Torah violation. The Rabbis did not impose a rabbinic prohibition, since in most cases putting water in a *keli sheni* doesn't effect cooking anyway. This resembles our earlier explanation of cooking in the sun.[9]

Perhaps the Rashba can be explained by applying the concept of "not the normal way to cook" as well. The Rashba's expression "not because the cold water reached *yad soledet bo*" is not a physical description of the heat of the added water. Rather, it is a statement of the person's goal in adding cold water to the *keli sheni.* Normally, when cold water is added to hot water in a *keli sheni,* the goal is to yield a mixture which is not *yad soledet bo.* The phrase "because the original water did not cool off" means that, in this case, the goal was not reached, and the combination is *yad soledet bo.* Since this is not a normal way of cooking, there is no Torah prohibition. And, since usually there is no cooking, because the goal of reaching a temperature beneath *yad soledet bo* is usually achieved, no rabbinic prohibition was imposed, just like cooking in the sun.

The reason the goal is a mixture beneath *yad soledet bo* is simple. The Rashba[10] holds that a typical person does not drink liquids which are *yad soledet bo.* Therefore, it is normal to have a mixture which is beneath *yad soledet bo.* If, in a given case, the mixture is *yad soledet bo,* it

5. *Ofeh* 91.
6. *O.C.* 318:13.
7. *Mishnah Berurah* 318: 81.
8. Fn. 459.
9. Chapter 9, section C.
10. *Shabbat* 42a.

is not the way of cooking. Therefore, it is permitted by Torah law, and, as we have explained, even rabbinically.

B. PROHIBITION OF COOKING FOODS THAT ARE NORMALLY COOKED IN A *KELI SHENI* OR *KELI SHELISHI*

Based on this analysis, if a food is normally cooked in a *keli sheni*, it may be prohibited by Torah law to do so. This is why we are stringent regarding bread.[11] It is not normally cooked in a *keli rishon*. Therefore, cooking it in a *keli sheni* is the normal way. If, in fact, cooking takes place, it is a Torah prohibition.

If so, tea in a *keli sheni* may be a Torah prohibition, since, in the modern era, it is very normal to cook tea in a *keli sheni*. Actually, it is normal even in a *keli shelishi*, when water is transferred from a kettle to a pitcher to a cup.

Indeed, *Sefer Yere'im*, the source of the Mordechai,[12] prohibits placing bread even in a *keli shelishi*. Based on our analysis, that cooking depends on whether the method is normal, tea may also not be placed in a *keli shelishi*. The *Yere'im* declares that we are not expert in defining soft and hard foods. We do not know which can be cooked in a *keli sheni* or *shelishi*, and which cannot. Therefore, no food should be placed in either *keli sheni* or *keli shelishi*.

The *Sefer Yere'im* is the source for the *Magen Avraham* who prohibits *keli sheni* for all foods. The leniency for *keli shelishi*[13] is based on the Mordechai's partial citation of the *Yere'im*. The Mordechai quotes only the *Yere'im*'s prohibition to put bread in a *keli sheni*, but does not quote the prohibition to put bread in a *keli shelishi*. According to our analysis, the leniency for a *keli shelishi* should not be relied upon, unless it is clear that it is not normal to cook this food in a *keli shelishi*.

The Rashba[14] prohibits placing cold water into a bathtub even if the bathtub is a *keli sheni*. He explains that this is different than a regular *keli sheni*, because it is normal to heat bath water more than necessary.

---

11. See chapter 10, section C.
12. See above, chapter 8, section A.
13. See *Mishnah Berurah O.C.* 318:45.
14. *Shabbat* 42a.

This phrase means that although people do not actually bathe in water that is *yad soledet bo,* it is normal to heat bath water to a higher temperature than *yad soledet bo,* and then have it cool off before bathing in it.

The words "because it is normal (*darkah*)" prove that "normally" is the Rashba's criterion for defining cooking. We must, therefore, understand his statement about water in a *keli sheni* cup cited above in the same light. As we explained, the phrase "not because the cold water reached *yad soledet bo*" means that it is not normal for the mixture of water in a *keli sheni* to reach *yad soledet bo*. Therefore, if it happened to reach *yad soledet bo,* no Torah violation exists, and since it is rare for the combined waters to reach *yad soledet bo,* the Rabbis did not prohibit pouring cold water into a *keli sheni.*

C. SUMMARY

It is permitted, even rabbinically, to pour cold water into a *keli sheni,* even if the cold water reaches *yad soledet bo,* because it is not the normal way of cooking. If, however, it is normal to cook an item in a *keli sheni,* such as bread or tea, it is a Torah prohibition to put that item into a *keli sheni.* If it is normal to cook in a *keli shelishi,* as with tea, that is a Torah prohibition as well.

13

Pouring

A. THREE OPINIONS ABOUT POURING HOT ONTO COLD

Tosafot[1] mention three opinions about pouring hot onto cold. The Rashbam says that this action is considered like *keli sheni*, and does not cook. The Ri says that it is considered like *keli rishon* and cooks the entire cold food. *Tosafot* conclude, based on a statement in the Talmud,[2] that the bottom food overpowers the top. Therefore, the hot water does not cook the entire cold food on the bottom. However, as the bottom cools the top, the bottom's upper peel absorbs the heat of the top. In a case of pouring hot non-kosher liquid onto kosher food, the upper peel of the kosher food is rendered non-kosher. By the same token, regarding a case of pouring hot liquid over cold food on *Shabbat*, the upper peel of the bottom food is cooked by the hot water poured over it. As a result, pouring from a *keli rishon* on *Shabbat* onto cold food is prohibited.

The Rama[3] rules that, for *kashrut* purposes, pouring affects only a thin peel, as *Tosafot* concludes. The *Shemirat Shabbat KeHilkhatah*[4]

1. *Shabbat* 42b, s.v *aval notein hu.*
2. *Pesachim* 76a.
3. *Yoreh De'ah* 92:7.
4. 1 fn. 139.

extends this ruling to the laws of *Shabbat*. He thus allows pouring hot water over a bottle which contains cold liquids. The bottle is like a peel, and the liquid inside is unaffected by the hot water.

This extension is questionable. The Rama may be lenient only post facto (*bedi'eved*). Under optimal circumstances, (*lekhatchilah*) we should be stringent and follow the Ri, who rules that pouring can cook the entire food, especially regarding *Shabbat*, a more serious potential violation than *kashrut*.

Tosafot rule that since pouring affects only the outer peel, pouring is insufficient to purge (*kasher*) a pot that absorbed non-kosher food completely by cooking. The *Taz*[5] states that pouring is like a *keli rishon* only *lechumra* (for purposes of stringency, but not to rely on for leniency). We cannot be lenient and allow pouring hot water as a method of koshering a pot in which non-kosher food was cooked. This leniency would assume the Ri's view that pouring is like a *keli rishon* and affects the entire bottom surface, thereby eliminating non-kosher absorption from the entire pot. By rejecting only the leniency of the Ri, the *Taz* apparently requires that we be strict and follow the Ri *lechumra*. This would disallow pouring hot water over a bottle containing cold liquids.

B. THE CONTRADICTION IN THE RAMA: TWO CASES IN *HILKHOT KASHRUT*

As noted,[6] the Talmud[7] prohibits placing a jug with oil into a bathtub. The Talmud establishes that the bath is in the hot springs of Teverya. Rashi explains that the hot water emerges from the spring, is "pulled" along the ground, and gathers in a bath-like crater. Only if the water is placed in a *keli sheni* may the jug of oil be placed in it.

The *Terumat HaDeshen*[8] proves from the prohibition of placing a jug of oil in the bathtub of the hot springs that an uninterrupted flow has the stringencies of pouring even if the flowing liquid slides along a cold

5. *O.C.* 318:16.
6. Chapter 5, section 1.
7. *Shabbat* 40b.
8. No. 181.

surface. The Rama[9] quotes this ruling regarding hot milk which slides onto a cold meat pot. The hot milk renders the meat pot non-kosher.

Elsewhere,[10] however, the Rama discusses one who poured hot water over dirty meat and dairy utensils. He rules that the utensils are kosher, since pouring is not like a *keli rishon* with regard to the ability of the utensils to absorb from one another. This seems to contradict the Rama's earlier ruling, based on the *Terumat HaDeshen,* that hot milk which slides onto a cold meat pot renders the pot non-kosher.

The *Shakh*[11] notes that the source of the Rama's leniency is the *Issur VeHeter HaArokh,* who rules like the Rashbam,[12] that pouring has the status of a *keli sheni.* Since we do not accept the Rashbam's leniency, we must reject the *Issur VeHeter HaArokh* and the Rama's lenient opinion about pouring hot water over dirty meat and dairy utensils, as well.

The *Shulchan Arukh*[13] prohibits pouring from a *keli rishon* onto spices. R. Akiva Eiger cites the *Issur VeHeter HaArokh,* who allows pouring water along the sides of the cup onto the spices. This leniency is based on the view of the Rashbam. Since pouring has the status of *keli sheni,* we prohibit only direct pouring onto spices, as a mere stringency, but allow pouring along the sides of the cup. As mentioned in the name of the *Shakh,* we do not rely on the Rashbam, and, therefore, cannot accept R. Akiva Eiger's leniency.

C. THE *CHAVVAT DA'AT*'S RESOLUTION OF THE CONTRADICTION IN THE RAMA

Of course, one can argue that we follow the Rama's lenient opinion, and not the *Shakh.* This requires that we resolve the contradiction in the Rama in *Yoreh De'ah* (where in the case of pouring hot water on both meat and dairy utensils the Rama says the water does not cause the utensils to become non-kosher, but in the case of milk sliding onto

9. *Yoreh De'ah* 92:7.
10. *Yoreh De'ah* 95:3.
11. *Y.D.* 95:20.
12. See above, section A.
13. *Orach Chaim* 318:10.

a meat pot the Rama says it does render the pot non-kosher), and see how we can apply the Rama's view to the laws of *Shabbat*.

The *Chavvat Da'at*[14] resolves the contradiction between the two cases in the Rama by distinguishing between absorbing and cooking. In *Yoreh De'ah* 92:7, the Rama rules that hot milk which slides along a cold surface onto a meat pot is absorbed in it, rendering it non-kosher. However, the hot milk sliding along the meat pot cannot achieve actual cooking, which requires hot walls, as *Tosafot*[15] explains. Cooking is the simultaneous extracting and absorption of taste. Pouring along a cold surface, which cannot cook, cannot extract and absorb taste simultaneously. Therefore, if water is poured on meat and dairy dishes, the hot water which slides from the meat dish onto the dairy dish cannot effect the transfer of taste from one to the other, so all the dishes are kosher. But in the hot milk case, even when it slides along a cold surface, the hot milk can nevertheless cause absorption in the meat pot.

The *Chavvat Da'at* cites two precedents for the distinction between absorption and cooking. In the Talmud, Rav[16] assumes absorption in a *keli sheni* from a higher positioned hot food, but agrees that a *keli sheni* cannot cook. In the later literature, the Maharshal[17] rules that although *keli sheni* does not absorb, because the cold walls cool its contents, this applies only to liquids, which assume the shape of the *keli sheni* and are, therefore, greatly affected by the cold walls. Solids, however, are not affected that much by the cold walls, and can absorb while in a *keli sheni*. The ruling differentiating between liquids and solids in a *keli sheni*, according to *Minchat Yaakov*,[18] does not extend to cooking, which requires hot walls. Thus, according to the *Minchat Yaakov*, the Maharshal distinguishes between absorption and cooking.

On that basis, the *Chavvat Da'at* concurs with the *Issur VeHeter HaArokh* and R. Akiva Eiger: Hot water which slides along the sides of

14. *Y.D.* 92:23.
15. *Shabbat* 40b.
16. *Pesachim* 76a.
17. *Yam Shel Shelomoh, Chullin* 7:42.
18. 61:45.

a cup cannot cook the food at the cup's bottom. Hot water sliding on a cold surface can cause absorption only, not cooking.

The view, cited in *Yoreh De'ah*,[19] that a *keli sheni* itself causes absorption,[20] as well as the view that heat that is less than *yad soledet bo* causes absorption[21] clearly make a distinction between absorbing and cooking, because a *keli sheni* and heat less than *yad soledet bo* do not cook.

The Rama, however, apparently rejects these views. Presumably, he accepts *Tosafot*, who equate cooking and absorption. Only a *keli rishon* cooks and absorbs completely. As *Tosafot* have concluded, pouring cooks and absorbs only the upper peel. Despite the pouring affecting only the upper peel, both cooking and absorption do occur. Therefore, the *Chavvat Da'at*'s resolution of the contradiction in the Rama, which distinguishes between absorption and cooking (and its equivalent: simultaneous extraction and absorption) is difficult.

Moreover, as *Chavvat Da'at* notes, the Rama's source for his ruling that flowing hot milk renders a meat pot non-kosher is the *Terumat HaDeshen*, who bases his ruling on the statement of the Talmud[22] which discusses cooking on *Shabbat* by placing a jug of oil in a bathtub. The *Chavvat Da'at* is forced to assume that the Rama accepts the *Terumat HaDeshen*'s ruling only regarding absorption and not cooking, based on logic and not based on the proof from the Talmud, which discusses actual cooking. This is difficult. We will examine alternative resolutions to this contradiction in the next chapter.

D. SUMMARY

Pouring hot liquid onto cold food on *Shabbat* is prohibited, as one is cooking the upper peel of the food (*Tosafot*), or the entire food (Ri). We do not follow the opinion of the Rashbam, that pouring is like a *keli sheni* which does not cook, for either the purposes of *Shabbat* or *kashrut*. The Rama, however, seems to hold like the Rashbam in one *kashrut* case, that of pouring hot water over both meat and dairy utensils.

19. 105:2.
20. *Be'ur HaGra Y.D.* 105:14.
21. *Shakh Y.D.* 105:5.
22. *Shabbat* 40b.

This is a contradiction with another case where he rules that hot milk sliding onto a meat pot renders the pot non-kosher. The *Chavvat Da'at* attempts to resolve the contradiction by distinguishing between absorbing (which occurs in the hot milk sliding onto the meat pot) and cooking or the simultaneous extracting and absorbtion of taste (which does not occur when hot water is poured over both meat and dairy utensils). However, this is inconsistent with the Rama's source, which discusses cooking, and with the Rama's apparent acceptance of *Tosafot,* who equate absorbing and cooking.

14

Further Issues of Pouring

A. THE *PERI MEGADIM*'S RESOLUTION OF THE CONTRADICTION IN THE RAMA

As mentioned,[1] the Rama[2] prohibits a meat pot if hot milk overflows an adjacent pot and spills onto it. Elsewhere,[3] he permits dirty meat and dairy dishes upon which hot water from a *keli rishon* was poured. These rulings seem contradictory. The first assumes pouring causes absorption. The second assumes that there is no absorption.

The *Peri Megadim*[4] offers a resolution. The *Terumat HaDeshen* and the Rama in the first instance refer to a hot liquid which slides from a *keli rishon,* or a hot spring, which is on the fire. This causes both cooking and absorption and would render a meat pot non-kosher if the hot milk was poured from a *keli rishon* which was on the fire. The Rama in the second instance, in the case of pouring hot water on both meat and dairy utensils, refers to a kettle which is no longer on the fire. Pouring from it along a cold surface cannot effect cooking or absorption.

1. Chapter 13, section B.
2. *Yoreh De'ah* 92:7.
3. *Yoreh De'ah* 95:3.
4. *Yoreh De'ah* 95:18.

The *Peri Megadim* notes, however, that the Rama elsewhere[5] applies the ruling of the *Terumat HaDeshen* (hot liquid poured on a cold surface achieves cooking, at least of the upper peel) even to a *keli rishon* which is not on the fire, and concludes that pouring from a *keli rishon,* even if the *keli rishon* is not on the fire, is prohibited on *Shabbat,* against the *Issur VeHeter HaArokh* and R. Akiva Eiger.

B. THE *IGGEROT MOSHE*'S RESOLUTION OF THE CONTRADICTION IN THE RAMA

The *Iggerot Moshe*[6] resolves the contradiction in the Rama differently. Pouring along a cold surface can cause cooking and absorption within the thickness of a peel. Therefore, *Tosafot*[7] prohibits the part of an unsalted chicken upon which hot water is poured. Blood is absorbed from one capillary to an adjacent one within the thickness of a peel. This blood is not withdrawn by a subsequent salting, and that part of the chicken is prohibited.

In contrast, two dishes can never be so close to one another. The water which slides along the meat dish cannot impact the dairy one which is more than a peel's width removed. For this reason, the Rama permits the dishes even if they were dirty. The flow of hot water cannot transport the meaty grease and cause it to be absorbed in a dairy dish more than a peel's width away. (This analysis is based on the *Iggerot Moshe,* but differs in some details.)

This seems to be the best resolution of the contradiction in the Rama. The result is that on *Shabbat* one may not pour water along the sides of the cup onto spices. Pouring along the sides of the cup will cause cooking of a peel's width. The leniency of R. Akiva Eiger and the *Issur VeHeter HaArokh* is based on the view of the Rashbam that pouring even directly does not cook. As mentioned, this view is not accepted.

5. *Torat Chatat* 56:7.
6. *Yoreh De'ah* I, 42.
7. *Shabbat* 42b, s.v *aval notein hu.*

C. A "BATH" FILLED FROM A HOT SPRING: *KELI RISHON* OR *KELI SHENI*?

The *Magen Avraham*[8] cites the ruling of the Talmud[9] which prohibits placing a cold liquid into a "bath" which was filled by the hot springs of Teverya. The *Peri Megadim* cites Rashi[10] and the *Taz*[11] who, based on the *mishnah*,[12] state that a *keli rishon* cooks even after it is removed from the fire. So, too, one may not place cold liquid in the bath which was filled by the hot springs, because the bath is a *keli rishon* even though it is off the fire (that is, the bath is not on the hot spring itself).

The *Shemirat Shabbat KeHilkhatah*[13] notes that, if so, a cup filled from an urn has a status of *keli rishon*, a view attributed to the *Chazon Ish*. The cup is analogous to the "bath" and the urn is analogous to the hot springs. However, the Rama[14] describes a case of milk which overflows a pot, which presumably is on the fire. The Rama limits the milk's impact to the peel of the pot upon which it spilled, permitting the contents of the pot onto which the milk spills. It seems that milk overflowing from the pot is considered "pouring," that cooks only a peel. This is against the view of the *Chazon Ish* that gathered water from a pot on the fire is not "pouring," but is itself a *keli rishon*.

It could be suggested that Rashi is proving from the *mishnah*[15] that a *keli rishon* need not be on the fire. If it was on the fire and was removed, it is still a *keli rishon*. Similarly, if the "bath" was never on the fire which heats the nearby hot springs, but is connected to the hot springs by an ongoing flow along the intervening ground, the bath is a *keli rishon*. However, once the flow stops, the bath is no longer a *keli rishon*. The Talmud requires removing the water into a *keli sheni* before placing the jug of oil into the bath because the flow from the spring was ongoing, and the bath never lost its status as a *keli rishon*.

---

8. *O.C.* 318:33.
9. *Shabbat* 40b.
10. *Shabbat* 40b, s.v *bekeli rishon*,
11. *O.C.* 318:12.
12. *Shabbat* 42a.
13. 1 fn. 122.
14. *Yoreh De'ah* 92:7.
15. *Shabbat* 42a.

We can attempt to prove the idea that the Talmud, Rashi and the *Terumat HaDeshen,* when prohibiting placing a jug into a bath that is filled by hot springs, refer to a case where the water is still flowing from the spring to the bath. If we are dealing with a regular case of pouring, (i.e., when the water flowed into the baṭh and then stopped) a major question arises. Why may the jug not be placed in the bath? After all, pouring only cooks the peel. Since the jug is thicker than a peel, the oil cannot be cooked.

The answer may be found in the words of the *Terumat HaDeshen*: "Since the flow slides from the hot liquid which is on the fire [on the hot spring], each later drop prevents the earlier one from cooling off." This unique *halakhah,* which applies only as long as the flow continues and gathers in a bath, cooks all of the contents, not merely a peel's width. If the flow doesn't continue and gather, it only affects a peel, as *Tosafot* and Rama rule. Therefore if the flow stops, the gathered water is a *keli sheni,* against the view of the *Chazon Ish.*

D. SUMMARY

The *Peri Megadim* attempts to resolve the contradiction in the Rama by distinguishing between a *keli rishon* that is on the fire (which causes the hot milk to render the meat pot non-kosher) and a *keli rishon* which is not on the fire (hot water from which cannot cause the meat and dairy utensils to become non-kosher). For the purposes of *Shabbat,* however, the *Peri Megadim* concludes that the Rama is strict and prohibits pouring even from a *keli rishon* which is off the fire. The *Iggerot Moshe* offers the best resolution. He resolves the contradiction by distinguishing between contact that reaches a peel's width (the case of the hot milk and the meat pot) and contact between objects that are more than a peel's width apart (meat and dairy utensils). The Rama would thus agree that in the case of pouring along the sides of a cold cup onto spices on *Shabbat,* the contact occurs within the width of a peel and is prohibited. A bath filled by hot springs, or a cup filled by an urn, maintains its status as a *keli rishon* only as long as the flow is ongoing. When the flow stops, the cup or bath becomes a *keli sheni* , and thus a jug with cold liquid may be placed in it.

15

Ladles and Solids

A. THE *CHAVVAT DA'AT*: LADLES AND SOLIDS ABSORB BUT DO NOT COOK

The *Chavvat Da'at*[1] equates the status of a ladle containing hot liquid removed from a pot on the fire with that of a solid removed from a pot on the fire and placed onto a cold plate. In both, he rules that there is absorption but not cooking. There is no cooking since there are no walls heated by a *keli rishon* that can cook. There is absorption since there are no cold walls which prevent absorption. The walls of the ladle are not cold. Similarly the cold plate, which merely touches the food at the food's bottom but does not surround the food and touch every surface the way cold walls surround liquids, has only a minimal effect on solids that are on the plate. Therefore, there is absorption from the solid.

B. THE RAMA: LADLES ABSORB BUT SOLIDS DO NOT

As mentioned,[2] the Rama seems to equate cooking and absorption of taste. The Rama rules that a ladle is a *keli rishon* for absorption, so we

1. *Y.D.* 92:27.
2. Chapter 13, section C.

must treat it as a *keli rishon* for cooking on *Shabbat* as well.[3] If a solid on a plate has the status of *keli rishon* for absorption as the *Chavvat Da'at* states, we should infer that a solid on a plate can cook on *Shabbat* as well.[4]

However, the Rama[5] disagrees with the Maharshal,[6] who rules that although a *keli sheni* does not absorb liquids, solids can absorb while in a *keli sheni*.[7] The Rama rules that a solid on a *keli sheni* does not absorb. He denies the *Chavvat Da'at*'s equation between ladles and solids. Solids on a plate do not absorb because the cold plate cools off solid food even though the plate touches the food only from the food's bottom. A ladle, which does not have cold walls at all, can indeed absorb.

C. A LADLE: *KELI RISHON* OR *KELI SHENI*?

The *Mishnah Berurah*[8] states that a ladle may possibly be a *keli rishon*. If the ladle remained in the *keli rishon* until steam rises from the ladle's contents, the ladle is certainly a *keli rishon*.

The source for the criterion of steam rising from the ladle is *Tosafot*.[9] However, *Tosafot* is in doubt only as to whether water with steam rising in a ladle is effective for koshering. In addition, the requirement that steam rise from the ladle may be limited to using the ladle for koshering, which requires boiling water. It may be irrelevant to the question of whether a ladle is a *keli rishon* or a *keli sheni*.

The *Mishnah Berurah*'s view that the ladle is a *keli rishon* if steam rises from it must be based on the view of the Maharil, cited by the *Taz*.[10] The reason may be that if the ladle remained for a long time in the *keli rishon*, the walls of the ladle are considered heated by the fire, so the ladle is a *keli rishon*. The criterion to determine whether the walls of the ladle are considered heated by the fire is steam rising. If the ladle

3. *Yoreh De'ah* 107:2; see *Shakh* 7.
4. *Magen Avraham* 318:45, *Mishnah Berurah* 118.
5. *Darkei Moshe Yoreh De'ah* 105:5.
6. *Yam Shel Shelomoh, Chullin* 7:42.
7. See above, chapter 13, section C.
8. *O.C.* 318:87.
9. *Avodah Zarah* 33b, s.v. *kinsa*.
10. *Yoreh De'ah* 92:30.

did not remain that long, the Maharil considers it a *keli sheni,* and the *Mishnah Berurah* is undecided .

The *Chazon Ish*[11] rules that if one placed a ladle in a *keli rishon* which is no longer on the fire, the ladle is a *keli sheni.* Here the walls of the ladle are certainly not heated by the fire. Since we generally remove the pot from the fire before inserting the ladle,[12] the ladle is a *keli sheni.*

D. SUMMARY

The *Chavvat Da'at* distinguishes between cooking and absorption, but equates ladles with solids which were placed on a *keli sheni.* According to the *Chavvat Da'at,* both ladles and solids absorb but do not cook. The Rama equates cooking and absorption, but distinguishes between ladles and solids which were placed on a *keli sheni.* According to the Rama, ladles absorb (and, therefore, cook) but solids do not absorb (and, therefore, do not cook). According to the *Mishnah Berurah,* a ladle which remained for a long time in a *keli rishon* on the fire is also a *keli rishon.* If the ladle remained for a short time, the *Mishnah Berurah* is doubtful whether it is a *keli rishon.* If the ladle was placed in a *keli rishon* that was off the fire, the ladle is a *keli sheni.*

11. *O.C.*122:3.
12. *O.C.* 318:18, *Mishnah Berurah* 113.

Section II: Warming

16

"Leaving": The Dispute Between Chananyah and *Rabbanan*

A. THE DISPUTE OVER LEAVING A POT ON THE STOVE ON *EREV SHABBAT*

The *mishnah*[1] prohibits placing a pot onto a stove which is heated with wood, unless the coals are shoveled away or covered with ashes. The *gemara* questions whether such placing is prohibited only when done on *Shabbat* itself, known as *hachzarah,* "returning," or even when left on from *erev Shabbat,* known as *shehiyah,* "leaving."

The first view, which permits leaving a pot on the stove on *erev Shabbat* with no precautions of shoveling or covering, follows Chananyah. Once food gets cooked to the degree of *ma'achal ben derusa'i,*[2] it may be left on an open fire on *erev Shabbat.* Covering is necessary only to permit returning the pot onto the stove on *Shabbat,* or to permit leaving food which did not reach *ma'achal ben derusa'i* on *erev Shabbat.*

1. *Shabbat* 36b.
2. See chapter 4, section A for the definition of this term.

The second view, which requires covering the fire even to leave *ma'achal ben derusa'i* foods on the stove on Friday, follows *Rabbanan* who argue with Chananyah. According to *Rabbanan,* leaving food on a fire on Friday going into *Shabbat* is prohibited for fear that one may stoke the coals on *Shabbat.* This prohibition applies unless the food is fully cooked and deteriorates if moisture is removed. At that stage, we do not fear that he will stoke the coals, because doing so might burn the food.

The Ran[3] explains that by covering the coals, one creates a recognizable reminder not to stoke them. Similarly, the *mishnah* allows leaving a pot on the stove on Friday if the stove is heated with straw or stubble. Since there are no coals, there is no concern for stoking on *Shabbat.*

The dispute between Chananyah and *Rabbanan* is whether we are concerned about stoking coals if the food has already reached the point of *ma'achal ben derusa'i.* Chananyah holds that since the food is edible, there is no concern about stoking, and the fire need not be covered. *Rabbanan* are concerned about stoking even if the food has reached *ma'achal ben derusa'i,* and require that the fire be covered. The dispute over whether it is permitted to leave *ma'achal ben derusa'i* food on an uncovered fire on *erev Shabbat* is a dispute over a rabbinic prohibition.

B. THE DISPUTE OVER HEATING PARTIALLY COOKED FOODS ON *SHABBAT*

However, the dispute between *Rabbanan* and Chananyah can also be understood as a dispute over whether there is a Torah prohibition to heat *ma'achal ben derusa'i* foods on *Shabbat.* The *Mirkevet HaMishneh*[4] writes that if the food is edible raw, *Rabbanan* agree with Chananyah, that it may be left on an uncovered fire on *erev Shabbat.* As noted above[5] the *Mirkevet HaMishneh* equates, for this purpose, *Shabbat* to the prohibition of *bishul akum,* which likewise does not apply to food which can be eaten raw. The *Mirkevet HaMishneh*'s statement that Chananyah and *Rabbanan* both permit leaving edible raw foods on an uncovered fire on *erev Shabbat* implies that Chananyah and *Rabbanan* argue about

---

3. *Shabbat* 15b.
4. *Hilkhot Shabbat* 9:3.
5. Chapter 1, section B.

whether there is a Torah prohibition of reheating partially cooked foods on *Shabbat*.

Chananyah allows returning onto a covered fire on *Shabbat* whatever can be left on an uncovered fire on Friday. Therefore, if food reached the degree of *ma'achal ben derusa'i*, it may be returned onto a covered fire on *Shabbat*. This proves that according to Chananyah there is no violation of cooking foods which had reached only *ma'achal ben derusa'i*.

The Rambam[6] holds that it is a Torah prohibition to heat food unless it had been fully cooked. The *Mirkevet HaMishneh* writes that *Rabbanan* and Chananyah argue on this very point. Chananyah, who permits returning *ma'achal ben derusa'i* foods to a covered fire on *Shabbat*, permits heating food that is only partially cooked on *Shabbat*. *Rabbanan*, who prohibit returning *ma'achal ben derusa'i* foods to a covered fire on *Shabbat* (since they prohibit leaving *ma'achal ben derusa'i* foods on an uncovered fire on *erev Shabbat*), prohibit heating food unless it was fully cooked. The Rambam rules like *Rabbanan*. However, if the food is edible in a raw state, there is no Torah prohibition to cook it, and therefore, *Rabbanan* agree with Chananyah that it is permitted to leave food that is edible in its raw state on an uncovered stove on *erev Shabbat*.

The Rashba[7] understands the dispute differently. The Rashba says that one may cook food which had reached *ma'achal ben derusa'i*, even according to *Rabbanan*. *Rabbanan* and Chananyah only dispute whether we are concerned with stoking the coals when *ma'achal ben derusa'i* food is left on the fire on *erev Shabbat*, but not whether *bishul* is violated when *ma'achal ben derusa'i* food is heated on *Shabbat*. The Rashba questions whether we follow *Rabbanan* or Chananyah regarding whether it is permitted to leave *ma'achal ben derusa'i* food on an uncovered fire on *erev Shabbat*, but not the leniency to cook *ma'achal ben derusa'i* food on *Shabbat*. If so, *Rabbanan* and Chananyah's dispute is only over a rabbinic prohibition.

According to those who reject the *Mirkevet HaMishneh*'s assumption that cooking edible raw foods is not a Torah violation,[8] the Rambam

6. *Hilkhot Shabbat* 9:3; see chapter 2, section B.

7. *Shabbat* 38a, 39a.

8. See chapter 1, section B.

agrees with the Rashba that Chananyah and *Rabbanan*'s dispute is only over a rabbinic prohibition. When Chananyah requires covering a fire to permit returning food onto a fire on *Shabbat,* Chananyah obviously requires that the food be fully cooked to avoid the *melakhah* of cooking. The requirement that the food be must be fully cooked to be returned, even to a covered fire, is not found in the passage in the Talmud,[9] since the requirement relates to cooking, whereas Talmudic passage deals only with a rabbinic prohibition to avoid stoking the coals.

According to the *Mirkevet HaMishneh,* the Rambam does not accept this answer (that the requirement that the food be fully cooked is omitted because the Talmud deals only with the rabbinic prohibition to stoke the coals). Therefore, since Chananyah permits leaving *ma'achal ben derusa'i* before *Shabbat* on an uncovered fire, and states that covering is required only for returning on *Shabbat,* this implies that no violation of cooking occurs when *ma'achal ben derusa'i* food is heated on a covered fire on *Shabbat. Rabbanan* permit leaving food on an uncovered fire on *erev Shabbat* only if the food is fully cooked, and permit returning food to a covered fire on *Shabbat* only if the food is fully cooked. Therefore returning *ma'achal ben derusa'i* food, even to a covered fire, is prohibited by Torah law.

C. SUMMARY

Shabbat 36b records a dispute between *Rabbanan,* who prohibit leaving *ma'achal ben derusa'i* foods on an uncovered fire on *erev Shabbat,* and Chananyah, who permits leaving *ma'achal ben derusa'i* foods on an uncovered fire on *erev Shabbat.* The Rashba understands the dispute to be only about the possible rabbinic prohibition to leave *ma'achal ben derusa'i* food lest the coals be stoked. The *Mirkevet HaMishneh,* however, believes the dispute may also be understood as a dispute over whether it is a Torah prohibition to heat foods that have not been fully cooked on *Shabbat* (*Rabbanan*), or is not a Torah prohibition to heat up heat foods that have not been fully cooked on *Shabbat* (Chananyah). The Rambam decides like *Rabbanan,* that it is a Torah prohibition to heat up food that it has not been fully cooked.

9. *Shabbat* 36b.

17

Returning

A. THE REASON THAT RETURNING FOOD ONTO AN UNCOVERED FIRE IS PROHIBITED ON *SHABBAT*

The *Rishonim* dispute the reason that no food may be returned onto an uncovered fire on *Shabbat*. Rabbenu Tam[1] is concerned that since the pot was removed from the fire the pot has cooled off, and one might stoke the coals to reheat the food even though the food had reached *ma'achal ben derusa'i*.

The *Ba'al HaMa'or*[2] agrees with Rabbenu Tam. He states that all the stringencies regarding an oven were enacted out of concern that one might stoke the coals. "All" must include the rabbinic prohibition of leaving food on an uncovered fire on Friday and the prohibition of returning food to an uncovered fire on *Shabbat*. Maharam[3] attributes this position to *Tosafot*,[4] who are concerned with stoking the coals even if the fire is covered.

1. *Sefer HaYashar* 235, cited in *Sha'ar HaTziyun* 253:37.
2. *Shabbat* 15b.
3. *Shabbat* 36b.
4. 38b s.v. *pina*.

The Ran[5] and the Rashba argue with Rabbenu Tam and hold that returning food on to an uncovered fire on *Shabbat* is prohibited because it has the appearance of cooking. If the fire is covered, however, returning a pot does not appear like cooking. This is against the position of the Maharam who assumes that covering is ineffective if the reason for the prohibition of returning is that it looks like cooking.

B. RETURNING FOOD JUST BEFORE *SHABBAT*

Tosafot[6] prohibit returning food onto an uncovered fire just before *Shabbat,* at a time when cold food can no longer be heated before *Shabbat* arrives. Rabbenu Tam[7] explains that the prohibition is based on the concern that one may stoke the coals after *Shabbat* arrives.

The Ran[8] rejects the prohibition to return cold food to an uncovered fire just before *Shabbat.* If one may cook at this time (since it is not yet *Shabbat*), he may certainly do something which only has an appearance of cooking. *Tosafot,* however, maintain that the prohibition is unrelated to cooking. It was enacted to prevent stoking the coals, a violation of lighting a fire.

The Rosh,[9] like *Tosafot,* prohibits returning food just before *Shabbat,* but for a different reason. If one returns food just before *Shabbat,* he might come to do so on *Shabbat* as well. The prohibition to return just before *Shabbat* is simply an aspect of the *gezeirah* (rabbinic prohibition) of returning food on *Shabbat* itself. However, if the food was not fully cooked, it may be returned just before *Shabbat.* This seems somewhat counterintuitive; why is the Rosh more lenient in the case of food that is not fully cooked?

The *Beit Yosef*[10] explains that if the food is not fully cooked, a Torah prohibition is violated if it is returned on *Shabbat.* The prohibition of returning just before *Shabbat* applies only when it is part of the *gezeirah* of returning on *Shabbat.* If returning is permitted right before

5. *Shabbat* 15b, 19a.
6. *Shabbat* 36b, s.v. *u'Beit Hillel.*
7. *Sefer HaYashar* 235.
8. *Shabbat* 15b in pages of the Rif, s.v. *Beit*.
9. *Shabbat* 3:2.
10. *O.C.* 253:2.

Shabbat, Chazal feared that one may violate the rabbinic prohibition of returning on *Shabbat.* However, if the food is not fully cooked, returning on *Shabbat* constitutes a Torah violation of cooking, not a rabbinic violation of returning. Chazal did not fear that people would violate Torah prohibitions. Therefore, they did not prohibit returning food which is not fully cooked just before *Shabbat.*

The explanation of the *Beit Yosef* is difficult, since the Rosh[11] does not believe that there is a Torah violation in returning food that reaches *ma'achal ben derusa'i.* Moreover, the Rosh never mentioned the prohibition of cooking in discussing which foods may be returned just before *Shabbat.*

The *Bach*[12] explains the Rosh differently. Typically, a pot is not removed from the fire until it is fully cooked. Extending the prohibition of returning fully cooked food from *Shabbat* until late Friday just before *Shabbat* is logical. The two cases are comparable, and it is all one enactment. Returning food not yet fully cooked on Friday is not comparable to returning fully cooked food on *Shabbat,* and cannot be viewed as part of the same enactment. To prohibit returning not yet fully cooked food on Friday would be a *gezeirah ligezeirah,* one enactment protecting another, which is generally outside the scope of rabbinic legislation.

It seems at first glance that, according to the Rosh, we should prohibit returning cooked food on Friday, against the aforementioned view of the Ran that such a prohibition is inconceivable. Since the Rosh prohibits returning cooked food on Friday out of concern one may return it to the fire on *Shabbat* (unlike Rabbenu Tam who says: "lest he stoke the coals on *Shabbat*"), returning food on Friday should be prohibited even if the reason that returning food on *Shabbat* is prohibited is the appearance of cooking. In reality, however, this is not the case, as we shall see below.[13]

---

11. See *Shabbat* 3:11.
12. *O.C.* 253:2.
13. See chapter 18, section B.

C. SUMMARY

According to Rabbenu Tam and *Tosafot,* it is prohibited to return food to an uncovered fire on *Shabbat* lest one stoke the coals. According to the Ran it is prohibited to return food to an uncovered fire because it looks like cooking. Returning food to an uncovered fire just before *Shabbat* is permitted according to the Ran because there is no concern about the appearance of cooking before *Shabbat.* Returning food to an uncovered fire just before *Shabbat* is prohibited according to the *Tosafot* lest one stoke the coals on *Shabbat,* and prohibited according to the Rosh lest one return food to an uncovered fire on *Shabbat* itself. The Rosh permits returning food that is not fully cooked to a fire right before *Shabbat,* either because it was never included in the *gezeirah* against returning fully cooked food on *Shabbat* (*Beit Yosef*) or because returning not fully cooked on Friday is a *gezeirah ligezeirah,* which is not enacted (*Bach*).

18

Placing

A. DEFINITION AND REASON FOR THE PROHIBITION OF "PLACING"

The *gemara*[1] limits the *mishnah*'s[2] permission to return food onto a covered fire. If one placed the pot on the floor and/or removed it without the intention to return it, the pot may not be returned onto a covered fire. This prohibition, called *hanachah* (placing, rather than returning, *hachzarah*), is based on the appearance of cooking, according to the Ran and the Rashba. When the pot is placed on the floor, the original status of "on the fire" is cancelled.[3] Hence, it is now viewed as starting from scratch. Placing the pot on the fire then looks like cooking even if the fire is covered.

As mentioned, the Ran and the Rashba prohibit returning onto an uncovered fire because it looks like cooking. If even on an uncovered fire the Ran and the Rashba are not concerned for stoking the coals[4] if the food was cooked to the point of *ma'achal ben derusa'i*, then the

1. *Shabbat* 38b.
2. *Shabbat* 36b.
3. See Rashi 38b, s.v.*aval.*
4. See chapter 17, section A.

concern over stoking coals certainly does not exist if the fire is covered. Perforce, placing food onto a covered fire is prohibited because it looks like cooking.

Tosafot and Rabbenu Tam prohibit returning food onto an uncovered fire "lest he stoke the coals." What about placing food onto a covered fire? *Tosafot*[5] cites Rabbenu Tam that this, too, is prohibited "lest he stoke the coals." Even though the fire is covered, since it is a new "placing," not a return, we fear that he might remove the covering and stoke the coals.

Tosafot HaRosh[6] disagrees with *Tosafot* and Rabbenu Tam about the reason for the prohibition of placing. Even though returning onto an uncovered fire is prohibited lest he stoke the coals, and placing onto a covered fire is prohibited lest he stoke the coals according to the *Tosafot* and Rabbenu Tam, the *Tosafot HaRosh* believes that placing food onto a covered fire after the food had been on the floor is a new placement which is, i.e., looks like, cooking on *Shabbat*. The *Ba'al HaMa'or*[7] also prohibits placing onto a covered fire because it looks like cooking on *Shabbat*, even though returning onto an uncovered fire is prohibited "lest he stoke the coals."[8]

B. PLACING FOOD ONTO A COVERED FIRE JUST BEFORE *SHABBAT*

The *Hagahot Mordechai*,[9] like *Tosafot*, prohibits returning onto an uncovered fire just before *Shabbat*. He is uncertain, however, about placing food onto a covered fire just before *Shabbat*.

As mentioned,[10] Rabbenu Tam prohibits returning the food just before *Shabbat*, lest he stoke the coals on *Shabbat*. Since Rabbenu Tam prohibits placing onto a covered fire for the same reason, lest he stoke the coals, presumably placing onto a covered fire, too, is prohibited just before *Shabbat*. According to the Rosh and the *Ba'al HaMa'or*, who are not concerned with stoking the coals of a covered fire, and prohibit

5. *Shabbat* 38b, s.v. *pinah*.
6. *Shabbat* 38b.
7. *Shabbat* 16b.
8. See chapter 17, section A.
9. *Shabbat* 55b.
10. Chapter 17, section B.

placing onto a covered fire because it looks like cooking, placing food onto a covered fire should be permissible just before *Shabbat.*

The Gra[11] indeed understands the Rosh[12] to permit placing just before *Shabbat,* writing, "by day, he may return in any case," including if the food was placed on the floor. The *Korban Netan'el,*[13] based on a later comment of the Rosh,[14] disagrees and interprets "by day" as meaning when it is not just before *Shabbat.* The Gra says that that comment of the Rosh merely records the language of *Tosafot,* as is his wont, but that the Rosh himself disagrees with the *Tosafot* about whether placing is prohibited just before *Shabbat.*

At first glance, the *Korban Netan'el* is correct. The Rosh[15] prohibits returning food just before *Shabbat,* not lest he stoke the coals on *Shabbat,* but rather lest he return the food on *Shabbat.* If so, he should prohibit placing onto a covered fire just before *Shabbat* lest he place food onto a covered fire on *Shabbat.*

Perhaps the Gra holds that we only extend *gezeirot* from *Shabbat* to late Friday. A *gezeirah* is a rabbinic enactment prohibiting one action lest one violate a different, prohibited action. According to *Tosafot* and Rabbenu Tam, placing on a covered fire is such a *gezeirah,* lest one stoke the coals on *Shabbat.* Therefore it can be extended from *Shabbat* to late Friday. This entire time period is the time of the prohibition of returning, which is prohibited lest he stoke the coals.

However, according to the Rosh, placing onto a covered fire is prohibited for an entirely different reason. As *Tosafot HaRosh* explains, it looks like cooking. This is an intrinsic prohibition, a rabbinically proscribed *melakhah* called "the appearance of cooking," and not a *gezeirah* lest one stoke the coals.[16] Since we do not prohibit cooking just before *Shabbat,* we cannot prohibit "the appearance of cooking" before Shabbat

11. *Be'ur HaGra, O.C.* 253:51.
12. *Shabbat* 3:2.
13. Ch. 3, *mem..*
14. *Shabbat* 4:2.
15. See chapter 17, section C.
16. Compare the two reasons to prohibit placing uncooked food into a *keli sheni* (chapter 10, sections B and C).

either. The Rosh[17] cites *Tosafot,* who prohibit placing onto a covered fire lest he stoke the coals. As a *gezeirah,* the prohibition of placing "lest one stoke the coals" can be extended to Friday just before *Shabbat;* but if placing is prohibited due the "appearance of cooking," that prohibition is limited to *Shabbat* itself, just as is actual cooking.

The Rama[18] says that one should follow *Tosafot* and not return food onto an uncovered fire just before *Shabbat.* The *Mishnah Berurah,*[19] citing the Gra, permits placing from scratch onto a covered fire just before *Shabbat.* According to our analysis, this means that returning onto an uncovered fire is prohibited "lest he stoke the coals," whereas placing onto a covered fire is prohibited because it looks like cooking.

C. SUMMARY

"Placing" is defined as putting a pot back onto a covered fire after one removed it and put it down and/or had no intention to put it back.[20] Consistent with their position on "returning," the Ran and the Rashba prohibit placing because it looks like cooking. Consistent with their position on "returning," *Tosafot* and Rabbenu Tam prohibit placing because one might come to stoke the coals. The Rosh and the *Ba'al HaMa'or,* however, prohibit returning because one might come to stoke the coals (like *Tosafot*), but prohibit placing because it looks like cooking (like the Ran and the Rashba).

Placing just before *Shabbat* is prohibited according to the *Tosafot* lest one come to stoke the coals on *Shabbat.* According to the Gra, the Rosh permits placing just before *Shabbat* because one is permitted to do an act that looks like cooking before *Shabbat.* According to the *Korban Netan'el,* however, the *Rosh* prohibits placing just before *Shabbat* as an extension of the *gezeirah* of placing on *Shabbat* itself. Based on rulings of the Rama and *Mishnah Berurah,* we follow the *Tosafot*'s reasoning

17. *Shabbat* 4:2.
18. *O.C.* 253:2.
19. *O.C.* 253:72.
20. See chapter 26, section A.

regarding returning – that it is prohibited because of concern over stoking the coals, and we follow the reasoning of the Ran, Rashba and Rosh regarding placing – that it is prohibited because it looks like cooking.

19

Asking a Non-Jew to Heat Food

A. ASKING A NON-JEW TO VIOLATE A RABBINIC PROHIBITION

The Rama[1] prohibits telling a non-Jew to do "all these things." Therefore one may not tell a non-Jew to heat (liquid) foods that cooled off. The *Mishnah Berurah,*[2] citing the Gra,[3] explains "all these things" to include rabbinic prohibitions, since one may not tell a non-Jew to do something which is a rabbinic violation for a Jew.

The *Be'ur Halakhah* cites the *Peri Megadim,*[4] who quotes the Rama,[5] who allows telling a non-Jew to do a rabbinically prohibited act for the purpose of a *Shabbat* meal in an exigent situation. If so, one who tells a non-Jew to reheat dry food should not be rebuked.

1. *O.C.* 253:5.
2. *O.C.* 253:94.
3. See *Sha'ar HaTziyun* 94.
4. *Eishel Avraham* 253:38.
5. *O.C.* 325:10.

The *Be'ur Halakhah* says that we allow telling a non-Jew to do a rabbinically prohibited act *lekhatchilah,* even if there is no exigency, for a *Shabbat* need. This is based on *Mishnah Berurah*[6] quoting *Darkei Moshe.*[7] However, this ruling is limited to the prohibition of carrying, which can be avoided by the person going to the object. Otherwise, we allow telling a non-Jew to do a rabbinically prohibited act for a *Shabbat* need, as for a *mitzvah* or a great need,[8] only in an extreme situation. While we should do our best to avoid relying on this leniency, one who is lenient is "not rebuked" if he does so on occasion, but it should not be done regularly.[9]

B. ASKING A NON-JEW TO DO AN ACT OF RETURNING OR PLACING

The *Be'ur Halakhah* equates the prohibition of returning and placing with respect to asking a non-Jew. This equation is questionable based on our earlier analysis.[10] Returning is prohibited lest one stoke the coals, whereas placing is prohibited because it looks like cooking.

The *Chazon Ish*[11] limits leniency in telling a non-Jew to prohibitions that are defined as "actions." The performance by a non-Jew of a rabbinically prohibited act is permitted for a *mitzvah* if there is no alternative. However, returning onto an open fire, like placing uncooked food onto an open fire on Friday, is not prohibited as an *action,* but rather as a *result.* It is the situation of such a pot on the fire that is prohibited, "lest one stoke the coals." Even if a robot put the pot there it must be removed; the act of placing itself is of no consequence. Having the action done by a non-Jew is of no avail.

Yet, according to our analysis, this is true only for returning

---

6. *O.C.* 325:63.
7. *O.C.* 325:8.
8. *O.C.* 307:5.
9. This is based on our analysis (see *Am Mordechai* on *Shabbat,* p. 204), that this leniency is based on an unresolved question in the Talmud (*Bava Metzi'a* 90a). We are lenient based on the rule that rabbinical uncertainties are resolved leniently. This rule should not be relied upon if there is no pressing necessity.
10. Chapter 17, section B.
11. *O.C.* 37:21.

onto an uncovered fire. In that case, there is a *gezeirah* "lest he stoke the coals," and the *gezeirah* applies even if a non-Jew placed the pot on the uncovered fire. However, placing onto a covered fire is prohibited only because it looks like cooking. It is not a *gezeirah* but a rabbinically prohibited act, which may be done by a non-Jew in a pressing case for a *Shabbat* need.

C. SUMMARY

It is permitted to ask a non-Jew to perform a rabbinically prohibited act only for a *Shabbat* need in an extreme situation. Nevertheless, one should not rely on this leniency with regularity. Contra the *Be'ur Halakhah,* it is always prohibited to ask a non-Jew to return a pot to an uncovered fire, for there is a *gezeirah* lest one stoke the coals that prohibits a pot being on an uncovered fire, no matter who put it there. It is permitted to ask a non-Jew to place a pot on a covered fire in a difficult case of *Shabbat* need, however, because placing is a rabbinically prohibited act because it looks like cooking, and not a *gezeirah* "lest one stoke the coals."

20

A Pot on Top of a Pot

A. PLACING FOOD ON TOP OF A HOT POT ON *SHABBAT*

The Rashba[1] permits placing dry cooked food on top of a pot to be reheated, since placing food on top of a pot is not "the manner of cooking." The *Shulchan Arukh*[2] quotes this law and its reason.

The *Hagahot Mordechai*[3] discusses a stew which may burn if it remains directly on the fire. He allows removing a pot from the fire, placing an empty pan on the fire, and returning the pot onto the empty pan which is covering the fire. However, if he puts the pot on the ground, he may not return it, since it would be an act of placing. The *Shulchan Arukh*[4] quotes this ruling as well. The prohibition of placing onto an empty pan seems to contradict the other ruling[5] in which the *Shulchan Arukh* allows placing onto a pot, presumably even if the pot being placed had been put on the ground.

---

1. *Shabbat* 40b, s.v. *meivi,* cited in Ran, 19a in pages of the Rif, s.v *v'khein*
2. *O.C.* 253:5.
3. 3, 80a.
4. *O.C.* 253:3.
5. *O.C.* 253:5.

The *Be'ur Halakhah*[6] answers by quoting the *Peri Megadim.*[7] An empty pan on a fire is simply a covered fire. The Talmud[8] prohibits placing a pot onto an empty pan, i.e., onto a covered fire, if the pot had been put on the floor.[9] Placing on a pot which has cooked food in it, however, is permissible even if the pot that is being placed had been put on the floor. This is because placing a pot on top of another pot which has cooked food in it is not "the way of cooking." The *Be'ur Halakhah* adds that the top of a pot that has food in it is not considered on top of the oven at all.

B. LEAVING COLD FOOD ON TOP OF A HOT POT ON *EREV SHABBAT*

Elsewhere, however, we find an opposite distinction between an empty pan on the fire and a pot full of food on the fire. The pot being full creates a stringency, not a leniency.

There exists a violation of *hatmanah,* placing a pot on Friday on or within a hot item which adds to its heat.[10] The Rama[11] rules that the prohibition exists only if a pot is enclosed. The *Shulchan Arukh* extends the prohibition to any case in which the pot is placed directly on a heat source.

Nonetheless, the *Shulchan Arukh*[12] allows placing a pot containing cold food onto a hot pot on Friday. It is not a violation of *hatmanah* with respect to the pot of cold food, since the bottom pot has no independent source of heat, and its heat dissipates.[13] The *Be'ur Halakhah* equates the case of placing a pot of cold food onto a hot pot on Friday with the case leaving a pot on an open fire. Citing *Magen Avraham* and *Peri Megadim,* the *Be'ur Halakhah* requires that the food being placed onto the hot pot reach the point of *ma'achal ben derusa'i* before *Shabbat.*

---

6. *O.C.* 253:3.
7. *Eishel Avraham* 253:33.
8. *Shabbat* 38b.
9. See above, chapter 17.
10. See *O.C.* 257.
11. *O.C.* 253:1.
12. *O.C.* 258:1.
13. *Mishnah Berurah* 258:2.

In such a case, we rely on the view of Chananyah, who permits leaving *ma'achal ben derusa'i* foods on an uncovered fire on *erev Shabbat,*[14] as the Rama[15] rules.

This raises a powerful question. Chananyah does not require the fire to be covered if the food being left on *erev Shabbat* has reached the point of *ma'achal ben derusa'i.*[16] The *Be'ur Halakhah,*[17] who requires the food to have reached the point of *ma'achal ben derusa'i* when the cold pot is placed on a hot filled pot on the fire on Friday, does not consider the hot pot a cover of the fire at all. He equates leaving cold food on a hot filled pot with leaving cold food on an uncovered fire, which is prohibited unless the food reaches *ma'achal ben derusa'i.* Thus, the *Be'ur Halakhah* treats a hot filled pot more stringently than a plain cover. Yet the *Be'ur Halakhah*[18] accepts the *Peri Megadim*'s lenient distinction regarding placing. A filled pot on the fire is a situation treated even more leniently than a plain cover, and allows placing anew on *Shabbat.*

This complete contradiction in the *Be'ur Halakhah* and the *Peri Megadim* can be resolved as follows. A full pot is better than a plain cover insofar as it is not "the way of cooking" to place another pot on top of it. Therefore, the prohibition of placing anew on *Shabbat,* which looks like cooking, does not apply to a full pot; however, the prohibition of placing does apply to a plain cover.

By contrast, the prohibition of leaving a pot on an open fire on Friday has a different reason, namely a concern that the one doing so may stoke the coals on *Shabbat.* If the fire is covered, it serves as a recognizable reminder not to stoke the coals. Since the cover is usually not there, its presence is a reminder not to stoke the coals. An empty pot is usually not on the fire, and thus can serve as an effective reminder. However, a filled pot, which is usually on the fire, cannot serve as a reminder. It is equivalent to an open fire, and the food placed on a full pot must reach *ma'achal ben derusa'i* before *Shabbat.*[19]

---

14. See above, chapter 15, section A.
15. *O.C.* 253:1.
16. *O.C.* 253:1, see *Be'ur Halakhah* s.v. *ela.*
17. *O.C.* 258.
18. *O.C.* 253:3.
19. See *Shulchan Arukh, Hadrat Kodesh, Yalkut Mefarshim* 258.

The prohibition of leaving food on a hot pot "lest one stoke the coals," however, presumes that a pot on top of a pot is considered to be on the oven. In the *Be'ur Halakhah*'s formulation, in which the top of a full pot is not considered on top of the oven at all, there can be no prohibition of leaving food on top of a pot on Friday, and the aforementioned resolution is not correct. However, the *Peri Megadim* does not employ the formulation that the top of a pot is not considered the top of an oven. Rather, the *Peri Megadim* simply says that the top of a pot is not considered the way of *bishul.* This avoids the prohibition of placing cooked food anew on *Shabbat,* but not the prohibition of leaving uncooked food on Friday, which is prohibited "lest he stoke the coals" unless the food reached the point of *ma'achal ben derusa'i.*

C. CONCERN LEST ONE STOKE THE COALS: THE POSITION OF THE *MAGEN AVRAHAM* AND THE *PERI MEGADIM*

The assumption of the previous section, namely that a full pot is not a reminder not to stoke the coals because such pots are usually on the fire, is a matter of dispute. The *Magen Avraham*[20] says that a full pot does serve as a reminder. The *Peri Megadim, Shulchan Arukh HaRav* and *Machatzit HaShekel* debate the issue, as well as the opinion of the *Magen Avraham* elsewhere[21] on the issue, as will now be explained.

Shulchan Arukh HaRav[22] disagrees with the *Peri Megadim.* He maintains that a full pot does remind a person not to stoke the coals. Although its mere presence is not unusual, leaving a second pot on top of it is. The idea that a full pot does serve as a reminder lest one stoke the coals is also the view of the *Magen Avraham* in the first comment cited above. There is no fear of stoking the coals if the pot is on another pot; since it is not "the way of cooking," there is a reminder not to stoke the coals.[23] Therefore, the food need not reach the point of *ma'achal ben derusa'i.*

---

20. *O.C.* 253:33.
21. *O.C.* 258:1.
22. 258:1 fn 1.
23. The *Magen Avraham* attributes this to the *Maggid Mishnah* (22:4). However, the *Maggid Mishnah* never discusses stoking the coals.

Shulchan Arukh HaRav, however, writes that his position is against that of the *Magen Avraham* later on, despite the *Magen Avraham's* position earlier that a full pot can serve as a reminder. In the later reference, the *Magen Avraham* writes that if the bottom pot is on the fire, the top pot has the status of "leaving." The *Peri Megadim* and *Shulchan Arukh HaRav* both understand this to mean that the *Magen Avraham* requires that the food left on a hot pot on Friday must be *ma'achal ben derusa'i,* an apparent contradiction to the *Magen Avraham's* earlier position. The *Peri Megadim* agrees with the later comment of the *Magen Avraham* as he understands it, that the food should be *ma'achal ben derusa'i,* while the *Shulchan Arukh HaRav* disagrees and says the food does not have to be *ma'achal ben derusa'i* when left on a hot pot on Friday.

The *Machatzit HaShekel,* however, understands the *Magen Avraham* differently. In his view, the *Magen Avraham* merely means that, in accordance with the Rama,[24] since the top pot is not enclosed, the laws of *hatmanah* do not apply. Rather than being a case of *hatmanah,* it is a case of "leaving." In his discussion of leaving, the *Magen Avraham* maintains that a pot on top of a pot serves as a reminder not to stoke the coals. If so, he does not necessarily require that the food be *ma'achal ben derusa'i.* In fact, according to his logic,[25] that a full pot removes the concern for stoking the coals, the food need not be *ma'achal ben derusa'i.*

Shulchan Arukh HaRav notes that the *Shulchan Arukh*[26] cites a dispute regarding placing food on a pot which is on the fire. Since the *Magen Avraham*[27] is lenient in viewing a pot on top of a pot as a reminder not to stoke the coals, placing food on a pot on the fire should be permissible on Friday even if the food is not *ma'achal ben derusa'i.* If the *Magen Avraham* requires food to be *ma'achal ben derusa'i,* as the *Shulchan Arukh HaRav* and *Peri Megadim* understood, we must distinguish, as mentioned, between leaving uncooked food on on an uncovered fire on Friday, where there is a concern that he may stoke the coals, and placing anew cooked food on a covered fire on *Shabbat,* where the only

24. *O.C.* 253:1.
25. In 253:33.
26. *O.C.* 318:7,8.
27. 318:26.

concern is that it looks like cooking. The latter concern does not apply if the food is on top of a full pot, since this is not "the way of cooking."

D. RETURNING COOKED FOOD ON TOP OF A POT

This analysis assumes that the concern for stoking the coals is limited to uncooked foods. This is the view of the *Shulchan Arukh*[28] and the Rashba. Only leaving uncooked food on an open fire on Friday is prohibited "lest he stoke the coals." The prohibitions of returning cooked foods and placing cooked foods anew on *Shabbat* are only because of the appearance of cooking.

As mentioned,[29] the *Tosafot* disagree and prohibit returning cooked food on an open fire "lest he stoke the coals." If the *Peri Megadim* is correct, that a full pot does not allay this concern the way an unusual cover does, we should not accept the lenient ruling of the Rashba and the *Shulchan Arukh* that the concern over stoking coals applies only to uncooked foods. Concern over stoking the coals also applies to cooked foods, according to *Tosafot,* and a full pot on the fire is not a good reminder according to the *Peri Megadim.* Therefore, returning cooked food to a pot on top of a pot should be prohibited.

The Rama,[30] who extends the prohibition of returning to Friday just before *Shabbat,* presumably accepts *Tosafot.*[31] If so, the stringent view, disallowing a pot on a pot on Friday right before *Shabbat* and placing it anew on *Shabbat,* should be accepted if the *Peri Megadim*'s concern for stoking the coals exists. Although the Rama[32] is silent on this, his comment in his *Darkei Moshe*[33] implies that the stringent view in the *Shulchan Arukh,*[34] which prohibits placing a pot on a pot, should be followed.

In practice, we may rely on the *Machatzit HaShekel* who is not concerned about stoking the coals if a pot is placed anew on top of a full

28. *O.C.* 253:5.
29. Chapter 18, section A.
30. *O.C.* 253:2.
31. See chapter 15, section B.
32. *O.C.* 253:5.
33. *O.C.* 258:2.
34. *O.C.* 318:7,8.

pot on the oven. One who wants to be stringent should place the bottom pot on a covered fire. The covering (e.g., a *blech*) removes the concern for stoking the coals, and the full pot removes the appearance of cooking.

E. SUMMARY

The *Shulchan Arukh* in 253:5 permits placing dry cooked food on top of a pot to be reheated, since placing food on top of a pot is not the manner of cooking. The *Shulchan Arukh* in 253:3 prohibits placing food anew onto an empty pot. The *Be'ur Halakhah* and *Peri Megadim* believe that the case permitting placing refers to a full pot, and the case prohibiting placing refers to an empty pot on a fire. An empty pot on a fire is considered merely a covered fire.

The *Be'ur Halakhah* and the *Peri Megadim* seem to regard a hot full pot more leniently than a covered fire regarding placing on *Shabbat* (placing on *Shabbat* is permitted onto a hot full pot), but more stringently than a covered fire regarding leaving on *erev Shabbat* (leaving on a hot full pot is prohibited unless the food is *ma'achal ben derusa'i*). This can be resolved by examining the reasons for the prohibitions of placing and returning. Since placing is prohibited because it looks like cooking, a pot on a hot, full pot does not look like cooking and placing is permitted. Leaving, however, is a *gezeirah* "lest one stoke the coals," and a hot full pot on the fire, which is not unusual, cannot serve as a reminder the way a covered fire can, so leaving food on a hot pot is prohibited unless the food is *ma'achal ben derusa'i*.

According to the *Shulkhan Arukh HaRav* and the *Magen Avraham*, however, a hot full pot on a fire can indeed serve as a reminder that one not stoke the coals, since it is unusual to have another pot on top of it. According to the *Shulchan Arukh HaRav*, food may be left on a hot full pot on *erev Shabbat* even if the food has not reached *ma'achal ben derusa'i*. According to the *Peri Megadim*'s interpretation of the *Magen Avraham*, however, food that did not reach *ma'achal ben derusa'i* may still not be left on a hot full pot on *erev Shabbat*. Combining the view of *Tosafot* that returning cooked food to an open fire just before *Shabbat* is prohibited lest one stoke the coals, and the view of the *Peri Megadim* that a pot on top of a pot does not alleviate the concern over stoking the coals, yields the position that returning cooked food on top of a pot is prohibited. In practice, however, we accept the *Machatzit HaShekel*'s understanding of the *Magen Avraham*, that a pot on top of a pot serves as a reminder lest one stoke the coals, in addition to not looking like cooking. Therefore, returning and placing a pot on top of a pot is permitted. One who wants to be extra stringent should cover the fire that the bottom pot is on, to alleviate the *Peri Megadim*'s concern lest one stoke the coals.

21

Other Devices and Views

A. PRACTICAL EXAMPLES: DEVICES THAT MAY OR MAY NOT BE CLASSIFIED AS A "POT ON A POT"

A double boiler has two parts. The lower part is filled with water. The upper part rests on the rim of the lower part. A double boiler is used to reheat the contents of the upper part. It is also used to steam-cook vegetables. *Hilkhot Shabbat*[1] notes that one may not reheat food in a double boiler. Since it is the way of cooking, the leniency of a pot on a pot does not apply.

The *Iggerot Moshe*[2] prohibits placing food anew onto a steam table. Why does the leniency of a pot on a pot not apply? A steam table, unlike a double boiler, is not used for cooking at all.

Perhaps the "pot on a pot" dispensation views the fire as cooking the bottom pot, while the top pot is a mere secondary entity. As such, it does not appear that one is cooking the contents of the top pot. However, this is true only when the contents of the bottom pot are eaten. If the contents of the bottom pot are discarded, then it appears that one is cooking the contents of the top pot which will be eaten.

---

1. Fn. 562.
2. *Orach Chaim* IV, 74:35.

Therefore, placing food anew onto a steam table whose water is discarded looks like cooking and is prohibited according to *Iggerot Moshe*. The same would apply to a double boiler, and to a "*kedeirah blech*," which consists of two "*blechs*" with water between them, since the water is discarded. A "*pelle plate*," which is a box-like urn, whose water is used for tea, would be permitted.

If the top pot is not considered on the oven at all, as the *Be'ur Halakhah* states,[3] it must be because the food is heated only indirectly via the steam generated by the water in the lower pot. Although, as mentioned, the *Peri Megadim* does not accept this definition, the *Chazon Ish*[4] does. If so, a *kedeirah blech* and a steam table would have the leniency of a pot on a pot.

All of the foregoing is based on the *Peri Megadim*'s distinction, accepted by the *Be'ur Halakhah*, between *Orach Chaim* 253:3 (an empty pan covering the fire) and 253:5 (a full pot on top of the fire).[5] A full pot is not "the way of cooking," so cooked food may be placed on it anew. An empty pan is merely a covered fire, so placing anew is prohibited.

B. DISTINCTION BETWEEN LIQUIDS AND SOLIDS

The *Machatzit HaShekel*[6] offers a different distinction. In 253:3 (which prohibits placing onto an empty pan) he refers to a stew containing liquids.[7] Although the person fears that the liquid will dry out and the stew will burn, at present there is liquid, and placing is prohibited. In 253:5 (which permits placing dry cooked food on top of a pot to be reheated) he refers to a dry *kugel*, which has no liquid.[8]

The source for the distinction between liquids and dry foods is the *Magen Avraham*.[9] The *Shulchan Arukh*[10] decides in favor of the

3. See chapter 20, section B.
4. *O.C.* 37:9, end.
5. See chapter 20, section A.
6. *O.C.* 253:34.
7. See chapter 20, section A.
8. *Mishnah Berurah O.C.* 253:86.
9. *O.C.* 318:26.
10. *O.C.* 318:8.

lenient view, found as well elsewhere,[11] that allows placing anew on a pot which is on the fire. Earlier,[12] the *Shulchan Arukh* quotes both views but does not decide which is normative. The *Magen Avraham* explains that the ruling permitting placing anew on a pot which is on the fire refers to cold food, which must be solid, for otherwise there is violation of cooking.[13] Solids may be placed anew on a pot which is on the fire. The comment in which the *Shulchan Arukh* quotes both views but does not decide which is normative refers to warm foods, which may contain liquid. The *Shulchan Arukh* does not render a definitive ruling in that comment, but earlier[14] he quotes the stringent view, prohibiting placing warm liquids anew on a pot which is on the fire.

The *Yechaveh Da'at*[15] accepts the distinction between solids and liquids as the distinction between permitted placing and prohibited placing, and allows taking cold food from the refrigerator and placing it on top of the *blech*. This requires explanation: how does a *blech* differ from a covered fire, on which placing anew is prohibited?[16]

The *Yalkut Yosef*[17] answers that since cooking would occasionally take place on a covered fire, placing anew is prohibited. Nobody ever cooks on a *blech*, a pot, or a pan, and, therefore, one may place dry food onto it.

The *Magen Avraham* offers the distinction between solids and liquids to explain the position of the *Shulchan Arukh*, and this may be the ruling for *Sefardim*. The *Magen Avraham* himself,[18] however, equates solids and liquids. If the *Peri Megadim*'s answer that the distinction between the two cases in the *Shulchan Arukh* is between a full pot (placing is permitted) and an empty pan (placing is prohibited) is accepted, *Ashkenazim* may not place cold dry food onto a *blech*.

11. *O.C.* 253:5.
12. *O.C.* 318:7.
13. *O.C.* 318:4.
14. *O.C.* 253:3.
15. II, 45.
16. *Shabbat* 38b, *O.C.* 253:23, *Mishnah Berurah* 55,81.
17. *O.C.* 253:9.
18. *O.C.*318:26, and 253:36.

The *Shemirat Shabbat KeHilkhatah*[19] suggests that it may be permissible to place cold dry food onto an inverted pan. This seems to be against the *Be'ur Halakhah* that he quotes there. The other sources are all based on the Rama,[20] who cites the Ran, based on the Yerushalmi, who allows placing cold dry food onto a covered fire if the food was on the fire when *Shabbat* entered. Both the Rama and the *Shemirat Shabbat KeHilkhatah*[21] advise not to rely on this leniency.[22]

The *Shemirat Shabbat KeHilkhatah*[23] adds that one should place an inverted plate under the pan. R. S.Z. Auerbach[24] explains that an additional cover achieves that it is not "the way of cooking."

In reality, however, even on a single covering, such as a *blech,* is not "the way of cooking," as *Yalkut Yosef* writes. Nonetheless, we are stringent and do not allow placing anew on a *blech.* Only on a full pot, when the source of heat – the steam – is itself unusual and the fire only indirectly heats the food do we allow placing anew, as the *Chazon Ish* states. Two coverings seem to be no better than one.

C. SUMMARY

Food may not be reheated in a double boiler since doing so is "the way of cooking." According to the *Iggerot Moshe,* food may not be reheated on a steam table or *kedeirah blech* on *Shabbat* because the bottom water is discarded and the device looks like cooking. By contrast, a "*pelle plate,*" a box-like urn, whose water is used for tea, is permitted. However, if one accepts the *Be'ur Halakhah*'s position that placing on a hot pot is not like placing on an oven, a steam table or a *kedeirah blech* is permitted.

Revisiting the two cases in the *Shulchan Arukh* discussed in the beginning of chapter 20, the *Shulchan Arukh* in 253:5 permits placing dry cooked food on top of a pot to be reheated, since placing food on top of a pot is not the manner of cooking. The *Shulchan Arukh* in 253:3 prohibits placing food anew onto an empty pot. According to *Mach-*

19. Ch. 1 fn. 112.
20. *O.C.* 253:2.
21. 1:20.
22. See Chapter 24B.
23. Ch. 1 fn. 66.
24. *Shemirat Shabbat KeHilkhatah* vol. 3, fn 112.

atzit HaShekel, the distinction between the two cases is not between a full and empty pot. Placing on an empty pot is prohibited for liquids and permitted only for solids. An empty pot is not equal to a covered fire, because a covered fire is occasionally used for cooking, but a fire with an empty pot, or a *blech,* on it is not the manner of cooking at all. *Sefardim* may place dry food directly on a *blech,* but *Ashkenazim* accept the *Peri Megadim*'s understanding of the distinction between the two cases (full pot – permitted; empty pot – prohibited) in the *Shulchan Arukh* and may not place dry food directly on a *blech.* The *Shemirat Shabbat KeHilkhatah* proposes that that one may place dry food onto an inverted pan, preferably with an inverted plate underneath as well, so it is not the way of cooking.

In practice, for *Ashkenazim,* it is permitted to place anew only onto a full pot, which preferably should be on a fire that is itself covered.

22

The Status of "Near the Oven"

A. RELEVANCE OF THE HALAKHAH OF "NEAR THE OVEN" TO THE DISPUTE BETWEEN *RABBANAN* AND CHANANYAH

The Talmud[1] questions whether or not placing a pot near the oven (*semikhah*), not on top of it, is permitted. After citing and debating several proofs, the Talmud permits placing a pot near the oven, not on top of it. In order to be considered near the oven, rather than on top of it, *Tosafot* require that the wall of the oven separate between the fire and the pot. The *Hagahot Mordechai*[2] disagrees and maintains that a wall is not required. The *Shulchan Arukh* is silent, while the *Magen Avraham*[3] requires a separating wall, unless the pot is somewhat distant from the fire. When one of these factors is present – there is a separating wall or the pot is somewhat distant from the fire – there is a recognizable reminder not to stoke the coals.

1. *Shabbat* 37a.
2. *Shabbat* 55b.
3. O.C. 318:38.

The Rif[4] infers that only placing the pot *near* the oven is permitted. *On* the oven is prohibited, which, according to the Rif, proves the position of *Rabbanan* against Chananyah.[5] The *Ba'al HaMa'or*[6] asks what the proof is. As the *Tosafot*[7] say, "placing near" applies to returning as well as to leaving. Chananyah prohibits returning onto an uncovered fire. The Talmud permits returning near the oven, but not on the oven. This does not contradict Chananyah at all.

The Ran[8] offers a textual answer. The Talmud contrasts into and onto an oven, with near the oven. Just as onto the oven is prohibited if the fire is uncovered, so too into the oven. Now, returning into the oven is prohibited even if the fire is covered.[9] Leaving in the oven on Friday, by contrast, is permitted if the fire is covered. By limiting the prohibition to an uncovered fire, the Talmud must be referring to leaving, not returning, since returning is prohibited whether the fire is covered or not. The Talmud's statement is thus that only leaving *near* the oven is allowed. Leaving *on* it is prohibited, against Chananyah.

We can still ask, perhaps the Talmud refers to leaving uncooked food on the oven, which even Chananyah prohibits. The *Korban Netan'el*[10] gives a textual answer. The Talmud resolves the question of whether or not putting a pot next to the oven is permitted from a *beraita* which allows returning. The *beraita* allowing returning must refer to cooked food, to avoid a violation of cooking on *Shabbat*. The Ritva[11] asserts that the *beraita* allowing returning must refer to cooked food to explain why the Talmud did not suggest that the *mishnah* refers to putting uncooked foods next to the fire. Since the end of the *mishnah* permits returning, it must refer to cooked foods only.

4. *Shabbat* 16a.
5. See above, chapter 16.
6. *Shabbat* 15b.
7. *Shabbat* 37a.
8. *Shabbat* 16a.
9. *Shabbat* 37a, *O.C.* 253:3.
10. *Shabbat* 3:1:3.
11. *Shabbat* 36b.

Based on the *Or Same'ach,*[12] a conceptual explanation of the Rif can be given. If returning is prohibited because it looks like cooking, near the oven is identical to on the oven with respect to returning, since cooking can take place near the oven as well. The Rif, like the Rashba and Ran,[13] prohibits returning because it looks like cooking. Perforce, the statement of the Talmud which permits placing near the fire refers to leaving before *Shabbat.* This proves that leaving food *on* the fire is prohibited, like *Rabbanan* against Chananyah.

The *Ba'al HaMa'or* questions this proof, which is based on the premise that returning is prohibited because it looks like cooking, because the *Ba'al HaMa'or* holds, like *Tosafot,* that returning is prohibited lest one stoke the coals.[14] Placing food near, rather than on, the fire is a recognizable reminder not to stoke the coals, both for leaving and for returning the food. Therefore, the Talmud's permission to put a pot near the fire can refer to returning, which Chananyah prohibits on, but not near, the fire, and there is no proof against Chananyah.

B. RETURNING NEAR THE FIRE ON *SHABBAT*

The *Magen Avraham*[15] cites the Rambam[16] who, like the Rif, prohibits returning near the fire. However, according to the second opinion in the *Shulchan Arukh,*[17] which follows Chananyah, even returning on *Shabbat* near the fire is permitted, as the Rama[18] states. The *Magen Avraham*'s statement is understood in two different ways by later authorities. The two different understandings of the *Magen Avraham* depend on whether the later authority views the Talmud's discussion on *Shabbat* 37a to be only about leaving near the oven, or about both leaving and returning near the oven.

The *Dagul MeRevavah* maintains that returning is certainly permitted near the fire. Placing anew, *hanachah,* depends upon the two

12. *Hilkhot Shabbat* 3:1.
13. See chapter 17, section A.
14. See chapter 17, section A.
15. 253:5
16. *Hilkhot Shabbat* 3:10.
17. *O.C.* 253:1.
18. *O.C.* 253:5.

opinions in the *Shulchan Arukh.* According to *Rabbanan* it is prohibited; according to Chananyah it is permitted.

R. Akiva Eiger disagrees. In his view, placing anew near the oven is certainly prohibited. It is returning that depends upon the two opinions in the *Shulchan Arukh.* According to *Rabbanan* it is prohibited. According to Chananyah it is permitted.

The Talmud[19] cites a *beraita* concerning two adjoining ovens, one covered and one uncovered. One may leave [a pot] on the covered one – even though the covered oven is near the uncovered one. This proves that leaving near an uncovered fire is permissible.

The *Machatzit HaShekel*[20] states that the Rif proved that the Talmud refers to leaving,[21] and not returning, from the proof from the *beraita* about adjoining ovens, which deals with leaving. The *Ba'al HaMa'or* and *Tosafot* hold that leaving and returning are equivalent, since both are prohibited "lest he stoke the coals." If leaving is permitted, so is returning, according to Chananyah. According to the Rif, who maintains that returning is prohibited because it looks like cooking, one cannot derive returning from leaving. The Talmud's proof from the *beraita* about leaving indicates that the entire discussion is limited to leaving *near* the fire. This proves that leaving *on* the fire is prohibited, like *Rabbanan* and against Chananyah.

The *Dagul MeRevavah* proves that returning near a fire is permissible from the aforementioned *beraita* permitting leaving near an oven. R. Akiva Eiger retorts that the *beraita* refers to leaving, but not returning. R. Akiva Eiger believes returning cannot be derived from leaving since the reason for returning is that it looks like cooking. The *Be'ur Halakhah*[22] answers for the *Dagul MeRevavah* that the end of the *beraita,* cited earlier in the Talmud, deals with returning as well, a point noted by the Ramban. The Talmud's discussion of a pot near the fire is therefore about both leaving and returning.

---

19. *Shabbat* 37a.
20. O.C. 253:5.
21. See section A of this chapter.
22. O.C. 253:2.

The Ramban writes that the *Ba'al HaMa'or* could have rebutted the Rif's proof on the basis of the fact that the *beraita* about adjoining ovens discusses returning. The Rif cannot claim that the Talmud's discussion of a pot near the fire is limited to leaving. The Rif would counter that since the Talmud, in its proof, cites only the first part of the *beraita*, dealing with leaving, the discussion of a pot near the fire is limited to leaving. If the discussion of a pot near the fire in the Talmud is limited to leaving, we can say, like R. Akiva Eiger, that returning next to a fire is not automatically permitted by the Talmud. Rather, returning depends upon the dispute between Chananyah and *Rabbanan*, and placing anew is prohibited. If we follow Chananyah, the Talmud's question must deal with returning near a fire, since leaving is permissible even on the fire. The proof from two adjoining ovens permits returning, which can be derived from leaving, as we shall see. If we follow *Rabbanan*, the Talmud's question deals with leaving, and returning is prohibited.

The Talmud's final proof is from the very beginning of the *beraita*,[23] which allows placing near but not leaving on (*mash'hin*, in the Rif's text). This proves that the Talmud only deals with leaving. The *Ba'al HaMa'or* refutes this. He believes that although the Talmud might deal only with leaving, we can derive returning from leaving. From leaving according to *Rabbanan*, whose concern regarding leaving is lest he stoke the coals, we derive returning according to Chananyah, whose concern regarding returning is also lest he stoke the coals. Therefore from the position of *Rabbanan* regarding leaving, we derive Chananyah's position regarding returning, because both positions have the same reason.

The Ramban asks against the view of the *Ba'al HaMa'or* as follows. How can returning be derived from leaving? Returning is treated more stringently than leaving according to Chananyah. For example, leaving in an oven is permitted, but returning into the oven is prohibited.[24] The Talmud may permit leaving near the fire, but permission for returning near the fire may not be derived from the permission for leaving, since Chananyah is more stringent about returning. The Ran defends the *Ba'al*

23. *Tosefta Shabbat* 3:1.

24. *Shabbat* 37a; see section A of this chapter.

HaMa'or: with respect to near the fire, leaving and returning are equivalent and one can indeed derive returning from leaving.

The Ran can be explained as follows. In the oven is treated more stringently than on the oven because it looks like cooking, a factor relevant to returning, not leaving. As mentioned, the *Ba'al HaMa'or*[25] holds that returning onto an oven is prohibited not because it looks like cooking, but lest one stoke the coals. Therefore, leaving near an oven and returning near an oven are equivalent regarding the concern for stoking. The distinction between leaving and returning regarding in the oven is based on returning into the oven looking like cooking, and is irrelevant to the status of leaving and returning onto or near the oven if one believes that the only concern is stoking the coals.

As mentioned, the *Magen Avraham*[26] cites the Rama. The Rama writes: "It has already been explained that the custom is to be lenient and return on *Shabbat* even if it was put down on the ground. The same applies to placing it near an uncovered oven."

R. Akiva Eiger proves his position, that placing anew is definitely prohibited, from this citation. The citation permits only situations classified as returning, not classified as placing anew. The custom to which the Rama refers is the aforementioned leniency of the Ran[27] based on the Yerushalmi. Only if the pot is removed before *Shabbat* is placing anew on *Shabbat* prohibited. If the pot was on the fire when *Shabbat* entered, even if it is put down on the floor, it is treated like returning and is permissible onto a covered fire.

The Rama applies this to placing near an uncovered oven. Near an uncovered oven, too, returning is permissible since we follow Chananyah,[28] and placing anew is prohibited. Our custom is to consider putting a pot near an uncovered oven to be returning, not placing anew, even if the pot was put on the ground. Therefore, the pot may be placed near an uncovered fire. Had putting a pot near an uncovered fire been considered placing anew, it would be prohibited.

---

25. *Shabbat* 17a.
26. *O.C.* 253:5.
27. Cited in *O.C.* 253:2; see chapter 21, section B.
28. *O.C.* 253:1.

Despite his citation of the leniency regarding returning, the Rama[29] in fact says one should be strict and not rely on the custom to follow the Ran. Therefore, one should not place anew onto a covered fire, and one should not place anew near an uncovered oven as well.

C. RETURNING FOODS WHICH DETERIORATE ONTO AN UNCOVERED FIRE

The *Sha'ar HaTziyun*[30] quotes the "Ran,"[31] a work which was attributed to the famous Ran, author of the commentary on the Rif, but in reality was written by a different, unknown author. He agrees with R. Akiva Eiger that placing anew is prohibited and returning depends on the dispute between *Rabbanan* and Chananyah. We now know that the real Ran, Rabbenu Nissim, did not write the so-called "Ran."

Interestingly, the "Ran"[32] permits returning foods which deteriorate when they lose moisture onto an uncovered oven. The real Ran prohibits returning even foods which deteriorate onto an uncovered fire, based on the statement of the Talmud,[33] which derives that food may be returned onto a covered fire on *Shabbat* from a case of water. Water deteriorates by losing volume when placed on the fire. If there is a difference between foods which improve and those which deteriorate, we cannot prove from water, which deteriorates by losing volume, that foods which improve may be returned onto a covered fire. Since there is no difference between foods which improve and foods which deteriorate, as the Talmudic proof establishes, neither food which deteriorates, and certainly not food which improves, may be returned onto an uncovered fire.

The "Ran,"[34] however, writes that water may indeed be placed on an uncovered fire. We are not concerned that one may stoke the coals. Stoking hastens the loss of moisture, and the equivalent loss of volume of water, so a person will not do so for water or other foods which will

29. *O.C* 253:2.
30. *O.C.* 253:20, 21.
31. *Shabbat* 38a.
32. *Shabbat* 38a.
33. *Shabbat* 38b.
34. *Shabbat* 38b.

deteriorate. This proves that even foods which improve may be placed on a covered fire. If the fire is covered, there is similarly no concern of stoking the coals.

As mentioned,[35] the real Ran prohibits returning because it looks like cooking, unless the fire is covered. Therefore, even if the food deteriorates, returning to an uncovered fire still looks like cooking and is prohibited.

D. SUMMARY

Authorities (such as the Rif and the Ran) who believe that the reason for the prohibition of returning is that returning looks like cooking, understand the Talmud on *Shabbat* 37a to permit *leaving* a pot near the fire, but not returning a pot near the fire, because returning near the fire looks like cooking. Authorities (such as the *Tosafot* and *Ba'al HaMa'or*), who believe that the reason for the prohibition of returning is lest one stoke the coals, understand the Talmud on *Shabbat* 37a to permit both returning and leaving a pot near the fire, because the pot being near, not on, the fire is a reminder not to stoke the coals. According to the Rif and Ran's understanding, the Talmud on *Shabbat* 37a disproves Chananyah who permits leaving on an uncovered fire and returning to a covered fire, since *Shabbat* 37a permits leaving next to the fire only, but not on the fire. According to the *Ba'al HaMa'or*'s understanding, the Talmud on *Shabbat* 37a does not disprove Chananyah, since *Shabbat* 37a permits returning next to the fire, which is equivalent to returning to a covered fire in alleviating the concern lest one stoke the coals.

According to the *Dagul MeRevavah*'s understanding of the *Magen Avraham*, returning near the fire is permitted according to both Chananyah and *Rabbanan*. Permission for returning near the fire can be derived from the Talmud's (*Shabbat* 37a) position permitting leaving near the fire, since both leaving and returning are prohibited lest one stoke the coals, and there is no concern lest one stoke the coals when the pot is near the fire. Placing anew new the fire, however, is permitted only if one follows Chananyah's opinion.

According to R. Akiva Eiger's understanding of the *Magen Avra-*

35. Chapter 17, section A.

ham, however, placing anew near the fire is prohibited according to both Chananyah and *Rabbanan.* Returning near the fire is permitted according to Chananyah (near the fire alleviates the concern lest one stoke the coals), but prohibited according to *Rabbanan* (since near the fire still looks like cooking). Permissibility of returning cannot be derived from the permissibility of leaving, since each is prohibited for a different reason.

Returning foods which deteriorate when they lose moisture may be permitted even onto an uncovered fire if the reason that returning is prohibited is lest one stoke the coals. One will not stoke the coals if the food will deteriorate. Returning foods which deteriorate when they lose moisture onto an uncovered fire is prohibited if the reason that returning is prohibited is that it looks like cooking. Whether the food will deteriorate or not, returning to an uncovered fire still looks like cooking and is prohibited.

23

Returning into the Oven

A. THE REASON FOR THE PROHIBITION OF RETURNING INTO AN OVEN

As mentioned,[1] the Talmud[2] prohibits returning food into an oven on *Shabbat*. The *Mishnah Berurah*[3] cites the Ran and the Rashba who explain that since we usually cook in the oven, returning into an oven appears like cooking even if the fire is covered.

It is possible that the Ran and the Rashba, who prohibit returning onto an uncovered fire because it looks like cooking,[4] give the same reason for returning into an oven with a covered fire. However, those who prohibit returning onto an uncovered fire "lest he stoke the coals" may explain the stringency of returning into an oven with a covered fire lest one stoke the coals as well. Since we established[5] that the Rama and the *Mishnah Berurah* hold that returning is prohibited lest one stoke the coals, our question, whether the stringency of returning into an oven is

1. Chapter 22, section A.
2. *Shabbat* 37a.
3. *O.C.* 253:58.
4. See chapter 17, section A.
5. Chapter 18, section B.

based on a fear "lest he stoke the coals," or based on the appearance of cooking, has particular relevance.

B. WARMING DRAWERS AND STOVETOP KNOBS

A warming drawer is used only to reheat and not to cook. Its temperature is adjustable. May one return food into a warming drawer if the fire is covered? This does not have the appearance of cooking, since no one cooks in a warming drawer. On the other hand, there may be a concern of stoking the coals, i.e., adjusting the heat setting.

The *Rishonim* who argue with the Ran and the Rashba, and prohibit returning onto an uncovered fire lest he stoke the coals, include, as mentioned, the *Ba'al HaMa'or*, *Tosafot*, and the so-called "Ran."[6] The "Ran"[7] explains that inside an oven is treated more stringently because it looks like cooking. It is not treated more stringently regarding the concern that one may stoke the coals of the covered fire.

Similarly, the real Ran, in his aforementioned defense of the *Ba'al HaMa'or*,[8] equates inside the oven to on the oven with respect to leaving food there on Friday, since they are equivalent with regard to the concern of stoking the coals. If so, it should be permissible to return food into a warming drawer if the fire is covered. We are not concerned with stoking the coals, as we derived from the "Ran" and the real Ran, and it does not look like cooking since no one cooks in a warming drawer.

There may be a technical problem, however. A cover must be a recognizable reminder serving as a deterrent to adjusting the fire. Covering the floor of the warming drawer might not suffice if the adjustable setting is reached before the cover can even be seen. (This problem may perhaps be solved by covering the surface with aluminum foil which then extends upwards and is seen before the adjustable setting. However, this solution is sometimes impractical.)

It is a matter of dispute whether merely covering the knob is sufficient on a standard stovetop. *Iggerot Moshe*[9] rules that such covering

6. See chapter 22, sections A and C.
7. *Shabbat* 37a.
8. Chapter 22, section B.
9. *Orach Chaim* I, 93.

is insufficient; one must create the reminder required by the Talmud, namely, covering the fire. Others disagree, and rule that covering the knob suffices, since the knob is the point of adjustment.[10] Generally, the *Iggerot Moshe*'s view is accepted.

Nevertheless, the Talmud[11] says that if one plasters over the opening of the oven, there is no concern for stoking the coals. According to the Rama,[12] this applies to all foods. The *Be'ur Halakhah* explains that one will not go through the bother of undoing the plaster in order to stoke the coals. This is a possible solution for the warming drawer.

However, the *Chazon Ish*[13] asserts that the Talmud's ruling that there is no concern for stoking the coals on a plastered oven refers only to leaving on Friday. Therefore, one may not place food on *Shabbat,* even if there is a covering of the plaster. This seems to rule out plastering as a solution to the problem of returning or placing anew into a warming drawer on *Shabbat.* However, the *Shevut Yitzchak*[14] writes that the *Chazon Ish* only prohibits placing anew, but would permit returning.

The reason for the *Shevut Yitzchak*'s distinction is as follows. The *Chazon Ish* rules that returning is prohibited only lest one stoke the coals. Stoking the coals is not a concern if there is a plaster cover. However, placing anew in an oven looks like cooking, and plastering does not remove this prohibition.

Placing anew in a warming drawer, however, does not look like cooking, since no one cooks there. If so, if there is a plaster cover, or its equivalent, on the adjustable knob, which prevents the concern for adjusting, one may place cold dry food anew into a warming drawer. Many pieces of tape, placed in a way that they cannot all be pulled off at once so that it is a bother to undo them, is the equivalent of a plaster covering. (*Orchot Shabbat*[15] considers even one piece of tape to be like plastering. This seems very questionable.)

---

10. *Hilchos Shabbos,* fn. 63, citing R. Aharon Kotler.
11. *Shabbat* 18b.
12. O.C. 254:1.
13. O.C. 38:2.
14. P. 126-7.
15. P. 68-9.

C. CROCKPOTS

The Talmud[16] permits placing completely raw meat in a pot on an uncovered fire just before *Shabbat*. One raw piece permits placing other food as well. The *Shulchan Arukh*[17] quotes this leniency, and the *Mishnah Berurah*[18] explains that raw meat cannot be cooked for the evening meal, so there is no fear that one would stoke the coals.

Nowadays, our ovens can cook very quickly, so this leniency should not be relied upon. *The Shabbos Kitchen*[19] permits raw food in a crockpot which cooks slowly.

Most crockpots have a circular insert which is surrounded by a circular base. Only the top is exposed. The simple reading of the Rama[20] is that as long as the top is exposed there is no violation of *hatmanah*, or insulating.

However, the *Peri Megadim*[21] suggests that the Rama permits leaving only if the pot is completely exposed, in contrast to the *Shulchan Arukh*[22] who prohibits leaving even if the pot is completely exposed, if the pot is directly on top of the fire.

Rabbenu Tam[23] defines *hatmanah* as a pot covered mostly or completely by the insulation. If so, a crockpot may not be used because of *hatmanah*.

However, there is a way to change the configuration of the crockpot so that the insert is not mostly covered. According to Rav Y.S. Elyashiv,[24] if one raises the insert (with marbles or the like), the bottom is not considered enclosed, since there is visible space between the pot and the fire.[25] The part of the insert that is elevated above the walls of the base (by the marbles), together with the top and the bottom,

---

16. *Shabbat* 18b.
17. *O.C.* 253:1.
18. *O.C.* 253:9.
19. P. 56.
20. *O.C.* 253:1.
21. 254, *M.Z.* 3.
22. *O.C.* 253:1.
23. *Sefer HaYashar* 235.
24. See *Orchot Shabbat*, p. 540.
25. See *Shulchan Arukh* 253:1, 257:8.

likely constitute a majority which is "uncovered" and is permissible according to Rabbenu Tam. In a tapered crockpot, elevating the insert may create a visible space along the entire surface of the insert.

D. OUR OVENS AND CROCKPOTS

The Ramban[26] explains that the inside of the oven is treated more stringently because it is hotter than on the oven. This would apply to our ovens as well, as the *Iggerot Moshe*[27] rules.

The *Arukh HaShulchan,*[28] however, interprets the *Shiltei HaGibborim,* cited in *Magen Avraham,*[29] as follows. If there are two ways to heat the food, on or in the oven, on the oven is permitted and in the oven is prohibited. If one can only use the inside of the oven, it is treated like on the oven. This is relevant to our ovens and to crockpots. Since one cannot place foods on our ovens and crockpots[30] the inside is treated like on the oven.

Once again, however, in practice the *Iggerot Moshe* is followed.

E. SUMMARY

Returning into a oven if the fire is covered is prohibited because it looks like cooking. A warming drawer does not look like cooking, so returning into it is permitted if the concern "lest one stoke the coals" (in this case, adjust the temperature setting) is alleviated by taping up the temperature knob in such a way that it would be extremely inconvenient to remove the tape to adjust the temperature. The *Iggerot Moshe* rules that one must cover the actual fire on a stovetop in a clearly recognizable way to avoid the concern lest one stoke the coals. This is sometimes impractical in the case of a warming drawer. However, the dispensation of "plastering" applies to a warming drawer. Therefore, one may place dry, cooked food anew into a warming drawer, if the adjustable knob is convered with many pieces of tape.

---

26. *Shabbat* 37a.
27. *Orach Chaim* IV, 74:20.
28. *O.C.* 253:17.
29. *O.C.* 253:22.
30. The stovetop is a completely different fire, but see *Hilchos Shabbos* (fn. 963) quoting R. Aharon Kotler.

One may place raw food in a crockpot right before *Shabbat* since it cooks slowly and there is no concern lest one stoke the coals. A crockpot's configuration should be changed to avoid the prohibition of *hatmanah* (insulating) by elevating the insert so that the entire insert is not covered by the sides of the crockpot.

Though the *Arukh HaShulchan,* based on the *Shiltei HaGibborim,* rules that the inside of our ovens today is treated like on the oven, since there is no way to place food on top of our ovens, the Ramban rules that the inside of the oven is treated more stringently because the heat is greater than on the oven. The *Iggerot Moshe* applies the Ramban's rule to our ovens today. We follow the *Iggerot Moshe*'s ruling in practice.

24

Permissible Cases of Leaving, Returning and Placing

A. LEAVING FOOD ON AN UNCOVERED FIRE ON *EREV SHABBAT*: THE POSITION OF THE *SHULCHAN ARUKH*

As mentioned, the Rif[1] rules like *Rabbanan* against Chananyah.[2] In order to leave food on Friday on an uncovered fire, the food must be fully cooked and must deteriorate if moisture is removed.[3] The *Shulchan Arukh*[4] quotes the Rif, and then quotes *Tosafot* who rule like Chananyah. The Rama says that we follow the lenient, second opinion, like Chananyah. If the food reached the point of *ma'achal ben derusa'i*, it may be left on an uncovered fire. The *Shulchan Arukh* adds that if the fire is covered, even uncooked food may be left on the covered fire before *Shabbat*.

1. *Shabbat* 16a.
2. See chapter 21, section A.
3. See chapter 16, section A.
4. *O.C.* 253:1.

R. Akiva Eiger questions the *Shulchan Arukh*'s ruling that even uncooked food may be left before *Shabbat* if the fire is covered. The Rif[5] quotes the Talmud:[6] "How much must it be roasted [before *Shabbat*]? *Ma'achal ben derusa'i.*" The Rosh[7] asks: The use of the term *ma'achal ben derusa'i* in the statement of the Talmud links this statement to Chananyah. However, the Rif rejects Chananyah. Why then does the Rif mention the *ma'achal ben derusa'i* criterion? R. Yonah answers that the Rif means that if the food reached *ma'achal ben derusa'i* it may be placed on a covered fire according to *Rabbanan*. Why, asks R. Akiva Eiger, does the *Shulchan Arukh* ignore R. Yonah and permit leaving even uncooked food on a covered fire?

We can answer as follows: The *Shulchan Arukh* permits leaving uncooked food on a covered fire when quoting the second opinion, of Chananyah. For those who adhere to the first, strict opinion, as the *Be'ur Halakhah* (s.v. *venahagu*) advises, the view of R. Yonah, that a covered fire should be used only for food that has reached *ma'achal ben derusa'i,* should be followed.

The Ran[8] answers the Rosh's question differently. Since roasted food has no separation between it and the fire (as does food cooked in a pot), stoking the coals can easily ruin the food. Therefore, the Rif allows leaving *ma'achal ben derusa'i* roasted food on an open fire. The *Shulchan Arukh* quotes this view.[9] Thus, even according to the Rif we do not accept the opinion of R. Yonah, that a covered fire should be used only for food that has reached *ma'achal ben derusa'i.*

R. Akiva Eiger asks another question. The Rashba[10] is concerned that one will stir the pot if it is not *ma'achal ben derusa'i,* thereby violating the *melakhah* of cooking. For that concern, covering the fire is ineffective. Why does the *Shulchan Arukh* allow placing uncooked food on a covered fire?

---

5. *Shabbat* 8a.
6. *Shabbat* 20a.
7. *Shabbat* 3:1.
8. *Shabbat* 6b.
9. O.C. 254:1.
10. *Shabbat* 18b.

We can answer in the following manner: The Rashba holds that once food reaches *ma'achal ben derusa'i,* further cooking is permissible.[11] However, the *Shulchan Arukh,*[12] following the Rambam,[13] requires that the food be fully cooked. Hence, the *Shulchan Arukh* cannot possibly be concerned with stirring, for if he were concerned with stirring, we should prohibit leaving *ma'achal ben derusa'i* food even on a covered fire, something which the Talmud[14] permits. We must, therefore, follow the Ramban[15] who is not concerned about stirring at all.

B. RETURNING TO AN OVEN NOT FUELED BY COALS

The *mishnah*[16] permits placing food on an oven fueled with straw. According to Chananyah, permitting placing food on an oven fueled by straw refers to returning food on *Shabbat.* If returning is prohibited "lest he stoke the coals," this is readily understandable, as there are no coals. But if returning is prohibited because it looks like cooking, why is it permissible when the oven is fueled by straw?

We must answer that since the fire is not as strong when there are no coals, it is not "the way of cooking," and, therefore, returning does not look like cooking.

Similarly, the Rama[17] quotes the *Kol Bo* who permits placing anew food into an oven which was baked in on Friday. There is only a small amount of residual heat from the Friday baking, so there is no concern of the appearance of cooking.[18]

The *Be'ur Halakhah*[19] compares a fire fueled by straw to a covered fire. If so, placing anew is prohibited, as *Shemirat Shabbat KeHilkhatah*[20]

11. See chapter 4, section A.
12. *O.C.* 318:4.
13. See chapter 4 section A.
14. *Shabbat* 36b.
15. *Shabbat* 18b.
16. *Shabbat* 36b; see chapter 16, section A.
17. *O.C.* 253:5.
18. *Mishnah Berurah* 253:90.
19. *O.C.* 253, s.v. *mutar.*
20. 1 fn. 71.

rules. Why does the Rama permit placing anew into an oven which has residual heat from Friday's baking?

The answer is found in the *Darkei Moshe HaArokh.*[21] He quotes the Ran and the Yerushalmi that if the food was on the fire when *Shabbat* entered, placing anew after the pot was placed on the floor is considered returning.[22] "And so wrote the *Kol Bo,* etc." The view of the *Kol Bo* is based on the Ran who treats placing a pot which was removed on *Shabbat* and put on the floor as returning, and not as placing anew which is prohibited even if the oven is fueled by straw or, presumably, residual heat.

The *Mishnah Berurah*[23] concludes that the *Kol Bo,* permits placing anew in an oven only if it has a little residual heat from Friday's baking. But the Rama[24] records a custom to place anew into an oven in all cases, although he recommends that one act stringently on the matter.

C. PLACING ANEW FOODS THAT ARE NOT USUALLY BAKED IN AN OVEN

The *Magen Avraham*[25] quotes the *Darkei Moshe HaArokh* at length. He understands the Rama as permitting placing anew into any oven, as long as the pot was in the oven when *Shabbat* began. The *Magen Avraham* asks: The Rama, based on the Ran and the Yerushalmi, treats placing anew as returning. However, even returning into the oven is prohibited.[26] Why does the Rama seem to permit placing anew into any oven?

A careful reading of the *Darkei Moshe* yields a completely different understanding of the Rama. The *Beit Yosef* quotes the Ran,[27] who allows placing kugel on an oven, since it is not ordinarily baked on the oven. Therefore, it is obvious that the kugel is placed on the oven only to heat, and it does not look like cooking. The *Beit Yosef* adds that the kugel may not be placed inside the oven because it is usual to bake it there.

21. *O.C.* 253:4.
22. See chapter 21, section B, and chapter 22, section B.
23. *O.C.* 253:90.
24. *O.C.* 253:2, and *Darkei Moshe HaArokh,* 4.
25. *O.C.* 253:35.
26. *Shabbat* 37a, *O.C.* 253:2.
27. *Shabbat* 19a in pages of the Rif.

Later, the *Beit Yosef* cites the Ran[28] and the Yerushalmi, who permit returning to a covered fire, and equates an oven whose coals have dimmed to a covered fire. But the custom was to place into an oven, a practice which the Ran and Yerushalmi cannot justify, since they permit only placing onto the oven.

The *Beit Yosef* then quotes the aforementioned *Kol Bo*[29] who permits placing into an oven in which food was baked on Friday. The *Beit Yosef* rejects the *Kol Bo,* since the permissible level of residual heat is arbitrary. He adds that the *Kol Bo*'s permission to place into an oven does not apply if the oven was heated to keep food hot for *Shabbat,* even if the coals were removed. Finally, he quotes the Ran who rules that kugel may be placed on the oven since it is not usually cooked on the oven, and applies this ruling even inside an oven for foods that are not usually baked inside the oven. However, it is still proper to prohibit placing inside the oven foods which are not usually baked in an oven, since it is controversial and can lead to prohibited activity.

Commenting on this, the *Darkei Moshe* says that the *Beit Yosef* was strict regarding the placing inside an oven of foods which are not usually baked in an oven only for cold foods, and our custom is to rely on the Ran for hot foods. The *Beit Yosef*'s earlier addition, that the Ran permits only on the oven and not in it, has no source in the Ran. (In reality, the *Beit Yosef* added that placing in the oven is prohibited since the food is baked in the oven. At the end the *Beit Yosef* permits the placing in the oven only food which is not usually baked there.)

It emerges that the *Darkei Moshe* permitted placing inside an oven only food which is usually not baked there, as the Ran ruled. The *Magen Avraham* understood that the Rama relied on the Ran quoting the Yerushalmi. This cannot permit placing in an oven, as the *Magen Avraham* asks. In truth, the Rama relied on the Ran's own ruling that foods may be placed where they are not usually baked, which can apply even inside the oven.

For foods which are baked in ovens, such as chicken and kugel, there is no early opinion which permits the food to be placed into the

28. *Shabbat* 17b in pages of the Rif.

29. See section B of this chapter.

oven. The *Magen Avraham,* who understood the Rama as permitting it, himself rejected this opinion. In reality, the Rama never permitted it. The *Mishnah Berurah,*[30] who says that the Rama permitted it, is difficult, as *Chazon Ish*[31] notes.

Perhaps those who place cold dry food into an oven rely on the aforementioned *Arukh HaShulchan*[32] that treats in the oven like on the oven if there is no way to cook food on the oven.[33] But this is a minority view and should not be relied upon, especially since even if in the oven is treated as on the fire, the Rama writes that, despite the custom to rely on the Ran based on the Yerushalmi, one should be stringent.

D. AMOUNT OF HEAT IN THE OVEN: *YAD SOLEDET BO* OR BELOW?

After quoting the *Kol Bo* permitting returning food into the oven which was baked in on Friday,[34] the Rama[35] adds: "Only if the food is not totally cooled off. Some are stringent; if the heat in the oven is *yad soledet bo* it is prohibited."

The *Mishnah Berurah*[36] cites the Gra[37] who emends the text: "Some are stringent that if," etc. In *Sha'ar HaTziyun*[38] he proves the validity of the Gra's emendation. Otherwise, the stricter view prohibits even when the heat is less than *yad soledet bo*. There is no reason to prohibit returning when the heat is less than *yad soledet bo*. The Rama[39] permits returning food when it remains cooler than *yad soledet bo*. The stringent view, in the *Beit Yosef,*[40] says we do not rely on an arbitrary *shi'ur* of temperature, but *yad soledet bo* is well established. Hence, the *Kol Bo* must prohibit returning only to *yad soledet bo* heat.

---

30. 253:90.
31. *O.C.* 37:8.
32. *O.C.* 253:17.
33. See chapter 23, section B.
34. See section B of this chapter.
35. *O.C.* 253:5.
36. *O.C.* 253:93.
37. *Be'ur HaGra O.C.* 253:65.
38. *O.C.* 253:93.
39. *O.C.* 253:2.
40. See section C of this chapter.

Our text assumes that there is a prohibition even when the food remains cooler than *yad soledet bo*. This is implied by the Ramban[41] quoting the Yerushalmi. The additional stringency of in the oven as opposed to on the oven does not apply when the temperature is under *yad soledet bo*. This implies that the regular prohibition of on the oven does apply when the temperature is cooler than *yad soledet bo*.

The Rama[42] permits returning when the food remains less than *yad soledet bo* only if one places food near the oven, not on it. We cannot prohibit placing near the oven food that remains cooler than *yad soledet bo* because there would be no end to this prohibition.

The Rama apparently understood the *Kol Bo*'s expression, "its heat is small (*me'at*)," as cooler than the point of *yad soledet bo*. The *Beit Yosef* is stringent since originally the oven's heat was *yad soledet bo*. A person may err and think that it is no longer *yad soledet bo*. (Compare *Chazon Ish*[43] who prohibits returning food to a part of the oven that is less than *yad soledet bo* if part of the oven is *yad soledet bo*; we cannot rely on people to draw a precise line. So, too, regarding a precise time when the fire cools to beneath *yad soledet bo*.)

The Rama permitted returning into an oven only in a case where the food did not cool off completely. The *Magen Avraham*[44] explains that if the food cooled off completely, the initial leaving is canceled. It is not considered returning but placing anew and is prohibited even for solids. The *Magen Avraham* cannot explain that the Rama refers only to liquids which may not be reheated. Our text prohibits less than *yad soledet bo*, and liquids cannot be cooked at that level of heat.

The Gra[45] comments on the Rama – "as above" – referring to the prohibition to heat liquids which were completely cooled off. This is based on the Gra's emendation that the Rama quotes a stringency prohibiting food that will reach *yad soledet bo*, which can cook, but permits returning food that is below *yad soledet bo*.

---

41. *Shabbat* 37a.
42. *O.C.* 253:2.
43. *O.C.* 37:8; see chapter 25, section B
44. *O.C.* 253:36.
45. *O.C.* 253:64.

E. SUMMARY

The *Shulchan Arukh* permits leaving uncooked food on a covered fire before *Shabbat.* When quoting the opinion of Chananyah, however, the *Be'ur Halakhah* advises adhering to the first, stringent opinion in the *Shulchan Arukh,* following *Rabbanan,* that the food must be fully cooked to be left on an uncovered fire. If so, R. Akiva Eiger requires that the food be *ma'achal ben derusa'i* to be left on a covered fire. According to the Ran's understanding of the *Rif,* which is quoted in the *Shulchan Arukh,* however, the food may be left on a covered fire even if it has not reached *ma'achal ben derusa'i.* In addition, we are not concerned that one will stir the pot when uncooked food is left on a covered fire or *ma'achal ben derusa'i* food is left on an uncovered or covered fire before *Shabbat.*

According to the *Kol Bo,* placing a pot anew into an oven fueled by residual heat from a Friday use is permitted. According to the Rama, it is permitted to place anew into an oven only foods which are not usually baked in the oven, because if the food is usually baked in the oven, placing anew looks like cooking.

One version of the text of the Rama in *Orach Chaim* 253:5 definitively prohibits returning food if the heat in the oven is *yad soledet bo* and is stringent that it is prohibited even if the oven is below *yad soledet bo.* The Ramban does indeed prohibit returning even if the oven is below *yad soledet bo.* The Gra's emended version of the Rama, supported by the *Sha'ar HaTziyun,* however, states that the strict view prohibits returning food only if the heat in the oven is *yad soledet bo;* the lenient view permits returning into the oven even if the heat in the oven is *yad soledet bo.* According to the emended text, returning to an oven below *yad soledet bo* is definitively permitted. The Rama clearly permits returning next to an oven if the food will not reach *yad soledet bo,* as opposed to returning into the oven, which, according to our text, is prohibited.

25

The *Blech*

A. WHAT MAY SERVE AS A HALAKHIC COVERING FOR A FIRE?

The *mishnah*[1] permits placing uncooked food on coals covered with ashes. As mentioned,[2] the *Shulchan Arukh*[3] allows covering with a pan. Our custom is to cover the fire with a flat covering, known as a *blech*.

However, the *Be'ur Halakhah*[4] proves from Rashi[5] that a flat cover is not like covering with coals. In defense of our practice of using a *blech*, we can suggest that the ovens of the Talmudic era had wide openings. One could not cook on top of the oven unless there was a cover to prevent the pot from falling to the bottom. Since this cover was used regularly, its presence would not remind a person not to stoke the coals. A *blech*, however, is not used during the week and thus can serve as a reminder.

---

1. *Shabbat* 36b.
2. See chapter 20, section A.
3. *O.C.* 253:3.
4. *O.C.* 253, s.v. *liten*.
5. *Shabbat* 37a.

The *Chazon Ish*[6] says that an inverted pan and a covering of ashes reduce the heat of the fire. A *blech* does not reduce the heat of the fire. Ashes do not serve as a covering inside the oven[7] presumably for the same reason. Ashes cannot reduce the intense heat inside the oven. This would seem to support the view of the *Chazon Ish*.

However, the *Peri Megadim*[8] explains that ashes are common inside ovens to prevent the food from being singed by the intense heat. Therefore, they cannot serve as a reminder. By contrast, a *blech*, which is not used during the week, can serve as a reminder and is a proper covering, even though it does not reduce the heat of the fire.

B. PLACING FOOD ON THE *BLECH*: ON THE FIRE OR NEAR THE FIRE?

As mentioned,[9] the *Chazon Ish*[10] prohibits placing food in a part of an oven that is not the temperature of *yad soledet bo* if another part of it is. *Hilchos Shabbos*[11] applies this to a *blech*. One may not place anew food on the part of the *blech* less than *yad soledet bo*, lest he place it in the part that is *yad soledet bo*. The *Hilchos Shabbos*'s prohibition assumes that the entire *blech* is considered on the fire. If part of the *blech* is considered near the fire, we cannot prohibit less than *yad soledet bo* endlessly. Indeed, *Hilchos Shabbos*[12] permits sliding a pot that had been on the *blech* since *Shabbat* began, along the *blech*, from the part of the fire to the part directly on it, since the entire *blech* is considered on the fire. He compares sliding a pot from one part of the *blech* to another to moving a pot from atop, not near, one oven to another.

Elsewhere[13] *Hilchos Shabbos* suggests that the part of the *blech* that is not on the fire is considered near the fire. Nevertheless, one may

6. *O.C.* 37:11.
7. *Shabbat* 37a, 38b.
8. *O.C.* 253, *Eishel Avraham* 8.
9. Chapter 24, section D.
10. *O.C.* 37:8.
11. Fn. 1073.
12. Fn. 1078.
13. Fn. 1061.

move a pot from there to the part on the fire. *Chazon Ish*[14] allows moving a pot from near the oven to on the oven. Since one may not place a pot anew near the fire,[15] one may move a pot from near the fire, where it has already crossed the "border" separating between permissible and prohibited with respect to placing anew, onto a covered fire.

By contrast, *Chazon Ish*[16] forbids moving a pot from atop another pot onto the covered stove. Since one may place food anew atop another pot, one may not move a pot from there across the "border" onto a covered fire. This is consistent with the view of *Chazon Ish*[17] that atop another pot is considered off the fire, since it is heated only indirectly by the steam of the bottom pot, and not directly by the fire.[18]

The *Chazon Ish*[19] prohibits moving a pot from the part of the inverted pan which is not *yad soledet bo* to the part that is *yad soledet bo*. The *Orchot Shabbat*[20] cites R. Nissim Karelitz who considers the *blech* near, not on, the fire. One may place anew onto the part that is not *yad soledet bo* (in contrast to in the oven), since to say otherwise would be to create an unlimited prohibition, which is not possible. Since the part of the *blech* that is not *yad soledet bo* is considered off the fire, one may not move from there onto the part which is *yad soledet bo*. This follows the view of the *Chazon Ish*.

R. Yosef Shalom Elyashiv disagrees. He considers the entire *blech* to be on, not near, the fire. Therefore, one may not place food anew on the part that is not *yad soledet bo*, just as one may not do so (based on *Chazon Ish*) in an oven. Since we give the part of the *blech* that is not *yad soledet bo* a status of on the fire, one may move the pot from there to the part of the *blech* which is *yad soledet bo*.

---

14. *O.C.* 37:10.
15. As R. Akiva Eiger maintains; see chapter 22, section B.
16. *O.C.* 37:11.
17. *O.C.*37:9
18. See chapter 21, section A.
19. *O.C.* 37: 10.
20. 2:62, 69.

C. SUMMARY

A flat covering, a *blech,* can serve as a covering for a fire even though it differs from the covering used in Talmudic times, because a *blech* is not used during the week and can serve as a reminder not to stoke the coals.

If the part of the *blech* that is not directly on the fire and is not *yad soledet bo* is considered "on the fire," one is prohibited to place food anew on the part that is not *yad soledet bo,* but it is permitted to slide a pot from the part of the *blech* that is not *yad soledet bo* to the part of the *blech* that is directly on the fire (R. Elyashiv, *Hilchos Shabbos*). Conversely, if the part of the *blech* that is not directly on the fire and is not *yad soledet bo* is considered "off the fire," one is permitted to place food anew on the part that is not *yad soledet bo,* but it is prohibited to slide a pot from the part of the *blech* that is not *yad soledet bo* to the part of the *blech* that is directly on the fire (R. Nissim Karelitz, cited in *Orchot Shabbat*).

26

The Definition of Placing Anew

A. CRITERIA NECESSARY TO PERMIT RETURNING FOOD TO A COVERED FIRE

The Talmud[1] prohibits returning food to a covered fire if the food is placed on the ground. Since the original status of "on the fire" is cancelled (Rashi), it is deemed placing anew and is not allowed. Only if the pot is still in his hand may it be returned to a covered fire.

The Talmud adds a second criterion, that the individual had in mind to return the food to the fire. The Talmud asks if both criteria are required to permit returning, or if either one is sufficient. This question is not resolved.

The Rama[2] rules strictly, that the pot must be in his hand and there must be intention to return it. The *Be'ur Halakhah* cites *Rishonim* who rule leniently. If it is in his hand, the *Shulchan Arukh*, following the Rambam, allows returning it, even if the individual did not have in mind to return it. One may rely on this view in cases of necessity. The

1. *Shabbat* 38b.
2. *O.C.* 253:2.

Beit Yosef suggests that if it is placed on a bench it may be returned. One may rely on this view, if the intention was to return it, in case of necessity.

The *Beit Yosef*'s position is based on the Talmud's unresolved question: If the food was placed on a bench, may it be returned? While the Rama is stringent and requires that the pot be in his hand, the Rambam prohibits returning only if the pot is placed on the ground. The *Beit Yosef* rules like the Rambam.

B. RETURNING COLD FOODS

There are two ways to explain the difference between the ground and a bench. First, the ground is cold and a bench is not. In that regard, a refrigerator is like the ground, and a counter is not. Second, the ground is a place where pots were placed to cool, and a bench is not. According to that reasoning, a counter is like the ground.

The Ritva[3] proves from a statement of the Talmud that cold food may not be returned because it has the appearance of cooking. This would apply even to solids. The proof is from the Talmud's insistence that the water that is being returned be hot. Since the Ritva[4] holds that one may reheat liquids which cooled off, there is no difference between solids and liquids regarding cooking.[5] Therefore, just as liquids must be hot in order to be returned, even though there is no violation of cooking when reheating cold liquids, so too must solids be hot in order to be returned.

The *Magen Avraham*[6] permits returning cold solids. Elsewhere,[7] however, he prohibits it. The *Peri Megadim*[8] raises this apparent contradiction. The *Machatzit HaShekel*[9] answers that the *Magen Avraham* is stringent only with respect to returning inside the oven.

3. *Shabbat* 38b.
4. *Shabbat* 39a.
5. See chapter 3, section A.
6. O.C. 253:19
7. O.C. 253: 36
8. O.C. 253 *Mishbetzot Zahav* 13.
9. O.C. 259, end.

C. OPENING AN OVEN DOOR

Opening the door of an oven inevitably causes the fire to increase earlier than otherwise, as the cold air which enters affects the thermostat. Some authorities require that all the food be removed at once. In this case, the earlier increase of the fire is an unwanted consequence (*pesik reishei delo neicha lei*), since there is no longer food to be heated.

Hilchos Shabbos[10] permits opening the oven door as long as it is possible that the fire will not increase immediately.[11] This leniency can be found in the *Shiltei HaGibborim*,[12] who permits a *pesik reishei* if the consequence happens only later. Presumably it applies even when the consequence is desired by the person, such as one who leaves some of the food in the oven. This explains why it is permissible to open the door to one's house in the winter, even though the cold air that enters inevitably causes the thermostat to activate the central heating earlier than otherwise.[13]

D. SUMMARY

The Talmud notes two criteria that permit returning onto a covered fire: (1) the pot must be in one's hand (2) one must have the intention to return the pot. The Rama requires that both criteria be met. One may be lenient in a case of necessity to return even if only one criterion is met.

The "ground" may be a cold place, which is analogous to a refrigerator; the counter would then be like a "bench" – permitted, in a case of necessity, to return if one had intention. We are lenient and do not consider a counter like the "ground," even though the other possible definition of the ground is "a place where food is put to cool off." The Ritva prohibits returning cold solids onto the fire, but the *Magen Avraham* permits returning cold solids onto the fire, and only prohibits returning cold solids into the oven.

10. P. 380.
11. In fact, the fire did not increase when the oven door was opened briefly until it was opened eight times (fn. 1261).
12. To *Shabbat* 120b. See chapter 3, section E.
13. See the comments of Rabbi Yaakov Neuburger at the end of the Hebrew section of this volume.

The *Shiltei HaGibborim* permits a *pesik reishei* if the consequence happens only later, even if the consequence is desirable. This explains why it is permissible to open the oven door and leave some food inside, even though the cold air coming through the open door will cause the oven thermostat to increase the fire, and why it is permitted to open the door to one's house in the winter, even though the cold air coming through the open door will cause the house thermostat to increase the fire.

27

A Hot Plate

A. CONCERN FOR THE APPEARANCE OF COOKING

We have seen two reasons for the prohibitions of returning and placing anew. One is the concern that a person may adjust the flame, and the second concern is the appearance of cooking. A non-adjustable hot plate should not need to be covered, then, as there is no concern of adjusting the heat. Since people do not usually cook on it, there is no appearance of cooking, and cold dry food may be returned onto it. The *Shemirat Shabbat KeHilkhatah*[1] equates the hot plate to a fire fueled by straw and stubble upon which food may be returned.[2]

Others disagree and require a covering on the hot plate for leaving or returning. According to this perspective, the rabbinic prohibitions exist even if the reasons do not apply, as a general rule that no distinctions are made in such prohibitions (*lo plug*).[3] Only if the source of heat is different, such as straw, or liquid fuel,[4] are we lenient when stoking

1. Ch. 1 fn. 71.
2. See chapter 24, section B.
3. R. Y.S. Elyashiv in *Shevut Yitzchak*, p. 99
4. *O.C. Sha'arei Teshuvah* 254:2.

is impossible. A hot plate, though, has an electric heat source, which is used for cooking on other devices.

We can argue that the opposite is true. The hot plate is a case in which we can more easily be lenient than the case of straw, which has a remote possibility of stoking a single spark.[5] The *Shemirat Shabbat KeHilkhatah*,[6] who compares a hot plate to straw, prohibits placing anew. However, the reason of stoking does not apply to hot plates at all; therefore, the *Shemirat Shabbat KeHilkhatah* must be concerned that it looks like cooking.

The *Shemirat Shabbat KeHilkhatah* is not concerned, however, that returning looks like cooking, and thus permits returning onto a hot plate even though he prohibits placing anew. A similar distinction exists if the fire is covered. Returning does not look like cooking, as the Ran explained, but placing anew does.[7] So, too, for an oven fueled by straw and for a hot plate. Nonetheless, we can argue that in the cases of a covered fire or an oven fueled by straw, food is often cooked, so placing anew looks like cooking. However, a hot plate is never used for cooking, so placing anew should be permitted.

B. IS IT POSSIBLE TO COOK ON A HOT PLATE?

The *Iggerot Moshe*[8] was asked about a hot plate and a hot tray, as this is not "the way of cooking." He responded that if it is impossible for the food to be cooked there, and it is non-adjustable, one may place anew upon it.

Piskei Teshuvot[9] and *The Shabbos Kitchen*[10] understood that *Iggerot Moshe* is more lenient than the *Shemirat Shabbat KeHilkhatah* and permits placing anew all cold dry food on a hot plate. However, *Iggerot Moshe* only permits placing anew all cold dry food on a hot plate if it is impossible for food to be cooked there. Moreover, regarding steam tables, the *Iggerot Moshe* writes that it is possible for food to be cooked there, so consequently it is "the way of cooking" – even though no one

5. *Mishnah Berurah O.C.* 254:22.
6. 1:25 fn. 72.
7. See chapter 18, section A.
8. *Orach Chaim* IV, 74:35.
9. *O.C.* 253:16.
10. P. 43.

cooks in steam tables. In fact, Rav Reuven Feinstein reports that his father prohibited even returning on a hot plate because it looks like cooking. *Iggerot Moshe*, then, is more stringent than *Shemirat Shabbat KeHilkhatah*.

Iggerot Moshe's position is difficult. He permits a non-adjustable hot plate when cooking is impossible. However, if the hot plate is *yad soledet bo*, by definition cooking water is possible. If it is not *yad soledet bo*, then, according to the *Mishnah Berurah* even placing on an adjustable fire is permitted.[11]

This question is based on the view of the *Mishnah Berurah*[12] that *yad soledet bo* is measured by the temperature of the food that heats up to the point of *yad soledet bo*. However, *Shulchan Arukh HaRav*[13] maintains that *yad soledet bo* depends upon the oven surface. If so, we can explain the view of the *Iggerot Moshe* as applying in a case in which the surface is *yad soledet bo* but the food cannot reach *yad soledet bo*.

Alternatively, the *Iggerot Moshe* writes "it can be cooked there" and not "one can cook there." While water can be cooked at *yad soledet bo*, chicken and kugel cannot. This is similar to the aforementioned view of the Ran who permits placing anew when it is not the way to cook this particular food there.[14] The *Iggerot Moshe* asserts that if this particular food can be cooked there it looks like cooking. Otherwise, it does not, even though it is *yad soledet bo* and water can be cooked there.

Most American hot plates cannot cook chicken and kugel, whereas Israeli hot plates, which are very hot, can cook kugel and perhaps even chicken. If our understanding of the *Iggerot Moshe* is correct, one may place kugel and chicken anew on an American hot plate but not on an Israeli one.

The simple meaning of the Rashba, cited in *Shulchan Arukh*,[15] is that if it is not the usual way to cook on a surface, such as on top of a pot, one may place food anew on that surface, even if that surface can cook some foods. The Ran permits placing anew as long as that particular food

11. See chapter 24, section D.
12. 253:67, 68
13. 253:21.
14. See above, chapter 24, section C.
15. *O.C.* 253:5.

is not usually cooked there. While *Be'ur Halakhah*[16] states that the *Beit Yosef* and *Shulchan Arukh* do not accept the Ran, we have shown[17] that the Rama accepts the Ran and explains that customary practice relies on his opinion.

The *Shemirat Shabbat KeHilkhatah* prohibits placing anew on a hot plate that is usually not cooked upon. Elsewhere[18] he writes that *Sefardim* do indeed cook on hot plates. Similarly, the *Shevut Yitzchak*[19] writes that the very hot Israeli hot plates are used to complete the cooking of kugel. The ones that only reach *yad soledet bo,* such as the American ones, do not have the appearance of cooking, so that placing anew upon them should be permitted. It seems that in America, even the very hot hot plates are not used for cooking.[20]

C. SUMMARY

There is no concern for stoking the coals on a non-adjustable hot plate. Some *poskim,* such as the *Iggerot Moshe,* are concerned that placing anew on a hot plate, and even returning on a hot plate, looks like cooking. However, according to the Ran, it does not look like cooking if one usually does not cook that particular food there.

In sum, one may use the hot plates whose surfaces reach *yad soledet bo* but which cannot cook the foods that are placed anew upon them. The very hot ones are controversial, but seem permissible based on the plain meaning of the Rashba and the Ran.

16. O.C. 253:3.
17. Chapter 24, section C.
18. See the introduction to *Am Mordechai,* p. 7.
19. P. 103.
20. The OU *Daf HaKashrus* (19:10) suggests that over 180 degrees can be used for cooking.

28

Timers

A. THE POSITION OF THE *CHAZON ISH*

The *Chazon Ish*[1] prohibits leaving food on, or returning food onto, a surface which will be heated later by a timer. The prohibition is not the act of returning the pot, but the reality of a cold pot on an uncovered fire; thus, even if a robot put it there it must be removed.[2] Others permit leaving, and even returning, in such a case.[3]

In a situation which seems analogous to a timer, the Rama[4] permits a non-Jew to place a pot on the oven which is not lit. Later, a non-Jew is permitted to light the oven. We may instruct a non-Jew to do *melakhah* in cases of illness, and we are all considered potentially "sick" if the room is extremely cold. As a result of the non-Jew lighting the oven for the purpose of heating the room, the food will be heated, together with the room.

1. *O.C.* 38:2.
2. See chapter 19, section B.
3. *Hilchos Shabbos* fn. 657,660.
4. *O.C.* 253:5.

The *Chazon Ish* asks:[5] Shouldn't the Jew be required to remove the pot from the oven once it is lit? His second answer to explain why it is not required to remove the pot is that it is not the usual way to cook on top of the oven; it is comparable to a pot on a pot. If so, even a Jew could place a hot pot, when there is no violation of cooking, on top of the oven, as the *Mishnah Berurah*[6] rules, even after it is lit, since it is not the way of cooking, although we are customarily stringent.

The Rama adds that it is permissible to place the hot pots near the oven. If only near the oven is permitted, this proves that placing on the oven is prohibited, against the view of the *Chazon Ish* who permits hot pots on the oven. Rather, we must accept the *Chazon Ish*'s first answer why one is not required to remove the pot once the oven is lit: since the fire is off at the time the pot was put on the oven, it is treated as leaving, not returning.

If so, it should be permissible to place dry, cold food onto a covered electric range which will go on with a timer, as *Hilchos Shabbos* quotes from R. Moshe Feinstein. This is consistent with the *Mishnah Berurah*, who rules that a Jew may place hot food on an oven which will be lit by a non-Jew. Since it is treated as leaving, not returning, it is permitted since the food is fully cooked, beyond the *ma'achal ben derusa'i* minimum.

The Rama permits leaving only near the oven, because he refers to a case where the oven is already lit. Earlier he prohibits a Jew to put uncooked or partially cooked food on before the oven is lit because of a cooking violation.[7]

B. THE POSITION OF THE *MAGEN AVRAHAM*

The *Magen Avraham*[8] prohibits placing a pot before the fire is lit lest he stoke the coals later. He notes a lenient custom, and bases it on the words of the *Shulchan Arukh*.[9] The *Machatzit HaShekel* explains that the

5. O.C. 37:21.
6. O.C. 253:103.
7. *Mishnah Berurah* O.C. 253:100.
8. O.C. 253:43.
9. O.C. 253:3.

Magen Avraham refers to his earlier comment,[10] that the roof of an oven is like an empty pan. Food may be returned, and, according to the Rama based on the Ran and the Yerushalmi,[11] placed anew.

The *Machatzit HaShekel* asks: The *Magen Avraham* (31) requires a recognizable reminder of wood or a shelf on top of the oven. Here (43) there is none. The *Machatzit HaShekel* answers that before the fire is lit we are lenient.

Apparently, it is not the usual way to cook on top of the oven. Therefore, placing food onto the top of the oven does not have the appearance of cooking. The reminder is needed so that the individual should not stoke the coals at the moment of the placing of the pot. The custom is to be lenient before the fire is lit. To address the concern of the appearance of cooking, which applies when one places a pot and another lights the fire, the *Magen Avraham* refers to his words that the roof of an oven is like a pan in terms of not having the appearance of cooking. The leniency described by the *Magen Avraham* would not apply to an electric range, where one normally cooks, because it looks like cooking.

As a result, it is prohibited to place food on an electric range which will go on with a timer because it looks like cooking. The *Iggerot Moshe,* and the *Chazon Ish* in his first answer, must hold that it does not look like cooking if the fire is not on yet.

C. COFFEE MAKERS

An electronic coffee-maker can be set on a timer to cook fresh coffee in the morning, mixing coffee and water which were placed in the machine the previous day. If it is set to cook on *Shabbat* morning, no violation of cooking occurs, since the person who set it and placed the coffee and water in it did so on Friday and is passive on *Shabbat.*

However, since it is possible to tamper with the machine when it goes on, which could lead to a Torah violation of cooking, this machine should not be used. For this reason, Rav Moshe Feinstein[12] prohibited placing water into a non-adjustable urn just before *Shabbat*. Removing

10. *O.C.* 253:31

11. See chapter 21, section B.

12. *Hilchos Shabbos,* p. 348 fn.408.

water or re-covering the urn before the water cooks completely is a Torah violation of cooking. These same concerns may exist regarding a coffee-making machine.

Furthermore, if the heat setting on the machine is adjustable, then, according to one answer in the *Chazon Ish*,[13] there is a prohibition of *hachzarah*. The mere fact that uncooked food is on an adjustable source of heat constitutes *hachzarah* even though the person is passive.

D. SUMMARY

Based on the first answer of the *Chazon Ish*, it is permissible to place dry, cold food onto a covered electric range which will go on with a timer, as the *Iggerot Moshe* indeed permits. Based on the *Magen Avraham*, however, it is prohibited to place food on an electric range which will go on with a timer because it looks like cooking, since we normally cook on an electric range. Coffee-makers and placing water in a non-adjustable urn just before *Shabbat* are both prohibited, since removing water or re-covering an urn before the water cooks completely is a Torah violation of cooking. Coffee-making machines that are adjustable have an additional problem of *hachzarah*, since according to the *Chazon Ish* uncooked food being on an adjustable heat source is a violation of *hachzarah*, even if the person is passive.

13. See above, section A.

29

Food Improperly Left on an Uncovered Fire

A. FOOD LEFT KNOWINGLY VS. FOOD LEFT UNKNOWINGLY

The Talmud[1] discusses the situation of one who forgot a pot on the fire and its contents cooked on *Shabbat*. The Talmud cites a *beraita* that states: If one cooks on *Shabbat* by mistake, the food may be eaten; if one cooks knowingly, though, it may not be eaten. (This is the opinion of R. Meir, *Terumot* 2:3.) If one leaves the pot on the fire on Friday by mistake, however, which is a rabbinic prohibition, there is no such distinction. The food may not be eaten, lest the individual leave it knowingly and claim he forgot. By contrast, we are not concerned that he will cook knowingly, since that is a Torah prohibition, and thus the food is permitted if he cooked by mistake.

Even though the Talmud seems to have reached a conclusion prohibiting food left on Friday, later the Talmud asks what seems to be an identical question: If one left food on the fire on Friday, do we penalize him and prohibit the food or not? This time, the question is unresolved.

1. *Shabbat* 38a.

The *Shulchan Arukh*[2] rules: If he forgot and left it, if it had been fully cooked it may be eaten, even if it improves when it loses moisture. If it was not fully cooked, it is prohibited until after *Shabbat*. If he left if knowingly, both are prohibited.

This ruling is puzzling. The *Shulchan Arukh* generally prohibits leaving food unless it deteriorates when it loses moisture. Why may the food be eaten if it is fully cooked, even if it improves, but not if it is not fully cooked, when in both cases he forgot and left food improperly?

Furthermore, the Talmud in its first discussion proves from the fact that if he left food knowingly the food is prohibited, that if one forgot, the food is prohibited, since regarding the rabbinic prohibition of leaving we are concerned one may leave the food knowingly and claim he forgot. This proves that the two cases, leaving knowingly and forgetting, are equivalent with respect to the status of the food which was heated improperly. How can the *Shulchan Arukh* distinguish between one who forgot and one who left food knowingly? (The Tur asks this question against the Rambam, the source of the *Shulchan Arukh*.)

Rav Soloveitchik answered that the *Shulchan Arukh* (and the Rambam) hold[3] that one violates cooking unless the food had been fully cooked beforehand. The Talmud discusses one who forgot a pot and its contents cooked on *Shabbat*, because we treat it as if he cooked it on *Shabbat*. In that case, it is prohibited to all even if he cooked mistakenly.[4] (This is the opinion of R. Yehudah, *Terumot* 2:3.)

This applies only if the food was not fully cooked. If the food was fully cooked before *Shabbat*, we cannot treat it as if he cooked it on *Shabbat*. The Talmud, in its first question, compares forgetting to a knowing violation only if the food was not cooked. Since it is treated as if it was cooked on *Shabbat*, in which case mistaken and knowing violations are equivalent, the comparison is valid.

The Talmud's second question, however, concerns fully cooked food. Here, it cannot be treated as if it were cooked on *Shabbat*, since it was already cooked before *Shabbat*. The Rif (the source of the Rambam

2. *O.C.* 253:1.
3. *O.C.* 318:4.
4. *O.C.* 318:1.

and the *Shulchan Arukh*) explains that the individual forgot the fully cooked food, and that since the second question in the Talmud is unresolved, we are lenient in a rabbinic matter.

The Rif's text in the second question, "he violated and forgot," in contrast to the first question, "he forgot and cooked," confirms this interpretation. In the first question, the food was not fully cooked, and is treated as if it was cooked on *Shabbat.* In the second question, the food was fully cooked. This food is prohibited, as a separate penalty, if he left it knowingly. The Talmud then asks if the penalty applies if he forgot. The matter is left unresolved, and the Rif, Rambam and *Shulchan Arukh* rule leniently.

B. MAY OTHERS EAT THE FOOD?

The *Magen Avraham*[5] states that the status of the food for others (not the one who left it) depends upon the aforementioned dispute between R. Meir and R. Yehudah[6] about food cooked on *Shabbat.* The *Machatzit HaShekel* asks: The Talmud says that leaving is worse than cooking, lest he leave it there knowingly. Since leaving is a separate enactment, why should the status of the food for others depend on the dispute between R. Meir and R. Yehudah about food cooked on *Shabbat*?

According to R. Soloveitchik's interpretation, we can answer as follows. The definition of the enactment of leaving uncooked food on an uncovered fire is that we treat the food as if it was cooked on *Shabbat.* Therefore, its status regarding others depends on the dispute regarding food which was actually cooked on *Shabbat.*

C. WHEN IS THE FOOD PERMITTED?

The *Peri Megadim*[7] derives from the Rambam's language that if the food was left knowingly, it is prohibited after *Shabbat* until such time as the food could have been heated after *Shabbat* ended. If he forgot it, it is permitted immediately after *Shabbat.*

5. *O.C.* 318:11.
6. see *Shabbat* 38a.
7. *O.C.* 318, *Eishel Avraham* 11.

This distinction can be explained based on the above. If the individual forgot, the definition of the prohibition on the food is that it is treated as if it was cooked on *Shabbat*. In such a case, it is permitted immediately after *Shabbat*.[8]

If the food was left knowingly, there is a separate penalty, which applies even to cooked food. This is similar to the statement of the Talmud[9] where, in a case of a separate rabbinic enactment lest one stoke the coals, the food is prohibited after *Shabbat* until the time that it could have been heated after *Shabbat* if the enactment was violated knowingly.[10] The separate penalty is applied to the separate enactment of leaving food on Friday, as well.

D. SUMMARY

The Talmud discusses two cases of leaving food. The first case is one who leaves uncooked food on an uncovered fire on *erev Shabbat*. The food is prohibited on *Shabbat*. The food is prohibited whether he left the food knowingly or unknowingly, lest one leave it knowingly and claim he forgot. Rav Soloveitchik understands that leaving uncooked food on *erev Shabbat* is treated as if the food was cooked on *Shabbat*. Therefore, whether others can eat the food is dependent on the dispute between R. Meir and R. Yehudah regarding food cooked on *Shabbat*; and, after *Shabbat*, if one left uncooked food knowingly one must wait until such time as the food could have been heated after *Shabbat* ended, but if one forgot one may eat it immediately after *Shabbat*.

The second case in the Talmud is that of one who leaves fully cooked food on an uncovered fire on *erev Shabbat*. It cannot be treated as if it was cooked on *Shabbat* if the food was fully cooked before *Shabbat*. According to the *Shulchan Arukh*, therefore, in the case of fully cooked food left on *erev Shabbat*, the food is prohibited on *Shabbat* as a separate penalty if it was left knowingly, but permitted on *Shabbat* if it was left unknowingly.

---

8. Rambam, *Hilkhot Shabbat* 6:23.
9. *Shabbat* 18b.
10. Rambam, *Hilkhot Shabbat* 3:12.

30

Food Improperly Returned to the Fire

A. FOOD WHICH DETERIORATES VS. FOOD WHICH IMPROVES

The *Hagahot Oshri*[1] is uncertain as to the status of food returned mistakenly. Perhaps only if one forgot a pot on Friday, and it cooked on *Shabbat,* is the food prohibited, because it was made edible on *Shabbat.*[2] However, if the food was returned, it was edible beforehand, (because otherwise a Torah prohibition of cooking would have been violated) and he does not receive that much benefit from the violation. For this reason, if a non-Jew returned the food mistakenly, it is permitted to be eaten. If a Jew returned it mistakenly, perhaps he is penalized.

The *Chazon Ish*[3] assumes that the food was fully cooked before *Shabbat.* He is uncertain as to whether the *Hagahot Oshri* refers to food which improves when it loses moisture or food which deteriorates with less moisture.

---

1. *Shabbat* 3:2.
2. See above, chapter 29.
3. *O.C.* 37 :24.

The Rama[4] writes: If a non-Jew returns food on *Shabbat*, it is comparable to one who forgot and left it on Friday (based on the *Hagahot Oshri*). If a Jew returned it on *Shabbat*, it is comparable to one who knowingly left it on Friday (based on the *Hagahot Mordechai*). If it deteriorates when it loses moisture, it may be eaten, since the individual does not benefit from the violation.

The *Chazon Ish* notes that according to the Rambam and the *Shulchan Arukh*,[5] who permit fully cooked food which was mistakenly left on Friday, there is no source to prohibit such food if it was returned on *Shabbat*. The Rama prohibits food returned by a Jew based on the *Hagahot Mordechai*.

The comparison that the Rama makes between returning on *Shabbat* and leaving on *erev Shabbat* is difficult. The *Hagahot Mordechai* argues with the Rambam and prohibits fully cooked food which improves when it loses moisture even if it was left mistakenly on Friday.[6] Since the *Shulchan Arukh*, based on the view of the Rif and the Rambam, permits fully cooked food which improves when it loses moisture, and the Rama is silent, indicating his consent, why does the Rama follow the *Hagahot Mordechai* in prohibiting such food which was returned on *Shabbat*?

The *Mishnah Berurah*[7] answers that returning is treated more stringently than leaving, since the individual did a prohibited action on *Shabbat* itself. However, the Talmud[8] suggests this point, that we are more strict concerning the food if an individual did a prohibited action on *Shabbat* itself, only regarding cooking. If returning is like cooking, then, as the *Chazon Ish* suggests, perhaps we should not be concerned that he will do it knowingly, and thus its status could be more lenient than food which was left mistakenly before *Shabbat*.

4. O.C. 253:1.
5. See chapter 29, section A.
6. See *Magen Avraham*. O.C. 253:14.
7. O.C. 253:35.
8. *Shabbat* 38a.

B. FOOD WHICH REACHED *MA'ACHAL BEN DERUSA'I*

Moreover, while the *Chazon Ish* was uncertain as to whether the *Hagahot Oshri* prohibited fully cooked food which deteriorates or only that which improves, as the Rama says, one can suggest that *Hagahot Oshri* prohibits only food which was not fully cooked. Presumably, he holds that once the food reaches *ma'achal ben derusa'i* there is no violation of cooking (only one of leaving), like the Rosh.[9] Further, he does not receive that much benefit since the food was edible as well when it had reached the point of *ma'achal ben derusa'i.*

In practice, with respect to fully cooked food which improves when it loses moisture, we follow the Rama who prohibits it if a Jew returned it. If a non-Jew returned it, it is permissible. The *Magen Avraham*[10] explains that he did not receive that much benefit since the food was edible originally. The *Magen Avraham* refers to the *Shulchan Arukh*[11] who rules as follows: If there was a candle in the house, and a non-Jew lit another candle, one may use the light, since he could have used the original light. So, too, if he could have eaten the food before it was returned, he may eat it even if a non-Jew returned it. Perhaps *ma'achal ben derusa'i* suffices to meet this criterion.

C. A VIOLATION OF A DISPUTED PROHIBITION

The Rama[12] writes: One may not tell a non-Jew to heat a cold pot that has already been cooked. If he did so, the food may not be eaten even after it has cooled. The *Magen Avraham*[13] cites the Rashba as the source: If one told a non-Jew to do a Torah *melakhah,* the Jew is penalized in that the food is prohibited even after it cooled. The Rashba is referring to the *melakhah* of lighting a fire. The Rama extends the idea to the *melakhah* of cooking liquids which cooled completely. The *Magen Avraham* himself

9. *Shabbat* 3:11 against the view of the Rambam and the *Shulchan Arukh,* 318:4; see chapter 4, section A, and chapter 17, section B.

10. *O.C.* 253:13.

11. See *O.C.* 276:4.

12. *O.C.* 253:5.

13. *O.C.* 253:37.

suggests, however, that eating the food may be permissible since some *poskim* permit even a Jew to reheat cooked liquids which cooled.[14]

Elsewhere, the *Magen Avraham*[15] permits using an item produced through the commission of a violation, if the existence of the relevant prohibition is controversial. The *Mishnah Berurah*[16] quotes the *Magen Avraham* and applies it to any disputed *melakhah*. If that is the case, even if a Jew reheated cold liquids, they may be eaten, as the reheating of liquids is a matter of dispute.

The *Be'ur Halakhah,*[17] based on the *Magen Avraham*[18] extends this rule from disputes concerning a *melakhah* to disputes regarding the returning of food to an open fire. This extension is questionable; perhaps the separate enactment regarding one who left food improperly[19] applies even when there is a lenient opinion. Moreover, the proof from the *Magen Avraham* is difficult. The *Magen Avraham* refers to a dispute as to whether the food is prohibited, and relies on lenient opinions. The *Be'ur Halakhah,* however, refers to a dispute over whether one may return the food in the first place or not. If we are stringent and disallow returning the food, perhaps the separate enactment prohibiting the food sets in, notwithstanding the fact that a lenient opinion allows it. The *Mishnah Berurah*[20] applies only to the general prohibition of items made available by a *melakhah* done on *Shabbat.*

This may be the position of the *Chazon Ish.*[21] He prohibits food returned to the fire by a non-Jew because the Jew violated the *halakhah* by not removing it. The *Orchot Shabbat*[22] explains that the *Chazon Ish* holds that the reason that returning is prohibited is "lest he stoke the coals."[23] Apparently, he does not rely on the opinion that the reason is

---

14. See chapter 3, section A.
15. *O.C.* 323:11.
16. *O.C.* 318:2.
17. 253:1 s.v. *ve'im.*
18. *O.C.* 253:14.
19. See chapter 29, section A.
20. *O.C.* 318:12.
21. *O.C.* 37:27.
22. Chapter 2 fn59.
23. See chapter 19, section B and chapter 23, section B

that it looks like cooking, which would permit the food if a non-Jew returned it.

A separate enactment is found in the Talmud only with respect to food left on the fire on Friday. This is not a *melakhah,* but a *gezeirah* "lest he stoke the coals." The Rama extends this enactment based on his view that returning, like leaving, is prohibited lest he stoke the coals.[24]

The *Shulchan Arukh* is silent on the matter. This indicates that he is of the opinion that returning is prohibited because it looks like cooking. Food that is returned is governed by the rules of food that is cooked.[25] The *Mishnah Berurah*[26] writes that a rabbinic prohibition violated mistakenly does not prohibit the food.

The Rama did not rely on the Ran and the Rashba who prohibit returning because it looks like cooking. This indicates that relying on a lenient view to allow the food applies to *melakhah,* but not to separate enactments of leaving and returning, against the view of the *Be'ur Halakhah.*[27]

D. SUMMARY

If a Jew returned fully cooked food which improves when it loses moisture, we follow the Rama who prohibits it. If a non-Jew returned it, it is permissible, since the food was edible before it was returned. Perhaps even *ma'achal ben derusa'i* food is permitted if returned by a non-Jew, since it, too, was edible before it was returned.

According to the Rama, if someone told a non-Jew to return food improperly, the food is prohibited even after it has cooled. According to the *Magen Avraham,* the food is permitted, because an item produced through the commission of a violation is permitted if the existence of the relevant prohibition is controversial. The *Magen Avraham*'s principle only applies to certain kinds of prohibitions. If the prohibition is a *melakhah,* such as the appearance of cooking, we rely on a lenient view is to permit the food. If the prohibition is a separate enactment, such as

24. See chapter 18, section B.

25. *O.C.* 318:1.

26. *O.C.* 318:3.

27. *O.C.* 253:1.

"lest one stoke the coals" however, we do not rely on a lenient view to permit the food. Returning and leaving are separate enactments.

Glossary

Acharonim – the leading Rabbis and halakhic decisors that lived approximately from the 16th century to the present.

Av Melakhah – the primary labors performed in the building of the *Mishkan*. The *mishnah* lists thirty-nine such categories of labors.

Bedi'eved – post facto, after the event.

Beraita – an oral Tannaitic tradition not included by R. Judah HaNasi in the *mishnah*.

Bishul – the *melakhah* of cooking.

(*Ein*) *Bishul Achar Bishul* – (There is no) [halakhic status of] cooking after cooking. This refers to one who attempts to cook a food that has already been cooked.

Bishul Akum – the prohibition to eat food cooked by non-Jews.

Blech – a covering for the fire on an oven.

Challah – the biblical obligation to separate a portion of bread and give it to the *Kohanim*.

Eino Mitkaven – an unintended consequence that results from an intentional action (including a non-inevitable consequence, as opposed to a *pesik reishei*).

Gemara – the compilation of Ammoraic discourse regarding the statements found in the Tannaic sources of the oral law. This was recorded by Ravina and R. Ashi in Babylon around 500 CE.

Gezeirah – a rabbinic decree, usually enacted to distance the populace from violating a biblical commandment.

Gezeirah LiGezeirah – a rabbinic decree on a rabbinic decree. Generally the Rabbis did not enact a decree to protect their own decrees.

Grogeret – a dried fig. This is the *shi'ur* that is used for the food-related *melakhot*.

Hachzarah – literally "returning." This refers to returning items to a heat source.

Halakhah – Jewish law

Hanachah – literally "placing." This refers to placing an item back on a heat source, if its original status of "on the fire" was cancelled, because there was originally no intention to return it, or because it was placed on the floor or other surface (see *Hachzarah*).

Hatmanah – literally "hiding/concealing." This refers to (totally) insulating a hot item with something that adds to or maintains its heat, such as a blanket.

Kashrut – Jewish dietary laws.

Keli Rishon – a utensil that was heated on a fire.

Keli Sheni – a utensil that was never heated on a fire that contains food that was previously held in a utensil that *was* on a fire (*Keli Rishon*).

Keli Shelishi – a utensil that was never heated on a fire that contains a food previously held in a *Keli Sheni*.

Korban Pesach – the Paschal offering.

Kotzer – the *melakhah* of reaping.

Lekhatchilah – the *halakhah* as applied to optimal circumstances.

Lo Plug – literally "they did not separate/distinguish." When the Rabbis enacted a *gezeirah* for a specific reason, they often extended the *gezeirah* to apply to other items/issues that are similar but do not necessarily share the original reason for the *gezeirah*.

Ma'achal Ben Derusa'i – literally "the food of Ben Derusa'i." Ben Derusa'i was a bandit in the time of the Talmud who used to eat his food undercooked. The Sages therefore state that however cooked his food was is the minimum amount of cooking required to render a food edible and thus one who cooks a food to this degree has violated the *melakhah* of *bishul*.

Matzah – unleavened bread eaten on Pesach.

Matzah Ashirah – literally "rich *matzah*." This refers to *matzah* that is made with more than just the basic ingredients of flour and water.

Melakhah – creative and constructive labor that was performed in order to build and erect the *Mishkan*.

Melekhet Machashavet – This refers to the fact that the Torah only prohibited purposeful actions on *Shabbat*, namely those actions (*melakhot*) performed in the *Mishkan*.

Mishkan – the Tabernacle that the Jews were commanded to build as a sanctuary in the desert. It served as the center of Jewish spiritual and ritual life while the Jews were in the desert.

Mishnah – the written compilation of oral Tannaitic statements redacted by R. Judah HaNasi around 220 CE in Israel.

Pasuk – a biblical verse.

Pat – bread.

Patur – exempt from punishment. In *hilkhot Shabbat* this usually connotes the existence of a prohibition but one with an exemption from punishment if transgressed.

Pesik Reishei – literally "cutting off the head." The Talmud uses this idiom to describe an inevitable consequence that results from an intentional action. The Talmud asks rhetorically: If one cuts off the head of a chicken (to use as a sort of toy), will it not die? Though one did not intend to kill the chicken, the intention was merely to acquire a new toy, the chicken will inevitably die. The

Rishonim discuss two types of *pesik reishei: Pesik reishei denicha lei* and *pesik reishei delo nicha lei. Pesik reishei denicha lei* refers to a case that one benefits from the unintended consequence. *Pesik reishei delo nicha lei* refers to a case that one does not benefit from it.

Poskim – halakhic decisors.

Rishonim – the leading Rabbis and halakhic decisors that lived approximately during the 11th to 15th centuries.

Semikhah – closeness/proximity. In the context of cooking on *Shabbat,* this refers to placing an item close to, but not directly on, a heat source.

Shehiyah – literally "leaving." This refers to leaving items on a heat source before *Shabbat.*

Shi'ur – a measurable quantity that is halakhically significant.

Shulchan Arukh – the code of Jewish law. Written by R. Joseph Karo in Safed, Israel, it has been accepted as the most authoritative source of Jewish Law. R. Moses Isserles, the Rama, living in Krakow, Poland added his glosses to the *Shulchan Arukh.* His comments generally provide the Ashkenazic custom on the issue discussed.

Talmud – the primary text of the oral law. It is comprised of the *mishnah* and the *gemara.*

Tochen – the *melakhah* of grinding.

Toladah – labors that were not specifically performed in the building of the *Mishkan* but are similar to the *avot melakhah.*

Yad Soledet Bo – literally "a hand is recoiled by it." This is the minimum amount heat required to halakhically cook a liquid.

Yoreh De'ah – the section of the *Shulchan Arukh* that discusses the laws of *issur veheter* (lit., prohibited and permissible things).

List of Sources Cited

A. THE TALMUD AND ITS COMMENTARIES

The following commentators wrote on the Talmud.

Hagahot Mordechai. Attributed to R. Samuel ben Aaron of Schlettstallt (end of 14th century). Addenda to the Mordechai including Ashkenazi rabbinical sources.

Hagahot Oshri. R. Yisrael of Krems (14th century), Austria. Addenda to the halakhic decisions of the Rosh according to Ashkenazi rabbinical sources.

Korban Netan'el. R. Netanel ben Naphtali Zvi Weil (1687–1769), Germany. Comprehensive commentary to the Rosh's commentary on the orders of *Mo'ed* and *Nashim.*

Maharsha. R Shmuel Eidels (1555–1631), Krakow, Poland. *Chiddushei Aggadot* and *Chiddushei Halakhot.*

Maharshal. R. Shlomo Luria (1510–1574), Prague, Czechoslovakia. Author of *Yam Shel Shlomo* and the Talmudic commentary *Chokhmat Shlomo.*

Mordechai. R. Mordechai ben Hillel HaKohen (1240–1298) of Germany. In Vilna editions of Talmud Bavli. Often quotes the rulings of the Ashkenazi rabbis, especially those of his rebbe, the Maharam.

Rabbenu Yonah. R. Yonah ben Avraham Gerondi (d. 1263), Gerona, Spain. Authored many works including (probably most famously) the ethical treatise *Sha'arei Teshuvah.*

Ramban. R. Moshe ben Nachman (1194–1270) of Gerona, Spain. Authored *Chiddushim* to the Talmud and many other works.

Ran. Rabbenu Nissim Gerondi (1290–1375) of Barcelona, Spain. Author of *Chiddushim* to the Talmud and *Derashot HaRan.* His comments on the code of the *Rif* appear in the Vilna Talmud.

Rashba. R. Shlomo ben Aderet (1235–1310) of Barcelona, Spain. Authored *Chiddushim* to the Talmud and many volumes of responsa.

Rashi. R. Shlomo ben Yitzchak (Yitzchaki) (1040–1105) of Troyes, France. Printed in most Hebrew editions of the Torah. Preeminent biblical and Talmudic commentator; also authored responsa.

Rif. R. Yitzchak Al Fasi (1013–1103) of Fez, Morocco. Authored a code of the halakhically relevant portions of the Talmud.

Ritva. R. Yom Tov ben Ishbilli (1250–1330), Seville, Spain. Authored works on the entire Talmud. Also authored responsa.

Rosh. Rabbenu Asher ben Yechiel (1250–1327), Germany and Spain. Code to halakhically relevant sections of the Talmud, and running commentary to *Masekhet Nedarim.* Father of the *Tur.* Also authored *Tosafot HaRosh.*

Sefer HaMa'or. R. Zerachiah ben Isaac HaLevi Gerondi (approx. 1125–1186), known as *Ba'al HaMe'or,* originally of Gerona, Spain then of Provence, France. A commentary on the Rif. The book is split into two parts – *HaMa'or HaGadol* on *Berakhot, Mo'ed,* and *Chullin,* and *HaMa'or HaKatan* on the orders of *Nashim* and *Nezikin.*

Shiltei HaGibborim. R. Yehoshua Boaz (16th century), Italy; commentary to the Rif and the Mordechai.

Tosafot. Talmudic comments of eleventh- and twelfth-century French and German scholars, printed alongside the text in the Vilna Talmud.

B. CODES OF *MITZVOT* AND HALAKHIC CODES OF *RISHONIM*

Issur VeHeter HaArokh. Unknown authorship. Compendium of the Jewish dietary laws and forbidden foods, and various other topics.

Kol Bo. R. Aharon HaKohen (fourteenth century) of Lunel, France.

Maharam MiRottenberg. R. Meir ben Baruch HaLevi of Rottenberg (1215–1293). Author of many responsa. Rebbe of the Rosh and the Mordechai.

Maharil. R. Yaakov ben Moshe Moelin (c. 1365–1427), Worms, Germany. Authored a compendium of Ashkenazic practices and customs called *Minhagei Maharil* often used as a source by the Rama in the *Shulchan Arukh.*

Or Zaru'a. R.Yitchak ben Moshe (d. 1260) of Vienna.

Sefer HaYashar. R. Yaakov ben Meir, known as Rabbenu Tam (1100–1171). One of the most renowned *Ba'alei HaTosafot,* he was a leading halakhic authority and a grandson of Rashi. His opinions are recorded in the works of the *Tosafot* and in this book.

Sefer Mitzvot Gadol. R. Moshe of Coucy (early 13th century). Known as the *Semag,* this work is divided into two sections, *Lavin* (prohibitions) and *Essin* (positive commandments).

Sefer Ra'avyah. R. Eliezer ben Yoel HaLevi (1140–1225). A prominent Germanic Tosafist and a grandson of the Ra'avan. His major work, also called *Sefer Avi HaEzri,* contains various *halakhot.*

Sefer Yere'im. R. Eliezer of Metz (c. 1115–1198). A discussion of the *mitzvot* following the listings of R. Yehudai Gaon and the *Ba'al Halakhot Gedolot,* divided into seven *amudim* (pillars). Also known as the Re'em. A French Tosafist and student of Rabbenu Tam.

Terumat HaDeshen. R. Yisrael Isserlein (1390–1460) of Germany.

C. THE RAMBAM'S *MISHNEH TORAH* AND COMMENTARIES

Rambam. R. Moshe ben Maimon (1138–1204), Egypt. Authored a codification of the laws in the Talmud, entitled *Mishneh Torah,* or *Yad HaChazakah.* The latter name is a reference to the organization of the work, which is arranged in fourteen volumes (the numerical value of the word *Yad* is fourteen). The following works are commentaries to the Rambam's code.

Even HaAzel. R. Isser Zalman Meltzer (1870–1953). Commentary on Rambam's *Yad HaChazakah.*

Hagahot Maimoniot. R. Meir HaKohen (13th century), Rottenberg. Student of Maharam of Rottenberg.

Lechem Mishneh. R. Avraham de Boton (1545–1588). Also authored *Responsa Lechem Rav.* In standard editions.

Maggid Mishneh. R. Vidal Yom Tov (d. 1370) of Tolosa, Spain. In standard editions.

Mirkevet HaMishneh. R. Shlomo of Chelm (d. 1781).

Or Sameach. R. Meir Simchah of Dvinsk (1843–1926). Also authored *Meshekh Chokhmah.*

Radbaz. R. David ben Zimra (1479–1573), Chief Rabbi of Egypt. Authored commentary to *Mishneh Torah.*

D. THE *TUR* AND *SHULCHAN ARUKH* AND COMMENTARIES

R. Ya'akov ben Asher (c. 1270–1340; son of the Rosh) of Germany and Toledo, Spain, authored a codification of Jewish law entitled the *Arba'ah Turim* (the "four rows"; see *Shemot* 28:17), so named as it is divided into four sections: *Orach Chayim,* covering daily life, prayer, and festivals; *Even HaEzer,* on marital law; *Choshen Mishpat,* on civil law; and *Yoreh De'ah,* covering the remaining areas of Jewish law, such as *kashrut, niddah,* mourning, vows, and other topics. Two centuries later, R. Yosef Karo (1488–1575), who authored the commentary *Beit Yosef* on the *Turim* (as well as *Kessef Mishneh* to *Mishneh Torah*), earned the title "the *Mechaber*" ("the Author") with his *Shulchan Arukh* ("set table"), which followed the organization of the *Turim* and took into account the rulings of the Rif, the Rosh and the Rambam. However, the rulings are reflective primarily of the Sephardic background of their author, and were supplemented by the Rama with glosses, known as *Mappah* ("tablecloth"), representing Ashkenazic practice. Together with the Rama's glosses, the *Shulchan Arukh* has become accepted as the standard text of Jewish law, and the titles listed below are commentaries to that work (or the *Turim*, when indicated as such).

Arukh HaShulchan. R. Yechiel Michel Epstein (1829–1908), Lithuania. Comprehensive code on all sections of the *Shulchan Arukh*, adding *Arukh HaShulchan HeAtid* to those areas not covered (ritual impurity, laws of agriculture relevant only in the land of Israel, sacrificial order, etc.). Rav of Novardok and father of *Torah Temimah*.

Bayit Chadash (*Bach*). R. Yoel Sirkes (1561–1640), Poland. Commentary to the *Tur*; also author of responsa and Talmudic emendations. Rav of Belz, Brest-Litovsk, and Krakow, and father-in-law of *Turei Zahav*.

Be'ur HaGra. R. Eliyahu ben Shlomo Zalman of Vilna (1720–1797). Towering scholar known as the *Vilna Gaon*, or *Gra* (an acronym for Gaon R. Eliyahu). Author of more than eighty works.

Chavvat Da'at. R. Ya'akov Loerbaum of Lissa. To *Yoreh De'ah*. Author of several works, including *Netivot HaMishpat, Derekh Chaim, Beit Ya'akov, Torat Gittin, Emet LeYa'akov, Mekor Chayyim*, and others.

Chazon Ish. R. Avraham Yeshayah Karelitz (1878–1953), Bnei Brak, Israel. This seven-volume halakhic work combines the sections of the Talmud and the *Shulchan Arukh* and defies easy categorization. Also authored *Emunah UBitachon*.

Dagul MeRevavah. R. Yechezkel Landau (1713–1793). Commentary to the *Shulchan Arukh*. Rav of Prague and a leading authority of his time, he also authored *Responsa Noda BiYehudah* and *Tziyyun LeNefesh Chayyah* to the Talmud.

Kaf HaChaim. R. Ya'akov Chaim Sofer (1870–1939) of Baghdad and Jerusalem. Commentary to *Orach Chaim* and *Yoreh De'ah*.

Magen Avraham. R. Avraham Gumbiner (1637–1683) Poland. In standard editions.

Machatzit HaShekel. R. Shmuel HaLevi of Kellin (c. 1720–1806), Bohemia. In standard editions.

Mishnah Berurah. R. Yisrael Meir Kagan (1838–1933) of Radin, Poland. Commentary to the *Orach Chaim* section of the *Shulchan Arukh*, evaluating the positions of earlier authorities and arriving at conclusions. Includes the more in-depth *Be'ur Halakhah* and the *Sha'ar HaTziyun*, listing sources. One of the preeminent moral authorities of the late eighteenth and early nineteenth centuries, he authored *Chafetz Chaim* (a name he came himself to be identified with) and *Ahavat Chesed* as well as many other works, including *Likkutei Halakhot*, a three-part commentary to the Talmudic order *Kodoshim*, written in the style of *Mishnah Berurah*.

Peri Megadim. R. Yosef Teomim (1727–1792), Poland. Super-commentary to *Shulchan Arukh* commentaries, including *Aishel Avraham* to *Magen Avraham* and *Mishbetzot Zahav* to *Turei Zahav*. Author of several other works, such as *Tevat Gomeh, Petichah HaKolelet, Shoshannat HaAmakim*, and *Matan Sekharan Shel Mitzvot*, and *Responsa Megadim*.

Piskei Teshuvot. R. Simcha Rabinovitz (contemporary) Jerusalem, 1991.

R. Akiva Eiger (1761–1837), Austria and Poland. Authored several works, including a commentary to the *Shulchan Arukh*.

Sha'arei Teshuvah. R. Chaim Mordechai Margolios (18th–19th century), Dubno, Ukraine. On *Orach Chaim*. In standard editions.

Siftei Kohen (*Shakh*). R. Shabtai HaKohen (1621–1662), Lithuania. In standard editions of *Shulchan Arukh* in the volumes of *Yoreh De'ah* and *Choshen Mishpat*. Also authored a commentary to the Torah.

Shulchan Arukh HaRav. R. Shneur Zalman of Liadi (1745–3813). First Rebbe of Lubavitch (Chabad) and author of the *Tanya*.

Turei Zahav (*Taz*). R. David ben Shmuel HaLevi (1586–1667) of Krakow, Poland. Also authored a commentary to the Torah.

E. COLLECTIONS OF RESPONSA AND HALAKHIC AND TALMUDIC ESSAYS, AND CONTEMPORARY AUTHORITIES

The following works are either responsa, written to answer halakhic inquiries, or collections of essays on topics of halakhic and Talmudic analysis. The titles of the works of responsa are generally preceded by the term *She'elot UTeshuvot* ("Questions and Answers"), translated in the text as Responsa and omitted in this listing.

39 *Melochos*. R. Dovid Ribiat (contemporary). Authored a comprehensive work on the laws of *Shabbat*.

Az Nidberu. R. Binyamin Yehoshua Zilber (1906–2008), Bnei Brak. Fourteen volumes. Also authored several volumes of *mussar*, some anonymously.

Chut Shani. R. Nissim Karelitz (full name R. Shmaryahu Yosef Nissim Karelitz, contemporary). Head of the *Beit Din Tzedek* in Bnei Brak. A nephew and student of the *Chazon Ish*.

Eglei Tal. R. Avraham Bornstein (1839–1910). Pietrkov, Poland, 1905. Hassidic Rebbe of Sochatchov, Poland; also authored *Responsa Avnei Nezer*. Innovator of a distinct style of Talmudic analysis continued by such students as *Chelkat Yoav*, *Kli Chemdah*, *Torat Michael* (R. Michael Forshlager), and *Eretz Tzvi* (R. Tzvi Hirsch Frimer, Kozaglover Rav).

Elyashiv, R. Yosef Shalom (1910 –2012), Jerusalem. Considered by most to be the *Posek HaDor* (the contemporary leading authority on *halakhah*). Though he himself authored only a few works, his numerous ideas and rulings have been disseminated throughout the world.

Feinstein, R. Reuven (contemporary). *Rosh Yeshiva* of the Yeshiva of Staten Island. Youngest child of R. Moshe Feinstein (see *Iggerot Moshe*).

Halachos of Shabbos. R. Shimon Eider (d. 2007), Lakewood. A student of R. Moshe Feinstein, authored numerous halakhic works on various topics, including the laws of *Shabbat.*

Iggerot Moshe. R. Moshe Feinstein (1895–1986) of Luban, Poland, and New York, NY. Eight volumes of responsa, beginning in 1959, New York. Considered one of the leading authorities of the late twentieth century, he was *Rosh Yeshiva* of Mesivta Tiferet Yerushalayim in the Lower East Side of Manhattan and also authored *Dibrot Moshe* to several volumes of the Talmud.

Kotler, R. Aharon (1891–1962). *Rosh Yeshiva* of Kletsk, Poland; founded and headed Beth Medrash Govoha in Lakewood, New Jersey.

Megillat Sefer. R. Uriel Eisenthal (contemporary), Israel.

Minchat Kohen. R. Avraham HaKohen Pimentel (d. 1697). Amsterdam, 1668.

Minchat Shlomo. R. Shlomo Zalman Auerbach (1910–1995). *Rosh Yeshiva* of *Yeshivat Kol Torah* of Jerusalem and considered one of the leading authorities of his time. Also authored *Me'orei Esh* to the laws of electricity on *Shabbat,* and *Ma'adanei Aretz.*

Minchat Yitzchak. R. Yitzchak Yaakov Weiss (1902–1989). Ten volumes of responsa. Rabbinical court judge in Manchester, England, and later Rav of *Edah HaChareidis* in Jerusalem.

Or LeTziyon. R. Ben Zion Abba Shaul (1924–1998). Served as *Rosh Yeshiva* of Yeshivat Porat Yosef in Jerusalem.

Orchot Shabbat. R. Shalom Yosef Gelber and R. Yitzchak Mordechai Rubin (contemporary).

Shevut Yitzchak. R. Yitzchak Drazi (contemporary).

Shemirat Shabbat KeHilkhatah. R. Yehoshua Yeshaya Neuwirth (1927–2013), Jerusalem. A compendium of the laws of *Shabbat,* with an emphasis in modern day application. A close student of R. Shlomo Zalman Auerbach and *Rosh Yeshiva* of Chochmas Shlomo.

Shevitat HaShabbat. R. Yitzchak Maltzan. Jerusalem, 1913.

The Shabbos Kitchen. R. Simcha Bunim Cohen (contemporary), United States.

Soloveitchik, R. Joseph B. (1903–1993) of Boston. Known as "the Rav," he was *Rosh Yeshiva* at Rabbi Isaac Elchanan Theological Seminary and one of the most influential figures of modern Orthodoxy. Author of many volumes of Talmudic lectures and philosophical writings.

Yechaveh Da'at. R. Ovadiah Yosef (1920–2013). Former Sephardic Chief Rabbi of Israel. Also authored *Shut Yabi'a Omer, Yalkut Yosef,* and other halakhic works.

Notes by Rabbi Hershel Schachter

1.3.B

There is a debate amongst contemporary authorities regarding the actual temperature of *yad soledet bo*. The *Rishonim* explain (based on a biblical verse, *Iyov* 6:10) that *yad soledet* refers to a temperature that, if touched, one's hand would pull back from. R. Soloveitchik maintained that this temperature was anywhere from 140-160 degrees Fahrenheit. *Shemirat Shabbat KeHilkhatah* 1:3 asserts that the temperature is 114 degrees; however, this is questionable, as one's hand would not recoil at such a low temperature. While R. Moshe Feinstein offers a number of different suggestions, these seem to be too high. The generally accepted position is to be stringent and to assume that anything above 120 degrees would be considered *yad soledet bo*.

1.6

We determine the status of an item as being either a solid or a liquid based on whether it is a solid or a liquid at room temperature (in accordance with the view of the *Magen Avraham*).

I.9

While one may cook with the heat of the sun, a pot that was heated up with the sun is considered a derivative of the sun, which is prohibited to use, because it may not be clear to onlookers that the pot was heated up by the sun as opposed to with fire. The *Magen Avraham* quotes the position of the Maharshal, who maintains that if the vessel is still in the sun, it would be permissible to have it cook there because that is still considered cooking with the heat of the sun rather than a derivative of the sun. Other authorities, however, argue with this approach. This argument has a practical application to cooking water in a "*Dud Shemesh*" (solar water heater). The Maharshal's position would indicate it would be permissible to use the *Dud Shemesh* during the day, when the sun is beating, because that would be cooking directly with the sun, which is considered an abnormal method of cooking. R. Soloveitchik, however, felt that today, cooking with a *Dud Shemesh* is considered a normative way of cooking and is thus forbidden by the Torah. (See *MePeninei HaRav*, page 94; this is also the view of R. Moshe Feinstein in *Iggerot Moshe.*)

I.11

Regarding making tea on *Shabbat*: The Talmud says that even though *bishul* generally cannot occur in a *keli sheni*, "*kalei habishul*" are an exception and can be cooked in a *keli sheni*. For this reason, the *Responsa Binyan Tzion* (I, 18) asserted that one should be stringent to not make tea with tea bags on *Shabbat,* even in a *keli sheni,* because of the concern that perhaps the tea leaves are also *kalei habishul.* However, this view, to question perhaps everything is included in *kalei habishul,* has not been generally accepted, since the Talmud has a very short list of *kalei habishul.* Accordingly, one may make tea on *Shabbat* using the hot water of an urn. One should first place the water into a *keli sheni* and only afterwards place the tea bag in the water. However, one should be careful about squeezing out the tea bag because of concerns of the *melakhah* of *sechitah* (squeezing). (See *Nefesh HaRav* page 170.)

It is permissible to warm a bottle of baby formula or milk in a *keli sheni.*

I.12

R. Soloveitchik noted that the leniencies of a *keli sheni* ought not apply if the soup bowls were preheated before the soup was placed into them.

I.15

One can consider a ladle a *keli sheni* and the bowl from which one eats a *keli shelishi*. Therefore, it is permissible to dip *challah* in soup that was served with a ladle, which was not heated to the temperature of the *keli rishon*, because the stringency of "*yeish bishul achar afiyah*" doesn't apply to a *keli shelishi*. (See *Mishnah Berurah* 318:45)

II.19

The Maharit writes that, since returning cooked food to the fire is only a rabbinic prohibition, and telling a non-Jew to perform a *melakhah* (*amirah lenokhri*) is a rabbinic prohibition, it is therefore permissible to ask a non-Jew to put food back on the fire on *Shabbat*, due to the principle that the combination of two rabbinic prohibitions is permitted if done for the sake of a *mitzvah* (*shevut deshevut bemakom mitzvah*). In this case, the relevant *mitzvah* would be having hot food for the *Shabbat* meal. However, the *Be'ur Halakhah* (*O.C.* 253:5) asserts that the *halakhah* does not follow this leniency of the Maharit. The reasoning may be as follows: The *Magen Avraham* maintains, citing the Radvaz, that if the prevalent custom is to always have music at a *sheva berakhot* celebration, then one may ask a non-Jew to play music at a *sheva berakhot* which falls on *Shabbat*, as it would be a situation of "*shevut deshevut bemakom mitzvah*." The view of the Radvaz is not currently followed, perhaps for the following reason: The *Eglei Tal* explains that the prohibition of (non-urgent) medicine usage on *Shabbat* applies even when the medicine is applied by a non-Jew. This is because the prohibition of applying medicine on *Shabbat* is a *gezeirah*, a protective measure that was enacted by the Rabbis in order to prevent a Torah prohibition from being violated. The *gezeirah* itself has no similarity to the Torah prohibition (i.e., *tochein*, in the sense of grinding ingredients to manufacture the medicine) that it was designed to protect. This is distinct from a different type of rabbinically prohibited act, a "*melakhah derabbanan*," which is an act which is similar to the Torah prohibition, and the Rabbis were concerned that if people were allowed to perform this act then they would come to violate the Torah prohibition itself.

The rule is that utilizing the services of a non-Jew can only decrease the severity of a *melakhah derabbanan*, but not necessarily that of a *gezeirah*. Each *gezeirah* must be judged individually. Some can only be violated *bekum ve'aseh* (actively), in which case the *amirah lenokhri* would lower it to the level of a *shevut dishevut*, while other *gezeirot* were formulated in such a way that they can be violated even *bishev v'al ta'aseh* (passively), in which case the *amirah lenokhri* would be irrelevant, and would not lower the level of the violation. Similarly, one could argue that the prohibition of playing music on *Shabbat* is a *gezeirah* and thus would not be obviated when performed by a non-Jew on behalf on a Jew.

Working within this framework, it can be understood that the Maharit maintains, consistent with the view of the Sephardic sages, that returning a food to the fire on *Shabbat* is a rabbinic form of cooking, a *melakhah derabbanan*, and thus the level of its prohibition can be lowered by instructing a non-Jew to replace the food on the fire. However, the general consensus of Ashkenazim is that that returning the food is a *gezeirah*, out of concern that one may stoke the fire, and therefore the act of a non-Jew will not lower the status of the prohibition of returning food in any case. Nevertheless, if one did follow the view of the Maharit, the food would be permissible *ex post facto*. (See *Eretz HaTzvi* 6:5)

11.20

It is proper to be stringent for the opinion of the *Mishnah Berurah* to not replace food on the fire unless the food will be placed on top of a full pot. There does not have to be a *blech* underneath the bottom pot (which is full of food) unless the flame could touch the bottom of the pot (due to the concern of *hatmanah*).

11.23

The Talmud states that "returning" is only permitted onto a stove, but not into an oven. Rabbi Soloveitchik, in explaining this statement, said that returning is only permitted in certain situations because it is being viewed as a continuation of the previous cooking. If there is no continuation of the previous cooking process then we view the placing of the food on the cooking area as initiating an act of reheating on *Shabbat*, which is clearly not allowed. There is only a continuation of the cooking process when the cooking is going on outside the oven. However, if food is outside of an oven and then returned back in, then the stark change of location creates a *hefsek* (break) in the cooking process and the permissibility to return to the food to the heating element ceases to exist. Therefore, it is always forbidden to return food into an oven. This is considered a new placement which is not allowed; only *hachzarah*, returning, is allowed.

R. Moshe Feinstein considered the question of whether the deterrent to the adjusting of the flame is applied to the fire or the knobs of the stove. R. Moshe maintained that at a minimum, the fire must be covered, with covering the knobs a reasonable stringency. This stringency is based on an opinion in the Ran that the purpose of creating a deterrent from adjusting the flame is to make it practically difficult to stoke the coals, and not simply to serve as a reminder. However, Rabbi Shimon Eider (*Hilchos Shabbos* page 338) quotes R. Aharon Kotler who felt that it is more important that one should cover the knobs, and as a stringency to also cover the fire. This was also the opinion of R. Soloveitchik.

One may only return food to a warming drawer on *Shabbat* if the temperature cannot be adjusted; merely taping up the dial is not adequate. (See the *Daf HaKashrus* vol. 19 no. 10)

11.25

A *blech* is a reliable cover for a fire, as the practice is to not follow the *Chazon Ish* on this matter.

11.26

The *Be'ur Halakhah* 253:2 understands the Rama to require that one have in mind to return the food that has been removed from the oven, and that the food has not left the individual's hand, to allow the food to be returned to the oven. In the event that the individual did not have in mind to return the food after it was removed, the *halakhah* is subject to an argument amongst the *Rishonim*, as the *Be'ur Halakhah* notes. The

Beit Yosef only records one early opinion who was lenient if one did not have in mind to return the food while it was in hand. The *Be'ur Halakhah* adds the Ra'ah, the Riaz and the Meiri who were lenient in this situation. However, these opinions are disputed by many major Rishonim, such as Rashi, Tosafot, Rashba and the Rambam, who all require both conditions. Surprisingly, the *Shemirat Shabbat KeHilkhatah* (I, 73) brings the *Be'ur Halakhah* as the accepted *halakhah,* without mentioning the difficulty of relying on this minority opinion. Despite the *Be'ur Halakhah*'s inclination toward leniency, it is questionable to rely on those Rishonim when such major authorities are in disagreement, and thus this leniency should only be utilized in pressing circumstances.

II.27

It is problematic to place food onto a hot plate on *Shabbat* if there are dials on the hot plate to change the temperature. In that circumstance, one could only place food onto the hot plate if the food that is being returned will be placed on another pot that is full of food. However, if there is no way to change the temperature, one may take the food directly from the refrigerator and place it on to the hotplate on *Shabbat.*

II.28

The Talmud (*Shabbat* 17b) cites an argument between Beit Hillel and Beit Shammai regarding a *melakhah* that began on *erev Shabbat* and continued into *Shabbat.* Beit Shammai maintained that one was not allowed to start such a process on Erev *Shabbat,* while Beit Hillel argued it was permissible. As usual, the law follows the opinion of Beit Hillel. However, the Rambam in his commentary to the *gemara* of *Massekhet Shabbat* writes that even Beit Hillel only allowed this if the actual *melakhah* begins before *Shabbat,* but it would be forbidden to do an act on *erev Shabbat* if it will result in a *melakhah* beginning in the middle of *Shabbat.* Rabbi Shlomo Yosef Zevin (*Soferim uSefarim* vol. 1 page 92) explains that this understanding of the Rambam would indicate that one may not use a timer that will cause a *melakhah* to be performed on *Shabbat* (however, Rabbi Zevin finds room to be lenient based on other considerations). Rabbi Moshe Feinstein felt that you could only use a *Shabbat* clock for the service of "*kavod Shabbat,*" such as, for example, having lights on for *Shabbat*. However, it cannot be used for things that are not for the enhancement of *Shabbat,* such as watching television. It may be that there was a period in time when it was too expensive to run the lights all *Shabbat,* and therefore the alternative to a timer was that people kept the lights off all *Shabbat* which would decrease the enjoyment of *Shabbat* . However, in contemporary times it is not that expensive to run the lights all *Shabbat,* and therefore it maybe questionable to use a *Shabbat* clock nowadays, in light of the above opinion of the Rambam.

II.29

The *Magen Avraham* (*O.C.* 318:2, also brought in *Mishnah Berurah* ibid. 4) writes in the name of the *Teshuvot HaRashba* that if a Jew cooks purposefully on *Shabbat,* not only is the food forbidden, but even the taste imparted into the pot is forbidden (known as "*beli'at keilim*"), and therefore the pot itself cannot be used until a proper *hagalat keilim* is done. Based on this, there were and are rabbis who propose that the bread from Jewish bakeries which bake on *Shabbat* is forbidden during the week, because the bread contains the *issur* of something cooked on *Shabbat,* transmitted through the utensils. In addition, each time the bakery bakes, the *issur* in the vessels is renewed and the *issur* never passes the required 24 hours of rest to make them permissible.

However, R. Moshe Soloveitchik questioned this applicability of "*beli'at keilim*" in this context. "*Ma'aseh Shabbat*" – the result of a *melakhah* performed on *Shabbat* – likely does not fall under the category of foods that are inherently forbidden, where the principle of *beli'at keilim* would logically be applied. Rather, "*Ma'aseh Shabbat*" is a penalty from the Rabbis to derive any benefit, in the normal fashion of benefit, from the food cooked on *Shabbat.* If one uses the vessels that were used for cooking on *Shabbat* within twenty-four hours, this would not be considered as benefiting from food cooked on *Shabbat.* (See *Nefesh HaRav* page 171.)

II.30

In a situation in which a caterer has a hot box plugged in over *Shabbat* in order to keep food warm for an event, and a non-Jewish waiter tripped over the cord, thereby unplugging it, and then immediately plugged the hot box back in, a question exists as to whether this is considered prohibited *melakhah* on behalf of a Jew on *Shabbat*. It is likely that this is indeed the case, and as a result the food in the hot box cannot be warmed up to be eaten later.

ADDITIONAL COMMENTS REGARDING CHOLENT POTS

If it appears likely that the cholent will dry out, one may add water which is *yad soledet bo* from a *keli rishon*. For example, one may position the cholent pot under the urn and then fill it from the urn. However, if it is very difficult to transfer the water from the urn directly into the crock-pot, it is an unanswered question in the Talmud as to whether one may transfer the hot water with a *keli sheni*. The *Mishnah Berurah* is lenient on this matter, but the custom is to not be lenient about pouring from a *keli sheni* into a *keli rishon* that is on the fire.

Me'ikkar hadin, there is no problem stirring the cholent if it is fully cooked, because of the principle of *ein bishul achar bishul*. However, the *Shulchan Arukh* records a stringent opinion to not stir a pot on the fire. If the cholent pot is no longer on the fire, there would be no problem placing the ladle into the pot.

The *Shulchan Arukh* (*O.C.* 253:1) rules that if there is no way to possibly cook the food in time for the evening meal, as it is raw, then one does not require a *blech*, and the food may be placed on the fire before *Shabbat*. The *Be'ur Halakhah* (*O.C.* 253, s.v. *lehashoto*) quotes the *Elyah Rabbah*, who maintains that if the food is designated for *Shabbat* day, then a *blech* is not required. However, the *Be'ur Halakhah* asserts that this opinion is not followed. R. Soloveitchik felt that if the food would not be ready until after *chatzot* at night, then a *blech* would not be needed to place the raw food on the fire before *Shabbat*. However, he thought, like Rav Henkin, that our stoves are such that the food probably could be ready for the nighttime meal with a little regulating of the knobs, and therefore this whole *heter* of *kedeirah chayta* ought not apply.

If the cholent pot is touching the heating element, something should be placed in between the crockpot and the element to avoid the issue of insulating the food (*hatmanah*). One may place a *challah* on top of the cholent pot, or on any full pot of food.

The Rama (*O.C.* 253:2) maintains that one is not allowed to return food to the oven unless the food is fully cooked (in addition to the four other conditions, i.e., the flame is covered, the food must be warm when returned, the pot cannot leave the hand, and the original intent is to return the food to the fire). Therefore, if one tastes the cholent on Friday night and sees that the potato isn't fully cooked, the lid may not be placed back onto the cholent pot, because doing so would speed up the cooking process, which is Biblically prohibited.

There is a debate among the *poskim* regarding the question of whether food that was cooked before *Shabbat* can be warmed with a heating device set to go on in the middle of *Shabbat*. The *Responsa Melamed LeHo'il* (I, 49) seems to allow it in the context of hospital usage. The *Shemirat Shabbat KeHilkhatah* allows it, while the *Chazon Ish* (*O.C.* 37:21) raised the possibility that this constitutes *chazarah* on Shabbat. It is proper to be stringent for the view of the *Chazon Ish* and to not use a timer to turn on a hotplate on *Shabbat*.

Index

T

U

W

Y

The Laws of Cooking and Warming Food on Shabbat

ספר בישול בשבת

Michael Scharf
Publication Trust
Yeshiva University Press
RIETS

מגיד
MAGGID

תוכן העניינים

Note to the Reader

For the full text of *The Laws of Cooking and Warming Food on Shabbat,* turn to the other end of this volume.

פרקים מתוך ספר
"עם מרדכי"

סימן א

שהייה והחזרה

א. שני טעמים לאיסור החזרה

תנן (לו:), כירה שהסיקוה בקש או בגבבא נותנין עליה תבשיל. בגפת או בעצים לא יתן עד שיגרוף או עד שיתן את האפר.

ובגמרא (שם) איבעיא להו, האי לא יתן לא יחזיר הוא, אבל לשהות משהין אע"פ שאינו גרוף ואינו קטום ומני חנניה היא דתניא חנניה אומר כל שהוא כמאכל בן דרוסאי מותר להשהותו על גבי כירה אע"פ שאינו גרוף ואינו קטום. או דילמא לשהות תנן ואי גרוף וקטום אין אי לא לא, וכ"ש להחזיר, ע"כ.

מבואר בגמרא שיש ב׳ גזירות חז"ל בענין זה, שהיית קדירה על גבי כירה מערב שבת, והחזרת קדירה על גבי כירה בשבת. ובטעם איסור שהייה והיתר גרופה וקטומה פירש הר"ן (טו: בדפי הרי"ף ד"ה כירה) דאסור להשהות מערב שבת שמא יחתה בגחלים בשבת, ומשום הכי כל שגרוף וקטום דאיכא היכרא שמסלק דעתו מלחתות שרי, וכן בקש וגבבא לא חיישינן שמא יחתה בגחלים, משום דקש וגבבא אין בהם גחלת. וכן כתבו שאר הראשונים (שם), וכן היא בשו"ע (או"ח סי׳ רנג ס"א).

ובטעם איסור החזרה נחלקו הראשונים, דר"ת בספר הישר (סי׳ רלה, ומובא בשעה"צ שם סקל"ז) פירש שיש חשש גדול יותר שיחתה בגחלים מכיון שנצטננה קצת כשהסיר מן האש. ולכן אינו מחזיר על גבי אש מגולה

אע"פ שהמאכל הגיע לכמאכל בן דרוסאי וקיי"ל כחנניה דמותר בשהייה, דהחזרה חמורה יותר.

ונראה דכן דעת בעה"מ (ריש פ"ג, טו: בדפי הרי"ף) שכתב וז"ל, שכל שאנו מחמירים ואוסרים וכו' בכירה בענין הזה איננו אלא משום גזירה שמא יחתה בגחלים, עכ"ל. ומלשונו נראה דכל האיסורים, כלומר שהייה והחזרה, משום שמא יחתה הם. וכן נראה בתוס' (לח: ד"ה פינה), וכמש"כ המהר"ם (לו: ד"ה אבל).

אבל הר"ן (טו: בדפי הרי"ף ד"ה גמ') כתב דלא מחזירין משום דמיחזי כמבשל בשבת. וגם רש"י פירש במתני' כדברי הר"ן דאין מחזירין משום דמיחזי כמבשל.

אמנם המהר"ם כתב דע"כ פירש רש"י כן רק לשיטת ב"ש (שם), דהחזרה אסורה גם בגרוף וקטום. אבל למאי דקיי"ל כב"ה דמותר להחזיר בגרוף וקטום, ע"כ טעם האיסור משום שמא יחתה, ולזה מהני ההיכר בגרוף וקטום, דאילו לענין נראה כמבשל לא מהני גרוף וקטום, עכ"ד.

אך נראה דאף אם נאמר כן לרש"י, מכל מקום הר"ן בודאי לא ס"ל כן, שבאיבעית הגמ' הנ"ל כתב (שם) וז"ל, האי לא יתן לא יחזיר הוא, משום דס"ל דמחזיר בשבת נראה כמבשל אם אינה קטומה, עכ"ל. הרי שקטומה מהני להסיר איסור נראה כמבשל, וא"כ זהו טעם האיסור אף לב"ה.

עוד כתב הר"ן (שם ד"ה ותו) דאסור להחזיר אע"פ שמצטמק ורע לו, ואין כ"כ חשש חיתוי בגחלים. ואזיל לשיטתו דהחזרה אסורה משום דנראה כמבשל. אבל לפי הטעם דשמא יחתה, יתכן דמותר להחזיר במצטמק ורע לו (עי' לקמן, סי' ד אות ד).

וז"ל הר"ן (יט. בדפי הרי"ף בשם הרשב"א), צונן שנתבשל מותר להניחו כנגד המדורה, שאין דרך בישול בכך, אבל על גבי האש ממש אסור [להחזיר] אא"כ גרוף וקטום, דהא אסקינן לעיל דאפילו תבשיל המצטמק ורע לו אסור להחזירו על גבי כירה שאינה גרופה וקטומה, הלכך דוקא כנגד המדורה הוא דשרי. וכן נמי מותר לתת ע"פ קדירת חמין בשבת תבשיל שנתבשל מערב שבת כל צרכו לחממן ... לפי שאין דרך בישול בכך. ואע"פ שהקדירה נתונה על האש, עכ"ל.

וגם מזה נראה דטעם איסור החזרה הוא משום דנראה כמבשל, וכנ"ל. ולכן מותר להחזיר על גבי קדירה, דכיון דאין דרך בישול בכך אינו נראה

כמבשל. ולפי הטעם דשמא יחתה יתכן דאסור להחזיר על גבי קדירה (עי׳ לקמן, סי׳ ג אות א).

ב. החזרה בערב שבת

והנה ר״ת (בספר הישר שם, ובתוס׳ לו: ד״ה וב״ה) סובר דאסור להחזיר על גבי אש מגולה בנתבשל כמאכל בן דרוסאי, אף בערב שבת סמוך לחשיכה, כל שאילו היה צונן לא היה שהות ביום כדי להתחמם.

והר״ן במשנה (טו: בדפי הרי״ף ד״ה ב״ש) חולק, דהא קיי״ל כב״ה (יז:) דמתירין בכולן עם השמש, וכיון שמותר לבשל בערב שבת ק״ו דמותר להחזיר. ונראה דהר״ן אזיל לשיטתו, דהחזרה אסורה משום דנראה כמבשל, ומותר בערב שבת ק״ו ממבשל ממש. אבל לתוס׳, דהחזרה אסורה משום שמא יחתה, שפיר י״ל דאסור אף בערב שבת, וכשהייה, די״ל דאסרו שהייה והחזרה בערב שבת שמא יחתה בגחלים בשבת.

אמנם אין הכרח שיש איסור החזרה בערב שבת במאכל שנתבשל כשיעור מאכל בן דרוסאי לטעם שמא יחתה. אבל לטעם נראה כמבשל בודאי אין איסור בערב שבת, וכמש״כ הר״ן.

והרמ״א (סי׳ רנג ס״ב) שכתב שטוב להחמיר ולאסור החזרה סמוך לשבת, ע״כ חושש לטעם שמא יחתה. ואף להמקילים שנהגו כמותם, עיי״ש, י״ל דזהו טעם איסור החזרה, וכנ״ל, שאף אם טעם איסור החזרה הוא משום שמא יחתה, אין הכרח שאסרו בערב שבת.

וז״ל ר״ת בספר הישר (שם) והא דאמרינן בכירה לא יחזיר עד שיגרוף, אפילו מבעוד יום קאמר, כי כיון שהוא נותנן עליה או בתוכה, מגלה דעתו שצריכה חימום. לכן יש לחוש שמא יחתה, ולכן צריך לעשות היכרא דגרוף וקטום, עכ״ל.

ובתוס׳ (לו: ד״ה וב״ה) הוכיחו כן מלשון הגמ׳ (לח:) ׳דלדברי [ב״ה] האומר מחזירין, מחזירין אפילו בשבת׳, ומוכח דנחלקו גם בחול. ופירשו דר״ל בערב שבת סמוך לחשיכה, כל שאילו היה צונן לא היה יכול להרתיח מבעוד יום.

ובתוס׳ ישנים (לו:) כתב, דרש״י (לח:) פירש ׳אפילו בשבת׳, ביום המחרת, לא תימא פלוגתייהו משחשיכה, כלומר רק בלילה דמוכח שדעתו להחזיר. ולפ״ז אין שום הכרח לפרש שיש איסור החזרה מערב שבת.

ובאמת לרש״י לשיטתו במשנה (כפשוטו דקאי אהחזרה, דלא כדעת המהר״ם, וכנ״ל אות א), דאיסור החזרה משום נראה כמבשל, מסתבר שאין איסור בערב שבת, שהרי מותר לבשל ממש בערב שבת, וק״ו לעשות פעולה שרק מיחזי כמבשל. וכ״כ הר״ן במשנה דמותר להחזיר מערב שבת לב״ה, דאזלי לשיטתם (יז:) דמתירין מלאכה ממש עם השמש, וכנ״ל.

אבל התוס׳ אזלי לשיטתם, דאיסור החזרה נגזר שמא יחתה בגחלים, דומיא דאיסור שהייה. וא״כ כמו שגזרו שהייה מערב שבת, שמא יחתה בגחלים בשבת, כן גזרו בהחזרה מערב שבת (אף במבושל כמאכל בן דרוסאי, דאין איסור שהייה לחנניה), שמא יחתה בגחלים בשבת מאחר שנצטננה כשהסירה מן האש, וכנ״ל.

והנה ברא״ש (סי׳ ב) אסר בערב שבת מטעם אחר לגמרי, שאם יחזיר בערב שבת יבא להחזיר בשבת. ולפ״ז אסר רק כשנתבשל כל צרכו, דאז אין איסור בישול החמור, ויש לחוש שיעבור על איסור קל דהחזרה בשבת, וכולה חדא גזירה היא. משא״כ בלא נתבשל כל צרכו, דלא גזרינן שיחזיר בשבת, כי יש איסור בישול, ולכן מותר בערב שבת. כן פירש הב״י (סי׳ רנג) את דברי הרא״ש.

ולכאורה צ״ע דאיסור חיתוי דאורייתא הוא (כמו איסור בישול), ואעפ״כ גזרו שמא יחתה בשבת. וצ״ל שגזרו שמא ישכח ששבת היום ויחתה, אבל בערב שבת אטו שבת גזרו רק שיטעה בדין ויחשוב שמותר להחזיר בשבת.

וכ״כ הט״ז (סקט״ו), וז״ל דהגזירה רק שמא ילמוד היתר מן סמוך לחשיכה, וזה לא שייך במקום שיש ודאי בישול, עכ״ל. כלומר, דבזה בודאי לא יטעה בדין.

אבל עיקר פירוש הב״י בדברי הרא״ש צ״ע, דהרא״ש (סי׳ יא) ס״ל דמשהגיע המאכל לשיעור כמאכל בן דרוסאי, שוב אין בו איסור בישול. וא״כ קשה למה מותר להחזיר בערב שבת כשלא נתבשל כל צרכו, הלא אין איסור בישול דאורייתא אם יחזיר בשבת. וכן הקשה הב״ח (שם). [ואין לומר דמיירי בלא הגיע לשיעור כמאכל בן דרוסאי, דבזה אסור לכו״ע משום שהייה.] ועוד קשה, שהרא״ש לא הזכיר איסור בישול כלל.

לכן נראה כדברי הב"ח (שם), וז"ל, דהחזרה בשבת מסתמא אינה אלא בקדירות שכבר הן מבושלות כל צרכן, ונתנן בכירה להשהותן שם עד זמן האכילה, ואם היו גוזרין זו שאינה מבושלת כל צרכה ומבעוד יום אטו שבת, ה"ל גזירה לגזירה. אבל קדירה שמבושלת כל צרכה, ומבעוד יום הניחה עומדת על הכירה עד לערב להחזיק חומה, דמיא להך קדירה שהיא כבר מונחת בכירה ונכנס השבת. דאם אתה מחזיר זו שמבעוד יום, דאינה מתבשלת עוד על הכירה, והוי כתחילת שהייה, אתא להחזיר גם זו בשבת, דדמיא לה, וכולה חדא גזירה היא, עכ"ל.

וזוהי כונת הרא"ש וז"ל, דכיון דאינה מתבשלת עוד על הכירה, הוי כתחילת שהייה, עכ"ל. כלומר דהרגילות היא שהתבשיל כבר מבושל כל צרכה כשמשהה מתחילה מערב שבת, ונוטל ומחזיר. ובזה גזרו ערב שבת אטו שבת להצריך גרוף וקטום, דדומה לרגילות דשבת, והכל גזירה אחת. משא"כ כשאינו מבושל כל צרכו, דאין רגילות להחזיר בשבת, דרגילין להשאירו שם עד שיתבשל כל צרכו. ולכן לא גזרו בערב שבת כשאינו מבושל כל צרכו, דלא דמי להחזרה הרגילה בשבת.

ובב"ח (שם) כתב דלפי ההגמ"י (פ"ג סק"ב, והסמ"ג, ועוד), כל שנתבשל כמאכל בן דרוסאי אסור להחזיר סמוך לשבת בכירה שאינה גרופה וקטומה. וכן נראה מדברי התוס' (לו:) דחנניה מתיר רק שהייה בשיעור כמאכל בן דרוסאי, ולא החזרה בערב שבת, כלומר, בשיעור כמאכל בן דרוסאי. ולדבריהם, שפיר יש לפרש כדעת הב"י, שאסרו בערב שבת אטו שבת רק באופן שאין איסור בישול בשבת, דהיינו משהגיע לשיעור כמאכל בן דרוסאי.

ולפ"ז, אף אם החזרה אסורה משום דנראה כמבשל, אפשר לכאורה דאסורה מערב שבת, אף דבישול ממש מותר, דגזרו ערב שבת אטו שבת באיסור דרבנן דהחזרה, ולא באיסור דאורייתא דבישול. וכתב כן בספר נחל זרד (ח"ג עמ' סה). [אך עיין בסמוך (סי' ב אות ב), דלפי הגר"א נראה דאינו כן.]

היוצא מכל הנ"ל שלפי הר"ן אין איסור החזרה בערב שבת כלל. ולפי ר"ת אסור להחזיר בערב שבת שמא יחתה בשבת עצמה. ולפי הרא"ש אסור להחזיר בערב שבת שמא יחזיר בשבת עצמה.

סימן ב

הנחה לכתחילה

א. איסור הנחה לכתחילה

בגמרא (לח:) מבואר דהיתר החזרה על גבי כירה גרופה וקטומה נאמר רק בעוד הקדירה בידו וגם דעתו להחזיר, וי"א דדי בעודה בידו או דעתו להחזיר (עי' לקמן סי' ז אות א).

ופי' רש"י (שם ד"ה מחזירין), דבהניח על גבי קרקע בטלי לה הטמנה דאתמול, והוי כמטמין לכתחילה. ולשון הטמנה ברש"י נאמרה לשיטתו (לו:) דאיסור שהייה משום הטמנה. ולפי שאר הפוסקים אמרינן דבטלה שהייה הראשונה, וכלשון המ"ב (סקנ"ה), והו"ל כמושיב לכתחילה על גבי הכירה בשבת, וזה אסור משום שנראה כמבשל, וכמש"כ הר"ן והרשב"א (שם).

והנה הרשב"א והר"ן ס"ל דהחזרה על גבי כירה שאינה גרופה וקטומה אסורה משום דנראה כמבשל וכנ"ל (סי' א אות א). וכנראה ס"ל דמשנתבשל כמאכל בן דרוסאי לחנניה, ובמצטמק ורע לו לרבנן דחנניה, שוב אין חשש חיתוי, אף באינו גרוף וקטום, וע"כ אסור רק משום דנראה כמבשל. ובגרוף וקטום לא נראה כמבשל, וכנ"ל (שם).

וא"כ לפי הרשב"א והר"ן, ק"ו דאיסור הנחה לכתחילה על גבי כירה גרופה וקטומה אינו משום חשש חיתוי, אלא משום דנראה כמבשל. וטעמם, דרק כשלא הניחו על גבי קרקע ונידון כהמשך המצב הקודם, לא נראה

כמבשל כשהאש קטומה. משא"כ בבטלה שהייה הראשונה ע"י הנחה על גבי קרקע, דאז נראה כמבשל גם באש קטומה.

אבל יש לעיין לפי ר"ת ותוס', דההחזרה אסורה משום שמא יחתה בגחלים, וכנ"ל, מה טעם איסור הנחה לכתחילה על כירה גרופה וקטומה. די"ל דבגרוף וקטום לכו"ע לא חיישינן לחיתוי, וע"כ האיסור משום נראה כמבשל. והטעם, דרק בהחזרה אינו נראה כמבשל, דנידון כהמשך של המצב הקודם מערב שבת, משא"כ במניח לכתחילה דבטלה שהייה הראשונה, ולכן נראה כמבשל, דרק מטעם זה אסור בגרוף וקטום.

אך עוד י"ל דבמניח לכתחילה חששו לחיתוי אף בכירה גרופה וקטומה, דגם אם האש קטומה, עדיין יכול לחתות. ובהחזרה לא חשו לזה, אבל במניח לכתחילה, שבטלה שהייה ראשונה, גזרו שמא יחתה בגחלים אף באש קטומה.

ולפי צד הב' יש לחלק בין החזרה להנחה ע"פ דברי השעה"צ (סקל"ז, הנ"ל שם). וז"ל, משום דכשנוטלה מן האש פעמים שמצטננת קצת, וחיישינן שמא יחתה בחזרתו, עכ"ל בשם ר"ת. ועפ"ז י"ל דבהחזרה, שמצטננת קצת, לא גזרו באש קטומה. אבל בהנחה לכתחילה, שמצטננת יותר, גזרו שמא יחתה אף באש קטומה.

ונראה דכן מבואר בתוס' (לח: ד"ה פינה), דבגמ' (שם, לצד א' באיבעיא) איתא, דאם פינה ממיחם למיחם בטלה שהייה ראשונה ואסור להניחו על גבי כירה גרופה וקטומה. והתוס' פירשו בשם ר"ת דאסור משום שמא יחתה בגחלים.

מאידך, בתוס' הרא"ש (שם) כתב דאם נסתלקה שהייה ראשונה, הוי כמו שהייה חדשה ובשיל בשבת, כלומר דנראה כמבשל. ומשמע דבהחזרה אינו אסור מטעם זה, אלא שמא יחתה בגחלים באינו גרוף וקטום.

ונראה דגם בעל המאור מחלק כן, שכתב בריש פירקין דכל איסורי משנתנו, שהייה וההחזרה, משום שמא יחתה בגחלים, וכנ"ל (שם). אבל בהניח על גבי קרקע כתב (טז: בדפי הרי"ף) דאסור משום דנראה כמבשל לכתחילה בשבת. ועי' לקמן (סי' ד אות ד) דגם בעל חידושי הר"ן ס"ל כן. ונפק"מ טובא בין שתי שיטות אלו, וכמו שיתבאר.

ב. הנחה בערב שבת

כתב בהגמ״ר (פ״ג, עט: בדפי המרדכי) וז״ל, חזרה היינו שמניח את הקדירה על גבי כירה סמוך לחשיכה, שלא היה סיפק ביום כדי להרתיח אם היתה צוננת, וזה ודאי אסור להניח או להחזיר על גבי כירה שאינה גרופה וקטומה ... אבל על גבי גרוף וקטום ... מותר להניח שם לכתחילה סמוך לחשיכה ... מיהו היא גופא צ״ע אם מותר להניח הקדירה לכתחילה על גבי גרופה וקטומה סמוך לחשיכה, דדילמא לא שרינן אפילו מבעוד יום אלא להחזיר, אבל להניח לכתחילה לא. ולשון חזרה משמע הכי, שכבר היתה שם ורוצה להחזירה. ועוד, מבעוד יום דומיא דשבת, ובשבת אסור להניחה על גבי מיחם לכתחילה וכו׳, עכ״ל.

ונראה לבאר אריכות דברי ההגמ״ר, דלענין החזרה בערב שבת יש ג׳ שיטות, וכמש״כ לעיל (סי׳ א אות ב). לפי הר״ן, דאיסור החזרה משום נראה כמבשל, אין שום איסור בערב שבת כי מותר לבשל אז. לפי הרא״ש, דגזרו ערב שבת אטו שבת, יש איסור החזרה גזירה שמא יחזיר בשבת. ולפי ר״ת יש איסור החזרה שמא יחתה בגחלים בשבת.

ומעתה ההגמ״ר ע״כ לא ס״ל כהר״ן, מדאסר החזרה בערב שבת על גבי כירה שאינה גרופה וקטומה. ובהנחה לכתחילה בערב שבת על גבי כירה גרופה וקטומה נסתפק, ולכאורה לפי הרא״ש אפשר לומר שאסור גזירה אטו הנחה לכתחילה בשבת. ונראה דזוהי הסברא האחרונה בהגמ״ר ׳ועוד מבעוד יום דומיא דשבת׳.

ובתחילה הקיל ההגמ״ר בפשיטות בהנחה לכתחילה בערב שבת על גבי גרוף וקטום. ונראה דזוהי כשיטת הבעה״מ (הנ״ל, אות א), שהחזרה אסורה באש מגולה שמא יחתה בגחלים, וא״כ י״ל דאסרו בערב שבת שמא יחתה בשבת עצמה. אבל בגרוף וקטום אין חשש חיתוי כלל, ואסרו להניח לכתחילה משום דנראה כמבשל, וזה לא שייך בערב שבת. ולא ס״ל בתחלה כהרא״ש דגזרו ערב שבת אטו שבת.

ובאמצע, נסתפק ההגמ״ר (בדין הנחה על גבי כירה גרופה וקטומה בערב שבת) ע״פ לשון הגמרא, שמותר להחזיר על גבי כירה גרופה

וקטומה, וקאי גם אמבעוד יום, וכדעת התוס׳ (לו:). ומשמע קצת דרק להחזיר מותר, אבל הנחה לכתחילה אסור.

ולכאורה ספק זה קיים רק לפי ר״ת והתוס׳ (לח:), ששני האיסורים, איסור החזרה על גבי אינו גרוף וקטום, ואיסור הנחה לכתחילה על גבי גרוף וקטום, משום שמא יחתה בגחלים הם. ולפ״ז יש להסתפק אם גזרו בהנחה לכתחילה בערב שבת על גבי כירה גרופה וקטומה שמא יחתה בשבת, כמו שגזרו בהחזרה על גבי כירה אינה גרופה וקטומה. או דילמא לא גזרו, דרק בשבת גזרו באש קטומה שמא יחתה במניח לכתחילה, אבל לא בערב שבת. וה״ט, דעד שיגיע שבת יתחמם קצת, ואין כ״כ חשש חיתוי. וההגמ״ר נוטה לחומרא ע״פ לשון הגמ׳, וכנ״ל.

עוד י״ל, דלפי ר״ת שאיסור הנחה לכתחילה על גבי כירה גרופה וקטומה הוא משום שמא יחתה בגחלים, בודאי גזרו בערב שבת סמוך לחשיכה, כמו שגזרו בהחזרה. וההגמ״ר באמצע נסתפק אם טעם איסור הנחה לכתחילה הוא כר״ת, וא״כ אסור בערב שבת, וכנ״ל, או דטעם האיסור הוא כשיטת הבעה״מ, דנראה כמבשל, וזה לא שייך בערב שבת, וכנ״ל.

והנה בקרבן נתנאל על הרא״ש (פ״ג סי׳ ב סק״מ) כתב כמש״כ לעיל, דלפי הרא״ש אסרו הנחה לכתחילה על גבי כירה גרופה וקטומה בערב שבת אטו הנחה בשבת (כמו דאסרו החזרה על גבי כירה שאינה גרופה וקטומה בערב שבת אטו החזרה בשבת), וכמש״כ הרא״ש בהדיא (פ״ד סי׳ ב). ומש״כ הרא״ש (פ״ג שם) ׳אבל מבעוד יום מחזירין בכל ענין׳ ר״ל כשאינו סמוך לחשיכה.

אבל הגר״א (סי׳ רנג סקנ״א) כתב שהרא״ש בפרק ג׳ מקיל בהנחה לכתחילה על גבי גרוף וקטום, כלומר, דלשון ׳אבל מבעוד יום מחזירין בכל ענין׳, ר״ל אפילו סמוך לחשיכה, דלא כדברי הק״נ. ואע״ג דבפרק ד׳ לא כתב כן, שם העתיק הרא״ש את לשון התוס׳ וכדרכו, אבל בעצמו ס״ל דמותר. וכ״פ המ״ב (סקע״ב) ע״פ דברי הגר״א.

[ובתפארת שמואל (פ״ד סק״ב) ג״כ כתב דלפי הרא״ש מותר להניח על גבי כירה גרופה וקטומה בערב שבת. ופירש שאוסר הרא״ש כשמניח בתוכה, ושם (פ״ד) כתוכה דמי. וכנראה ס״ל דתוכה חמור שמא יחתה בגחלים, ולא משום נראה כמבשל (עי׳ לקמן סי׳ ד אות ו), שהרי בערב שבת אין איסור נראה כמבשל כלל.]

ולכאורה צ"ע לפי הבנת הגר"א (שהרא"ש ס"ל שלא גזרו הנחה לכתחילה על גבי כירה גרופה וקטומה בערב שבת), שהרי לפי הרא"ש דגזרו החזרה בערב שבת אטו החזרה בשבת, נימא דנגזור גם בהנחה לכתחילה בערב שבת אטו הנחה לכתחילה בשבת עצמה (וכהבנת הק"נ בדברי הרא"ש).

ואולי י"ל, דאע"פ דאפשר לגזור ערב שבת אטו שבת גם באיסור מלאכה דרבנן שאינו חמור כ"כ ויש לחוש שיעבור בשבת, מ"מ לא מצינו כן בשאר מלאכות דרבנן. וא"כ י"ל דהרא"ש הדגיש דכולה חדא גזירה היא, ורק באיסור שיסודו גזירה שמא יחתה גזרו ערב שבת אטו שבת, כבהחזרה, דהכל גזירה אחת.

אבל בהנחה לכתחילה על גבי כירה גרופה וקטומה, אין האיסור משום שמא יחתה לפי תוס' הרא"ש (לח: הנ"ל אות א), אלא משום דנראה כמבשל, וכנ"ל. וזה אינו גזירה, אלא מלאכה מדרבנן. ולכן לא גזרו ערב שבת אטו שבת, דבשבת אינה גזירה, ובערב שבת לא מצינו איסור מלאכה דרבנן או גזירה שמא יעשה מלאכה דרבנן זו בשבת, ודו"ק.

וזוהי כונת הגר"א שכתב שהרא"ש (פ"ד) 'העתיק לשון התוס' וכדרכו', דלפי תוס' (לח:, הנ"ל) גם הנחה לכתחילה אסורה משום גזירה שמא יחתה בגחלים, ולא משום נראה כמבשל כדברי הרא"ש. ולכן לתוס' גם הנחה על גבי כירה גרופה וקטומה איסור גזירה היא, וגזרו ערב שבת אטו שבת, והכל גזירה אחת. אבל לדעת הרא"ש עצמו, דהנחה על גבי כירה גרופה וקטומה אסורה משום דנראה כמבשל, מותר בערב שבת.

ולפ"ז, לפי הגר"א והמ"ב נראה, דהרמ"א ס"ל דהחזרה אסורה משום חשש חיתוי מהא דהביא השיטה שהחזרה אסורה בערב שבת, וכנ"ל (סי' א אות ב), והנחה לכתחילה על כירה גרופה וקטומה אסורה משום נראה כמבשל. ומה שסתם המ"ב (סקל"ז) דאיסור החזרה משום דמיחזי כמבשל, י"ל דכ"כ רק אליבא דהמחבר, שכתב מפורש (ס"ה) שטעם איסור החזרה הוא משום דנראה כמבשל. ובשעה"צ (סקל"ז) כתב הטעם דשמא יחתה בגחלים, כר"ת. ולמש"כ זוהי שיטת הרמ"א לדינא, וכדרכו לפסוק כבעלי התוס', והשו"ע פסק כהרשב"א והר"ן.

והנה במ"ב (סי' שיח סקצ"ח) כתב ב' טעמים לאיסור הנחה באינו גרוף וקטום, נראה כמבשל (כדעת הר"ן) ושמא יחתה (כדעת הרא"ש, סי'

י). ולפי מש"כ מודה הרא"ש דיש איסור נראה כמבשל בהנחה, ויש גם איסור שמא יחתה באינו גרוף וקטום, ק"ו מהחזרה.

ויש להעיר, דכאן הזכיר שמא יחתה במ"ב עצמו, ולעיל (סי' רנג סקל"ז) הזכיר טעם זה רק בשעה"צ, וכנ"ל (סי' א אות א). ואולי י"ל דכאן (סי' שיח) מפרש דברי הרמ"א. ולפי הרמ"א שאוסר החזרה בערב שבת, ע"כ טעם האיסור הוי משום שמא יחתה, וכנ"ל. ולעיל הזכיר טעם שמא יחתה רק בשעה"צ (סי' רנג סקל"ז), משום דשם מפרש דברי השו"ע. ולפי השו"ע (שם ס"ה) טעם איסור החזרה הוא משום דנראה כמבשל. (עי' בסמוך סי' ג אות א).

ג. על ידי נכרי

והנה הרמ"א (שם ס"ה) כתב וז"ל, וכל הדברים שאסור לעשות מדברים אלו אסור לומר לאינו יהודי לעשות, עכ"ל. ובבה"ל (שם ד"ה להחם) כתב בשם הפמ"ג, דכיון דקיי"ל דשבות דשבות לצורך שבת שרי לכתחילה, אפשר דהמיקל להחזיר ע"י גוי אין גוערין בו, ובמהרי"ט מתיר לכתחילה. וסיים הבה"ל וז"ל, ובסימן זה משמע מכמה פוסקים דאין סוברין כן. ועיין במג"א (סקל"ז, כצ"ל) ובתו"ש. ומ"מ יש לסמוך עליו לצורך שבת להקל בזה, וכנ"ל בשם הפמ"ג, עכ"ל.

והנה הרמ"א עצמו אסר בפירוש, וכנ"ל, ואף בדיעבד אסר המאכל (ס"א). אבל זהו בדבר לח, שיש בו איסור בישול דאורייתא, וכמש"כ המג"א (סקל"ז). ולכן בדבר יבש כתב הבה"ל דרק 'כמה פוסקים' אסרו, ולא הרמ"א עצמו. וכוונתו, דבמג"א (שם) התיר דבר יבש (שהחזירהו נכרי) רק בדיעבד, ומוכח דאסור לכתחילה. ומ"מ מלשון הרמ"א 'וכל הדברים' משמע דהכל אסור עכ"פ לכתחילה ע"י נכרי, כדמשמע במג"א. אך צ"ב, דהלא שבות דשבות מותר לצורך שבת, וכמש"כ הפמ"ג.

ונראה, דהרמ"א אזיל לשיטתו, דטעם איסור החזרה הוא משום גזירה שמא יחתה. ובזה אין היתר דע"י נכרי, דיש לחוש שהנכרי יחזיר והישראל יחתה. ורק כשהמעשה אסור בפ"ע יש להקל ע"י נכרי. וכ"כ בחזו"א (סי' לז סקכ"א), וכתב שאפילו אם החזירו הקוף חייב להסירו שמא יבוא לחתות בעצמו. וכ"כ מו"ר הג"ר צבי שכטר שליט"א (ארץ הצבי סי' ו

סק"ד). והמקילים כנראה ס"ל כטעם נראה כמבשל בלבד, אבל אנן קיי"ל לחומרא, וכדעת הרמ"א.

והנה בבה"ל (שם, בתחילת דבריו, לפני שהביא מחלוקת הפמ"ג ו'כמה פוסקים') אוסר להניח לכתחילה על גבי כירה גרופה וקטומה ע"י נכרי, דומיא דאיסור החזרה ע"י נכרי על גבי כירה אינה גרופה וקטומה שברמ"א.

ולפי הנ"ל יש מקום לחלק ביניהם, דהחזרה באינו גרוף וקטום אסור שמא יחתה בגחלים, ובזה אין שום היתר דשבות דשבות במקום מצוה, כי הגוי יחזיר והישראל יחתה, וכנ"ל. אבל בכירה גרופה וקטומה, כשבטלה שהייה ראשונה, נראה דלשיטת בעה"מ ותוס' הרא"ש (הנ"ל אות א) שהאיסור הוא רק משום נראה כמבשל, דלא חיישינן שיסיר הכסוי שעל האש ויחתה, א"כ שפיר י"ל דע"י נכרי מותר מדין שבות דשבות לצורך מצוה.

אמנם לתוס' (לח:), דאיסור הנחה לכתחילה על גבי כירה גרופה וקטומה הוא משום שמא יסיר הכסוי ויחתה בגחלים, אסור ע"י נכרי כדין החזרה על גבי כירה אינה גרופה וקטומה. אבל לפי מה שנתבאר (לעיל אות ב), ע"פ דברי הגר"א והמ"ב, נראה דלא קיי"ל כתוס', אלא כבעה"מ ותוס' הרא"ש. וא"כ בהנחה לכתחילה ע"י נכרי על גבי כירה גרופה וקטומה, י"ל דמותר לצורך שבת. ומ"מ אין לסמוך לכתחילה על היתר זה, דמקילים בשבות דשבות רק כאשר נזדמן ולא בקביעות.

אכן בהחזרה קשה לסמוך על דברי המהרי"ט (שמתיר החזרה ע"י נכרי לכתחילה על גבי כירה אינה גרופה וקטומה), אף לצורך שבת, דהרי אין היתר שבות דשבות בגזירה דשמא יחתה, ודלא כדעת הפמ"ג והבה"ל (הנ"ל).

סימן ג

קדירה על גבי קדירה

א. מליאה וריקנית

בשו"ע (סי' רנג ס"ה) כתב דמותר לתת דבר יבש על גבי קדירה בשבת, לפי שאין דרך בישול בכך, וכשיטת הר"ן הנ"ל (סי' א אות א).

ובבה"ל (ס"ג ד"ה ויזהר) הקשה, דבר"ן ושו"ע (ס"ה) מוכח שמותר ליתן לכתחילה בשבת ע"ג קדירה, ועדיפא מכירה גרופה וקטומה, והוי כמעמיד נגד המדורה. אבל בשו"ע (ס"ג) כתב דמותר להחזיר 'ע"ג קדירה ריקנית ויזהר שלא ישים קדירתו ע"ג קרקע', וכמבואר בגמ' (לח:) ושו"ע (ס"ב) לענין החזרה ע"ג כירה גרופה וקטומה, ודלא כמש"כ שם (ס"ה) דמותר אף בהניחו ע"ג קרקע וצ"ע, עיי"ש.

ותירץ בשם הפמ"ג, וז"ל, דבסעיף ה' שאיירי בעומדת ע"ג קדירת חמין או תבשיל, לא נחשב כלל כעומד ע"ג כירה, ולהכי מותר אף ליתן לכתחילה בשבת. משא"כ בענינו שהקדירה ריקנית ועומדת רק לסתום את חום הכירה שלא יהיה כ"כ חום, נעשית הכירה עי"ז רק כשאר כירה גרופה וקטומה, דאסור ליתן עליה בשבת תבשיל לכתחילה, עכ"ל. וכתב בבה"ל דתירוץ זה נאמר בטוב טעם, עיי"ש.

וכל הנ"ל נאמר לענין החזרה והנחה. ולענין שהייה כתב בבה"ל (סי' רנח ס"א ד"ה מותר) בשם הפמ"ג (שם א"א סק"א) דעל גבי קדירה

יש דין שהייה, וצריך שיהיה מבושל כמאכל בן דרוסאי לפי הרמ״א (סי׳ רנג ס״א) שפסק כחנניה. והקשה הפמ״ג (שם) על דין זה, דהא קיי״ל דע״ג קדירה לא גרע מע״ג כירה גרופה וקטומה, ובזה קיי״ל דמותר להשהות אף בלא נתבשל כמאכל בן דרוסאי. ותירץ וז״ל, דזהו בריקנית וצוננת, משא״כ כשהתחתונה חמה ע״ג אש, יש לעליונה ג״כ דין שהייה, עכ״ל.

ולכאורה צע״ג, דהפמ״ג בעצמו פסק דע״ג קדירת חמין קל יותר מע״ג קדירה ריקנית. ומותר ליתן מאכל שנתבשל כל צרכו על קדירת חמין לכתחילה בשבת, כלומר אף שלא היה ע״ג האש בשבת כלל, אף שאסור לעשות כן בקדירה ריקנית. ולמה פסק להפך לענין שהייה במאכל שלא הגיע לשיעור מאכל בן דרוסאי, דע״ג קדירה ריקנית מותר, וע״ג קדירה מליאה חמין אסור, וצ״ע.

ועוד צ״ע, דאם ע״ג קדירה לא נחשב כלל כעומד ע״ג כירה, וכמש״כ בבה״ל בשם הפמ״ג, וכנ״ל, לא יתכן שיש איסור שהייה ע״ג קדירה בפחות משיעור כמאכל בן דרוסאי, כדברי הפמ״ג (סי׳ רנח), שהרי אינו ע״ג האש.

ובאמת, הפמ״ג (א״א סקל״ג) לא כתב כלל לשון ׳לא נחשב כלל כעומד ע״ג כירה׳ שכתב הבה״ל, אלא כתב דאין זה דרך בישול, וכמש״כ הר״ן. ולפ״ז על גבי קדירה נידון כעל גבי האש, ולכן יש איסור שהייה. ודברי הבה״ל צ״ע.

אבל גם לפ״ז (דמתיר הפמ״ג להניח קדירה ע״ג קדירה דוקא מטעם שאין דרך בישול בכך ולא מטעם דלא נחשב כלל כעומד ע״ג כירה) יש סתירה בפמ״ג, וכנ״ל. שו״ר קושיא זו בילקוט מפרשים בשו״ע הדרת קודש (סי׳ רנח).

ונראה, דלענין נראה כמבשל יש להקל רק בקדירה מליאה, דאין הדרך לבשל כשהחום עולה מהאש באמצעות החמין שבקדירה. משא״כ בקדירה ריקנית (שהחום עולה בלי אמצעי) דאין להקל.

אבל לענין שמא יחתה בגחלים, הוי היכר רק בקדירה ריקנית שאינה רגילה להיות עומדת ע״ג האש, ודין הכירה שתחתיה כקטומה דמי. משא״כ קדירה מליאה חמין, שתמיד מצויה ע״ג הכירה, דאיננה היכר. ולכן חששו שיחתה בגחלים, אא״כ הגיע התבשיל לכמאב״ד, שבכה״ג מותר אף באש מגולה לדעת חנניה ולפי הרמ״א שפסק כוותיה.

נמצא דבשהייה (שאסור משום שמא יחתה), קדירה מליאה חמין לא מהני להיכר כקטומה, ובעינן שהגיע המאכל לשיעור כמאכל בן דרוסאי. אבל בהנחה, שאסור להר״ן משום דנראה כמבשל, מותר ע״ג קדירה מליאה אף בהניח ע״ג קרקע, כי לא נראה כמבשל, משא״כ בקדירה ריקנית.

אמנם במג״א (סקל״ג) כתב בשם המ״מ (פכ״ב ה״ד) שאין חשש חיתוי ע״ג קדירה מליאה, שאין דרך בישול בכך. אך דבריו צ״ע, וכנ״ל, ובמ״מ (שם) לא דן בחשש חיתוי כלל.

ולפי המג״א צ״ל, דאף דקדירה מליאה חמין מצויה תמיד ע״ג הכירה, מ״מ כיון שאין הדרך לבשל על גבה, זה גופא נידון כהיכר להסיר חשש חיתוי בגחלים, ודו״ק. ובשו״ע הרב (ריש סי׳ רנח) חולק מה״ט על הפמ״ג וס״ל דשהייה מותרת ע״ג קדירה מליאה דלא חיישינן לחיתוי בגחלים, וכנ״ל.

ולכאורה יוצא מכל הנ״ל דאסור להחזיר ע״ג קדירה מליאה, אם קיי״ל כהשיטה דהחזרה אסורה משום שמא יחתה, וגם כשיטת הפמ״ג הסובר דשהייה במאכל שנתבשל פחות מכמאכל בן דרוסאי אסורה ע״ג קדירה מליאה. וכ״כ בשו״ע (סי׳ שיח ס״ז,ח) בדעה הב׳, ומקור ב׳ הדעות בב״י (סי׳ רנח) בשם ר׳ ירוחם. ואף שסיים וראשון נראה עיקר, וכדסתם לעיל (סי׳ רנג), לכאורה למאי דקיי״ל כהרמ״א, שהאיסור משום שמא יחתה, יש להחמיר בזה, וצ״ע לדינא.

ובילקוט מפרשים (שם) תירצו הקושיא על הפמ״ג כנ״ל, ומ״מ כתבו דמודה הרמ״א לדברי השו״ע (סי׳ רנג ס״ה), כדמוכח מזה דלא חלק עליו. וצ״ל, דקדירה מליאה יש בה קצת היכר. ולכן בדבר שנתבשל כל צרכו, שאין חשש חיתוי חמור כ״כ, מהני להיכר, ומותר לתת לכתחילה ע״ג קדירה מליאה. אבל לקמן (סי׳ רנח) מיירי במאכל שלא נתבשל אפילו כמאכל בן דרוסאי, ובזה חשש חיתוי חמור יותר. ולכן מותר לשהות רק בהיכר גמור דגרופה וקטומה, ולא בהיכר קצת דקדירה מליאה, ודו״ק.

והנה בד״מ (שם סק״ב) כתב דלפי הטור אסור להניח קדירה ע״ג קדירה. ולפי מש״כ לעיל, קיי״ל כן לדינא (דלא כמש״כ בילקוט מפרשים). והרמ״א לא הגיה על דברי המחבר מפני שסמך על הדעה הב׳ בשו״ע (סי׳ שיח סע׳ ז,ח) הנ״ל, וגם על מש״כ בד״מ. ודוחק הוא, אבל ע״כ צ״ל כן לפי הפמ״ג. ועיין בסמוך (אות ב), דנראה דלא קיי״ל כוותיה בזה.

ומ"מ לפי מש"כ לעיל (סי' ב אות ב) דבכירה גרופה וקטומה אין חשש חיתוי, והנחה לכתחילה אסורה רק משום נראה כמבשל, מותר לכו"ע להניח לכתחילה ע"ג קדירה העומדת ע"ג כירה גרופה וקטומה. והיינו טעמא, דע"ג קדירה מתיר איסור נראה כמבשל, וע"ג גרוף וקטום מתיר איסור שמא יחתה בגחלים, וכנ"ל.

ובקדירה כפולה הנהוגה אצלנו, אף דהמאכל מתחמם באמצעות חום המים, מכל מקום אסור להחזיר עליה לכו"ע, כיון דהיינו הדרך לבשל בה ירקות בחול. וא"כ לא שייך טעם של הר"ן (הנ"ל, סי' א אות א), בשם הרשב"א דאין דרך בישול בכך.

אמנם הר"ן כתב סברא נוספת, דמאכל שאין דרכו לבשל שם מותר, שהדבר מוכיח שאינו מחזיר אלא בשביל שיתחמם. ולפי"ז יש להתיר בנידון דידן בבשר ושאר מאכלים שאין הדרך לבשלם בקדרה כפולה. אבל הבה"ל (ס"ג הנ"ל) כתב, דלפי המחבר לא קיי"ל כסברא זו, וס"ל דכיון שהדרך לבשל מקצת מאכלים במקום זה, נראה כמבשל בכל המאכלים, ודלא כדעת הר"ן. וכ"כ בהלכות שבת לר"ש איידר (הע' תקסב).

עוד י"ל, דטעם ההיתר דע"ג קדירה מליאה הוא דאז אינו נראה כמבשל את האוכל שהניח לכתחילה ע"ג הקדירה, דעיקר הבישול הוא ביחס לתבשיל שבתוך הקדירה, והאוכל שע"ג הקדירה מתחמם בדרך אגב.

[ומצינו כיו"ב באיסור בישול בכלי שני משום מיחזי כמבשל, לתוס' (לט. ד"ה כל), דבתבלין מותר (משנה מב:), כי עשויין למתק את הקדירה, ולא מיחזי כמבשל. וכוונת התוס' בזה היא דנראה כמבשל את התבשיל, ולא את התבלין (לפי ספר הלכות שבת הע' נה, ועי' לקמן סי' י אות ב פירוש אחר בדבריהם ע"פ האו"ז). וכן בנד"ד, דנראה כמבשל את התבשיל, ולא את האוכל שע"ג הקדירה.]

ולפ"ז בקדירה כפולה אסור להניח עליה גם מטעם אחר, דהיינו שאינו שותה את המים שבחלקה התחתון. וא"כ א"א לומר שנראה כמבשל את המים, והבשר שבחלק העליון מתחמם בדרך אגב. ולפי סברא זו נראה, דאין להניח לכתחילה על גבי ה"קדירה בלעך" שיש בה מים בין שני טסי מתכת רחבים. והיינו טעמא, דכיון שאינו שותה את המים, נראה כמבשל

את הבשר, ולא כמבשל את המים והבשר מתחמם דרך אגב, וא״כ אין כאן ההיתר דהנחה לכתחילה ע״ג קדירה מליאה.

והנה באג״מ (ח״ד סי׳ לד, בישול סקל״ה) אוסר הנחה ע״ג שלחן מחומם באדים (סטי״ם טייב״ל), מכיון שאפשר לבשל עליו. וצ״ע, דלכאורה האש מחמם את המים, והמים מחממים את האוכל, ויש היתר דע״ג קדירה מליאה. ואולי ס״ל כסברא הנ״ל, דמותר רק כשהאוכל למעלה מתחמם בדרך אגב, דבזה לא נראה כמבשל. משא״כ שלחן מחומם באדים, דאינו שותה את המים, ונראה כמבשל את האוכל, וכנ״ל.

ובחזו״א (סי׳ לז סוף סק״ט) פירש ההיתר דע״ג קדירה ע״פ מה שמתחמם רק באמצעות החמין שבקדירה, וכנ״ל. אך כתב דעי״ז אינו נידון על גבי האש כלל. וז״ל, ואפשר שאם יש חום עולה לקדירה עליונה להרתיחה וכו׳, והעליונה מרתיחה לפני התחתונה, ודאי חשיבא כעומדת על הכירה. אלא היה כאן היתר של הגמ״ר, ודוקא להחזיר, אבל לא ליתן לכתחילה בשבת. אבל באמת כל שהתחתונה מליאה היא, בולעת חום הכירה, ואין החום עולה לעליונה אלא מחום הקדירה. והלכך גרע ממפסיק בקדירה ריקנית, דהתם חום הכירה סלקא למעלה, עכ״ל.

ביאור דבריו, דאם החום עולה מהאש בלי אמצעי, והעליון מרתיח קודם, נחשב כעומד על גבי הכירה. אבל אם חום הקדירה מחמם את העליון, נידון כאינו ע״ג האש כלל, ומקורו בבה״ל (ס״ג), וכנ״ל. ולכן אם חום האש מחמם, יש רק היתר קדירה ריקנית שבהגמ״ר. ולפי״ז י״ל דקדירה כפולה ו׳קדירה בלעך׳ (אם אין חום האש מחמם) מותרים, דלא כהנ״ל, דכל שחום הקדירה מחמם במציאות, אינו נידון כע״ג האש, ולשון השו״ע (סע׳ ה) ׳שאינו דרך בישול בכך׳ לאו דוקא.

אבל מדברי הפמ״ג (סי׳ רנח סק״א, הנ״ל), דיש דין שהייה כשמונחת ע״ג קדירה מליאה מע״ש, מוכח דנידון כמונח ע״ג האש.

ומכל מקום נראה כעיקר סברת החזו״א (דתלוי באמצעות המים), דיש קולת ׳אין דרך בישול בכך׳ רק אם חום הקדירה מחמם (כשבאמת אינו דרך בישול, משא״כ בקדירה כפולה). אבל בבלעך אסור, כיון דחום האש מחמם, אף דבמציאות אינו דרך בישול בזמנינו, וכמש״כ בילקוט יוסף (סי׳ רנג סק״ט). וב׳קדרה בלעך׳ מותר לפי״ז, אם במציאות החום

בא ע"י המים ולא בא ישר מן האש. ואסור רק לפי הסברא השניה הנ"ל (ע"פ ס' הלכות שבת והאג"מ). וצ"ע לדינא.

ב. לח ויבש

והנה כל מה שנתבאר מיוסד על שיטת הפמ"ג, שפסק כן בבה"ל, שמחלק בין קדירה מליאה לריקנית. אבל במחצית השקל (סקל"ד) חילק בענין אחר לתרץ הסתירה בין סעיף ג לסעיף ה. והוא, דבס"ג מיירי בתבשיל, ואף שהתחיל להקדיח, יש בו רוטב, ובזה הנחה לכתחילה ע"ג קדירה אסורה. ובס"ה מיירי בפנאדי"ש, דאין בו רוטב (מ"ב סקפ"ו), ובזה הנחה לכתחילה ע"ג קדירה מותרת.

ומקורו במג"א (סי' שיח סקכ"ו), שכ"כ לפרש הא דבשו"ע (שם ס"ח) הכריע להקל בדבר קר שנתבשל, דמותר להניחו לכתחילה ע"ג קדירה, ואילו בדבר חם (שם ס"ז) כתב ב' שיטות מבלי להכריע. ופירש המג"א, דדבר קר ע"כ יבש הוא, דאל"כ יש איסור בישול אחר בישול בלח (שם ס"ד), ובזה הכריע השו"ע להקל (שם ס"ח וסי' רנג ס"ה). ודבר חם מיירי בלח, ובזה לא הכריע (שם ס"ז), ולכן כאן (סי' רנג ס"ג) מצריך שלא יניחנה ע"ג קרקע.

ובשו"ת יחוה דעת (ח"ב סי' מה) מתיר עפ"ז לחמם מאכל יבש שהיה מונח במקרר ע"ג פח מתכת או אזבסט, וכבלעך הנהוג אצלנו. ולכאורה קשה, דבכיסוי כזה נראה דדין האש כאש קטומה, ובגרוף וקטום קיי"ל דאסור להניח לכתחילה בשבת.

שו"ר בספר ילקוט יוסף (סי' רנג סק"ט) שנשמר מקושיא זו, ותירץ, דהיה הדרך לבשל לפעמים על אש קטומה, ולכן אסרו הנחה לכתחילה. משא"כ בפח הנקרא בלעך, דאין הדרך לבשל עליו כלל, ולכן מותר להניח דבר יבש עליו לכתחילה.

וראיתי בספר נחל זרד (עמ' קפב) שפקפק בהוראה זו, דאף דבמג"א חילק בין לח ליבש אליבא דהב"י והשו"ע, המג"א עצמו לא ס"ל חילוק זה, שהרי לבסוף מקיל גם בדבר לח שעדיין חם ע"ג קדירה. וא"כ עכצ"ל כהפמ"ג לחלק בין מליאה לריקנית, ובריקנית אסור להניח לכתחילה אפילו בדבר יבש.

וכ״כ המג״א (סי׳ רנג סקל״ו) אליבא דהרמ״א. כלומר, דאף אם השו״ע מחלק בין לח ליבש (כדעת המחצית השקל ע״פ המג״א אליבא דהב״י) יש לנו לפסוק כדעת המג״א הפמ״ג והבה״ל, דאין חילוק בין דבר לח לדבר יבש אלא בין קדירה מליאה לקדירה ריקנית. וא״כ לפי הספרדים (הפוסקים כהשו״ע) יש מקום להקל בזה, וכמש״כ ביחוה דעת.

והנה מקור הפמ״ג (סי׳ רנח) הנ״ל, דבקדירה מליאה יש דין שהייה ואסור בלא הגיע למאכל בן דרוסאי, הוא המג״א (שם סק״א). וא״כ הקושיא הנ״ל (אות א), דשם קדירה מליאה חמורה מריקנית, ולעיל (סי׳ רנג) קדירה מליאה קלה מריקנית, היא בעצם קושיא על המג״א להבנת הפמ״ג.

ובנחל זרד (עמ׳ קצ) הקשה כן, ותירץ דלא כדעת הפמ״ג, אלא דבסימן רנח מיירי שהאש נוגעת בקדירה, ובזה הכל גוף חימום אחד, ואין שום היתר דע״ג קדירה. ולעיל (סי׳ רנג) מיירי שהאש אינה נוגעת בקדירה, ובזה יש היתר דע״ג קדירה. והוסיף, דלפי השו״ע א״א לומר כן, דכשהאש נוגעת אסור משום הטמנה, וע״כ מדובר כשאינו נוגעת, ולכן צריך לחלק בין לח ליבש, וכמש״כ המג״א אליבא דהשו״ע.

ולכאורה תירוץ זה, דבסימן רנח מדובר כשהאש נוגעת בקדירה ורק בזה אין קולא דע״ג קדירה, אוקימתא היא, ואין לה שום רמז בדברי המג״א. והנחל זרד הוכרח לדחוק כן מחמת הקושיא העצומה על הפמ״ג, שסותר את עצמו מן הקצה אל הקצה. ולמש״כ ליישב, דבנראה כמבשל מליאה עדיפא, ובשמא יחתה ריקנית עדיפא, אין שום הכרח לאוקימתא זו ולסברא זו. ולכן נראה עיקר לדינא כדעת הפמ״ג, וכדברי הבה״ל שהביאו וקלסו.

אבל במש״כ הפמ״ג (סי׳ רנח), דקיי״ל דגזרו שמא יחתה בגחלים כשמשהה על גבי קדירה מליאה, נראה דלא קיי״ל כוותיה. ולדינא קיי״ל לענין הנחה על גבי קדירה כדעת הבה״ל, דנידון כשלא על גבי האש, או כדעת המג״א דאין חשש חיתוי. ולכן לפי הרמ״א מותר להניח על גבי קדרה מליאה, וכמש״כ השו״ע (סע׳ ה), אף שחושש לחיתוי באינו גרוף וקטום. [וא״צ לדחוק שהרמ״א חולק עליו, וכנ״ל (אות א) לדעת הפמ״ג.] ולפ״ז צ״ל דלא כדעת הפמ״ג (סי׳ רנח), אלא כדברי השו״ע הרב (שם), דס״ל דשהייה ע״ג קדירה מליאה מותרת.

והנה בשו״ע הרב (שם) כתב דדבריו הם דלא כדעת המג״א. אך י״ל, דלשון המג״א (שם) היא, ׳דאם הקדרה התחתונה עומדת על גבי האש יש

לה דין שיהוי.׳ ופירש הפמ״ג דר״ל לחומרא להצריך גרוף וקטום בלא הגיע לשיעור מאכל בן דרוסאי. אך יותר נראה דר״ל לקולא, וכדברי המחצית השקל (שם) דאפילו עומדת על האש ליכא דין הטמנה. וכן נראה מדברי המג״א עצמו (סי׳ רנ״ג סקל״ג, הנ״ל, אות א), שכתב שאין חשש חיתוי על גבי קדירה מליאה, וכנ״ל.

ג. קדירה ריקנית ובלעך

והנה בספר שמירת שבת כהלכתה (פ״א הע׳ קיב) צדד דמותר להניח לכתחילה על גבי קדירה ריקנית, ע״פ מש״כ המ״ב (סי׳ רנג סקפ״א, סוף סי׳ רנט, וסי׳ שיח ס״ק מא,צד). וצ״ע, דבבה״ל (סי׳ רנג ס״ג ד״ה ויזהר, הנ״ל אות א) מפורש דאסור, וכמש״כ השמירת שבת כהלכתה (שם), וסיים בצ״ע.

והנה המג״א (סוף סי׳ רנט, דיני שהייה בקיצור) כתב, וז״ל, ולהניח תבשיל חם ... אם נתן לבינה או ד״א על התנור ואח״כ נותן הקדירה עליה, שרי אפילו הוסק ... ודבר שאין בו רוטב, אפילו קר כחם דמי, עכ״ל.

והקשה רע״א, דלבינה וד״א כגרוף וקטום, ומהני רק לענין חזרה כמו בגרוף וקטום. ובנצטנן לא מיקרי חזרה והוי כמניח לכתחילה, כמש״כ המג״א (סי׳ רנג סקל״ו), וממילא אסור אף בגרוף וקטום, עכ״ד רע״א.

ונראה דכתב המג״א לשון ׳ולהניח׳, כלומר, להניח לכתחילה. וע״כ כשכתב דיני שהייה בקצור סמך על מנהג הרמ״א (ס״ב) והר״ן ע״פ הירושלמי, שכל שסלק בשבת, אף בהניחו ע״ג קרקע לא בטלה שהייה ראשונה, ונידון כמחזיר ולא כמניח בתחילה. (עי׳ לקמן סי׳ ז אות א.)

ולפ״ז המ״ב (סקפ״א) שמקיל ע״פ המג״א (סוף סי׳ רנט) ע״כ סומך על מנהג הרמ״א והר״ן. ובבה״ל (ד״ה ויזהר) אוסר לפי דברי השו״ע (ס״ג) שחולק על הר״ן. וכ״ה לפי מש״כ הרמ״א עצמו דטוב להחמיר שלא כדעת הר״ן.

וא״כ קשה על מש״כ בשמירת שבת כהלכתה, שהרי סומך על הרמ״א והר״ן רק בדיעבד כשאין לו מאכל חם (ס״כ). וכאן (סל״ח והע׳ קיב) מתיר להניח ע״ג קדירה ריקנית בכל ענין כדברי המ״ב (סקפ״א). וכתב ׳וע״ע בבה״ל׳ (וכוונת ׳וע״ע׳ לדעה חולקת כמש״כ שם בשש״כ, עמ׳ 11). והיה

לו לפסוק כדעת הבה״ל ולאסור, ולהתיר רק בדיעבד כשאין לו מאכל חם, וכדעת המ״ב והרמ״א והר״ן, וצ״ע.

והנה בשש״כ (הע׳ סו) כתב, במי שסומך על הרמ״א בדיעבד, וז״ל, טוב יעשה אם יניח צלחת הפוכה מתחת לקדירה, עכ״ל. וצ״ע, דהאש כבר מכוסה בבלעך, ומה מוסיף הצלחת. שו״ר בשש״כ (ח״ג הע׳ קיב) שהגרשז״א ס״ל דכיסוי שני פועל שאינו דרך בישול. ודייק כן מלשון הבה״ל (ס״ג הנ״ל), ׳דקדירה ריקנית עומדת רק לסתום את חום הכירה׳, כלומר שאינו שינוי מדרך בישול. וא״כ כשיש כיסוי שני, כצלחת הפוכה, שלא נצרך לסתום את החום, אינו נידון כדרך בישול, ומותר בהנחה.

ולפי מש״כ לעיל (אות א) נראה דאסור, דהלא אף בבלעך עצמו אינו דרך בישול, וכמש״כ בילקוט יוסף. ואעפ״כ קיי״ל דאסור, וכקדירה ריקנית, אם הניח ע״ג קרקע. וההיתר דקדירה מליאה נאמר רק כשמקור החום עצמו משונה, שחום התבשיל מחמם, ולא חום האש, וכמש״כ החזו״א. אבל אין הבדל בין כיסוי אחד לשני כיסויים, דשניהם רק סותמים את החום כקדירה ריקנית.

סימן ד

סמיכה ותוכה

א. סמיכה בשהייה והחזרה

איתא בגמ׳ (לז.), תא שמע, ב׳ כירות המתאימות, אחת גרופה וקטומה ואחת שאינה גרופה ואינה קטומה, משהין על גבי גרופה וקטומה ואין משהין על שאינה גרופה ואינה קטומה, וכו׳, וב״ה אומרים אף מחזירין, ע״כ.

ועוד איתא (שם), איבעיא להו, מהו לסמוך בה. תוכה וגבה אסור, אבל לסמוך בה שפיר דמי. או דילמא לא שנא. תא שמע, שתי כירות המתאימות אחת גרופה וקטומה ואחת שאינה גרופה וקטומה, משהין על גבי גרופה וקטומה, ואף על גב דקא סליק ליה הבלא מאידך. דילמא שאני התם, דכיון דמידליא שליט בה אוירא, וכו׳. מאי הוי עלה. תא שמע, כירה שהסיקוה בגפת ובעצים, סומכין לה ואין מקיימין אא״כ גרופה וקטומה, ע״כ.

המבואר בגמ׳ דקיי״ל דמותר לסמוך קדירה אצל הכירה. ובתוס׳ (ד״ה תא) פירשו דמותר רק כשדופן הכירה מפסיק בין הקדירה להאש. ובהגמ״ר (ריש פ. בדפי המרדכי) חולק וסובר דא״צ דופן מפסיק. ובשו״ע (סי׳ רנג ס״א) כתב וז״ל, ואפילו אינו גרוף וקטום מותר לסמוך לה קדירה בסמוך חוצה לה, עכ״ל. ובפוסקים שם לא נזכר דין דופן מפסיק כלל. ואולי ס״ל דנלמד מלשון חוצה לה, כל׳ לכירה, וע״כ דופן הכירה מפסיק. ובמג״א

(סי׳ שיח סקל״ח) מצריך דופן המפסיק אא״כ מרחיק קצת מהאש, דאז יש היכירא ולא אתי לאחתויי, וצ״ע לדינא.

והנה הרי״ף הוכיח דשהייה ע״ג כירה שאינה גרופה וקטומה אסורה אף בנתבשל כמאכל בן דרוסאי (ודלא כחנניה), מהא דהתירו רק בסמיכה, וש״מ דע״ג אסור. והקשה בעה״מ וז״ל, מה ראיה יש בזה, והלא יש סמיכה בחזרה כמו שיש סמיכה בשהייה. והכי קאמר, מהו לסמוך הקדירה בחזרתה לכירה שאינה גרופה וקטומה וכו׳, עכ״ל. וכ״כ התוס׳ (ד״ה מהו), דאיבעית הגמ׳ אהחזרה נמי קאי.

ובר״ן כתב דראית הרי״ף היא מלשון ׳תוכה וגבה אסור׳. ומשמע דאסור רק באינו גרוף וקטום, והיינו רק בשהייה. אבל בהחזרה תוכה אסור אף בגרוף וקטום, וכמבואר בגמ׳ (שם).

אולם, באור שמח (שבת ריש פ״ג) ביאר שראיית הרי״ף היא ע״פ סברא ולא מדיוק הלשון. והיינו, דאם החזרה אסורה משום מיחזי כמבשל (כ״כ בתחילת דבריו, ואח״כ כתב ׳שמא יבשל׳, עיי״ש), כל שאסור להחזיר אסור לסמוך. ורק אם אסור משום שמא יחתה בגחלים, אפשר להתיר סמיכה בהחזרה, דבדופן מפסיק ליכא למיחש שמא יחתה בגחלים, עכ״ד.

המבואר מדברי האו״ש, דע״כ אסור להחזיר סמוך לכירה לפי הרי״ף והרמב״ם דס״ל דהחזרה אסורה משום נראה כמבשל. [והאו״ש כתב דע״כ צ״ל לפי הרמב״ם, לשיטתו בבישול אחר בישול בדבר שהגיע לשיעור כמאב״ד (עי׳ בסמוך וסי׳ ט אות א).] וא״כ איבעית הגמ׳ מהו לסמוך ע״כ אשהייה קאי, ודלא כבעה״מ ותוס׳.

[וכעין זה כתב הצל״ח (לז.) ע״פ לשון הגמ׳, שנראה שהסיקו לחומרא, ואח״כ שאלו מאי הוי עלה והסיקו לקולא. וע״כ החמירו בהחזרה והקילו בשהייה, עיי״ש].

ולפ״ז התוס׳ ובעה״מ אזלי לשיטתם (סי׳ א אות א), דאיסור החזרה הוא משום שמא יחתה בגחלים. וא״כ בעית הגמ׳ בסמיכה קאי גם לחנניה, ובהחזרה, וממילא אין שום ראיה לפסוק נגד חנניה, ולכן פסקו כמותו. והרי״ף והרמב״ם אזלי לשיטתם, דס״ל דאיסור החזרה הוא משום נראה כמבשל. וא״כ איבעית הגמ׳ בסמיכה היא רק בשהייה, וממילא מוכח דשהייה על גבה אסורה ודלא כחנניה, וכנ״ל.

אמנם סברת האו"ש, דבנראה כמבשל אין שום חילוק בין ע"ג לסמיכה, אינה מוסכמת לכו"ע. דהרשב"א ס"ל דאיסור החזרה הוא משום נראה כמבשל, וכנ"ל (סי' ג אות א). ואעפ"כ פירש איבעית הגמ' בסמיכה דהחזרה ג"כ, ועפ"ז נוטה לפסוק כחנניה, עיי"ש.

ועדיין קשה, דבתוס' (שם) כתבו דהגמ' ד'מהו לסמוך' קאי גם כחנניה, ומיירי בשהייה בנתבשל פחות ממאכל בן דרוסאי, ובטלה ראית הרי"ף דהגמ' דלא כחנניה. וכבר הקשה הריטב"א כן על הגמ' (לו:), דנימא דמתני' לשהות תנן, וכחנניה, ובפחות משיעור כמאכל בן דרוסאי. ותירץ, דבסיפא תנן 'ומחזירין', וע"כ קאי דנתבשל כמאכל בן דרוסאי, דאל"כ יש איסור בישול דאורייתא. וא"כ גם ברישא ע"כ הגיע לשיעור מאכל בן דרוסאי.

ובקרבן נתנאל (סק"ג) כ"כ לענין ראית הרי"ף, דמדפשטו מברייתא שבסיפא שלה נזכר 'אף מחזירין' (וכנ"ל), ע"כ מיירי בהגיע לשיעור מאכל בן דרוסאי, ורישא דומיא דסיפא, וכמש"כ הריטב"א.

אכן לפי הרמב"ם (פ"ט ה"ג) דס"ל דיש איסור בישול דאורייתא בהחזרה עד שמבושל כל צרכו, ע"כ בסיפא, דמתני' ודברייתא, קאי במבושל כל צרכו, וברישא, דשהייה מותר, קאי בנתבשל כמאכל בן דרוסאי. וע"כ אין רישא כסיפא, ודלא כדעת הריטב"א, וכמש"כ שם בהערות (הע' 25). וא"כ לפי האו"ש (ריש פ"ג, הנ"ל) דהרי"ף והרמב"ם שיטה אחת הן, שוב קשה על ראית הרי"ף לפי הרמב"ם, וצ"ע.

ב. סמיכה בהנחה לכתחילה

והנה במג"א (סי' רנג סק"ה) הביא שיטת הרמב"ם, דסמיכה מותרת רק בשהייה ולא בהחזרה. וכתב וז"ל, דאיבעית הגמ' לא הוי אלא בע"ש, וכ"מ ברי"ף [ר"ל כנ"ל, דזוהי ראית הרי"ף לפסוק דלא כחנניה]. אבל לסברא השניה [שבשו"ע, לפסוק כחנניה] שרי אפילו בשבת [כלומר, לסמוך בהחזרה], כמ"ש הרמ"א סוף סי' זה, עכ"ל.

ונחלקו הדגול מרבבה ורע"א (שם) בכונת דברי המג"א, דלדעת הדגמ"ר סמיכה בהחזרה מותרת לכו"ע, ובהנחה לכתחילה תלוי בב' השיטות שבשו"ע. ולדעת רע"א סמיכה בהנחה לכתחילה אסורה לכו"ע,

ובהחזרה תלוי בב׳ השיטות בשו״ע. ובמ״ב (סקט״ו) כתב ב׳ השיטות, ומלשונו נראה קצת שנוטה לפסוק כשיטת הדגמ״ר.

והנה בגמ׳ (לז.) פשטו איבעית הגמ׳ בסמיכה לקולא מהברייתא דב׳ כירות המתאימות משהין ע״ג גרופה וקטומה, אף שסמוך לאינו גרופה וקטומה (וכנ״ל אות א). וכתב במחצית השקל (סק״ה), דמזה דפשטו ממשהין ע״ג גרופה וקטומה, ע״כ איבעית הגמ׳ היא בשהייה ולא בהחזרה, וזוהי ראית הרי״ף [והוא פירוש שלישי לתרץ קושיית בעה״מ על ראית הרי״ף, דנימא דאיבעית הגמ׳ היא לענין החזרה. והיינו בנוסף לפירוש האו״ש והר״ן הנ״ל (אות א).] ולפי תוס׳, דקיי״ל כחנניה, צ״ל דהאיבעיא היא בהחזרה, ואפ״ה שפיר פשט כנ״ל דסמיכה מותרת.

הרי מבואר דלפי הרי״ף א״א לפשוט החזרה משהייה, ולפי תוס׳ אפשר. ולפי הנ״ל (אות א) ה״ט, דלפי תוס׳, לשיטתם דההחזרה אסורה משום שמא יחתה, טעם איסור שהייה והחזרה שוין הן, ויש ללמוד זה מזה. אבל לפי הרי״ף, דהחזרה אסורה משום נראה כמבשל, א״א לפשוט דין החזרה מהברייתא דסמיכה בשהייה.

ובבה״ל (ד״ה מותר לסמוך) כתב דהדגמ״ר (הנ״ל) הוכיח דמותר להחזיר בסמיכה (לכו״ע, וא״כ ע״כ מתיר המג״א לפי חנניה, אף בהנחה) מברייתא דב׳ כירות המתאימות. והקשה רע״א על דברי הדגמ״ר, דהברייתא מיירי בשהייה, וכדברי המחה״ש הנ״ל. ותירץ הבה״ל דבסיפא דהברייתא (מובא בגמ׳ לעיל שם, וכנ״ל אות א) מיירי בהחזרה, וא״כ ע״כ סמיכה מותרת בהחזרה, וכ״כ במלחמות (טו: בדפי הרי״ף), ומוכח כדעת הדגמ״ר.

והנה במלחמות כתב כן לפי בעה״מ (שם), וז״ל, דהיה לו לדחות ראית הרי״ף דמסיפא דמילתא ראיה דקתני אף מחזירין, עכ״ל. ולפ״ז להרי״ף, שלא דחה כן, צ״ל דבגמ׳ לא הביאו הסיפא, וש״מ דהראיה מהרישא היא, דמיירי בשהייה. וע״כ האיבעיא היא בשהייה, וכדעת רע״א דכן היא להרי״ף ושיטה ראשונה בשו״ע. וא״כ לחנניה, ושיטה שניה בשו״ע, התירו רק החזרה ולא הנחה, ודלא כדעת הדגמ״ר.

ומסקנת הגמ׳ היא, ת״ש כירה שהסיקו בגפת ובעצים סומכין לה ואין משהין על גבה [כ״ה ברי״ף, וכן צ״ל לגירסתינו, ׳ואין מקיימין עליה׳], ע״כ. ומוכח כדברי הרי״ף דהגמ׳ מיירי בשהייה. ודחה בעה״מ, דמשהייה דרבנן נשמע להחזרה דחנניה. והקשה הרמב״ן, דהחזרה חמורה

משהייה אף לחנניה, דתוכה מותר בגרופה וקטומה בשהייה ולא בהחזרה. ותירץ הר"ן אליבא דבעה"מ, דלענין סמיכה כי הדדי נינהו, כלומר, שהייה והחזרה. וצ"ב.

ונראה בכונת הר"ן, דתוכה חמורה מעל גבה משום נראה כמבשל (עי' בסמוך אות ו), וזהו רק בהחזרה. אבל לענין חשש חיתוי שוים הם, ולכן בשהייה דין תוכה כדין על גבה. ולפ"ז לבעל המאור לשיטתו (דהחזרה אסורה משום שמא יחתה) סמיכה בהחזרה כסמיכה בשהייה, דטעמם שוה. ומשהייה דרבנן נשמע לחזרה דחנניה (וכנ"ל), ואין קושיא מתוכה, דטעמו משום נראה כמבשל.

ג. שיטת הרמ"א

והנה רע"א הביא ראיה לדבריו מהרמ"א (ס"ה) וז"ל, וכבר נתבאר שנהגו להקל בחזרה בשבת אפילו הניחה ע"ג קרקע, וה"ה לסמוך לתנור שאינו גרוף וקטום, עכ"ל.

ונראה בכונת רע"א, דהרמ"א (ס"ב) כתב דנהגו להקל בהניח ע"ג קרקע, אם היה על האש בכניסת השבת, וכשיטת הר"ן (לח:), דרק כשסלקה מע"ש בטלה שהייה ראשונה (עי' לקמן סי' ז אות א).

וא"כ יש נ"מ גם לסמיכה, דמותרת בהחזרה, ואסורה בהנחה לכתחילה כשבטלה שהייה ראשונה. וכיון שנהגו להקל כדעת הר"ן בהחזרה (דלא אמרינן בטלה שהייה ראשונה אם היה ע"ג האש בכניסת השבת), נהגו להקל אף בסמיכה בהניח ע"ג קרקע, כל שהיה על האש בכניסת השבת. ולפ"ז למש"כ הרמ"א דטוב להחמיר דלא כהר"ן בהחזרה, ה"ה נמי בסמיכה בהניחה ע"ג קרקע.

ובבה"ל (ס"ה ד"ה וכבר) כתב דהבית מאיר נתקשה מאד בדברי הרמ"א. ונראה דאזיל לשיטתו, דס"ל כהדגמ"ר, וכמש"כ בשעה"צ (סקכ"א). אבל לרע"א ניחא כנ"ל, דרע"א מפרש דברי הרמ"א (ס"ה) בהנחה לכתחילה, ומותר רק לפי הר"ן דס"ל דאין ביטול שהייה הראשונה בשבת, וכל הנחה לכתחילה דינה כהחזרה אם היה על האש בכניסת השבת. אבל כשסלקה מע"ש, ולרוב הפוסקים, שחולקים על הר"ן, גם בהניחה ע"ג קרקע בשבת, אסור להניחה סמוך לכירה. ואולי זוהי כונת הבה"ל (שם ד"ה לסמוך).

וז"ל הרמ"א (שם), אבל אם הקדירות עדיין חמין, מותר להעמידן אצל תנור בית החורף מאחר שנתבאר דתנורים שלנו יש להם דין כירה, וסמיכה בכירה שאינה גרופה וקטומה כדין גרופה וקטומה לענין נתינה עליה, וכבר נתבאר וכו' [וכנ"ל], עכ"ל. ובמ"ב (סקק"ה) כתב, וז"ל, וכבר נתבאר וכו', הוא ענין בפנ"ע, עכ"ל. כלומר, דלעיל מיירי בהחזרה, שלא הניחן ע"ג קרקע, וכמש"כ שם (סקק"ד). ועפ"ז כתב הבה"ל (ד"ה וכבר, לסמוך), דאין קשר בין תחילת דברי הרמ"א, דמיירי בהחזרה, להנחה ע"ג קרקע, וניחא קושית הבית מאיר, ומוכח כדעת רע"א.

אך עוד י"ל, דגם תחילת דברי הרמ"א מיירי בהנחה, וכגון שהיו הקדירות ע"ג קרקע ומעמידן אצל התנור. ולפ"ז 'וכבר נתבאר וכו',' הוא המשך דבריו, וכרע"א. כלומר, דאף דסמיכה אסורה בהנחה, מ"מ נהגו להקל, דמותר להחזיר בהניח ע"ג קרקע, וכדברי הר"ן והירושלמי. וא"כ למנהג זה הנחה כהחזרה וסמיכה מותרת, וכנ"ל. ולדברי הבית מאיר לשיטתו, דסמיכה בהנחה מותרת, א"א לפרש כן, וכנ"ל.

ד. שיטת חידושי הר"ן והריטב"א

והנה בשעה"צ (שם) כתב דבחידושים המיוחסים להר"ן (מ:) אוסר סמיכה לכתחילה בשבת, אף דמקיל בהחזרה (לז.), ומוכח כרע"א. ובחידושי הר"ן (לח.) מתיר החזרה על גבי כירה שאינה גרופה וקטומה במצטמק ורע לו (ודלא כדעת הר"ן על הרי"ף שאוסר, דהרי ידוע שחידושי הר"ן אינם להר"ן).

ונראה דע"כ ה"ט, דס"ל דאיסור החזרה הוא משום שמא יחתה בגחלים, וס"ל דלא גזרו במצטמק ורע לו, דומיא דשהייה לרבנן דחנניה. אבל אם האיסור הוא משום נראה כמבשל, אין חילוק בין מצטמק ורע לו למצטמק ויפה לו, דלעולם אסור [וכמש"כ הר"ן על הרי"ף]. עכ"פ מוכח דלפי חי' הר"ן החזרה אסורה מטעם שמא יחתה, ולכן מתיר בסמיכה, וכדעת האו"ש (הנ"ל, אות א).

אמנם הריטב"א (לז:) כתב וז"ל, אבל מצטמק ורע לו מותר אפי' בכירה שאינה גרופה וקטומה (והיינו כשיטת המיוחס להר"ן), דכיון שהצמוק רע לו, לא מיחזי כמבשל, ולחיתוי נמי ליכא למיחש, עכ"ל.

משמע דס״ל דיש ב׳ איסורים בהחזרה, שמא יחתה ונראה כמבשל. וס״ל דבמצטמק ורע לו אינו נראה כמבשל. וכנראה דעת יחיד היא.

ויש לעיין אם ס״ל להריטב״א דהחזרה על גבי כירה שאינה גרופה וקטומה אסורה גם מטעם שמא יחתה, וכדעת התוס׳, וכנ״ל. או דילמא דס״ל דהחזרה אסורה רק מטעם נראה כמבשל, כדעת הר״ן. ולפי צד הב׳, ׳ולחיתוי נמי ליכא למיחש׳ ר״ל דכל שנתבשל כמאכל בן דרוסאי לא חיישינן לחיתוי (ולא רק בדבר שמצטמק ורע לו, דבזה מיירי הריטב״א), וכדמצינו לענין שהייה.

ונראה לפשוט ספק זה מהא דכתב הריטב״א (לז.) דהחמירו טפי בהחזרה, כיון דנראה כמבשל (כדעת הר״ן). ואילו במשנה (לו:) כתב דהחזרה אסורה מע״ש (כדעת התוס׳ ודלא כדעת הר״ן). ומוכח דס״ל דיש ב׳ טעמים לאיסור החזרה, דהיינו, נראה כמבשל וחשש שמא יחתה.

[אבל מוכח כן רק אם לא אמרינן דגזרו החזרה בע״ש שמא יחזיר בשבת ויעבור על איסור מלאכה דרבנן, ועיין לעיל (סי׳ ב אות ב) דבאמת לא אמרינן כן.]

ובגמ׳ (לח:) הוכיחו דמחזירין על כירה גרופה וקטומה אף בשבת מקומקום של חמין. ובר״ן (טז: בדפי הרי״ף ד״ה ותו) כתב דמוכח דיש איסור החזרה ע״ג כירה שאינה גרופה וקטומה במצטמק ורע לו, דאל״כ א״א להוכיח דהחזרה ע״ג כירה שאינה גרופה וקטומה מותרת מהא דקומקום של חמין (דמצטמק ורע לו) לתבשיל דמשנתינו (דמצטמק ויפה לו).

ובמיוחס להר״ן (לח:) דחה, וז״ל, ומדחמין באינה גרופה, תבשיל נמי שרי בגרופה להחזיר, עכ״ל. וכונתו, דהחזרה אסורה שמא יחתה בגחלים. ואין חשש חיתוי במצטמק ורע לו ע״ג כירה שאינה גרופה וקטומה. וגם בתבשיל ע״ג כירה גרופה וקטומה אין חשש חיתוי, ויוצא דדינם שוה.

ולדעת הר״ן (על הרי״ף) לשיטתו, דהחזרה אסורה משום נראה כמבשל, א״א להשוותם. ובאמת בחמין דמצטמק ורע לו, אסור להחזיר באינו גרוף וקטום משום דנראה כמבשל. ובתבשיל דמצטמק ויפה לו וגרוף וקטום מותר, כיון דאינו נראה כמבשל, וכנ״ל (סי׳ א אות א). אבל את״ל דבמצטמק ורע לו מותר באינו גרוף וקטום, וכדעת הריטב״א הנ״ל, א״א ללמוד משם דבמצטמק ויפה לו מותר בגרוף וקטום, די״ל דעדיין נראה כמבשל, וכדעת מהר״ם במשנתינו (הנ״ל, שם).

וז"ל חי' הר"ן (מ:), וכל שנתבשל מבעוד יום, היה מותר לבשלו לכתחילה ע"ג כירה, אלא משום מראית העין. ולפיכך התירו בחזרה בגרוף וקטום, דכיון שאינו מחזירה אלא כדי שלא תצטנן והיא גרוף וקטום, תו לא מיחזי כמבשל דבר חי לכתחילה, עכ"ל.

ובספר תיבת משה הקשה, דכאן משמע שאיסור החזרה משום נראה כמבשל, ולעיל (לו:) כתב דטעמו משום שמא יחתה. ולכאורה לא קשה כל כך, די"ל דאסור משני טעמים. אבל מהא דהתיר החזרה במצטמק ורע לו מוכח דלא ס"ל טעם נראה כמבשל, וכנ"ל. ויש לתרץ דחידושי הר"ן ס"ל כדעת הריטב"א (הנ"ל), דיש שני טעמים דאסור להחזיר, ולא נראה כמבשל בדבר שמצטמק ורק לו.

אך יותר נראה, דהר"ן (מ:) אוסר רק הנחה לכתחילה משום דנראה כמבשל. [והיינו לשיטתו (שם, וכנ"ל סי' ד אות ד), שסמיכה אסורה בהנחה לכתחילה, וכסברת האו"ש (הנ"ל, שם אות א) דבנראה כמבשל סמיכה אסורה.] וכונת 'היה מותר לבשלו לכתחילה', ר"ל להניחו לכתחילה. וכונת 'אלא משום מראית העין', ר"ל דנראה כמבשל.

מאידך החזרה, שהיא רק 'כדי שלא תצטנן', כי לא בטלה שהייה הראשונה, אסורה רק משום שמא יחתה אבל לא משום מיחזי כמבשל. והא דהצריכו גרוף וקטום בהחזרה הוא כדי למנוע חשש חיתוי. ובהנחה לכתחילה אסור אף בגרוף וקטום, משום שנראה כמבשל, וניחא הכל.

[ואף דקצת קשה בלשונו, צ"ל דעיקר כונתו היא לחלק בין החזרה להנחה, דרק בהנחה נראה כמבשל. והזכיר גרוף וקטום ב' פעמים, דאל"כ אסור בין בהחזרה ובין בהנחה מטעם אחר לגמרי, דשמא יחתה בגחלים. והוא כמאמר מוסגר, ואינו ענין לנראה כמבשל.]

ה. כנגד המדורה

ת"ר (מ:) מביא אדם קיתון מים ומניחו כנגד המדורה, לא בשביל שיחמו, אלא בשביל שתפיג צינתן, ע"כ.

והקשה הרא"ש (סי' י) וז"ל, תימה, מאי שנא הכא דשרינן להשים קיתון של מים אצל המדורה בשביל שתפיג צינתן. ואי לאו משום דמבשל בשבת הוה שרי אפילו יד סולדת בו, וכו'. ולעיל אסרינן להשים ע"ג

כירה אע״פ שגרופה וקטומה, וכו׳. וי״ל דיש לחלק בין להשים ע״ג כירה, למדורה. דהא קדירה ע״ג כירה אסור, אבל אצל המדורה שרי, משום דדמי לסומך, ושרי. ומיהו לא דמי כולי האי לסומך, דהתם מפסיק כותלי הכירה, אבל הכא שהוא אצל המדורה ה״ל למיחש שמא יחתה. וי״ל כיון שהצריכו חכמים להרחיק מן המדורה, מדנקט ׳כנגד המדורה׳, ולא נקט ׳אצל המדורה׳ איכא הכירא, ולא אתי לחתויי, עכ״ל.

והר״ן (הנ״ל סק״ב) מתיר כנגד המדורה כי אין דרך בישול בכך, ואפילו במקום שהיד סולדת בו. ודלא כדעת הרמב״ן שמתיר אפילו ע״ג המדורה מפני שרק מפיג צינתן.

והנה הר״ן אזיל לשיטתו, דאין חשש חיתוי במצטמק ורע לו, וכל האיסור הוא משום נראה כמבשל. והרא״ש דן מצד חשש חיתוי, שקיים לשיטתו בהחזרה באינו גרוף וקטום, וק״ו בהנחה. אבל לא דן מצד נראה כמבשל, אע״פ שלדבריו (הנ״ל סי׳ ב אות ב) יש איסור זה בהנחה.

ואולי קאי כאן כשיטת התוס׳, דהנחה אסורה רק משום שמא יחתה, ועל דרך דברי הגר״א (הנ״ל שם). ורק לפי שיטת התוס׳ התיר הרא״ש להניח לכתחילה בסמיכה, כדמוכח מהא דהשוה סמיכה לכנגד המדורה. אבל לשיטת הרא״ש עצמו, שיש איסור נראה כמבשל בהנחה (וכנ״ל שם), לכאורה סמיכה בהנחה לכתחילה אסורה, כיון דנראה כמבשל. ורק כנגד המדורה לא נראה כמבשל, וכמש״כ הר״ן.

עוד יש לפרש דברי הרא״ש כדברי הגר״א (סי׳ שיח סקכ״א) שפירש מסקנת הרא״ש שכנגד המדורה אינו כסמיכה, כי אין דופן המפסיק. וע״כ דינו כאינו ע״ג האש, מכיון שמרחיק כנגד המדורה ולא אצלה. ולכן גם הנחה מותרת, וכקדירה ע״ג קידרה לשיטה א׳ בשו״ע (שם ס״ז,ח) דדינו כאינו ע״ג האש (וכנ״ל סי׳ ג אות א, לפי הבה״ל).

[כתב הגר״א (שם) דלפי הר״ן (יט. בדפי הרי״ף) והמגיד משנה (פכ״ב ה״ד) כנגד המדורה הוא כסומך. אבל בר״ן ובמ״מ לא כ״כ כלל, וכן נראה מדהתירו בהנחה, אף דהנחה בסמיכה אסורה לפי הר״ן, ק״ו מהחזרה. וי״ל דכונת הגר״א היא רק דא״צ להרחיק מן האש כדעת הרא״ש, אלא דמותר אצל האש. והא דאין איסור סמיכה הוא משום דאין רגילין לבשל על המדורה, ולכן בסמוך לה אינו נראה כמבשל, משא״כ בכירה דסמיכה אסורה בהנחה לכתחילה.]

ו. תוכה

והנה בגמ׳ (לז.) ושו״ע (ס״ב) אסרו החזרה לתוך הכירה. ובמ״ב (סקנ״ח) כתב שהאיסור להחזיר בתוכו הוא משום נראה כמבשל וכמש״כ הרשב״א והר״ן. ולפ״ז מותר להחזיר לתוך כלי שאין מבשלין בו כמגירת חימום המצויה בתנורים חדשים, ומיועדת רק לחמם ולא לבשל, והחום מגיע לשיעור יד סולדת בו (מה שקורין ווארמינ״ג דרא״ר).

ויש לפקפק בזה, דהרשב״א והר״ן אזלי לשיטתם דס״ל דכל איסור החזרה הוא משום נראה כמבשל, וכנ״ל (סי׳ א אות א). ולכן כתבו שהאיסור להחזיר לתוך הכירה הוא משום נראה כמבשל. אבל לפי הרמ״א, שאיסור החזרה הוא משום שמא יחתה בגחלים (וכנ״ל שם אות ב), אולי אסרו להחזיר לתוך הכירה, אף בגרופה וקטומה, משום שמא יחתה בגחלים. ולפ״ז במגירת חימום, שאפשר לשנות מידת החום, אסור להחזיר לתוכה משום שמא יחתה, אף אם האש קטומה.

ונראה לפשוט ספק זה משיטה המיוחסת להר״ן (דקיי״ל כוותיה וכדעת הבעה״מ והתוס׳ הרא״ש, וכנ״ל, אות ד), דס״ל דההחזרה אסורה משום שמא יחתה בגחלים. ומכל מקום פירש דלתוך הכירה אסור משום נראה כמבשל. ומוכח מזה שלתוך הכירה אינו חמור מעל גבי כירה ביחס לחשש חיתוי אלא דאסור משום נראה כמבשל בלבד. וכיון שעל גבי כירה מכוסה לא חיישינן לחיתוי, ה״ה כאשר מחזירים לתוך הכירה. וכן מוכח מדברי הר״ן (על הרי״ף) אליבא דבעה״מ (וכנ״ל, אות ב) דתוכה כע״ג בשהייה כי דינם שוה לענין חשש חיתוי.

ולפ״ז במגירת חימום (הנ״ל), שאין מבשלין בו כלל, מותר להחזיר לתוכה אם יש לה דין קטומה. אבל קשה לעשות היכר במגירת חימום, כדי שייחשב קטומה. דהרי אם מכסה רק את קרקעית המגירה בפנים, והכפתור לשינוי מידת החום נמצא מבחוץ, אין הכיסוי מועיל כלום. ואולי אם מכסה את הקרקעית בנייר כסף, וחלק מן הכיסוי בולט החוצה וניכר מיד, יש לה דין קטומה.

והנה הרמב״ן וסיעתו פירשו דתוכה אסור משום דנפיש הבליה, ונראה כמבשל. ולפ״ז תנור שלנו אסור, דנפיש הבליה יותר מע״ג האש, אע״פ ששניהם דרך בישול, כי יש לתנור מחיצות מכל הצדדים. וכן פסק באג״מ (ח״ד סי׳ עד סק״כ).

ובמ"ב (שם) כתב וז"ל, תוכה אסור, דכיון שהוא מעמיד לתוכה כדרך שמבשלין בה תדיר נראה כמבשל, עכ"ל. ועיי"ש (סי' שיח סקצ"ד) וז"ל, דאסור להכניס קדירה לתוך התנור. אך אם אינו מעמיד את הקדירה על קרקעית התנור כ"א על איזה כלי המפסיק, אז יש להקל, וכנ"ל (סי' רנג ס"ג), עכ"ל. ובשעה"צ (ס"ק קי"ח) כתב שהחיי אדם (כלל כ סי"ד) מפקפק בזה.

ובחיי אדם כתב דבקדירה ריקנית מותר לפי המג"א (סקכ"ב), דאינו כיושב בקרקעית הכירה. וטעמו, דאויר הקדירה הכפויה מפסיק, ועדיף מדבר המפסיק שאין לו תוך (כגון טס ובלעך). ואף שבשו"ע (ס"ג) השוה קדירה ריקנית לקטומה, זהו להתיר איסור החזרה. [והח"א והמ"ב התירו, אף שהניח ע"ג קרקע, לפי מנהג הרמ"א (ס"ב), דהנחה שלנו כהחזרה, עי' בסמוך (סי' ז אות א).] אבל לענין איסור תוכה, קדירה ריקנית עדיפה מדבר המפסיק שאין לו תוך, וכנ"ל. אך לכאורה מסברא הכל תלוי בדרך בישול תדיר (וכמש"כ המ"ב, סקנ"ח, הנ"ל).

ובשלט"ג (יז: בדפי הרי"ף, סוף סק"א) כתב וז"ל, שלא אסרו להחזיר בתוכה אלא בכירה שיש לה תוך וחלל כעין תנור. אבל הכירות שלנו שהן פשוטות, ואין להן תוך וחלל, הרי תוכה ועל גבה אחד ומותר להחזיר בה, עכ"ל. וכתב המ"ב (שם) וז"ל, ואותן כירות שאין להן תוך וחלל אלא הן פשוטות, ותוכן וגבן אחד, מותר להחזיר להן, דאין עליהם שם תוך, עכ"ל. ומקורו בשלט"ג הנ"ל (שעה"צ סקנ"ג).

וצ"ע דלפי מש"כ המ"ב ע"פ החיי אדם, ע"כ 'תוכה', ר"ל עיקר דרך בישולה. ואין דינו כ'תוכה' אם אינו עיקר דרך בישולה, אע"פ שבמציאות מחזיר הקדירה לתוך הכירה (שהרי התירו להחזיר לתוכה ע"ג קדירה ריקנית). וא"כ מסברא נימא דאסור כשאין תוך וחלל, דזהו דרך בישול העיקרית והיחידית, ודלא כדעת השלט"ג.

ונראה דהשלט"ג ס"ל כדעת הרמב"ן, ולכן מתיר להחזיר בכירה פשוטה, כיון דלא נפיש הבליה. והמ"ב ס"ל דאסור רק כשיש תרתי לריעותא (כלומר, דנפיש הבליה וגם החזיר בעיקר דרך בישולו). לכן מותר להחזיר בכירה פשוטה ומותר להחזיר גם בתוכה על גבי דבר המפסיק.

עוד י"ל דסובר השלט"ג דלא אסרו אלא כשיש ב' דרכים, דאסרו בדרך העיקרי כי אפשר לחמם בדרך שאינו עיקר דרך בישול. אבל כשיש

רק דרך אחת התירו. וכ"כ בערוה"ש (סי"ז). ולפ"ז בתנורים שלנו אין דין תוכה אע"פ שיש חלל, מכיון דא"א לבשל על גבן.

וגדולה מזו כתב בספר הלכות שבת (הע' תתקסג) בשם הגר"א קוטלר זצ"ל, דמותר להחזיר לתוך תנורים שלנו אם הכפתורים מכוסים. וז"ל, דעיקר בישול שלהם היה בתוכו, לפיכך יותר מיחזי כמבשל בתוכו מעל גביו, משא"כ בשלנו על גביו הוא כמו בתוכו, עכ"ל. ועפ"ז התיר להחזיר לתוך תנורים שלנו. וכנראה ס"ל דכאשר נמצא על האש המגולה שעל גבי התנור שלנו (מה שקורין ריינג'), נידון כ'על גבי התנור', אע"פ שמדובר (בשלנו) באש אחר לגמרי.

[אך אולי כונת הגר"א קוטלר היא דאמנם על האש המגולה· אינו נידון כעל גבי תנור. ומכל מקום מכיון שמבשלים גם על האש המגולה כמו תוך התנור, א"כ שניהם עיקר במטבח שלנו. ולכן אין לתנור שלנו דין 'עיקר בישולו', שהוא יסוד דין תוכה.]

והנה הערוך השלחן הנ"ל כתב דאין דין תוכה רק כאשר אי אפשר לבשל על גביו. ולפי הגר"א קוטלר, מותר אף אם אפשר לבשל על גביו, כל שאין הבישול בתוך התנור יותר עיקר מבישול שעל גביו.

ויש נפק"מ גם למכשיר החדש שנקרא סיר בישול איטי (מה שקורין קראקפא"ט), שמבשלין רק בתוכו ולא על גבו, דלפי מש"כ לעיל על פי הרמב"ן והאגרות משה אסור להחזיר לתוכו, ולפי הערוך השלחן והגר"א קוטלר מותר להחזיר לתוכו. וכן כתב בספר הלכות שבת במטבח (עמ' 60).

והקשה בהלכות שבת (שם), דאם כיסה את הכפתורים ולא את האש, יש לאסור משום נראה כמבשל (אף אם לא חיישינן לחיתוי), דהלא אינו גרוף וקטום. וכ"כ באג"מ (ח"א סי' צג) דאסור להחזיר על אש מכוסה כאשר הכפתורים מכוסים. ואם מכסה את האש, אין צורך לכסות את הכפתורים מדינא. ולכאורה צ"ל דהגר"א קוטלר פסק דהחזרה אסורה רק שמא יחתה בגחלים, וכדעת התוס', ודלא כדעת הר"ן. ומשום הכי ס"ל דמותר להחזיר אם מכסה את הכפתורים, מכיון דאין חשש חיתוי.

הרמב"ן כתב דבירושלמי י"א דדינו כדין תוכה רק אם נכנס ג' טפחים לתוכה, וי"א רק במקום שעושה חריץ, ופירש שעושין חריץ בכירה.

ונחלקו מפרשי הירושלמי, דלפי הפני משה החריץ נמצא בתוך הכירה למעלה, ואפשר לתלות הקדירה שם. ובכה"ג מותר, אבל אם נמצא

הקדירה למטה מהחריץ אסור. ולפי הפני משה דעה הב׳ בירושלמי חומרא היא, כיון דס״ל דאוסרת אף אם לא נכנס ג׳ טפחים לתוכה. [וע״פ הנ״ל פירש בעל הפנ״מ (במראה הפנים) את סתימת הרמב״ם (פ״ג ה״י), דאין מחזירין אלא על גבה.]

ולפי הקרבן העדה החריץ נמצא בגחלים למטה, ומותר אם לא נגעה הקדירה בגחלים. ולפי הקרבן העדה, דעה הב׳ בירושלמי קולא היא כיון דס״ל דמותר אף אם נכנס לתוכה יותר מג׳ טפחים. ומכאן יש מקור לדברי המג״א (סקכ״ב, הנ״ל) שאסר תוכה רק על קרקעית התנור, ולא על קדירה המפסקת. ושו״ר שכ״כ בגליון הש״ס בירושלמי שם. [ומקור המג״א מדברי הב״ח צ״ע, שהב״ח כ״כ ע״פ דברי רש״י, וי״ל דרש״י אזיל לשיטתו דשהייה כעין הטמנה.]

ובירושלמי סיימו, מפני שהוא שליט במקום שהיד שולטת, דמותר להפשיר במקום שהיד שולטת (כגמ׳ מ:, כלומר במקום שאין היד סולדת בו). וברמב״ן נראה, דבזה אין חומרת תוכה (שרב אסר להחזיר תוכה רק במקום שהיד סולדת בו מפני רוב החמימות), ועדיין נידון כ׳על גבה׳. ומוכח דיש איסור החזרה גם כשאין יד סולדת בו. ותלו איסור תוכה בשיעור יד סולדת בו דבישול, אבל יש איסור החזרה אפילו אם החום הוא פחות משיעור יד סולדת בו.

והנה הרמ״א (ס״א) כתב דאסור רק כל זמן שהיד סולדת בו. ובמג״א (סק״ט) צדד דהוא הדין בהנחה על גבי כירה. אבל י״ל דקאי רק אלשון השו״ע ׳אפילו לסמוך לו׳, דבסמיכה ע״כ מותר כשלא הגיע לשיעור יד סולדת בו, דאל״כ אין לדבר סוף. [ובגר״א (סקט״ז, הנ״ל) כ״כ לענין החזרה כנגד המדורה. ולפי הגר״א, כנגד המדורה אינו דין בפ״ע, אלא דאז לא הוי יד סולדת בו.] ואולי מודה הרמ״א דלעולם על גבה ותוכה אסור אף אם החום פחות מיד סולדת בו, וכדנראה בירושלמי. וכן כתב הרמ״א (ס״ה), לגירסא שלנו, ודלא כהגר״א (סקס״ה), וכמש״כ במג״א (שם). ולפ״ז ע״כ הרמ״א קאי רק אסמיכה, וכנ״ל.

אמנם בהגמ״ר (פ.) מתיר בפחות מיד סולדת בו גם ע״ג התנור. ולדבריו יל״פ דברי הירושלמי דבפחות מיד סולדת בו אין איסור כלל, ולא כמש״כ לעיל ע״פ הרמב״ן שפירש דאין חומרת תוכה, ומ״מ נידון כע״ג האש.

עוד יש לפרש דברי הירושלמי כדעת החזו״א (עי׳ לקמן סי׳ ו אות ב) שאסרו כל תוך התנור כשמקצתו הגיע ליד סולדת בו. אבל אם כל ע״ג התנור אינו יד סולדת בו, מותר, וכדעת ההגמ״ר. וא״כ יש מקור לדעת החזו״א מדברי הירושלמי. אך צ״ע, דלפי סברתו דאין מחיצה מגדרת, הוה לן למימר דיש לכל התנור דין תוכה, ודלא כדברי הירושלמי, וצ״ע. וי״ל דלענין תוכה מצינו חילוק, בין ג׳ טפחים לבין פחות מג׳ טפחים, וכן מקום שעשה חריץ. אבל לענין עיקר דין החזרה, מחמירים בכל התנור, ודו״ק.

סימן ה

שהייה והחזרה המותרת

א. בדבר שנתבשל כמאב"ד ופחות ממנו

נחלקו הראשונים בענין המחלוקת בין חנניה לרבנן (הנ"ל, סימן א). דהרי"ף פסק לחומרא וס"ל דאסור להשהות ע"ג כירה אינה גרופה וקטומה אא"כ מבושל כל צרכו ומצטמק ורע לו. ובתוס' (לז. ד"ה לעולם) פסקו כחנניה. ובשו"ע (ס"א) כתב שתי השיטות, והרמ"א כתב דנהגו להקל. ועיי"ש בשו"ע, דלשיטה זו א"צ גרוף וקטום אלא כשלא הגיע לשיעור כמאכל בן דרוסאי.

והנה לשון השו"ע לשיטה זו היא, וי"א שכל שנתבשל כמאכל בן דרוסאי או שנתבשל כל צרכו ומצטמק ויפה לו מותר להשהותו ע"ג כירה. ודייק רע"א (שם) מלשון זה דהשו"ע ס"ל כשיטת הבעל המאור, דאף דקיי"ל כחנניה, מ"מ אם מצטמק ויפה לו אסור. ולא התיר אלא כמאכל בן דרוסאי ומצטמק ורע לו, או במבושל כל צרכו ומצטמק ויפה לו, עיי"ש. ולכן השו"ע הזכיר מצטמק ויפה לו רק במבושל כל צרכו, להורות דכמאכל בן דרוסאי ומצטמק ויפה לו אסור.

ויש לדחות, דהרמב"ן כתב על דברי בעל המאור וז"ל, ואלו דברי תוהו, שכל מאכל בן דרוסאי מתבשל ומצטמק ויפה לו הוא עד שיתבשל כל צרכו, עכ"ל. הרי שבמציאות אין אפשרות של כמאכל בן דרוסאי ומצטמק ורע לו להרמב"ן. ולפי"ז ניחא לשון השו"ע שהזכיר מצטמק ויפה לו רק

במבושל כל צרכו, דכשאין מבושל כל צרכו פשיטא דמצטמק ויפה לו. ולעולם ס"ל דמותר בכמאכל בן דרוסאי בכל אופן, אף במצטמק ויפה לו, וכדעת התוס' דלא כבעל המאור.

והקשה רע"א (שם), דהרא"ש כתב בשם רבינו יונה דאסור להשהות על גבי כירה גרופה וקטומה אלא א"כ הגיע לכמאכל בן דרוסאי, ולכן הזכיר הרי"ף (כ.) שיעור כמאכל בן דרוסאי להורות דבפחות מזה אסור להשהות אף אם הכירה גרופה וקטומה.

ולכאורה לק"מ, דהרא"ש כ"כ אליבא דהרי"ף, וכאן השו"ע מביא שיטת התוס' דקיי"ל כחנניה, ודלא כשיטת הרי"ף. ובלא"ה, הלא הר"ן כתב דהרי"ף נקט שיעור כמאכל בן דרוסאי לענין צלי, דכיון דאין דופן קדירה המפסיק בין האש לתבשיל יחרך התבשיל אם יחתה, ולכן לא חיישינן לחתוי בכמאכל בן דרוסאי. ומותר אף אם אינה גרופה וקטומה. וכ"כ בשו"ע (סי' רנד ס"א), וא"כ לא קיי"ל כסברת הרא"ש אף אליבא דהרי"ף, וניחא קושיית רע"א.

עוד הקשה רע"א (שם) על הא דהשו"ע מתיר שהייה בפחות מכמאכל בן דרוסאי בגרוף וקטום, דהיה לו לחוש לשיטת הרשב"א (יח:) שאסור משום חשש מגיס. ונראה דע"כ לא קיי"ל כן, דהרשב"א אזיל לשיטתו (שם, לט.) דאין בישול אחר בישול אם כבר הגיע לכמאב"ד. אבל השו"ע (סי' שיח ס"ד) פסק דיש בישול אחר בישול אא"כ נתבשל כל צרכו. א"כ אם נחוש להגסה, ע"כ אסור בגרוף וקטום אף בכמאכל בן דרוסאי, וזה א"א דהרי מפורש בגמ' (לו:) דמותר. וע"כ ס"ל דלא חיישינן להגסה כלל, וכמש"כ ברמב"ן (יח:).

והנה במשנה מבואר דנותנין תבשיל ע"ג כירה שהסיקוה בקש וגבבא, וכנ"ל (סי' א אות א), ובגמ' (לו:) מבואר דלחנניה נותנין ר"ל מחזירין. ולכאורה צ"ע, דבשלמא אם החזרה אסורה משום שמא יחתה בגחלים, מובן הא דמותר בקש וגבבא, כי אין גחלים. אבל למ"ד דאסור משום נראה כמבשל, מ"ש קש וגבבא מגפת ועצים. וצ"ל דס"ל דקש וגבבא, מפני שאין גחלת, אין האש חזקה כ"כ, ואינו דרך בישול כ"כ, ולכן לא אסרו משום נראה כמבשל, ודו"ק.

ב. אפו בו בע"ש

וכעין סברא זו מצינו ברמ"א (ס"ה) וז"ל, ויש מתירין ליתן לתוך תנור שאפו בו מבעוד יום וכו' דלא נשאר בו רק הבל מעט ואין לחוש לבישול, עכ"ל. ובמ"ב (סק"צ) פירש דכיון דיש רק חום מועט, אינו נראה כמבשל. ובשעה"צ (סקפ"ח) הוסיף, וז"ל, דאף דיש חום שהיד סולדת בו, מ"מ אין דרך לבשל בתנור כזה שחומו הוא רק מאפייה דאתמול, עכ"ל.

אמנם, הרמ"א מתיר אף להניח לכתחילה כאשר אפו בו מבעוד יום, אבל בקש וגבבא נראה דאסור להניח בתחילה, וכ"כ בשש"כ (פ"א הע' עא). וכ"נ בבה"ל (ס"א ד"ה מותר לשהות), דמותר להחזיר בשבת על גבי כירה שהוסקה בקש וגבבא, 'דכגרופה וקטומה דמיא', וא"כ אסור להניח לכתחילה.

אכן נראה דהרמ"א אזיל לשיטתו (סע' ב, ע"פ הירושלמי והר"ן) דהנחה שלנו נידון כהחזרה שבגמרא (עי' מש"כ לקמן סי' ז אות א). ולפ"ז דברי הכל בו מבוססים על שיטת הר"ן הנ"ל.

וכן נראה מהמשך דברי הד"מ הארוך (סי' רנג סק"ד) שהביא שיטת הר"ן והירושלמי, 'וכן כתב הכל בו'. ולכאורה צ"ע דנראה דב' התירים נפרדים הם (דהר"ן מתיר הנחה על כירה רגילה, והכל בו מתיר הנחה תוך תנור שאפו בו מבעוד יום). ולפי הנ"ל, הכל בו מתיר רק בהחזרה ולכן ע"כ סומך על הר"ן, דהנחה שלנו נידון כהחזרה, ודו"ק.

וצ"ע בעיקר ההיתר של הכל בו, דבכל כירה גרופה ע"כ הסיר הגחלים מבעוד יום, דאסור לגרוף בשבת, וכתוס' (ד"ה ובה"ה). ולרוב הפוסקים גרופה ר"ל דהסיר הגחלים חוץ לכירה לגמרי (מ"ב סקי"ד), ודלא כבעל המאור שפירש שגרפם לצד אחד. וא"כ מ"ש הוחם מאתמול מסתם כירה גרופה דאסור להחזיר לתוכה, וכגמ' (לז.) ושו"ע (ס"א).

ובב"י תירץ, דההיתר דאפו בו מבעוד יום נאמר רק כשאחרי שהוציאו הפת לא חממו התנור עוד. אבל כל שחממוהו כדי להכניס בו קדירת חמין לצורך מחר, אסור להחזיר לתוכו אפילו אם גרפו כל הגחלים. עכ"פ מבואר במ"ב דבהוחם מאתמול אינו נראה כמבשל, שאין דרך בישול בכך. וכעין זה צ"ל בקש וגבבא אם קיי"ל כחנניה וקיי"ל כטעם נראה כמבשל.

ובמ״ב (סק״צ) סיים וז״ל, אבל בד״מ, וכן מהרמ״א לעיל (ס״ב), מוכח דנוהגים להקל להחזיר לתוך התנור בכל גווני, עכ״ל. ובמג״א (סקל״ה) כתב שבד״מ סמך על הר״ן, ופירש דר״ל הר״ן (לח:) שכתב ע״פ הירושלמי שבסלק בשבת דינו כהחזרה ולא כהנחה מתחילה. והקשה וז״ל, וצ״ע, דהר״ן לא כתב היתר זה אלא כשהניחה ע״ג קרקע, דלא הוי כתחלת הטמנה, כיון שהיה שם בשבת. אבל לענין היתר תוכה לא מהני זה, עכ״ל. כלומר, דלפי הר״ן והירושלמי, הנחה נחשבת כהחזרה (אם היה על האש בכניסת השבת, עי׳ סי׳ ז אות א). אבל הרי החזרה גופא בתוך הכירה אסורה היא.

ונראה דהב״י (סוף סי׳ רנג) כתב דברי הר״ן (מ: הנ״ל, סי׳ ג אות א), שמותר לתת פנאדי״ש ע״ג כירה, שאין דרכו לאפות שם, והדבר מוכיח שאינו נעשה אלא בשביל שיתחמם. וכתב הב״י וז״ל, ומשמע דדוקא ע״ג כירה קאמר, אבל ליתן בתנור אסור, כיון שדרכו ליאפות שם, עכ״ל. וכתב הד״מ (סק״ח) וז״ל, ונוהגין היתר כדברי הר״ן, ומה שחילק [הב״י] בין נתינה על הכירה או לתוכה, זה לא נזכר בדברי הר״ן, אלא שהב״י חילק מעצמו בכך. ואפשר דלא סבירא לן לחלק בהא, עכ״ל.

הרי מבואר שהד״מ לא סמך על דברי הר״ן (לח:) ע״פ הירושלמי, שהנחה שלנו הוי כהחזרה, דבזה בודאי אין היתר ב׳תוכה׳, וחילוק זה איתא בגמ׳ (לז.) עצמה, ולא חידש כן הב״י מעצמו. ולא היה כותב הד״מ בענין חילוק זה ׳שהב״י חילק מעצמו בכך׳.

לכ״נ דסמך הד״מ על הר״ן (מ:) דבמאכל שאין רגילים לבשל שם, כגון פנאדי״ש, אין איסור דנראה כמבשל. וס״ל דהדין כן גם בתוכה, דמ״ש, דהרי כל החומר דתוכה הוא דנראה כמבשל, ולא שייך בפנאדי״ש כיון דאינו מבשלו שם. ואף הב״י, דאסר בתוכה לא כ״כ ע״פ הגמ׳ (לז.) אלא מסברא, ׳כיון שדרכו ליאפות שם׳. ובמקום הד״מ לא אפו הפנאדי״ש שם. ולכן ׳לא סבירא לן לחלק בהא׳.

ולפי פירושנו בדברי הד״מ, לכאורה אין מחלוקת בדין, אלא שהב״י אוסר רק באופן שהדרך לאפות שם, ובזה מודה הרמ״א. וניחא קושית המג״א שהקשה לפי הבנתו שהד״מ סומך על הר״ן (לח:) ע״פ הירושלמי, ובאמת סומך על דבריו (מ:) בפנאדי״ש, וכנ״ל.

ולפירוש המג״א בדברי הדרכי משה צ״ל דלפי הר״ן והירושלמי, אם היה על האש בע״ש והניחו על גבי קרקע, מותר להניחו לכתחילה על

גבי האש, אף באופן שאסרו החזרה (כגון בתוכה). והגמ' אסרה להחזיר לתוכה, אבל לפי הר"ן והירושלמי, הנחה באופן שהיה על האש בע"ש עדיפא מהחזרה.

ולפ"ז הב"י הוא שאסר הנחה לכתחילה בתוכה לפי סברת הר"ן. ואמנם כן נראה מסברא, דהר"ן כתב רק דהנחה שלנו נידון כהחזרה, והרי החזרה לתוכה אסורה. אבל אין זה מפורש בגמ', די"ל דהנחה דידן עדיף מהחזרה שבגמ'. וזוהי כונת הדרכי משה (לפי המג"א) 'שהב"י חילק מעצמו בכך', ודו"ק.

ולפירוש המג"א, כונת לשון הד"מ הארוך הנ"ל 'וכן כתב הכל בו' היא להפך ממש"כ לעיל. כלומר, דלפי מש"כ לעיל הכלבו מקיל יותר מהר"ן. אבל להבנת המג"א בדברי הד"מ, שהר"ן מתיר הנחה לכתחילה לתוך תנור רגיל, הכל בו מחמיר יותר מהר"ן, ומתיר להניח רק לתוך תנור שאפו בו מבעוד יום.

ולפי פירושנו הנ"ל, עדיין קצת קשה, דסברת הר"ן (מ:) בפנאדי"ש מהני לשיטתו, דבדבר המבושל כל צרכו אין חשש חיתוי, והחזרה אסורה רק משום נראה כמבשל. אבל לפי הרמ"א שצדד שאסור להחזיר מע"ש (עי' לעיל סי' א אות ב), נראה שיש חשש חיתוי, ולמה אינו אסור מה"ט כאשר מניח בתחילה בתוך התנור, והרי ק"ו הוא מהחזרה (מאחר דהנחה חמורה יותר מהחזרה). וי"ל, דהד"מ קאי אדברי הב"י, דמיירי באפו בו מבעוד יום, ופירש הב"י שדינו כגחלים שעממו, שאין חשש חיתוי, דהוי כקטומה (לז.).

והנה המ"ב (סוף סק"צ, הנ"ל) צירף דברי הד"מ למש"כ הרמ"א (ס"ב), ועפ"ז כתב דהרמ"א מקיל להחזיר לתוכה בכל גווני. והמ"ב כתב כן ע"פ הבנת המג"א. אבל לפי פירושנו הנ"ל, הד"מ מקיל רק באפו מבעוד יום, וכ"כ הרמ"א (ס"ה). וכבר כתב החזו"א (סק"ח) שהרמ"א (ס"ב) לא התיר החזרה לתוכה.

ג. פחות משיעור יד סולדת בו

עוד כתב הרמ"א וז"ל, ויש מחמירין בזה, ואם החום כ"כ בתנור שהיד סולדת בו אסור, עכ"ל. ובמ"ב (סקצ"ג) כתב דצ"ל שאם החום וכו', דאל"ה

אפילו להיש מחמירין שרי. ובשעה"צ (סקצ"ג) מבואר שכ"כ הגר"א (סקס"ה), ועכצ"ל כן, דלא מצינו איסור החזרה כשאין היד סולדת בו. ובמקור הדין בכלבו, מובא בב"י, כתב דלא נתנו חכמים דבריהם לשיעורים, אבל בפחות מיד סולדת בו פשוט דהתירו.

ולגירסא שלנו ברמ"א י"ל ע"פ הירושלמי, דיש איסור בתנור כשאין היד סולדת בו, וכדנראה ברמב"ן (לז.), ודלא כדעת ההגמ"ר, וכנ"ל (סי' ד אות ו). ולפי הירושלמי, דבפחות מיד סולדת בו דינו כעל גבה ולא כתוכה, אף תוך התנור, יש ליישב המנהג להניח בתוך התנור בפחות מיד סולדת בו כפשוטו, וא"צ לסמוך על הר"ן (מ:) הנ"ל. אך הרמ"א לא הביא דברי הירושלמי.

לכן נראה שהרמ"א כתב כן (לפי גירסתנו) ע"פ לשון הב"י בשם הכלבו, דהבלו מעט, ופירש דר"ל פחות מיד סולדת בו, וס"ל דאסור מסברא. וקושית המ"ב (סקצ"ג), דהרמ"א מקיל בסוף סעיף ב, בפחות מיד סולדת בו, לק"מ, דשם מיירי בסמיכה, ובזה א"א לאסור, דאין לדבר סוף. אבל על גבה ובתוכה אסור [לולא סברת הר"ן (מ:) הנ"ל], אף דבאש שפחות מיד סולדת בו א"א לבשל, וכדנראה בירושלמי, ודו"ק.

ובמג"א (סקל"ו) פי' חומרת הרמ"א בזה בנצטנן לגמרי, משום דבטלה שהייה ראשונה, ואינו החזרה אלא הנחה. ולא פירש משום בישול, דלגירסתו דמיירי בפחות מיד סולדת בו, א"א להגיע לידי בישול בדבר לח. והגר"א (סקס"ד) שפי' דברי הרמ"א - 'וכנ"ל', כל' משום איסור בישול בדבר לח, אזיל לשיטתו (סקס"ה) דמיירי שהיד סולדת בו.

סימן ו

דיני הבלעך

א. הנחה על הבלעך

הנה לענין אש קטומה, נהגו לכסות האש בכיסוי של ברזל שקורין בלעך, ודלא כדעת החזו״א (סי׳ לז סקי״א) שמצריך קדירה ריקנית דוקא, וכשו״ע (סי רנג ס״ג), כדי למעט חומו יותר, עיי״ש.

ובבה״ל (שם ס״א ד״ה ליתן) הוכיח מרש״י (לז.) דכיסוי אינו כקטום. ולפי מנהגנו צ״ל דבכירה שלהם היה רגיל לכסותו, כדי לבשל ע״ג הכירה קדירה שאינה רחבה כל כך, והיתה נופלת לתוך הכירה לולא הכיסוי. אבל בתנורים שלנו, שאין חלל שפתוח מלמעלה, אין רגילות לכסותו כדי לבשל עליה, ולכן כיסוי הוא היכר טוב, וכגרוף וקטום שלהם.

וכתב הרמב״ם (פ״ג ה״ד) דע״י קטימה מסיח דעת, והר״ן כתב דהוי היכירא, ולא הצריכו שימעט חומם. והחזו״א (סק״ט) כתב דקדירה ריקנית אין דרך בישול בכך, ולכן דינו כסמיכה. ולשון ההגמ״ר (פ.), ׳ולהניח קדירה ריקנית על פי הכירה והו״ל כירה כגרופה וקטומה׳, לאו דוקא הוא.

והחזו״א אזיל לשיטתו (שם), דעל גבי קדירה מליאה (דהתירו הר״ן והשו״ע כי אין דרך בישול בכך) אינה נחשבת כעל גבי האש כלל, ולכן אפשר לומר דע״ג קדירה ריקנית (דג״כ אין דרך בישול בכך) חמיר ממנו. אבל בכיסוי כתב (שם) דדרך בישול בכך, והוי בכלל על גבה, כלומר ואינו כקטום.

ונראה דאה"נ, דכיסוי שנמצא שם תדיר אינו כקטומה, דאינו היכר. [ולכן אסור להחזיר על מכשיר חשמלי שהאש מכוסה בו תמיד, דאינו גרוף וקטום.] אבל בלעך לא נמצא שם תדיר. א"כ אף לסברת החזו"א (דבעינן שיהא אינו דרך בישול בכך), י"ל דבלעך הוי כגרוף וקטום (אף דהחזו"א עצמו כנראה אסר החזרה על גבי בלעך).

ומ"מ בפשוטו אין הקולא בבלעך משום שאין דרכו בכך [כמש"כ הילקוט יוסף הנ"ל (סי' ג אות א), ולדבריו בלעך עדיף מכירה גרופה וקטומה דהיה דרכו בכך, עיי"ש]. אלא דדינו כגרוף וקטום, דהיכירא הוא, וכמש"כ הר"ן (במשנה לו:). ולכן הנחה ע"ג הבלעך אסור, וכדעת הבה"ל והפמ"ג (הנ"ל סי' ג אות א), כיון שהמאכל מתחמם ע"י האש בלי אמצעי.

עוד כתב החזו"א (שם) דקדירה ממעט את החום הרבה, משא"כ כיסוי. [וגם הטור (סי' רנג) כתב דקטום ממעט את חום האש.] וכנראה ס"ל דהאויר שתחת הקדירה הכפויה מרחק את התבשיל מן האש. אבל לפי שו"ע הרב (קו"א סק"י), שהקדירה אינה כפויה, ונותנים את התבשיל בתוך הקדירה הריקנית, אינו ממעט החום יותר מכיסוי רגיל.

והנה גרוף וקטום לא מהני להתיר שהייה בתנור, ולכאורה משמע כדעת החזו"א, דבעינן שימעט חומו, ובתנור שחומו רב, אינו ממעט. אבל בפמ"ג (א"א סק"ח) פירש דאם גרוף וקטום הוא, יש גילוי דעת שמסיח דעתו, וכשיטת הרמב"ם. אבל בתנור אין גילוי דעת, דקטם כדי שלא יתחרך בהבל הרב של התנור. ולפי הפמ"ג יש לומר דא"צ מיעוט החום, וסגי בהיכירא בלבד.

ובמג"א (סק"ג) כתב וז"ל, ואפילו הובערה אח"כ שרי (גמ' לז:), כיון שגילה דעתו דלא בעי לגחלים סגי, עכ"ל.

ובפני יהושע (לז: ד"ה ומה) חולק משום דהרמב"ם והשו"ע השמיטו דין קטמה והובערה. ופירש, דבגמרא הוכיחו דמותר במצטמק ויפה לו, ודחו, דקטמה והובערה כקטומה דמי. וקיי"ל לחומרא בשניהם, דאסור במצטמק ויפה לו [לשיטה א' בשו"ע, דלא כחנניה] וגם אסור בקטמה והובערה.

ובשש"כ (הע' מו) צדד הגרשז"א דקטמה והובערה מותר בשהייה ואסור בהחזרה. ולכאורה תלוי במחלוקת בין הר"ן והתוס', דקטמה והובערה הוי גלוי דעת דלא בעי לגחלים, וכמש"כ המג"א, ולא גזרינן שמא יחתה.

ולכן מותר לדעת התוס׳ (כיון דהחזרה אסורה משום שמא יחתה, וכנ״ל, סי׳ א אות א), ושפיר י״ל דתלוי בשעת הכנת האש, ובאותה שעה היתה קטומה. אבל לדעת הר״ן (דאסור משום דנראה כמבשל), קטמה והובערה לא מהני להחזרה, כיון דבשעת החזרה הקדירה אין היכירא.

והגרש״ז אויערבך (ח״ג שם) חזר בו על פי דברי הגמ׳, כלומר דבברייתא (לז.) התירו להחזיר על גבי האש כשקטמה ונתלבתה, ומוכח שלענין זה אין חילוק בין שהייה להחזרה.

אמנם, יש לקיים דברי הגשרז״א הראשונים, דהנה קשה גם לדברי הפני יהושע מברייתא זו. וצריך לחלק בין הובערה לנתלבתה, דלא חמור כל כך [ודלא כדעת רש״י (לז. ד״ה ונתלבתה) שדינם שוה, אלא כדעת התוס׳ (ד״ה שמע)]. וא״כ יש לומר כדעת הגרשז״א (ח״א), ולא היה צריך לחזור בו.

ודין גחלים שעממו, שדינם כקטומה (לז.), ניחא לפי הטור, שסובר שבקטומה נתמעט חומם, וכדעת החזו״א, דגם בעממו נתמעט חומם. והר״ן (במשנה) כתב דבקטומה יש היכר, וכתב דין עממו, וכנראה ס״ל דגם זה היכר. ולפי הרמב״ם צ״ל כמש״כ הרשב״א, ומובא במ״ב (סקי״ד), דכיון דלא חש ללבותן כדי שלא יעוממו, מוכח דאינו רוצה לחתות, והוי כהיסח הדעת.

ב. הנחה על הבלעך שלא ע״ג האש

והנה מצוי שבחלק מהבלעך אין היד סולדת בו בברזל עצמו, וק״ו במאכל שהושם על גבי הבלעך, שזהו באמת הקובע, וכמש״כ החזו״א (סק״ח) והמ״ב (סקס״ז וס״ח). ומעתה יש לעיין אם מותר לתת קדירה לכתחילה בשבת על חלק זה מהבלעך שאין היד סולדת בו. ובספר הלכות שבת (הע׳ תתרעג) אסר ע״פ החזו״א (שם, הנ״ל, סי׳ ד אות ו) שאסר להחזיר לחלק מהתנור שאין היד סולדת בו, דאין למסור לכל אחד תורתו בידו, ואין מחיצה המבדלת בין יד סולדת בו לאין היד סולדת בו.

ולכאורה נראה דדין זה תלוי בהגדרת חלק הבלעך שאינו ע״ג האש ממש אבל הוא יד סולדת בו. שאם דינו כע״ג האש, שפיר י״ל כנ״ל, דלא חילקו בע״ג האש בין יד סולדת בו לאין היד סולדת בו, כמו שלא חילקו

בתוך התנור לפי החזו"א. אבל אם דינו כסמוך לאש, לכאורה מוכרח דמותר, דאל"כ ייאסר עד סוף העולם, להאוסרים סמיכה בהחזרה, או עכ"פ בהנחה בתחילה. וע"כ שבסמיכה א"א לומר שאסרו כשאין היד סולדת בו, וכ"נ ברמ"א (ס"א וסוף ס"ב, וכנ"ל שם).

אמנם בהלכות שבת (הע' תתרעח) התיר להעביר מחלק הבלעך שלא ע"ג האש לחלק שע"ג האש, דלא גרע מכירה אחרת שברמ"א (ס"ב). ומזה נראה דחלק הבלעך שלא ע"ג האש דינו כע"ג כירה, ולא כסמוך לה. וא"ש הא דאסר להחזיר אף כשאין היד סולדת בו, וכמש"כ החזו"א לענין תוך התנור וכנ"ל.

ונראה דאם נידון כסמיכה רק כשדופן מפסיק, וכשיטת התוס' (לז.), א"כ כאן, שאין דופן מפסיק, נידון כע"ג האש. וכ"נ במג"א לדינא, וכמש"כ לעיל (שם אות ה). וכ"כ בנחל זרד (עמ' קיח). אך למסקנה פסק (שם) דאף דאין דופן המפסיק, מ"מ הרשב"א (מ:) פירש דכנגד המדורה מותר מפני שהדרך רק לחמם שם ולא לבשל, וכ"ה בבלעך שלנו שלא ע"ג האש, דכיון שהאש נמצא למעלה, המקום שלא על גבי האש נידון כסמיכה. ולא דמי לתוך הכירה, שיש דפנות מסביב, שהדרך לבשל גם שלא ע"ג האש.

והנה אם נידון כמו כנגד המדורה, ולא כסמיכה, מותר אפילו להניח לכתחילה. ונראה דזוהי כונת המ"ב (סי' שיח סקצ"ד), דמותר להניח על גבי קדירה ריקנית סמוך לאש, אף בתוך התנור, דדינו כמו כנגד המדורה.

נמצא דאם נידון כסמיכה, אסור להניח לכתחילה וכדעת רע"א, וכנ"ל (שם אות ב). ורק אם נידון כמו כנגד המדורה מותר להניח לכתחילה. אמנם להמ"ב, שנטה לפסוק כדעת הדגמ"ר (ודלא כדעת רע"א, וכמש"כ לעיל, שם), דסמיכה מותרת בהנחה לכתחילה, א"כ ניחא דבריו (סקפ"א הנ"ל) גם אם נידון כסמיכה בגרופה וקטומה, ולא כמו כנגד המדורה.

והנה השו"ע (סי' שיח סט"ו) מתיר להניח דבר יבש כנגד המדורה. והרמ"א (שם) הוסיף וז"ל, ואפילו נצטנן כבר. אבל אם הוא רותח, אפילו בדבר שיש בו מרק מותר. ויש מקילין לומר דכל שאין נותנו על גבי האש או הכירה ממש רק סמוך לו אפילו נצטנן מותר. ונהגו להקל בזה אם לא נצטנן לגמרי וכמו שכתבתי לעיל סימן רנג, עכ"ל.

ולכאורה מוכח מדברי הרמ"א דהנחה לכתחילה מותרת בסמיכה דומיא דכנגד המדורה (אא"כ נאמר ד'סמוך' לא ר"ל סמיכה כלשון הגמ'

אלא הכונה היא כנגד המדורה). ומש"כ הרמ"א 'וכמו שכתבתי לעיל סימן רנג' קאי אדין בישול אחר בישול בדבר לח (ס"ה).

אבל לפי מש"כ לעיל (שם) דהנחה לכתחילה אסורה בסמיכה, צ"ל דהרמ"א מקיל רק ע"פ שיטת הר"ן (עי' לקמן סי' ז אות א), דכל שסילק את הקדירה בשבת, אף בהניחה ע"ג קרקע לא בטלה שהייה ראשונה, ונידון כהחזרה ולא כהנחה לכתחילה. ואף שלא כתב בפירוש דמיירי בכה"ג, מ"מ כיון שלא נצטנן לגמרי, מובן שסילקה רק בשבת.

ולפ"ז לשון הרמ"א, 'וכמו שכתבתי לעיל סימן רנג', קאי גם אשיטת הר"ן הנ"ל (ס"ב). ולמסקנת הרמ"א דטוב להחמיר ולאסור, גם בסמיכה אסור. וא"כ קשה לצרף שיטת ההגמ"ר (דדינו כסמיכה בלי דופן המפסיק), כדי להניח לכתחילה על הבלעך סמוך לאש, אף אם נידון כסמיכה, וכ"ש אם דינו כמו על גבי האש.

ג. הזזת קדירה על הבלעך

והנה בספר הלכות שבת (הע' תתרסא) צדד דהחלק מהבלעך שלא ע"ג האש נידון כסמוך להאש, ולא כמקום שעל גבי האש. [והיינו דלא כדבריו (הע' תתרעח), הנ"ל (אות ב).]

ומ"מ י"ל דמותר להעביר משם לע"ג האש וכדעת החזו"א (סק"י), שכתב דמסמיכה לע"ג מותר, כלומר, דמותר להעביר קדירה שהיתה סמוכה לכירה מערב שבת ולהניחה ע"ג הכירה בשבת עצמה. ולפי"ז נראה דאין לאסור להחזיר ע"ג חלק הבלעך שאין היד סולדת בו, וכנ"ל, דבסמיכה אין לגזור באינו יד סולדת בו אטו יד סולדת בו.

ובעיקר ההיתר דמסמיכה לע"ג מותר צע"ק, דבחזו"א (שם) כ"כ מסברא, דכל שיהוי אחד הוא (דראייתו מהירושלמי שלא הזכירו איסור מסמיכה לע"ג יש לדחות, דלא דנו שם על סמיכה כלל, עיי"ש), ואינו מוכרח, די"ל דסמיכה אינה בכלל שיהוי. וראיה לזה מהא דקיי"ל דמותר לסמוך בשהייה מערב שבת, אף בכירה אינה גרופה וקטומה.

ועיי"ש בחזו"א (סקי"א) דקדירה שהשהה על גבי קדירה מע"ש, אסור לתת אותה על גבי הבלעך בשבת עצמה, דכאשר הניחה על גבי הקדירה אין דינה כשהייה. ובאמת דין זה צ"ע, לפי מש"כ לעיל (סי' ג אות א)

בשם הפמ"ג (בבה"ל סי' רנח), דאסור להשהות על גבי קדירה בלא הגיע לכמאכל בן דרוסאי, ומוכח דדינו כשהייה, והיה נראה דמותר להורידה על גבי הבלעך בשבת, וצ"ע. ומאידך, בסמיכה, דא"צ כמאכל בן דרוסאי לשהות, דאין דינו כשהייה, יתכן דאסור להעביר לעל גבי האש, וכמש"כ לעיל. וזהו להיפך מפסקי החזו"א, וצ"ע.

ונראה דהחזו"א ס"ל דכל מקום שאסור להניח עליו לכתחילה, נידון כע"ג האש, ומותר להעביר ממנו לע"ג אש גרוף וקטום. ולכן מותר להעביר מסמיכה לעל גבה. אבל אסור להעביר מע"ג קדירה, שהוא מקום שמותר להניח עליו לכתחילה, ולא נידון כע"ג האש, לע"ג אש גרוף וקטום.

וכבר נתבאר (לעיל, שם) שלפי החזו"א קדירה ע"ג קדירה נחשב כמונח שלא ע"ג האש כלל, מכיון שחום הקדירה מחמם, ולא חום האש.

ולפי מש"כ (שם) ע"פ דברי הפמ"ג דעל גבי קדירה נידון כעל גבי האש (מהא דאסרו שהייה ע"ג קדירה), י"ל דמותר להעביר מעל גבי קדירה לעל גבי האש, ודלא כדעת החזו"א. אמנם לפי מש"כ שם (אות ב), דמותר להשהות על גבי קדירה מליאה (ודלא כדברי הפמ"ג), אולי על גבי קדירה נחשב כמונח שלא על גבי האש.

וסברת החזו"א בסמיכה היא, דא"א לעבור על איסור הנחה לכתחילה על גבי כירה גרופה וקטומה, אם נוטל מסמוך לה, שהוא מקום שיש איסור להניח שם לכתחילה, דאין הנחה אחר הנחה. ואינו ענין לאיסור שהייה, שהוא שמא יחתה בגחלים, וחשש זה קיים על גבי קדירה ולא בסמיכה. ולשון החזו"א, וכל שיהוי אחד הוא, לא ר"ל דתלוי באיסור שהייה, דבאמת תלוי באיסור הנחה, וכנ"ל.

ובנחל זרד (עמ' קכ) כתב, דהחזו"א מתיר להעביר רק מסמיכה אצל כירה שאינה גרופה וקטומה ולתת אותה ע"ג כירה שהיא גרופה וקטומה. ובזה י"ל דהכל שיהוי אחד הוא כיון דדינם שוה, דבשני מצבים אלו קיי"ל דההחזרה מותרת והנחה לכתחילה אסורה. אבל אם מותר הוא להניח לכתחילה ע"ג הבלעך שלא על האש, נמצא דאין דינו שוה לע"ג כירה גרופה וקטומה. וא"כ אסור להעביר קדירה על הבלעך מסמוך לאש לעל גבה. ולפ"ז, למנהג העולם להקל בזה, ע"כ כל הבלעך נידון כע"ג האש.

וכן היא לפי מש"כ לעיל לצדד דאסור להעביר מסמיכה לעל גבה, ודלא כדעת החזו"א. ולכאורה יוצא דאסור להניח לכתחילה ע"ג הבלעך שלא על האש.

ועיי"ש בחזו"א (סק"י), דאסור להעביר מהחלק שאין היד סולדת בו להחלק שהיד סולדת בו, דכשאין היד סולדת בו לא חשיב שיהוי והו"ל משהה בתחלה בשבת. אבל בהלכות שבת (הע' תתרעו) כתב דהגרמ"פ זצ"ל מתיר, דלא נחשב חזרה מכיון שהוא על הבלעך שעל התנור, וצ"ב.

ואולי ס"ל דכל הבלעך נידון כעל גבי האש ממש, וכצד א' הנ"ל. והטעם הוא משום שכאן יש טס רחב המונח על האש, והקדירה מונחת עליו [משא"כ בקדירה על גבי קרקע או דבר אחר וסמוכה לאש.] ולפ"ז נידון כקדירה רחבה מאד, שהאש בצדה האחד, ובצדה השני יתכן דאין היד סולדת בו, ואעפ"כ אין איסור להעביר מחלק אחד שבקדירה להאחר, ודו"ק.

אולם יתכן דכוונת הגרמ"פ למש"כ באג"מ (ח"ב סי' ס), להקל לכתחילה בהניח ע"ג ספסל ודעתו להחזיר כשלא נצטנן לגמרי, ודלא כנראה ברמ"א (ס"ב) דבעינן עודה בידו דוקא, עיי"ש. ומיירי כשהיה ע"ג האש ממש בכניסת השבת. וכ"כ בספר הלכות שבת במטבח (עמ' 46). והגרש"ז אויערבך בשש"כ (פ"א הע' קיא) צדד דבנ"ד נחשב כעודה בידו, עיי"ש.

שו"ר בספר ארחות שבת (פ"ב סע' סב,סט, ובהערות שם), שלפי הגרי"ש אלישיב שליט"א כל הבלעך נידון כע"ג האש, ואסור להניח לכתחילה ע"ג המקום שאין היד סולדת בו (וכמש"כ החזו"א לענין תנור), ומותר להעביר משם למקום שהיד סולדת בו. ואילו לפי הגר"נ קרליץ שליט"א, אינו נידון כע"ג האש. ולכן מותר להניח במקום שאין היד סולדת בו, וכדין סמיכה, ואסור להעביר משם למקום שהיד סולדת בו, עיי"ש.

סימן ז

דיני הנחה למעשה

א. בטלה שהייה ראשונה

גרסינן (לח:), לא שנו אלא שעודן בידו, אבל הניחן ע"ג קרקע אסור, וכו'. הא דאמרת עודן בידו מותר, לא אמרן אלא שדעתו להחזיר, אבל אין דעתו להחזיר אסור. איכא דאמרי וכו', הא דאמרת על גבי קרקע אסור, לא אמרן אלא שאין דעתו להחזיר, אבל דעתו להחזיר מותר. מכלל שבעודן בידו, אע"פ שאין דעתו להחזיר מותר. ע"כ.

הרמ"א (סי' רנג ס"ב) פסק בזה לחומרא, דצריך ב' התנאים, עודה בידו ודעתו להחזיר, וכנ"ל (סי' ו סוף אות ג). ובבה"ל (ד"ה ודעתו), הביא דיש מקילים דדי באחד מהם, והקיל לעת הצורך בצירוף שיטת הרמב"ם שסובר שבעודה בידו א"צ דעתו להחזיר. וכן הקיל בהניחה ע"ג ספסל ודעתו להחזיר, בצרוף שיטת הב"י דהניחה ע"ג קרקע דוקא מבטל שהייה ראשונה, אבל ע"ג ספסל דינה כעודה בידו. וכ"ז לעת הצורך, ודלא כדעת האג"מ הנ"ל (סי' ו' אות ג') שמתיר באופן זה אפילו לכתחילה, וכנ"ל.

ומקור דין ע"ג ספסל הוא באיבעיא בגמ' (שם) בהניחה ע"ג מטה ועלה בתיקו, והרמ"א מחמיר ומצריך עודה בידו דוקא. אבל הרמב"ם (פ"ג ה"י) כתב, והוא שלא הניח הקדירה ע"ג קרקע, וכתב הב"י קרקע דוקא, שפסק להקל בתיקו דרבנן. והגר"א (סקמ"א) הביא דברי הירושלמי

כמקור להרמב"ם וז"ל, נתנו ע"ג ספסל נאמר אם היה מפוחם מותר ואם לאו אסור. א"ר יוחנן ברם בשלא העביר את ידו ממנו, אבל אם העביר את ידו ממנו אסור, עכ"ל. אך הקשה הגר"א, שהירושלמי מקיל רק בלא העביר את ידו ממנו, והרמב"ם לא הזכיר דבר זה.

אולם כתב הרמב"ם (בפיהמ"ש) וז"ל, בתנאי שלא תונח הקדירה על דבר אלא שתהיה באויר עד שישפך ממנה ויחזירנה, עכ"ל. ומזה נראה להפך, דאסור אף בלא העביר את ידו ממנו ומונח ע"ג ספסל. וע"כ צריך לומר דהרמב"ם חזר בו, וכמש"כ הגרמ"פ, מובא בהל"ש (הע' תתקמ). אך מש"כ שם (בהע') דבהניחה ע"ג קרקע ולא העביר ידו ממנה מותר להירושלמי, בקרבן העדה (שם) נראה דרק ע"ג ספסל התירו בכה"ג, וכמש"כ בשש"כ (הע' נב). ובנחל זרד (עמ' צח) כתב דלפי הגר"א אסור אף בהניחה ע"ג ספסל ולא העביר ידו ממנה, ודלא כדברי הדמשק אליעזר שכתב שהגר"א סובר כהקרבן העדה.

ובהא דמצריך הירושלמי שיהיה מפוחם, י"ל דמיירי בדבר לח, וכמ"ד יש בישול אחר בישול בלח. ולפי"ז בעינן יד סולדת בו, וכשיטת הקרבן העדה (שם) דבעינן רותח גמור, וכמג"א (סקי"ט) לפי השו"ע (ס"ב וסי' שיח ס"ד). ולפי"ז בדבר גוש א"צ מפוחם כלל. ובבה"ל (סע' ה ד"ה ובלבד) כ"כ בשם הגר"א.

אך המג"א (סקל"ו) פירש את דברי הרמ"א (סע' ה, לענין אפו בו מבעוד יום) 'ובלבד שלא שנצטנן לגמרי', דלא ר"ל בדבר לח ומשום בישול, וכשיטתו (סי' שיח ס' ט"ו), אלא וז"ל, ואפילו בדבר שאין בו מרק דלית ליה משום בישול אסור אם נצטנן, דה"ל כמניח לכירה לכתחילה בשבת, דלא התירו אלא חזרה, עכ"ל. כלומר דכמו דע"י הניחו ע"ג קרקע בטלה שהייה ראשונה ושוב אינו נידון כהחזרה, ה"ה נמי בנצטנן. ועיין לעיל (סי' ה אות ג) דלפי גירסתנו ברמ"א ע"כ צ"ל כן.

וכ"כ הריטב"א (לח:) וז"ל, ומ"מ מוכחא מסוגיין דבעינא שיחזירנה קודם שתצטנן לגמרי דלא ליחזי כמבשל, עכ"ל. וכונתו היא דבגמ' (שם) התירו להחזיר קומקומוס של חמין, הא אם נצטננו אסור.

ונראה דהריטב"א אזיל לשיטתו (לט.) דאין בישול אחר בישול בדבר לח, וע"כ בנצטנן אסור רק משום דבטלה שהייה ראשונה, ונראה כמבשל. אבל אם יש בישול אחר בישול בלח, אסור להחזיר משנצטננו החמין משום

בישול, ולכן התירו בקומקומוס של חמין דוקא. ולעולם בדבר יבש מותר, וכצ״ל להגר״א שמתיר החזרת יבש קר. [אא״כ נאמר דקומקומוס של חמין ר״ל מים שהוחמו אע״פ שנצטננו אח״כ, ודלא כהריטב״א.]

עכ״פ י״ל דבהחזרה ע״ג כירה בעינן שלא יצטנן ביבש (וכדעת הריטב״א, ודלא כדעת הגר״א). ואף דהירושלמי הזכיר מפוחם רק בהניח ע״ג ספסל, לעולם בעינן לא נצטנן אף בעודה בידו.

והנה הקשה בפמ״ג (מ״ז סקי״ג) שהמג״א (סקי״ט) כתב דבדבר יבש מותר אף בנצטנן, וכ״כ (סוף סי׳ רנט) וז״ל, ודבר שאין בו רטוב אפי׳ קר כחם דמי, עכ״ל. וסותר לדבריו (סקל״ו) הנ״ל.

וי״ל דרק בתוכה החמיר המג״א, דרק בלא נצטנן אמרינן דהבל מועט אינו נראה כמבשל. אבל היינו רק משום שלפי פירוש המג״א (סקל״ה, הנ״ל סי׳ ה אות ב) בדברי הרמ״א, החזרה בתוכה קולא מיוחדת היא [כיון שבגמ׳ (לז.) מוכח דאסור בכה״ג, וכנ״ל (שם)]. ולכן החמיר המג״א אף בדבר יבש, וס״ל דרק כשלא נצטנן מותר להחזיר לתוכה. משא״כ על גבה, דמותר מדינא דגמרא בגרוף וקטום, דס״ל להמג״א דנידון כהחזרה (ולא כהנחה) אף בדבר יבש שנצטנן. ושו״ר במחה״ש (סוף סי׳ רנט) שמחלק בין תוכה לע״ג, לפי המג״א.

והנה המג״א (סקי״ט) קאי אדברי השו״ע, שמתיר החזרה רק אם עודה בידו, ולא אם הניח על גבי קרקע. וי״ל דרק בזה לא בטלה שהייה הראשונה, ומותר להחזיר אף בנצטנן. אבל לפי הרמ״א (סע׳ ב, הנ״ל), ע״פ הר״ן והירושלמי, דס״ל שאם היה על האש בכניסת השבת מותר להחזירו לתוך התנור (לפי הבנת המג״א), אולי מודה המג״א דבטלה שהייה הראשונה, ואסור להחזירו אם נצטנן, וצ״ע.

ורע״א (שם) הקשה, דכאן (סי׳ רנג ס״ה) אוסר הרמ״א (בשם יש מחמירים) בהבל מועט, דר״ל פחות מיד סולדת בו, וכגירסא שלנו, דלא כגירסת הגר״א (עי׳ לעיל סי׳ ה אות ג). ואילו הרמ״א לעיל (סע׳ א,ב) מתיר בתנור בפחות מיד סולדת בו. ויש לתרץ, דלעיל (שם) מיירי בסמיכה, ובזה א״א לאסור בפחות מיד סולדת בו, דאין לדבר סוף, וכנ״ל (שם). אבל כאן אוסר בפחות מיד סולדת בו בתוך התנור. וכ״נ בירושלמי, וכנ״ל (סי׳ ד אות ו).

ואם כונת הרמ״א (סע׳ א,ב, עיי״ש בלשונו) היא להתיר לגמרי (ולא רק סמיכה) בקדירה על גבה בפחות מיד סולדת בו, עדיין י״ל (כמש״כ

לעיל לתרץ קושית הפמ"ג) דבתוכה, שהיא קולא מחודשת, התירו (לפי היש מחמירים, הנ"ל) בפחות מיד סולדת בו רק להחשיבו כגרוף וקטום, ואסור להניח לכתחילה. והרמ"א לעיל (סע' א,ב) דמיירי בנתן על גבה, התירו אף להניח לכתחילה, ודו"ק.

והנה המג"א (סק"ט) כתב דמשמע בסעיף ה' דאסור לתת בתוכו, כלומר בפחות מיד סולדת בו [כן פי' בהגהות על הפמ"ג (סקע"ג), וכ"נ. ובפמ"ג ומחה"ש (סק"ט) כנראה לא פירשו כן. ומ"מ לפי הגירסא שלנו 'ואם' שהיא בכל הדפוסים, וכמש"כ שם (בהגהות והערות סקמ"ח), מוכח כן]. ולשיטתו הוכרח לפרש שאסור כשנצטנן לגמרי משום הנחה מתחילה שבטלה שהייה ראשונה, דא"א לפרש משום בישול, שהרי אין היד סולדת בו. והגר"א (סקס"ד) שפירש משום בישול, אזיל לשיטתו (סקס"ה), שהגירסא ברמ"א היא 'שאם', ומיירי כשהגיע ליד סולדת בו, שבכה"ג יש איסור בישול (עי' לעיל, סי' ה אות ג).

ויש שמקילים להחזיר דבר יבש ע"ג הבלעך אפילו הושם במקרר בליל שבת. ולכאורה לפי האג"מ הנ"ל, דכשלא הניח ע"ג קרקע, ודעתו להחזיר, מותר לכתחילה. וא"כ אם נפסוק כדעת הגר"א הנ"ל, דבדבר יבש מותר להחזיר אף בנצטנן, יש מקום לקולא זו. אכן נראה, דבאמת קרקע לאו דוקא אלא דיש יותר היסח הדעת בקרקע מבספסל, וא"כ כשהושם במקרר כל הלילה מסתבר דגרע מע"ג קרקע.

ומ"מ יש מקילים כשהיה על האש בכניסת השבת, ע"פ פירוש הר"ן בירושלמי, דא"צ עודה בידו אלא כשסלקו מהאש בע"ש, דהרמ"א (סע' ב) כתב דנהגו כהר"ן. אך עיי"ש שהרמ"א מסיק שטוב להחמיר, דבבבלי לא נראה כן, ותוס' והרמב"ם לא ס"ל כן, וכמש"כ הב"י. ואף בירושלמי יש לפרש בענין אחר, וכמש"כ בשירי הקרבן (שם), שהר"ן גרס אם וכו' (עיי"ש), ולגירסתנו מימרא בפ"ע הוא. וכ"כ בחזו"א (סק"ח), ועכ"פ לכתחילה אין להקל.

[הר"ן (יט. בדפי הרי"ף) הביא דברי הגמ' (מ:) דמותר להניח כנגד המדורה. ואח"כ כתב וז"ל, אבל על גבי האש ממש אסור, אא"כ גרוף או קטום, עכ"ל. ובאגלי טל (סקמ"ח אות ב) הבין שהרן מתיר להניח לכתחילה על גבי כירה גרופה וקטומה. והקשה דהרי זה נגד דברי הגמ' (לח:). ותירץ דהר"ן אזיל לשיטתו (לח:), דאסור רק אם סלק מן האש לפני שבת, וכאן מיירי כשסילק בשבת.

ועדיין צע"ק, דהר"ן השוה ע"ג כירה גרופה וקטומה לכנגד המדורה, ובזה מותר אף אם סילק לפני שבת. ועוד קשה, דהר"ן כתב הדין דמותר להניח ע"ג כירה גרופה וקטומה בשם הרשב"א, והרשב"א אוסר בפירוש. וכן הקשה בהערות לחידושי הר"ן (הע' 237), וצ"ע.

ונראה דעיקר כונת הר"ן היא להוכיח דמותר רק להניח כנגד המדורה ולא ע"ג האש. והוכיח כן מק"ו, דאף החזרה אסורה ע"ג האש כשאינו גרוף וקטום, וק"ו בהנחה. וכשכתב הר"ן 'אבל ע"ג האש ממש אסור אא"כ גרוף או קטום' קאי רק אהחזרה. וכן נראה מראייתו (שם) דאסור להחזירו ע"ג כירה שאינה גרופה וקטומה במצטמק ורק לו. ולעולם הנחה אסורה ע"ג האש, אף בגרוף וקטום, וכדברי הגמ' (לח:) הנ"ל, ודו"ק.]

ב. פלטה חשמלית

ולענין פלטה חשמלית המיוחדת לחמם מאכלים ולא לבשל כלל, לכאורה לא שייך הטעם דנראה כמבשל. וכשיש לה רק מדת חום אחת וא"א לשנות מדת חומה כלל, לא שייך הטעם דשמא יחתה. ולכן נראה דמותר לתת דבר יבש מבושל קר עליה בתחלה בשבת, דהא לא שייכים טעמי האיסור. וכ"כ בהלכות שבת (הע' תקסו). וכן כתב בספר ל"ט מלאכות (עמ' 667).

ובספר הלכות שבת הוכיח דמותר כשלא שייכים טעמי האיסור מהמ"ב (סק"צ) הנ"ל לענין תנור שאפו בו מבעוד יום, דיש מתירין, עי' רמ"א (ס"ה), וטעמם דיש רק חום מועט ואין נראה כמבשל עי"ז. ובשעה"צ (סקפ"ח) כתב וז"ל, דאף שיש חום שהיד סולדת בו, מ"מ אין דרך לבשל בתנור כזה שחומו הוא רק מאפייה דאתמול, עכ"ל. וא"כ ה"ה בפלטה.

והא דאסור ע"ג תנור בית החורף, אף דאין הדרך לבשל עליו, וכמש"כ המ"ב (סקצ"ט), פירש בהלכות שבת שהוא משום שמא יחתה, כיון שאינו גרוף וקטום, וכמש"כ המ"ב (ס"ק קג), אבל מותר בפלטה כיון דא"א לחתות, עכ"ד.

[עוד י"ל, דשם יש אש גדולה, ויתכן חשש נראה כמבשל (אף שהמ"ב כתב רק שמא יחתה, וכנ"ל), משא"כ בפלטה, שחומו מועט ביחס לכירה ותנור רגילים.]

והנה יש מחמירים (ברמ״א שם) כשאפו בו מבעוד יום, ובמ״ב (סקצ״ב) פירש דלא נתנו חכמים דבריהם לשיעורים. אך י״ל דכל זה בתנור, דרגילים לבשל בו, משא״כ בפלטה. ויש לצרף שיטת הר״ן (מ:), שהוא באמת טעם המקילים ברמ״א, וכנ״ל (סי׳ ה אות ב), דאין דרך לבשל מאכל זה במקום ההוא, וק״ו בפלטה שאין הדרך לבשל עליו כלום.

ובספר שמירת שבת כהלכתה (הע׳ עב) החמיר בזה, וצ״ע, דלא שייכים טעמי האיסור, וכנ״ל. ומש״ש בשש״כ (הע״א) דדומה לקש וגבבא, דמותר להחזיר ולא ליתן לכתחילה, יל״ח, דשם יש חשש חיתוי קצת, כדמוכח מדאסור לשהות בתנור, משא״כ בנד״ד.

ובשש״כ (שם) מתיר החזרה ע״ג פלטה, ואוסר רק הנחה בתחילה. והנה אם החזרה אסורה רק משום שמא יחתה ניחא. [וכ״נ בדברי החזו״א (סי׳ לז), וכמש״כ בספר ארחות שבת (סקנ״ט) שלא הזכיר טעם נראה כמבשל כלל. וכ״נ מדברי הגר״א קוטלר, וכנ״ל (סי׳ ד אות ו).]

אבל השש״כ, דרכו לפסוק כדעת המ״ב, דס״ל (סקל״ז) שהחזרה אסורה גם משום נראה כמבשל. [וכ״נ מלשונו (הע׳ עא), ׳וגם לא שייך הטעם של שמא יחתה׳]. וא״כ מהא דמקיל בהחזרה בפלטה, ע״כ לא נראה כמבשל בפלטה, ולמה אסור בהנחה, וצ״ע.

ונראה לתרץ שיטת השש״כ, שהרי לא אסרו החזרה בכירה קטומה לפי הר״ן, משום דלא נראה כמבשל. ומ״מ אסרו הנחה מתחילה משום מיחזי כמבשל. הרי דבקטומה הנחה נראה כמבשל ולא החזרה. וכן הדין בקש ובגבבא לפי השש״כ (שם), וא״כ הוא הדין ע״ג פלטה חשמלית לפי השש״כ. ומ״מ מסברא נראה דכל זה באש רגיל (שמבשלים עליה) שאז אפילו בקטומה (או בקש וגבבא) נראה כמבשל בהנחה. משא״כ בפלטה חשמלית שלא מבשלים עליה כלל.

והנה ז״ל שאלת ר״ש איידר (המובא באג״מ ח״ד סי׳ עד אות לה), האם מותר לחמם קדרה שנתבשלה, והיא חמה קצת, ע״ג מכשירים שנועדו לחימום ולא לבישול, כפלטה חשמלית (האט פלייט והאט טריי) ... גם בלא הפסק קדרה, דאין דרך בישול בכך, עכ״ל.

וז״ל תשובת האג״מ (שם), על פלטה חשמלית אם א״א להתבשל שם אז מותר להעמיד קדרה חמה אם אין שם אלא מדה אחת להחום. ואם יש שתי מדות אסור, עכ״ל.

ועפ״ז כתבו בפסקי תשובות (סי׳ רנג סקט״ז) ובספר הלכות שבת במטבח (עמ׳ 43) שהאג״מ מתיר הנחה לכתחילה על גבי פלטה שיש בה מדת חום אחת. וכן שמעתי מר״ש איידר שהאג״מ מקיל בזה. ואע״פ שהאג״מ מתיר בזה רק ׳אם א״א להתבשל שם׳, כונתו היתה להשיב על השאלה, ומותר כל ׳דאין דרך בישול בכך׳. ולפ״ז האג״מ מקיל יותר מהשש״כ.

אך מלשון האג״מ ׳אי אפשר׳ לא משמע כן. ולגבי ׳סטים טייבל׳ כתב שם, וז״ל, שאפשר להתבשל שם, וא״כ הוא ממילא דרך בישול, עכ״ל. ומשמע שאוסר בפלטה אם אפשר לבשל עליה, אף אם אין הדרך לבשל שם. וכן שמעתי מבנו הג״ר ראובן פיינשטיין שליט״א, שאביו אוסר אפילו החזרה על גבי פלטה אם אינה מכוסה מטעם נראה כמבשל. ולפ״ז האג״מ מחמיר יותר מהשש״כ.

ומ״מ קשה קצת, דאם אוכל אינו יכול להגיע לשיעור יד סולדת בו בפלטה, מותר להניח לפי המ״ב (סקצ״ג), כיון דלא חיישינן לחיתוי. וא״כ מותר אף אם יש ב׳ מידות חום. ואם אפשר להגיע לשיעור שהיד סולדת בו בפלטה, ממילא אפשר לבשל בו מים. וא״כ צ״ב מהי המציאות של פלטה שא״א לבשל עליה שהתיר האג״מ להניח עליה ׳אם אין שם אלא מדה אחת להחום׳.

ואולי כונת האג״מ היא, דמיקרי דרך בישול אם אפשר לבשל מאכל זה בפלטה זו, אף דאין רגילין לעשות כן. אבל מותר להניח על הפלטה אם א״א לבשל מאכל זה שם, אף דאפשר לבשל מים שם, דהרי ע״כ מיירי בפלטה שאפשר לחמם עד לשיעור שהיד סולדת בו. וכ״נ קצת מלשון האג״מ ׳אפשר להתבשל שם׳, כלומר מאכל זה.

ויסוד לחילוק זה נמצא בשיטת הר״ן לענין פנאדי״ש (כנ״ל, סי׳ ה אות ב), דס״ל דכאשר אין דרכו לבשל מאכל זה לא נראה כמבשל, אף שהדרך לבשל מאכל אחר שם. ולפי האג״מ אסור להניח שם כל שאפשר לבשל מאכל זה שם.

ומ״מ נראה מלשון הר״ן דמותר להניח כל שאין דרכו בכך, וא״צ שיהיה ׳אי אפשר להתבשל׳. וז״ל, דמה שאין דרכו לאפות על גבי כירה וכו׳ שהדבר מוכיח שאינו נעשה אלא בשביל שיתחמם, עכ״ל. וכן היא לשיטת הרשב״א (שהביא הר״ן שם) דמותר אם אין דרכו לבשל שום מאכל על

גבי הפלטה. והשש"כ (פ"א סכ"ה) אוסר להניח על גבי פלטה כאשר 'אין רגילים לבשל עליה'. ואולי כונתו לאסור רק כשיש אלו שמבשלים עליה, וכמש"כ במכתבו (מובא לעיל, עמ' ז) 'מצאנו אצל ספרדים שרגילים לבשל בכה"ג'. [וצ"ע במש"כ שם לגבי קראקפאט, דכו"ע מבשלים בקראקפאט.]

ולפ"ז במדינתנו, שכמדומה אין הדרך לבשל על פלטה כלל וכלל, לא נראה כמבשל. ולכן מותר להניח עליה מאכל יבש קר שהוציא מן המקרר. וכן נראה לדינא, בצירוף שיטת הר"ן, וכנ"ל.

ג. שעון שבת

ולענין תנור חשמלי שידלק ע"י שעון שבת, החזו"א (סי' לח סק"ב) אוסר בין בשהייה בין בהחזרה משום דשמא יחתה, כלומר שישנה מדת חומו, אח"כ כשנדלק. ואזיל לשיטתו שאין מעשה ההחזרה אסור, אלא המצב של קדירה שנצטננה ע"ג האש, אף אם הוחזר ע"י קוף, והוה"נ בהוחזר כשאין התנור פועל, וכן הדין בשהייה, עכ"ד.

אבל יש מקילים עכ"פ בשהייה, ויש מקילים אפילו בהחזרה. וכן מבואר בספר הלכות שבת (הע' תרנז, תרס).

והנה הרמ"א (ס"ה) כתב שמותר לגוי להושיב קדירה אצל תנור בית החורף או עליו, ומבערת השפחה אח"כ התנור ההוא (דהכל חולים אצל הצינה), וע"י זה הקדירות (שנצטננו לגמרי) חוזרים ונרתחים. אבל ע"י ישראל אסור בכה"ג. ובמג"א (סקמ"א) באר הדין מצד איסור בישול, דע"י נכרי מותר, דעיקר כונתו לחמם את הבית, ואף דפסיק רישי' שיתחמם התבשיל, אין איסור אמירה לנכרי בפ"ר. ואסור לישראל להניח את הקדירה ע"ג התנור לפני שהסיקו הנכרי, דהוי כאחד נותן את הקדירה ואחד נותן את האור, דהראשון פטור אבל אסור.

ובחזו"א (סי' לז סקכ"א) הקשה, איך מותר ע"י גוי, הלא נוצר מצב של החזרה כשתדליק השפחה את התנור. ותירץ דאין דרך לבשל ע"ג תנור כזה שפתוח מן הצד, וא"כ דומה לנותן כנגד המדורה, או ע"ג מיחם, או כסומך. וכן נראה מהמ"ב (סקצ"ה) ושעה"צ (סקצ"ו) דעל התנור אינו כעל האש. ולפי"ז מובן מש"כ במ"ב (ס"ק קג) דמדינא מותר לישראל

ליתן קדירה חמה ע"ג התנור גם לאחר שהוסק, אלא שנהגו להחמיר ליתן קודם היסק.

אך עיי"ש ברמ"א שסיים וז"ל, אבל אם הקדירות עדיין חמין מותר להעמידן אצל תנור בית החורף ... [כדין] סמיכה בכירה שאינה גרופה וקטומה, עכ"ל. ומוכח שאסור להעמידן על התנור, אף שאין איסור בישול, ומזה נראה דאינו כנותן כנגד המדורה, ודלא כדברי החזו"א הנ"ל. לכ"נ כתירוץ הראשון בחזו"א (שם) וז"ל, וע"כ צ"ל דחשבו הדבר לשהייה מע"ש ולא כחזרה, כיון שבשעת הנחה התנור צונן, עכ"ל. עוד י"ל דכשאין אש אינו בכלל גזירת חז"ל כלל, אף שידלק ע"י נכרי או שעון אח"כ, וכן נראה מדברי הגרמ"פ (ספר הלכות שבת שם).

ולכאורה לפי"ז מותר להחזיר מאכל יבש קר כשידלק אח"כ ע"י שעון שבת, וכהגרמ"פ. אמנם הוא אסר מטעם אחר, דאין להשתמש בשעון שבת כלל (אג"מ ח"ד סי' ס), אך נראה דלא נהגו כן. והחזו"א אסר לפי תירוצו השני הנ"ל, אבל לפי תירוצו הראשון לכאורה מותר וכנ"ל, דאף דמצב של קדירה שנצטננה ע"ג אש אסור, וכנ"ל, זהו רק כשאש דולק בשעה שהוחזר.

ולפי"ז מוכח כמנהג העולם שבמ"ב (סקק"ג), דמותר אף ע"י ישראל קודם היסק כשאין חשש בישול, דדינו כשהייה, וכדעת החזו"א. ואין איסור שהייה בהגיע לכמאכל בן דרוסאי לחנניה, ולרבנן במבושל כל צרכו ומצטמק ורע לו. ולדעת הגרמ"פ, 'דלא חשיב שהייה כשאין שם אש' (ס' הלכות שבת, שם), מותר גם לפי רבנן אפילו במצטמק ויפה לו.

ולדברי שניהם (החזו"א והאג"מ) לא אסרו משום שמא יחתה או משום נראה כמבשל אם מחזיר כשאין שם אש. והרמ"א, שהתיר רק בסמיכה, מיירי כשכבר הוסק התנור. ולעיל, שאסר ע"י ישראל קודם היסק, היינו משום איסור בישול, וכמש"כ המ"ב (סק"ק), דמיירי בנצטנן. וכן מוכח במקור הדין בתרוה"ד המובא בב"י, שדן על איסור בישול, ולא על איסור החזרה.

וכל הנ"ל הוא דלא כדברי המג"א (סקמ"ג) שכתב שהרמ"א אוסר להניח קודם היסק, שמא יחתה בגחלים אח"כ. ולפי דבריו אינו מובן הא דהתיר הרמ"א ע"י נכרי, וכנ"ל. והוסיף המג"א וז"ל, ומיהו העולם נוהגין היתר בזה. ועמ"ש ס"ג דיש להם על מה שיסמוכו, עכ"ל. ובמחה"ש (שם)

פירש דכונת המג"א לדבריו (סקל"א), דגג התנור כקדירה ריקנית שמותר להחזיר עליה, ולפי הר"ן אף להניח עליה לכתחילה כשסילקה בשבת, וכנ"ל (אות א).

והקשה במחה"ש, דשם מצריך המג"א עץ או דף על התנור להכירא, וכאן אין עץ או דף. ותירץ דקודם היסק הקילו. וזה צ"ב, דאם יש איסור החזרה כשיווצר מצב של קדירה ע"ג האש אח"כ, מסתבר דדינו שוה להחזרה ע"ג האש, דלא מצינו שני איסורים. וא"כ קשה איך נהגו להחזיר ע"ג התנור בלי דף או עץ לפני היסק התנור. ואם אין איסור החזרה כלל לפני שהוסק התנור, אין צריך לדברי המג"א (ס"ג סקל"א), וצ"ע.

וי"ל דבמג"א (סקל"א) כתב דלפי הרמ"א (ס"ה) צריך היכירא, בנוסף על המעזיבה המפסיק בין האש להקדירה שע"ג התנור. ופירש (סקמ"ג) דבלי היכר חשש הרמ"א שמא יחתה. אבל י"א (סקל"א) דכשיש מעזיבה אין צריך היכר נוסף להניח ע"ג התנור. ועל זה סמכו העולם קודם היסק. והיינו משום דס"ל דמהני המעזיבה לענין נראה כמבשל, דאין הדרך לבשל שם. ולענין שמא יחתה, בעינן היכירא. אבל קודם היסק, אף דע"ג אסור משום נראה כמבשל (דהרי אסרו בא' נותן הקדירה וא' נותן האש), מ"מ לא חיישינן לחיתוי אלא בשעה שמניח, ולא כשיוסק אח"כ, ולכן מותר ע"ג מעזיבה, ודו"ק.

ולפ"ז אסור להניח ע"ג תנור חשמלי שיידלק משום דנראה כמבשל, שהרי אסור בלי מעזיבה מה"ט, אף אם יידלק האש רק לאחר זמן. ולדעת הגרמ"פ ע"כ דאין חשש נראה כמבשל כשאין שם אש בשעה שמניח. ולדעת החזו"א כל החזרה אסורה רק משום שמא יחתה, וכנ"ל (אות ב), ואולי גם בהנחה ס"ל כן. ואף שאסרו (הגרמ"פ והחזו"א) בשעון שבת מטעמים אחרים, וכנ"ל, מ"מ יש צד להקל. ולפי המג"א אסור משום נראה כמבשל. וצ"ע לדינא.

והנה החזו"א (שם) אוסר אף לפי תירוצו הראשון, דשעון שבת גרע מנכרי, דבנכרי מחוסר מעשה של בן בחירה, משא"כ כשסוף החום לבא מעצמו ע"י השעון, דנראה דחשיב כמשהה, כל' כמחזיר ע"ג האש. וצ"ב, דאם מדובר באיסור מעשה, שפיר יל"ח כן. אבל מכיון שהאיסור הוא המצב של קדירה ע"ג האש, ואף אם העמיד הנכרי או הקוף חייב להסירו

וכמש״ש, ואעפ״כ מותר כשהניחו לפני ההיסק דע״י נכרי, א״כ נראה דמותר גם אם האש יודלק ע״י שעון.

ואם האש החשמלי מכוסה, לפי מש״כ לעיל (סי׳ ב אות ב) דאין חשש חיתוי, נראה דמותר אפילו לפי החזו״א. אבל אם יש איסור משום נראה כמבשל (וכמה שכתבנו לפי המג״א), עדיין אסור, דבהנחה לכתחילה נראה כמבשל אף בקטומה. ויש עוד נ״מ מכל הנ״ל בהפסקת חשמל, דדומה לשעון שבת כאשר שוב נדלק החשמל.

הפמ״ג (א״א סס״ק מ״א) הקשה על המנהג להשאיר מים ע״ג האש כשהוחם מבעוד יום, וז״ל, ומה בכך, הא בלילה נתקררו המים, ואיך שרי שהייה בשבת [כשהשפחה מבערת את התנור] בכירה שאין גרופה. ואפשר דסומכין כה״ג על גדולי הפוסקים המתירים בלח, דאין בישול אחר בישול, עכ״ל.

וקשר זה בין גזירה שמא יחתה לאיסור בישול צ״ע, דבפרי חי קיי״ל (סי׳ רנד ס״ד, ע״פ תוס׳ מח. ד״ה בזיתים) דאין איסור שהייה, דל״ג שמא יחתה כיון דנאכלין טפי כמו שהן חיין מתבשיל שנתבשל כמאכל בן דרוסאי. ומ״מ קיי״ל (שעה״צ סי׳ שיח ס״ק קיד) דהמבשל פרי חי חייב. ולהרמב״ם והשו״ע (שם ס״ד) הדין כן במאכל שנתבשל כמאב״ד, לחנניה. הרי שלא גזרו שמא יחתה אף אם יש איסור בישול.

א״כ מסתבר שבמקום שגזרו, אסור אף אם אין איסור בישול. ובמים, אם גזרו כשנצטננו, כצוננים מעיקרא, וכמש״כ המג״א (סי׳ רנד סקכ״ו), דגרע מפרי חי, נימא כן אף לפי הפוסקים הסוברים דאין בישול אחר בישול בדבר לח, וצ״ע.

ובחזו״א (סקכ״ז) כתב דלא גזרו איסור שהייה בתבשיל שנצטנן, אף לשיטה דיש בישול אחר בישול בדבר לח. ואם הדין כן אף במים ניחא קושיית הפמ״ג. ובשש״כ (ס״מ) אסר במים שנצטננו.

ולפי השש״כ יש לתרץ קושית הפמ״ג, דמכיון שכאשר שהה מע״ש היה חם, לא גזרו אע״פ שבאמצע הלילה התקרר. ונ״מ גם להפסקת חשמל, דאם שוב נדלק החשמל וחזרו ונתחממו המים, המים מותרים. וגם לפי החזו״א מותר אם מים נידונים כתבשיל, וכנ״ל, אם דינו כשהייה. ואם דינו כהחזרה אסור להחזו״א שמא יחתה, וכנ״ל. אבל מותר בדוד מים, כיון שא״א לשנות מידת חומו.

סימן ח

דין המאכל בדיעבד

א. שהה באיסור

גרסינן (לח.), שכח קדירה ע"ג כירה ובשלה בשבת וכו', המבשל בשבת בשוגג יאכל, במזיד לא יאכל. ולא שנא וכו', לאיסורא. מבשל הוא דלא אתי לאיערומי, בשוגג יאכל. אבל האי דאתי לאיערומי, בשוגג נמי לא יאכל, וכו'. איבעיא להו, עבר ושהה מאי, מי קנסוהו רבנן או לא, וכו', ע"כ.

ופסק בשו"ע [(סי' רנג ס"א) ע"פ הרי"ף והרמב"ם, והם פסקו כרבנן דלא כחנניה] וז"ל, ואם שכח ושהה אם הוא תבשיל שבישל כל צרכו מותר אפילו הוא מצטמק ויפה לו, ואם לא בישל כ"צ אסור עד מוצ"ש. ואם עבר ושהה אסור בשניהם, עכ"ל.

ושיטת הרי"ף והרמב"ם והשו"ע הנ"ל צ"ב, דמכיון שאסור להשהות לכתחילה אף במבושל כ"צ כל שמוי"ל, למה מותר בשכח ושהה בדיעבד במבושל כ"צ ואסור באינו מבושל כ"צ. וגם קשה קו' הטור, דלמה מחלק הרמב"ם בין עבר ושהה לשכח, הא בגמרא מייתי ראיה מעבר ושהה לשכח.

ושמעתי בשם מו"ר הגרי"ד, זצ"ל, דהרמב"ם ושו"ע אזלי לשיטתם, דס"ל דיש בישול אחר בישול במאכל שנתבשל כמאכל בן דרוסאי (פ"ט ה"ג, סי' שיח ס"ד). וא"כ י"ל דגדר גזירת חז"ל (שאסרו בדיעבד אם השהה מאכל שאינו מבושל כ"צ) הוא דנידון כאילו בישלו בשבת,

דקיי"ל דאסור אף לאחרים אפילו בשוגג [לפי הרמב"ם (פ"ו הכ"ג) והשו"ע (סי' שיח ס"א) שפסקו כרבי יהודה]. אבל כשכבר נתבשל כל צרכו, א"א לומר שכאילו עבר על איסור בישול בשבת. וזוהי האבעיא השני' בגמ' (לח.), אם יש גזירה בפ"ע בדיעבד בשכח (וכקנס מיוחד), או רק בעבר במזיד.

ופסקו הרמב"ם והשו"ע לקולא, דקנסו רק בעבר ולא בשכח, דבקנס זה המיוחד שפיר יש לחלק ביניהם. ובגמ' הביאו ראי' מעבר לשכח רק באבעיא הראשונה, דמיירי בלא נתבשל כל צרכו וכמש"כ הב"י, דגדר הגזירה הוא דנידון כאילו בשלו הישראל בשבת, ובזה (בנתבשל רק כמאב"ד ואינו מבושל כ"צ) באמת דינם (בין עבר בין שכח) שוה לאיסור, וכפסק הרמב"ם (פ"ו), עכ"ד.

והנה בתוס' (ד"ה עבר) פירשו כשיטת הרי"ף, דהאיבעיא הב' היא בשכח ושהה מאכל שמבושל כל צרכו. והקשו, וז"ל, ומיהו לשון עבר ושהה משמע במזיד, עכ"ל. ולגירסת הרי"ף, עבר ושכח, ע"כ אינו מזיד. אבל עדיין צ"ע, דבב' האיבעיות הרי שכח, וההבדל ביניהם הוא דבאיבעיא הא' לא נתבשל כל צרכו, ובאיבעיא הב' נתבשל כל צרכו. ולמה נקט 'שכח ובשל' באיבעיא הא', ובאיבעיא הב' נקט 'עבר ושכח'.

ולדברי מו"ר הגרי"ד זצ"ל ניחא, דבאיבעיא הא' דנים על החפצא כאילו מבושל בשבת לאסור בדיעבד (וכדעת רבי יהודה), אף לאחרים בשוגג, וה"ה בשכח. ולכן נקטו 'שכח ובשל', אף דשהה מע"ש, דהחמירו להחשיבו כמבשל בשבת בשוגג. אבל באיבעיא הב' (שכבר נתבשל כל צרכו לפני שבת), א"א להחשיבו כמבשל בשבת, ודנו על קנס מיוחד על הגברא. ולכן נקטו לשון 'עבר ושכח', ו'עבר' לא ר"ל מזיד אלא קנס מיוחד על הגברא.

ובפמ"ג (א"א סקי"א) דייק מלשון הרמב"ם (פ"ג ה"ט, לגבי מאכל שלא נתבשל כ"צ), דאם עבר ושהה אסור במוצ"ש בכדי שיעשו, משא"כ בשכח, וכ"כ במרכבת המשנה (שם). וצ"ב. וי"ל דבשכח ולא נתבשל כל צרכו, נידון כמעשה שבת, וכפירוש מו"ר הגרי"ד (הנ"ל). ובזה קיי"ל (עי' ברמב"ם פ"ו הכ"ג) דמותר במוצ"ש מיד. אבל מלשון האיבעיא הב' ('עבר ושכח מהו'), שנפשטה לקולא, משמע שאם עבר והזיד בודאי יש קנס מיוחד על הגברא, וכנ"ל. ובזה אסור במוצ"ש בכדי שיעשו, דאיתא

בברייתא (יח:), לא ימלא נחתום חבית של מים ויניח לתוך התנור ע״ש עם חשיכה [שמא יחתה בגחלים], ואם עשה כן, למוצאי שבת אסורין בכדי שיעשה, ע״כ. וגם שם מיירי רק במזיד (עי׳ ברמב״ם שם הי״ב).

ובמג״א (סקי״א) תלה דין איסור בדיעבד לאחרים במחלוקת ר״מ ור״י. וצ״ע דכאן גזירה מיוחדת היא, ובמחצית השקל (שם) נדחק בזה. אכן לפירוש מו״ר הגרי״ד ניחא, דאמנם טעם האיסור הוא משום גזירה, אבל גדר הגזירה היא דנחשב כאילו נתבשל בשבת. ושפיר תלה המג״א דין איסור בדיעבד לאחרים במחלוקת ר״מ ור״י.

ב. החזיר באיסור

כתב בהג״א (סי׳ ב) וז״ל, צ״ע אם החזיר באיסור בשוגג אם מותר באכילה או לא, דדלמא דוקא שכח קדירה ובשלה שנתקן המאכל בשבת באיסור, אבל בהחזרה כבר היה ראוי לאכילה ואינו נהנה כ״כ. ואע״ג דאם נכרי עשה לצורך ישראל מותר כה״ג, שאין הישראל נהנה ממנו כ״כ, מ״מ כשישראל בעצמו עשה איסור אפשר דקנסוהו רבנן, עכ״ל. וההגמ״ר אוסר בעבר והחזיר, כל שמצטמק ויפה לו.

ובחזו״א (סקכ״ד) נסתפק אם ההג״א מיירי במצטמק ויפה לו או במצטמק ורע לו, ומסיק לדינא דמיירי במוי״ל. וכ״כ הרמ״א (שם) וז״ל, ואם החזירה גוי בשבת דינו כשכח ושהה, ואם החזירו ישראל דינו כעבר ושהה, ואם מור״ל מותר, שהרי לא נהנה מן האיסור, עכ״ל. והוסיף החזו״א וז״ל, ומיהו לדעת הר״מ דבשהה בשוגג תבשיל שנתבשל כל צרכו שרי אפי׳ מצטמק ויפה לו, אין לנו מקור לאסור את המוחזר המבושל כל צרכו ומוי״ל. ואמנם אחרי שה[הגהות] מרדכי אסר והעתיקו הרמ״א כבר איכא הוראה לאיסור, עכ״ל.

ובאמת הוראה זו צע״ג, דאף דבהגמ״ר כ״כ, הלא ההגמ״ר אזיל לשיטתו (מובא במג״א סקי״ד), דגם בשהייה אסור במבושל כל צרכו ומצטמק ויפה לו. אבל השו״ע פסק כהרמב״ם שמתיר, והרמ״א לא חלק עליו בזה, ואיך אסר בהחזרה. ובמ״ב (סקל״ה) באר דהרמ״א מחמיר בהחזרה טפי משהייה משום דקעבד מעשה, כלומר דמה״ט פסק כדעת ההגמ״ר בהחזרה ולא בשהייה, עי׳ מג״א (שם).

וקשה, דבגמ׳ (לז.) נאמרה סברא זו דקעבד מעשה רק בבישול, ולא בהחזרה. ואדרבה, בחזו״א (שם) צדד דכיון שהחזרה חמורה משהייה לבני אדם, ולא אתי לאערומי, לא גזרו בה בדיעבד כלל. ואף לפי ההג״א, דס״ל דגזרו, וכנ״ל, ובחזו״א נסתפק אם מיירי במצטמק ויפה לו או במצטמק ורע לו, וכנ״ל, באמת נראה דמיירי בלא נתבשל כל צרכו, דההג״א מסתמא ס״ל כהרא״ש (סי׳ א,יא), דקיי״ל כחנניה, ושאין בישול אחר בישול דכמאכל בן דרוסאי.

וזה שכתב ההג״א שם ׳דאינו נהנה כ״כ׳, דבשהייה ע״כ מיירי בלא הגיע לכמאכל בן דרוסאי, דאל״כ מותר לכתחילה. ובהחזרה הרי לא נהנה כ״כ, דע״כ הגיע לכמאב״ד, דאל״כ אסור משום בישול. וא״כ אף בהג״א אין מקור לאסור בדיעבד במבושל כל צרכו ומצטמק ויפה לו. וההגמ״ר שאסר אזיל לשיטתו בשהייה, ולא קיי״ל כן, ודברי הרמ״א צ״ע.

ובהא דמקיל הרמ״א בדיעבד ע״י נכרי, וכההג״א הנ״ל, כתב הגר״א (סקכ״ה), דמזיד דגוי כשוגג דישראל, כדמוכח מהא דמותר לו בשניהם במוצ״ש. וצ״ע, דאם השוואה זו נכונה, ע״כ החזרת נכרי במזיד כהחזרת ישראל בשוגג, והרמ״א בעצמו אסר החזרת ישראל בשוגג. וכתב דבהחזיר גוי דינו כשכח ושהה, דמותר בנתבשל כל צרכו ומצטמק ויפה לו.

ויותר נראה דכיון דההג״א נסתפק אף ע״י ישראל כיון שלא נהנה כ״כ, התיר עכ״פ בנכרי. וכן נראה במג״א (סקי״ג) שכתב ׳שלא נהנה כל כך, עי׳ סי׳ רעו׳. ושם מיירי שנכרי הדליק נר במקום שכבר היה נר אחר. ולא מצינו היתר זה מפורש בעבר ישראל על איסור מלאכה. וכן בהחזרה יש לחלק בין עשה ישראל לעשה נכרי.

ובבה״ל (ד״ה ואם) כנראה פירש דברי הגר״א ע״פ מש״כ במ״ב (סקל״ה), דיש בו מעשה חמיר טפי. וס״ל דמזיד דנכרי בהחזרה, דינו כשוגג דישראל בשהייה, דהרי הישראל לא עשה מעשה. אבל במקורו של הגר״א (דאסור בשבת ומותר במוצ״ש), השוו אותה פעולה שנעשית ע״י ישראל בשוגג להא דנעשית ע״י גוי במזיד, וצ״ע.

ג. הוחם באיסור ומצטמק ורע לו

כתב החזו״א (שם) דאם מחזיר דבר יבש קר שמצטמק ורע לו, אסור לאכלו כי נהנה מן החימום. וכן נראה בב״י (שהוא מקור הרמ״א שמתיר במור״ל),

שכתב 'דאין שום הנאה בחזרה זו דהא מור"ל'. ואם המאכל היה קר, הרי יש הנאת חימום.

והנה הרמ"א (שם) אוסר כשמחמם הגוי לצורך ישראל אף כשנצטנן אח"כ. ובחזו"א (סקכ"ז) כתב דמיירי גם במור"ל, ובאר דהרי נהנה מעצם החימום, וכמש"כ השו"ע (סי' רנז ס"א) לענין הטמנה. ולפ"ז הרמ"א (סי' רנג ס"א) שמתיר במור"ל ע"כ מיירי בלא נצטנן עדיין בשעה שהחזירו באיסור. וצ"ע, דלולא החזרתו היה מצטנן, וכמש"ש, וא"כ למה נחשב כלא נהנה, ודומה להטמנת דבר חם בשבת בדבר המוסיף הבל, דאסור (שעה"צ סי' רנז סק"ו).

והחזו"א (שם) פירש דלא מינכר שבחא, ולכן אע"פ שהיה מתקרר לולא החזרתו, אין איסור בדיעבד, וגם בהטמנה אין איסור בדיעבד. ובשעה"צ (שם) אסר ע"פ רע"א שכתב דבמטמין בשבת בדבר המוסיף הבל אף בעומד בחמימותו אסור, שהרי המג"א (שם סק"ו) מתיר בדיעבד רק במטמין בשבת בדבר שאינו מוסיף הבל.

ולפי החזו"א, דע"כ חולק ארע"א, נראה דהמג"א כ"כ משום איסור בישול, דבשו"ע (ס"ב) כתב אפילו תבשיל שנתבשל כל צורכו וכו', ומשמע דלעיל (ס"א) לא נתבשל כל צורכו. ורק בזה אסור בדיעבד בהטמין בשבת בדבר המוסיף הבל, דעבר על איסור בישול (עי' סי' שיח ס"א). אבל בעבר על איסור הטמנה, או החזרה, אין איסור בדיעבד בעומד בחממימותו, דלא מינכר שבחא.

ונראה עוד, דהמג"א אזיל לשיטתו (שם סקי"ג, וכדברי הפמ"ג שם), דכשמטמין בדבר שאינו מוסיף הבל אינו מבשל, וכיסוי גורם למאכל להתבשל (ס"ד) רק כשיש אש מתחתיו, וכשו"ע (ס"ח), דע"י האש מוסיף הבל. ובבה"ל (ד"ה גורם) פסק כהבית מאיר, דדבר שאינו מוסיף הבל גורם בישול, דכל שעה שמאריך הרתיחה מתבשל יותר. ולפ"ז כשהביא במ"ב (סק"ח) את דברי המג"א (סק"ו הנ"ל), ע"כ פירש במבושל כל צורכו, דאל"כ אסור בדיעבד משום בישול, גם באינו מוסיף הבל. וא"כ מוכח דבמוסיף הבל אסור בדיעבד משום איסור הטמנה, אף דעומד בחמימותו, וכרע"א ושעה"צ הנ"ל.

אבל מכיון שכל דיוקו של רע"א הוא מלשון המג"א, יותר נראה כמו שכתבנו, שהמג"א אזיל לשיטתו (סקי"ג), דאין איסור בישול באינו

מוסיף הבל, ומיירי בלא נתבשל כל צורכו. ולעולם אין שום איסור בדיעבד כשעבר על איסור הטמנה, או החזרה, כשעומד בחמימותו, ודלא כדעת רע"א, וניחא שיטת החזו"א.

ד. הוחם באיסור ונצטנן

והנה יש לדחות עיקר דין החזו"א (ע"פ הרמ"א, הנ"ל אות ב), דבהחזיר הגוי באיסור אסור אף כשנצטנן. דהרי במקור הדין ברשב"א המובא בב"י ובמג"א (סקל"ז) מבואר שקנסוהו אף לאחר שנצטנן מפני שצוה לגוי להבעיר, והבערה אסורה מדאורייתא. אבל כשהגוי רק החזיר ולא הבעיר, מותר לאחר שנצטנן. ולפי מש"כ לעיל (שם) לדעת הלבוש עכצ"ל כן, כיון דמיירי כאן כשאינו ע"ג כירה ממש, ואין איסור החזרה. ובאמת יש להקשות על לשון הרמ"א, דהיה לו להזכיר דמיירי שאמר לגוי להבעיר, וכמש"כ הרשב"א, במקום לסתום שאמר לגוי להחם הקדירה, וצ"ע.

וכתב המג"א (סקל"ז) דאסר הרמ"א בדיעבד באמר לגוי להחם דבר לח צונן, אף שנצטנן אח"כ, דומיא דהרשב"א שאסר בנצטנן כשאמר לגוי להדליק אש.

וז"ל המג"א, דס"ל דלדידן דס"ל דאסור לחממו מדאורייתא אסור לומר ג"כ לעכו"ם, ואם עשה כן אסור אפילו בדיעבד ... ומיהו י"ל דאם לא חממו העכו"ם ע"ג האש או הכירה ממש, דיש להקל [בדיעבד דלא כרמ"א, כן נראה בכוונתו], מאחר שגדולי הפוסקים מתירין אפילו לישראל לעשותו [דס"ל אין בישול אחר בישול בדבר לח, ולפ"ז לכאורה גם אם חממו ישראל מותר] וכו' [והמרדכי, סי' שכג כתב] דאם צוה לעכו"ם לעשות לו מלאכה דרבנן אין אוסרין התבשיל, עכ"ל.

והנה בחזו"א (שם) אוסר בדיעבד בעבר והחזיר דבר יבש קר, אף לאחר שנצטנן, ע"פ הרשב"א. אבל במג"א מוכח, דרק כשנעשה מלאכה דאורייתא ע"י הנכרי קנסו בנצטנן להרשב"א. ולכן הזכיר המג"א דבישול אחר בישול בדבר לח אסור להרמ"א מדאורייתא, דאם היה אסור מדרבנן היה מותר בדיעבד עכ"פ בנצטנן, ולהמרדכי אף בעודו חם. הרי מוכח מדברי המג"א דלא קנסוהו בנצטנן אח"כ אא"כ הנכרי עשה מלאכה דאורייתא, ובהחזיר דבר יבש נראה דמותר כשנצטנן, ודלא כהחזו"א.

ולכאורה אף אם ישראל שהה או החזיר באיסור, מותר לאוכלו כשנצטנן, שהרי לא נהנה כלל, וקנסו רק באמר לנכרי לעשות איסור דאורייתא.

מאידך, במחה"ש (שם) כתב ע"פ המרדכי והמג"א, דכיון דאיסור החזרה דרבנן, מותר בדיעבד גם בעודו חם. וצ"ע, דבשהייה יש גזירה מיוחדת בדיעבד, נוסף על איסור מעשה שבת בכל המלאכות, וכגמ' (לח.), וכנ"ל (אות א). ואם החזרה בכלל גזירה זו וכהרמ"א (עי' לעיל אות ב), ע"כ אסור בדיעבד אף שנעשה רק איסור דרבנן, ולא דמי לאיסור בישול או הבערה דרבנן שדנו בהם המג"א והמרדכי [ובפרט לפי מש"כ השעה"צ (סקצ"ו) שלדעת הפמ"ג והגר"א אסור בעודו חם כשעשה מלאכה דרבנן אף לפי המרדכי].

והנה המג"א צדד להקל בדיעבד כשהנכרי חימם דבר לח, דיש גדולי הפוסקים המתירים לישראל לחממו. ואזיל לשיטתו, דס"ל (סי' שכג סקי"א), דכל שיש מתירין לכתחילה, יש להקל בדיעבד, ומובא במ"ב (סי' שיח סק"ב). ולכאורה לפ"ז אף אם ישראל חימם דבר לח, מותר לאוכלו.

ויש לעיין במחלוקת בדיני שהייה החזרה ונתינה לכתחילה, דיש גזירה מיוחדת, וכנ"ל, האם יש להקל בדיעבד כשיש מחלוקת לכתחילה, וככל המחלוקות הנ"ל, וצ"ע. שו"ר בבה"ל (סוף ס"א ד"ה ואם) שמותר בדיעבד כאשר יש מחלוקת בהחזרה, וכעין שכתב במג"א (סי' רנג סקי"ד).

וצ"ע, דבמג"א שם מיירי במחלוקת בענין איסור בדיעבד, ולא כתב שיש לסמוך על המקילים כשיש מחלוקת בזה. וכן בדין, שהרי נחלקו לענין בדיעבד. ויש ראיה לזה שהרי ההג"א צדד שמותר בהחזיר בשוגג, ולא קיי"ל כן.

ומש"כ המג"א אינו ענין למחלוקת הפוסקים אם מותר לשהות לכתחילה, דשם יש לעיין אם קיי"ל דמותר בדיעבד, כמו באיסור מעשה שבת. ובבה"ל מיקל, אבל לכאורה אין שום ראיה לדברי הבה"ל מדברי המג"א.

ובחזו"א (סקכ"ז) אסר בדיעבד בהחזיר גוי, משום דפסק דהאיסור מוטל על הישראל שלא הסירו, שמא יחתה בגחלים, וכנ"ל (אות ב). ולכאורה קשה, דלדעת הר"ן דהחזרה אסורה משום נראה כמבשל, לא עבר הישראל על האיסור. ובספר ארחות שבת (סקנ"ט) כתב שהחזו"א פסק דלא כדעת הר"ן, וכנ"ל (סי' ז אות ב). אך קשה, דלענין בדיעבד

סומכין על המקילין, והרי כאן מקיל הר"ן. ואולי החזו"א חולק על הבה"ל, וס"ל דסומכים בדיעבד על המקילים רק באיסור מעשה שבת, ולא באיסור המיוחד דשהייה והחזרה.

אכן נראה, דמצינו איסור מיוחד בדיעבד רק אם עבר על הגזירה שמא יחתה בגחלים. וכ"ה בגמרא (לח.) בשהייה, ובהחזרה קיי"ל דאסור בדיעבד מה"ט. אבל לפי המ"ד דהחזרה אסורה משום נראה כמבשל, נראה דאסור בדיעבד רק משום מעשה שבת, וא"כ מותר בדיעבד באופן שיש מחלוקת. וכ"נ לדינא באיסור הנחה לכתחילה ע"ג כירה גרופה וקטומה, לפי מש"כ לעיל (סי' ב אות ב) דאסור רק משום נראה כמבשל.

והנה הרמ"א (סי' רנג ס"א) דן באיסור בדיעבד אם החזיר בשוגג או במזיד (כנ"ל, אות ב). ובשו"ע השמיטו לגמרי. ולפי הנ"ל ניחא, דהשו"ע ס"ל דהחזרה אסורה מטעם נראה כמבשל, וכנ"ל (סי' ב אות ב). ולכן הדין הוא כשאר מעשה שבת, והרי נתבאר בהלכות בישול (סי' שיח ס"א). אבל הרמ"א ס"ל דיש איסור מיוחד בדיעבד בהחזרה כמו בשהייה, דהרי ס"ל דהחזרה אסורה מטעם שמא יחתה כמו בשהייה, וכנ"ל (שם).

סימן ט

בישול אחר בישול

א. בנאכל חי ובנתבשל במקצת

תנן (שבת קמה:) כל שבא בחמין מערב שבת שורין אותו בחמין בשבת. וכל שלא בא בחמין מערב שבת מדיחין אותו בחמין בשבת חוץ מן המליח הישן וקולייס האיספנין, שהדחתן זו היא גמר מלאכתן. ועפ"ז כתב הרמב"ם (הל' שבת פ"ט ה"ג) המבשל על האור דבר שהיה מבושל כל צרכו או דבר שאינו צריך בישול כלל פטור.

ובמ"מ (שם) הביא שהרשב"א חולק על מש"כ הרמב"ם דרק במבושל כל צרכו פטור, וס"ל שכל שנתבשל כמאכל בן דרוסאי, שהוא שיעור חיוב בישול [ולהרמב"ם (ה"ה) הוא חצי בישולו], שוב אין בו משום חיוב בישול דבר תורה.

ונראה שהרמב"ם כתב שני הדינים האלו ביחד, כי טעם אחד להם, דיש חיוב בישול רק כשמתקן ומשביח את המאכל. וכאשר נתבשל כל צרכו לפני שבת אין בישולו השני בשבת מתקנו, וכמו כן בדבר שאינו משתבח כלל ע"י בישול פטור.

והנה כתב השער הציון (סי' שיח ס"ק קיד) בדעת הרמב"ם, דרק באינו משתבח כלל פטור, משא"כ פרי הנאכל חי דחייב, כיון דמשתבח ע"י הבישול. [והיינו כצד הא' בספקו של הברכי יוסף, עיי"ש.]

ולפ"ז יוצא, שלפי הרמב"ם גדר בישול בשבת הוא שמשביח ומתקן המאכל במציאות. וגדר אין בישול אחר בישול הוא שכיון שכבר נשתבח לגמרי ע"י האש, במציאות א"א להשביחו יותר.

אולם הרדב"ז (ח"א סי' ריג) כתב דכל דבר שנאכל חי אין בו משום בישול מן התורה. [והיינו כצד הב' בברכי יוסף שדחה השעה"צ.] וכ"כ במרכבת המשנה (שם) בדעת הרמב"ם, והשוה לדין בישול עכו"ם, דלא שייך כשנאכל חי. והרדב"ז הוכיח כן משיטת הרשב"א, דכל שנתבשל כמאכל בן דרוסאי אין בו בישול מן התורה, ומשום דכיון דאיכא מאן דאכיל ליה שוב לא מיחייב על בישולו, וכל שכן דברים הנאכלים לכל אדם כשהם חיים. ולפ"ז גדר איסור בישול הוא שמכשיר לאכילה מאכל שכעת אינו ראוי לאכילה.

ויש לדחות ראיה זו, דנראה דלפי הרשב"א דין אין בישול אחר בישול אינו משום שאינו מתקנו ומשביחו, וכמש"כ לעיל לדעת הרמב"ם. אלא דאע"פ שמשביחו, וכגון שגומר בישולו ממבושל כמאכל בן דרוסאי למבושל כל צרכו, מ"מ פטור מכיון שכבר נתבשל ע"פ דין. ולפ"ז בדבר שמעולם לא נתבשל, אע"פ שנאכל חי, נראה דחייב לפי הרשב"א, ודלא כהרדב"ז שכתב דפטור לדעת הרשב"א בנאכל חי אף במשביח טעמו.

לפ"ז יוצא שלפי דעת הרשב"א, גדר בישול בשבת הוא שפועל בו פעולת בישול ע"פ דין ע"י חום האש. וגדר אין בישול אחר בישול הוא שכיון שכבר נתפעל בו פעולת בישול ע"פ דין פעם א', שוב א"א לחייבו משום מעשה בישול שני.

ב. במתכת ובנתבשל בחמה

ואולי יש נ"מ בנתבשל בחמה (דאינו בישול ע"פ דין) וחזר ובישלו באש בשבת. ובפמ"ג (מ"ז סק"ו) נסתפק בזה, ומסיק וז"ל, ויראה דפטור הוא דכבר נתפעל בבישולו ואפשר מותר לגמרי, עכ"ל.

ונראה דלדעת הרמב"ם בודאי פטור, כיון שנתבשל במציאות וכמסקנת הפמ"ג. אבל לדעת הרשב"א, שאין בישול אחר בישול כמאכל

בן דרוסאי, ומוכח שאינו משום שבמציאות אינו משביחו, אלא שפטור מכיון שנתבשל כבר בשיעור חיוב דמאכל בן דרוסאי, א"כ יתכן דבנתבשל בחמה, דע"פ דין אינו בישול בשבת, המבשלו אח"כ בשבת חייב.

ויש בזה נ"מ למעשה לפי השיטות דבישול בתנור מיקרו-גל הוי כבישול בחמה (עי' לקמן סי' י אות א), דאסור לחמם על גבי האש מאכל שנתבשל בתנור מיקרו-גל לפי שיטת הרשב"א.

ומ"מ גם לפי הרשב"א י"ל דפטור אם אינו משביחו, אף לפי מש"כ לעיל (דלא כדברי הרדב"ז) דס"ל להרשב"א דחייב במבשל ומשביח מאכל שנאכל חי. והיינו, די"ל שלפי הרשב"א צריך ב' עניינים כדי לחייבו, א', בישול ע"פ דין במאכל שעדיין לא הפעיל בו פעולת בישול ע"פ דין, וב', בישול שמשביחו במציאות. ובנתבשל בחמה, חסר בו תנאי ב' (כיון שאינו משביחו), אף שקיים בו תנאי הא' (כיון דבישול בחמה אינו בישול ע"פ דין).

והנה הרמב"ם (שם ה"ו) כתב דהמתיך אחד ממיני מתכת חייב משום בישול. והמ"מ כתב דמקורו ביבמות (ו.) מה לי בישול פתילה מה לי בישול סממנין. ובאגלי טל (סקי"א אות ו) כתב דבגמ' (שם) מוכח שחייב אף בכבר היה מהותך וחזר ונתקשה, דלא משכחת לה הבערת בת כהן בלי איסור בישול הפתילה, ובאמת כל מתכת מהותך בעת עשייתו.

והקשה האג"ט, דנימא דאין בישול אחר בישול. ותירץ דדוקא בשאר בישול, דאף שנצטנן מ"מ בישולו עליו, אמרינן אין בישול אחר בישול. משא"כ במתכת, שהתכתו הוא בישולו, וכשחוזר ומתקשה אזל ליה בישולו, ולכן כשחוזר ומתיכו שנית מתחייב.

ודין זה דחייב במתכת מובן לשיטת הרמב"ם, דס"ל דאין בישול אחר בישול משום דבמציאות אינו מתקנו. וא"כ במתכת, שהתכתו הוא בישולו וכעת מתיכו מחדש, חייב. אבל לפי הרשב"א, דמשנתבשל ע"פ דין פטור אף במשביחו, כמו בגומר בישולו, לכאורה צ"ב. וי"ל דאם נתבטל הבישול הראשון לגמרי, כמו בנתקשה המתכת, מודה הרשב"א דחייב במבשלו אח"כ, ולא דמי לנתבשל כמאב"ד, דלא נתבטל בישול הראשון.

ג. לפי חנניה ולפי רבנן

והנה ז"ל המרכבת המשנה (פ"ט ה"ג, הנ"ל אות א), ואע"ג דלענין נתבשל כמאכל בן דרוסאי לא מדמה רבנו בישול שבת לבישול עכו"ם ממש, מ"מ מה דחזי חי לגמרי מודים רבנן לחנניה, עכ"ל.

ונראה בכונת המרכבת המשנה, דדבר שנאכל חי לכל אדם קל יותר מדבר שכבר נתבשל כמאכל בן דרוסאי (וכסברת הרדב"ז הנ"ל, אות א). ולכן הרמב"ם מתיר בדבר הנאכל חי, אע"פ שאוסר בדבר שנתבשל כמאכל בן דרוסאי. ואילו לענין בישול עכו"ם, מותר בשניהם (כלומר, בדבר שנאכל חי וגם בדבר שנתבשל כמאכל בן דרוסאי).

והנה רבנן וחנניה נחלקו (לו:) בענין איסור שהייה בערב שבת בדבר שנתבשל כמאכל בן דרוסאי. דלפי חנניה שהייה מותרת דסובר דאין חשש דשמא יחתה בגחלים (וכנ"ל, סי' א אות א), ולא הצריכו שיהא האש גרוף וקטום אלא כדי להתיר החזרה בשבת. ואילו לרבנן שהייה אסורה מחשש שמא יחתה בגחלים. ולכאורה נחלקו רק לענין שהייה, ולא מצינו שנחלקו לענין בישול.

אך המרכבת המשנה סובר, דחנניה מצריך שהאש יהא גרוף וקטום כדי להתיר החזרה, אבל אין צריך להיות גרוף וקטום כדי להתיר שהייה. ומשמע שחנניה מתיר החזרה באש שגרוף וקטום בכל מאכל שמתיר שהייה כשאין האש גרוף וקטום. ולפ"ז כמו שמתיר שהייה בדבר שנתבשל כמאכל בן דרוסאי כאשר האש אינו גרוף וקטום, ה"ה דמתיר החזרה בדבר שנתבשל כמאכל בן דרוסאי כאשר האש גרוף וקטום.

ועפ"ז הקשה המרכבת המשנה על שיטת הרמב"ם שסובר דיש בישול אחר בישול בדבר שנתבשל כמאכל בן דרוסאי, דא"כ איך התיר חנניה החזרה, הרי אסור מן התורה משום בישול. ותירץ דע"כ צריך לומר דנחלקו חנניה ורבנן גם בדין דאורייתא, דלפי חנניה אין איסור בישול בדבר שהגיע לשיעור כמאכל בן דרוסאי, ואילו לפי רבנן יש איסור בישול אא"כ נתבשל כל צרכו. ולפי הרמב"ם קיי"ל כרבנן, ומ"מ מודים רבנן לחנניה שאינו חייב במבשל דבר שנאכל חי (שהוא קל יותר), וכנ"ל.

והנה הרשב"א סובר דאין בישול אחר בישול בדבר שנתבשל כמאכל בן דרוסאי, וכנ"ל. וכתב כן מסברא, ולא הוכיח משיטת חנניה, ולדבריו

מותר אף לרבנן. [שהרי נסתפק אם קיי"ל כחנניה או כרבנן, ובסוף נטה לפסוק כחנניה. אבל מקיל בבישול אחר בישול בדבר שנתבשל כמאכל בן דרוסאי בפשיטות.]

ולפ"ז נחלקו חנניה ורבנן רק בגזירה דשמא יחתה בגחלים. ובפשוטו גם הרמב"ם סובר כן (ודלא כדעת המרכה"מ), אלא שלפי הרמב"ם חנניה ורבנן סוברים דיש בישול אחר בישול אא"כ המאכל נתבשל כל צרכו. וכשחנניה מצריך אש גרוף וקטום כדי להתיר החזרה, פשוט דמצריך גם שיהא המאכל מבושל כל צרכו מדין בישול. ודין זה לא נזכר בגמרא (לו:), דדנים שם רק באיסור דרבנן דשהייה והחזרה, ולא באיסור בישול דאורייתא.

ד. במצטמק ויפה לו

עכ"פ לפי הרדב"ז והמרכבת המשנה בשיטת הרמב"ם, נמצא דחייב רק כשמבשל דבר שאינו ראוי לאכילה לגמרי, לאפוקי דבר שנאכל חי, ולאפוקי דבר שנתבשל כל צרכו.

ולפ"ז לשון הרמב"ם 'שאינו צריך בישול כלל' ר"ל שראוי לאכול לגמרי לפני שמבשלו בשבת. ואע"פ שמבשיחו, כגון בדבר שנאכל חי, מ"מ פטור. וא"כ ניחא הא דקיי"ל (מ"ב סי' שיח סק"נ בשם המאמ"ר), דמותר לחמם דבר שנתבשל כל צרכו בשבת, אע"פ שיהיה מצטמק ויפה לו ע"י העמדה זו אצל האש. ולכאורה צ"ע, דהרי משביחו. ולפי המרכבת המשנה דסובר שפטור אף במשביחו, כל שראוי לגמרי לכל אדם (כמו בנאכל חי), ה"ה בנתבשל כל צרכו, אף שמשביחו ע"י שמצטמק ויפה לו.

[אלא דק"ק דאם נחלקו חנניה ורבנן גם בדין בישול דאורייתא (ולא רק בגזירה שמא יחתה, וכנ"ל ע"פ המרכבת המשנה), הרי קיי"ל דלפי רבנן אסור לשהות אא"כ נתבשל כל צרכו ומצטמק ורע לו (סי' רנג ס"א). וא"כ הול"ל דבאמת אסור לבשל מאכל שמבושל כל צרכו ומצטמק ויפה לו, כמו שאסור להשהותו (ודלא כדעת המ"ב ומאמ"ר הנ"ל). ובאמת בעולת שבת (סקכ"ג) פסק שאסור לחמם תבשיל שנתבשל כל צרכו ומצטמק ויפה לו. ובמאמ"ר (שם) רמז לדבריו וחלק עליהם. ואולי מקור שיטת העולת שבת הוא ע"פ שיטת המרכבת המשנה.]

ולפי השעה"צ הנ"ל (אות א), דס"ל דהמבשל פרי שנאכל חי ומשביחו חייב (ודלא כדעת המרכה"מ), צ"ע מאי שנא פרי שנאכל חי (שחייב) מדבר שמבושל כל צרכו ומצטמק ויפה לו (שפטור).

ואולי יש לומר דבדבר שמצטמק ויפה לו, השבח שיש בו אין דינו כבישול. וכן משמע מדברי הבעל המאור (עי' לעיל סי' ה אות א), דלפעמים יש תבשיל שלא נתבשל כל צרכו, ומ"מ מצטמק ורע לו. ואם צימוק דינו כבישול, הרי טוב לו כדי שיתבשל יותר. אלא ע"כ דשני ענינים הם, צימוק ובישול, ולכן מצטמק ויפה לו אין בו שום שבח מדין בישול.

ה. בדבר לח

והנה נחלקו הראשונים אם אמרינן אין בישול אחר בישול בדבר לח, דהרא"ש (פ"ג סי' יא) כתב בשם רש"י דהא דאמרינן דאין בישול אחר בישול היינו בדבר יבש, אבל בדבר לח שנצטנן אמרינן יש בישול אחר בישול. [ומקורו בגמ' (לה.) דאין טומנין משחשיכה גזירה שמא ירתיח, ופרש"י, קדירה שנצטננה כשירצה להטמינה וירתיחנה בתחלה באור, ונמצא מבשל בשבת.] ולפ"ז המשנה (קמה: הנ"ל, אות א), דאין בישול אחר בישול, מיירי רק בדבר יבש.

אבל בתחילה (סי' י) כתב הרא"ש דאין בישול אחר בישול אף בדבר לח. ובב"י כתב שכ"נ מסתימת הרמב"ם ושאר ראשונים. אך לדינא החמיר בשו"ע (ס"ד), דבתבשיל שיש בו מרק יש בישול אחר בישול אם נצטנן.

ונראה לפרש שלפי הסוברים שאין בישול אחר בישול בדבר לח, גדר בישול בדבר לח שוה הוא לבישול דבר יבש, דהיינו הכשרת האוכל לאכילה ע"י חום האש. ואף אם נצטנן, ובדבר לח אין אוכלין אותו כך, לא אמרינן אזיל ליה בישולו (עי' לעיל, אות ב), כיון שכבר נתפעל בו בישול הראשון שלא נתבטל ממנו, ועכשיו רק צריך לחזור ולחממו כדי לאכלו. ואין זה נחשב כמעשה בישול, ודומה לדבר יבש שלא נאכל אלא חם, דמותר לחממו לכו"ע.

מאידך, לפי הסוברים שיש בישול אחר בישול בדבר לח, גדר בישול בדבר לח שונה לגמרי מבישול בדבר יבש. והיינו, שהגדר בבישול בדבר

לח הוא חימום, שהרי זוהי הפעולה שעושה בדבר לח. ולכן כשנצטנן, בודאי אמרינן אזיל ליה בישולו, כיון שאינו חם.

והנה ז"ל הרמב"ם (פ"ט ה"א), האופה כגרוגרת חייב. אחד האופה את הפת או המבשל את המאכל או את הסממנין או המחמם את המים, הכל ענין אחד הוא. שיעור המחמם את המים כדי לרחוץ בהן אבר קטן, ושיעור מבשל סממנין כדי שיהיו ראויין לדבר שמבשלין אותן לו, עכ"ל.

ולכאורה משמע מדברי הרמב"ם שחימום מים הוי דין בפני עצמו. ויש לדחות, דהרמב"ם נקט חימום מים כדין בפני עצמו רק משום ששיעורו שונה משיעור מבשל, וכן נקט סממנים בנפרד מה"ט. אך א"כ הוה ליה למימר 'מבשל מאכל סממנים ומים'. ומדנקט 'מחמם מים', משמע שדין חימום הוא.

ובפמ"ג (א"א סי' רנד סק"א) כתב וז"ל, ולכאורה נראה דווקא מים ויין ושמן, שאין האש פועל בו להכשיר כ"כ, דנאכל חי ג"כ, והבישול הוא החימום, הלכך כל שנצטנן יש בו בישול. משא"כ שומן אווז ומוהל הבשר, דא"א לאכול כי אם ע"י בישול, תו אף נצטנן אין בו בישול. אלא מסתימת הפוסקים משמע כל שהוא צלול ולח יש בישול אחר בישול בנצטנן, עכ"ל.

והנה סברת הפמ"ג היא דבמים החימום הוא הבישול. ומראיתו מנאכל חי נראה שסובר כמו הרדב"ז ומרכבת המשנה הנ"ל (אות א), דפרי שנאכל חי אין בו בישול מן התורה. והוקשה לו ממים דפסק הרמב"ם (ה"א) דמחמם את המים חייב. ותירץ, דמים שאני, שחימומו הוא בישולו, וכלשון הרמב"ם. וצדד דרק בזה י"ל דיש בישול אחר בישול בנצטנן, דאזיל ליה בישולו. וכ"כ האג"ט הנ"ל (אות ב) לענין מתכת ומים.

והנה אם המחייב בדבר לח אינו בישול אלא חימום, וכלשון הרמב"ם, מסתבר דיש חימום אחר חימום. וא"כ נראה דלפי הרמב"ם יש בישול אחר בישול בדבר לח, ודלא כמש"כ הב"י (הנ"ל) ע"פ סתימת הרמב"ם. ולפי סברת הפמ"ג י"ל דהרמב"ם לא סתם, שהרי כתב דחייב משום מחמם, וממילא מוכח דיש בישול אחר בישול בדבר לח, ודו"ק.

אך לפי השעה"צ (סי' שיח ס"ק קיד, הנ"ל, אות א), דבמשביחו חייב לפי הרמב"ם אף דנאכל חי, אין ראיה דמים שאני משאר מאכלים. ואמנם כ"כ המ"ב (סק"א) וז"ל, אף דמים ראוי לשתייה בלא בישול, מ"מ חייב כיון שמשתבח ע"י הבישול, עכ"ל. ובשעה"צ (שם) כתב וז"ל, דמים יש

בו משום בישול והרי מים ג"כ שותה אותו כשהוא חי, עכ"ל. הרי דהשוה מים לשאר מאכלים. ולפי הפמ"ג, דס"ל דמים שאני, אינו ראיה, וכנ"ל, דלפי הפמ"ג החיוב במים הוא משום חימום ולא משום בישול.

והנה ראית השעה"צ שיש בישול במים היא מהגמ' (מ:). אולם לא מבואר שם שחייב מן התורה. ויש שהוכיחו שחייב מהגמ' (ביצה לד.) אחד נתן המים ואחד נתן המאכל כולם חייבים משום מבשל. אבל בתפא"י (כלכלת השבת סקי"א) כתב, דלפי הרמב"ם שפוטר בדבר שהוא טוב חי כמבושל, כמו מים, צ"ל דחייב בגמ' ביצה משום שמבשל רוטב, משא"כ מים. ואף דצ"ע מדברי הרמב"ם עצמו (ה"א), דמחמם מים חייב, מ"מ מסברא יתכן דפטור.

והנה השעה"צ פירש הגמ' (מ:) דיש איסור דאורייתא בבישול מים, וכנ"ל. ובגמ' (שם) נזכר שיעור יד סולדת בו. וצ"ע דבבישול בעינן כמאכל בן דרוסאי, וכדעת הרמב"ם (ה"ה) ע"פ הגמ' (מנחות נז.). ולכאורה צ"ל דמים שאני, דחימומו הוא בישולו, ושיעור חום בכל התורה כולה הוא שיעור יד סולדת בו, וכדמצינו לענין בליעת איסורים (יו"ד סי' קה ס"ב). ולפ"ז צע"ק ראית שעה"צ הנ"ל ממים, דע"כ אף לדבריו מים שאני, מדמחייב כשיעור יד סולדת בו.

ו. שיטת ה"ר יונה

וז"ל הר"ן (ריש פ"ד) בשם רבינו יונה, ומכשלה גדולה תחת יד קצת העם, שטומנים קומקום של מים חמים ליתן לתוך הקדירה בשבת כאשר התבשיל מצטמק, ופעמים שהאחד אין יד סולדת בו והאחר יד סולדת בו ומתבשל זה בזה ונמצאו מבשלין בשבת. ואפילו אם שניהם יד סולדת בו איכא מ"ד בירושלמי עירוי אינו ככלי ראשון. וכשמערין המים לאלתר שיצאו מן הכלי אע"פ שהן רותחין, פסק כח רתיחתן מלבשל כדין כלי שני שאינו מבשל, ומתבשלין בתוך כלי ראשון. ומים מבושלים אם פסקה רתיחתן יש בהם משום בישול, עכ"ל.

המבואר מדבריו דסובר רבינו יונה דיש בישול אחר בישול בדבר לח אם נצטנן, וגם סובר דשיעור חמימות המים לפטור המחממו יותר הוא יד סולדת בו. וכן מסתבר לפי מש"כ לעיל (אות ה) דבדבר לח חימומו הוא בישולו. ושיעור חום ע"פ דין הוא יד סולדת בו בין לחומרא (לחייב

המבשל דבר לח עד שיעור יד סולדת בו), ובין לקולא (לפטור המחמם דבר לח שכבר הגיע לשיעור יד סולדת בו).

והוסיף רבינו יונה דאם המים שיצאו מן הכלי לתוך האויר דינם ככלי שני, וכדעה א׳ בירושלמי, חייב אף ביד סולדת בו. ומוכח מזה כמש״כ לעיל (אות ה), דהוא שיעור ע״פ דין (אם הוא בגדר חם) ולא במציאות (אם נאכל או לא), שהרי אף אם במציאות רותח ממש חייב, אם דינו ככלי שני וחוזר לכלי ראשון.

עוד מוכח מלשון רבינו יונה ׳ומתבשל זה בזה׳, דשיעור יד סולדת בו לא נאמר במים בלבד אלא גם במרק, שהרי חשש גם שתבשיל פחות מיד סולדת בו יתחמם ע״י מים רותחים. [והיינו דלא כדעת האג״ט (סקי״א אות ו) שכתב שלפי רבינו יונה חייב רק במים ולא בתבשיל.]

ולכאורה קשה, שהרי במרק גדר בישולו אינו חימום בלבד, שהרי משנה כל המאכלים ביחד להיות מקשה אחת שאינו משתנה כשמצטנן, וכסברת הפמ״ג הנ״ל. וא״כ קשה, למה נקט שיעור יד סולדת בו גם במרק. וע״כ צ״ל דבמרק וכדומה יש שני ענינים - בישול וחימום, ואם בטל אחד מהם (דהיינו חימום), אז יש בישול אחר בישול. ובשו״ע (סי׳ רנג ס״ד) הביא דברי רבינו יונה. והרמ״א כתב ׳עיי״ל סי׳ שיח׳, ופי׳ המ״ב (סקפ״ד), דאנו מקילים (שם סט״ו) דאין בישול אחר בישול בדבר לח כל שלא נצטנן לגמרי, וא״כ לא קיי״ל כרבינו יונה. והשו״ע אזיל לשיטתו (שם ס״ד), דיש בישול אחר בישול בדבר לח שאין היד סולדת בו.

וכתב הפמ״ג (א״א סי׳ שיח סקי׳, מובא בבה״ל שם ס״ד ד״ה אם) דלפי השו״ע אם הדבר לח הורק לכלי שני, יש בישול אחר בישול, אף דעדיין היד סולדת בו, דדינו כמו נצטנן, וכשיטת רבינו יונה. אבל האג״ט כתב (השמטה לסקי״ד בסופה) דהשו״ע אינו פוסק כרבינו יונה בזה, אף אם אמרינן יש בישול אחר בישול בדבר לח.

ז. שיטת הרמ״א בנצטנן לגמרי

כתב הרמ״א (סי׳ שיח סט״ו) וז״ל, אם הוא רותח אפילו בדבר שיש בו מרק מותר. ויש מקילין לומר וכו׳ [ד]אפילו נצטנן מותר. ונהגו להקל בזה אם לא נצטנן לגמרי, וכמו שכתבתי לעיל סי׳ רנג, עכ״ל.

ונחלקו האחרונים בביאור דברי הרמ"א. המג"א (סי' רנג סקל"ז) כתב וז"ל, דס"ל [להרמ"א] דלדידן דס"ל דאסור לחממו [דבר לח שנצטנן] מדאורייתא, אסור לומר לעכו"ם, ואם עשה כן אסור אפילו בדיעבד, עכ"ל. הרי שפירש שיטת הרמ"א, דאם נצטנן לגמרי יש בישול אחר בישול בדבר לח מדאורייתא.

והנה הרמ"א (שם ס"ה) אסר לישראל להושיב קדירה אצל תנור שהשפחה תבער וע"י זה הקדירות חוזרים ונרתחים. ובמ"ב (סק"ק) כתב דהו"ל כאחד נותן את הקדירה ואחד האש, דראשון פטור אבל אסור. ומקורו (שעה"צ ס"ק קה) בתה"ד (סי' סו). ושם הוסיף וז"ל, ויש לדמותו להא דכתב המרדכי (סי' רנג), דנותנין מזונות לפני הנכרים בחצר, דאם יודע בודאי שיוציאנו הנכרי אסור לתת לפניו. וא"כ בנ"ד, כיון דיודע דהשפחה מבערת את התנור בוודאי, הוא כנותן ע"מ לבשלן, ואב מלאכה היא כמו הוצאה, עכ"ל. הרי שכתב התה"ד שאסור מדאורייתא, כאב מלאכה. ומפורש כדעת המג"א.

ויש לדחות, דלשון אב מלאכה לאו דוקא, ואף איסור מלאכה דרבנן בכלל. והרי כתב (שם) 'כמו הוצאה', והמרדכי אסר לדינא בזמנו, אף דס"ל (עירובין סי' תקט) דאין רה"ר דאורייתא בלי ששים ריבוא. וא"כ אפשר דאיסור מלאכה דבישול הוי כמו הוצאה, כלומר דאסור רק מדרבנן. [ואף דשבות דשבות מותר במקום מצוה דעונג שבת, לא רצה התה"ד להתירו בקביעות.] ומ"מ בפשטות נראה דלפי התה"ד אב מלאכה היא.

והא דמותר כשלא נצטנן לגמרי, פירש בתה"ד (שם) בשם המרדכי (סי' תנו), וז"ל, אם היורה מתקררת, ועבדים נכרים מחממין אש תחתיה [כלומר, דזה מותר כי הכל חולים אצל הקור, וצרכי חולה נעשין ע"י נכרים], ואם ראויה שיאכל בלא חימום כמאכל בן דרוסאי אין קפידא במה שחיממוה נכרי בשבת, עכ"ל. וכ"כ בשם ההגמי"י (פ"ג סק"ב) וז"ל, אם לא נתקררה כל כך שלא היתה ראויה לאכילה דוגמת טעם מאכל בן דרוסאי קודם שחממוה נכרים, א"כ אין חוששין בחימום ושרי, עכ"ל. והכונה, דמצד איסור בישול מותר אף לישראל בכה"ג, ורק משום איסור הבערה, דמותר ע"י נכרי לחולה, הוצרכו לנכרים.

ולכאורה מוכח מהמרדכי ההגמי"י והתה"ד, דס"ל כדעת הרשב"א (עי' לעיל אות א), דכל שנתבשל כמאכל בן דרוסאי אין בו איסור בישול.

ולכן לענין חימום מותר להרתיחו כל שנתבשל כמאכל בן דרוסאי (דהיינו שנאכל בדוחק כחמין בחום כזה, כמו שבשר נאכל בדוחק בחצי בישולו שהוא כמאכל בן דרוסאי), כמו שמותר לבשל בשר שהגיע לשיעור מאכל בן דרוסאי עד לבישול כל צרכו.

אך לפ"ז קשה, שבתה"ד (שם) כתב דגם הסמ"ג כתב כדעת המרדכי והגמי"י. ובבה"ל (שם ד"ה אפילו) כתב שהסמ"ג ס"ל כדעת הרמב"ם, שאסור מדאורייתא לבשל מאכל שלא נתבשל כל צרכו. וא"כ א"א לפרש שיטת הסמ"ג ע"פ דברי הרשב"א שאין איסור בישול כשגומר בישולו של מאכל שהגיע לכמאכל בן דרוסאי, וצ"ע.

ונראה, דכל זמן שהתבשיל חם דוגמת כמאכל בן דרוסאי, א"א לומר שנתבטל הבישול הראשון, שעדיין ראוי לאכול מחמת חמימותו (וכלשון שו"ע הרב, סי' שיח ס"ט). ולכן אף לפי הסמ"ג (דס"ל שהמבשל מאכל שהגיע לשיעור מאכל בן דרוסאי חייב) מותר לחמם דבר לח שנתבשל כל צרכו ונצטנן קצת (אם עדיין נאכל מחמת חמימותו, דוגמת שיעור מאכל בן דרוסאי), דלא נתבטל בישולו הראשון.

והנה ז"ל האור זרוע (סי' ח, מובא בד"מ סי' רנג סק"ז), פעמים מתקררים השאלינ"ט שלהם, ובשבת קודם האוכל מדליקין העבדים אש סמוך לקדרות כדי שיתחממו בטוב. ויש שמסלקין אותם ונותנים אותם סמוך לאש. ומפרשים להתיר מפני שאין לחוש לאוסרן, דמסתמא חמין הן קצת קרוב להיד סולדת בו, וכשמוסיפין להם חום מותר, שהרי גם בישול אין בהן, עכ"ל.

ונראה לפרש דס"ל להאו"ז ד'בישול אין בהן' משום דאין בישול אחר בישול. ולענין חימום כתב דב'קצת קרוב להיד סולדת בו' מותר להוסיף להם חום. ולכאורה זוהי שיטת המרדכי וההגמי"י והתה"ד, וסוברים דבקרוב להיד סולדת בו נאכל מחמת חמימותו. [וראיה לדבר שבכל הראשונים הנ"ל מבואר שהיו רגילין העבדים לעשות כן בחופות, ומוכח דהכל שיטה אחת.]

ומכל הנ"ל מוכח דלפי הרמ"א יש בישול אחר בישול בדבר לח מן התורה אם נצטנן לגמרי. ורק בקצת קרוב להיד סולדת בו, לא נחשב נצטנן לגמרי. וזוהי כונת הרמ"א (סי' שיח סט"ו, הנ"ל) שכתב 'ונהגו להקל בזה אם לא נצטנן לגמרי וכמו שכתבתי לעיל סי' רנג'. וע"כ לשון 'לגמרי' לאו דוקא הוא.

ח. פירושים אחרים בשיטת הרמ״א

והנה באג״ט (סקי״ד) מפרש שיטת הרמ״א דבחשש דאורייתא מחמירין דיש בישול אחר בישול בדבר לח. אבל כשראוי לאכול מחמת חמימותו, לא גרע מנתבשל כמאכל בן דרוסאי, דשוב אין בו בישול דאורייתא (אף לדעת הרמב״ם והשו״ע, לשיטתו סק״י אות טו). ולענין איסור דרבנן דבישול סומכין על הסוברים דאין בישול אחר בישול בדבר לח, עכ״ד.

ומדברי הסמ״ג לא נראה כן, שכתב בודאות שיש בישול אחר בישול בדבר לח כשנצטנן לגמרי, ולא כשעדיין חם דוגמת כמאכל בן דרוסאי, אף דס״ל כדעת הרמב״ם דאסור לבשל מאכל שהגיע לשיעור כמאכל בן דרוסאי, וכנ״ל (אות ז). וע״כ צ״ל דחילוק הסמ״ג בין נצטנן לגמרי ללא נצטנן לגמרי הוא מעיקר הדין. דהיינו, אם לא נצטנן לגמרי לא פקע הבישול הראשון, אבל אם נצטנן לגמרי יש בישול אחר בישול מדינא, ולכאורה איסור דאורייתא הוא. וא״כ נראה דזוהי גם שיטת הרמ״א (ע״פ המרדכי ההגמי״י והתה״ד), ודלא כדעת האג״ט.

ובמנחת כהן (שער ב׳ פ״ב, מובא באג״ט שם) כתב שהרמ״א תופס בעיקר שאין בישול אחר בישול בדבר לח. וכן כתב בחזו״א (סי׳ לז סקי״ג) בפשרת הרמ״א להתיר בישול אחר בישול בדבר לח ולאסור בנצטנן לגמרי. וז״ל, וע״כ שאנו תופסין לעיקר הדין כדעת הרמב״ם והרשב״א והר״ן שאין איסור לחמם את הצונן המבושל. אלא מפני שלא יבואו להקל בחמים, לא נהגו להקל בצונן שאין חמימותו ניכרת. ואפשר דהוא משום גדר חזרה ע״ג גרופה, דבנצטנן לגמרי לדעת המג״א בטלה שהיה ראשונה. ומיהו משמע דבדבר יבש מקילין אפילו בנצטנן לגמרי, עכ״ל.

וכ״נ מדברי המ״ב (סי׳ שיח סקצ״ט) וז״ל, אף דלדעת המחבר כיון שנצטנן מעט מחמימותו ואין היס״ב שוב יש בו משום בישול, וכמו שכתבנו לעיל בס״ד, המנהג להקל בזה דסומכין בזה איש מקילין כ״ז שלא נצטנן לגמרי, עכ״ל. ומשמע שמעיקר הדין קיי״ל כהיש מקילין דאין בישול אחר בישול בדבר לח.

וכן כתב באג״מ (או״ח ח״ד סי׳ עד, בישול סק״ב). וכתב עוד (שם סקי״ט) שאם נשארו כמה טיפות של משקין שנתבשלו ונצטננו לגמרי, המותר לערות עליהם עוד מים רותחין. ופירש שבטיפות אלו לא נהגו

להחמיר כיון שמעיקר הדין קיי"ל דאין בישול אחר בישול בדבר לח. ולפי מה שנתבאר (אות ז) שבאמת הרמ"א סובר דיש בישול אחר בישול מעיקר הדין, יש לפקפק בהוראה זו (אלא שיש עוד כמה צדדים אחרים להקל, ואכמ"ל).

ט. שיעור יד סולדת בו

נחלקו הפוסקים בשיעור יד סולדת בו, דיש מחמירין משיעור ק"ד מעלות, ויש מקילים עד ק"י, קי"ג או ק"כ. אבל כשיד סולדת בו קולא הוא, שמותר לחזור ולחממו, מצריכים ק"ס מעלות. וכ"ז מובא בספר הלכות שבת לר"ש איידער (הע' יט). וכתב שהפוסקים הגיעו לשיעור ק"י וק"כ ע"י בדיקה והבחנה.

וקשה, דבמחה"ש (סקל"ז) כתב בשם הדרישה, דאין לשער בחזקת היד, אלא בשיעור כריסו של תינוק נכוית בו, וכמבואר בגמ' (מ:), ופרש"י דיש סולד מרתיחה מועטת ויש שאינו סולד, וע"כ מודדים ע"פ שיעור כריסו של תינוק נכוית, ששוה כמעט בכל התינוקות. ואולי הפוסקים בדקו ע"י הרבה בני אדם, וקבעו שיעור יד סולדת בו כהבינוני.

והנה בגמ' (שם) אסרו להשתטף בצונן כנגד המדורה, ופירש בעה"מ (שם) דהמים מתחממים והוי כמבשל. וכן משמע מהרמב"ם (פכ"ב ה"ד) שאוסר להניח ידיו הרטובות אצל האש רק אם יגיעו המים לשיעור יד סולדת בו. והרמב"ן חולק על בעה"מ, ופירש משום איסור רחיצה. ולכאורה סובר הרמב"ן כדעת הרשב"א (מב.) שאין אדם רוחץ במים חמין שהוא מסלד בהן, וע"כ אין לאסור משם בישול, דבודאי לא יתן המים שעליו להגיע לשיעור יד סולדת בו, ואסרו רק משום רחיצה. ואיסור זה ע"כ נאמר בפחות מיד סולדת בו, דאין רוחצים במים שהיד סולדת בו, וכנ"ל. אבל מהרמב"ם ובעה"מ מוכח דאדם רוחץ במים שהיד סולדת בו, וצ"ע במה נחלקו.

ונראה, דלשיטת הרמב"ם ובעה"מ שיעור יד סולדת בו נאמר באדם שאינו מצפה לנגוע בדבר חם, ויד סולדת בו כתגובה טבעית שאינו חושב עליה מראש. והוא שיעור חום נמוך, וכשמכין את עצמו לכך, יכול לרחוץ במים כאלו. ולפ"ז יש לפרש דהא דמשערים בשיעור דכריסו של תינוק

נכוית בו הוא משום דקשה מאד לשער בשיעור דיד סולדת בו, דהרי אם מכין את עצמו לשער, איננו השיעור הנכון. ורק כשמופתע אפשר למדוד, וקשה לסדר בדיקה כזו, ולכן משערים בכריסו של תינוק.

ולפ״ז יש לומר דרש״י (שלא פירש כן, אלא שיד סולדת בו אינו שוה בכל אדם וכנ״ל) סובר כדעת הרמב״ן והרשב״א דיד סולדת בו נמדד כאשר היד סולד אפילו במכין את עצמו לכך. והוא שיעור גבוה, וא״א לרחוץ בו כשסולד בו אף אחר הכנה, וכמש״כ הרשב״א (וכן נראה קצת מרש״י שם שפירש סולדת, נמשכת אחריה מדאגה שלא תכוה, ומלשון דאגה משמע דמיירי דמכין את עצמו לכך).

ולפי הביאור הנ״ל, יל״פ הספק בפוסקים אם שיעור יד סולדת בו הוא ק״ד או ק״ס מעלות. דלפי בעה״מ והרמב״ם, שמודדים במופתע, שיעורו ק״ד מעלות. ובשיעור זה רגילים להתרחץ באמבטיא, וכעדות המומחים, דכאשר מכין את עצמו אינו סולד מחום כזה. אבל לרש״י הרמב״ן והרשב״א, דמודדים במכין את עצמו, שיעורו ק״ס מעלות, ובשיעור זה א״א לרחוץ, וכנ״ל. והרשב״א (שם) כתב עוד דאין אדם שותה חמין גמורין אלא פושרין, וכשיטתו הנ״ל, ולפי הרמב״ם נראה דאדם שמכין את עצמו שותה חמין.

והנה רגילים להגיש תה חם מאד, ממים שכמעט רותחים, ודלא כמש״כ הרשב״א דאין אדם שותה חמין גמורין. אך י״ל, דמים בכוס מתקררים מהר מאד, וכששותים את התה הוא פחות מק״ס מעלות. עוד י״ל שבזמנם שתו את החמין, כדרך שאנו שותים מים קרים, וזה א״א בחמין גמורין. ומה שנוהגים עכשיו, שמוצצים כמה טיפות מהחמין הגמורין, אינו בכלל השתייה דהרשב״א, ודו״ק.

כתב בכף החיים (ס״ק קמג) וז״ל, כל היכא שזה החמין ראוי לשתיה או לאכילה שאין האדם נמנע ממנו מכח ריבוי חמימותו, ה״ז לא חשוב יד סולדת בו. אבל אם נמנע מלשתותו או לאוכלו מרוב חומו, ה״ז נחשב בכלל יד סולדת בו, עכ״ל.

ומדבריו מוכח שאם המים הגיעו ליד סולדת בו, אין בנ״א שותים אותו, וכשיטת הרשב״א. והוסיף הכף החיים שאם שותין אותו, מוכח דלא הגיעו המים לשיעור יד סולדת בו. (כלומר, דשיעור שהיד סולדת בו

ושיעור שהפה סולד בו, שוין הם.) והוספה זו לא נמצא בדברי הרשב"א, ויתכן דמש"כ הרשב"א שאין אדם שותה חמין גמורין היינו גם אם שיעור החום פחות קצת משיעור שהיד סולדת בו.

י. במים שהגיעו לשיעור יד סולדת בו

בשביתת השבת (פתיחה סקי"ח) כתב שמדברי הב"י נראה שאם הגיעו המים לשיעור יד סולדת בו לפני השבת, דמותר להרתיחם בשבת. והקשה, דהא אנו רואים כאשר מבשלים מים, שמקפידים שלא לשתות עד שתהיה מעלה רתיחה, וא"כ יתחייב כשגומר רתיחתו, ובפרט לשיטת הרמב"ם והשו"ע (ס"ד) דהמבשל מאכל שכבר נתבשל כמאכל בן דרוסאי חייב.

ולפי מש"כ לעיל (אות ה) לדעת הפמ"ג יש לתרץ, דבמים חייב משום חימום, ולא משום בישול שתלוי בראוי לאכול ולשתות. ולכן שיעור חימום מים, בין לחייב המחממו בשבת ובין לפטור המחממו בשבת אם הוחם מע"ש, הוא יד סולדת בו, שהוא שיעור ע"פ דין.

ובשבה"ש צדד דמיירי הב"י שהורתחו המים לגמרי, ואח"כ נצטננו קצת ועדיין יד סולדת בו, דפטור אף לאלו הסוברים יש בישול אחר בישול בדבר לח. וכתב שכ"נ מלשון המג"א (סקי"ב, עיי"ש במחה"ש). ובשביתת השבת דחה דברי המג"א.

ונראה בזה, דאמנם לפי רבינו יונה והשו"ע (הנ"ל, אות ו) דס"ל דיש בישול אחר בישול בדבר לח, הכל תלוי בשיעור יד סולדת בו, שהוא שיעור חום ע"פ דין, וכנ"ל. וה"ט, שהם סוברים שגדר בישול במים ודברים לחים הוא חימום, ולכן תלוי בשיעור שנחשב חם ע"פ דין. ומותר להרתיחו משהגיע לשיעור יד סולדת בו, וכמסקנת השביתת השבת.

אבל לדעת הרמ"א, דאין בישול אחר בישול בדבר לח (כל שלא נצטנן לגמרי), בעינן שהמים והמרק יתבשלו כל צרכם, ורק בכה"ג מותר לחזור ולחמם אותם אם נצטננו. ובמרק, נתבשל כל צרכו היינו שנאכל כך לרוב בני אדם, וכדין דבר גוש. ואף במים תלוי במנהג המקום, וכמש"כ בספר ברית עולם (סי' ז). ועיי"ש, שמנהגנו שמרתיחין את המים עד שמעלה כמו אבעבועות, וכ"ז שלא הגיע לשיעור בישול כזה אסור לחממו בשבת.

ולפ"ז יש לקיים שיטת המג"א [הנ"ל, דאסור להרתיח מים שמעולם לא הגיעו לרותחין, אבל אם הגיעו לרותחין וירדו לשיעור יד סולדת בו מותר לחזור ולהרתיחן], דיש שני ענינים במים, חימום - שתלוי בשיעור יד סולדת בו, ובישול - שתלוי בשיעור כל צרכו לפי הזמן והמקום. ולכן אם הגיע ליד סולדת בו וחממו יותר חייב משום בישול. אבל אם הורתח וירד לשיעור יד סולדת בו מותר לחזור ולהרתיחו, דלענין בישול הרי אמרינן דאין בישול אחר בישול. ולענין חימום (דיש חימום אחר חימום, וזהו יסוד מה שנקרא יש בישול אחר בישול בדבר לח) הרי לא נתבטל חומו מפני שעדיין הוא חם כשיעור יד סולדת בו.

אולם באג"מ (או"ח ח"ד סי' עד, בישול סק"א) מתיר לחמם מים שהגיעו ליד סולדת בו לפני השבת לדינא, ומקורו בשו"ע הרב (סי"ט). וז"ל האג"מ, משו"ע הגר"ז משמע שמתיר אפילו להרתיח מים שהיד סולדת בו, ואף שאיירי בנצטנן, הרי איירי אליבא דהסוברין יש בישול אחר בישול בדבר לח אף לחייב כשלא היה יד סולדת בו ובשלו עד שנעשה יד סולדת בו [וכשו"ע ס"ד], דלא כקולת הרמ"א, עכ"ל. ולמש"כ המג"א אינו ראיה, דעדיין י"ל לפי השו"ע דאם היה רותח וירד ליד סולדת בו מותר להרתיחו, אבל אם מעולם לא היה רותח, אסור להרתיחו משום דהוי כגמר בישולו.

עוד יש לדחות ראית האג"מ, דלעולם מותר לחמם מים מיד סולדת בו לרותחים לפי רבינו יונה והשו"ע, וכהבנת האג"מ. וכ"נ מדברי הב"י (סי' רנח, וכמש"כ שם בשבה"ש הנ"ל סק"ג בסוף). [ובפרט ממש"כ שם בב"י, 'ובלא"ה צ"ל כן', לדעת הטור דס"ל יש בישול אחר בישול בדבר לח. ומוכח דלעיל מזה לא דן בבישול אחר בישול, ומ"מ מתיר לחמם מים שהיד סולדת בו.]

ומ"מ י"ל דזהו רק לשיטת השו"ע, דיש בישול אחר בישול בדבר לח כי חימומו הוא בישולו, ושיעור חום ע"פ דין הוא יד סולדת בו, ומשהגיע לחום זה שוב א"א לחייבו, עכ"פ במים, וכנ"ל. אבל לפי הרמ"א, דאין בישול אחר בישול בדבר לח (כל שלא נצטנן לגמרי), י"ל כדעת המג"א, דיש ענין של בישול כל צרכו אחרי שיעור יד סולדת בו, וכנ"ל. ולפ"ז קולת הרמ"א מביאה ליד חומרא, ודו"ק.

יא. בישול אחר אפיה

המרדכי (סי׳ שב) כתב שיטת היראים, וז״ל, יש בישול אחר אפיה וצליה כדאמרינן בפסחים (מא.) צלאו ואח״כ בשלו חייב. ומוקי לה כר׳ יוסי דאמר יוצאין ברקיק השרוי אבל לא במבושל אע״פ שלא נימוח. אלמא דיש בישול אחר אפיה. וה״ה דיש בישול אחר צליה, עכ״ל.

והראבי״ה דחה, דאיתא בגמ׳ ברכות (לח:), ע״כ לא קאמר ר׳ יוסי אלא גבי מצה, דבעינן טעם מצה בפיו וליכא. ומוכח דבישול אינו מבטל אפיה (אלא דשאני מצה כיון דבעינן טעם מצה), וא״כ אין בישול אחר אפיה בשבת.

וביישוב דחייה זו לשיטת היראים, מצאנו ב׳ יישובים באחרונים, שיוצא מתוכם ב׳ הבנות שונות לגמרי בביאור שיטתו. שהנה באגלי טל (אופה סקט״ו אות ב) כתב דלפי היראים צ״ל דלעולם בישול מבטל אפיה לאשוויי מצה עשירה, וזוהי כונת הגמ׳ דבעינן טעם מצה, וכתוס׳ (פסחים מא. ד״ה אבל), ורבינו יונה ותוס׳ הרא״ש (ברכות שם).

אבל הט״ז (סי׳ שיח סק״ו) כתב וז״ל, דכי נמי תימא משום דטעם מצה בעינן, ה״נ אזלינן בתר טעם התבשיל. וכיון דנשתנה הטעם ע״י בישול אמרינן דנתכון לזה בשבת וכו׳ דמלאכת מחשבת אסרה תורה, עכ״ל. ולכאורה לפ״ז אינו תלוי בשם בישול צליה ואפיה ע״פ דין, אלא בשינוי טעם שבא ע״י הבישול הצליה או האפיה אחרי סוג בישול אחר. ומאידך משמע מדברי האג״ט (שלא תירץ כן) שבאמת תלוי בשם חדש ע״פ דין ולא משום שנשתנה הטעם.

ונראה דיש כמה נפק״מ לדינא בין ב׳ הבאורים. דהנה הפמ״ג (מ״ז סק״ז) אוסר צליה אחר אפיה. ובס׳ ארחות שבת (פ״ה הע׳ ס׳) כתב שלפ״ז אסור לעשות צנימים אם מקבלים טעם חדש ע״י חום האש. כלומר, דקאי הפמ״ג (במ״ז) לשיטת הט״ז, דכל שנתכוון לטעם חדש ע״י חום האש הוי מלאכת מחשבת דבישול.

אבל המג״א (סקי״ז) כתב שמותר לתת דבר אפוי אצל האש. ופירש במחה״ש דס״ל להמג״א דאפוי כצלי לכל דבר. [ואף אם נאמר שאפיה

יותר חשובה היא מצלי, מפני שיוצרת שם לחם (עי׳ להלן בסמוך), בודאי אין צלי יותר חשוב מאפיה.] ולפ״ז אין צליה אחר אפיה, ומותר לעשות צנימים. וזהו כשיטת האג״ט הנ״ל דאסור רק אם יש סוג חדש של בישול ע״פ דין (דהחדוש ע״פ דין שיש בו נחשב כבישול).

והנה בשלט״ג (סא: בדפי הרי״ף) צדד דיש בישול אחר אפיה וצליה, אבל אין צליה אחר בישול, וכ״נ בטור, וצ״ב. ולפי הט״ז ששינוי טעם מחייב, נראה דצליה אחר בישול דינו כבישול אחר צליה. אך לפי האג״ט יש לחלק, דבישול עדיף מצלי (ע״פ דין), מדמבשל בכולו, וצליה פועלת רק בכדי נטילה (עי׳ גמ׳ חולין צו:). ולכן יש בישול אחר צליה ואין צליה אחר בישול. ויש בישול אחר אפיה, דבישול במים פועל יותר מאפיה באש.

מאידך, נראה דאפיה (שיוצרת שם לחם שהוא סוג מיוחד ע״פ דין), עדיף מבישול, ולכן יש אפיה אחר בישול, אף אם אין צלי אחר בישול. ובאג״ט (שם אות טו) מצדד שאפילו אם אין בישול אחר אפיה, יש אפיה אחר בישול, עיי״ש. ואזיל לשיטתו, דתלוי בסוג הבישול ע״פ דין, ולא בשינוי טעם כדעת הט״ז.

וז״ל השו״ע (סי׳ שיח סט״ו), דבר שנתבשל כ״צ והוא יבש שאין בו מרק מותר להניחו כנגד המדורה אפילו במקום שהיס״ב. ובבה״ל (ד״ה והוא) הקשה בשם הבית מאיר, דהלא יש צליה אחר בישול. ולפי הט״ז ניחא, שאין שינוי טעם בחימום זה, וכ״כ החזו״א (סי׳ לז סקי״ד). והבית מאיר אזיל לשיטתו (ס״ה), שתירץ קושיית הראבי״ה (הנ״ל) דלא כדעת הט״ז.

ולפי האג״ט והבית מאיר (שחולקים על הט״ז וס״ל דיש בישול אחר בישול ע״פ דין), יש לפרש שיטת השו״ע דס״ל כדעת הטור והשלט״ג (הנ״ל), דאין צליה אחר בישול. עוד י״ל דסובר השו״ע דיש ב׳ דינים, ולכן יש צלי אחר בישול רק בשינוי טעם, וכדעת הט״ז. ויש בישול אחר צלי גם בלי שינוי הטעם, דבישול עדיף ע״פ דין, וכדעת האג״ט. ומ״מ בצלי אחר בישול בלי שינוי טעם מותר (כיון שצלי אינו יותר חשוב מבישול ע״פ דין).

והנה בבה״ל (ס״ה ד״ה יש) כתב דלפי הפמ״ג אין בישול אחר צלי אחר בישול (וה״ה דאין צלי אחר בישול אחר צלי). ובבה״ל צדד דאסור, וז״ל, דנהי דמוכח [מגמ׳ פסחים (מא.) דקרבן פסח שבשלו ואח״כ צלאו

חייב] דלא נתבטל שם הראשון [כלומר מבושל], הרי שם השני [כלומר צלי] בודאי קיים, ושפיר י״ל דמיקרי עתה בישול אחר צלי, עכ״ל.

[אולם האג״ט (הנ״ל) ע״כ חולק אדברי הפמ״ג, שהרי פירש שיטת ר״א ממיץ שבישול מבטל אפיה ע״פ דין, וכנ״ל. וקשה על האג״ט מגמ׳ פסחים (מא.) דמוכח דשם בישול לא נתבטל ע״י צלי, מדחייב בקרבן פסח שנתבשל ואח״כ נצלה.

ונראה לתרץ, דאף דבתחילת הגמ׳ שם איתא, ׳בשלמא בשלו ואח״כ צלאו חייב דהא בשליה׳ (ומוכח כסברת הפמ״ג הנ״ל, דלא נתבטל שם הראשון, וכמש״כ בבה״ל להדיא), מ״מ כשתירצו (לענין צלאו ואח״כ בשלו חייב) ׳הא מני ר׳ יוסי היא׳, דבישול מבטל אפיה במצה וצליה בפסח, א״כ מסברא י״ל דבשלו ואח״כ צלאו פטור. ואף דמבואר בברייתא דחייב, י״ל דנלמד מגזה״כ דבשל מבושל מ״מ. דבתוס׳ (שם ד״ה אמר) הקשו האי בשל מבושל, שדרש ר׳ מאיר, מאי עביד להו ר׳ יוסי, כיון שלמד מסברא דבישול מבטל צלי, ונדחקו, דלמד מהריבוי דבישול מבטל צלי. ולפי מש״כ י״ל דמהריבוי נלמד דאע״פ דמסברא צלי מבטל בישול, עדיין חייב, ודו״ק. ולפ״ז נדחית ראית הפמ״ג לפי מסקנת הגמ׳ שהיא המקור לשיטת ר״א ממיץ, וכנ״ל.]

ובעיקר השגת הבה״ל על שיטת הפמ״ג, לפי הנחתם דשם הראשון קיים, נראה דאדרבה, מסברא י״ל כדעת הפמ״ג, דכל ששם הראשון קיים אין חיוב בבישול נוסף, ומה בכך ששם השני בודאי קיים. אכן לפי הט״ז (דס״ל דהכל תלוי בשינוי טעם) שפיר י״ל כדעת הבה״ל, דכיון שטעם שם השני קיים, כשמבשל וחוזר לטעם הראשון ונתכוון לכך יש מלאכת מחשבת דבישול.

ועדיין צ״ע, שהבה״ל (סט״ו) מחמיר דלא כדעת הט״ז, בחימום אחר בישול בלי שינוי בטעם. ואולי ס״ל דיש ב׳ דינים (וכמש״כ לעיל לפי השו״ע סט״ו), ובהא דהפמ״ג (בישול אחר בישול צלי אחר בישול) חייב משום שינוי הטעם, ובחימום אחר בישול חייב כי חל שם צליה ע״פ דין. (ולית ליה סברת השלט״ג הנ״ל, דכיון דצליה אינו חשוב יותר מבישול, אין צלי אחר בישול.)

ובס׳ ארחות שבת (פ״א הע׳ סה) כתב, וז״ל, גם במקרה שהאבקות הנמסות עברו תהליך של בישול, יש מקום לדון שתהליך הייבוש שלהן

ייחשב כמין אפיה או צליה, ואם יבא ליתנן בכ"ש ה"ז בכלל הנידון של בישול אחר צליה אחר בישול. אמנם, אפשר שסתם ייבוש אינו נותן לאבקה תואר של דבר אפוי או צלוי, עכ"ל.

ולפי הנ"ל נראה להסביר שמותר ממ"נ, דמצד שינוי הטעם, אינו כאפוי או צלוי, וכמש"כ שם. ומצד בישול אחר אפיה ע"פ דין, אין חיוב מכיון שכבר נתבשל מתחילה, ודו"ק.

סימן י

בישול שלא בכלי ראשון

א. בישול בחמה

איתא בגמ׳ (לט.), בחמה דכ״ע לא פליגי דשרי, בתולדת האור כ״ע לא פליגי דאסור. כי פליגי בתולדת חמה, מר [ת״ק] סבר גזרינן תולדת החמה אטו תולדת האור, ומר [ר׳ יוסי] סבר לא גזרינן, ע״כ. ופרש״י דשרי, דאין דרך בישולו בכך.

ובאג״מ (ח״ג סי׳ נב) מסיק דחייב אף בחמה אם דרך בישול בכך. ונ״מ לתנור מיקרו-גל. ובשש״כ (פ״א הע׳ קכז) כתב בשם הגרשז״א דפטור ומותר. וכ״נ בגמ׳ (שם), שהקשו רבנן על רבי יוסי, מדאסרו רבנן לבשל בחמי טבריה. ורבי יוסי השיב, ההוא תולדת אור הוא, דחלפי אפיתחא דגיהנם. ונראה שלא נחלקו במציאות, דלכו״ע האש שבתוך כדור הארץ מחמם חמי טבריה. ולפי רבנן נידון כחמה, מכיון שהוא אש טבעי שלא ע״י אדם, שהרי גם החמה עצמה היא כדור אש גדול. ולפי רבי יוסי, כל אש שבארץ בכלל אור הוא, ולשון פיתחא דגיהנם מליצה בעלמא היא.

ולכאורה מוכח דההיתר דבישול בחמה אינו הפטור הכללי דמלאכה הנעשית כלאחר יד הנלמד ממלאכת מחשבת. דא״כ אם הדרך הוא לבשל בחמי טבריה, חייב לכו״ע. ואם אין הדרך כן, פטור לכו״ע. (ואינו תלוי אם דינו כתולדות אש או כתולדות החמה.) ובלא״ה בשלא כדרך פטור

אבל אסור, ובחמה מותר. [ובאג"מ (שם) צדד עפ"ז דפטור משום שלא היה במשכן, ולפי טעם זה פטור אף אם דרכו בכך. ולטעם ב' (שם) כתב דאם דרכו בכך חייב אף שלא בשלו בחמה במשכן, וצ"ב.]

ובספר הלכות שבת (הע' תנט) פירש שבישול בחמה דומה לכלי שני, שאין הדרך לבשל כי ברוב מקרים אינו מבשל במציאות. ולכן פטור אף אם מבשל במציאות. ועפ"ז י"ל דהא דקיי"ל דבישול בחמה מותר (ולא אמרינן דפטור אבל אסור, ככל המלאכות הנעשות שלא כדרכן) ה"ט, דכיון דברוב המקרים אינו מבשל במציאות, השוו מידותיהם והתירו בכל ענין. [והיינו דלא כמש"כ בהלכות שבת (שם), שפירש הא דמותר (ולא פטור) בענין אחר, ופירש דברי האג"מ (הנ"ל) כן. ולפי מש"כ לקמן (סימן כו), לא נראה כן.] משא"כ בקלי הבישול (ובישול אחר אפייה) דהדרך הוא לבשל בכלי שני, דאסור מדאורייתא (עי' בסמוך, אות ג).

וא"כ הוא הדין בבישול בחמה, דפטור ומותר, כי אין דרך לבשל בחמה, וכפרש"י, וגם אינו מבשל במציאות ברוב מקרים. אבל אם הדרך לבשל כן, כתנור מיקרו-גל, אסור מדאורייתא.

ולפ"ז יש לפרש דבחמי טבריה אין הדרך לבשל. ולפי רבי יוסי (דחמי טבריה הוי תולדת האור) פטור אבל אסור, וככל מלאכה שנעשית שלא כדרכה. אבל לפי הת"ק (דהוי תולדת החמה), הרי בישול בחמה מותר, כי השוו מידותיהם להקל, כיון שברוב המקרים אינו מתבשל בחמה במציאות. ובתולדת חמה (כחמי טבריה) אסור רק משום שגזרו אטו תולדת האור.

הגרשז"א (מנחת שלמה ח"א סי' יב הע' 4) הוכיח דבישול בחמה אינו בישול ע"פ דין, מזה שנזכר גם לענין פסח מצה וחלה, ושם מאי נ"מ אם רגילים בכך או לא. וע"כ כונת רש"י (לט. הנ"ל) היא דאין בישול בחמה נקרא בישול.

אמנם מבואר בגמ' (פסחים לז.) דעשאן בחמה פטורין, כלומר מן החלה. אבל י"ל דדין מיוחד הוא, דאינו לחם. והרי לדעת ריש לקיש (שם) עשאן באילפס פטורין, ופרש"י דאין לחם אלא האפוי בתנור, כדכתיב לחמכם בתנור אחד. ואף לדעת ר' יוחנן (שם) דאילפס הוי כתנור (משום דיש שם אש), חמה בודאי אינו כתנור. וממילא אין ראיה משם דבישול בחמה אינו בישול.

ולענין קרבן פסח כתיב (שמות יב,ט), אל תאכלו ממנו נא, ובשל מבושל במים, כי אם צלי אש. וא״כ פשוט דצלאו בחמה פסול, דאינו צלי אש, ואין ראיה דבישול בחמה אינו בישול. ואולי י״ל דמלשון ׳אש׳ למדין דכוונת ׳בשל מבושל במים׳ היא רק במים שהוחמו ע״י אש, דההבדל היחידי בין צלי לבין בישול הוא המים, ובשניהם החום בא ע״י אש דוקא. וא״כ גזיה״כ היא שבישול בחמה אינו בישול, ודו״ק.

ב. כלי שני

תנן (מב.), האילפס והקדרה שהעבירן מרותחין לא יתן לתוכן תבלין, אבל נותן הוא לתוך הקערה. ופירש רש״י, דכלי שני אינו מבשל (וכמובאר בגמ׳ מ:).

ובתוס׳ (לט. ד״ה כל) הקשו, שבמשנה (קמה: ומובא בגמ׳ שם) התירו להדיח דבר חי בשבת. וז״ל, אבל לפר״ת דמפרש דעירוי הוי ככלי ראשון, ע״כ מדיחין אותו מכלי שני קאמר, וא״כ מאי איריא מדיחין, אפילו שורין נמי. ואומר ר״י דאפילו בכלי שני אין שורין, דהואיל דהמים חמין מיחזי כמבשל. ואע״ג דתנן לקמן (מב.) אבל נותן לתוך הקערה, היינו דוקא תבלין שהן עשויין למתק את הקדירה ולא מיחזי כמבשל. א״נ ה״ה שורין אותו כיון דאיירי בכלי שני וכו׳, עכ״ל.

ובמג״א (סקט״ו) החמיר כתירוץ ראשון בתוס׳, דבכלי שני מיחזי כמבשל. ולקמן (סקי״ח) דייק מלשון השו״ע (ס״ה) דרק בפת החמירו בכלי שני, שהביא מחלוקת אם מותר לתת פת בכלי שני לפי המ״ד דיש בישול אחר אפיה.

וטעם המחמירים הוא, דכיון שהוא דבר רך אפשר דדינו כקלי הבישול שמתבשלים בכלי שני, כמו מליח הישן וקולייס האיספנין דמתניתין, (עיי״ש במחצית השקל). אבל בשאר דברים לא הזכיר השו״ע איסור בכלי שני כלל, דס״ל להשו״ע כתירוץ השני שבתוס׳. וסיים המג״א דיש להחמיר.

וז״ל המג״א (סקי״ח) אפילו בכלי שני, דיש דברים שמתבשלים בו, ואין אנו בקיאים, וא״כ בשאר דברים נמי יש להחמיר, עס״ט, עכ״ל. וכוונתו דהשו״ע (ס״ט) מתיר לתת מלח בכלי ראשון שלא על האש, והרמ״א אוסר

אף בכלי שני, והן ב׳ לשונות בגמ׳ (מב:). ומוכח מדברי הרמ״א דיש דברים המתבשלים בכלי שני, כמו מלח, והשו״ע החמיר בפת, וא״כ יש לנו להחמיר בשאר דברים.

ולכאורה זוהי שיטת המג״א בעצמו, דיש להחמיר בכלי שני מחשש קלי הבישול. ונמצא דלדבריו, יש שני טעמים להחמיר - מיחזי כמבשל והחשש דקלי הבישול. אבל השו״ע מקיל בדברים שאינם רכים, וכנ״ל. וע״כ ס״ל כתירוץ הב׳ בתוס׳ והיינו דאין זה מיחזי כמבשל (וכמש״כ המג״א, סקי״ט), ועוד ס״ל דאין אנו חוששים לקלי הבישול (כיון דבקיאים אנו בדברים שאינם רכים - שאינם מתבשלים בכלי שני).

והנה במים, מפורש בגמ׳ (מב.) דלד״ה מותר לחממו בכלי שני, וכ״כ השו״ע (סי״ב,יג). ולענין שאר משקים, השו״ע הרב (סי״ב) מקיל, והמ״ב (סקל״ט) מחמיר (אא״כ נתבשלו ונצטננו). ובשמירת שבת כהלכתה (פ״א הע׳ קנא) הוכיח כדברי שו״ע הרב ממש״כ בשו״ע (סי״ג), שמתיר ליתן קיתון של מים או שאר משקים בכלי שני שיש בו מים חמים.

ויש לדחות, דמחלוקת הגר״ז והמ״ב היא אליבא דהמג״א, דאין אנו בקיאים בקלי הבישול, והכל אסור חוץ ממה שמפורש בגמ׳, דהיינו תבלין ומים, ונחלקו אם שאר משקין דינם כמים. אבל לפי השו״ע, שסובר שאנו בקיאים בקלי הבישול, ומחמירים רק בדבר רך, מודה המ״ב שאין להחמיר בשאר משקים. וא״כ א״א להוכיח מלשון השו״ע כשיטת הגר״ז אליבא דהמג״א.

וז״ל הšש״כ (שם), ואין לחלק דשאני התם דהמשקין נמצאין בקיתון המפסיק בינם לכלי שני, דהא כל המקור דשמן מותר בכלי שני הוא מהגמ׳ (מ:), והתם השמן נמצא בתוך הקיתון. ואם נחלק כך אין לנו מקור להקל בשמן בתוך כלי שני עצמו, עכ״ל.

אבל המהרש״א (לט.) באמת חילק כן, שכתב (ביישוב תירוץ הא׳ בתוס׳ שיש חשש מיחזי כמשבל, שלא תיקשי משימת שמן בכלי שני) שלענין מיחזי כמבשל מותר בשמן רק משום דמפסיק כלי (כשאין היתר דתבלין). וקמ״ל הגמ׳ (מ:) רק דאין בישול ממש בכלי שני.

ולענין בישול ממש ע״כ אין לחלק בין שמן בתוך קיתון לבין שמן בתוך כלי שני בלי הפסק קיתון. ובס׳ ארחות שבת (פ״א הע׳ קל) פירש שהטעם שאינו מיחזי כמבשל כשיש קיתון הוא, דהדרך לבשל בכלי

ראשון הוא בלי הפסק קיתון, ולכן לא מיחזי כמבשל בכלי שני כשיש קיתון המפסיק.

ואין להקשות על שיטת הגר״ז מדברי המהרש״א הנ״ל שכתב שבהפסק כלי לא מיחזי כמבשל, ומשמע שבמשקין בלי הפסק כלי מיחזי כמבשל. דאדרבא, המהרש״א הקדים, וז״ל, ושמן בעין לא שייך ביה למתק, עכ״ל. כלומר, דשמן בפך נראה כמחמם את השמן ולא כמקרר את המשקה הנמצא בפך, ובזה אסור לולא הפסק כלי. אבל בחלב בקפה נראה כמקרר את הקפה ולא כמחמם את החלב, ודומה לתבלין שכונתו למתק, ולא לבשל ולא לחמם.

ולפ״ז יש לחלק, דשאר משקין בכלי שני ממש בלי הפסק כלי אסור אפילו לדעת השו״ע (סי״ג), ודלא כדעת השש״כ. והשו״ע מתיר נתינת שאר משקין בכ״ש רק בהפסק קיתון. ונראה דכן סובר המ״ב, דהרי לא חלק על דברי השו״ע (סי״ג), אף דפסק (סקל״ד) כדברי המג״א דמיחזי כמבשל בכלי שני, ודלא כדעת השו״ע. וכן כתב בספר הלכות שבת במטבח (פ״ב הע׳ 21).

ולענין קפה ותה, בהלכות שבת (הע׳ נה) כתב דלפי המ״ב (סקל״ט) אסור בכלי שני. ולפי האג״מ (שם, ובאג״מ ח״ד סי׳ עד סקי״ח) מותר, וכדין תבלין, ותמה על המ״ב. ובהלכות שבת כתב דתבלין דזמן חז״ל לא היו מקלי הבישול, משא״כ בזה״ז. וכ״כ בשש״כ (הע׳ קנב), דתבלין שלנו דקים מאד ומתבשלים בכלי שני.

ובהלכות שבת (שם) הוסיף דקפה הוא דבר העיקרי במים. ונראה בכוונתו, דהתוס׳ (לט.) כתבו דבתבלין לא מיחזי כמבשל, כי עשויין למתק את הקדירה, וכנ״ל. ופירש בהלכות שבת דהתבלין לא ניכר כלל בתבשיל, ונראה כמבשל את האוכל העיקרי, ולא את התבלין. אבל תבלין כמו קפה בודאי ניכר, ושייך בו סברת נראה כמבשל, ואסור בכלי שני.

והנה באור זרוע (סי׳ ז) כתב דברי התוס׳ (לט. הנ״ל) והוסיף, וז״ל, שהרי יש שנותן תבלין גם במשקה קר, ולכן אינו נראה כמבשל, עכ״ל. כלומר, שאין כונתו לבשל את התבלין, כדמוכח מהא דנותן תבלין גם למשקה קר. וכן מוכח משקית תה, שהרי זורק את התבלין שבשקית לאשפה. ומכיון שכונתו רק למתק את הקדירה ולא לבשל את התבלין עצמם, אינו בכלל חומרת נראה כמבשל, וכמש״כ האג״מ.

ולפ"ז יש לפרש מחלוקת הגר"ז והמ"ב הנ"ל, דבמים לא אמרינן דנראה כמבשל, דאדרבה, הוספת מים קרים לכלי שני נראה כמקרר את המשקין, ולא כמבשל את המים. ובשאר משקין, לפי המ"ב נראה כמחמם את המשקה הקר, ולפי הגר"ז נראה כמקרר את המשקה החם.

ולענין מי שמוסיף חלב קר לכוס קפה חם, מלשון בנ"א משמע כשיטת הגר"ז, דכונתו לקרר את הקפה כדי שיוכל לשתותו (בנוסף על טעם החלב שמוסיף), ולא לחמם את החלב. ובפמ"ג (א"א סקל"ב) כתב דמים מתערבים ואינם עומדים בפ"ע, ולכן אינו נראה כמבשל. ולפ"ז הוא הדין בשאר משקים, וכדעת הגר"ז.

ג. מים בכלי שני

והנה בגמ' (מב.) מבואר דלכל הדעות מותר לחמם מים בכלי שני, וכנ"ל, אף אם מגיעים לשיעור יד סולדת בו.

וכתב הרשב"א (שם) וז"ל, ואפילו היו מים שהיד סולדת בו לאחר שנתערבו צונן לתוכן, אינו מחמת הצוננין שבו להיות יד סולדת בו, אלא מחמת הראשונים שלא נצטננו, עכ"ל. כלומר, שהוקשה לו, איך י"ל דכלי שני אינו מבשל מים, הלא גדר בישול מים הוא חום יד סולדת בו, ורואים בחוש שהצוננים שניתנו בכלי שני מגיעים לשיעור יד סולדת בו. ותירץ, דבאמת לא הגיעו הצוננים ליד סולדת בו, ומרגישים יד סולדת בו ע"י החמין שלא נצטננו.

ודבריו צ"ע במציאות, דיש בילה בתערובת לח, וברור שהכל יד סולדת בו. ובשבה"ש (ס"ק צ"א) הקשה מהשו"ע (סי"ג) שמתיר להניח קיתון מים בכלי שני, ובפשוטו מיירי גם כשהמים בקיתון מגיעים ליד סולדת בו, ושם א"א לפרש משום החמין, שהרי לא נתערבו. ותירץ וז"ל, וצ"ל דתולדות האור לא מקרי רק מה שהוחם באור עצמו, ולא כאשר הורק מכלי אל כלי, עכ"ל. וצ"ע, דמצינו בקלי הבישול שחייב בכלי שני, ומוכח דכלי שני דינו כתולדת האור, וצע"ג.

ובספר הלכות שבת (הע' תנט) תירץ הקושיא על היתר נתינת מים בכלי שני, וז"ל והנראה בזה (ע"פ תוס' מ:) דכלי ראשון, כיון דדופנותיו חמין, לפיכך ראוי לבשל ודרך בישול בכך, משא"כ כלי שני, כיון שהולך

ומתקרר, אין דרך לבשל בו, חוץ מקלי הבישול שהדרך לבשל אותם בכלי שני, עכ"ל. ולפ"ז אף אם כלי שני מבשל במציאות אין איסור מן התורה, דאין דרכו בכך, ורבנן לא אסרוהו, עיי"ש.

וכבר נתבאר לעיל (סי' ט אות יא, לענין בישול בחמה), דע"פ סברת ספר הלכות שבת י"ל דחכמים השוו מדותיהם והקילו בכל אופן, כל שאינו דרך בישול. וגם בכלי שני יש לומר כן. ולפ"ז ניחא סתימת הראשונים והשו"ע להתיר בכלי שני חוץ ממה שנזכר בגמ'. ולא חששו שאין אנו בקיאים, דכל שאינו דרך בישול מותר אפילו אם מתבשל במציאות. ואדרבה צ"ע למה אסר השו"ע פת בכלי שני (ס"ה). וי"ל דדרך בישול בכלי שני נמדד לעומת כלי ראשון, וכיון שאינו מצוי כ"כ להשים פת בכלי ראשון, א"א לומר דבכלי שני לא נחשב דרך בישול.

ולפ"ז נראה להחמיר בתה בכלי שני, וכדעת המ"ב ודלא כדעת האג"מ, עיין לעיל (אות ב), דכיון שדרכו בזמנינו לבשל תה בכלי שני, יש איסור דאורייתא כיון דהוא מקלי הבישול, כדנראה במציאות.נמצא דתבלין שבגמ' דהתירו בכלי שני, יותר קל משאר מאכלים שאסרו בכלי שני לדעת התוס'. מאידך, שקית תה חמור טפי משאר מאכלים ואסור מדאורייתא לבשלה בכלי שני גם לפי השו"ע. משא"כ בשאר מאכלים (שאין דרכם לבשלם בכלי שני) דמותר להניחם בכלי שני.

ולפי הנ"ל יתכן לחלק בין כלי שני לכלי שלישי, אף אם במציאות שוים הם לענין בישול, אם כלי שני דרכו בכך וכלי שלישי אין דרכו בכך. אך נראה שתה דרכו בכך גם בכלי שלישי, ע"י הורקת מים מקדירה לכד של כסף, ומהכד לכוס, ואח"כ מכניסים התה. ומ"מ נ"מ לשאר דברים שאין דרכם לבשל בכלי שלישי, דלפי הנ"ל מותר, ודלא כדעת החזו"א (סי' נב סקי"ט) שכתב דאין לחלק בין כלי שני לכלי שלישי, כיון דבמציאות שוים הם, וכנ"ל.

והנה היראים כתב וז"ל, ואין בישול תלוי לא בכלי ראשון ולא בכלי שני, אך לפי שהוא דבר המתבשל. פעמים שהוא דבר רך ומתבשל אף בכלי שני, ויש דבר קשה שאפילו בכלי ראשון אינו מתבשל. ויש דבר המתבשל בכלי ראשון ולא בכלי שני וכו'. למדנו לפי רכיכותן הוי בישולן. הילכך יזהר אדם שלא להכניס בשבת שום דבר בכלי שני ואף בכלי שלישי שהיד סולדת בו, שאין אנו בקיאים בדברים רכים וקשים מי הוא מתבשל ומי

שהוא אינו מתבשל וכו׳, עכ״ל. ומכאן מקור לשיטת המג״א להחמיר בכל מאכלין בכלי שני, וגם מקור לשיטת החזו״א להחמיר בכל מאכלים אפילו בכלי שלישי, משום חשש קלי הבישול.

ולפי זה יש לפרש מחלוקת הגר״ז והמ״ב [מצד החשש דקלי הבישול, דלעיל (אות ב) בארנו מחלוקתם מצד נראה כמבשל], דהמג״א מחמיר בכל מאכלים, כיון שיש מאכלים שדרכם לבשל בכלי שני. ואיננו בקיאין בקלי הבישול, ובקלי הבישול שדרכן לבשל בכלי שני אסור מן התורה. אבל לא מצינו במשקין שדרכן לבשל בכלי שני, ולכן מותר לפי הגר״ז. ולפי המ״ב, מקילים רק בתבלין ומים, שמפורש הוא בגמ׳ שמותר. אבל במשקין החמירו כבאוכלין, אף אם החשש דקלי הבישול לא שייך, דלא פלוג חז״ל.

והרשב״א (מב.) הנ״ל אסר לתת מים באמבטי בכלי שני, וז״ל, דא״א לבא לידי הפשר אלא לידי בישול, ואע״פ שהוא כלי שני ובעלמא אינו מבשל, הכא שאני, לפי שדרכן לחממן יותר מדאי, עכ״ל.

[ואף שלפי הרשב״א אין אדם רוחץ במים שהיד סולדת בו וכנ״ל (סי׳ ט אות ט), י״ל שנכנס לזיעה שעולה מהאמבטי שחם יותר מדאי, ודו״ק.]

והנה מלשון הרשב״א נראה, דהכל תלוי בכדרכו, וכמש״כ לעיל ע״פ ספר הלכות שבת (אלא ששם כתב כן ע״פ תוס׳ (מ:) ומשמע שלא פירש כן דברי הרשב״א). ולכן בכוס, שדרכו רק להפשיר ולא לבשל, מותר לתת מים קרים בכלי שני אף אם במציאות מתבשל, משום דאינו נחשב דרך בישול. והיינו טעמא, דכאשר מפשיר, בדרך כלל התערובת הוי פחות משיעור יד סולדת בו. ואף אם במקרה נמצא דמגיע ליד סולדת בו, הרי אין זה דרך בישול.

ולפ״ז לשון הנ״ל ברשב״א, ׳אינו מחמת הצוננין שבו להיות יד סולדת בו׳, לא ר״ל במציאות. דבאמת במציאות הצוננין מגיעים לשיעור יד סולדת בו. אלא שאין הדרך לחמם הצוננין עד יד סולדת בו, אלא להגיע לפושרין, כלומר פחות מיד סולדת בו. ולשון הרשב״א, ׳אלא מחמת הראשונים שלא נצטננו׳, ר״ל, שהדרך היא לצנן החמין עד לפחות מיד סולדת בו. ובמקרה זה הראשונים החמין לא נצטננו כ״כ, והתערובת יותר מיד סולדת בו, ופטור ומותר מפני שאינו דרך בישול, וכנ״ל.

ונראה שהרשב״א אזיל לשיטתו דאין אדם שותה חמין גמורין אלא פושרין, וכנ״ל (שם). וע״כ הדרך לצנן החמין היא שמורידין החום עד פחות משיעור יד סולדת בו.

סימן יא

עירוי

א. מכלי ראשון

בתוס׳ (מב: ד״ה אבל) כתבו ג׳ שיטות בעירוי מכלי ראשון. לפי הרשב״ם דינו ככלי שני ואינו מבשל, לפי הר״י דינו ככלי ראשון ומבשל בכולו, ולמסקנת התוס׳ עירוי מבשל כדי קליפה, דתתאה גבר, אבל אדמיקר ליה בלע כדי קליפה, וה״ה דמבשלו. ולפי הרשב״ם י״ל דמבליע כדי קליפה אבל אינו מבשל. ושיטה ד׳ לרבינו יונה, עיין לעיל (סי׳ ט אות ו), דעירוי ככלי שני אף לפני שגבר עליו התתאה, ולכן אסור לערות מכלי לכלי, וכנ״ל.

וכתב הרא״ש (סי׳ טז), שהרשב״ם מתיר לערות מכלי ראשון על התרנגולת למלגה. ובק״נ (אות א) הקשה, דאף דתתאה גבר, מ״מ אדמיקר ליה בלע כדי קליפה. ותירץ דהעירוי מבליע כדי קליפה אבל אינו מפליט או מבשל. ויותר נראה דעירוי מפליט ג״כ, אבל אינו מפליט ומבליע כאחד. דכמו שאינו מבשל לדעת הרשב״ם, כן אינו מפלט ומבליע כאחד, שגדר בישול הוא תערובת הטעמים, וכדברי החוו״ד (סי׳ צב סקכ״ז). ולכן כאשר מערה מכלי ראשון על התרנגולת למולגה, אין דם יוצא ממקום למקום (שרק בכה״ג אינו יוצא אח״כ ע״י מליחה) והתרנגולת מותרת.

ולפי הרשב״ם דעירוי אינו מבשל, ע״כ צריך לחלק בין בליעה לבישול. והגר״א (יו״ד סי׳ קה ס״ק יג) הביא שהרמב״ן והרשב״א מחלקים בין בליעה לבישול לענין כלי שני. וכמו שעירוי לפי הרשב״ם מבליע ואינו

מבשל, כן סוברים הרמב"ן ורשב"א בכלי שני ממש [דלדבריהם עירוי מבשל מדטעון מריקה]. והוסיפו, דאף אם אין יד סולדת בו, מבליע, וכראייתם מחום בית השחיטה.

והנה לדינא, מקילים כאשר אין היד סולדת בו, וכמש"כ הפ"ת (שם סק"ו), ומשמע דקיי"ל דכל מקום שאין בישול אין בליעה. וא"כ נראה דלענין בליעת איסור יש להקל כדעת הרמ"א בכלי שני אף כאשר היד סולדת בו, ודלא כדעת הט"ז (שם סק"ד). [אולם קושית הנקוה"כ (שם) לק"מ, דלר"ת לשיטתו, בישול ובליעה שוים, ועירוי אוסר רק כדי קליפה. ולפי הרשב"ם, דיש בליעה בלי בישול, כלי שני אוסר כולו.]

ובשש"כ (הע' קלט) פסק דמותר לערות ע"ג בקבוק חלב, דהבקבוק במקום כדי קליפה וכנ"ל. אך נראה דיש להחמיר לכתחילה, דלפי הרבה פוסקים עירוי מבשל בכולו. וכך נראה לפרש כוונת הט"ז (סי' שיח סקט"ז) דקיי"ל כדעת רש"י ור"ת דעירוי ככלי ראשון לחומרא. כלומר, דלפי רש"י ור"ת עירוי מבשל בכולו, וכמש"כ הרשב"א (מב:). ולדבריהם עירוי מהני ככלי ראשון אף לקולא, כדי להגעיל כלי שבשלו בו בכלי ראשון. וכתב הט"ז, דלא קיי"ל כרש"י ור"ת לקולא, ולכן אין להגעיל בעירוי אם בשלו בו בכלי ראשון.

וז"ל המ"ב (סקע"ד), העירוי מכלי ראשון קיי"ל דהוא מבשל כדי קליפה, עכ"ל. ויש לפרש דעירוי מבשל עכ"פ כדי קליפה, ואולי אף בכולו, ובנידון שם אין נ"מ בזה. ואף דהרמ"א (סי' צב ס"ז) פסק דמבליע רק כדי קליפה, וכנ"ל, י"ל דזהו בדיעבד, אבל לכתחילה אולי יש להחמיר, ובפרט באיסור חמור דבישול בשבת.

ובמ"ב (שם) אסר תבלין שעירה עליהם מכלי ראשון, אף בדיעבד, וכדעת המג"א (סקל"ב). ובשבה"ש (סקנ"ח) הקשה, דבמ"ב (סק"ב) כתב דכל שיש מחלוקת מותר בדיעבד, וכאן הלוא מתיר הרשב"ם. ובספר הלכות שבת (הע' נב) כתב דקיי"ל בהחלט דעירוי ככלי ראשון עכ"פ לענין כדי קליפה, וכמש"כ הפמ"ג ביו"ד (סי' סח). אבל נראה, דרק לענין בליעה עירוי אוסר כדי קליפה לכו"ע וכנ"ל. אבל בבישול מקיל הרשב"ם, וכן פסקו הרשב"א (כאן) והגר"א (יו"ד סי' סח סקכ"ז). ואף דלא קיי"ל כן, מ"מ אינה שיטה דחוייה. ולכ"נ כדעת השבה"ש, דמותר בדיעבד, ודלא כדעת המג"א. והמ"ב עצמו (ססק"ב) הקשה על המג"א וסיים וצע"ק, עיי"ש.

ב. נפסק הקילוח

והנה המ״ב (סקע״ה, הנ״ל) מתיר עירוי שנפסק הקילוח עכ״פ בדיעבד. ובאליה רבה (שהביא שם בשעה״צ ס״ק קב) מוכח דמותר לכתחילה, וז״ל, הרמ״א (יו״ד סי׳ סח ס״י) כתב דבנפסק הקילוח שרי. ובש״ך (סי׳ קה סק״ה) כתב דאף למ״ד דאסור היינו שמבליע, אבל אינו מבליע ומפליט כאחת. ומזה פשוט דלענין בישול בשבת דאין חשש כלל, עכ״ל.

ומקור דין עירוי שנפסק הקילוח הוא בגמ׳ פסחים (עו.), דנטף מרוטבו [של קרבן פסח] על החרס [ושוב חזר על הקרבן] יטול את מקומו [שאינו צלי אש]. ובר״ן (ע״ז עה:) הקשה מכאן על ר״ת הסובר דבלע בכולו. [התוס׳ הביאו שיטה זו בשם הר״י, והר״ן מביאו בשם ר״ת.] ותירץ דנטף ר״ל שקילוחו נפסק. ובש״ך (שם) הוכיח משם דעכ״פ מבליע כדי קליפה, וכתב שהרמ״א (סי׳ סח) מקיל רק שאינו מפליט ומבליע כא׳, וכנ״ל. אבל ברמ״א (סי׳ צב ס״ז) נראה שאינו מבליע כלל אלא דינו ככלי שני. ובמטה יהונתן (שם) דחה ראיית הש״ך מפסחים, דלמ״ד תתאה גבר פירשו בגמ׳ דמיירי בחרס רותחת, ולעולם בנפסק הקילוח ונפל על דבר צונן אינו מבליע כלל.

ולכאורה קשה להש״ך (שם) מדברי הרמ״א הנ״ל, וכן הקשה בהגהה (שם). ובדגמ״ר (סי׳ צב ש״ך סקל״ח) תירץ, דהרמ״א מקיל רק בעירוי שנפסק וגם נזחל ע״ג הכירה, אבל בלא נזחל מודה דאוסר כדי קליפה, עיי״ש. ויותר נראה כדעת החזו״א (יו״ד סי׳ ט סק״ה), דבישול ובליעה שוים לדינא, וכנ״ל. ולפי הרמ״א אין בישול ואין בליעה בעירוי שנפסק הקילוח (ודלא כדעת הש״ך). ורק בעירוי שלא נפסק הקילוח מבשל ומבליע כדי קליפה.

[והקשה האג״ט (סקל״ב) על היסוד הנ״ל, דעירוי שנפסק הקילוח אינו מבשל את מה שנפל עליו. דבגמ׳ (שם) נראה דלפי רב שסובר עילאה גבר, רוטב הנוטף מרתח ליה לחרס, והחרס מבשל הפסח ואוסרו, וק״ו דהרוטב מבשל את מה שנופל עליו, אע״פ שנפסק הקילוח. ותירץ האג״ט, שהרוטב עצמו נצלה באש ודינו כדפנות שהוחמו באש, משא״כ בקילוח מן הקדירה, שהדפנות מפסיקין בינו לבין האור, עיי״ש. וזהו חידוש גדול, ומשאר פוסקים לא נראה כן, ולדבריהם צ״ע כנ״ל. ועוד צ״ע, דלכאורה

אף בעירוי שלא נפסק הקילוח שנפל על החרס, החרס שנפל עליו נידון ככלי שני, ואילו בגמ' משמע דהוי ככלי ראשון, וצ"ע.

ואולי י"ל, דבתוס' (שם) ד"ה בשלמא הקשו וז"ל, וא"ת למ"ד עלאה גבר, למה הפסח אינו נאסר מחמת השפוד, עכ"ל. והקשה המהרש"א (שם), דקשה גם לשמואל דס"ל תתאה גבר, כיון דהשפוד הוא באמצע הפסח. ותירץ הצל"ח (שם), דלמסקנה, ששמואל פירש מתני' בחרס רותח, עיי"ש, גם רב מודה לפירוש זה, להנצל מקושית התוס'. וכ"נ קצת בגמ', דרק בקומץ פירש שמואל ברותח, דלרב אצ"ל כן. משא"כ בחרס, דלכו"ע הוי רותח. והתוס' הקשו רק להס"ד דרב חולק, עיי"ש. ולפי"ז למסקנה אף לרב א"צ ליטול מקומו בנטף הרוטב על חרס צונן, דנפסק הקילוח אינו מבשל, וניחא קושית האג"ט.]

ג. נזחל

ובעירוי שנזחל ולא נפסק כתב הרמ"א (סי' צב ס"ז) דמבליע כדי קליפה, וכמש"כ בתה"ד (סי' קפא), ומובא בבהגר"א (שם סקל"ו). ומקורו בגמ' (מ:), בקשתי להניח לרבי פך של שמן באמבטי ואמר לי טול בכלי שני ותן. ואע"ג שהאמבטי נמשך מן היורה בקרקע, אעפ"כ הוי ככלי ראשון. ואין לדחות דחמי טבריא שאני שטבען בקרקע, דא"כ למה הוצרך להוכיח (שם) דמיירי בחמי טבריה מהא דמעשה דרבי לאחר גזירה היה, כלומר דלולא גזירת מרחצאות היה אפשר לפרש המעשה בחמי האור. הלוא בלא"ה אין לפרש המעשה בחמי האור אם עירוי שנזחל אינו מבשל. אלא ע"כ מוכח דאע"פ שנזחל דינו ככלי ראשון, עכ"ד התה"ד.

אבל לקמן (סי' צה ס"ג) כתב הרמ"א בשם האו"ה וז"ל, אם עירה מים רותחים על כלים של בשר ושל חלב ... הכל שרי, דאין עירוי ככלי ראשון ממש שיעשה שהכלים שמערה עליהם יבלעו זה מזה, עכ"ל. ומוכח דעירוי שנזחל אינו ככלי ראשון, וצ"ע.

ותירץ החוו"ד (סי' צב סקכ"ג) דעירוי שנזחל מבליע, וכדברי הרמ"א (שם), אבל אינו מבשל, ולכן אינו מפליט ומבליע כאחד, וכדברי הרמ"א (סי' צה) שכתב שהכלים אסורים רק אם יש פליטה מכלי אחד ובליעה לכלי אחר. אך קשה דראיית התה"ד היא מהגמ' (מ:), ומוכח שמבשל ולא

רק מבליע. ותירץ החוו"ד, דהתה"ד עצמו כתב שהראייה דחוקה קצת, ומ"מ מסברא נראה דדינו ככלי ראשון, וא"כ שפיר יש לחלק בין בליעה ובישול. ועדיין צע"ק, דעיי"ל דלפי רוב הפוסקים, שסוברים דעירוי מבשל (ולא רק מבליע) כדי קליפה, דין בישול ובליעה שוים.

ובפמ"ג (ש"ד סי' צה סקי"ח) הוכיח מראית התה"ד דעירוי שנזחל מבשל, וא"כ יש סתירה בדברי הרמ"א. וצדד דבתה"ד מיירי בעירוי מכלי ראשון שעל גבי האש, אבל באו"ה מיירי בעירוי מכלי ראשון שאינו על גבי האש. אך הקשה מדברי הרמ"א בת"ח שאוסר אף בעירוי מכלי ראשון שאינו על גבי האש.

ובספר חימום מים בשבת (עמ' 58) תירץ דעירוי שנזחל מבליע אף אם הקדירה איננה על גבי האש. אבל לענין בישול, וכן להפליט ולהבליע כאחד, בעינן עירוי שנזחל מקדירה שעל גבי האש. וניחא שיטת הרמ"א על דרך הפמ"ג. ועדיין צע"ק כנ"ל, דלפי רוב הפוסקים דיני בישול ובליעה שוים הם, וכנ"ל.

ובאמת הש"ך (סי' צה סק"כ) פסק כנגד הרמ"א (שם), וכתב שהאו"ה אזיל לשיטתו, דס"ל דעירוי נחשב ככלי שני כדעת הרשב"ם, ואינו מבשל אפילו כדי קליפה [ורק החמיר בתורת חומרא כנגדו (עי' לקמן), ולכן בנזחל הקיל]. אבל למאי דקיי"ל דעירוי מבשל כדי קליפה מדינא ולא כחומרא בעלמא, ומפליט ומבליע כא' כדי קליפה, ע"כ אסור, דאין חילוק בין עירוי באויר לעירוי שנזחל. ונדחק ליישב שיטת הרמ"א, דס"ל דמפליט ומבליע כאחד כשמערה על תרנגולת למלגה, וכמש"כ לעיל (סי' סח), שהוא דבר רך, משא"כ בכלי (סי' צה), עיי"ש.

ואולי יש לפרש שיטת הרמ"א בענין אחר, דכבר נתבאר ע"פ החוו"ד דגדר בישול הוא תערובת טעמים. ומהא דעירוי מבשל כדי קליפה נלמד דמפליט ומבליע כא' כדי קליפה, כמו במערה על תרנגולת למלגה. אך י"ל שאין בכח העירוי להפליט ממקום אחד ולהבליע במקום אחר, דיכול לערב רק טעמים שהם תוך כדי קליפה אחד לשני, כמו בתרנגולת. אבל במערה מים על כלי בשר וכלי חלב, א"א לעירוי להוליך הטעם מכלי בשר לכלי חלב המרוחק ממנו יותר מכדי קליפה ולהבליעו שם.

ועיי"ש ברמ"א שמתיר אף אם שומן דבוק בכלים. וצע"ג, דא"כ א"צ להפליט ולהבליע, דיש שומן בעין ודי להבליעו, ואיך מתיר הרמ"א, וכן

הקשה באג"מ (יו"ד ח"א סי' מב), עיי"ש. ולפי מש"כ י"ל דעירוי אינו יכול להוליך השומן ולהבליעו במקום אחר, דכאשר המים עוברים כדי קליפה ממקום נגיעתם בשומן, אינם מבליעים השומן בכלי האחר, וכנ"ל, וכ"כ האג"מ (שם).

אמנם אף דיש ליישב שיטת הרמ"א בדרכים הנ"ל, מ"מ במקור הדין באו"ה (כלל לד סי"ח, כא) מוכח דסובר כהרשב"ם, וכמש"כ הש"ך. אלא דאנו מחמירין לומר שמבליע כדי קליפה, דאדמיקר ליה בלע, ולפי האו"ה החמירו גם שמבשל כדי קליפה. אבל כיון שאינו אלא חומרא, הקילו בעירוי שנזחל שאינו מבליע ואינו מבשל.

ולפ"ז לרוב הפוסקים החולקים על הרשב"ם אסור לערות על צדו של הכוס כדי שהמים יתפשטו על התבלין, ודלא כרע"א (ס"י) שהביא דברי האו"ה שמקיל בזה. ואף דלפי החוו"ד והפמ"ג יש סמך להקל, וכפירושם ברמ"א, מ"מ אסור לפי הש"ך. ואף לפי הרמ"א אסור לפי מה שתרצנו לעיל (בדעתו), ויש להחמיר.

ד. נתמלא מכלי ראשון שעל האש

וז"ל רש"י (מ: ד"ה בכלי), דהך אמבטי שהחמין נמשכין לה מן המעיין חשיב לה ככלי ראשון שנרתחו בו שאע"פ שהעבירו מעל האור מבשל, עכ"ל. ובפמ"ג (א"א סקל"ג) פסק כן, ומשמע (בפשוטו) שפירש שהמים נמשכים מן המעיין אל האמבטי, ומ"מ המים שבאמבטי נידונים כמים בכלי ראשון, כיון שנמשכו מהמעיין (שדין המעיין הוא כעומד על גבי האש). ובשש"כ (הע' קכב) כתב כן בשם החזו"א. ועפ"ז פסק שכאשר ממלאים כוס מדוד חשמלי הכוס נידון ככלי ראשון. ובשש"כ הקשה מדברי הרמ"א (סי' צב הנ"ל, דמיירי בקדירה על גבי האש), דמוכח דדינו כעירוי ואוסר רק כדי קליפה.

ויש לדחות הראיה מרש"י, דאין כוונת רש"י כפשוטו, וכהבנת הפמ"ג (שם) דיש לאמבטי דין כלי ראשון גם לאחר שנפסק זחילת המים לתוכו. ומה שהזכיר דין כלי ראשון שהעבירו מעל האור היינו כדי להוכיח שיש דין כלי ראשון אף אם איננו על האש עכשיו, כיון שהיה על האש ועי"ז יש קשר בינו לבין האש אחרי שהוסר. והוה"נ באמבטי דמעולם לא היה על האש, כל זמן שהמים נזחלים לתוכו וקשור הוא לאש. והיא ראיה ע"ד

דמיון. משא"כ אחרי שנפסק זחילת המים, דהאמבטי והכוס אינם קשורים להאש, ודינם ככלי שני.

והנה ז"ל התה"ד (סוף סי' קפא), הואיל והיה הקילוח נוזל והולך מתוך הרתיחה העומדת אצל האש, כל טיפה וטיפה אחרונה אינה מנחת את הראשונה להתקרר. שהרי פירשו התוספות פ' כירה דהא דיד סולדת בו בכלי שני אינו מבשל, היינו משום דאינו עומד אצל האש אינו מחזיק חומו והולך ומתקרר, משמע דאם עוד היה כח האש שולט שם אינו מתקרר, עכ"ל. ולפ"ז נראה דכל זמן שהמים נזחלים, כל המים שבאמבטי ושבכוס נידונים כמים בכלי ראשון. אבל כשנפסקה הזחילה נידונים כמים בכלי שני, וכנ"ל.

והנה לכאורה סובר התה"ד דעירוי מבשל בכולו, דאם עירוי מבשל רק כדי קליפה, מותר להניח פך שמן באמבטי, דהרי הפך הוא הכדי קליפה וא"כ השמן לא יתבשל. ולפ"ז א"א לפרש כדברי התה"ד לפי דעת הפוסקים דעירוי מבשל רק כדי קליפה, וכסתימת המ"ב (סקע"ד).

אך אפשר ליישב את שיטת התה"ד, אף לדידן (דקיי"ל דעירוי מבשל רק כדי קליפה). די"ל דעירוי מבשל כדי קליפה רק כשנופל על דבר קר. אבל כשמתאספים המים באמבטי או כוס, 'טיפה אחרונה אינה מנחת את הראשונה להתקרר'. ולכן כל זמן שהמים נזחלים הוי ככלי ראשון ממש, אף לדידן.

[עוד י"ל (ליישב שיטת הרמ"א דבנזחל מכלי ראשון שעל גבי האש אינו ככלי ראשון) כמש"כ התה"ד עצמו, דחמי טבריא שאני, שיש שם קרקע חם. ולכן האמבטי נידון ככלי ראשון, דיש אש טבעי סמוך לו השומר על חימומו. ואף שהעמידוהו בחמי טבריה רק משום גזירת מרחצאות, כבר כתב בתה"ד דיש לדחות, דחמי טבריא שאני. ונראה לפרש דלפי ההו"א בגמ', דמיירי בחמי האור, א"כ מסתמא אמבטי ר"ל כלי ראשון שעל האש, וכגמ' (מב., לפי רש"י עי' שעה"צ סקק"ה), ואין ראיה כלל לענין עירוי שנזחל. ויש ראיה רק לפי המסקנה, שהעמידוהו בחמי טבריא. ויש לדחותה כנ"ל, דחמי טבריא שאני.

ובאמת לולא דברי רש"י היה נראה לפרש דאמבטי ר"ל בריכה העומדת ע"ג החור שממנו יוצאים המים, ונידון כע"ג האש ממש, וכמבואר בגמרא (לט., ובתה"ד שם כתב דרש"י לא פירש כן מפני שאינו מצוי,

עיי"ש). וכ"נ בחדושים המיוחסים להר"ן, שבתחלה פירש אמבטי, בריכה העשוי בבית המרחץ שהמים החמין נמשכין בה ונאספין שם. ובסוף פירש, אבל לא באותה בריכה שחמי טבריה שם, ולא הזכיר שנזחל או נמשך כמש"כ לעיל, ומשמע דמיירי בבריכה שע"ג החור שממנו יוצאים חמי טבריא, וכנ"ל. ודו"ק.]

ה. כלי ששואבים בו

הקשו התוס' (מ: ד"ה ושמע) וז"ל, תימה מ"ש כלי שני מכלי ראשון, דאי יד סולדת בו אפילו כלי שני נמי, ואי אין יד סולדת בו אפילו כלי ראשון נמי אינו מבשל. וי"ל לפי שכלי ראשון מתוך שעמד על האור דופנותיו חמין ומחזיק חומו זמן מרובה, ולכך נתנו בו שיעור דכ"ז שהיד סולדת בו אסור. אבל כלי שני אע"ג דיד סולדת בו מותר, שאין דופנותיו חמין, והולך ומתקרר, עכ"ל.

ובחוו"ד (סי' צב סקכ"ז) פירש, דלפי שמואל הסובר (פסחים עו.) תתאה גבר, קושית התוס' לק"מ, דבכלי ראשון האש הוא התתאה וגבר, ובכלי שני הכלי הקר הוא התתאה וגבר. אבל לפי רב, דעילאה גבר, קשה בתרתי, דנימא דכלי שני מבשל ולא כלי ראשון. ולכן הוצרכו התוס' לתרץ ב' תירוצים, דבכלי ראשון תירצו דדפנות שהוחמו באור לא מתקררות ע"י עילאה. ובכלי שני תירצו דדפנות מקררות ואינו מבשל אף לדעת רב.

ולפ"ז מחלוקת רב ושמואל היא כשאין דפנות מחממות או מקררות, כגון עירוי שנפסק הקילוח, דאין לו קשר עם דופן שהוחם כעירוי סתם. ולכן לפי שמואל אם נפל רוטב של איסור על סולת צונן א"צ לקמוץ את מקומו, וע"כ פי' מתני' (עה:) בסולת רותחת. ולפי רב אף בסולת צוננת יקמוץ, דעילאה גבר.

וכתב החוו"ד, דכלי ששואבים בו מכלי ראשון, שדופנותיו הוחמו ע"י המים ולא ע"י האור, דינו ככלי ראשון ובולע מזבוב שנפל לתוכו, וכמש"כ הש"ך (סי' קז סק"ז) ע"פ הרמ"א (שם). ופירש כנ"ל, דאין לו דפנות מקררות, וגם לא דפנות שהוחמו ע"י האור. וא"כ קיי"ל תתאה גבר, ובנפל לתוכו דבר צונן יש בליעה. וכתב החוו"ד דיוצא לפי התוס' (מ:)

דלפי מאי דקיי״ל כשמואל דתתאה גבר, אם נתן אוכל לתוך כלי ששאבו בו מכלי ראשון, ע״כ מבשל ג״כ.

אך עיי״ש בחוו״ד דנ״מ בזה גם לדבר גוש, שאין דפנות קרות מקררות אותו. ונחלקו המהרש״ל והרמ״א אם בולע או לא, וכמבואר בט״ז (סי׳ צד סקי״ד). ושם נראה דלפי המהרש״ל דבר גוש מבשל. אבל הסכימו הפוסקים (האו״ה והמ״י) דמבליע ואינו מבשל. ועפ״ז מסיק החוו״ד דלא כתוס׳, אלא דאין בישול אא״כ יש דפנות מחממות. ולפ״ז נמצא דכלי ששואבין בו מכלי ראשון ג״כ מבליע ואינו מבשל. ובחוו״ד השוה לעירוי שנפסק הקילוח, דמבליע ואינו מבשל, וכדברי הש״ך (סי׳ קה סק״ה, הנ״ל אות ב).

ולכאורה קשה לדחות דברי התוס׳ ע״פ הסכמת הפוסקים אליבא דמהרש״ל [בפרט משום דלא ס״ל להרמ״א כשיטת המהרש״ל בכלל. ולדברי הרמ״א ע״כ צריך לחלק בין כלי שואב ודבר גוש (עי׳ לקמן אות ו), ודלא כשיטת החוו״ד שהשווה כלי שואב לדבר גוש]. וגם קשה לחלק בין בליעה לבישול, לפי רוב הפוסקים, דעירוי מבשל ומבליע כדי קליפה.

והנה החוו״ד אזיל לשיטתו שחילק ביניהם לענין עירוי שנזחל (כנ״ל אות ג). וגם המהרש״ל חילק ביניהם לענין כלי שני. והש״ך חילק ביניהם לענין עירוי שנפסק הקילוח. אבל לדינא נראה דאין לחלק (וכנ״ל). וא״כ אם כלי שואב מבליע (וכשיטת הרמ״א) ע״כ גם מבשל, אף דאין דפנות מחממות.

ובמ״ב (סקפ״ז) כתב וז״ל, אם שואב בכלי ריקן מתוך כלי ראשון, י״א דדינו ככלי ראשון, ובפרט אם משהה הכלי הריקן בתוכו עד שמעלה רתיחה, ודאי מיקרי כלי ראשון, עכ״ל. ומקורו בט״ז (סי׳ שיח סקי״ט), שכתב שדינו ככלי ראשון לחומרא ולא לקולא, וכמש״כ ביו״ד (סי׳ צב סק״ל), דבזה מסופק ר״י בתוס׳ (ע״ז לג: סוף ד״ה קינסא). וז״ל התוס׳, ויש משימין קערה בתוך מחבת על האש עד שהרתיחות עולות תוך הקערה ומאותה קערה מגעילין. ובזה מסופק ר״י אם זה מועיל ככלי ראשון אם לאו, ותלה הדבר להחמיר וכו׳, עכ״ל.

ובחוו״ד (שם) כתב, דבעוד המים בכלי השואב בודאי מבליע (וכעירוי שנפסק הקילוח) ובודאי אינו מבשל (דלא הוחמו דפנות כלי השואב ע״י האור). ולכן א״א להגעיל ע״י עירוי ממנו מאחר דבעינן כח הראוי לבשל.

והיינו דלא כדעת הט"ז שכתב שאם כלי שואב ככלי ראשון הוא, שפיר מגעיל ע"י עירוי ממנו. והט"ז מסיק דדבר זה גופא הוא ספק של הר"י הנ"ל, ולכן יש להחמיר שלא להגעיל בכה"ג.

ולפ"ז דברי המ"ב (סקפ"ז הנ"ל, דבמעלה רתיחה ודאי מיקרי כלי ראשון), צ"ע. דלפי מסקנת הט"ז גם במעלה רתיחה הוי רק ספק כלי ראשון. ועוד, דנראה דמעלה רתיחה הוא תנאי רק לגבי הלכות הגעלה, ונצרך אף בכלי ראשון ממש. משא"כ בבישול ובליעה דא"צ מעלה רתיחה כלל, וכסתימת הש"ך (ס' קז) הנ"ל, וצ"ע.

אמנם הש"ך (שם) כתב דהוי ככלי ראשון רק לחומרא אף בעודו בכלי השואב, ודלא כדברי החוו"ד, שכתב שמבליע בודאי. ונראה לפרש שיטת הש"ך (הנ"ל) דאולי האויר הקר מקרר את הכף, ולכן לצד זה אינו מבשל ואינו מבליע, וכהניחו ע"ג קרקע לפי החוו"ד, עיי"ש, ודו"ק.

ולפ"ז נמצא, דלפי מש"כ ע"פ התוס' דבישול ובליעה דינם שוה (ודלא כדברי החוו"ד ע"פ האו"ה והמ"י), א"כ ספק של הש"ך בכלי השואב עצמו שייך גם בבישול, וכדברי המ"ב (סקפ"ז). אך מש"כ שם דבמעלה רתיחה ודאי מיקרי כלי ראשון, צ"ע, דהר"י מסופק גם בזה. וגם מסברא לכאורה אין חילוק, חוץ מבהלכות הגעלה, וכנ"ל.

ונראה לתרץ שיטת המ"ב, דבט"ז (שם) כתב דלפי המהרי"ל כשאינו מעלה רתיחה כלי השואב ככלי שני, וכשמעלה רתיחה הוי כלי ראשון. וצ"ב. ואולי ס"ל למהרי"ל דאם מעלה רתיחה, ע"כ שהה זמן רב בתוך הקדירה, והדפנות של כלי השואב נחשבים כהוחמו ע"י האור שמתחת הקדירה. והמ"ב (סקפ"ז) פסק כדעת המהרי"ל במעלה רתיחה (ודלא כמסקנת הט"ז ע"פ התוס'), ובאינו מעלה רתיחה פסק דספק הוא.

ובמ"ב (סקמ"ה) כתב דאם שואב בכף ומריק לקערה דדינו ככלי שלישי, ואין בישול אחר אפייה. וצ"ע, דלקמן (סקפ"ז) פסק דדינו ככלי ראשון. ולפי החוו"ד ניחא, דהוי ככלי ראשון בעודו בכלי השואב, אבל אין עירוי ממנו כעירוי מכלי ראשון. ובשש"כ (הע' קפ) כתב דמותר רק בצירוף השיטה דאין בישול אחר אפייה אף בכלי ראשון. ובמעלה רתיחה פסק דאסור, וכדעת המ"ב (סקפ"ז), משום דבודאי נחשב ככלי ראשון.

ועוד כתב השש"כ (שם), שהחזו"א (סי' קכב סק"ג) מקיל כאשר שאב מכלי ראשון שלא על האש. ולפי הנ"ל יל"פ, דס"ל דבעינן דפנות

שהוחמו ע״י האור (וכדעת המהרי״ל ודלא כשיטת החוו״ד). ולכן אם שאב מהכלי ראשון אחר שכבר סילקוהו מן האש, בודאי לא הוחמו הדפנות ע״י האור ומתקרר מהאויר, ורק בשאב מכלי ראשון על האש נחלקו אם דינו כהוחמו ע״י האור. ולפ״ז למנהגנו להחמיר לסלק הקדירה מן האש לפני ששואבים בכלי (סי׳ שיח סי״ח ומ״ב ס״ק קיג) כלי השואב הוי ככלי שני.

ו. דבר גוש

כבר נתבאר (אות ה) דנחלקו המהרש״ל והרמ״א אם דבר גוש המונח בכלי שני מבליע או לא. ונחלקו אליבא דמהרש״ל אם מבשל (כדברי המג״א, סקמ״ה) או לא (כדברי החוו״ד). ובחוו״ד השוה דין דבר גוש לדין כלי שואב, דבשניהם אין דפנות מחממות או מקררות, ופסק בשניהם דמבליע ואינו מבשל. אך נראה דע״כ יש לחלק ביניהם, דהא הרמ״א מקיל בדבר גוש ומחמיר בכלי שואב, וכנ״ל (שם).

ונראה דסברת הרמ״א היא, דאמנם אין דפנות הכלי שני מקררות דבר גוש באותה מדה שמקררות דבר לח הנוגע בדפנותיו מכל צד. אבל מכיון שיש תתאה צונן המקררו קצת, דינו ככלי שני. משא״כ בכלי שואב, דדינו ככלי ראשון כיון דאין האויר מקררו ואין כאן תתאה צונן.

הגר״א (סי׳ קה סקי״ז) הביא ראית המהרש״ל (מובא בד״מ שם סק״ד) מדין דגים שעלו בקערה, דבולעים ממנה אף שהקערה כלי שני. ודחה הרמ״א, דשם הוי כמו חם לתוך צונן, כיון שהדגים לא היו בכלי שני עד שנגעו בקערה, משא״כ במאכל שהיה כבר בכלי שני. ולפ״ז אם נטלו נבילה במזלג מהקדירה ושמו אותה בקערה, נאסרה הקערה אפילו לפי הרמ״א. והרמ״א מתיר רק בבשר המונח בקערה ששמו עליה גבינה, שדינו ככלי שני.

הגר״א (שם) הביא ראיה לשיטת הרמ״א מדברי הגמ׳ (חולין קד:) סוף סוף כלי שני הוא, ומיירי בבשר וגבינה בקערה. ועוד ראיה מהר״ש (מעשרות ספ״א).

ובנשמ״א (כלל כ׳ סק״ג) דחה ע״פ התוס׳ יו״ט (חולין רפ״ח) שלא גרס כן בגמ׳ (קד:), ופהמ״ש להרמב״ם (שם), שפירש דלא כהר״ש. ולפי

החוו"ד אצ"ל כן, דמראיות אלו מוכח רק דאינו מבשל, ולעולם י"ל שמבליע.

ולדינא, המ"ב (ס"ק קי"ח) מחמיר לכתחילה כשיטת המג"א, ומקיל בדיעבד כהרמ"א. ובשעה"צ (ס"ק קמ"ב) כתב דאם טח על הצלי קודם שהניחו בכלי, אסור אף בדיעבד. ור"ל כדברי הרמ"א הנ"ל בדגים בקערה, דלכו"ע מבליע, וכדין חם לתוך צונן. ואולי יש להקל בדיעבד אף בזה, דלכאורה לא חמור מעירוי ממש, ולפי הרשב"ם מבליע אבל אינו מבשל.

והמ"ב לשיטתו אזיל (סקע"ד) דאוסר בדיעבד, דס"ל דשיטת הרשב"ם דחויה לגמרי. אבל לפי דעת השביתת השבת (סקנ"ח, עיי"ל סוף אות א), דמותר בדיעבד, י"ל דהה"ה נמי בנד"ד.

אבל בחזו"א (יו"ד סי' ט סק"ה) הוכיח מהגמ' (פסחים עו.) דדבר גוש קודם שהניח בכלי דינו ככלי ראשון, עכ"פ בצלי (ונסתפק בדבר לח לפי הרמ"א). ואע"כ ע"כ אסור בדיעבד, וכדעת השעה"צ, אא"כ נסמוך בדיעבד על שיטת הרשב"ם דעירוי מבליע ואינו מבשל, וכנ"ל.

חימום מאכלים בשבת

א. שיטת הרמב"ם בבישול אחר בישול

תנן (שבת קמה:) כל שבא בחמין מערב שבת שורין אותו בחמין בשבת. ובגמ' שם כגון מאי א"ר ספרא כגון תרנגולתא דר' אבא. וז"ל תוס' הרא"ש שם: פרש"י שורין אותו זמן מרובה, משום דזמן מועט מילתא דפשיטא היא, ולא אצטריך למתני', כיון דכבר נתבשל אין בישול אחר בישול. אבל שריית זמן מרובה איצטריך לאשמועינן, דכיון דמתקן מנא ע"י שריי' זו היא גמר מלאכתו וליתסר, עכ"ל. המבואר מדבריו דדין אין בישול אחר בישול (אבא"ב) נלמד מסברא, ומילתא דפשיטא היא, וא"צ ללמוד ממשנתנו.

אבל המרדכי (סי' ש"ב) הביא דברי ר"א ממיץ וז"ל מכאן (ממשנתנו) דאין בישול אחר בישול, וא"כ כל דבר שנתבשל כל צרכו מותר להחזירו לכלי ראשון להתחמם או ליתנו אצל האש, עכ"ל. הרי דאינה סברא פשוטה אלא שנלמדת ממשנתנו. ומ"מ מדברי הפוסקים נראה שאין שום חולק על דין זה.

וז"ל הרמב"ם (שבת פ"ט ה"ג) המבשל על האור דבר שמבושל כל צרכו או דבר שאינו צריך בישול כלל פטור, עכ"ל. וצ"ע דפטור בלשון הרמב"ם כונתו שאסור מדרבנן (פ"א ה"ג), ואם אבא"ב למה כתב הרמב"ם פטור ולא מותר. ובאגלי טל (אופה סי' יט סק"ח) תירץ שאסור משום שמחזיר על האור ואסור אם אין הכירא דגרופה או קטומה (פ"ג ה"י).

ותירוץ זה נראה דחוק, שהרמב"ם לא הזכיר אם האור קטום או לא, ובכלל אינו עוסק באיסור החזרה אלא באיסור בישול עצמו.

והנה בשו"ע (סי' שיח ס"ד) כתב וז"ל, דבר שנתבשל כבר והוא יבש מותר לשרותו בחמין בשבת, עכ"ל. ובתבשיל שיש בו מרק כתב דיש בו בישול אחר בישול. ובבה"ל (ד"ה יש) כתב דלהרמב"ם, הרשב"א, והר"ן אבא"ב בדבר לח אף אם נצטנן לגמרי. ומקורו בב"י שהרשב"א והר"ן כתבו כן בפירוש, והרמב"ם לא חילק בין לח ליבש [ובב"י נראה שכ"כ בשם המגיד משנה, אבל גם הרמב"ם לא חילק, וכמש"כ הבה"ל].

ובמג"א (סקי"ד) כתב וז"ל, ומשמע מלשון השו"ע דאם לא נתבשל מערב שבת, רק נשרה בחמין, אסור לשרותו בחמין בשבת, עכ"ל. אבל הרמב"ם (פכ"ב ה"ח) כתב וז"ל, דבר שנתבשל קודם השבת או נשרה בחמין מלפני השבת, אע"פ שהוא עכשיו צונן מותר לשרותו בחמין בשבת, עכ"ל. ובמחצית השקל פירש דלהרמב"ם די בנשרה מלפני השבת, אבל השו"ע אוסר, וטוב להחמיר כהשו"ע.

וז"ל הב"י (שם): ונראה שדבריו [של הרמב"ם] דאפילו לא נתבשל כמאכל בן דרוסאי נמי, כיון שנשרה במים רותחים חשיב מבושל לענין שלא יחשב כמבשל בשבת כששורה אותו בשבת בחמין, עכ"ל. ובד"מ (סק"ג) הקשה וז"ל, וצ"ע דהא לעיל כתב בשם הרמב"ם דאפילו לשרות אסור אלא בנתבשל כל צרכו, ואין לחלק לדעת הרמב"ם בין דבר לח לדבר יבש כמשנ"ת לעיל וצ"ע, עכ"ל.

ולולא דברי הב"י נראה שהרמב"ם מחלק בין מבשל בשבת לשורה בשבת, דבמבשל חייב אא"כ היה מבושל כל צרכו מלפני השבת, וכדבריו (פ"ט ה"ג) הנ"ל. אבל מותר לשרות בשבת כל שנשרה במים רותחים מלפני השבת אף שלא נתבשל כלל.

וכ"כ באבן האזל (פכ"ב), וז"ל: דהא דאסור לשרות בחמין בשבת דבר שלא נשרה מלפני השבת אינו משום התחלת בישול וכו', אלא נראה דאיסורו הוא משום דשריית הבשר בחמין הוה תיקון קצת דעי"ז ראוי כבר לאוכלו, ואיסורו משום תיקון האוכלין, וגדר האיסור הוא כמו כובש כבשים דאסור מדרבנן משום דהוי כמו מבשל, שע"י נתקן הדבר לאכילה, וכמש"כ הרמב"ם (ה"י) והכובש אסור מפני שהוא כמבשל וכו', א"כ כיון שנשרה מע"ש וכבר נתקן, שוב אין בו משום תיקון דשריי',

ולכן שורין אותו בשבת, והוה כמו בישול, דאחרי שנתבשל כל צרכו תו לא שייך בישול, עכ״ל.

והנה מסיום דברי האבן האזל נראה דס״ל דלהרמב״ם אבא״ב, ומותר לחמם דבר יבש שנצטנן, וכמש״כ דלכאורה אין שום חולק על זה. אבל אין שום מקור לדין זה לפי הרמב״ם, שהרי משנתנו עוסקת בדין מיוחד דשריי׳, שאיסורו תיקון אוכלין, ומנ״ל שמותר לחמם דבר יבש שנצטנן.

לכן נראה, דבאמת הרמב״ם חולק וסובר שאסור אם נצטנן אף בדבר יבש, וכדבריו (פ״ט ה״ג) הנ״ל דפטור, אבל אסור. וההיתר להחזיר קדירה נאמר רק כל זמן שהיא רותחת (סי׳ רנג ס״ב). וכ״כ במגילת ספר (סי׳ ג׳ סק״ד), דלפי הרמב״ם אין מקור לדין אבא״ב מהמשנה (קמה:). אבל מצינו בביאור הגר״א (סי׳ רנג סקל״ט) שהביא מקור אחר להא דאבא״ב, ממה שמותר להחזיר בשבת קדירה לאש, וזו ראי׳ ברורה שאפילו על האש אבא״ב, עכ״ד.

וצ״ע, דנימא דמותר להחזיר רק כשהמאכל עדיין חם, ואין זה נחשב בא״ב, דבא״ב אינו שייך אלא כשנצטנן. והרי הריטב״א (לט.) ס״ל דאם נצטנן, אין היתר להחזיר, דבטלה שהייה ראשונה ונראה כמבשל (עי׳ עם מרדכי עמ׳ מו), ודלא כהגר״א (עיי״ש). וא״כ י״ל דגם להרמב״ם החזרה מותרת רק כשהמאכל חם, לא מפני שנראה כמבשל כהריטב״א, אלא מפני שסובר שבישול אחר בישול אסור מדרבנן. נמצא דלפי הרמב״ם אין מקור כלל לדין אבא״ב. ולעולם י״ל דלהרמב״ם בא״ב אסור מדרבנן, בין בלח ובין ביבש, שלא חילק ביניהם, וכדיוק הבה״ל, אבל לא מפני **שמתיר** בשניהם כמו שסובר הבה״ל, אלא, להיפך, משום **שאוסר** בשניהם. והא דאין חיוב מן התורה, סברא היא, וכדברי תוס׳ הרא״ש (קמה:) הנ״ל.

וז״ל המ״מ (שם), ומש״כ וכן דבר שאינו צריך בישול כלל, פשוט הוא, ונלמד ממה שנחלקו פ׳ כירה (מ:) שמן אם יש בו משום בישול אם לאו. מכאן שדבר שאינו צריך בישול אין בו בישול לדברי הכל, עכ״ל. ולשון המ״מ, ׳פשוט הוא׳ ר״ל מסברא, שהרי א״צ בישול, וכעין לשון תוס׳ הרא״ש הנ״ל, לענין בישול אחר בישול, ׳מילתא דפשיטא היא,׳ והרי הרמב״ם כתב שני הדינים ביחד.

והנה סיום דברי המ״מ, דנלמד משמן, צ״ע, דלפי מש״כ שבא״ב אסור להרמב״ם עכ״פ מדרבנן, ה״ה דבר שא״צ בישול כלל. אבל בשמן

מותר לגמרי וכלשון הגמ' (מ:) שמן אע"פ שהיס"ב מותר, וכאן הרמב"ם כתב דפטור משמע אבל אסור מדרבנן, וצ"ע. וכ"כ רעק"א (סי' רנד מג"א סקי"ד) דלפי הרמב"ם דבר שא"צ בישול אסור לבשלו בשבת מדרבנן. והאג"ט (סקי"ט הנ"ל) חולק על רעק"א, לשיטתו דהאיסור שברמב"ם הוא רק משום החזרה על האור, וכנ"ל. ולפמש"כ נראה כרעק"א שאסור מדרבנן, ושגם בא"ב אסור מדרבנן, ולכן הרמב"ם כתב דיני שניהם ביחד וסיים פטור. וגם בשמן קיי"ל דאסור (פכ"ב הל' ד,ה), ואולי גם כונת המ"מ דאין בישול מדאורייתא לדברי הכל כשא"צ בישול, ולעולם אסור מדרבנן כשמן, ודו"ק.

וז"ל הרמב"ם (פ"ד ה"ו) אבל אין מניחין כלי שיש בו דבר צונן על גבי כלי חם בשבת, שהרי מוליד בו חום בשבת, עכ"ל. ומקורו בגמ' (מח.), ובספר מגילת ספר (שם סק"ג) פירש שהוא איסור בפ"ע וכמש"כ הב"י (סי' רנח) ולא משום בישול. אבל לפמש"כ נראה דאיסור בישול דרבנן הוא, וכנ"ל.

ובזה ניחא קושית המגילת ספר שם מהגמ' (מב.) דמותר לתת מים צוננים בכלי שני, והרי מוליד חום. ולמש"כ ניחא, דאינו איסור בפ"ע, אלא איסור בא"ב מדרבנן, והרי כלי שני אינו מבשל, ולכן מותר לתת מים צוננים בכלי שני. ולדינא לא קיי"ל כהרמב"ם, ומותר לחמם דבר יבש ומבושל שנצטנן ע"ג קדירה העומדת ע"ג האש (סי' רנג ס"ה, עיי"ש).

ב. בדבר לח

והנה בדין בא"ב בדבר לח, הב"י כתב שלפי הרמב"ם מותר, מדלא חילק בין לח ליבש. ולפמש"כ, אדרבה, ס"ל דבשניהם אסור, אמנם רק מדרבנן. ובחזו"א (סי' לז סקי"ג) פירש כן שיטת הרמ"א (סי' שיח סט"ו) בדבר לח, דנהגו להקל בלא נצטנן לגמרי, כדעת הב"י בדעת הרמב"ם, וז"ל, והנה מעיקר הדין אין שום מקום לחלק בין נצטנן לגמרי ללא נצטנן לגמרי, דכל שאין היס"ב חשיב מן הדין כצונן, וע"כ שאנו תופסין לעיקר הדין כדעת הרמב"ם והרשב"א והר"ן שאין איסור לחמם את הצונן המבושל, עכ"ל.

ונראה דהחזו"א אזל לשיטתו (שם) שפירש שיטת רש"י והרא"ש דיש בא"ב בלח וז"ל, דיש חילוק בין דבר יבש לדבר לח, דדבר יבש כיון

שנתבשל אין בו עוד בישול, אבל דבר לח, דאינו מתרכך בבישולו, אלא חמימותו זהו תיקונו, וכל שנצטנן חוזר לקדמותו ויש בו בא״ב, עכ״ל. ובאור דבריו, דבגמ׳ (עד:) נראה דבישול היינו ריכוך, וחייבים במרכך עץ. ובדבר לח, שאין ריכוך, ע״כ דין בפ״ע הוא, דחייב אם מחממו. ונ״מ גם לבא״ב, דבדבר יבש כיון שאף אם נצטנן עדיין רך הוא, אבא״ב. אבל בדבר לח שנצטנן, שאינו חם, יבא״ב. וע״כ תלוי בגדר חום ע״פ דין, שהוא יס״ב. ואם הרמ״א מקיל באינו יס״ב כשלא נצטנן לגמרי, ע״כ ס״ל דמדאורייתא אבא״ב בדבר לח, ורק החמיר בנצטנן לגמרי משום גזירה, וכמש״כ החזו״א שם.

והנה המג״א (סי׳ רנג סקל״ז) כתב שלפי הרמ״א אסור לחמם דבר לח שנצטנן מדאורייתא. ומ״מ כל שלא נצטנן לגמרי מותר, דראוי׳ שיאכל בלא חימום וכעין מאכל בן דרוסאי, וכמש״כ התה״ד (סי׳ סו) ע״פ ההגמ״ר (סי׳ תמ) וההגמי״י (פ״ג סק״ב). ולפ״ז אין הבדל יסודי בין יבש ללח, אלא דביבש אף אם נצטנן לגמרי ראוי שיאכל בלא חימום דוגמת מאב״ד, ובלח מותר רק אם לא נתקררה כל כך שלא היתה ראוי׳ לאכילה דוגמת טעם מאב״ד [כלשון ההגמי״י שם, ועיין עם מרדכי על מס׳ שבת עמ׳ סא].

והנה הפמ״ג (סי׳ רנד א״א סק״א) צידד וז״ל, דדוקא במים יין ושמן שאין האש פועל בו להכשיר כל כך, דנאכל חי ג״כ, והבישול הוא החימום, הלכך כל שנצטנן יש בו בישול. משא״כ שומן אווז ומוהל בשר, שא״א לאכול כי אם ע״י בישול, תו אף נצטנן אין בו בישול עכ״ל. וכתב דמסתימת הפוסקים משמע שכל שהוא צלול ולח יבא״ב בנצטנן. ובמג״א (הנ״ל) מיירי במחמם קדירה שנצטנן, כל שיש בו מרק וכדומה, ומוכח דאף בזה אסור מדאורייתא. וזהו דלא כמש״כ בספר שבות יצחק (עמ׳ שלט) בשם הגרי״ש אלישיב (שליט״א) זצ״ל, שאף אם יבא״ב מדאורייתא במים, האיסור בשומן רק מדרבנן. וכתב שכ״כ בחזו״א (הנ״ל) דבלח, חמימותו הוא תיקונו, וכל שנצטנן חוזר לקדמותו. וע״כ בשומן שאינו חוזר לקדמותו כשנצטנן אין בישול דאורייתא בחימומו.

ולפי המג״א והתרומת הדשן הנ״ל נראה דכל שאינו ״ראוי לאכול מחמת חמימותו״ (כלשון הגר״ז סי׳ שיח ס״ט) בעצם חזר לקדמותו, דשוב אינו נאכל אף כדוגמת מאב״ד. ורק בדבר יבש, שאף אם נצטנן לגמרי ראוי לבן דרוסאי (כלו׳ בשעת הדחק), אבא״ב בנצטנן לגמרי. וכ״כ השבות יצחק

בעצמו (עמ' שמב בהערה) ע"פ הריטב"א (לט.), דבדיעבד המרק אסור והבשר מותר "מפני שהבשר בלא"ה נמי ראוי לאוכלו". וכ"כ המ"ב (סי' רנג סקצ"ח). וכתב השבות יצחק (בהערה שם) מיהו א"כ בדבר לח וחם שאיס"ב, וראוי הוא לאכילה, לא יהא בישול כאשר מחמם אותו ליס"ב. ולדברינו אה"נ, דזוהי שיטת הרמ"א.

ועיי"ש (עמ' שמא), שבטור מוכח דבתבשיל שיש בו מרק יבא"ב מדאורייתא, וכמש"כ. אך פירש שזהו משום שהמים שבמרק נתבטל חומם, משא"כ בשומן. וצ"ע דמסברא נראה דהמים שבמרק נשתנו, ואינם חוזרים לקדמותם, ודינם כשומן ומוהל בשר שבפמ"ג. וא"כ מהטור נראה דיבא"ב מדאורייתא, וכסתימת הפוסקים הנ"ל.

ובספר ארחות שבת (עמ' יד) כתבו כסברא הנ"ל, דדבר יבש בדרך כלל ראוי הוא לאכילה בהיותו צונן, משא"כ בדבר לח, שאין רגילין לאוכלו כלל כשהוא צונן. ולפ"ז אפשר דלענין דרגת הסמיכות להקרא דבר יבש תלוי באם ראוי לאכילה בהיותו צונן. ונ"מ לענין קעטשופ, דבאג"מ (ח"ד סי' ע"ד, בישול סק"ה) צידד דדינו כדבר לח, כיון שזב וצריך כלי להחזיקו. אבל כיון שראוי לאכילה בצונן, נראה דדינו כדבר יבש, וכדברי הגריש"א (שליט"א) זצ"ל והגרשז"א זצ"ל, עיי"ש.

וכתבו עוד שם וז"ל: ומ"מ פשוט דמאכל נוזלי לגמרי יבא"ב אף אם הוא ראוי לאכילה בהיותו צונן, ומאכל מוצק לגמרי אבא"ב אף אם אינו ראוי לאכילה מחמת שהוא צונן, עכ"ל. אבל כתבו (עמ' טו) וז"ל, מרק עוף שבהיותו במקרר נעשה קפוי כמין ג'לי, או קפוא כקרח כשהיה בהקפאה, אין היתר ליתנו על האש ולחממו, דדיינינן ליה כבישול בדבר לח וכו', כיון שבמצב הזה אין המרק נאכל כלל אלא רק בהיותו לח, עכ"ל. ואף שבמג"א (סי' שיח סק"מ) מתיר לחמם שומן שנקרש אף שחוזר ונימוח, צ"ל דבהיותו קרוש יש לו תואר ושם של דבר מבושל, וצ"ב.

ונראה דיש לומר להיפך בב' מקרים אלו (כלומר מאכל נוזלי לגמרי ומאכל מוצק לגמרי). דכל שאינו ראוי לאכול אא"כ יחזור ויחממו באש, הרי חזר לקדמותו ויבא"ב, וכ"ה במרק קפוי. אבל בשומן שנקרש, אם יעמוד בקערה עם הבשר בלי חום של אש, יהיה ראוי לאכילה עם הבשר. ומטעם זה גם בבשר מבושל קפוי, שא"א לאוכלו כלל, אבא"ב, דאם יעמוד בקערה בלי חום של אש יגיע לדרגת מאב"ד וכנ"ל. אבל לו יצוייר

מאכל יבש שנצטנן ואינו ראוי לאכול כלל עד שיחזור ויחממו באש, נראה דבאמת אסור, וכמרק קפוי.

מאידך, בדבר צונן לח שראוי לאוכלו בלי שיחממנו על האש (וכמרק פירות), יתכן דמותר. ובזה ניחא הא דמותר לחמם דבר יבש אף שיש עליו שמן טופח ע״מ להטפיח, וכמש״כ (שם עמ׳ טו), דבכה״ג ראוי לאכילה אף אם לא יחזור ויחממנו על האש. ואף שיטת המנחת כהן, דכל שרובו יבש ומיעוטו לח מותר, נראה לפרש כן, ודו״ק.

והנה הרמ״א (סי׳ שיח ס״ד) כתב די״א דיבא״ב בדבר לח דוקא אם מצטמק ויפה לו. וצ״ב, ובט״ז (סק״ד) האריך, ובמ״ב (ס״ק כ״ה) אוסר במצטמק ורע לו כהב״ח והגר״א. ואולי יש לפרש שיטת הרמ״א, דחימומו דדבר לח הוא תיקונו וכנ״ל. ולכן אסור רק בתיקון גמור, משא״כ במצטמק ורע לו דאינו תיקון גמור, אף שתיקן אותו ע״י שחזרו וחממו, ודו״ק.

והנה רע״א (על המג״א סי׳ רנג סקמ״א) הקשה על המג״א שלא אסר לשפוך רותחים על כלים מלוכלכים בשומן מדין בישול, דכאן גרע מהנחת שומן אצל האש הנ״ל, דשם אח״כ כשנימוח אינו עושה שום דבר, משא״כ כאן, כיון שבא מעט רותחין על השומן נמס ונימוח, וכששופך אח״כ עוד רותחין הוא מבשל להלח, וא״כ אף בשאינו מתכוין אלא לצחצחן ליתסר דהוי מבשל ופ״ר.

ואולי י״ל לפי מש״כ דיסוד איסור בא״ב בלח הוא שחמימותו הוא תיקונו, וכנ״ל, דבהיותו צונן אינו ראוי לאכילה וע״י החימום נעשה ראוי לאכילה. ובשומן שאינו אלא לכלוך, והמים המלוכלכים שמתערבים עמו אינם ראויים לאכילה גם לאחר שיתחממו יותר ע״י ששופך עוד רותחין עליהם, והכל הולך לאיבוד, א״כ אינו מלאכה כלל, ועדיף מפ״ר דלא ניחא ליה, ודו״ק.

ובמגילת ספר (עמ׳ רד) תירץ, דבשומן שבמצבו הטבעי הוא יבש, אבא״ב אף אם נימוח אח״כ. וכ״כ בשע״ת (סי׳ שיח ס״ט) דאבא״ב בדבר יבש כסוכר, ואף שהסוכר נימוח יש לו דין יבש, וצ״ב. ולפי מש״כ י״ל דסוכר ראוי למתק את המאכל או המשקה גם בהיותו צונן, וכל כה״ג יש לו דין יבש, אע״פ שעכשיו נעשה לח, דגם בדבר לח ממש הדין כן, וכשמן על דבר יבש, וכנ״ל.

והנה בערוה"ש (סי' שיח סכ"ח) אוסר לעשות תה או קפה, אף אם נתבשלו, ולא אמרינן אבא"ב, ומותר רק אם מכין סענ"ס מבעוד יום. וז"ל, אין הבישול [בבית החרושת] לבשלו, אלא לעשותו פירא שיהא ראוי לבישול. ואיך נאמר על זה שהוא כבר מבושל, והרי מוכרין אותו עתה בכסף מלא כדי לבשלו, עכ"ל. ולכאורה צ"ב, דכשהיה מבושל במים היה ראוי לשתותו, ונימא דאבא"ב בעלי תה וקפה טחון. ולפי מש"כ לעיל י"ל דאינו ראוי לאכול כלל בלי שיתערבו במים חמים, ובזה קיי"ל יבא"ב, וכדבר לח. ולא דמי לסוכר, דראוי להיות תבלין גם למאכלים ומשקים קרים. ונראה דאבקת תה שלנו נמכרת כך לעשות תה קר (אייס-טי), ויש דעושים קפה קר (אייס-קאפי) מאבקת קפה (אינסטנט). וכיון שראוים לאכול בלי שתערבו במים חמים מותר לחזור ולחממם ע"י הוספת מים חמים, כמנהג העולם, כיון דאבא"ב, וכנ"ל.

ג. בדבר יבש

כתב השו"ע (סי' רנד ס"א) וז"ל ואם הוא בתנור, וטח פיו בטיט וכו' מותר, דלא חיישינן לחיתוי, עכ"ל. וברמ"א שם כתב דהכל שרי, כלו' כל מיני מאכל, ודלא כשו"ע. ופי' המ"ב (סקי"א) דכיון דאינו מוכן לחתות שהרי סתום הוא בטיט לא יבוא לחתות. ובבה"ל (ד"ה אע"פ) כתב דמקורו בגמ' (יח:), ולרמ"א, ע"פ הרא"ש והטור, לא טרח כולי האי לסתור הטיחה שסביב פי התנור.

והנה הגמ' והרמ"א התירו בשהיי'. ובחזו"א (סי' לח סק"ב) כתב דלא מצינו היתר זה ליתן בשבת. ובספר שבות יצחק (דיני שהייה וחזרה עמ' קכו-קכז) כתב דהחזו"א אסר רק בנותן בתחלה בשבת, כלו' הנחה, ולא בהחזרה. ונראה לפרש דהחזו"א ס"ל דהחזרה אסורה רק משום שמא יחתה, ובטח בטיט אין לחוש, וכמש"כ הרמ"א לענין שהיי'. אבל הנחה בתחלה אסור משום נראה כמבשל, ובזה טח בטיט לא מהני.

ולפ"ז נראה דמגירת חימום (ווארמינ"ג דרא"ר) שאין מבשלין בו כלל, אין דין נראה כמבשל [עי' עם מרדכי עמ' לו]. ואם קשה לעשות היכר בקטומה כדי למנוע חשש חיתוי [עיי"ש], יש לכסות את הכפתור בהרבה ניירות דבק נפרדים, באופן שיש טירחא מרובה להסירו, כלו' דא"א

להסירם במשיכה אחת, ובזה יש היתר דטח בטיט אף בהנחה מתחלה, כיון דאין דין נראה כמבשל, ודומה להחזרה להחזו"א, וכנ"ל. [ובארחות שבת עמ' סח-סט התיר אף הנחת נייר דבק אחד מדין טח בטיט לגבי שהייה.]

הר"ן (במשנה לו: ד"ה עד) הקשה למה אסור בתנור גרוף, הלא אין חשש חיתוי. ותירץ דנפיש הבלי' ומחזי כמו שיש שם גחלים לוחשות, ואתו לשהויי בכירה ולחתויי. והקשה הר"ן דשמא יחתה גזירה היא, ואינו דין לגזור גרוף אטו אינו גרוף. ומסיק כבעה"מ, דגרוף ר"ל לצד אחד, אבל אם הסיר הגחלים לגמרי מותר, דאין חשש חיתוי. והרשב"א תירץ דאתי לחתויי בתנור גופי' דאינו גרוף.

ובספר שבות יצחק (עמ' צו) כתב דלפי הגריש"א (שליט"א) זצ"ל אסור להשהות על פלטה חשמלית, אף דא"א לחתות, וכתירוץ הראשון שדחה הר"ן. ואף לשאר התירוצים (בעה"מ ורשב"א), י"ל דהתירו כל שאין חשש חיתוי בכלי זה, רק אם עשה מעשה גריפה כתקנת חז"ל, משא"כ בפלטה, ולפ"ז רעק"א (סי' שיח ס"ג) מתיר רק בתולדות אור, כי א"א לחתות, אבל באור ממש אסור משום לא פלוג.

וכתב (עמ' צט) דבשע"ת (סי' רנד סק"ב) בשם הפנים מאירות משמע דכל שא"א לחתות מותר, וכן משמע בבה"ל (סי' רנג ס"א ד"ה אפילו) שבקש וגבבא מותר כל שא"א לחתות. ודחה הגריש"א ראי' זו, דאש זו שונה שאין בה גחלים. משא"כ אש חשמלי שאפשר להגדילו בכלי אחר. ובפשוטו, פלטה עדיף מקש וגבבא, דיתכן בהם חיתוי, וכן בגרופה, דיתכן שמשהו נשאר (עי' מ"ב סקכ"ח). וכ"כ בשש"כ (פ"א הע' עא), דמותר להשהות ע"ג פלטה שא"א לשנות מדת חום שלה, דאין חשש חיתוי כלל.

וכתב (עמ' קג) דפלטות של א"י, שיכולים להרתיח תבשיל צונן, פעמים נותנין עליהן קודם שבת קדירת חמין או קוגל שלא נתבשלו כל צרכם ונגמר בישולם בשבת, ובזה אסור להחזיר משום מחזי כמבשל, משא"כ בפלטות שמגיעות רק ליס"ב, דאין הדרך לחמם דבר שאינו מבושל, וא"כ י"ל דלא מיחזי כמבשל. וכמדומה שבמדינתנו אין רגילות כלל לבשל אף בפלטות שיכולות להרתיח, ובטלה דעת העושה כן אצל כל בני אדם, וא"כ י"ל דלא מחזי כמבשל [ועי' עם מרדכי עמ' מט].

והנה באג"מ (ח"ד סי' עד אות לה) מקיל רק כשא"א להתבשל שם. ואם ר"ל שאין יס"ב בתבשיל צ"ע, דמותר גם ע"ג אש שאפשר לחתות,

וכמש"כ המ"ב (ס"ק סז). וי"ל דהגר"ז (סכ"א, ובקו"א) חולק, וס"ל דשיעור יס"ב תלוי בחום התנור ולא בחום התבשיל. וא"כ כשחום הפלטה יס"ב ואפשר לשנות מדת החום שלה אסור אף אם א"א להתבשל, כלו' שהתבשיל לא יגיע ליס"ב. ובזה כתב האג"מ שכשא"א לשנות מדת החום מותר, ודו"ק.

ובאג"מ (שם) אסר להניח לכתחילה על סטי"ם טייב"ל, ומשמע שאין היתר דקדירה ע"ג קדירה כשהמים נשפכים, דאז נראה כמבשל את המאכל ולא את המים. ונ"מ ל"קדירה-בלעך" שלפי סברת האג"מ ג"כ ייאסר ליתן עליו בשבת [עי' עם מרדכי עמ' כח]. וכעת חידשו "פלא-פלטה", שהוא דוד מים בצורה של תיבה, עם ברז להוציא מים ממנה כמו בדוד רגיל, וגגה רחב ושוה, כמו בלעך רגיל. ולכאורה מותר להניח ע"ג פלא-פלטה זו, וכדין קדירה ע"ג קדירה.

מקורות

1

רמב"ם הלכות שבת פרק ט הלכה א

האופה כגרוגרת חייב, אחד האופה את הפת או המבשל את המאכל או את הסממנין או המחמם את המים הכל ענין אחד הוא, שיעור המחמם את המים כדי לרחוץ בהן אבר קטן, ושיעור מבשל סממנין כדי שיהיו ראויין לדבר שמבשלין אותן לו.

תלמוד בבלי מסכת שבת דף עד עמוד ב

והלש והאופה. אמר רב פפא: שבק תנא דידן בישול סממנין דהוה במשכן, ונקט אופה! - תנא דידן - סידורא דפת נקט. אמר רב אחא בר רב עוירא: האי מאן דשדא סיכתא לאתונא - חייב משום מבשל. פשיטא! מהו דתימא - לשרורי מנא קא מיכוין, קא משמע לן: דמירפא רפי, והדר קמיט. אמר רבה בר רב הונא: האי מאן דארתח כופרא - חייב משום מבשל. פשיטא! - מהו דתימא: כיון דהדר ואיקושא - אימא לא, קא משמע לן.

מגיד משנה הלכות שבת פרק ח הלכה טו

הטוחן כגרוגרת חייב וכו'. כל אלו השיעורין שהן במלאכת האוכלין נראה שהן שוין וכגרוגרת. ובפ' כלל גדול (שם ע':) קצר וטחן כגרוגרת וזה מבואר:

רמב"ם הלכות שבת פרק ט הלכה ו

המתיך אחד ממיני מתכות כל שהוא או המחמם את המתכת עד שתעשה גחלת הרי זה תולדת מבשל, וכן הממסס את הדונג או את החלב או את הזפת והכופר והגפרית וכיוצא בהם הרי זה תולדת מבשל וחייב, וכן המבשל כלי אדמה עד שיעשו חרס חייב משום מבשל, כללו של דבר בין שריפה גוף קשה באש או שהקשה גוף רך הרי זה חייב משום מבשל.

לחם משנה הלכות שבת פרק ט הלכה ו

בין שריפה גוף קשה באש או שהקשה גוף הרך וכו'. קשה דבפ' כלל גדול (דף ע"ד) אמרו האי מאן דשדא סיכתא לאתונא חייב משום מבשל. והקשו פשיטא. ותירצו מהו דתימא לשרורי מנא קא מכוין קמ"ל דמירפא רפי והדר קמיט ע"כ. ופירש"י דמירפא רפי ע"י חום האור והמים שבתוכו ולאחר שיצאו מימיו קמיט מתקשה וכי רפי ברישא הוי בישולו ע"כ. משמע דבסיכתא אי לאו דרפי בתחלה לא הוה חייב ואיך כתב שבכ"מ שהקשה גוף הרך שחייב. וי"ל דהוא סובר דכל דבר לח שמתבשל אע"פ שמתקשה חייב משום בישול דומיא דאופה ומה שאמרו בסיכתא שהוא כלי אדמה לפי דעתו ז"ל הפירוש מהו דתימא שאינו עושה שום מלאכה שהרי הם חזקים שהם מתחזקים יותר קמ"ל שחייב על הבישול מפני שבתחלה האש מרפה אותם ונעשה לח ואח"כ מקשה אותם ומש"ה חייב אבל לעולם דבכל דבר לח חייב בקישויו:

רמב"ם הלכות שבת פרק ט הלכה ג

המפקיע את הביצה בבגד חם או בחול ובאבק דרכים שהן חמים מפני השמש אע"פ שנצלית פטור, שתולדות חמה אינם כתולדות האש, אבל גזרו עליהן מפני תולדות האור, וכן המבשל בחמי טבריה וכיוצא בהם פטור, המבשל על האור דבר שהיה מבושל כל צרכו או דבר שאינו צריך בישול כלל פטור.

רע"א למג"א סימן רנד ס"ק י"ד

לא ידעתי מה כ"ש איכא הא הכא גרע לענין קירוב בשול הוי בשול גמור דאורייתא אלא דהכא הוי רק דרבנן כיון דנאכלים חיים וא"צ בשול

כמ"ש הרמב"ם פ"ט הל' ג' אבל עכ"פ הבשול הוי בשול מעליא דבעלמא כה"ג חייב ואלו להניחם סמוך לתנור קודם שהוסק בעלמא הוי ג"כ דרבנן דבעידנא דנותן שם הפירות עדיין ליכא אור וכדקיי"ל א' נותן מים וא' נותן אור דהנותן מים פטור א"כ קיל יותר מהך דהכא ומה כ"ש הוא.

רמב"ם הלכות שבת פרק א הלכה ג

וכל מקום שנאמר שהעושה דבר זה פטור הרי זה פטור מן הכרת ומן הסקילה ומן הקרבן אבל אסור לעשות אותו דבר בשבת ואיסורו מדברי סופרים הרחקה מן המלאכה, והעושה אותו בזדון מכין אותו מכת מרדות, וכן כל מקום שנאמר אין עושין כך וכך או אסור לעשות כך וכך בשבת העושה אותו דבר בזדון מכין אותו מכת מרדות.

מרכבת המשנה פרק ט הלכה א

ומ"ש או דבר שאינו צריך בישול כלל בעכו"ם דף לח כל שהוא נאכל כמות שהוא חי אין בו משום בשולי עכו"ם וה"ה לענין שבת, ואע"ג לבישולי עכו"ם ממש דלענין נתבשל כמב"ד לא מדמה רבנו בישול שבת לבישול עכו"ם ממש, מ"מ מה דחזי חי לגמרי מודים רבנן לחנניא.

תלמוד בבלי מסכת עבודה זרה דף לח עמוד א

אמר רב שמואל בר רב יצחק אמר רב: כל הנאכל כמות שהוא חי - אין בו משום בישולי עובדי כוכבים.

שער הציון סימן שיח ס"ק קיד

הנה ברמב"ם פרק ט הלכה ג כתב דהמבשל דבר שמבשל כל צרכו או שאין צריך בישול כלל פטור, ופשוט לעניות דעתי דהיינו דבר שאינו משתבח כלל על ידי הבשול, ולאפוקי פירות וכהאי גוונא שהוא משתבח על ידי הבשול, ותדע, דהלא מוכח בגמרא בשבת [מ' ע"ב] דמים יש בו משום בישול, והרי מים גם כן שותה אותו כשהוא חי [ויש לדחות קצת, דמים לא עדיף כמו פירות, עיין מגן אברהם בסוף רנ"ד לחד תרוצא]. ומצאתי בברכי יוסף שהוא מסתפק בזה אי חייב מן התורה או מדרבנן, ועיין לעיל בסימן רנ"ד סוף סעיף ד ובראשונים שכתבו דיש בזה משום מבשל, משמע מסתימת

הלשון דהוא דאורייתא, וגם בפרי מגדים בסעיף זה משמע דסבירא לה דהוא דאורייתא, וכן כתבו הגר"ז וחיי אדם:

תלמוד בבלי מסכת שבת דף מ עמוד ב

אמר רב יהודה אמר שמואל: אחד שמן ואחד מים, יד סולדת בו - אסור.

משנה ברורה סימן שיח ס"ק א

המבשל וכו' - אחד המבשל את המאכל או את הסממנין או המחמם את המים [ר"ל אף דמים ראוי לשתיה בלא בישול וה"ה חלב מ"מ חייב כיון דמשתבח ע"י הבישול] ואחד האופה את הפת הכל ענין אחד הוא [דאפיה הוא מענין בישול אלא שאפיה הוא בפת ובישול הוא בשארי דברים].

פרי מגדים אשל אברהם רנד:א

ולכאורה נראה דדוקא מים ויין ושמן שאין האש פועל בו להכשיר כל כך דנאכל חי גם כן והבישול הוא החימום הלכך כל שנצטנן יש בו בישול משא"כ שומן אווז ומוהל הבשר שאי אפשר לאכל כי אם ע"י בישול תו אף נצטנן אין בו בישול ומהא אמינא לה ביו"ד קי"ג בש"ך אות ה' וט"ז אות ב' "פנאדה" בשומן דגים דאלו שומן אווז אין בו בישול אחר בישול ולמה לא יצויר בצלול וכו' אלא מסתימת הפוסקים משמע כל שהוא צלול ולח יש בו בישול אחר בישול בנצטנן וא"כ הוא הדין צלי קדר המיחל וכו'.

2

תלמוד בבלי מסכת שבת דף קמה עמוד ב

משנה. כל שבא בחמין מערב שבת - שורין אותו בחמין בשבת. וכל שלא בא בחמין מערב שבת - מדיחין אותו בחמין בשבת. חוץ מן המליח הישן (ודגים מלוחין קטנים) וקולייס האיספנין, שהדחתן זו היא גמר מלאכתן.

מרדכי מסכת שבת פרק כירה שב

[דף לט] כל שבא בחמין מלפני השבת כו' פי' ה"ר אליעזר ממיץ מכאן

דאין [רמז שב] בישול אחר בישול וא"כ כל דבר שנתבשל כל צרכו מותר להחזירו לכלי ראשון להתחמם או ליתנו אצל האש ופי' כל שבא בחמין כו' שורין אותו בחמין בכלי ראשון ושלא בא בחמין מלפני השבת מדיחין אותו בחמין בכלי ראשון חוץ ממליח הישן וקולייס האספנין ודגים קטנים מלוחים שהדחתן זו היא גמר מלאכתן פירוש אלו ג' וכיוצא בהן שבהדחה בעלמא מתבשלין דבישול אין תלוי לא בכלי ראשון ולא בכלי שני אך לפי דבר שנתבשל כדלקמן בשמעתין [דף מב ב] גבי מלח דאיכא דאמרי דאפי' בכלי שני נמי בשלה ואיכא דאמרי דאפי' בכלי ראשון נמי לא בשלה ואע"פ שאין בישול אחר בישול מ"מ יש בישול אחר אפיה וצליה כדאמרי' בפסחים [דף מא א] צלאו ואח"כ בשלו חייב ומוקי לה כרבי יוסי דאמר יוצאין ברקיק השרוי אבל לא במבושל אע"פ שלא נימוח אלמא דיש בישול אחר (*צליה) [*אפיה] וה"ה דיש בישול אחר (*אפיה) [*צליה] הלכך יזהר אדם שלא ליתן פת אפוי אף בכלי שני במקום שהיד סולדת בו וגם מצלי *יש ליזהר כמו כן והמבושל לא יתן אצל האש בחום גדול שהיד סולדת בו ואם עושה חילל שבת מיהו ראבי"ה כתב דלאו מילתא היא דבפ' כיצד מברכין [ברכות ד' לח ב] מייתי לה ומסיק דע"כ לא קאמר ר' יוסי אלא לגבי מצה דבעינן טעם מצה בפיו וליכא:

שולחן ערוך אורח חיים סימן שיח סעיף ד

תבשיל שנתבשל כל צרכו, יש בו משום בישול אם נצטנן. הגה: וי"א דוקא אם מצטמק ויפה לו (רבינו ירוחם ח"ג); ואם לא נתבשל כל צרכו, ואפילו נתבשל כמאכל ב"ד =בן דרוסאי=, שייך בו בישול אפילו בעודו רותח; וה"מ שיש בו בישול אחר בישול, בתבשיל שיש בו מרק, אבל דבר שנתבשל כבר, והוא יבש, מותר לשרותו בחמין בשבת. ואם הוא דבר יבש שלא נתבשל מלפני השבת, אין שורין אותו בחמין בשבת אבל מדיחים אותו בחמין בשבת, חוץ מן המליח הישן ומן הדג שנקרא קולייס האספנין שאינם צריכים בישול אלא מעט והדחתן היא גמר מלאכתן. הגה: וה"ה כל דבר קשה שאינו ראוי לאכול כלל בלא שרייה, דאסור לשרותו בשבת, דהוי גמר מלאכה. (הגהות מרדכי).

משנה ברורה סימן שיח ס"ק לג

מותר לשרותו - אפילו בכלי ראשון רותח כדי שיהיה נימוח שם ויהיה דבר לח דאין בישול אחר בישול אבל לא יתנו לכ"ר שעומד על גבי האש:

תוס' הרא"ש קמה ע"ב

כל שבא בחמין מע"ש שורין אותו בחמין בשבת פרש"י שורין אותו זמן מרובה משום דזמן מועט מילתא דפשיטא היא ולא איצטריך למתנייה כיון דכבר נתבשל אין בישול אחר בישול אבל שריית זמן מרובה אצטריך לאשמועי' דכיון דמתקן הוא ע"י שרייה הוא גמר מלאכה וליתסר ולהכי בעי בגמרא כגון מאי אי זה דבר הוא שנתבשל כבר ומתוקן ע"י שרייה וקאמר כגון תרנגולתא דר' אבא.

אגלי טל אופה סימן יט ס"ק ח-ט

ואינו נ"ל וזה לשון הרמב"ם המבשל על האור דבר שהיה מבושל כל צורכו או דבר שאין צריך בישול פטור. וכתב המ"מ ומ"ש וכן דבר שאין צריך בישול נלמד ממה שנחלקו בפרק כירה בשמן אם יש בו משום בישול ולד"ה דבר שאין צריך בישול אין בו משום בישול. ע"כ. והנה מזה מוכח דאפי' לכתחילה מותר נגד המדורה או בתולדת האור כמו בשמן דמותר לכתחלה שם למ"ד דאין בשמן משום בישול ודינו כמו דבר המבושל כל צורכו. ועל זה כתב הרמב"ם המבשל על האור כו' דבכה"ג פטור אבל אסור הא כנגד המדורה או בתולדת האור אפי' לכתחילה מותר כמו במבושל כל צורכו והרי מפורש בכאן בתפוחים שאסור. אלא ודאי דבר שאין צריך בישול שכתב הרמב"ם לאו היינו תפוחים אלא דבר שאין הבישול מתקנו כלל ואינו משנה טעמו לטעם אחר וכדאיתא באו"ז שהעתקנו לעיל.

מ"מ אף שדעת הסה"ת המובא בש"ע הנ"ל ע"כ אינו כמו שפירש רעק"א לדעת הרמב"ם. מ"מ בדעת הרמב"ם עצמו גם בעל ספר מנחת כהן כתב דפירות הנאכלין חיים אין בהם משום בישול. וכתב דמ"ש הרמב"ם פטור אבל אסור היינו במבשל ע"ג האור אבל כנגד המדורה מותר.

רמב"ם הלכות שבת פרק ג הלכה י

כל שמותר לשהותו על גבי האש כשנוטלים אותו בשבת אסור להחזירו למקומו, ואין מחזירין לעולם אלא על גבי כירה גרופה או מכוסה או בכירה וכופח שהוסקו בקש וגבבה, והוא שלא הניח הקדרה על גבי הקרקע אבל משהניחה על גבי קרקע אין מחזירין אותה, ואפילו על גבי כירה גרופה או מכוסה, ואין מחזירין לתנור ולא לכופח שהוסקו בגפת או בעצים אף על פי שגרף או כסה מפני שהבלן חם ביותר, וכל שאין מחזירין עליו אין סומכין לו בשבת.

רמב"ם הלכות שבת פרק כב הלכה ח

דבר שנתבשל קודם השבת או נשרה בחמין מלפני השבת אע"פ שהוא עכשיו צונן מותר לשרותו בחמין בשבת, ודבר שהוא צונן מעיקרו ולא בא בחמין מעולם מדיחין אותו בחמין בשבת אם לא היתה הדחתו גמר מלאכתו אבל אין שורין אותו בחמין.

רמב"ם הלכות שבת פרק כב הלכה י

מערב אדם מים ומלח ושמן וטובל בו פתו או נותנו לתוך התבשיל, והוא שיעשה מעט אבל הרבה אסור מפני שנראה כעושה מלאכה ממלאכת התבשיל, וכן לא יעשה מי מלח עזין והן שני שלישי מלח ושליש מים מפני שנראה כעושה מוריס, ומותר למלוח ביצה אבל צנון וכיוצא בו אסור מפני שנראה ככובש כבשים בשבת והכובש אסור מפני שהוא כמבשל, ומותר לטבל צנון וכיוצא בו במלח ואוכל.

בית יוסף אורח חיים סימן שיח

אבל הרמב"ם כתב בפרק כ"ב (ה"ח) דבר שנתבשל קודם השבת או נשרה בחמין מלפני השבת אע"פ שהוא עכשיו צונן מותר לשרותו בחמין בשבת. ונראה מדבריו דאפילו לא נתבשל כמאכל בן דרוסאי נמי כיון שנשרה במים רותחים חשיב מבושל לענין שלא יחשב כמבשל בשבת כששורה אותו בשבת בחמין.

דרכי משה שם סק"ג

וצריך עיון דהא לעיל כתב בשם הרמב"ם דאפילו לשרות אסור אלא בנתבשל כל צרכו ואין לחלק לדעת הרמב"ם בין דבר לח לדבר יבש כמו שכתבתי לעיל. וצ"ע.

רמב"ם הלכות שבת פרק ט הלכה ה

הניח בשר על גבי גחלים אם נצלה בו כגרוגרת אפי' בשנים ושלשה מקומות חייב, לא נצלה בו כגרוגרת אבל נתבשל כולו חצי בישול חייב, נתבשל חצי בישול מצד אחד פטור, עד שיהפך בו ויתבשל חצי בישול משני צדדיו, שכח והדביק פת בתנור בשבת ונזכר מותר לו לרדותה קודם שתאפה ויבוא לידי מלאכה. /השגת הראב"ד/ אבל נתבשל כולו חצי בישול. א"א חצי בישול פי' כמאכל בן דרוסאי.

אבן האזל הלכות שבת פרק כב הלכה ח

ונראה לבאר דהא דאסור לשרות בחמין בשבת דבר שלא נשרה מלפני השבת אינו משום התחלת בישול (דהא שרי' בחמין פחות ממאכל ב"ד) ומגדר חצי שיעור הא בארנו דלא שייך בבישול גדר חצי שיעור אלא נראה דאיסורו הוא משום דשריית הבשר בחמין הוה תיקון קצת דעי"ז ראוי כבר לאוכלו ואיסורו משום תיקון האוכלין וגדר האיסור הוא כמו כובש כבשים דאסור מדרבנן משום דהוי כמו מבשל שע"י נתקן הדבר לאכילה וכמש"כ הרמב"ם בהל' י' והכובש אסור מפני שהוא כמבשל.

אלא דבאמת צריך ביאור דין דכבוש כמבושל גבי שבת דהא גם מבשל ממש בחמה מותר ורק בתולדות החמה גזרו אטו תולדות האור וא"כ אמאי אסיר מבושל ע"י כבישה וגם לפי דברינו דכבישה הוא משום דין תיקון האוכלין גם כן קשה דעכ"פ במבשל בחמה יהא ג"כ אסור משום תיקון אוכלין, והיה אפשר לומר דהא דמותר לההם בחמה היינו דוקא במידי דלא שייך תיקון וכמו שדייק הרמב"ם בהל' ט' לפיכך מותר ליתן מים צונן בשמש כדי שיחמו, וכן הוא לשון המשנה קמ"ו ע"ב ואת הצונן בחמה בשביל שיחמו משום דבמים לא שייך כ"כ תיקון אוכלין, אלא דקשה ע"ז מהסוגיא בדף ל"ט ע"א דמיירי בביצה דשייך בה תיקון

אוכלין וקאמר התם בחמה כו"ע לא פליגי דשרי ומבואר דבחמה מותר לבשל אף מידי דשייך בה תיקון אוכלין, וי"ל דשאני ביצה משאר מאכל דלא אמרינן דאסור משום תיקון אוכלין אלא במידי דאינו ראוי לאוכלו בלתי מבושל אבל ביצה אפשר לאכלה בלא בישול ואף דגם בשר חי אמרינן בגמ׳ דחזי לאומצא מ"מ רובא דעלמא אינם אוכלים כן אבל ביצה דרכה לגומעה חיה לכן ליכא בזה משום תיקון אוכלין, (ועוד נראה דשאני בישול בחמה דהא דלא שייך בזה בישול משום דאין דרך בישולו בכך לכן גם מטעם תיקון אוכלין ליכא דאין דרך תיקון בכך משא"כ בכבישה ובשרייה דרך תיקונו בכך.)

ולפימש"כ מיושבים דברי רבינו כיון דכל איסור שרייה בחמין בשבת אינו אלא משום תיקון אוכלין א"כ כיון שנשרה מע"ש וכבר תיקן שוב אין בו משום תיקון דשרייה ולכן שורין אותו בשבת והוה כמו בישול דאחרי שנתבשל כל צרכו תו לא שייך בישול.

מגילת ספר סימן ג סעיף כג ס"ק ד

עיין בב"י שרצה לדייק מל׳ הרמב"ם פכ"ב ה"ח שכל שנשרה בחמין בע"ש אף שלא נתבשל כל צרכו מותר לחזור ולשרותו בחמין בשבת ולכאורה כוונתו אפילו באופן שע"י השריה הנוספת יתוסף בבישולו ומ"מ התירו היות וכבר התחיל קצת להתבשל בע"ש וגם כעת כשמניחו בחמין שנית לא יגמר בישולו ורק באופן שלא בא בחמין בע"ש אסרו עליו לשרות בחמין בשבת אף שלא יגמר בישולו דלהתחיל בישול בשבת אסור וזה כעין שכתב הט"ז בסק"ט והובאו דבריו לעיל אות ב׳ והנה כל הראשונים הביאו המקור לזה שאין בישול אחר בישול מהמשנה פ׳ חבית וזה נכון אם נפרש כפרש"י שם שהמשנה מדברת על דבר שכבר נתבשל כל צרכו בע"ש אבל לפי מה שנקט הב"י בדעת הרמב"ם אין משם מקור לדין זה אבל מצינו בבהגר"א סי׳ רנ"ג ס"ב בד"ה כל זמן שהיא רותחת שהביא מקור אחר להא דאין בישול אחר בישול ממה שמותר להחזיר בשבת קדירה לאש וזו ראיה ברורה שאפילו על האש אין בישול אחר בישול אף שלגבי הגסה מצינו דעת הכלבו דיש הגסה אחר בישול כשהקדירה על האש ועיין בשעה"צ ס"ק מ"ו מש"כ בשם הא"ר וצ"ע.

ביאור הגר"א אורח חיים סימן רנג ס"ק לט

כ"ז שהיא רותחת. אע"ג דאין בישול אחר בישול מדמותר להחזירה בשבת בנצטנן יש בישול מדאמרינן שם ל"ד גזירה שמא ירתיח וערא"ש פ"ג ס"י:

רמב"ם הלכות שבת פרק ד הלכה ו

מניחין מיחם ע"ג מיחם בשבת וקדרה על גבי קדרה וקדרה ע"ג מיחם ומיחם על גבי קדרה וטח פיהם בבצק לא בשביל שיוחמו אלא בשביל שיעמדו על חומם, שלא אסרו אלא להטמין בשבת אבל להניח כלי חם על גב כלי חם כדי שיהיו עומדין בחמימותן מותר, אבל אין מניחין כלי שיש בו דבר צונן על גבי כלי חם בשבת שהרי מוליד בו חום בשבת ואם הניחו מבערב מותר ואינו כטומן בדבר המוסיף.

תלמוד בבלי מסכת שבת דף מב עמוד א

אבל נותן כו'. תנו רבנן: נותן אדם חמין לתוך הצונן, ולא הצונן לתוך החמין, דברי בית שמאי. ובית הלל אומרים: בין חמין לתוך הצונן, ובין צונן לתוך החמין מותר. במה דברים אמורים - בכוס, אבל באמבטי - חמין לתוך הצונן. ולא צונן לתוך החמין. ורבי שמעון בן מנסיא אוסר. אמר רב נחמן: הלכה כרבי שמעון בן מנסיא. סבר רב יוסף למימר: ספל הרי הוא כאמבטי. אמר ליה אביי, תני רבי חייא: ספל אינו כאמבטי. ולמאי דסליק אדעתא מעיקרא דספל הרי הוא כאמבטי, ואמר רב נחמן: הלכה כרבי שמעון בן מנסיא, אלא בשבת רחיצה בחמין ליכא? - מי סברת רבי שמעון אסיפא קאי? ארישא קאי: ובית הלל מתירין בין חמין לתוך צונן, ובין צונן לתוך החמין, ורבי שמעון בן מנסיא אוסר צונן לתוך חמין. - לימא רבי שמעון בן מנסיא דאמר כבית שמאי! - הכי קאמר: לא נחלקו בית שמאי ובית הלל בדבר זה. אמר רב הונא בריה דרב יהושע: חזינא ליה לרבא דלא קפיד אמנא, מדתני רבי חייא: נותן אדם קיתון של מים לתוך ספל של מים, בין חמין לתוך צונן ובין צונן לתוך חמין. - אמר ליה רב הונא לרב אשי: דילמא שאני התם

דמיפסק כלי? - אמר ליה: מערה איתמר, מערה אדם קיתון של מים לתוך ספל של מים, בין חמין לתוך צונן, בין צונן לתוך חמין.

תלמוד בבלי מסכת שבת דף מ עמוד ב

תנו רבנן: מביא אדם קיתון מים ומניחו כנגד המדורה, לא בשביל שיחמו, אלא בשביל שתפיג צינתן. רבי יהודה אומר: מביאה אשה פך של שמן ומניחתו כנגד המדורה, לא בשביל שיבשל אלא בשביל שיפשר. רבן שמעון בן גמליאל אומר: אשה סכה ידה שמן ומחממתה כנגד המדורה, וסכה לבנה קטן, ואינה חוששת. איבעיא להו: שמן מה הוא לתנא קמא? - רבה ורב יוסף דאמרי תרוייהו להתירא, רב נחמן בר יצחק אמר לאיסורא. רבה ורב יוסף דאמרי תרוייהו להתירא: שמן אף על פי שהיד סולדת בו - מותר, קסבר תנא קמא: שמן אין בו משום בשול. ואתא רבי יהודה למימר: שמן יש בו משום בשול, והפשרו לא זה הוא בשולו. ואתא רבן שמעון בן גמליאל למימר: שמן - יש בו משום בשול, והפשרו זהו בשולו. רב נחמן בר יצחק אמר לאיסורא: שמן אף על פי שאין היד סולדת בו - אסור, קסבר: שמן יש בו משום בשול, והפשרו זהו בשולו. ואתא רבי יהודה למימר: הפשרו לא זהו בשולו. ואתא רבן שמעון בן גמליאל למימר: שמן יש בו משום בשול, והפשרו זהו בשולו. רבן שמעון בן גמליאל היינו תנא קמא! - איכא בינייהו כלאחר יד. אמר רב יהודה אמר שמואל: אחד שמן ואחד מים, יד סולדת בו - אסור, אין יד סולדת בו - מותר. והיכי דמי יד סולדת בו? אמר רחבא: כל שכריסו של תינוק נכוית. אמר רבי יצחק בר אבדימי: פעם אחת נכנסתי אחר רבי לבית המרחץ ובקשתי להניח לו פך של שמן באמבטי, ואמר לי: טול בכלי שני ותן. שמע מינה תלת, שמע מינה: שמן יש בו משום בשול, ושמע מינה: כלי שני אינו מבשל, ושמע מינה: הפשרו זהו בשולו.

רש"י מסכת שבת דף מ עמוד ב

והיכי דמי - סלוד, יש שסולד מרתיחה מועטת, ויש שאינו סולד.

3

רא"ש מסכת שבת פרק ג

סימן י

והכי איתא בירושלמי מותר להפשיר במקום שהיד שולטת בו ואסור להפשיר במקום שאין היד שולטת עד היכן רבי שמעון בן פזי בשם רבי יוסי בר חנינא אומר עד שיהא נותן ידו לתוכה והיא נכוית והא דאמרי' בגמרא דידן לא בשביל שיחומו אם באנו להשוות לגמרא דבני מערבא נוכל לפרש לא בשביל שיחומו כלומר במקום שראוי להתחמם אלא כדי להפיג צינתו אלא במקום שראוין להפיג צינתו ולא להתבשל אפילו יעמוד שם כל היום והא דא"ר יהודה אמר שמואל יד סולדת בו אסור אין יד סולדת בו מותר ה"ק יד סולדת בו הוי בישול הלכך אסור להניחו במקום שאפשר שיחומו כדי שהיד סולדת בו מותר להניחו במקום שיחומו ולא תהא היד סולדת בו ולמאי דפרשינן דלא שייך בישול בתבשיל שנתבשל לא תקשה הא דאמרינן לעיל בבמה מדליקין (דף לד א) דאין טומנין בדבר שאינו מוסיף הבל [משחשיכה] גזירה שמא ירתיח. התם לאו משום בישול אלא משום שמא יחתה והאי דנקט הרתחה דבר הצריך להטמנה נקט:

סימן יא

ורש"י פירש לעיל גזירה שמא ירתיח קדירה שנצטננה כשירצה להטמינה וירתיחנה בתחלה באור ונמצא מבשל בשבת ופריך אי הכי בין השמשות נמי נגזר דהא שבות מעליא הוי דהא איכא גזירת איסור דאורייתא וכן לעיל בפרק קמא (דף יח ב) גבי יורה עקורה דפריך והלא מגיס ופירש רש"י ובמבושל הוי בשול מדרבנן למדנו שאף בתבשיל שנתבשל ונצטנן שייך ביה בישול כיון שיש בו משקה והא דאמרינן כל שבא בחמין לפני השבת שורין אותו בחמין בשבת היינו דבר יבש כגון תרנגולתא דרבי אבא לקמן בפרק חבית (דף קמה ב) ונראה לי להביא ראיה לדבריו מהא דתניא במסכת יו"ט בפרק המביא יין ת"ר אחד מביא האור ואחד מביא העצים ואחד שופת את הקדירה ואחד נותן לתוכה מים ואחד נותן לתוכה תבלין אחד מגיס בה כולן חייבין אע"פ שאותו שנתן לתוכה מים נתחייב משום

מבשל המגיס בה נמי חייב משום מבשל אלמא יש בישול אחר בישול ואע״פ שהרתיח ואיכא למידחי דעד שלא נתבשל כמאכל בן דרוסאי כל המקרב בישולו חייב ואחר שנתבשל כמאכל בן דרוסאי אפשר דאין בישול אחר בישול ומסתברא דעד שלא הגיע למאכל בן דרוסאי כל המקרב בישולו חייב ואחר שהגיע למאכל בן דרוסאי אם נצטנן והרתיחו חייב כדפי׳ רש״י לעיל גבי שמא ירתיח והא דפריך בפרק קמא והלא מגיס אפילו ביורה רותחת איכא למימר סמנין לצבוע בהן צריך בישול לעולם אי נמי לאו משום בישול פריך אלא משום צובע כשהוא מגיס מכניס הסממנין בצמר. ה״ד יד סולדת בו אמר רחבא כל שכריסו של קטן נכוית ממנו א״ר יצחק בר אבדימי פעם אחת נכנסתי אחר רבי לבית המרחץ ובקשתי להניח פך שמן באמבטי אמר לי טול בכלי שני ותן שמע מינה תלת שמע מינה שמן יש בו משום בישול ושמע מינה כלי שני אין בו משום בישול ושמע מינה הפשירו [לא] זהו בישולו:

בית יוסף אורח חיים סימן שיח סעיף ד

אבל הרמב״ם כתב בפרק ט׳ (ה״ג) המבשל על האור דבר שהיה מבושל כל צרכו או דבר שאינו צריך בישול כלל פטור. עד כאן לשונו. וכתב הרב המגיד שכתב כן מדתנן כל שבא בחמין מלפני השבת שורין אותו בחמין בשבת שאם היה בו משום בישול אפילו בחמי האור היה חייב אלא ודאי לית ביה משום בישול ומשום הכי שרי לשרותו בחמין ומיהו על האור ממש מיתסר מדרבנן וזה נלמד מדין חזרת מצטמק ורע לו. ומשמע מדברי הרמב״ם דכשלא נתבשל כל צרכו אף על פי שהגיע למאכל בן דרוסאי שייך ביה בישול וחיובי נמי מיחייב. והרב המגיד כתב שדעת הרשב״א (יח: סוד״ה צמר, לט. ד״ה גמרא) וקצת מפרשים שכל שנתבשל כמאכל בן דרוסאי שוב אין בו משום חיוב בישול דבר תורה. ונראה דלפי דבריהם כל שנתבשל כמאכל בן דרוסאי מותר לשרותו בחמין בשבת כיון שכשמבשלו על האור ליכא חיובא אבל לדעת הרמב״ם כל שלא נתבשל כל צרכו אם שורה אותו בחמין בשבת חייב חטאת כמבשל באור עצמה כמו שכתבתי למעלה. ומכל מקום לא חילקו בין תבשיל שיש בו מרק ליבש. וגם בפרק כ״ב (ה״ד) כתב הרב המגיד בשם הרשב״א (מ: ד״ה מביא) דלדברי הכל תבשיל שנתבשל מערב שבת ונצטנן מותר

לחממו כנגד המדורה אפילו במקום שהיד סולדת בו והוא שלא יתן על גבי המדורה או על גבי כירה. עד כאן לשונו. ולא חילק בין יש בו מרק לאין בו אלמא בכל גוונא שרי לתתו כנגד המדורה במקום שהיד סולדת ואם כן מתניתין דכל שבא בחמין מלפני השבת אפילו ביש בה מרק נמי היא. וכן נראה דעת הר"ן שכתב בפרק כירה (יט. ד"ה תנו רבנן מביא) גבי הא דאסרינן להניח קיתון של מים כנגד המדורה במקום שהיד סולדת מיהו הני מילי בדבר שלא נתבשל אבל צונן שנתבשל מותר להניחו אפילו בכלי ראשון או כנגד המדורה ואפילו במקום שהיד סולדת בו שאין דרך בישול בכך וראיה לדבר מדתנן כל שבא בחמין מלפני השבת שורין אותו בחמין בשבת כלומר אפילו בכלי ראשון אף על פי שתולדת האור כאור והמבשל בה חייב חטאת כמבשל על גבי האש ממש ומיהו דוקא בכלי ראשון או כנגד המדורה אבל על גבי האש ממש אסור דהא אסיקנא לעיל (ר"ן טז: ד"ה ותו) דאפילו תבשיל המצטמק ורע לו אסור להחזיר על גבי כירה שאינה גרופה וקטומה. עד כאן לשונו. הרי שסתם דבריו להתיר לתת כנגד המדורה במקום שהיד סולדת צונן שנתבשל ולא חילק בין יש בו מרק ליבש אלמא דבכל גוונא סבירא ליה דשרי. ומיהו לתתו כנגד המדורה במקום שאין היד סולדת פשיטא דלכולי עלמא שרי ואפילו יש בו מרק ונצטנן וכמו שיבוא בדברי רבינו לקמן (פה.) מותר ליתן קיתון של מים או של שמן כנגד האש וכו'. ואם יש בו שומן והוא נימוח מחום האש גם כן יבוא משפטו בדברי רבינו בסוף סימן זה:

שולחן ערוך אורח חיים סימן שיח סעיף ד כבר נמצא בפרק ב אות ב

משנה ברורה סימן שיח ס"ק כד

(כד) אם נצטנן - היינו שאין היד סולדת בו אף שהוא קצת חם עדיין אבל אם היד סולדת בו אף שנצטנן מרתיחתו לא שייך בו בישול עוד דבכלל רותח הוא ואין בישול אחר בישול [ודוקא לענין להחזירו לתנור כשהוא גרוף מן הגחלים או שהם עמומין אבל לתנור כשאינו גרוף וכ"ש על האש ממש אסור להחזיר לכו"ע אפילו רותח גמור וכדלעיל ברנ"ג] וכ"ז הוא דעת המחבר אבל הרמ"א לקמן בסט"ו בהג"ה כתב דכל זמן שלא נצטנן לגמרי נהגו להקל דאין בו משום בישול וע"ש:

שולחן ערוך יורה דעה סימן קה סעיף ב

חום של כלי ראשון שהיד סולדת בו, מבשל ואוסר כולו. אבל חום של כלי שני אינו מבשל. ויש אומרים שגם כן אינו מפליט ואינו מבליע. וי"א דמכל מקום הוא מפליט ומבליע, ואוסר כדי קליפה. וראוי לחוש ליזהר בדבר לכתחלה (ועי"ל סי' ס"ח סעיף י"ג), אבל בדיעבד מותר בלא קליפה, ובהדחה בעלמא סגי. (ועיין לעיל סימן ס"ח וצ"ב וצ"ה נתבארו דיני כלי שני ועירוי).

אגלי טל אופה סימן יא ס"ק ו

אמנם העיקר מה שנ"ל בדעת רבינו יונה דהנה הרמב"ם פ"ט מה"ש הל"ו כתב המתיך אחד ממיני מתכות כל שהוא או המחמם את המתכות עד שתעשה גחלת הר"ז תולדת מבשל. וכן הממסס את הדונג או את החלב או את הזפת והכופר והגפרית וכיוצא בהן הר"ז תולדת מבשל וחייב. ודבריו בהיתוך מתכות מפורשים בפ"ק דיבמות ובפרק האורג מה לי בישול פתילה מה לי בישול סממנין. והנה שם ביבמות איתא אהא דבעי למילף דעשה דוחה לא תעשה שיש בה כרת מדאיצרך קרא דלא תבערו דאין מיתת ב"ד דוחה שבת. ופריך דילמא ר' יוסי הוא דאמר הבערה ללאו יצאת. פי' והוה אמינא דדחי לא תעשה גרידא ומשני מה לי בישול פתילה וכו'. ולכאורה לדעת הפוסקים דאין בישול אחר בישול אפי' בדבר לח. ועוד דמתכת יבש הוא. א"כ אכתי איצרך קרא במתכות שכבר היה מהותך וחזר ונתקשה דשוב אין בו משום בישול. ואיצרך קרא לאסר מטעם הבערה והוא רק לאו גרידא לר' יוסי והוה אמינא דדחי. ובאמת כל מתכות בשעת עשייתו הוא מהותך וא"כ כשחוזרין ומתיכין אותו למה יתחייב משום מבשל. [ואפי' לדעת האומרים דבדבר לח יש בישול אחר בישול מ"מ בדבר יבש שמתיכין אותו ע"י בישול מודו אף שנעשה אח"כ לח. משום דבתר מעיקרא אזלינן דהי' יבש. ודנין אותו כדבר יבש כדמוכח בפשטיד"א וכמ"ש הגמ"א סי' שי"ח והוכיח ג"כ מפרש"י בתרנגולתא דר' אבא שכששורין אותו במים נמוח אלא ודאי הדבר ברור דדוקא בשאר בישול אף שנצטנן מ"מ בישולו עליו מה שאין כן במתכות שהתכתו הוא בישולו וכשחוזר ומתקשה אזל לי' בישולו וכשחוזר ומתיכו שנית מתחייב. וע"כ נראה דה"ה במים דחימומו הוא בישולו וכשנצטנן ואזל ליה בישולו והוא חוזר ומחממו שנית מתחייב. וכן משמע דבמים חימומו הוא בישולו. וכיון דמכל הני משמע דמים לא

שייך בהם לשון בישול אלא לשון חימום וחימומו הוא בישולו כמו התכת מתכת שהתכתו זהו בישולו. וכשנצטנן ואזל לי׳ בישולו חייב שנית על בישולו. וזה שדייק רבינו יונה וכתב ומים מבושלים אם פסקה רתיחתן יש בהם משום בישול. למימר שדין זה נוהג רק במים לבד כנ״ל מלתא בטעמא. ואין אנו צריכין לומר דתרי רבינו יונה הם.

משנה ברורה סימן שיח ס״ק פט

דהיינו מקום שכריסו וכו׳ - דלא נוכל לשער ביד דיש שסולד מרתיחה מועטת ויש שאינו סולד:

שמירת שבת כהלכתה פרק א׳ הע׳ ג׳

ובדבר שיעור החום שהיד סולדת בו עיין יו״ד סימן קה בפתחי תשובה ס״ק ז ובדרכי תשובה ס״ק נא ספר בן איש חי שנה שניה פרשת בא או״ק ה מצודת ציון על קצשו״ע סוף כלל עב ועיין בנעם ח״ו דעת הגרש״ז אויערבך שליט״א כי מה שנוהגים להקל עד 40 מעלות הוא מחמת הוכחת הד״ת הנ״ל מדברי הבה״ג שכתב כי חלב אפי׳ בשעה שחולבים אותו צונן הוא וידוע כי שיעור החום של חלב פרה ועז בשעת החליבה אינו עולה על יותר מארבעים מעלות והגרש״ז אויערבך שליט״א מוכיח שם דעד 45 מעלות אין לחוש וכן כתבתי בפנים וראיתו ברורה כי החום הרגיל של ברווז שהוא עוף טהור בשעת מאמץ הוא קרוב לארבעים וחמש מעלות ולדעת מומחים הדם היוצא מבית השחיטה עולה לפחות במעלה אחת וכשהוא חולה ג״כ עולה החום לפחות בשתי מעלות וכיון דקיי״ל שגם בית השחיטה של ברווז חולה השיב כצונן עיין חולין ח ב לכן אפשר לקבוע בפשיטות את השיעור של מעלות.

הלכות שבת (איידר) הע׳ יט

שמעתי שמו״ר הגר״א קטלר זצ״ל אמר שעד 120° אין יס״ב (בא לשיעור זה ע״י הבחנה). כתב הגרמ״פ שליט״א בתשובה בסוף הספר ״מהראוי להחמיר כמדומני בשיעור ק״י הוא כבר חום גדול שיש לחוש ליד סולדת כפי מה שבדקנו בעצמינו.

שו"ת אגרות משה אורח חיים חלק ד סימן עד

(ג) מהו שיעור החום שיש לחוש בו לחומרא ליס"ב =ליד סולדת בו=, ובאיזה שיעור הוי ודאי יס"ב.

תשובה: מהראוי להחמיר כמדומני בשיעור ק"י (מ"ג מעלות צלסיוס) הוא כבר חום גדול שיש לחוש ליד סולדת כפי מה שבדקנו בעצמנו. והספק יש לחוש עד ק"ס (ע"א מעלות צ') כי מדת ק"ס הוא ודאי יד סולדת אף לקולא.

פסקי תשובות סי' רנג הע' 5

אם אין נמנע מלאכול ולשתות מחמת חמימותו אין הוא בגדר יס"ב וע"כ כוונתם שיכול לשתות ולאכול היטב ובבת אחת בלי לנפוח על המאכל ובלי שהיות (וכן מפורש במנחת שי, הנהגת הנשאל), דאם ע"י נפיחה ולאט ובשהיות אפילו בחום של 80 מעליות יוכל להכניס לפה שרגיל בחמין, וכ"ה בברית עולם אופה סעי' צ"ג. והנה בגמ' ורש"י (שבת מ ע"ב) ושו"ע (סי' שי"ח סעי י"ד) ושאר פוסקים מבואר שיעור יס"ב 'כריסו של תינוק נכוית', דא"א לשער ביד, דיש סולד מרתיחה מועטת ויש שאינו סולד ואעפ"כ כתבו הפוסקים הנ"ל להקל לשער באצבעו. ובס' בירור הלכה שעפ"י המדידות הנ"ל מובן, כי עפ"י מומחי רפואה עולה שחום מים עד 44 מעלות אכן אינו גורם לכויה המשארת רושם בכריסו של תינוק, הגם שסולד ומצטער והוא שיעור שיד אדם עדיין אינו סולה, ומכאן ואילך כריסו של תינוק נכוית וידו של אדם סולדת ואידי ואידי חד שיעורא הוא.

חידושי הרשב"א מסכת שבת דף מב עמוד א

נותן אדם חמין לתוך צונן אבל לא צונן לתוך חמין. פירש רש"י ז"ל משום דתתאה גבר, ואינו מחוור דאם כן בפרק כיצד צולין (פסחים ע"ו א') דפליגי בהא מילתא רב ושמואל חד אמר תתאה גבר וחד אמר עילאה גבר, לותביה מהא למאן דאמר עילאה גבר, ועוד דהא אפילו למאן דאמר תתאה גבר מודה דכדי קליפה אסור דאדמקרר ליה תתאה לעילאה מיבלע בלע, ואם כן אפילו חמין לתוך צונן הרי מבשל כדי קליפה וליתסר, אלא ודאי נראה דבמים שהן מתערבין אלו לתוך אלו ליכא למימר בהו תתאה ועילאה.

ובתוספות פירשו שדרך המערה שנותן המועט לתוך המרובה והלכך חמין מועטין לתוך צונן מרובין אין בהם כח לבשל אבל צוננין מועטין לתוך חמין מרובין מתבשלין, וגם זה אינו מחוור בעיני דהכא סתמא קתני לא שנא מרובין ולא שנא מועטין, ולתוך הכוס ואפילו לתוך מיחם רגילות הוא לתת צונן הרבה כדי להפשיר מפני שהן עשוין לשתיה ואין אדם שותה חמין גמורין אלא פושרין, והוה ליה למיתני הכא צונן לתוך חמין כדי שיחמו אסור וכדי להפשירן מותר וכדתני במתניתין.

אלא נראה דכלים אלו בין כוס בין אמבטי וספל כולן כלי שני הם, וכן פירשו הגאונים ז"ל והרמב"ם ז"ל, והכי נמי משמע מדאקשינן לקמן אלא לרב נחמן רחיצה בחמין מי ליכא, ואי איתא משכחת לה בכלי שני, ואע"ג דאמבטי דלעיל (מ' ב') גבי עובדא דרבי משמע דכלי ראשון הוא מדאמר ליה טול בכלי שני ותן, אמבטי דהכא כלי שני הוא דהא אמבטאות הרבה יש והכא דבר הלמד מענינו אמבטי דומיא דכוס, ומהתם נמי משמע לי דהכא אפילו בנותן מים מרובין ואפילו כדי מלואו של אמבטי ושל ספל קאמר, דאי לא הא משכחת לה בנותן מים מרובין כדי להפשירן שהרי אין אדם רוחץ במים חמין שהוא מסלד בהן, והכא הכי פירושה נותן אדם חמין כל שהוא לתוך הצונן לפי שהן מתקררין בעירויין ומתערבין ממש בתוך הצונן ואין כח בהן לבשל ואפילו בבאין מכלי ראשון, דאפילו תימצי לומר בעלמא דעירוי דכלי ראשון ככלי ראשון, הני מילי כגון שמערה על גבי תבלין וכיוצא בהן שאין החמין מתערבין בתוכן אלא מכין עליהם בקילוחן ומבשלין, אבל מים במים הן מתערבין ממש בתוך הצונן ואין בהן כח לבשל, אדרבה כל שהן נופלין הן מצטננין וכל שכן הכא בכוס שהוא כלי שני שאינו מבשל, אבל צונן לתוך חמין אסור משום דגזור בית שמאי כלי שני אטו כלי ראשון הואיל ואפשר דאתי בכלי ראשון לידי איסורא דאורייתא דכלי ראשון מבשל, ובית הלל מתירין אפילו בצונן לתוך חמין דכלי שני אינו מבשל ואפילו נתן לתוכן צוננין מועטין דאין באין לתוכן לידי בישול אלא לידי הפשר, והא דתנן במתניתין אבל נותן לתוכו או לתוך הכוס כדי להפשירן ומפרשין עלה בגמ' אבל נותן לתוכו מים מרובין כדי להפשירן, משום מיחם הוא דאמרינן אבל בכוס כל שהוא נותן לתוכו היינו להפשירו, אבל באמבטי שעומדין לרחיצת אדם מחממן

הרבה והלכך צונן לתוך חמין אסור לעולם שאי אפשר לבא לידי הפשר אלא לידי בישול ואפילו נתן באמבטי כדי מלואו, ואע"פ שהוא כלי שני ובעלמא אינו מבשל הכא שאני לפי שדרכן לחממן יותר מדאי, וספל כיוצא בו למאי דהוה סבירא ליה לרב יוסף מעיקרא, אבל במסקנא לא מדתני ר' חייא ספל אינו כאמבטי, דמים שבספל אינן חמין כל כך ואינו אלא ככוס והואיל וכלי שני הוא לעולם מותר שאינו בא אלא לידי הפשר, ואפילו היו מים שהיד סולדת בהן לאחר שנתערבו צונן לתוכן, אינו מחמת הצונן שיש בו להיות יד סולדת אלא מחמת הראשונים שלא נצטננו.

כף החיים סימן שיח ס"ק קמג

וא"ת איך ידע האדם לשער כך בדעתו הנה נקיט האי כללא בידך כל היכא שזה החמין ראוי לשתיה או לאכילה שאין האדם נמנע ממנו מכח רבוי חמימותו ה"ז לא חשיב היס"ב אבל אם נמנע לשתותו או לאכלו מרוב חומו ה"ז נחשב בכלל יס"ב

שמירת שבת כהלכתה פרק א' סעיף לט

מיתקן לחימום מים המופעל בחשמל בוילר נפט וכדו' מכיון שכאשר מוציאים ממנו מים חמים באים במקומם של אלה מים קרים במיכל שלו ומתחממים שם הרבה אסור להוציא ממנו מים חמים אפילו כשאין המיתקן מופעל אלא אם כן המיתקן בנוי בצורה כזאת שניתן להוציא ממנו מים חמים אף אם אין מים קרים נכנסים במקומם.

שולחן ערוך אורח חיים סימן שיח סעיף יד

מותר ליתן קיתון של מים או שאר משקים כנגד האש להפיג צנתן, ובלבד שיתנם רחוק מהאש בענין שאינו יכול להתחמם באותו מקום עד שתהא היד סולדת (פי' מתחממת ונכוית) בו, דהיינו מקום שכריסו של תינוק נכוית בו; אבל אסור לקרבו אל האש למקום שיכול להתחמם שתהא היד סולדת בו, ואפילו להניח בו שעה קטנה שתפיג צנתו, אסור כיון שיכול להתבשל שם. הגה: וה"ה בפירות או שאר דברים לז הנאכלים כמות שהן חיין (מרדכי פ' כירה וע"ל ס"ס רנ"ד).

משנה ברורה סימן שיח ס"ק צ

כיון שיכול וכו׳ - וחיישינן דילמא מישתלי ליטלו:

שלט"ג קכ ע"ב [מה. סק"ב]

ומה שכ׳ הטוא"ח סי׳ של"ד טלית שאחז בה האור שרי לפושטו אע"פ שהוא נכבה כיון שאינו מכוין בפשיטותו זאת לכבות דמשמע שאם מכוין לכך שאסור לפושטו ואי[ן] שום אחד מהפוסקים שיזכיר דבר זה כי מדברי כולם מוכח דגרם כבוי שרי אפי׳ מכוין לכך מ"מ נראה דודאי כל גרם כיבוי דשרינן הוא בענין שאינו מכוין לכבות אלא הוא עושה שום דבר לחצוץ בפני הדליקה וע"י כך בא הכיבוי כההיא דפריס׳ עור או מחיצת כלים מלאים מים או נתינת כלי ריקן תחת הנר וכיוצא באלו שאינו מכוין לכבות אלא להגין והלכך אי בהאי מעשה שעושה בא ממילא הכבוי שפיר דמי דלא הוי אלא גרם כיבוי בלא מתכוין דאי מכוין לכך אפי׳ ע"י גרם אסור כמ"ש הטור ומיהו כשאינו מכוין לכך אע"פ דהוי פסיק רישיה שרי ע"י גרם שהרי התירו לחצות בכלי׳ מלאי׳ מים אע"פ שבודאי יתבקעו ויכבו והוי פסיק רישיה מ"מ שרי כיון שאינו אלא גרם ואינו מכוין לכך ועי׳ בתוס׳ פ׳ בתרא דיומא. ומסופקני בכל מלאכת שבת הנעשית בלא מתכוין ע"י גרם בפסיק רישיה כי האי דגרם כיבוי אי שריא או דלמא גבי דליקה הקילו.

4

רש"י מסכת שבת דף כ עמוד א

בן דרוסאי - לסטים היה, ומבשל בישולו שליש.

שו"ת רדב"ז חלק א סימן ריג

ולענין דבר הנאכל כמו שהוא חי אם יש בו משום מבשל בשבת לענין מלקות אינה לוקה אבל אסור מדרבנן ואם נתבשלו מאיליהן כגון שהניחם מערב שבת מותר לאוכלן בשבת. תדע שהרי דבר שנתבשל כמאכל בן דרוסאי אין חייב עליו בשבת וטעמא כיון דאיכא מאן דאכיל ליה הכי שוב לא מחייב על בישולו וכ"ש הדברים הנאכלין חיים לכל אדם.

פרי מגדים משבצות זהב סימן שיח ס"ק ו

נסתפקתי בישל בחמי טבריא ותולדות חמה אם מבשל אח"כ בחמי אור אם חייב ויראָה דפטור הוא דכבר נתפעל בבישולו ואפשר מותר לגמרי.

תלמוד בבלי מסכת שבת דף לט עמוד א

אמר רב נחמן: בחמה - דכוליה עלמא לא פליגי דשרי, בתולדות האור - כוליה עלמא לא פליגי דאסיר, כי פליגי - בתולדות החמה; מר סבר: גזרינן תולדות החמה אטו תולדות האור, ומר סבר: לא גזרינן.

ר"ן על הרי"ף מסכת שבת דף כב עמוד א

והרב ר' יונה ז"ל כתב בלשון הזה ומכשלה גדולה תחת יד קצת העם שטומנין קומקום של מים חמין ליתן לתוך הקדרה בשבת כשהתבשיל מצטמק ופעמים שהאחד אין יד סולדת בו והאחר יד סולדת בו ומתבשל זה בזה ונמצאו מבשלין בשבת ואפילו אם שניהם יד סולדת בהם איכא מאן דאמר בירושלמי עירוי אינה ככלי ראשון וכשמערין המים לאלתר שיצאו מן הכלי אף על פי שהן רותחין פסק כח רתיחתן מלבשל כדין כלי שני שאינו מבשל ומתבשלין בתוך כלי ראשון ומים מבושלין אם פסקה רתיחתן יש בהן משום בישול אלו דבריו ז"ל ולא ידעתי מנין לו שהרי כל שבא בחמין מלפני השבת שורין אותו בחמין בשבת אע"פ שהוא צונן גמור ולא ידעתי הפרש בין מים מבושלין למבושל אחר וצריך עיון ובדיקה:

5

שולחן ערוך אורח חיים סימן שיח סעיף טו

דבר שנתבשל כ"צ והוא יבש שאין בו מרק, לח מותר להניחו כנגד המדורה אפי' במקום שהיד סולדת בו. הגה: ואפי' נצטנן כבר. אבל אם הוא רותח, אפילו בדבר שיש בו מרק, מותר. ויש מקילין לומר דכל שאין נותנו ע"ג האש או הכירה ממש רק סמוך לו, אפילו נצטנן, מותר (המגיד פרק כ"ו). ונהגו להקל בזה אם לא נצטנן לגמרי, וכמו שכתבתי לעיל סי' רנ"ג.

מגן אברהם סימן רנג ס"ק לז

להחם הקדירה - כב"י בשם הרשב"א אסור לומר לעכו"ם להדליק אש לחמם הקדירה וכו' דאלו להחם הקדירה ס"ל להרשב"א דאפי' לישראל שרי לעשותו כמ"ש סימן שי"ח סט"ו כיון שאינו נותנו ע"ג האש או הכירה ממש ורמ"א כתב סתם אסור לומר לעכו"ם להחם וכו' דס"ל דלדידן דס"ל דאסור לחממו מדאורייתא אסור לומר ג"כ לעכו"ם ואם עשה כן אסור אפי' בדיעבד כמ"ש ס"א בדין החזיר עכו"ם ע"ג כירה ומיהו י"ל דאם לא חממו העכו"ם על גבי האש או הכירה ממש דיש להקל מאחר שגדולי פוסקים מתירין אפי' לישראל לעשותו ועמ"ש סי' רנ"ד ס"ג ועיין בב"י ס"ס רנ"ט בשם המרדכי דאם צוה לעכו"ם לעשות לו מלאכה דרבנן אין אוסרין התבשיל:

תרומת הדשן סימן סו

שאלה: יש בני אדם שאין להם תנורים מיוחדים לאפות בהן ולהטמין בהן החמין, ומטמינים באותו תנור שבבית החורף, ולמחרת בשבת באתה השפחה ומוציאה את החמין כולו מן התנור, ומושיבות ע"ג התנור ומבפנים בבית החורף. ואז מבערת את האש בתוך התנור, כדי לחמם בית החורף וע"י כך נרתחים החמין שע"ג התנור לכל צרכם, שרי למעבד הכי או לאו?

תשובה: יראה דאם לא נתקררו החמין כל כך בשעה שהוציאה אותם מן התנור, והבעירה האש בתנור דוגמת מאכל בן דרוסאי, אז ודאי שרי. והכי איתא בהדיא בסמ"ג ובמרדכי ובה"ג במיימוני, דרגילים בחופות לכסות החמין בנסרים, ולמחר באין עבדים נכרים ומחממים אותם, אם לא יתקררו כ"כ דוגמת מאכל בן דרוסאי שרי, עכ"ל. וא"ל דבחופה יש משום שמחת חתן וכלה מקילינן טפי, דבא"ז כתב וז"ל: כשמתקרר הצאלנ"ט / החמין/, ושפחה מחממתה מותר ובמדינה דלא שכיחי רבנן ראוי לאסור עכ"ל. הא קמן דבלא חופה נמי שרי, היכא דשכיחי רבנן. אמנם משמע דווקא אם לא נתקררו, אבל אם נתקררו לא שרי. ונראה דבנ"ד יש להתיר אפי' נתקררו לגמרי. דהא העבד או השפחה מתכונים לחמם התבשיל, ולכך היכא דנתקרר לגמרי אסור. אבל הכא עיקר כוונת השפחה לדבר היתר, לחמם בית החורף, דשרו רבנן בה אמירה לנכרי, משום דהכל חולים הם אצל הצינה. ונהי נמי דהחמין נרתחים ע"י כך מאליהם בודאי, וע"ד כן היא מושיבתם על התנור. מ"מ בשעה שהיא מושיבתו על התנור, אין שום

אש בתנור, וההבערה שהיא מבערת אח"כ, עיקר כוונה היא לבית החורף. ואף כי פסיק רישיה הוא לענין החמין, מ"מ יש חילוק בשבות דרבנן, בין מתכוין גמור ללא מתכוין דפסיק רישיה. והכי אשכחן בתשובת מהר"ם במרדכי, פ' הזורק במס' שבת, אההיא דגבי בית הכסא שע"ג חפירה שסביב העיר. אמנם נראה דאין להתיר כלל לישראל או לבת ישראל, שיושיבו מן החמים ע"ג התנור והשפחה מבערת אח"כ התנור. דהוי כאחד נותן את הקדירה ואחד הצית את האור, דהראשון פטור אבל אסור. וכן משמע מדברי הרמב"ם דכתב וז"ל: אחד שופת את הקדירה ואחד נתן את המים ואחד הצית את האור ואחד הגיס בה, שנים אחרונים לבד חייבים משום מבשל. מדאיצטריך לאשמועינן דהראשונים אינם חייבים, משמע קצת דאבל אסורים הן לעשות כן. [הגה"ה: והכי נמי תנן פ' המביא כדי יין (ביצה לד ע"א): האחרון חייב וכולן פטורין, וכל פטורי שבת פטור אבל אסור. והא דפריך השופת הקדרה מאי קעביד? אקדרה ריקנא קאי, כדפרש"י התם. אבל קדירה מליאה תבשיל, פשיטא דשופת הקדרה הוי כמו נתן את המים בקדרה, ע"כ.] ויש לדמותו להא דכתב במרדכי פ"ק דשבת, דנותנים מזונות לפני הנכרים בחצר, דאם יודע בודאי שיוציאנו הנכרי אסור לתת לפניו. וכן משמע התם בתוס' ובאשירי בריש המסכתא. וא"כ בנ"ד כיון דיודע דהשפחה מבערת את התנור, בוודאי הוא כנותן ע"מ לבשלו, ואב מלאכה היא כמו ההוצאה. ולכך צריך לה להניחה השפחה שתושיבה היא החמין על התנור, קודם שהיא מבערת אותו. ובענין זה יש פנים להתירו כדפרישית.

מרדכי מסכת שבת הגהות מרדכי פרק שלישי

ובחופה רגילין ליתן היורה מלאה תבשיל על הפטפוט מע"ש ולכסותה בנסרים ויש אש תחתיה ולהשהות שם עד למחר ביום השבת אם היורה מתקררת ועבדים נכרים מחממין אש תחתיה ואם ראויה שיאכל בלא חימום כמאכל בן דרוסאי אין קפידא במה שחיממוה נכרי בשבת ומותר וכן מנהג בחופות:

הגהות מיימוניות הלכות שבת פרק ג

ובחופה רגילים ליתן היורה מע"ש על הפטפוט והאש בוערת ומכסים בנסרים

את היורה ועבדים נכרים מחממין אותה בשבת אם לא נתקררה כל כך שלא היתה ראויה לאכילה דוגמת טעם מאכל בן דרוסאי קודם שחממוה נכרים א"כ אין חוששין בחימום ושרי

ספר מצוות גדול לאוין סימן סה

בחופה רגילין ליתן היורה מערב שבת על הפיטפוט שקורין טרפייד והאש בוערת ומכסין היורה בנסרים ועבדי הגוים מחממין אותה בשבת, אם לא (ד"ו דף יג, ד) נתקררה כל כך שלא היתה ראויה לאכילה דוגמת טעם מאכל בן דרוסאי קודם שחממו אותה הגוים, אם כן אין חששא בחימום ושריא לאכול (סה"ת שם):

שולחן ערוך הרב אורח חיים סימן שיח סעיף ט

כל דבר לח יש בו בישול אחר בישול דהיינו תבשיל לח שנתבשל כבר כל צרכו ונצטנן ואפילו לא נצטנן לגמרי אלא שאין היד סולדת בו וחממו בשבת עד שהיד סולדת בו חייב משום מבשל אבל אם הוא חם כל כך עד שהיד סולדת בו ומרתיחו יותר אין בזה משום בישול ומותר אפילו לכתחלה להרתיחו סמוך לאש במקום שאין לחוש לחיתוי כמו שיתבאר (ואם מותר ליתנו על גבי כירה או תנור נתבאר בסימן רנ"ג) ויש אומרים שאפילו נצטנן לגמרי אין בישול אחר בישול ומותר להרתיחו בשבת סמוך לאש במקום שאין לחוש לחיתוי.

ונהגו להקל אם לא נצטנן לגמרי אלא ראוי עדיין לאכול מחמת חמימותו אבל אם נצטנן לגמרי נוהגין כסברא הראשונה אפילו לענין דיעבד כמו שנתבאר בסימן רנ"ג ואפילו ליתנו על תנור בית החורף קודם שמסיקו הנכרי כדי שיתחמם כשיסיקנו אסור כמו שנתבאר שם וכן בכל דבר שיתבאר שיש בו משום בישול:

ספר אור זרוע ח"ב - הלכות ערב שבת סימן ח

ראיתי בצרפת בית מורי ר' יהודא בר' יצחק שפעמים מקררים צלנ"ט שלהם דהיינו טמון ובשבת טרם עת האוכל מדליקין העבדים אש סמוך לקדרות כדי שיתחממו בטוב ויש שמסלקין אותם ונותנים אותם סמוך לאש ומפרשים להיתר מפני שאין לחוש לאוסרן דמסתמא חמין הן קצת קרוב להיד סולדת

וכשמוסיפים להם חום מותר שהרי גם בישול אין להם ואפי׳ יתקררו הרבה אין לאוסרן שגם כונתן בעבורם הן ואפי׳ מתכוני׳ בעבור ישראל אין לחוש דמסתמא אין ישראל רוצה בכך שאילו ידעו שהקדירות נתקררו לגמרי לא היו מניחים לחמם אותם כלל וכשהעבדים עושים לאו כל כמינייהו לאסור לנו התבשילים בעל כרחנו ובחופות רגילים לעשות כן עבדיהם ואין איש נמנע מלאוכלן וגם ר״ת זצ״ל ושאר גדולי הדור כולם מתירין. מיהו נכון וראוי שלא לנהוג כן משום דאוושא מילתא ואיכא זילותא דשבתא וכל מדינה דלא שכיחי בה רבנן ראוי לאסור עליהם דבר זה:

אגלי טל סימן יד

ויראה לי דמים שנתבשלו ונצטננו כו׳. כי הכרעת הרמ״א להקל בלא נצטנן לגמרי כתב המנחת כהן משום דס״ל דהעיקר כדעת הפוסקים דלא מחלקין בין יבש ללח. ול״נ באיסור דאורייתא מחמירין כאינך פוסקים. וכשלא נצטנן לגמרי וראוי עדיין לקצת בני אדם לאכל מחמת חמימותו כבר יצאנו מחשש איסור דאורייתא דלא גרע מאם נתבשל כמאכל ב״ד בדבר יבש אף דלא נתבשל כל צורכו דשוב אין בו משום בישול מדאורייתא. ובדרבנן סמכינן על הפוסקים דלא מחלקין בין לח ליבש ובכולן אין בישול אחר בישול. וממילא במים שכתבנו דכל הפוסקים מודים דבנצטנן יש בהם משום בישול מה״ת א״כ אף אם לא נצטנן לגמרי רק שאין רוב בני אדם שותין כך. שוב הו״ל כמו שנתבשל כמאכל בן דרוסאי בדבר יבש דשוב אין בהם משום בישול מן התורה אבל יש בהן משום בישול מדרבנן מיהת.

אגלי טל סימן י ס״ק טו

ונאמר דמ״ש הרמב״ם המבשל על האור דבר שהיה מבושל כל צורכו פטור לאו להשמיענו דאם לא היה מבושל כל צורכו חייב אלא משום דכתב המבשל על האור וכו׳ פטור. ובא להשמיענו דדוקא על האור הוא דפטור אבל אסור אבל בתולדת האור או כנגד המדורה מותר לכתחלה. היה מוכרח לכתוב דבר שהיה מבושל כל צורכו דאם היה כתב דינו במבושל סתם והיה במשמע דאפילו בנתבשל רק כמאכל ב״ד דוקא על האור פטור אבל אסור. אבל בתולדת האור או כנגד המדורה מותר אפי׳ לכתחלה. ובאמת זה אינו כנ״ל בשם הפוסקים דעכ״פ מדרבנן יש בו משום בישול. וע״כ היה

מוכרח הרמב"ם לכתוב דינו בנתבשל כל צורכו לומר דדוקא בנתבשל כל צורכו דשוב אין בו משום בישול כלל אף מדרבנן הוא דע"ג האור פטור אבל אסור. הא בתולדת האור או כנגד המדורה מותר לכתחלה. אבל בלא נתבשל כל צורכו אפי' בתולדות האור או כנגד המדורה אסור דיש בו משום בישול מדרבנן מיהת.

משנה ברורה סימן שיח ס"ק צט

אם לא וכו' - אף דלדעת המחבר כיון שנצטנן מעט מחמימותו ואין היס"ב שוב יש בו משום בישול וכמו שכתבנו לעיל בס"ד המנהג להקל בזה דסומכין בזה איש מקילין כ"ז שלא נצטנן לגמרי:

שו"ת אגרות משה אורח חיים חלק ד סימן עד

(ב) מהו טעם הרמ"א /או"ח/ (שי"ח סט"ו) בדבר שיש בו מרק שכ' ונהגו להקל אם לא נצטנן לגמרי, ומהו שיעור זה.

תשובה: טעם הרמ"א משום שסובר לדינא כהרמב"ם והרשב"א דאין בשול אחר בשול גם בלח אבל מחמירין כשנצטנן לגמרי. ושיעור החמימות שצריך להיות בלח להרמ"א הוא שראוי לאכול לאלו שרוצין לאכול חמין כדכתב בש"ע הגר"ז ס"ט.

ומה שהביא כתר"ה מאג"ט ס"ק י"ד דכשראוי עדיין לקצת בנ"א =בני אדם= לאכול מחמת חמימותו כבר יצאנו מחשש איסור דאורייתא ובדרבנן סמכינן על הפוסקים דלא מחלקין בין לח ויבש, לא מובן כלל דבלא נתבשל מתחלה אלא פחות מיד סולדת אף שהוא בחום גדול הראוי לאכילת חמין חייב כשישלים לבשל עד שיהיה יד סולדת. וממילא להסוברים דיש בשול אחר בשול בלח כשנצטנן חייב אף אם נצטנן קצת שנעשה פחות מיד סולדת אף שהוא עדיין חם טובא כראוי ועוד יותר מאכילת בנ"א חמין חייב, וא"כ איך כתב דבראוי לאכול מחמת חמימותו לקצת בנ"א הוא רק בשול מדרבנן וצ"ע בכוונתו.

חזון איש אורח חיים לז:יג

וכתב הרמ"א דאנן נוהגין להקל כדעת הרשב"א והר"ן דאפילו בדבר לח אין בישול אחר בישול אף שנצטנן אלא שאין אנו מקילין אלא בלא נצטנן

לגמרי, והנה מעיקר הדין אין שום מקום לחלק בין נצטנן לגמרי ולא נצטנן לגמרי דכל שאין היס"ב חשיב מן הדין כצונן וע"כ שאנו תופשין לעיקר הדין כדעת הרמב"ם הרשב"א והר"ן שאין איסור לחמם את הצונן המבושל, אלא מפני שלא יבואו להקל בחיים לא נהגו להקל בצונן שאין חמימותו ניכרת.

שו"ת אגרות משה אורח חיים חלק ד סימן עד

(יט) האם מותר לערות מים מכ"ר לכלי שנותרו בו טיפי מים שנתבשלו ונצטננו.

תשובה: הנה יש חלוק בין טפות מים שלא מיתוסף בזה שום הנאה אף לא בכמות שאף במים קרים שהוא בשול דאורייתא אין בזה איסור להערוך והרבה פוסקים דפסיק רישא דלא ניחא לו שרי אף לכתחלה, ובטפות מים שהוא פחות מכשיעור אפשר אין להחמיר, אבל מ"מ כתבתי באג"מ ח"א ס"ס צ"ג שיש לאסור. שלכן בהיו מים רותחין שנצטננו שמעצם הדין אין בשול אחר בשול דכן סוברין רוב הפוסקים ודאי לא שייך להחמיר בהטפות. ואם יש מים הרבה מבושלים שנצטננו יש לאסור לערות עלייהו הרבה מים רותחין באופן שגם המים הצוננין יעשו רותחין כיון דהוא פסיק רישא דניחא לו.

שו"ת אגרות משה אורח חיים חלק ד סימן עד

(ה) האם מותר ליתן קעטשאפ בשבת על בשר רותח הנמצא בכלי שני, דיש כאן ב' חומרות א' לחוש לדעת מהרש"ל (בש"ך יו"ד סי' צ"ד ס"ק ל' ומ"א סי' שי"ח ס"ק מ"ה) שדבר גוש חם חשב כ"ר =כלי ראשון=. ב' לחוש שיש בישול אחר בישול בדבר לח (עי' רמ"א /או"ח/ סי' שי"ח סעי' ט"ו).

ועוד אולי הקעטשאפ לא חשיב משקה כיון שהוא עב ביותר.

וכן האם מותר ליתן מלח שלא נתבשל על דבר גוש חם בכ"ש =בכלי שני=, דהא מדינא אפי' בכ"ר שרי (עי' רמ"א סעי' ט' ומ"ב ס"ק ע"א).

תשובה: נראה לדינא כדעת כתר"ה דרשאין ליתן קעטשאפ על בשר רותח שניתן לכלי שני דאף אם נחמיר גם שתי חומרות הוא בשתי חומרות שהוא ספק ממש כל חומרא שאף שהוא ס"ס =ספק ספיקא= אולי יש להחמיר בשבת משום חומרתו. אבל הכא חומרא דיש בשול אחר

בשול בדבר לח הוא חומרא בעלמא שגדולי הפוסקים סברי דגם בלח אין בשול אחר בשול וכן הוא הכרעת הרמ"א ונוהגין כן דרק שבנצטנן לגמרי מחמיר. וגם החומרא בדבר גוש שאף בכלי שני הוא עדיין כרותח, הא פליגי הרבה על זה ובתוכם הרמ"א (יו"ד צ"ב ס"ז) אשר הוא עיקר גדול בהוראה והט"ז שם ס"ק י"ד מחמיר רק מצד דוחקא דסכינא שלא שייך כאן בהנחת הקעטשאפ, והח"ס הובא בפ"ת סק"ז מקיל כהרמ"א בהפ"מ =בהפסד מרובה= וכן כתב שהורה כן גם מורו הגאון להקל בדבר גוש בעת הצורך וא"כ גם דין זה אף דהש"ך בסימן ק"ה סק"ח פוסק כמהרש"ל וכן המג"א בס"ק מ"ה אין להחשיבו כספק השקול אלא שכיון שלא ברור להיתר מחמירין, לכן צדק כתר"ה דאין להחמיר שתי החומרות אלו אף באיסורי שבת.

ומה שנסתפקת בקעטשאפ שמא הוא אוכל מחמת שהוא עב אף שנירוק ע"י שפיכה מסתבר שלא תלוי זה בדין אוכל או משקה לגבי טומאה, אלא באם הוא דבר הזב או דבר שהוא חתיכה העומדת ומדובקת יחד אף בלא כלי המעמידן ומדבקן שלכן יש להחשיבו כלח.

חידושי הריטב"א מסכת שבת דף לט עמוד ב

ומ"מ אומר ר"י ז"ל שלא אסרו אלא דומיא דחמי טבריה שהועילו מעשיו בשבת אבל אם לא הועילו בשבת מותר, ומעשה היה בחופת חתנים שהטמינו בדבר המוסיף ואסר ריב"א ז"ל המרק והתיר הבשר מפני שהבשר בלאו הכי נמי ראוי לאוכלו.

טור אורח חיים סימן שיח

אפילו תבשיל שנתבשל כבר יש בו משום בישול אם נצטנן כבר אבל בעודו רותח לא ואם לא נתבשל כל צרכו ואפילו נתבשל כמאכל בן דרוסאי שייך בו בישול אפי' בעודו רותח וה"מ שיש בישול אחר בישול בתבשיל שיש בו מרק אבל דבר יבש שנתבשל כבר מותר לשרותו בחמין בשבת דתנן כל שבא בחמין מלפני השבת פי' שנתבשל כבר שורין אותו בחמין ומוקי לה בתרנגולת דר' אבא שנתבשלה כל צורכה והיתה יבשה וכל שלא בא בחמין לפני השבת אין שרין אותו בחמין בשבת דחשיב כמבשל אבל מדיחין

אותו כחמין חוץ ממליח הישן וקולייס האספנין פירוש דג קטן מליח שאין צריכין אלא בישול מעט הדחתן הוא גמר בישולן

שבות יצחק עמ' שמא

והנה כתב הטור וז"ל אפילו תבשיל שנתבשל כבר יש בו משום בישול אם נצטנן וכו' בתבשיל שיש בו מרק ומבואר דגם במרק יש בישול אחר בישול אע"פ שבישולו הראשון אינו מתבטל כשהוא מצטנן ומשמע שם שאסור מדאורייתא ויש לדחות דהבישול אחר בישול במרק הוא מפני המים המעורבים בו שנתבטל חומם וכן שמעתי מהגרי"ש אלישיב שליט"א.

6

ארחות שבת עמ' יד

והנה לכאורה עיקר החילוק ביז דבר לח שיש בו בישול אחר בישולן לבין דבר יבש שאין בו בישול אחר בישול הוא משום שבדבר לח יש חשיבות מרובה לחומו ופעמים שאין רגילים לאוכלו כלל כשהוא צונן ולכן החשיבו הפוסקים המחמירים את החימום כבישול משא"כ בדבר יבש שבדרך כלל הוא ראוי לאכילה אף בהיותו צונן ומעתה אפשר שלענין הנידון הנ"ל של דרגת הסמיכות להקרא דבר יבש יהא בזה חילוק בין מאכלים שונים דיש מאכל שבסמיכות מועטת נחשב ראוי לאכילה אף בהיותו צונן ויש מאכל שצריך לזה סמיכות מרובה ומ"מ פשוט דמאכל נוזלי לגמרי יש בו בישול אחר בישול אף אם הוא ראוי לאכילה בהיותו צונן ומאכל מוצק לגמרי אין בו בישול אחר בישול אף אם אינו ראוי לאכילה מחמת שהוא צונן.

ארחות שבת עמ' טו

והנה לכאורה טעמו של המג"א שהיקל בשומן קרוש צ̇ריך ביאור דסו"ס השומן עתיד להיות נימוח ובדבר נוזלי יש חשיבות מלאכה לחימומו וצ"ל דכיון שגם השומן הקרוש הוא אוכל ובהיותו קרוש יש לו תואר ושם של דבר מבושל שאין בו בישול כלל לכן אזלינן בתר שעת נתינתו על האש דנותן דבר יבש שאין בו בישול ולכן אף שלבסוף הוא נימוח מ"מ מעשה

האדם מתיחס לשומן הקרוש וכעי"ז כ' הגרשז"א זצ"ל במנחת שלמה ח"ב עמ' ל"ה ומעתה נראה שמרק עוף שבהיותו במקרר נעשה קפוי כמין ג'לי או קפוא כקרח כשהיה בהקפאה אין היתר ליתנו על האש ולחממו דדיינינן ליה כבישול בדבר לח ולא אמרינן דדינו כשומן קרוש דאזלינן בו בתר השתא ודיינינן ליה כבישול בדבר יבש כיון שבמצב הזה אין המרק נאכל כלל אלא רק בהיותו לח ומעשה האדם נידון בזה על שם סופו וחשיב כמחמם דבר לח ויש בו בישול אחר בישול וכן כתב לן מו"ר הגר"ש אויערבאך שליט"א וז"ל מסתמא פשוט דכל מעשה הבישול מתייחס רק לבישול המרק הלח ולא משנה כלל מה דבעת נתינתו ע"ג האש היה קפוי בגלל הסיבה שהונח במקום קר כדי שלא יתקלקל המרק הלח עכ"ד.

מגן אברהם סימן רנג ס"ק מא

מיהו כשהכלים מלוכלכים בשומן נ"ל דאסור לשפוך רותחים עליהם כמ"ש סי' ש"כ סי"ד ע"ש, ובשם מהר"ף מ"כ שמותר כיון שאינו מכוין אלא לצחצחן ול"נ שיניח הכלי תוך המים ולא יערה עליהם:

רבי עקיבא איגר שם

היינו מדין נולד וקשה לי אמאי אינו אסור מדין מבשל אף דשומן קרוש הוי כמו יבש אף דנימוח אח"כ עיין מג"א סי' שי"ח סק"מ היינו התם כשמניחו אצל האש הוא קרוש ואח"כ כשנימוח אינו עושה דבר אבל הכא כיון שבא מועט רותחים על השומן נמסה ונימוח וכששופך אח"כ עוד הרותחים הוא מבשל הלח א"כ אף באינו מכוין אלא לצחצחן ליתסר דהוי מבשל ופ"ר ואולי י"ל דע"י תחלת השפיכה שבא על השומן נעשה השומן רותח דכלי שני וסמכי' על הדין דבלא נצטנן לגמרי אין בשול אחר בשול כמ"ש המג"א כאן סקל"ב אף דנלע"ד דזהו רק כשלא נצטנן לגמרי מבשולו דלא פקע שם בשול ממנה אבל בנצטנן לגמרי דאזדא שם הבשול ממנו אם אח"כ הורתחו מעט הוי דבר חדש ואסור לגמור בשולם דמ"מ כיון דבתחלה כשהיה השומן קרוש אף דנצטנן לא אזדא שם מבושל ממנו וכשניחמו ונעשה לח הוי רותח קצת נשאר שם בשול עליו והוי אח"כ בכלל אין בשול אחר בשול ודו"ק ועדיין צ"ע לדינא.

שערי תשובה סימן שיח סעיף ט

בטל - עבה"ט וע' פמ"א סי' פ"ד אותם שמביאין בשבת מים רותחין בכ"ר מבושלים אם טעה ומערה מכ"ר לתוך הקערות קטנות שיש בהם ציקור אין כאן משום בישול כיון שהצוק"ר כבר נתבשל בבית האומן ואין בישול אחר בישול בדבר יבש אף שהציקור נימוח יש לו דין יבש ומותר ליתן הצוק"ר אף בכ"ר וכמש"כ המג"א לענין המלח ע"ש ובמח"ב כתב בשם זרע אמת שמגמגם קצת ומסיק שטוב לערות הקאווי בכוסות ואחר כך לתת בו הצוק"ר ע"ש, ופשוט דהיינו דוקא ברותח דכ"ר ושהיס"ב:

ערוך השולחן אורח חיים סימן שיח סעיף כח

וכיון שנתבאר דכל דבר שהדחתן זו היא גמר מלאכתן הוי בישול וחייב בשבת לפ"ז העשב שקורין טה שמערין עליהם חמין ודבר ידוע שבישולן קל ואפילו בכלי שני מתבשלים כמו שעינינו רואות המערה עליהן חמין בשבת אפילו ע"י כלי שני חייב חטאת ורבים נכשלים בזה בטענות של הבל יש שאומרים שהטי"י כבר נתבשל במקומו ואין בישול אחר בישול וטעות גדול הוא אפילו אם האמת כן הוא דבשם אין הבישול לבשלו אלא לעשותו פירא שיהא ראוי לבישול ואיך נאמר על זה שהוא כבר מבושל והרי מוכרין אותו עתה בכסף מלא כדי לבשלו וגם שמעתי ששקר הדבר שאין מבשלין אותו במקומו ויש שעושין ע"י כלי שני והיינו שמערין מים חמין מהכלי ראשון לצנצנת ונותנים עליו הטי"י ואח"כ נותנים המים והטי"י להטשאני"ק ואח"כ שופכין עליהם החמין מכלי ראשון וממ"נ חייבים חטאת ובפרט שעינינו רואות שמתבשלים בכלי שני ובכלי שלישי שבישולן קל ויש שנוהגים לערות עליהם רותחים מכלי ראשון מבעוד יום ועומד מעט ואח"כ שופכים המים והטי"י נשאר יבש ולמחרת בבוקר שופכים עליו חמין מכלי ראשון שהרי כבר נתבשל מאתמול ואין בישול אחר בישול בדבר יבש אך בזה האופן צריך להשהות החמין על הטי"י מבעוד יום מעט זמן כדי שיתבשל ולא לערות החמין על הטי"י ותיכף לשפוך החמין לחוץ דברגע אחת לא יתבשלו והדרך הישר הוא להכין הסענ"ס מבעוד יום וכן אנו נוהגים וכן הדין בקאוו"א ובשארי מיני בישולים כאלו כמו סאקאלאד"א וקאק"א:

שביתת השבת פתיחה לבישול י"ח

וכתב הב"י ומשמע לי כל שהיד סולדת בו מקרי רותח, וכתב על זה הער"ש כלומר דאם עשה אח"כ שיהיה הקדירה מרתיח פטור כיון שכבר ג"כ היתה היס"ב בו עכ"ל ודבר זה צריך טעם דהא אנו רואים כשמבשלים מים מקפידים שלא לשתות עד שתהיה מעלה רתיחה וכדאמרינן בב"מ כסא דחרשין ולא כסא דפושרין וה"מ דלא צויץ, וא"כ אם היה יס"ב והעמידו נגד האש עד שהרתיח מ"ט לא יתחייב ובפרט לד' הרמב"ם וש"ע דגם שנתבשל כמאב"ד חייב בבישולו עד שיתבשל כ"צ והיה אפשר לדחוק ולומר דכונת הב"י בנתבשל כבר והעלה רתיחה ונצטנן מעט ומ"מ היס"ב אז אף שהרתיחו פטור דהב"י איירי בדין בישול אחר בישול וכ"מ מל' המ"א אך מד' חדושי הר"ן משמע דגם בלא נתבשל הדין כן וצריך טעם, ואפשר דמ"ש גבי כסא דפושרין ואי צויץ ל"ל בה קאי דוקא שהעלה רתיחה רק כל שהוחם עד שהיס"ב שפיר דמי, וכן בפיר"ת בב"מ שם פירש כסא דפושרין שלא הוחמו כל צרכן (וכ"ה בערוך צייץ כתב זה עם הא דאמרינן (נדה מ"ב) גבי תינוק שנולד דצרייץ בין השמשות ועל צהלי קולך מתרגמינן צייצי בקליך נראה מכל זה שמפרש הא דאמרינן גבי פושרין אבל צייץ ל"ל בה היינו שהשמיע קול ברתיחתו וצ"ע) ועל כן כל שהוחם עד שהיס"ב הגם שהוסיף לחמם עד שהרתיח אין בו משום בישול (ובלבד שלא יהיה על האש וכדלקמן) וכן בסי' רנ"ח כתב הב"י כלי שיש בו דבר חם שיכול להניחו על הקדרה היינו כשהיד סולדת בו דאז אפי' אם ירתיח מחום התחתון וקומי מוקים הוי עכ"ל.

בית יוסף אורח חיים סימן שיח סעיף ד

והא דאמרינן דתבשיל שנתבשל כל צרכו ונצטנן יש בו משום בישול אם יש בו רוטב כתבו סמ"ק (סי' רפב עמ' רפח) וזה לשונו ומיהו בדבר לח וצלול לדברי הכל יש בישול לאחר בישול לאחר שנצטנן אם חוזר ומרתיחו כדאמרינן בפרק במה מדליקין שמא ירתיח וכדפירש שם בקונדריס. עד כאן. ומשמע דאפילו בנתבשל כל צרכו אסר דסתם קדרות כשמטמינין אותם בדבר שאינו מוסיף הבל כבר נתבשלו כל צרכן. וכן כתב רבינו ירוחם בחלק ג' (דנתיב יב סט ע"ג) וזה לשונו כי כל דבר שנצטנן אפילו מבושל כל צרכו ויש בו רוטב ומצטמק ויפה לו יש בו משום בישול ולפיכך אין מניחין אותו כל כך סמוך למדורה במקום שהיד סולדת בו אלא ברחוק שלא תהא היד סולדת בו. עד

כאן לשונו. וכן כתב עוד (שם סוף ע"א) בשם ה"ר יונה וזה לשונו וכל זה שאמרנו שמחזירין דוקא שהגיע למאכל בן דרוסאי ואפילו הגיע אם שהה בעודה בידו עד שנצטנן התבשיל אסור להחזירה אם יש בה רוטב דכל דבר שיש בו רוטב ומצטמק ויפה לו והוא צונן כשהחזירו על גבי כירה ומצטמק הוי מבשל גמור. עד כאן. ולמדנו מדבריו דאם מצטמק ורע לו אף על פי שיש בו מרק אין בו משום בישול ושרי ליתנו אצל המדורה אפילו במקום שהיד סולדת בו. וכתב עוד רבינו ירוחם (שם) ומכל מקום מוכח מהגמרא שאם לא נצטנן אפילו שינה מרתיחתו קצת מותר להחזירה. עד כאן לשונו:

השאר מובא בפרק ג אות א

7

מגן אברהם סימן שיח ס"ק יב

נצטנן - כב"י ומשמע ליה דכל שהיס"ב מיקרי רותח וכ"מ ס"ו וז"ל רי"ו אם לא נצטנן אפי' שינה קצת מרתיחתו מותר ועסט"ו בהג"ה:

מחצית השקל שיח ס"ק יב

ר"ל אפילו אינו עומד אצל האש ונח קצת מרתיחתו, מכל מקום כל זמן שהיד סולדת בו מיקרי חם ואין בו משום בישול.

שו"ת אגרות משה אורח חיים חלק ד סימן עד

(א) האם מותר לחמם דבר לח שנתבשל כדי יד סולדת, ונצטנן קצת, ואף להרתיחו.

תשובה: לאחר שהוא יד סולדת אמת שהוא כבר נחשב בשול, ואולי אין זה אף בחשיבות מצטמק ויפה לו, דאם היה זה כמצטמק ויפה לו אפשר לאסור מדרבנן עיין בעה"ש סי' שי"ח סעיף י"ט, ולדידיה יהיה אסור להעמיד במקום שאפשר לבא ליד העלאת רתיחות אלא במקום שיבא רק לידי יד סולדת אבל יותר מסתבר שכיון שאיכא דעדיפי להו שלא יהיה יותר מיד סולדת לא נחשב מצטמק ויפה לו. עכ"פ מש"ע הגר"ז סי' שי"ח ס"ט שמתיר אפילו להרתיח מים שהיד סולדת בהן, ואף שאיירי בנצטנן

הרי איירי אליבא דסוברין יש בשול אחר בשול בלח אף לחייב כשלא היה יד סולדת ובשלו עד שנעשה יד סולדת דלא כקולת הרמ"א, א"כ או דסובר דלא כעה"ש שבמצטמק ויפה לו אסור מדרבנן, או שסובר דלא נחשב מצטמק ויפה לו כהטעם שכתבתי, עכ"פ יש לסמוך ע"ז ויש להתיר דבר לח שנתבשל ליד סולדת כשנצטנן קצת שעדיין חם הוא וראוי לאכול מחמת חמימותו להעמיד אף במקום שירתיח, כדעת כתר"ה.

בית יוסף אורח חיים סימן רנח

וכתב רבינו בסימן שי"ח (פג.) דהא דאסור להניח כלי שיש בו תבשיל קר ע"ג קדרה טמונה דוקא כשהקדרה חמה בענין שהעליון יכול להתבשל אבל אם אינו יכול להתבשל מותר אם אין בו דבר קרוש ובקצת נוסחאות כתוב כן גם בסימן זה ונראה שטעמו משום דמשמע ליה דלא מיקרי אולודי מוליד אלא א"כ מרתיח ועוד דאם אין העליון יכול להתבשל כלומר להתחמם עד שתהא יד סולדת בו ודאי שרי כדשרי להניח כנגד המדורה קיתון של צונן במקום שאין יד סולדת בו כמו שיבא בסימן שי"ח (פה.) וכן כתבו התוספות (ד"ה מאי שנא ממיחם) והר"ן (כב. ד"ה ומקשו) שם אעובדא דרבה ורבי זירא שדין הנחה ע"ג מיחם שוה לדין הנחה כנגד המדורה וכן כתב הרב המגיד בסוף פ"ד (ה"ו) וז"ל ופירשו ז"ל שהקומקום היה חם כל כך שהיה בו כדי לחמם הכוזא שהיה בו צונן ולא שיעור להפשיר בלבד שאל"כ מותר היה אפילו נגד המדורה וכן מורה לשון רבינו עכ"ל ולפי זה כלי שיש בו דבר חם שיכול להניחו על הקדרה היינו דוקא כשהיד סולדת בו דאז אפילו ירתיח מחמת חום התחתון אוקומי מוקים הוי ובלאו הכי צ"ל כן לפי מה שכתב רבינו בסימן הנזכר (פב.) דיש בישול אחר בישול בתבשיל שיש בו מרק אפילו נתבשל כל צרכו אם אינו רותח ואין לומר דשאני הכא שאינו באור עצמו דהא מבשל בתולדת האור חייב כמבשל באור עצמה כדאיתא בפרק כירה (לט.).

משנה ברורה סימן שיח ס"ק קיח

וכתב הרב המגיד דלד"ה כל שאין בבישולו חיוב כגון במבושלת כל צרכו אין בהגסתו חיוב וב"י כתב בשם הכלבו דכשהיא על האש חייב בהגסה

אפילו במבושל כל צרכו. כלי בישול שלנו שקורין סאמאווא"ר שהוקם מע"ש אסור ליטול ממנו מים בשבת כשאינו גרוף מן הגחלים [כ"כ בספר תוספת ירושלים לעיל בסימן רנ"ג ע"ש שהביא זה בשם ירושלמי דקאמר שם דמוליאר שאינו גרוף אין שותין ממנו בשבת הטעם מפני שהוא עשוי פרקים הוא מתיירא שמא יתאכל פירוקו והוא מוסיף מים] ולפ"ז יש ליזהר כשישב לשתות מן הכלי בישול שלנו קודם שקיעה ובאמצע קידש עליו היום שלא לשתות ממנו עוד:

מגיד משנה הלכות שבת פרק ג הלכה יא

אסור להכניס מגרפה לקדרה והיא על האש. יתבאר פ"ט שהמגיס חייב כמבשל ובריתא היא ביום טוב (דף ל"ד) פ' המביא כדי יין ושם אכתוב דעת קצת מפרשים ז"ל שלא אמרו אלא בהגסה ראשונה וכאן נראה שרבינו כתב זה ממה שאמרו סוף פ"ק (שבת י"ח ב') ודילמא מגיס. ונ"ל שאין דברי רבינו אמורין במבושל כל צרכו דהתם ודאי אפילו מחזירן ע"ג האש ומבשלן פטור כמו שיתבאר פ"ט כיון שכן אין לגזור בהכנסת מגרפה אבל באינו מבושל ודאי יש לחוש לדעתו ז"ל שכתב פ"ט. ובהשגות א"א הפריז על מדותיו שאסור להוציא אפילו מן הקדרה במגרפה עכ"ל. ומה שנ"ל כתבתי והוא שכל שאין בהגסה ממש חיוב הכנסת המגרפה מותר וכל שיש בהגסה חיוב אסור להכניסה ובפ"ט אכתוב עוד בזה:

שער הציון סימן שיח ס"ק קמח

ולא אדע הטעם, דמאי עדיפא הגסה מבישול ממש, וכל הפוסקים מודים דבמבשל כל צרכו אין בו משום בישול, וכן איתא בתוספתא בהדיא, ועל כל פנים בדיעבד בודאי אין לאסור בזה, וכדעת שאר פוסקים:

מגן אברהם סימן רנג ס"ק כ

ועודה בידו - דהרב"י ס"ל דוק' כשהניח' עג"ק אסור אבל הניחם ע"ג מטה או ספסל או שפינן ממיח' למיחם שרי אבל רמ"א ס"ל דכל אלו אסור דה"ל כמושיב בשבת לכתחל' ועסי' רנ"ז ס"ה:.

שער הציון סימן רנג ס"ק מז

מגן אברהם לדעת הרמ"א. ולא הזכרתי פינה ממיחם למיחם שזכר המגן אברהם, משום דבלאו הכי יש דעות שמקילין במיחם שני, עיין בתוספות ור"נ, על כן לפי עניות דעתי פשוט דיש לסמוך על המקילין בבעיא זו:

שמירת שבת כהלכתה פרק א' סעיף טז

שתי קדירות העומדות על גבי האש והתבשילין שבהן הם מבושלים כל צורכם מותר להעביר מה שבהן מאחת לחברתה ולפיכך אם רואים שהתבשיל שבתוך הקדירה העומדת על גבי אש מכוסה (עיין להלן סעיף יח) הולך ומתייבש מותר ליצוק בו בנחת מן המים הרותחים שבדוד השבת העומד על גבי האש אף הוא.

שמירת שבת כהלכתה שם הע' מב

ולא אסרינן משום הגסה במה ששופך לתוכו מים וכן במה שמכסה אח"כ את הקדירה דלא אסרינן במבושל כ"צ רק הגסה ממש או להוציא בכף מן האוכל שבקדירה סימן שיח במ"ב ס"ק קיז ובלבד שיקפיד לשפוך בנחת דאל"כ יש לחשוש למ"ש הב"י סוסי' רנג מהכלבו דאסור שמעתי מהגרש"ז אויערבך שליט"א.

שמירת שבת כהלכתה שם הע' מד

ולענין לשפוך מים מן הדוד לתוך כוס וליתנם לקדירה העומדת על גבי האש שמעתי מהגרש"ז אויערבך שליט"א דאפשר שראוי להחמיר דכיון דבפינה ממיחם למיחם פסק המ"א סי' רנג ס"ק כ לאיסור ורק המ"ב בשעה"צ ס"ק מז מכריע להיתר נראה דאין להוסיף על דבריו ולא שרי אלא ליחן מהמיחם שעמד ע"ג האש לתוך קדירה שמעמידה ע"ג האש אבל אם עירה באמצעות כלי לתוך הקדירה אפשר דחשיב כהניח ע"ג קרקע ואסור עכ"ל אך שוב אמר לי הגרש"ז שליט"א דאעפ"כ נראה דמכיון שמותר להעמיד על האש את הכוס עם המים שבה לא מסתבר כלל לאסור להעמיד את המים בלבד ע"י עירוי לתוך הקדירה שעל האש עכ"ד ולהעביר ע"י מצקת או כף שמכניס בתוך הדוד דעת הגרש"ז אויערבך שליט"א דפשיטא דאין להחמיר דכיון שמכניס הכף בתוך הכלי העומד ע"ג האש י"ל דבכה"ג לא

דמי לפינה ממיחם למיחם שהמיחם השני לא היה בכלל על האש ומכיון דהוה ספק אם זה בכלל הבעיא של פינה ממיחם למיחם יש לסמוך על השעה"צ שכתב דמה שאנו מסופקים אם זה נכלל בהבעיא של מינה ממיחם למיחם פשוט דיש לסמוך על המקילין בבעיא זו ובפרט לשיטת הרא"ש דדין המצקת אחרי שהכניסה לכ"ר דינה כמו הכלי שנמצאת בתוכו.

8

מרדכי כבר נמצא בפרק ב

תלמוד בבלי מסכת פסחים דף מא עמוד א

אין מבשלין וכו'. תנו רבנן: (שמות יב) במים - אין לי אלא במים, שאר משקין מניין? אמרת: קל וחומר, ומה מים שאין מפיגין טעמן - אסורין, שאר משקין שמפיגין טעמן - לא כל שכן? רבי אומר: במים - אין לי אלא מים, שאר משקין מניין - תלמוד לומר (שמות יב) ובשל מבושל - מכל מקום. מאי בינייהו? - איכא בינייהו: צלי קדר. - ורבנן האי בשל מבושל מאי עבדי להו? - מבעי ליה לכדתניא: בשלו ואחר כך צלאו, או שצלאו ואחר כך בשלו - חייב. בשלמא בשלו ואחר כך צלאו חייב - דהא בשליה, אלא צלאו ואחר כך בשלו הא צלי אש הוא, אמאי? - אמר רב כהנא: הא מני - רבי יוסי היא, דתניא: יוצאין ברקיק השרוי, ובמבושל שלא נימוח, דברי רבי מאיר. רבי יוסי אומר: יוצאין ברקיק השרוי, אבל לא במבושל, אף על פי שלא נימוח. עולא אמר: אפילו תימא רבי מאיר, שאני הכא דאמר קרא ובשל מבושל - מכל מקום.

תלמוד בבלי מסכת ברכות דף לח עמוד ב

דרש רב נחמן משום רבינו, ומנו - שמואל: שלקות מברכין עליהם בורא פרי האדמה; וחברינו היורדים מארץ ישראל, ומנו - עולא, משמיה דרבי יוחנן אמר: שלקות מברכין עליהן שהכל נהיה בדברו; ואני אומר: במחלוקת שנויה. דתניא: יוצאין ברקיק השרוי ובמבושל שלא נמוח, דברי רבי מאיר, ורבי יוסי אומר: יוצאים ברקיק השרוי, אבל לא במבושל, אף על פי שלא נמוח. ולא היא, דכולי עלמא - שלקות מברכין עליהן בורא פרי האדמה,

ועד כאן לא קאמר רבי יוסי התם - אלא משום דבעינן טעם מצה וליכא, אבל הכא - אפילו רבי יוסי מודה.

אגלי טל סימן טו ס"ק ב

ואמנם ליישב דעת הר"א ממיץ נראה עפ"י מ"ש התוס' בפרק כל שעה בהא דמצה מבושלת פרש"י דבישול מבטל לי' מתורת לחם ולפיכך צ"ל דמיירי בבלילתו רכה דבלילתו עבה לא נפק מתורת לחם לפר"ת. ור"י מפרש דהכי מייתי דכי היכי דבישול מפיק ליה מתורת אפיה לשוי' מצה עשירה ה"נ גבי פסח דבישול עקר מיניה שם צליה. ובתלמידי ר' יונה למס' ברכות וכן בתוס' הרא"ש כתבו דהא דבעינן טעם מצה פי' דבבישלו הוי מצה עשירה והיינו דמעיקרא ס"ד דהש"ס דבישול מפיק ליה מתורת לחם וע"כ מייתי ראיה דה"ה דבישול מפיק ליה מתורת ירק. ובתר הכי דחי דהתם משום טעם מצה היינו דבישול מפיק ליה רק מתורת אפיה להחשב מצה עשירה אבל לא מפיק ליה מתורת לחם. וה"ה דלא מפיק ליה מתורת ירק. וזה דלא כמו שכתבו התוס' פסחים שם דבור המתחיל עולא אמר דהש"ס מדמי בברכות דכי היכי דמפיק בישול מאפיה ה"ה דמפיק בישול מתורת ירק. והם ס"ל דרק מתורת אפיה מבטל אבל לא מתורת ירק שהוא בעצם. וא"כ סוגית הש"ס פסחים אליבא דמסקנא משום טעם מצה והיינו דחשוב מצה עשירה משום דמבטל האפיה וה"ה דבישול מבטל הצליה. ומה שדחקו לתר"י לפרש משום מצה עשירה ולא כפשוטו דבעינן טעם מצה דק"ל דהא קיי"ל בלע מצה יצא. ובהכי ניחא דבתר דשני הש"ס בעינן טעם מצה וליכא הדר פריק ממרור ומשני בעינן טעם מרור וליכא ולכאורה כיון דמשני דבעינן טעם מצה כ"ש דבעינן טעם מרור דהא בלע מצה יצא בלע מרור לא יצא אך לפירושם ניחא דבמצה לא יצא משום מצה עשירה ע"כ פריך ממרור ומשני דבמרור לא יצא כמו דבלע מרור לא יצא.

ט"ז אורח חיים סימן שיח ס"ק ו

אם בישלו אח"כ כו'. - זה כתב הטור בשם הר"א ממיץ דאע"ג דאין בישול אחר בישול בדבר יבש מ"מ יש בישול אחר צלי וראייתו מההיא דפרק כ"ש דף מ"א בקרבן פסח אם צלאו ואח"כ בשלו חייב הא מני ר"י הוא דאמר יוצאין ברקיק השרוי במים בפסח אבל לא במבושל דלאו לחם

קרינא ביה אף ע״פ שכבר נאפה בתנור הואיל וחזר ובישלו ביטלו מתורת לחם ה״נ יש בישול לאחר אפייה לענין שבת וראבי״ה חלק עליו דבפ׳ כ״מ מייתי לההיא דר״י לענין ברכה דשלקות מברכין עליה שהכל ולא בפ״ה כבתחלה כמו במצה לר״י ומסיק עלה דעד כאן לא אמר ר״י אלא דבעינן טעם מצה וליכא וקלסה ב״י לראבי״ה דקושייתו חזקה דהא קיימא לן דברכתו בפ״ה וא״כ ע״כ קיימא הדחי׳ דבעי׳ טעם מצה אליבא דהלכתא וכ״כ התו׳ שם בפרק כל שעה דיש לדחות מחמת טעם מצה בעי׳ ול״ד לפסח כמו דדחי בפ׳ כ״מ לענין ברכה. ואני איני כדאי להכריע בין הרים גדולים מ״מ כנלע״ד לתרץ על נכון דברי הרא״מ בדרך זה דס״ל כרי״ו ור״י לעיל בס״א במצטמק ורע לו דאין בו בישול אחר שנתבשל כ״צ. וכבר ביארנו טעמו בסמוך דבמצטמק ויפה לו יש בו משום בישול כיון דנהנה ממלאכת שבת בטעם חדש משא״כ במצטמק ורע לו א״כ נאמר כאן ג״כ סברא זו דאף למאי דבעית למידחי ולפר׳ ההיא דר״י משום בעינן טעם מצה זה מועיל לדחות ההיא דצלאו לפסח והדר בשלו דשם גזירת הכתוב הוא דצלי בעינן ולא בטעם תליא מילתא ע״כ נוכל לומר דלא נתבטל ממנו שם צלי אבל במצה בעי׳ טעם מצה דלחם עוני בעינן כן נוכל לדחות ההיא דפסח לפי דעת התוס׳ אבל כאן לענין שבת לא מהני האי דחיה דכי נמי תימא משום דטעם מצה בעינן ה״נ אזלינן בתר טעם התבשיל וכיון דנשתנה הטעם ע״י בישול אמרינן דנתכוין לזה בשבת ולא עדיף מן מצטמק ויפה לו דיש משום בישול אפי׳ אחר בישול כ״ש אחר אפיה זה כתבנו לדעת התוס׳ דס״ל דגם לענין הפסח שייכה הדחייה דבעינן טעם מצה וא״כ צ״ל דבצלי אין שייך לומר טעם צלי בעינן וע״כ צ״ל דיש לימוד אצל מצה דשם דוקא בעינן טעם מצה דהיינו מדכתיב לחם עוני אבל נ״ל דהרא״מ ס״ל דלא שייכא דחי׳ זו גבי פסח כלל דגם גבי פסח נימא טעם צלי בעי׳ ומש״ה חייב במבשל אחר הצלייה אבל לענין ברכה שפיר הוה הדחיה בפרק כ״מ דודאי טעם ירק שהיה בו קודם הבישול ישנו ג״כ אח״כ אלא שנשתנה למעליותא ולמה יגרע הברכה ממה שהיה תחלה דהיינו בפ״ה ומ״ה לא דחה בגמרא בפ׳ כ״ש לשום מ״ד דחיה זו דבעינן טעם מצה וא״כ כאן לענין בישול בשבת פשיטא דליתא לדחיה זו כמ״ש דמלאכת מחשבת אסרה תורה כדאיתא בהרבה דוכתי וק״ו דנימא דאסור מדרבנן מחמת שינוי הטעם ומ״ש כאן אסור לד״ה כנ״ל נכון:

שולחן ערוך יורה דעה סימן קה סעיף ד

במה דברים אמורים, כשנפל לתוך התבשיל, מפני שהרוטב מוליך פליטת האיסור ומערבו בכל התבשיל. אבל איסור, בין חם בין קר, שנפל על הצלי שאצל האש, אינו אוסר אלא כדי נטילה, שהוא כעובי רוחב אצבע.

שולחן ערוך אורח חיים סימן שיח סעיף טו כבר מובא בפרק ה אות א

ביאור הלכה סימן שיח סעי' ה' ד"ה יש מי

יש מי שאומר וכו' משום בישול - עיין מ"ב דה"ה דיש צלי אחר בישול ועיין בפמ"ג שהביא מפסחים מ"א דלא נתבטל שם בישול הראשון והוליד מזה דמותר לשרותו בחמין בשבת [ר"ל אם עשה צלי אחר בישול בע"ש] כשאר דבר מבושל ונראה דה"ה לדידיה בבישול אחר צלי דמותר בשבת להניחו בלי רוטב בתנור אף שיצלה דלא נתבטל שם צלי ראשון ממנו דהא רבינו אליעזר ממיץ משוה אותם להדדי אך לענ"ד אין דין הפמ"ג מוכרח דנהי דמוכח שם דלא נתבטל שם הראשון הרי שם השני בודאי קיים ושפיר יש לומר דמקרי עתה בשול אחר צלי. אך זה נלענ"ד בבשלו ואח"כ צלאו בע"ש דמותר להניחו בתנור בשבת דפעולה אחרונה נקבע בו יותר ומקרי צלי אחר צלי:

ביאור הלכה סימן שיח סע' טו ד"ה והוא יבש

והוא יבש וכו' כנגד המדורה - צ"ע הא לעיל בס"ה מביא דעת הרא"ם וע"ש במ"א דלדעתו ה"ה דיש צלי אחר בישול ואיך מתיר הכא בסתם [מס' בית מאיר על או"ח וכן הקשה בספר מאמר מרדכי ע"ש שנדחק ליישב]

אגלי טל סימן טו ס"ק טו

ומה שהביא הר"א ממיץ ראיה מה דיבמות פרק החולץ אע"ג דחלטיה מעיקרא כיון דהדר אפיה בתנור לחם קרינא ביה. לפענ"ד יש להשיב שהרי בפרק כל שעה במעשה אלפס לר"ל דאמר דפטור מחלה דלא לחם הוא ואעפ"כ בהדר אפיה בתנור חייב בחלה ור' יהודה החולק ופוטר מחלה מפרש שם הטעם משום דכתיב ואפו עשר נשים לחמכם בתנור אחד לחם שאינו אפוי בתנור אחד אינו קרוי לחם. ולולי זה היה מודה לת"ק. וקשה

הא לכ"ע אין אפיה אחר אפיה וא"כ מה מועיל אפיית תנור אחר אפיית האלפס. אלא ודאי כיון דאפיית תנור חשוב מאפיית אלפס דמשוי' ליה לחם לכ"ע הוה אפיה. כעין שכתבו התוס' בכתב ע"ג כתב דלא הוה כתב מ"מ בגט שנכתב שלא לשמה והעביר עליו קולמוס לשמה הוי כתב כיון דכתב האחרון הועיל מה שלא הועיל הכתב הראשון וה"נ בזה שהועיל לשויי לחם שמפני חשיבות הלחם קבעו לו חכמים ברכה בפני עצמו. וכ"ש דמהני טעם זה להכשר מצה דכיון דהועיל האפיה להכשר מצה אפיה הוא.

ארחות שבת פרק א' הע' סה

גם במקרה שהאבקות הנמסות עברו תהליך של בישול יש מקום לדון שתהליך הייבוש שלהן יחשב כמין אפיה או צליה ואם יבא ליתנו בכלי שני הרי זה בכלל הנידון של בישול אחר צליה אחר בישול שיתבאר להלן סעיף ל"א וסעיף פ"ו ואמנם אפשר שסתם ייבוש אינו נותן לאבקה תואר של דבר אפוי או צלוי ורק בקפה נמס וכיוצ"ב שמעוניינים שהאבקה תקבל טעם של דבר קלוי חשיב כצליה אחר בישול.

9

תלמוד בבלי מסכת שבת דף לח עמוד ב

אין נותנין ביצה בצד המיחם בשביל שתתגלגל ולא יפקיענה בסודרין, ורבי יוסי מתיר. ולא יטמיננה בחול ובאבק דרכים בשביל שתצלה. מעשה שעשו אנשי טבריא והביאו סילון של צונן לתוך אמה של חמין, אמרו להם חכמים: אם בשבת - כחמין שהוחמו בשבת, ואסורין ברחיצה ובשתיה. אם ביום טוב - כחמין שהוחמו ביום טוב, ואסורין ברחיצה ומותרין בשתיה.

תלמוד בבלי מסכת שבת דף לח עמוד ב – לט עמוד א

גמרא. איבעיא להו: גלגל מאי? - אמר רב יוסף: גלגל - חייב חטאת. אמר מר בריה דרבינא: אף אנן נמי תנינא:

כל שבא בחמין מלפני השבת - שורין אותו בחמין בשבת, וכל שלא בא בחמין מלפני השבת - מדיחין אותו בחמין בשבת, חוץ מן המליח ישן וקולייס האיספנין שהדחתן זו היא גמר מלאכתן. - שמע מינה.

ולא יפקיענה בסודרין והא דתנן נותנין תבשיל לתוך הבור בשביל שיהא שמור, ואת המים היפים ברעים בשביל שיצננו, ואת הצונן בחמה בשביל שיחמו לימא רבי יוסי היא ולא רבנן! אמר רב נחמן: בחמה - דכוליה עלמא לא פליגי דשרי, בתולדות האור - כוליה עלמא לא פליגי דאסיר, כי פליגי - בתולדות החמה; מר סבר: גזרינן תולדות החמה אטו תולדות האור, ומר סבר: לא גזרינן.

ולא יטמיננה בחול. וליפלוג נמי רבי יוסי בהא! - רבה אמר: גזרה שמא יטמין ברמץ. רב יוסף אמר: מפני שמזיז עפר ממקומו. מאי בינייהו? - איכא בינייהו: עפר תיחוח, מיתיבי, רבן שמעון בן גמליאל אומר: מגלגלין ביצה על גבי גג רותח, ואין מגלגלין ביצה על גבי סיד רותח. בשלמא למאן דאמר גזרה שמא יטמין ברמץ - ליכא למיגזר. אלא למאן דאמר מפני שמזיז עפר ממקומו - ליגזר! - סתם גג לית ביה עפר. - תא שמע: מעשה שעשו אנשי טבריא והביאו סילון של צונן לתוך אמה של חמין וכו'. בשלמא למאן דאמר גזרה שמא יטמין ברמץ - היינו דדמיא להטמנה, אלא למאן דאמר מפני שמזיז עפר ממקומו - מאי איכא למימר? - מי סברת מעשה טבריא אסיפא קאי? ארישא קאי: לא יפקיענה בסודרין, ורבי יוסי מתיר. והכי קאמרי ליה רבנן לרבי יוסי: הא מעשה דאנשי טבריא דתולדות חמה הוא, ואסרי להו רבנן! - אמר להו: ההוא - תולדות אור הוא, דחלפי אפיתחא דגיהנם.

רש"י מסכת שבת דף לט עמוד א

דשרי - דאין דרך בישולו בכך, וחמה באור לא מיחלפא דליגזר הא אטו הא.

שו"ת אגרות משה אורח חיים חלק ג סימן נב

בענין בשול בחמה ז' מנחם אב תשל"א. מע"כ ידיד בן ידיד חשוב ונכבד בר אוריין ובר אבהן, מוהר"ר אליעזר נחום אייזענבערג, שליט"א.

הנה בדבר בשול בחמה דליכא איסור בשבת שפרש"י בשבת דף ל"ט וכן הר"ן מטעם דאין דרך בשול בכך, הוא פשוט משום דנהי שהבשול שהיה במשכן היה באש מ"מ היה שייך למילף גם בשול ע"י חמה להיות תולדה, דהא מכל האבות מלאכות שהיו במשכן הרי למדין לחייב גם כל הדומה להאבות באותו החיוב ממש ונקראו תולדות, שלכן הוצרך רש"י

לפרש שאין למדין בשול ע״י חמה מבשול ע״י האש שהיה במשכן משום שאין דרך בשול בכך. ואין הכוונה דאין דרך בשול בכך כהא דעושה מלאכה כלאחר ידו ושאר שנויים שפטור כדאיתא /בשבת/ בדף צ״ב בהוצאה וה״ה בכל מלאכה שצריך לעשותה כדרך שעושין בנ״א מלאכה זו כדאשכחן בכמה דוכתי. דהא חזינן שבתולדות החמה איכא גם אלו שדרך לבשל בהם ממש כמו בתולדות האור, דהרי המבשל בחמי טבריא תליא דלר׳ יוסי דסובר דתולדות אור הם דחלפי אפתחא דגיהנם חייב ולרבנן דתולדות חמה נינהו פטור כדאר״ח /בשבת/ בדף מ׳, ואם אין דרך מלאכה בכך מ״ט יתחייב כשהוא תולדות האור, דמ״ש מבורר בקנון ובתמחוי שפטור משום שאין דרך מלאכת בורר בכך בדף ע״ד ומנטל צפרניו בידו ובשניו שפטור משום דאין דרך גזיזה בכך /בשבת/ בדף צ״ד, אלא ודאי שהוא דרך מלאכה מאחר שהם חמים טובא שיכולין לבשל, ומ״מ לרבנן שחמי טבריא הם תולדות חמה פטור, וכן בסודר שהוחם באור הוא חייב בגלגל ביצה בהסודר דתולדות האור הם כאור שחייב ובהוחם הסודר בחמה באותו החום וגלגל ביצה פטור. אלא כוונתם דאף דאין להחשיב דלאו דרך מלאכה הוא לבשל בחמה דאם אין לו עצים והוא דבר המתבשל בחמה יבשלו בחמה, אבל כיון שעכ״פ אין מבשלין בחמה אלא כשאין לו עצים אין למילף אותו מבשול על ידי האור שהיתה במשכן להחשיבו תולדה מאחר שאינו דומה להבשול שהיה במשכן.

וממילא מאחר שלא ילפינן בשול חמה מבשול האור ליכא חיוב אף לא לתולדות החמה אף שדרך הבשול על ידם הוא כמו על ידי תולדות האור, דהסודר הא נתחמם בחמה באותה מדה שנתחמם באש, וחמי טבריא הא חמים כחמי האור, דמאחר דהבשול דחמה אינה מכלל המלאכה משום דלא דמו למבשל שהיה במשכן אין למילף שוב את התולדות דממילא גם הם לא דמו לבשול שבמשכן כיון שהם תולדות דבר שאין בו מלאכת בשול.

ואולי יש לומר בטעם אחר דתולדות החמה וגם תולדות האור אין הדרך כל כך לבשל בהם, שלכן אין למילף אותם שיהיו תולדה מצד חמום של עצמם אף לא לתולדות האור, אך שמ״מ חייב גם על הבשול דע״י תולדות האור מצד שנחשב זה כבשול מצד האש עצמו שהרי החמימות שבהמים והסודר הרי הוא מהאש וממילא הוא בכלל בשול האש עצמו שהרי חמום האש הוא המבשל, שלכן אף שלא היה בשול זה ממש במשכן

כיון שאין לחשוב זה שינוי מדרך המלאכה חייב, ודמי זה להעמיד הקדרה ברחוק קצת יותר מהאש מכפי דרך בנ"א אבל הוא עכ"פ מקום הראוי להתבשל במשך יותר זמן שודאי חייב אף אם במשכן לא היו עושין כן כדי למהר הבשול. וכמו כן הוא במבשל בתולדות האור שהוא בשול בחמימות האור לא שייך לחלק כל זמן שאין זה שינוי ממש מדרך המלאכה שיש אף רק מעט אינשי דמבשלין בהם, ולכן כשהם תולדות חמה אף ששוין ממש במדת החום כמו אם היו תולדות האור כהא דחמי טבריא וכהא דסודר שבחמימותו יכול לבשל ביצה, פטור דמצד עצמן הא אין למילף תולדות מבשול האש שהיה במשכן מאחר דאין הדרך כל כך לבשל בהן וכל החיוב בתולדות האור הוא מצד שהוא נחשב בשול בחמימות האש שזה הא ליכא בתולדות החמה, שאם נחשוב כן הרי מתבשל בחמימות דחמה שאין בו חשיבות מלאכה. וטעם זה הוא יותר מסתבר.

ולמה שבארתי כוונת רש"י והר"ן מסתבר שזהו גם כוונת קרית ספר דכתב דאין בשול מן התורה אלא באש, ולא פליגי כלל, אלא שלא כתב הטעם דפירשו רש"י והר"ן, דהא מוכרח כן דבלא טעם היה לן ודאי למילף מבשול אש שהיה במשכן כמו כל התולדות.

וא"כ בהמייקר - וייו אוועז /תנור מיקרוגל/ שטוב לבשל בו כמו באש ממש ואלו שיש להם תנור כזה משתמשים בו יותר מבשול דבאש ומה שלא נתפשטו תנורים אלו עדיין הוא משום דלא מצוי עדיין הרבה תנורים וכשיהיו מצויין ודאי ישתמשו בהם כו"ע דהא הוא יותר טוב, ודאי יש למילף מבשול דאור דהיה במשכן בחשיבות תולדה שהוא לכל הדינים כהאב דבשול ע"י האור לאיסור ולחיוב סקילה וחטאת, לא רק לרש"י והר"ן אלא אף לקרית ספר דהרי לא פליגי כלל לפ"מ שבארתי.

שו"ת מנחת שלמה חלק א סימן יב הע' 7

דאף שכתב רש"י בשבת (לט ע"א) אהא דמבשל בחמה לכו"ע שרי דהוא מפני "דאין דרך בישולו בכך", מ"מ נראה שגם באופן שכן רגילים לבשל בחמה כמו דוד שמש וכדומה ג"כ פטור, וכדחזינן מחמי טבריא דאי אמרינן דחלפי אפיתחא דגיהנם הו"ל תולדות אור וחייב ואם לאו הו"ל תולדות חמה ופטור, וגם חילוק זה שבין אור וחמה נזכר גם לענין פסח מצה וחלה וכו' והתם מאי נפק"מ אם רגילין בכך או לא, וע"כ דכוונת רש"י בדברים אלה

לומר דאין זה קרוי בישול [ואף שהמנ"ח מסתפק בנתבשל בחמה ואח"כ ע"י האש, ומביא מהפמ"ג שסובר דגם בזה אין בישול אחר בישול, עיי"ש. היינו מפני שכך היתה להם קבלה דלענין זה בעינן דוקא דומיא דמשכן שהבישול היה ע"י אש ותולדותיה ולא ע"י דבר אחר], ולפי"ז גם בישול החוט ע"י זרם ג"כ חשיב כמבשל בחמה.

תלמוד בבלי מסכת פסחים דף לז עמוד א

תנו רבנן: הסופגנין, והדובשנין, ואיסקריטין, וחלת המסרת, והמדומע - פטורים מן החלה. מאי חלת המסרת? - אמר רבי יהושע בן לוי: זה חלוט של בעלי בתים. אמר ריש לקיש: הללו מעשה אילפס הן. ורבי יוחנן: אמר מעשה אילפס חייבין, והללו שעשאן בחמה. מיתיבי: הסופגנין והדובשנין והאיסקריטין, עשאן באילפס - חייבין, בחמה - פטורין.

ויקרא פרק כו פסוק כו

בשברי לכם מטה לחם ואפו עשר נשים לחמכם בתנור אחד והשיבו לחמכם במשקל ואכלתם ולא תשבעו:

שמות פרק יב פסוק ט

אל תאכלו ממנו נא ובשל מבשל במים כי אם צלי אש ראשו על כרעיו ועל קרבו:

10

רש"י מסכת שבת דף מ עמוד ב

נכנסתי - בשבת, ובחמי טבריא הוה שלא נאסרו, כדאמר לעיל התירו להם חמי טבריא.

באמבטי - כגון בריכה עשויה בקרקע, שהמים נכנסים שם ונאספין.

ובקשתי להניח שם פך שמן - להפשיר, לסוך הימנו קודם הרחיצה.

טול - מן המים.

בכלי שני - שיצטננו מעט, דכלי שני אינו מבשל, ואחר כך תן הפך לתוך אותו כלי שני, דהך אמבטי שהחמין נמשכין לה מן המעיין חשיב

לה ככלי ראשון שנרתחו בו, שאף על פי שהעבירו מעל האור - מבשל, כדתנן לקמן /שבת/ (מב, א) האילפס והקדירה שהעבירן מרותחין - לא יתן לתוכן תבלין.

תוספות מסכת שבת דף מב עמוד ב

אבל נותן הוא לתוך הקערה כו׳ - מהכא ליכא למידק דעירוי ככלי שני מדקתני לא יתן לתוכה תבלין ולא אשמעינן רבותא אפילו שלא יערה על הקערה שתבלין בתוכה דאדרבה דוק מסיפא דקתני אבל נותן הוא לתוך הקערה ולא קתני מערה על הקערה שתבלין בתוכה ורבינו שמואל מביא ראיה דעירוי ככלי שני מהא דקי״ל תתאה גבר ולר״י נראה דעירוי ככלי ראשון ומביא ראיה דבזבחים בפרק דם חטאת (דף צה: ושם) ת״ר אשר תבושל בו אין לי אלא שבישל בו עירה לתוכו רותח מניין תלמוד לומר [אשר תבושל] בו ישבר אלמא דעירוי חשיב מבשל ובירושלמי בפרק כירה בעי מהו ליתן תבלין מלמטה ולערות עליהן מלמעלה ר׳ יונה אמר אסור דעירוי ככלי ראשון חיליה דר׳ יונה מן הדא אחד שבישל בו ואחד שעירה לתוכו רותח ודחי ר׳ יוסי תמן כלי חרס בולע תבלין אינו מתבשל השיב רבי יוסי בר בון והתניא מניין שבכלי נחשת כן תלמוד לומר ואם בכלי נחשת בשלה אית לן למימר כלי נחשת בלע בתמיה פי׳ ע״י עירוי אם אינו מבשל לא בלע אלמא דמסיק דעירוי ככלי ראשון ונראה דעירוי לא הוי ככלי ראשון ולא ככלי שני אלא מבשל כדי קליפה דהא קי״ל כשמואל דאמר תתאה גבר דתניא כוותיה בכיצד צולין (פסחים עו.) ומ״מ מבשל כדי קליפה דאמר התם תניא כוותיה דשמואל חם לתוך צונן או צונן לתוך צונן מדיח ופריך חם לתוך צונן אדמיקר ליה בלע אלא אימא חם לתוך צונן קולף צונן לתוך צונן מדיח וכן משמע בשילהי מסכת ע״ז (דף עו.) דאמר מר עוקבא זבן יורה מעכו״ם אהדר ליה גדנפא ומסיק כבולעו כך פולטו מה בולעו בניצוצות אף פולטו בניצוצות ואי עירוי ככלי ראשון מאי איריא משום דבלע בניצוצות אפילו בלע בליעה גמורה פלט בניצוצות שהוא עירוי אלא ודאי לא מבשל אלא כדי קליפה ואם עירו רותחים על התרנגולת צריכה קליפה וכלי שתשמישו ע״י עירוי כגון קערות יכול להגעילן ע״י עירוי דכבולעו כך פולטו אבל כלי שנתבשל בו איסור לא

סגי להגעילו על ידי עירוי והא דאמר בפרק בתרא דע"ז (דף עד:) דרש רבא נעוה ארתחיה דהתם מסתמא ע"י עירוי שאני התם דאותה נעוה לא בלעה ע"י רותח.

שולחן ערוך אורח חיים סימן שיח סעיף י

אסור ליתן תבלין בקערה ולערות עליהן מכלי ראשון.

תוספות מסכת שבת דף לט עמוד א

כל שבא בחמין מלפני השבת - פירוש שנתבשל לגמרי כדמפרש לקמן בפרק חבית (דף קמה:) כגון תרנגולת דרבי אבא שורין אותו בחמין אפילו בכלי ראשון וכל שלא בא כו' מדיחין אותו לפירוש רשב"א דמפרש דעירוי ככלי שני אתי שפיר הכא דאין שורין אותו בכלי ראשון אבל מדיחין אותו מכלי ראשון דרך עירוי אבל לפר"ת דמפרש דעירוי הוי ככלי ראשון ע"כ מדיחין אותו מכלי שני קאמר וא"כ מאי איריא מדיחין אפילו שורין נמי ואומר ר"י דאפילו בכלי שני אין שורין דהואיל דהמים חמין מיחזי כמבשל ואע"ג דתנן לקמן (דף מב:) אבל נותן לתוך הקערה או לתוך התמחוי היינו דוקא תבלין שהן עשויין למתק את הקדירה ולא מיחזי כמבשל א"נ ה"ה שורין אותו כיון דאיירי בכלי שני והא דנקט מדיחין לאשמעינן דאפילו הדחה הויא גמר מלאכה במניח /במליח/ הישן וקולייס האיספנין.

ספר אור זרוע ח"ב - הלכות שבת סימן סב

וכשורה אינו שורה אלא בכלי שני דדילמא יש בישול לאחר בישול וא"ת ויהי' מותר להשרות בכלי שני אפי' היכא שלא נתבשל הואיל שבכלי שני אינו מבשל כדתנן פ' כירה האלפס והקדירה שהעבירן מרותחין לא יתן לתוכן תבלין אבל נותן לתוך הקערה או לתוך התמחוי ופר"ת דהכא אסור משום דמיחזי כעין בישול ודילמ' אתי למיעבד אף בכלי ראשון אבל גבי תבלין אין נראה בישול אלא משום מתוקי טעמא דפעמים רגילין ליתן תבלין בתבשיל צונן למתקו וליתן בו ריח טוב אך זה תימא אפי' דבר שנתבשל מערב שבת יהא אסור בכלי שני להשרותו שמא ישרה אותו בכלי ראשון ואם יש בישול לאחר בישול וה"ר משה מיימן כתב דבר שנתבשל קודם

השבת או נשרה בחמין מלפני השבת אע"פ שהוא עכשיו צונן מותר לשרותו בחמין בשבת עכ"ל:

רמב"ם הלכות שבת פרק ט הלכה ב

הנותן ביצה בצד המיחם בשביל שתתגלגל ונתגלגלה חייב, שהמבשל בתולדת האור כמבשל באור עצמה, וכן המדיח בחמין מליח הישן או קוליס האספנין והוא דג דק ורך ביותר הרי זה חייב, שהדחתן בחמין זה הוא גמר בשולן וכן כל כיוצא בהן.

שולחן ערוך אורח חיים סימן שיח סעיף ה

יש מי שאומר דדבר שנאפה או נצלה, אם בשלו אח"כ במשקה יש בו משום בישול, ואסור ליתן פת אפילו בכלי שני שהיד סולדת בו, ויש מתירין. הגה: בכלי שני; ויש מקילין אפילו בכלי ראשון; ונהגו ליזהר לכתחלה שלא ליתן פת אפילו בכלי שני כל זמן שהיד סולדת בו.

מגן אברהם אורח חיים סימן שיח סעיף קטן יח

דיש דברים שמתבשלים בו ואין אנו בקיאין ואם כן בשאר דברים נמי יש להחמיר עס"ט:

שולחן ערוך אורח חיים סימן שיח סעיף ט

כלי ראשון (פי' הכלי שמשתמש בו על האש) אפילו לאחר שהעבירוהו מעל האש מבשל, כל זמן שהיד סולדת בו. לפיכך אסור ליתן לתוכו תבלין, אבל מלח מותר ליתן לתוכו כיון שהעבירו מעל האש, דצריכא מלחא בישולא כבשרא דתורא. ויש מי שאוסר לתת לתוך כלי זה בשר מלוח, אפילו הוא של שור. הגה: ונ"ל דבלא מלוח נמי אסור, אלא דנקט מלוח דבלאו הכי אסור משום דם שבו. ויש אוסרים לתת מלח אפילו בכלי שני כל זמן שהיד סולדת בו; והמחמיר תע"ב (תוספות ומרדכי פרק כירה). ואם עבר ונתן מלח, אפילו בכלי ראשון אפילו הוא על האש שעבד איסורא, מותר המאכל דהמלח בטל ע"ג המאכל. (ב"י בשם שבולי הלקט).

מגן אברהם אורח חיים סימן שיח סעיף קטן יט

דס״ל דאין כ״ש מבשל ולפי מ״ש ס״ד בשם תוס׳ יש להחמיר דמיחזי כמבשל אך היש מתירים סוברים להקל כתירוץ שני של התו׳ וכ״מ דעת הש״ע ויש להחמיר:

שמירת שבת כהלכתה פרק א׳ הע׳ קנב

סימן שיח במשנה ברורה ס״ק מה ו-עד וע״ע קצור שו״ע סי׳ פ סע׳ ג ומהם הדברים הנקראים תבלין, שמעתי מהגרש״ז אויערבך שליט״א דלא מסתבר שהם תבלינים הרגילים בינינו שהם באים להטעים התבשיל, דכיון שהם דקים מאד, כל שכן שהם מתבשלים גם בכ״ש.

ארחות שבת פרק א הע׳ צז

והנה הגרשז״א זצ״ל מובא בספר שש״כ פ״א הערה קנ״ב דן להחמיר דמה שאמרו במשנה שבת מ״ב דתבלין אינו מתבשל בכלי שני היינו דוקא כשאינו שחוק אך תבלין שחוק כגון פלפל שחור וכיו״ב לא מסתבר שאינו מתבשל בכלי שני ועפ״ז השיב הגרש״ז אויערבאך זצ״ל [במכתב שבסוף ספר מאור השבת ח״ב מכתב ל״ב ה׳] שאין ליתן חומוס המכונה ארבעס בתוך מרק שהוא כלי שני מחשש שהתבלין שבו לא התבשל שהרי התבלין ניתן בו אחרי הבישול ולכאורה הדברים צ״ע שהרי סתם תבלין שבגמרא איירי גם בתבלין שחוק וכמבואר במסכת ביצה שהיו רגילים לדוך את התבלין וכן בשבת דף קמ״א השוחק פלפלין חייב חטאת ואיך יתכן שהמשנה תכתוב בסתמא היתר ליתן תבלין ולא יהא היתר זה נאמר בתבלין שחוק.

משנה ברורה סימן שיח ס״ק מב

ואסור ליתן פת וכו׳ - הוסיף בזה דין אחר והטעם דסבירא ליה לדעה זו דיש דברים שמתבשלים אפילו בכלי שני מפני שהם רכים ואין אנו בקיאים וע״כ הוסיף לאסור ליתן פת האפוי דהוא רכיך אפילו בכלי שני וה״ה דלדעה זו יש להחמיר נמי בשאר דברים שלא ליתנם בכלי שני ועיין לקמן בס״ט אודות תבלין:

שער הציון סימן שיח

(סז) מגן אברהם:

(סח) חוץ ממים ושמן וכדלקמן בסימן זה:

11

משנה ברורה סימן שיח ס"ק כג

בישול - וע"כ אסור מן התורה להניח התבשיל הזה בשבת במקום חם שהיד סולדת בו ולערב אותו בתבשיל רותח בכלי שני יש להקל [אחרונים]:

משנה ברורה סימן שיח ס"ק לט

דאסור לשרותו - אפילו בכלי שני וה"ה אם הוא דבר שיהיה נעשה ראוי לאכילה ע"י הדחת חמין בעלמא גם ההדחה אסור וכנ"ל לענין דג מליח. ועתה נבאר דין בישול עלי הטיי"א השייך בכמה ענינים לסעיף זה. הנה טיי"א בשבת פשוט בפוסקים דיש בו משום בישול ובמזיד יש בו איסור סקילה ובשוגג חיוב חטאת וע"כ יש ליזהר בו מאד ובעו"ה רבים נכשלים בו ומקילין לעצמן בקולות שאין בהם ממש וע"כ מוכרח אני לבאר אופני ההיתר והאיסור בזה בעזה"י. הנה לערות מכלי ראשון על עלי הטיי"א יש בזה בודאי חשש אב מלאכה דקי"ל דעירוי מבשל כדי קליפה כדלקמן בסעיף יו"ד וכ"ש אם יעמידנו אח"כ על התנור או בתוך הקאכלין עד שיהיה היד סולדת בו בודאי יבוא לכו"ע לידי איסור סקילה ע"ז ואפילו אם ירצה ליתן את עלי הטיי"א לתוך הכלי אחר שיערה החמין לתוכה כדי שיהיה על המים שם כלי שני ג"כ אסור כדקי"ל בסעיף זה דדבר שלא בא בחמין מלפני השבת אין שורין בשבת אפילו בכ"ש וכ"ש לפי מה שמבואר בסעיף זה דיש דברים רכים קלי הבישול שמתבשלים אפילו בהדחה מכלי שני אפשר דיש בהעלים ג"כ חשש איסור דאורייתא אפילו באופן זה וע"כ הסכימו האחרונים דיש לערות עליהם מע"ש רותחין מכלי ראשון כדי שעי"ז יהיה נקרא הטיי"א מבושל במקצת דעירוי מבשל כדי קליפה ויהפך בעת העירוי את הטיי"א היטב בתוך הרותחים מלמעלה למטה ומלמטה למעלה [ויותר טוב שיהיה מבושל ממש ע"י העמדה במקום שמתבשל] ואח"כ יריק את העסענס לכלי אחר כדי שישארו עלי הטיי"א

יבשים ויהיה מותר לו לערות אח"כ בשבת עליהם מים חמין מכלי ראשון כיון שכבר נתבשלו מע"ש כדין דבר יבש דקי"ל בסעיף זה דאין בו בישול אחר בישול אפילו אם נצטנן [ואח"כ מותר לו להחזיר גם מי העסענ"ס אלו הצוננים לתוך הכלי זה גופא וכמו שכתבנו לעיל דדבר לח שנצטנן מותר לו ליתנו בתוך כלי שני רותח] דאם ישאר בו משקה העסענ"ס הרי קיי"ל דבלח יש בישול אחר בישול אם נצטנן אם לא שמי העסענס הצוננים הם מרובין שלא יתחממו ע"י המים שמערה עליהן למחר וכן הדין לענין קאווי' יזהר שלא יערה עליהם מים חמין מכלי ראשון אם לא שעירה עליהם מאתמול והריק את המים מעליהן והטעם ככל הנ"ל [עיין בתשובות חתם סופר סימן ע"ד ובפ"ת על או"ח]. ודע דאף שהתרנו לערות חמין על עלי הטיי"א והקאוו"י אם נתן עליהם מאתמול מים מכ"ר אעפ"כ יזהר שלא יעמיד את הטיי"א והקאוו"י בתנור או בקאכלין אחר ששפך עליהם מים דהא אין עירוי מבשל רק כדי קליפה וא"כ לא נתבשל אתמול רק כדי קליפה ועכשיו ע"י העמדה בתנור יתבשל לגמרי. והנה אופן זה שבארנו אף שאין למחות ביד הנוהגים בו מ"מ כתבו האחרונים עצה המובחרת מזה דהיינו שיתקן העסענס מע"ש לגמרי שלא יצטרך לערות לתוכו עוד רותחין למחר בשבת ולמחר כשיצטרך לשתות יתן העסענס הצונן לתוך הכוס ששותה בו אחר שעירו המים חמין לתוכו ונעשה כ"ש וה"ה שמותר לתת לתוך הכוס הזה שהוא כ"ש חלב שנצטנן אבל אסור לערות עליהם מכ"ר וכדלעיל בס"ד וכשהעסענס שלו אינו צונן הוא בודאי טוב לצאת בזה ידי כל הדעות:

שולחן ערוך הרב אורח חיים סימן שיח סעיף יב

ויש מי שמסתפק וחושש מחיוב חטאת גם בכלי שני שהיד סולדת בו מפני שיש דברים רכים שמתבשלים גם בכלי שני ואין אנו בקיאין בהן ושמא גם הלחם נקרא רך לענין זה ומתבשל גם בכלי שני שהיד סולדת בו וכן יש להסתפק ספק זה גם בשאר דברים ויש להחמיר בכולן לבד מבתבלין שהתירו חכמים בפירוש ליתנם בכלי שני וכן מים ושמן כמו שיתבאר והוא הדין לשאר משקין ואפילו בבשר צלוי יש להחמיר כיון שיש בישול אחר צליה אבל במבושל אין להחמיר כלל אפילו בכלי ראשון שלדברי הכל אין בישול אחר בישול בדבר יבש.

שולחן ערוך אורח חיים סימן שיח סעיף יג

מותר ליתן קיתון של מים או של שאר משקים בכלי שני שיש בו מים חמין, אבל בכ"ר אסור.

מהרש"א חידושי הלכות מסכת שבת דף לט עמוד א

בד"ה כל שבא כו' היינו דוקא תבלין שהן עשויין למתק את הקדירה כו' עכ"ל ק"ק דהא גבי שמן בעין אמרי' לקמן דאין כלי שני מבשל ושמן בעין לא שייך ביה למתק וי"ל דשאני התם דמפסיק כלי דכה"ג משני לקמן ודקאמר התם ש"מ דכלי שני אינו מבשל היינו נמי דבכה"ג אינו מבשל היכא דמפסיק כלי וק"ל:

ארחות שבת פ"א הע' קל

ועיין מהרש"א דף ל"ט שכתב דהטעם שהיות והכלי מפסיק בין המים החמים לבין המשקה שבכלי לכן לא מחזי כמבשל [ונראה כוונתו דגזרת מחזי כמבשל היא משום דנראה כמבשל בכלי ראשון ואין דרך לבשל בכלי ראשון אם מפסיק כלי אלא נותן את האוכל בתוך הכ"ר עצמו].

משנה ברורה סימן שיח ס"ק פ"ו

קיתון של מים - אף דמים בלבד בלא כלי ג"כ מותר לערב בתוך כלי שני וכנ"ל בסי"ב נקט ע"י כלי משום סיפא לאשמועינן דבכלי ראשון אפי' ע"י הפסקת כלי אסור:

שולחן ערוך אורח חיים סימן שיח

מיחם שפינה ממנו מים חמין, מותר ליתן לתוכו מים צונן (לו מרובים) כדי להפשיר; ומותר לצוק מים חמין לתוך מים צונן, או צונן לתוך חמין והוא שלא יהיו בכלי ראשון מפני שמחממין הרבה. הגה: ואם המים מרובים כל כך שא"א שיתבשלו, רק שיפיגו צנתן, אפילו בכלי ראשון שרי רק שלא יהיה על האש (טור).

הלכות שבת במטבח פרק ב הע' כא

ולפ"ז נראה ליישב דעת המ"ב, דס"ל דבאמת כל משקין לא הווין קלי

הבישול, ולהכי שפיר מותר לתת קיתון של משקה לתוך כלי שני, דליכא איסור בישול בכלי שני בשום משקה ומשום מיחזי כמבשל נמי ליכא דהא המשקין הם בתוך קיתון, והא דחילק המ״ב בין שאר משקין לשמן ומים היינו כשנותנן לתוך הכלי שני עצמו, דהתם אסור בשאר משקין משום דמיחזי כמבשל, אבל בשמן ומים אפילו זה מותר דבשמן ומים לא מיחזי כמבשל, והטעם הוא דשמן בכלל תבלין הוא ולא מיחזי כמבשל כמ״ש התוס׳, ובמים כתב הפמ״ג בא״א סי׳ שי״ח ס״ק ל״ד דכיון שהמים מתערבין יפה בהחמין שבכלי שני ואינם נכרים בפני עצמו לא מיחזו כמבשל.

פרי מגדים אשל אברהם סימן שיח ס״ק לב

והנה למ״ש באות ט״ו דהמחבר בתי׳ א׳ בתוס׳ שם דבכלי שני חי אסור דמחזי כמבשל אתי שפיר דנקיט כאן לערות אתבלין וכן הוא במשנה הא שאר בשר וכדומה אף בכלי שני שיד סולדת בו אסור דמחזי כמבשל. והא דסעי׳ י״א אמבטי בכלי שני שמחממן הרבה לא קשה מידי דמשמע שאר כלי שני שרי די״ל דדוקא להניח גוש בכלי שני לשרות מחזי כמבשל משא״כ מים במים שמתערבין יפה לא מחזי כמבשל אלא בהוחם לרחיצה אסור.

שו״ת אגרות משה אורח חיים חלק ד סימן עד

(יח) האם מותר ליתן בצלים או לימונים בכלי שני כתבלין.

ועל קאפע /קפה/ אינו מבושל וכן קאקאו שאין נאכלין והוא רק לתבלין לכאורה הם ודאי בכלל סתם תבלין וא״כ מפורש במתני׳ שבכלי שני אינם מתבשלין ומותר ליתן לכתחלה, ותמוה על מה שעה״ש מחמיר בכלי שני וגם בכלי שלישי לדעתו, וכן משמע ממ״ב ס״ק ל״ט שאוסר גם קאווי /קפה/ שהוא קפה בכלי שני מטעם דיש דברים המתבשלים בכלי שני הא בתבלין מפורש שאין מתבשלין בכלי שני. בשלמא בעלי טיי אפשר לא נחשבו בכלל תבלין דהם לא ניתנו לטעמא אלא למראה ואינם בכלל תבלין שבמתני׳ ושייך לאיסתפוקי בהו אבל קפה וקאקאו שהן תבלין בודאי הרי הם בכלל תבלין שבמתני׳ וליכא ספק וצ״ע. ולמעשה צריך עכ״פ להחמיר בכלי שני ומותר בכלי שלישי.

הלכות שבת (איידער) הע' נה

ועוד תבלין הוא דבר שמוסיפין לדבר אוכל אבל קאפע הוא דבר אוכל העיקרי המבסם מים.

12

משנה ברורה סימן שיח ס"ק פא

(פא) לתוך מים צונן או צונן וכו' - ובשניהן אפי' המים צוננים מועטין שעדיין היד סולדת בהן אחר התערובות ג"כ שרי כיון שהוא בכלי שני קי"ל דכלי שני אינו מבשל כדלעיל בס"ט:

תוספות מסכת שבת דף מ עמוד ב

ושמע מינה כלי שני אינו מבשל - תימה מאי שנא כלי שני מכלי ראשון דאי יד סולדת אפי' כלי שני נמי ואי אין יד סולדת אפילו כלי ראשון נמי אינו מבשל ויש לומר לפי שכלי ראשון מתוך שעמד על האור דופנותיו חמין ומחזיק חומו זמן מרובה ולכך נתנו בו שיעור דכל זמן שהיד סולדת בו אסור אבל כלי שני אף על גב דיד סולדת בו מותר שאין דופנותיו חמין והולך ומתקרר.

הלכות שבת (איידער) הע' תנט

ע' מ"ב (שם ס"ק ל"ה) שכ' "לתוך מים צונן או צונן וכו". ובשניהן אפי' המים צוננים מועטין שעדיין היד סולדת בהן אחר התערובות ג"כ שרי כיון שהוא בכלי שני קי"ל דכלי שני אינו מבשל וכדלעיל בס"ט. בס' תה"ל הקשה "הא דבכ"ש מותר בין חמין לתוך צונן בין צונן לתוך חמין כמ"ש המחבר בסי"ב וע"כ שהיס"ב לאחר שנתערבו דאל"כ אף בכ"ר שרי. ויקשה כיון שהיס"ב לאחר שנתערבו ונעשו הצוננין חמין שהיס"ב והוי כמבשל בתולדות האור. והעיר ה' את עיני ומצאתי להרשב"א ז"ל שכ' ואפילו היו המים יס"ב לאחר שנתערבו צונן לתוכן אינו מחמת הצונן ששבו להיות יס"ב אלא מחמת הראשונים שלא נצטננו וכו" ע"ש ובשבה"ש שם כ' "וצ"ל דתולדות האור לא מקרי רק מה שהוחם באור עצמו ולא כאשר הורק מכלי אל כלי ועיין". וע' בס' יסו"י (ח"ו דף תכ"ט ד"ה דף ת"ד) שהקשה

הגרשז"א "הרי עינינו רואות שיכולים להחם מים ע"י כלי בתוך כלי שני וכו'" כבר הקדימו התה"ל. והנראה בזה דכלי ראשון כיון שדופנותיו חמין מוסיף חום או מיהא מחזיק חומו זמן מרובה לפיכך ראוי לבשל ודרך בישול בכך, משא"כ כלי שני כיון שהולך ומתקרר אין דרך לבשל בו רק לפשר בו.

רשב"א מב עמוד א כבר מובא בפרק ג

משנה ברורה סימן שיח ס"ק מה

ונהגו ליזהר וכו' - פי' שאין נותנים לחם במרק של הטשאלינ"ט בקערה שהיא כלי שני וכ"ש שיזהר שלא לערות עליהם מכלי ראשון ואותם שחותכים הבצלים ונותנין לתוך המרק בקערה לא ישימו רק אחר שלא תהיה היד סולדת בהמרק דבלחם יש קולא מחמת שנאפה כבר ואפ"ה נזהרים כ"ש בבצלים שצריך ליזהר כי אין אנו בקיאין במידי דמקרי רכיך וכנ"ל וכ"ש לפי מה שנוהגין ליתן הבצלים לתוך התבשיל שהוא דבר גוש בודאי יש ליזהר בזה דיש פוסקים שסוברים דדבר גוש שמונח בכלי שני דינו ככ"ר. ואפילו אם ימתין עד שיהיה המרק שבקערה אין היד סולדת בו מ"מ יזהר שלא ישפוך אח"כ על שיורי בצלים שנשאר בקערה מן המרק שבקדרה אם היד סולדת בהן דעירוי מבשל כדי קליפה כדקי"ל בסעיף י' ויש בזה חשש דאורייתא. וכן מה שנוהגין איזה אנשים כשעושין חמין מרגלי בהמה לחתוך חתיכת פת בכלי ולערות עליהם המרק של הרגלים מכ"ר לא יפה הם עושין דאפילו אם לא יתן הפת בתחלה עד שיערה המרק תחלה בכלי כדי שיעשה כ"ש הלא כתב רמ"א דיש ליזהר בזה אלא אם רוצה ליתן פת ימתין עד שלא יהיה היד סולדת במרק או שלכל הפחות ישאב בכף מן הקדרה כדי שתהיה הקערה כלי שלישי וכ"ש אם רוצה ליתן בצלים ושומים לתוך החמין האלו בודאי יזהר מאד לעשות כן דאם יערה עליהם מכלי ראשון שהיד סולדת בהן יש בזה חשש אב מלאכה וכנ"ל:

ספר יראים סימן רעד [דפוס ישן - קב]

הלכך יזהר אדם שלא להכניס בשבת שום דבר בכלי שני ואף בכלי שלישי שהיד סולדת בו שאין אנו בקיאים בדברים רכים וקשים מי הוא מתבשל בכלי שני ומי הוא שאינו מתבשל.

13

תוספות מב עמוד ב כבר מובא בפרק י

תלמוד בבלי מסכת פסחים דף עו עמוד א

חם לתוך צונן, וצונן לתוך חם; רב אמר: עילאה גבר, ושמואל אמר: תתאה גבר.

שולחן ערוך יורה דעה סימן צב סעיף ז

יש מי שמתיר בשעת הדחק, כגון בערב שבת, אפילו שלא כנגד הרוטב, אפילו שלא כנגד האש, על ידי ס'. הגה: והכי נהוג (ארוך). ואם נשפך חלב או שאר איסור רותח על גבי קרקע, והעמידו עליו לא קדירה חמה; אם מה שנשפך אינו אצל האש, לא הוי רק כלי שני, ולכן הקדירה אסורה, דבולע קצת, והתבשיל מותר, דתתאי גבר. (הגהת ש"ד סימן כ"ה). וקלוח מן הקדירה רותחת שהלך אל קדירה צוננת, אם נפסק הקלוח מן הקדירה הרותחת קודם שהגיע אל הצונן, הוי נמי ככלי שני (כך משמע בשערים מתשובת מוהר"ם). ואם לא נפסק, הוי כעירוי והקדירה הצוננת נאסרה, אם היד סולדת בקלוח הנוגע בקדירה (ת"ה סי' קפ"א), והתבשיל שבתוכה שרי, דאין עירוי אוסר רק כדי קליפה. אבל אם הקדירה היא חמה, והוא כלי ראשון, וכ"ש עומד אצל האש, אפילו הקלוח הוא צונן, לו הכל אסור, דתתאי גבר, והוי כצונן לתוך חם דכולו אסור (כך משמע מב"י), כמו שנתבאר לעיל סימן צ"א. טפה הנופלת על גבי כיסוי קדירה, דינה כנפל על גבי קדירה נגד הרוטב, לז והוא שהתחילה הקדירה להרתיח, דאז עולה הזיעה תמיד ומגיע אל הכיסוי ויורד משם אל הרוטב. (ארוך כלל ל"א וש"ד).

ט"ז אורח חיים סימן שיח ס"ק טז

(טז) ולערות עליהם מכ"ה. - דקי"ל כרש"י ור"ת דעירוי ככ"ר היינו לחומרא אבל לא לקולא כגון להכשיר [כלי] שצריך הגעלה ע"י עירוי מכ"ר כמבואר בי"ד:

תרומת הדשן סימן קפא

שאלה: קדירה מליאה חלב רותח שפותה אצל האש על הכירה, ומחמת הרתיחה יצא החלב למעלה מאוגני הכלי והיה נזחל ונמשך בקילוח בלי

הפסק דרך דופני הקדירה ע"ג הכירה עד שהגיע אצל בשר שהיה ג"כ על גבי הכירה, מי חשבינן האי קילוח עדיין כעירוי מכלי ראשון ונאסר הבשר, או נימא כיון דנזחל ע"ג הכירה נתקרר ולא היה רותח?

תשובה: יראה דחשיב כה"ג כעירוי מכלי ראשון אם היתה היד סולדת בחלב במקום שנגע בבשר, ולא אמרינן שנתקרר ע"ג הכירה. וראייה מדאמרינן פ' כירה /שבת מ' ע"ב/ אר"י בר רב דימי פעם אחת נכנסתי אחר רבי לבית המרחץ כו' עד טול בכלי שני ותן, פי' רצה להפשיר פך שמן באמבטי שנאספו שם מים מחמי טבריא שהיתה בריכה עשויה בקרקע ואסר לו להניח הפך בתוך האמבטי בשבת, משום דהך אמבטי שהחמין נמשכין לה מן המעיין חשיב לה ככלי ראשון שנרתחו בו, אע"פ שהעבירו מעל האש מבשל כל זה מפרש רש"י התם. הא קמן דאע"ג דנמשכו הרותחים ע"ג קרקע כמו הני חמי טבריא שהיו נמשכין דרך קרקע חשיבי עדיין ככלי ראשון. וא"ת שאני חמי טבריא שאין בטבע שלהן שקרקע מקררתן שהרי כל רתיחתן עולה ונובע מן הקרקע ולא דמי לחמי האור. מטעם זה נראה דאין לחלק דהא אמרינן התם בההיא סוגיא /שבת מ' ע"ב/, אמר רב חסדא המבשל בחמי טבריא בשבת חייב, דהא מעשה דרבי לאחר גזירה הוי, וא"ל טול בכלי שני ותן, פי' כיון דלאחר גזירה שגזרו עלה רחיצה כחמי האור הוא א"כ ע"כ בחמי טבריא רחץ, ואפ"ה הוצרך לכלי שני דאי הוי ראשון הוי מבשל. והשתא מדמוכח משום דמעשה דרבי לאחר גזירה הוי, משמע דאי הוי קודם גזירה הוי מצי לאוקמי בחמי האור. ואע"ג דבהדיא קאמר התם ובקשתי להניח לו פך שמן באמבטי ואמר לי טול בכלי שני ותן, וע"כ המים חמין שהן באמבטי לא נרתחו בתוך האמבטי אלא נמשכו לתוכה מן היורה ע"ג קרקע, כי כן דרך האמבטי להיות כדמוכח מתוך פרש"י, דאל"כ מי הזקיקו לפרש שנמשכו מים מן המעיין לתוך האמבטי, נימא דאמבטי היתה ממש על ניקבי הנביעה של חמי טבריא מתוקנים כמו בריכה. אע"כ לא מיקרי אמבטי אלא הנמשך לה מים ממקום אחר שהוחמו שם. א"כ חזינן אע"ג דהוי בעי לאוקמי בחמי האור ונמשכין ע"ג קרקע חשיב כרותחים דכלי ראשון, מדקאמר טול בכלי שני כדפרישית. אף את"ל דהראייה קצת דחוקה, מ"מ הדעת נוטה בנ"ד אם נראה לנו שהיתה היד סולדת בחלב במקום שנגע בבשר, הואיל והיה הקילוח נוזל והולך מתוך הרתיחה העומדת אצל האש, כל טיפה וטיפה אחרונה אינה

מנחת את הראשונה שלפניה להתקרר. שהרי פירשו התוספות פ׳ כירה / שבת מ׳ ע״ב ד״ה וש״מ/ דהא דיד סולדת בו בכלי שני אינו מבשל, היינו משום דאינו עומד אצל האש /אינו/ מחזיק חומו והולך ומתקרר, משמע דאם עוד היה כח האש שולט שם אינו מתקרר, הלעד״כ.

שולחן ערוך יורה דעה סימן צה סעיף ג

קערות של בשר שהודחו ביורה חולבת בחמין שהיד סולדת בהן, אפילו שניהם בני יומן, מותר, משום דהוה ליה נותן טעם בר נותן טעם דהתירא. והוא שיאמר ברי לי שלא היה שום שומן דבוק בהן. ואם היה שומן דבוק בהן, צריך שיהא במים ס׳ כנגד ממשות שומן שעל פי הקערה. הגה: ויש אוסרים אפילו אין שומן דבוק בהן (טור בשם סה״ת וסמ״ג וסמ״ק וש״ד והר״ף ותוס׳ ומרדכי ור״ן והגמ״יי ופסקי מהרא״י ואו״ה), אלא א״כ אחד מן הכלים אינן בני יומן יג מבליעת כלי ראשון, ואז כל הכלים מותרים והמים נוהגין בהן איסור לכתחלה. אבל אם שניהם בני יומן, והדיח אותן ביחד בכלי ראשון, הכל אסור. טז והכי נוהגין, ואין לשנות. ודוקא שהודחו ביחד ובכלי ראשון, אבל אם הודחו זה אחר זה, או בכלי שני אפילו ביחד, הכל שרי (בארוך כלל ל״ד). ואם עירה מכלי ראשון של בשר על כלי חלב, דינו ככלי ראשון ואוסר אם היה בן יומו. אבל אם עירה מים רותחים שאינן של בשר ולא של חלב על כלים של בשר ושל חלב ביחד, ואפילו שומן דבוק בהם, הכל שרי, דאין עירוי ככלי ראשון ממש שיעשה שהכלים שמערה עליהם, יבלעו זה מזה (שם). ואם נמצא קערה חולבת בין כלי בשר, לא חיישינן שמא הודחו ביחד בדרך שנאסרים (הגהות ש״ד ואו״ה).

ש״ך יורה דעה סימן צה ס״ק כ

כ דאין עירוי ככלי א׳ ממש כו׳ - קשה לי דהא משמע מדברי הרב בהג״ה סי׳ ס״ח ס״י דעירוי מבשל כדי קליפה וכ״כ בת״ח כלל ל״ג ד״ב וצ״ל דס״ל להרב דנהי דמבשל כ״כ שהתרנגולת מפליט ומבליע מ״מ הכלי שהוא קשה אינו בולע דאינו מפליט ומבליע כאחת בכלי שהוא קשה אכן לענין דינא נראה כמ״ש בהגהת ש״ד סי׳ נ״ז בשם מהר״ש ומביאו בת״ח שם דנאסרו דכיון דקי״ל דעירוי מבשל וכמו שיתבאר בסי׳ ק״ה ס״ק ד׳

א״כ חשיב כבישול ממש ומבליע אפילו בכלי והכי מוכח מדברי המרדכי והגה״א סוף עבודת כוכבים דאפילו למ״ד כלי שני מבליע ומפליט אין סברא לחלק בכלי שכתבו על מ״ש ה״ר חיים כהן דתרנגולים שנמלגו בכלי שני אסורים וזה לשונו ולפי דבריו היו נאסרים כל הכלים שמולגין בהם התרנגולת מחמת הדם שפולטת התרנגולת ונבלע בכלי עכ״ל א״כ כ״ש דלמאי דקי״ל דעירוי מבשל דמבשל אפי׳ לכלי וכ״כ מהרש״ל בספרו פכ״ה ס״ס ס״ד וז״ל היכא שעירו מים רותחים על הקערות צריכים לדקדק ולשאול אם היו שם שיורי מאכל לפי שהעירוי מפליט ומבליע כדי קליפה עכ״ל וגם הרב בת״ח שם כ׳ שלא נהגו להקל בזה ושיש להחמיר במקום שאין הפסד מרובה ואו״ה דהתיר אפילו שומן דבוק בהן היינו משום דאזיל לטעמיה דס״ל דעירוי אינו מבשל ולא מפליט ומבליע אפי׳ כדי קליפה אלא בולע כדי קליפה קודם שמצננו וכמבואר בדבריו להדיא אבל למאי דקי״ל דעירוי מבשל כדי קליפה נראה כמו שכתבתי מיהו היכא דהם נקיים ודאי יש להתיר מטעם נותן טעם בר נותן טעם וכדמשמע מדברי מהרש״ל אבל היכא דהוי כלי של איסור דלא שייך ביה נותן טעם בר נותן טעם נראה דאפילו נקי אסור וצריך עיון בזה דאפשר דאפילו מבשל לא מבשל כולי האי שיפליט מן הכלי ויבליע לכלי ולפ״ז גם בכלים של בשר וחלב שאחד מהן נקי ואחד מהן אינו נקי שהנקי אסור ושאינו נקי צ״ע אי נימא כיון דהנקי נ״נ חוזר ואוסר השני כיון שמערה עליו כל פעם או נימא דעירוי לא מבשל כולי האי ויש להחמיר בשניהם במקום שאין הפסד מרובה כי נראה כיון דמבשל חשיב ממש כבישול והכי משמע בהגהת ש״ד הישנים שנדפסו בקושטנדינ״א שנת שוב״ה (סי׳ ל״ג) דאין חילוק ע״ש:

שולחן ערוך אורח חיים סימן שיח סעיף י

אסור ליתן תבלין בקערה ולערות עליהן מכלי ראשון.

רבי עקיבא איגר שם

באיסור והיתר הארוך כלל לד דין כא כתב דאין איסור אלא לערות על התבלין עצמן, אבל לשפוך בצדן לא עכ״ל.

שולחן ערוך יורה דעה סימן קה סעיף ב

חום של כלי ראשון שהיד סולדת בו, מבשל ואוסר כולו. אבל חום של כלי שני אינו מבשל. ויש אומרים שגם כן אינו מפליט ואינו מבליע. וי"א דמכל מקום הוא מפליט ומבליע, ואוסר כדי קליפה. וראוי לחוש ליזהר בדבר לכתחלה (ועי"ל סי' ס"ח סעיף י"ג), אבל בדיעבד מותר בלא קליפה, ובהדחה בעלמא סגי. (ועיין לעיל סימן ס"ח וצ"ב וצ"ה נתבארו דיני כלי שני ועירוי).

חוו"ד סי' צב ס"ק כג

ואם לא נפסק הקילוח ואף שנזחל על כירה צוננת קודם שהגיע אל הבשר, לא אמרינן דנתקרר מהתתאה, כיון דהקילות מקושר עדיין בכלי הראשון אינו מניחו להתקרר, כן הוא בתרומת הדשן סימן קפא. והנה לכאורה יראה סתירה לזה מהאיסור והיתר הארוך כלל ל"ד דין כ"א שכתב וז"ל דאותו כלי שאין העירוי בו בתחלת הניצוק בזה לא אמרינן שיהיה העירוי ככלי ראשון ואינו מבשל. וגם בשבת אינו אסור לערות הרותחין רק על התבלין, אבל בצידן לא. וכן פסק הש"ך בסימן צ"ה ס"ק י"ח ע"ש. וכן פסק עוד בסימן ס"ח ס"ק ל"ה שכתב שכבר נצטנן המים שנפלו על התרנגולת קודם שהגיע אל הכלי ע"ש לכן נראה דאף התרומת הדשן והרב לא קאמרי רק שאינו יכול להתקרר מהתתאה מאתר שהטפה האחרונה אינה מניחה הראשונה להתקרר כמו שכתב התרומת הדשן שם בתשובה ע"ש, ויכול להפליט או להבליע, אבל בהא מודים שבודאי אינו יכול לבשל, דלבשל אינו יכול רק מה שיש לו דפנות המחממות בכלי ראשון שדפנותיו הוחמו באור, כמו שכתבו התוספות בשבת דף מ' ע"ב בד"ה ושמע מינה בטעם שהכלי ראשון מבשל. והך דינא דתרומת הדשן והרב שבכאן אין לו דפנות המחממות אדרבה יש לו דפנות המקררות רק שהטיפות אינן מניחות להתקרר אינו מבשל רק שמבליע ומפליט כמו כלי שני לרב דאמר עילאה גבר, שאז ודאי דלא נתקרר מהתתאה, וחום כלי ראשון עליו להבליע ולהפליט, ואפילו הכי מודה רב דכלי שני אינו מבשל כיון שאין לו דפנות המחממות, וכן כתב המנחת יעקב בתורת תטאת כלל ס"א ס"ק מה דדבר גוש אף שיש לו דין כלי ראשון להרש"ל, אינו מבשל, מכל שכן הכא שיש לו אפילו דפנות המקררות מכל שכן שאינו מבשל. ואף דתרומת הדשן בסימן קפ"א

שם מביא ראיה להך דינא משבת דף מ׳ ושם קרי ליה מבשל מכל מקום הא סיים בעצמו דראיה זו דחוקה רק שסומך על הסברא מכח דאין הטפה השניה מניחה הראשונה להתקרר אין סברא זו נותנת רק לענין שיהיה מבליע או מפליט ככלי ראשון אבל לא לענין מבשל. ואף דתרומת הדשן סבירא ליה דמבשל מכל מקום האיסור והיתר הארוך והרב והש״ך חולקים עליו בהא וסבירא להו דאינו מבשל, ומשום הכי בכלים דסימן צ״ה וסימן ס״ח הנ״ל דבעינן שיהיה מפליט ומבליע כאחד, שזהו פעולת בישול דכל שאינו מבשל אינו מפליט ומבליע כאחד, עיין ש״ך סימן ק״ה ס״ק ה,׳ וכן לענין שבת מותר כמו שכתב האיסור והיתר הארוך וזה ברור. ועיין ט״ז ס״ק כ״ז שהביא בשם רש״ל שהקשה למה לי שהחלב רותת כיון שהבשר רותח אסור כדין קר וחם שנוגעין וכו׳, אין לתמוה על קושייתו דהא בעצמו פסק דבאיסור קר והיתר חם דאינו אוסר כמו במליחה, דזה אינו, דבאיסור צלול אפילו במליחה אסור.

ביאור הגר״א יורה דעה סימן קה ס״ק יד

[יד] וי״א כו׳. ממ״ש בפ׳ כ״ה קי״א ב׳ קערה שמלח בה כו׳ ובפ״ז דשבת (ע״ה ב׳) האי מאן דמלח בישרא כו׳ ואילו משום מבשל לכ״ע פטור אלמא אע״ג דאין מבשל מבליע ובסוף ע״ז הלוקח כלי תשמיש כו׳ שנשתמש בהן בחמין ומשמע אף בכלי שני ועבה״ג (עוד ב׳ ראיות):

(ליקוט) וי״א דמ״מ כו׳. וירושלמי הנ״ל פי׳ הרמב״ן ות״ה דמה שלמד מקדשים מדהצריכה תורה מריקה ושטיפה ולא סגי לה בהגעלה דכ״ש אלמא בלע טובא ככלי ראשון אבל בולע הוא אפילו כ״ש ואפילו כלי נחשת וצריך הגעלה וכ״כ בא״ח סי׳ תנ״א ס״ו (ע״כ):

ש״ך יורה דעה סימן קה ס״ק ה

וראוי לחוש ליזהר בדבר לכתחלה - פי׳ אפי׳ הוא דבר שדרכו להדיחו אח״כ דאז מותר להניחו ע״ג איסור צונן כדלעיל ר״ס צ״א מ״מ הכא יש ליזהר לכתחלה בדבר זה ובספרי הארכתי בדיני עירוי וכלי שני וכאן אכתוב בתכלית הקצור מה שנוגע בשרשי הדין דעת רשב״ם שהביאו התוס׳ פ׳ דם חטאת (דף צ״ה ע״א) ופ׳ כירה (דף מ״ב ע״ב) והרא״ש והר״ן לשם ומרדכי והגה״א סוף עבודת כוכבים וסה״ת דעירוי ככלי שני ואינו מבשל וכן אינו

מפליט ומבליע כאחד כמו כלי שני ודעת ר"ת שהביאו כל הנך פוסקים לשם דעירוי מבשל כדי קליפה כמו כלי ראשון ומוכח דעת רשב"ם דמ"מ עירוי מבליע כדי קליפה כגון אם עירה איסור רותח על היתר או חלב על גבי בשר אוסר כדי קליפה אלא דאינו מפליט ומבליע כאחד ולכך מותר לערות על התרנגולת למולגה וגם מוכח דעת רשב"ם דכלי שני אינו מבליע כלל אפילו כדי קליפה ודעת ר"ת שהביאו כל הנך פוסקים דלעיל מוכח דסבירא ליה דעירוי כמו שאינו מבשל בכולו כך אינו מבליע בכולו ודלא כמהרש"ל בתשו' סי' ס"ב שכתב דלר"ת שהביא הרא"ש מבליע בכולו ובפרישה סי' ס"ח כתב דלר"ת שהביא הרא"ש מבשל בכולו והוא תמוה ומוכח נמי דעת ר"ת דלעיל דכלי שני אינו מבליע כדי קליפה וא"כ דעת כל הפוסקים דלעיל והסמ"ג מכללם שעומדים בשטת ר"ת כן ודלא כמ"ש מהרש"ל באו"ש סי' ל"ג דלסמ"ג אפי' כלי חרס בולע בכלי שני וכ"ש דבר מאכל וכן דעת הרבה פוסקים ראשונים ואחרונים דכלי שני אינו מבליע כלל וכ"פ הרב בת"ח כלל ל"ג דין א' ותימא דבהג"ה בא"ח ר"ס תנ"א משמע דסובר דכלי חרס שנשתמש בו חמץ בכלי שני אסור ואולי משום חומרא דחמץ נגע ביה ומ"מ יש להחמיר ולאסור בכלי חרס במקום שאין הפסד כל כך בשגם שהרמב"ן והרשב"א בתה"א דף צ"ב סוברים דאפילו בכלי נחושת מבליע וגם יש פוסקים דאע"ג דכלי שני אינו מבשל מ"מ מבליע ומפליט וכן בדבר מאכל יש לקלוף במקום שאין הפסד כ"כ אבל על כל פנים אין לאסור כולו בכלי שני וכן מהרש"ל בתשו' שם לא כתב דמבליע אלא כדי קליפה ותימא על מ"ש בספרו פכ"ה סי' ע"א לאסור כולו, ובב"ח בסי' זה מחמיר ביותר דכלי שני מפליט ומבליע כאחד ואוסר כולו והוא תמוה ואנן קי"ל לחומרא דעירוי דכלי ראשון מבשל כדי קליפה והלכך לענין שבת ובשר בחלב אסור ואפי' בעירוי שנפסק הקלוח מבליע מיהא כ"ק לכ"ע וכמ"ש הפוסקים וכדמוכח בפרק כ"צ (דף ע"ו ע"א) ואע"ג דמדברי הרב סי' ס"ח ס"י נראה דאם עירה מכלי ראשון על התרנגולת למולגה ונפסק הקילוח א"צ אפי' קליפה היינו משום דאינו מפליט ומבליע כאחד אבל מ"מ מבליע והכי משמע להדי' מתוס' דזבחים והמרדכי והג"א והר"ן דסוף עבודת כוכבים מיהו ודאי דסגי בקליפה ואינו מבליע יותר והכי מוכח מהא דכתבו הפוסקים והט"ו סי' צ"א ס"ד בחלב רותח שנפל על בשר צונן דקולף הבשר ומותר וכן הוא בש"ס פכ"צ שם, וכל חום היינו דוקא כשהיד סולדת בו

אבל אין היד סולדת בו אפי׳ הוא כלי ראשון שעומד על האש אינו אוסר כלל וכ״פ הפוסקים ראשונים ואחרונים בדוכתי טובי וכ״כ מהרש״ל פכ״ה סימן ע״א אלא שאח״כ כתב אלא דמסתפינא להקל בכלי ראשון שעומד על האש כל זמן שהוא חם אפי׳ אין היד סולדת בו דעשו הרחקה לכלי ראשון כדאיתא בירושלמי כו׳ ולא ירדתי לסוף דעתו דהרי בירושלמי פרק כירה איתא דעשו הרחקה לכלי ראשון שאין היד שולטת בו והיינו שאין להיד שליטה בו דהיינו היד סולדת בו אבל כשהיד שולטת בו מוכח התם בירושלמי להדיא דשרי לכ״ע וכן הסכמת הפוסקים וכ״כ בת״ח כלל נ״ז דין י״ב אלא דבכלל כ״ג ד״ג פסק כהרשב״א וטור דצונן לתוך חם שאין היד סולדת בו צריך קליפה וצריך לומר דסבירא ליה דאע״פ שאין היד סולדת בו מבליע כדי קליפה וכן יש להחמיר אע״פ דמדברי שאר הפוסקים לא נראה כן ודו״ק:

14

פרי מגדים יורה דעה שפתי דעת סימן צה ס״ק יח

עירה. עש״ך עיין באו״ה כלל ל״ד דין כ״א דלשאר כלים שאין הנצוק נוגע בהן הוה כ״ש וכן לענין שבת דאין מערה רותחין על תבלין אבל בצידיהן שרי עוד כתב שם בדין י״ז בזה אחר זה אם היו נקיים שרי ופשוט הוא דאם כלי א׳ מלוכלך נאסר הב׳ אבל הכלי הב׳ מלוכלך אין מזיק כלום לשני לדידן דנצלו שרי עיין ברא״ש פכ״ה:

והוי יודע שמ״ש דהכלי שאין הנצוק בו שרי יש בו מהעיון לפי מ״ש הר״ב בצ״ב ס״ז דקלוח מהקדירה רותחת על צוננת אם לא נפסק הקלוח אף שנזחל על גבי כירה צוננת לא הוי כ״ש דנצוק חיבור ואין מניח לקרר ודין עירוי כדי קליפה יש עליו וכדבעינן למימר קמן א״כ כאן נמי כ״ז שלא נפסק העמוד אף שנזחל ונח המים על כלי צוננת ומגיע לכלי אחר הכל חשיב עירוי כאמור וכן לענין תבלין בשבת כל זמן שלא נפסק הקילוח אף בצידיהן אסור לערות כדכתיבנא וכי תימא נהי דדין כ״ש לא הוי מ״מ אין מבשל ולענין שבת מישרא שרי הא בורכא הוא דהא דין זה מדברי תה״ד בסימן קפ״א והביא ראיה משבת מ׳ ב׳ אמבטי הרי מבשל הוא יע״ש. וסבור הייתי אני העני לומר המעיין במהרא״י שם סיים קדירה על האש ומתוך

רתיחותיו נזחל וסיים וז״ל הואיל וקילוח נוזל ונזחל מקילוח העומד על האש כו׳ משמע דאם עוד כח ״אש״ שולט אין מתקרר יע״ש היטב משמע הא סלקו (ממש) [מהאש] כה״ג אף שלא נפסק הקילוח ונזחל ע״ג מקום קר קודם שהגיע לכלי הוי תו כלי שני ומה אעשה שהרי הר״ב לא אומר כן בצ״ב ס״ז אין אומר ואין דברים מהא דעל אש אלא סתם וכתב וקלוח מקדירה רותחת ואף אם נדחוק בזה מ״מ המעיין בת״ח כלל נ״ו דין ו׳ וז״ל ואם קדירה על האש או שאר ״כלי ראשון״ ולא נפסק הקילוח הוה כעירוי כמ״ש מהרא״י יע״ש הרי בביאור אף כ״ר שהוסר מאש דינא הכי ועמ״ש בצ״ב בט״ז אות כ״ו גם מ״ש הת״ח ס׳ נגד מה שנגע בקדירה הא הכל מחובר וצ״ל מ״מ משערין באומד יפה וצ״ע גם בזה:

ומה אעשה שעוונותי גרמו שלא זכיתי להבין כל זה כי לפ״ד תרומת הדשן דמדמה זה לערוי א״כ איך יפרנסו מעשה זו כת הפוסקים דאין עירוי מבשל כלל ובהכרח דיש חילוק בין עומד על האש ואפשר כה״ג אף הכל אוסר לא כדי קליפה עמ״ש בדיני עירוי בס״ח וצ״ב בשם הר״ן דאצל האש לא שייך תתאה יע״ש. גם מהמשנה האלפס והקדירה שהעבירן מרותחין [שבת] דף מ״ב ב׳ תוס׳ בד״ה אבל שכתבו דהדיוקים סתרי ליכא למידק מינה והא דיוקא דסיפא בהכרח לאו דווקא דאל״כ לאשמועינן רבותא דמערה מצידיהן. ואפשר היה לומר דהתנא מדבר בקצוות לתוכן וודאי אסור ולכלי שני וודאי שרי וע״י עירוי עליהן אסור ובצידיהן שרי (ואפשר בנפסק הקילוח שרי) והדברים ארוכים ואין להאריך:

סוף דבר הכל נשמע לענין דינא כל זמן שלא נפסק הקילוח אף שאין על האש ונח על כלי שני אפ״ה חשוב כעירוי לחומרא וה״ה בשבת לא יערה בצידיהן כ״ז שלא נפסק העמוד וכדאמרן ואם נזחל כלי ראשון על כירה צוננת שלא בהפסק ומשם ניתז צרורות על כלי קר נמי הוי עירה ואוסר כ״ק כדין חם לתוך צונן ונהי שאין מבשל כה״ג מפליט ומבליע מיהא. ונקוט האי כללא בידך כ״ז שלא נפסק הקילוח הוי עירוי ולא נתקרר אף שנח על גבי כלי קר אלא אם כן נפסק ונח על גבי כלי קר ומשם לכלי אחר אין אוסר:

שו"ת אגרות משה יורה דעה חלק א סימן מב

אך שיקשה מהא דבשומן דבוק בהכלים נמי מתיר ואף בכ"ח, הא סגי לאסור בהבלעה לבד שבזה כיון שמקושר עם הכ"ר מבליע. וצריך לומר דבר חדש דהרמ"א סובר דמה שמפליט ומבליע כאחת הוא תלוי בבשול, הוא משום שהם שתי עשיות שרק בשול יכול לעשות זה. ולכן סובר דאף לחמם השומן הצונן ולהבליעו נמי הם שני מעשים שרק בשול יכול לעשות זה, והוי גם להשומן הדבוק בהם דין מפליט ומבליע, שבכלי שני אף שלא נפסק הקלוח שמקושר עם הכ"ר אינו יכול לעשות. ול"ד לקלוח מקדירה רותחת שבסימן צ"ב דהתם איירי שהקלוח היה מחלב ורוטב של בשר ממש שהלך מקדירה הרותחת שלא היה צריך לעשות אלא מעשה הבלעה לבד, שבלא נפסק הקלוח מבליע אף שאינו מבשל, אבל הכא שהקלוח הוא ממים שאינן של חלב ושל בשר שהוא צריך לחמם את השומן הצונן ולהבליעו שהם שני מעשים אינו יכול כיון שאינו מבשל. וזה צריך לומר לתירוץ החו"ד. וכן גם להש"ך שתירץ להרמ"א בסק"כ דאינו מפליט ומבליע כאחת בכלי שהוא קשה, דג"כ קשה הא הרמ"א מתיר גם בשומן דבוק שא"צ להפליטו, אלא הוא מטעם דגם לחמם השומן הוא עוד עשיה כמו הפלטה כדכתבתי. וכן כשכתב הש"ך אח"כ בשם מהרש"ל שאוסר ביש שם שיורי מאכל דוקא, דבנקיים הא מתיר מטעם נ"ט בר נ"ט, כתב נמי לפי שהעירוי מפליט ומבליע כדי קליפה שלכאורה קשה דהא אין כאן הפלטה, אלמא כדבארתי דאף הבעיין כיון שצריך הקלוח לחממו נחשב כמפליט ואוסר רק משום שעירוי עושה תרוייהו כאחת מפליט ומבליע ולא היה אוסר אם לא היה עושה רק הבלעה לבד.

מגן אברהם סימן שיח ס"ק לג

מלאה מים חמין - ואפי' בחמי טבריא אסור ליתן צוננין באמבטי שהומשכה מן המעיין לתוכה אלא צריך ליטול מהאמבטי בכ"ש ואחר כך יתן המים לתוכה [גמרא]:

ט"ז אורח חיים סימן שיח ס"ק יב

אפי' לאחר שהעבירוהו כו'. - בב"י כתב וז"ל כתב בהגמ"ר שקרוב הדבר דלא מקרי כ"ר אלא עם סילוקו מן האש מיד אבל אם הניחו לעמוד להפיג רתיחתו ה"ל כ"ש ולי משמע ממ"ש בפ' כירה גבי נתינת קיתון של מים כנגד המדורה שכל זמן שהיס"ב חשיב כ"ר ואע"פ שגם בכ"ש היס"ב אין לו דין כ"ר דשאני כ"ר שנתחמם באור עצמו וכמ"ש התוס' כו' עכ"ל ואיני יודע מהיכן למד ב"י מגמרא שהביא לענין זה דשם לא מיירי כלל מהעבירוהו מן האש אלא מענין דין יד סולדת אבל תמהתי מאד דהא משנה מפורשת היא בפרק כירה האילפס והקדירה שהעבירן (פרש"י מן האור) מרותחין לא יתן לתוכן תבלין פירש"י מרותחין בין השמשות לא יתן לתוכן תבלין משתחשך דכ"ר כ"ז שהוא רותח מבשל עכ"ל הרי מבואר דלא כהגמ"ר:

15

חוו"ד סי' צב ס"ק כז

אבל חלק מהותך. עיין ט"ז ס"ק ל' שהאריך בדין אם הוציא הכף עם מאכל מכלי ראשון, שעדיין שם כלי ראשון עליו. וגם מתיר להגעיל מכלי שהוציאו עם מים מכלי ראשון, ע"ש. ולבבי לא כן ידמה, דמה שמביא ראיה מהא דכף שהוציאו עם זבוב שנאסר המאכל, אין בו שום ראיה, דודאי כל זמן שלא נתקרר מהתתאה לשמואל או מעילאה לרב, עדיין שם כלי ראשון עליו ויש בו כח להפליט ולהבליע, ומשום הכי נאסר גבי זבוב. בהא מודינא, שכל שהוציאו עם מאכל מכלי ראשון ולא העמידו על דבר צונן, שלא נתקרר עדיין שום דבר, שבודאי יש כח בו להפליט ולהבליע. אבל לענין שיהיה יכול להגעיל עם כלי כזה, נראה דאינו רשאי להגעיל, דלענין הגעלה בעינן שיהיה דוקא ע"י עירוי שלא נפסק הקילוח מכלי ראשון שדפנותיו הוחמו באור, כמו שכתבו התוס' בשבת דף מ' ע"ש, שיש בו כח לבשל,וכלי זה עם המים שבתוכו אין לו רק דין עירוי שנפסק הקילוח, דהכלי זה שנתבשל בכלי ראשון עם המים שבתוכו דינו כשאר בשר ועצמות שנתבשל בכלי ראשון שכשוציאם ונתנם על דבר צונן יש להם דין עירוי שנפסק הקילוח להרמ"א, דמה הפרש יש בין כלי או עצם שנתבשל בכלי ראשון. ואף להרש"ל שהביאו הט"ז בסימן צ"ד והש"ך בסימן ק"ה ס"ק ח' דדבר גוש

יש לו דין כלי ראשון כיון שאין לו דפנות המקררות, מכל מקום מודה הוא דאינו מבשל כדמוכח מאיסור והיתר הארוך כלל ל״ו וכן כתב המנחת יעקב בתורת חטאת כלל ס״א מאחר שאין לו דפנות המחממות. וא״כ הכא נמי, נהי דמבליע ומפליט, מכל מקום ודאי דאין מבשל. ומה שכתב הט״ז דהכא נמי יש לו דפנות המחממות שהרי הוחמו בבישול, אינו מובן כלל, דהא בהדיא כתבו התוס׳ שם בטעמא דכלי ראשון משום שדפנותיו הוחמו באור וכו׳, וזה ודאי דדופן שהוחם באור דהוי תולדות האור דאינו מתקרר לא מתתאה לשמואל ולא מעילאה לרב, ולעולם מבשל כל זמן שהיד סולדת בו, דהא גלגל ביצה על גבי דבר שהוחם באור חייב אפילו לרב, כדמוכח בשבת שם. מה שאין כן דבר שהוחם בבישול תוך כלי ראשון ודאי דמתקרר מתתאה, אפילו כלי שנתבשל מכלי ראשון. תדע, דהא כלי אינו מקבל חום כל כך בכלי ראשון כשאר דברים המתבשלים, דהא כלי כשמוציאו ריקן מהבישול שוב אינו מבליע ומפליט כלל, כמו שכתב הט״ז כאן, ושאר דברים גושים אפילו מוציאם ריקן יש להם דין כלי ראשון לרש״ל, וקודם שהונחו על צונן לכולי עלמא מבליעין ומפליטין. וקל וחומר הדברים, שאם שאר דבר גוש המתבשל אינו מבשל כשוציאו מכלי ראשון, כל שכן כלי ודאי דלא עדיף מהמים שבתוכו שעל ידן מחזיק הכלי חום ויש להמים והכלי כשנופלין על איזה דבר צונן דין עירוי שנפסק הקילוח, כיון שנפסק הקילוח מהכלי ראשון שדפנותיו הוחמו באור. גם מה שהביא ראיה מהא דשבת דאסור ליתן השמן לתוך כלי שנטל מים מתוך הכלי ראשון, נראה דלאו ראיה היא, דהנה יש להבין בדברי התוספות שבת דף מ ד״ה שמע מינה, שהקשו מאי שנא כלי ראשון מכלי שני, ותירצו דכלי ראשון מתוך שדפנותיו הוחמו באור, מה שאין כן כלי שני שיש לו דפנות המקררות וכו׳. ולכאורה הדיוקים שבתוספות סתרי אהדדי, דגבי כלי ראשון כתבו דוקא משום שיש לו דפנות שהוחמו באור מבשל, משמע דדבר שאין לו דפנות המחממות אף שאין לו ג״כ דפנות המקררות אינו מבשל, וכן כתב המנחת יעקב בתורת חטאת דדבר גוש אינו מבשל מטעם שאין לו דפנות המחממות אף שג״כ אין לו דפנות המקררות, וגבי כלי שני כתבו הטעם דאינו מבשל משום שיש לו דפנות המקררות, משמע כל שאין לו דפנות המקררות מבשל. והנראה בכוונתם דהנה על כרחך לא קאי קושייתם לשמואל דאמר תתאה גבר, דלשמואל החילוק מבואר, דכלי שני כבר נתקרר מהתתאה. רק קושייתם

הוא אליבא דרב, ואליבא דרב הקושיא בתרי אנפי, על כלי ראשון קשה דלמה מבשל הניתן לתוכו, הא העליון הניתן לתוכו הוא צונן, ולרב עילאה גבר. ועל כלי שני קשה, למה אינו מבשל כשמקלח מכלי שני על צונן כיון דלא נתקרר לרב, לא כשניתן מעיקרא לתוך כלי שני, ולא עכשיו כשמקלח על צונן מן הכלי שני, כיון דלרב עילאה גבר. ולזה הוצרכו התוספות לשני הטעמים, בכלי ראשון נתנו טעם דמבשל אפילו עילאה הצונן לרב, משום שיש לו דפנות המחממות אינו מתקרר לא מהעילאה לרב, ולא מהתתאה לשמואל כשהעמיד כלי ראשון על צונן כמו שכתבתי בסימן צ״א ע״ש. ובכלי שני כתבו הטעם דאינו מבשל אף להתתאה לרב, משום שיש לו דפנות המקררות. ודבר שיש בו חילוק בין כשהעליון צונן או התחתון צונן, הוא על כרחך בדבר שאין לו לא דפנות המחממות ולא המקררות, כגון עירוי שנפסק הקילוח על צונן דמבשל לרב, או דבר גוש וכיוצא בו, דאז יש חילוק לרב דכשהעילאה רותח מבשל, וכשהעילאה צונן אינו מבשל. ואם כן הכי נמי לדידן דקיימא לן כשמואל דתתאה גבר, יש לומר בדבר שאין לו לא דפנות המחממות ולא המקררות, כגון כלי שהוציאו עם מים כשהוא התתאה, ודבר אחר ניתן לתוכו, מבשל, כיון דלא נתקרר בשום פעם. מה שאין כן כשמערה ממנו על צונן, שהתחתון צונן, אינו מבשל, כדין שאר עירוי שנפסק הקילוח. והא דעירוי שלא נפסק הקילוח מבשל כדי קליפה, הוא מטעם שהקילוח מקושר בדפנות שהוחמו באור, כמו שכתבו הפוסקים. אבל כשאין לו שום קישור עם דופן שהוחם באור, ודאי דאינו מבשל כלל. ולפי זה היה אפשר לומר דדבר גוש מבשל לעילאה לשמואל, רק לתתאה אינו מבשל כיון שאין לו לא דפנות המחממות ולא המקררות כמו לרב. וכיון שהסכימו הפוסקים דאפילו לעילאה אינו מבשל אלמא דסבירא להו דהעיקר בטעם דמבשל תלוי דוקא ביש לו דפנות המחממות, א״כ ודאי דהך גוונא דט״ז ג״כ אינו מבשל על כל פנים, ואסור להגעיל ממנו. ואפילו דינו של מהרי״ל תמוה לי, שכתב דאם משהה אותו בתוך כלי ראשון דמותר להגעיל ממנו, דנראה לי דגם זה אינו מבשל בנפל על תחתון צונן דהוי כנפסק הקילוח, כיון שאינו מקושר בדופן שהוחם באור, כמו שאר דבר המתבשל בכלי ראשון שנפסק הקילוח שמתקרר מהתתאה. ואם העמיד כלי זו על קרקע או שאר דבר צונן ונפל דבר לתוכו, תליא בפלוגתא דדבר גוש אי מבשל, דהמים כיון שהוא בתוך כלי דמיא לדבר גוש הנ״ל.

שולחן ערוך יורה דעה סימן קז סעיף ב

זבוב, וכיוצא בו מדברים המאוסים שנפשו של אדם קצה בהם, שנמצא בתבשיל, זורקן, והתבשיל מותר, שאין פליטת דברים אלו הפגומים אוסרת. הגה: וכן המנהג פשוט. אף על גב דיש מחמירין, דברי המקילין עיקר. (ב"י שפסק כרשב"א ורוקח וטור סי' ק"ד). ואין לשנות המנהג. ואם לקח עם הכף דג טמא מן הקדרה, או שאר דבר שאינו פוגם, אסור להחזיר הכף לקדרה. ואם החזיר, צריך ס' מן הקדרה נגד האיסור,ולא נגד כל הכף. (ד"ע דלא אמרינן גבי כלי חתיכה נעשית נבלה). אבל אם היה מעט מן התבשיל עם האיסור בכף והוחזר לקדירה, צריך ס' גם נגד מעט התבשיל, דהרי נעשה נבילה בכף (ארוך כלל כ"ז).

ש"ך יורה דעה סימן קז ס"ק ז

דהרי נ"נ בכף - דאנו מחזיקין הכף ההיא שעתא כמו הקדרה עצמה מאחר שהוציאה עתה מהקדרה רותחת וחשיב כלי ראשון לחומרא כ"כ באו"ה כלל כ"ז ד"ב ולענין אי זבוב אוסר בטעמו הסכים הרב להמחבר וסייעתו אבל תימה דהרי רבו הפוסקי' ראשוני' ואחרוני' [לאיסור] וכ"כ האו"ה כלל כ"ז דכן נוהגים וכ"כ מהר"ם פדוואה דכן נוהגין וכ"כ מהרש"ל באו"ש ובספרו פרק ג"ה סי' מ"ט מקבלת מהר"ש דכן נוהגין מיהו במקום הפסד מרובה או שעת הדחק וכה"ג נראה דעת מהר"ם פדוואה בתשובה להתיר וכ"פ הב"ח מיהו בחלא ושיכרא לכ"ע אסור וכמו שנתבאר בס"ס ק"ד:

מגן אברהם סימן שיח ס"ק מה

כנגד המדור' - לאו דוקא דה"ה אם הוא רותח שיס"ב כמ"ש ס"ה וכ"ט וכ"מ מל' רש"י וכ"כ הפוסקים בי"ד דדבר שהוא גוש אפי' בכ"ש מבשל וכ"ש צלי ונ"ל דבשומן מותר לטוחו דאין בו משום בישול כמ"ש סי"ו.

משנה ברורה סימן שיח ס"ק קיח

כנגד המדורה - לאו דוקא דה"ה במעביר את השפוד שתחוב עליו הצלי מהאש כ"ז שהוא רותח שהיס"ב אסור לטוח עליו ואפילו אם הניח אח"כ על הקערה שהוא כ"ש ג"כ אסור דהא כמה פוסקים סוברים דדבר גוש כ"ז שהיס"ב אפילו בכ"ש מבשל ומ"מ בדיעבד אין לאסור כשהוא מונח בכלי

שני דסמכינן על הפוסקים דכלי שני אינו מבשל בכל גווני וכ"ז בשום ושמן דהוא דבר חי שלא נתבשל אבל בשומן שנקפא מותר לטוח אפילו כנגד המדורה דאין בו שוב משום בישול כיון שכבר נתבשל וכמו שכתבנו למעלה בסט"ז דדבר יבש שכבר נתבשל אין בו שוב משום בישול.

משנה ברורה סימן שיח ס"ק פז

(פז) בכלי שני - כ"ש מיקרי כשעירו מן כלי ראשון שהרתיחו החמין בתוכו לתוך כלי זה ומותר אפי' אם היד סולדת בו אבל אם שואב בכלי ריקן מתוך כלי ראשון י"א דדינו ככלי ראשון ובפרט אם משהה הכלי ריקן בתוכו עד שמעלה רתיחה ודאי מקרי כ"ר [אחרונים]:

תוספות מסכת עבודה זרה דף לג עמוד ב

וענין הגעלה התיר ר"ת להגעיל חבית לטהר מיין נסך אם פתח אחד משוליה וזורק רותחין לתוכה ומהפך המים על שוליה אילך ואילך דאע"ג דבשאר איסורין לא סלקא הגעלה בהכי דאפילו עירוי מכלי ראשון ליכא הכא מ"מ איכא למימר ביין נסך דתשמישו בצונן שרי ומביא ראיה מדקא"ר יוסי לקמן בפ"ב (עה.) חולטן במי זיתים ובשאר איסורין לא מהניא חליטת מי זיתים ור"י אומר כי מצוה מן המובחר להגעיל כל נסר לבד ולזרוק עליה מאותו כלי עצמו שהוא רותח על האור ודי בכך אע"פ שפסקה הרתיחה כשמעבירה מן האור ויש משימין קערה בתוך מחבת על האש עד שהרתיחות עולות תוך הקערה ומאותה קערה מגעילין ובזה מסופק ר"י אם זה מועיל ככלי ראשון אם לאו ותלה הדבר להחמיר ואסר בהן להגעיל דחשיב ככלי שני ולענין מליגת תרנגולת נמי אסר דחשיב ליה ככלי ראשון.

ט"ז יורה דעה סימן צב ס"ק ל

כתוב במהרי"ל הלכות פסח וז"ל והמגעיל על ידי עירוי ששופך הרותחין על הכלי להגעילו יזהר שישפוך המים הרותחין דוקא מן הכלי שבשלו בו והוא הנקרא כלי ראשון ואל ישאוב מן הכלי שבו הרותחין בכלי אחר ולערות ממנו להגעיל משום דכלי ששואב עמו הוא כלי שני ונתבטל בו בישול הרותחין טרם שמגעילן אכן אם שוהה את הכלי ששואב עמו תוך הכלי שמבשלין בו הרותחין ובעוד הוא שם מעלין המים רתיחות שפיר

מתקרי גם הוא כלי ראשון עכ"ל. מדברים אלו משמע שאם שואב מכלי ראשון והוציא רותחים מקרי אח"כ כלי שני ויש בו דין כ"ש ותמהתי מאד על זה דהא בעודו בכלי ראשון הכלי הזה שתוחב בו גם הוא כלי ראשון דהא מגעילין בכלי ראשון כלים ומפליט מהם הבלוע וכן קי"ל בתוחב כף איסור לקדירה דאוסר תכף אפילו אם מוציאו תכף ממנו והיאך נאמר כאן שכשמוציא הכלי ששואב מכלי ראשון נעשה כלי שני כיון שבא עליו שם כלי ראשון מי נותן לו אח"כ שם אחר והלא כלי ראשון שמו עליו אף אם נעקר מאש ה"ה נמי זה שנעקר מהרותחין שתוך כלי ראשון. ותו דאם שהה שם קצת מודה מהרי"ל דנשאר עליו שם כלי ראשון ואם כן מאן מפיס כמה תהא השהייה וכמ"ש הטור א"ח סי' תנ"ב וז"ל כתב רי"ף משהי למאני בגו יורה עד דפלטו וכתב אבי עזרי מי יודע לשער כו' ה"נ נימא כך מי יודע לשער שיעור השהייה בזה. ועוד ראיה מפ' כירה דאמר ר' (שמואל) [יצחק] בר אבדימי נכנסתי אחר רבי למרחץ בשבת כו' וא"ל טול בכלי שני כדי שיתמעט החום. ואין לטעות ולומר דהכי קאמר שבכלי שני ישאוב מן האמבטי שהוא כלי ראשון ונמצא למד שבכלי ששואב הוא כלי שני זה אינו דאם כן היה לו לומר סתם טול בכלי ותן ותו דאי תפרש דמה שאמר בכלי שני קאי על טול דהיינו שבשעת נטילה יהיה כ"ש הא ודאי אין שייך לומר כן דבשעת נטילה מן הרותחין הוי כלי ראשון שהרי בתוכה הוא וג"כ א"ל שיהיה כלי שני אחר שיצא מן המים דהא טול בכ"ש קאמר שמע מיניה שבשעת נטילה אמר לו ולא על ההוצאה שאחריה ותו דכשהוציאה מי שם עליו שם כלי שני דאטו כל כלי ראשון אחר שיתקרר יהיה עליו שם כלי שני. ותו דהתוספות כתבו התם דעיקר החילוק שבין כלי א' לכלי שני הוא דכלי שני מתקרר מחמת שאין דופנותיה חמין ע"כ הולך ומתקרר וזה ודאי דופנותיה רותחין שהרי הוחמו ברותחין דכלי ראשון אלא דבר פשוט דה"ק רבי טול מן המים באיזה דבר ותנהו לכלי שני דהיינו שיערה אותו לכלי שני ככל כלי שני שבתלמוד ותדע דאם היה כאן רבותא בהאי כלי ראשון שנעשה אח"כ שני היה לו שם לומר חידוש זה במקום דילפינן מינה כלי שני אינו מבשל טפי היה לו לומר דאפילו כלי ראשון נעשה כלי שני ואינו מבשל גם הטור א"ח סימן ש"ח כשהעתיק דין זה של טול בכלי שני כו' לא כתב אלא אם היה חמין בכ"ש יוכל ליתן לתוכו כו' ולא כתב שישאב מכלי ראשון ואפ"ה יתן לתוכו אלא פשוט שזהו אינו

וראיה מפורשת עוד ממ״ש באגודה הביאו באו״ה כלל (ס) [כ״ז] וז״ל זבוב הנמצא בקערה מותר דהוי ספק ספיקא שמא בכלי שני נפלה ואת״ל בכלי ראשון שמא כשהוציאו הזבוב והיינו בכף היה ס׳ בכף עכ״ל וכן לענין הוצאת ביצה טמאה בכף וכ״כ בש״ד ובטור לענין הוצאת זבוב בכף סי׳ ק״ז הרי שהצריך ס׳ במרק שבכף נגד הזבוב והיינו דחשביה לכלי ראשון אע״פ שהוציאו מן הקדרה דכל זמן שהיה בקדירה אין איסור מחמת זבוב דהיה שם ס׳ רק אחר שהוציאוהו בכף אוסרו ועל זה אמר שמא היה ס׳ בכף שמע מיניה דעדיין שם ראשון על הכף אע״פ שהוציאוהו וכן מוכח מפסק רמ״א בסי׳ ק״ז שכתב אבל אם היה מעט מהתבשיל עם האיסור בכף והוחזר לקדירה צריך ס׳ גם נגד מעט התבשיל דהוא נעשה נבילה בכף שמע מיניה דהכף הוא כלי ראשון במה ששואב מן הקדירה ואוסר מרק שבתוכו עד ס׳: ושוב ראיתי בת״ה סי׳ קפ״ג לענין שבלוע בתוך הכף יהיה נעשה נבילה כתב וז״ל י״ל דלאחר שהוציאו הכף מן הרותחין כל הבלוע בתוכה חשיב כמו כלי שני ולא פלט ולא בלע וכ״ש לטעמא דאין איסור בלוע אוסר היתר בלוע עכ״ל. נראה דלק״מ מזה על מה שכתבתי דהתם מוציא כף ריקן מהקדירה ואין שם אלא מה שבלוע בו בזה אמרינן ודאי דאין בכלי ריקן חום כ״כ שיפליט ויבליע במה שבתוכו בלוע ואפילו בכלי ראשון ממש שהוסר מן האור והורק מה שבתוכו נראה לומר כן מה שאין כן באם יש עדיין בתוכו הרוטב או התבשיל הרותח ודאי הוה על הכף שם כלי ראשון ממש כמו על הקדירה דאל״כ ודאי אין סברא לומר דהת״ה יחלוק מסברא בעלמא על הש״ד וטור ואגוד׳ שזכרתי אלא ודאי כמו שכתבתי. ושוב ראיתי בתוס׳ פרק א״מ דף ל״ג ד״ה קינסא וז״ל ור״י היה אומר כי מצוה מן המובחר להגעיל כל נסר לבד ולזרוק עליה מאותו כלי עצמו שהוא רותח על האור ודי בכך אע״פ שפסקה הרתיחה כשמעבירה מן האור ויש משימין קערה בתוך מחבת על האש עד שהרתיחה עולה תוך הקערה ומאותה קערה מגעילין ובזה מסופק ר״י אם זה מועיל ככלי ראשון אם לאו ותלה הדבר להחמיר ואסר להגעיל בהן דחשיב ככלי שני ולענין מליגת תרנגולת נמי אסור דחשיב ליה ככלי ראשון עכ״ל. הרי לפנינו דהתוס׳ נסתפקו בזה והעלו לחומרא אלא דהרא״ש שם כתב בשם ר״י דהוה ככלי ראשון כיון שהוציאו מן היורה מרותח וכ״כ הטור בי״ד סי׳ קל״ה בשם ר״י וא״כ צ״ל דגירסא אחרת היתה להם בתוס׳ ומדברי

רמ״א על פי הגהת מיימוני בא״ח סי׳ תנ״א משמע שפסק לחומרא דלא הוי ככלי ראשון דהא כתב שם ויערה עליהן רותחין מכלי ראשון כו׳ ע״כ נראה להחמיר כדברי התוספות:

חזון איש אורח חיים קכב:ג

סדר כלי הסעודה, ששופכין מן הקדירה לתוך קערה גדולה, ושואבין מן הקערה בכף ונותנים לצלוחית לכל אחד ואחד. ופעמים שואבין מן הקדירה ונותנים לתוך הצלוחית, ואם שואבין מתוך הקדירה בשעה שהוא על האש, כף עצמה נעשית כלי ראשון. והצלוחית נאסרת כדי קליפה. ואם שואבין מן הקדירה לאחר שהעבירה מעל האש, נראה מדברי הראשונים שהביא הט״ז שם שמה שבכף הוי דין כלי שני, ובדין כלי שני כבר הכריע מרן יו״ד סי׳ ק״ה ס״ב להתיר בדיעבד, וכש״כ אם מערין מקדירה לקערה ושואבין מקערה להצלוחית דהו״ל עירוי מכלי שלישי.

שולחן ערוך אורח חיים סימן שיח סעיף יח

האלפס והקדירה שהעבירן מרותחין מעל גבי האור, אם לא נתבשל כ״צ אין מוציאין בכף מהם שנמצא מגיס ואיכא משום מבשל ואם נתבשל כל צרכו מותר אבל צמר ליורה אע״פ שקלט העין אסור להגיס בו (פי׳ לנענע אותו בכף). הגה: ולכתחלה יש ליזהר אף בקדירה בכל ענין. (פסקי מהרי״ו).

משנה ברורה סימן שיח ס״ק קיג

(קיג) שהעבירן מרותחין - נקט שהעבירן לרבותא דאפי׳ בזה אסור כשלא נתבשל כל צרכו ובנתבשל כל צרכו אפי׳ עומד ע״ג האור מותר להוציא בכף כן משמע בב״י אבל בא״ר מסיק דיש לאסור בזה:

Section II

16

תלמוד בבלי מסכת שבת דף לו עמוד ב

כירה שהסיקוה בקש ובגבבא - נותנים עליה תבשיל. בגפת ובעצים - לא יתן עד שיגרוף, או עד שיתן את האפר. בית שמאי אומרים, חמין אבל לא

תבשיל ובית הלל אומרים, חמין ותבשיל. בית שמאי אומרים, נוטלין אבל לא מחזירין ובית הלל אומרים, אף מחזירין.

איבעיא להו: האי לא יתן - לא יחזיר הוא, אבל לשהות - משהין אף על פי שאינו גרוף ואינו קטום, ומני - חנניה היא. דתניא, חנניה אומר: כל שהוא כמאכל בן דרוסאי - מותר לשהותו על גבי כירה, אף על פי שאינו גרוף ואינו קטום; או דילמא: לשהות תנן, ואי גרוף וקטום - אין, אי לא - לא, וכל שכן להחזיר.

ר"ן על הרי"ף מסכת שבת דף טו עמוד ב

עד שיגרוף. הגחלים משום דמוסיף הבל וטעמא פרישית בפרקין דלעיל [דף לד ב] שמא יחתה בגחלים:

או עד שיתן את האפר. על גבי גחלים לכסותן ולצננן כך פירש רש"י ז"ל לפי שהוא מפרש זה הפרק (אף) בהטמנה דכל שגרוף וקטום ס"ל שאינו מוסיף הבל וכן כתב בהרבה מקומות בהלכה וכתב הר"ז הלוי ז"ל שהשיאו לרש"י ז"ל לפרש כן מפני שראה פרק כירה בין שתי הטמנות סוף במה מדליקין ותחלת במה טומנין ולא נהירא דהיאך אפשר שכירה קטומה אינה מוספת הבל והרי הוא עצמו ז"ל פירש לעיל בסוף פרק במה מדליקין [דף לד ב] מפני מה אמרו אין טומנין בדבר המוסיף הבל מבעוד יום גזירה שמא יטמין ברמץ ורמץ (היינו) אפר המעורב בגחלים אלמא אע"פ שנתן האפר מוסיף הבל הוא וכן הוא ודאי שהרמץ מחמם את הצונן וכל שמחמם את הצונן מוסיף הבל הוא וכיון שכן היאך אפשר דכי נתן את האפר דהויא נתינה כל דהו כמו שנפרש בסמוך בסייעתא דשמיא לא יהא מוסיף הבל ותו דאמרינן בגמרא [דף לז א] דגחלים עוממות הרי הן ככירה קטומה ובודאי דגחלים עוממות מוסיפין הבל טפי מרמץ אלא ודאי עיקרן של דברים כדברי רבינו האי גאון ורבינו אפרים גאון ז"ל שפי' דהכא לא איירי בהטמנה כלל אלא כגון שהקדרה יושבת על כסא של ברזל וכיוצא בו או שהיא תלויה באבנים שאין שולי הקדרה נוגעין בגחלים ומשום הכי כל שגרוף וקטום דאיכא היכרא שמסלק דעתו מלחתות בגחלים שרי:

מרכבת המשנה הלכות שבת פרק ט הלכה ג

ומ"ש או דבר שאינו צריך בישול כלל בעכו"ם דף לח כל שהוא נאכל

כמות שהוא חי אין בו משום בשולי עכו"ם וה"ה לענין שבת ואע"ג דלענין נתבשל כמב"ד לא מדמה רבנו בישול שבת לבישולי עכו"ם ממש מ"מ מה דחזי חי לגמרי מודים רבנן לחנניא

חידושי הרשב"א מסכת שבת דף לח עמוד א

ולענין פסק הלכה הרב אלפסי ז"ל פסק כמאן דאמר לשהות תנן דאפילו לשהות אי גרוף וקטום אין אי לא לא וכל שכן להחזיר, והלכך כירה שאינה גרופה וקטומה אסור להשהות עליה תבשיל שלא בישל כל צרכו וחמין שלא הוחמו כל צרכן ואפילו תבשיל מצטמק ורע לו, אבל תבשיל שבישל כל צרכו וחמין שהוחמו כל צרכן משהין ואע"פ שאינה גרופה ואינה קטומה, ודוקא מצטמק ורע לו אבל מצטמק ויפה לו אסור עד שיגרוף או עד שיתן את האפר, וראיותיו שהביא בהלכות אין הכרח באחת מהן, דכל אותן בעיות שנעשו במהו לסמוך שנסמך עליהן הרב ז"ל אין בהם כדי הכרע, דאפילו למאן דאמר להחזיר תנן איכא למיבעיא נמי לענין סמיכה בחזרה וכמו שכתבנו לעיל במקומה (ל"ז א' ד"ה איבעיא), וההיא דלקמן (ל"ח ב') נמי דאביי דאמר אילימא על גבה ובמאי אי בשאינה גרופה על גבה מי שרי, לא מכרעא אי בשהייה ואי בחזרה, וכי תימא מכל מקום איכא לסיועה להא דרב אלפסי ז"ל מדאצטרכינן לדחוקי ולחסורי למתניתין אליבא דחנניה ולרבי יהודה אתיא מתניתין כפשטה, לא היא דאדרבה דוק מינה מדדחקינן לחסורי מתניתין כי היכי דתיקום כחנניה שמע מינה דכחנניה קיימא לן ומשום הכי מהדרינן לאוקומה לסתמא דמתניתין כוותיה, דאי לא לא טרחינן ולא משכנינן נפשין אדידיה לדחוקי מתניתין ולחסורה ולפרוקה.

חידושי הרשב"א מסכת שבת דף לט עמוד א

גמרא כל שבא בחמין מלפני השבת שורין אותו בחמין בשבת. פירוש שבא בחמין מלפני השבת ונתבשל כמאכל בן דרוסאי דשוב אין בו משום בישולי גוים והלכך שורין אותו אפילו בחמין בכלי ראשון, אבל אם לא נתבשל כמאכל בן דרוסאי והוי דבר שמתבשל בכלי ראשון כתבלין וכיוצא בזה אסור, וכדתנן בפרקין (מ"ב א') האילפס והקדירה שהעבירן מרותחין לא יתן לתוכן תבלין.

17

ספר הישר לר"ת סימן רלה

והא דאמרי' בכירה לא יחזיר עד שיגרוף אפילו מבעוד יום קאמר כי כיון שהוא נותנן עליה או בתוכה מגלה דעתו שצריכה חימום. לכך יש לחוש שמא יחתה ולכך צריך לעשות היכרה בגרופה וקטומה.

שער הציון סימן רנג ס"ק לז

ובספר הישר איתא דלכך בעינן גרופה משום דכשנוטלה מן האש פעמים שמצטננת קצת וחיישינן שמא יחתה בחזרתו.

בעל המאור מסכת שבת דף טו עמוד ב

שהסיקוה בקש ובגבבא וכו'. תחלת כל דבר אתה צריך לדעת שכל המשניות השנויות בענין הזה וכל השמועות האמורות עליהם בגמרא אין בהם שום הטמנה כלל ואין טעם מה שאנו אוסרים בענין הזה משום דקא מוסיף הבלא כמו שפי' רש"י ז"ל שאין הטעם הזה אמור אלא בדברים שאין טומנין בהם וכאן אין זה הטמנה וכל שאנו מחמירין ואוסרים בו בין בתנור בין בכירה בענין הזה איננו אלא משום גזירה שמא יחתה בגחלים.

מהר"ם דף לו ע"ב ד"ה רד"ה אבל לא תבשיל

וכן משמע בתוס' לקמן בדף לח ע"ב ד"ה פינה ממיחם למיחם דבחזרה נמי שייך טעם גזירת חיתוי.

תוספות מסכת שבת לו ע"ב ד"ה וב"ה אומרים אף מחזירין

ועוד אומר ר"י דמצינו למימר דבערב שבת נמי אסור להחזיר אפילו רותח משעה שאם היה קר לא היה יכול להרתיח מבע"י

ר"ן על הרי"ף מסכת שבת דף טו עמוד ב

בית שמאי אומרים נוטלין ולא מחזירין. דמיחזי כמבשל בשבת:

וב"ה אומרים אף מחזירין. הואיל וגרוף וקטום: ואמרי' בגמ' [ד' לח ב] לדברי האומר מחזירין מחזירין ואפי' בשבת ומדאמרינן אפי' בשבת

מכלל דעיקר פלוגתייהו בחול היא וכי תימא א״כ לב״ש למה לא מחזירין פי׳ בתוס׳ דכל שהוא סמוך לחשיכה כל כך שכשהתבשיל צונן אינו יכול להתחמם מבעוד יום לב״ש אסור וכל כי האי גוונא מיקרי חזרה וכי יהיב לה על גבי כירה מקמי הכי מקרי שהייה ואפשר ג״כ שאפי׳ היה התבשיל חם כל שאילו היה צונן לא היה שהות ביום כדי להתחמם אסור לב״ש משום גזירת הרואין וב״ה שרו והיינו דאמרינן בגמרא דאע״ג דעיקר פלוגתייהו בחול לדברי האומר מחזירין מחזירין ואפי׳ בשבת וכתבו בתוס׳ דמדב״ש אסרי כי האי גונא אפי׳ בגרופה נשמע לב״ה בשאינה גרופה כל שהוא סמוך לחשיכה כל כך אסור ולא נראה לי כן משום דב״ש לטעמייהו אזלי דבעו בכולהו מלאכות שאדם מתחיל מבעוד יום (הוא) אם יעשה מקצת מעשה שלהם קודם לחשיכה אבל לב״ה דמתירין בכולן עם השמש כדאיתא בפרקא קמא אפי׳ אין שהות ביום כדי להתחמם שרי. ומשום הכי אמרינן בגמרא לדברי האומר מחזירין מחזירין אפילו בשבת משום דלהחזיר סמוך לחשכה לא איצטריך להו לבית הלל דהא בכל מלאכות כולן הן מתירין עם השמש אלא משום דחזרה דשבת גופיה הוא דאצטריכו לאפלוגי אבל אין הכי נמי דאפילו בשאינה גרופה מבעו״י שרי:

רא״ש מסכת שבת פרק ג סימן ב

ולישנא דמחזירין אף בשבת משמע הכי דכי היכי דפליגי בשבת פליגי בערב שבת הלכך נראה דבערב שבת נמי [אפילו] הוא רותח אסור להחזירו כל היכא דאם היה קר לא היה יכול להרתיחו מבעוד יום. ונ״ל הא דאסור מבעוד יום להחזיר לבית שמאי אף בגרופה וקטומה היינו מבעוד יום דומיא דמשחשיכה דכמו משחשיכה דהיינו אחר שנתבשלה נתנה בכירה להשהותה שם. כן נמי מבעוד יום דאסור להחזיר היינו אחר שנגמר בישולה ומניחה עומדת על הכירה עד לערב להחזיק חומה ואם נטלה אז מן הכירה אסור להחזירה אטו שבת. וכולה חדא גזירה היא דכיון דאינה מתבשלת עוד על הכירה הוי כתחלת שהייה ואי שרינן להחזיר מבעו״י אתי נמי להחזיר משחשיכה. אבל כל זמן שלא נתבשלה כל צרכה נוטל ומחזיר כל היום.

בית יוסף סימן רנג אות ב

ונראה לי דטעמא דכל זמן שלא נתבשלה כל צרכה מותר להחזיר אפילו

סמוך לחשיכה ולא גזרינן דילמא אתי להחזיר משחשיכה משום דאם היה מחזיר משחשיכה הוי מבשל בשבת ופשיטא דמזדהר בהכי אפילו אי שרית להחזיר מבעוד יום

ב"ח רנג אות ב ד"ה ואם אינה עד ודוק

ואם אינה וכו'. כתב הרא"ש בפרק כירה. וכתב ב"י ונראה לי דטעמא דכל זמן שלא נתבשלה כל צרכה מותר להחזיר אפילו סמוך לחשיכה ולא גזרינן דילמא אתי להחזיר משחשיכה משום דאם היה מחזיר משחשיכה הוי מבשל בשבת ופשיטא דמיזדהר בהכי אפילו אי שרית להחזיר מבעוד יום עכ"ל ותימה אדרבה טפי הוה לן למיגזר בלא נתבשל כל צרכה דלא ליתי לידי איסור דאורייתא כי היכא דגזרו וחששו לשמא יחתה דהוי נמי איסורא דאורייתא ועוד דאף בלא נתבשל כל צרכה אם נתבשל כמאכל בן דרוסאי ליכא משום מבשל להרא"ש כמ"ש בסמוך ואם כן איכא למיגזר לפי דעת ב"י. אבל לפע"ד נראה מדברי הרא"ש דהכי קאמר דבלא נתבשל כל צרכה עוסק הוא בבישולה מבעוד יום ורגיל ליטלה מן הכירה ולהחזירה כמה פעמים עד שתתבשל ובקדרה זו לא חששו חכמים לאסור חזרה מבעוד יום אטו חזרה בשבת דהחזרה בשבת מסתמא אינה אלא בקדרות שכבר הן מבושלות כל צרכן ונתנן בכירה להשהותן שם עד זמן האכילה ואם היו גוזרין זו שאינה מבושלת כל צרכה ומבעוד יום אטו שבת ה"ל גזירה לגזירה אבל קדירה שמבושלת כל צרכה ומבעוד יום הניחה עומדת על הכירה עד לערב להחזיק חומה דמיא להך קדרה שהיא כבר מונחת בכירה ונכנס השבת דאם אתה מחזיר זו שמבעוד יום דאינה מתבשלת עוד על הכירה והוי כתחלת שהייה אתא להחזיר גם זו בשבת דדמיא לה וכולה חדא גזירה היא ודו"ק.

18

תלמוד בבלי מסכת שבת דף לח עמוד ב

מחזירין - אפילו בשבת. ואף רבי אושעיא סבר: אף מחזירין - אפילו בשבת; דאמר רבי אושעיא: פעם אחת היינו עומדים לעילא מרבי חייא

רבה, והעלנו לו קומקמוס של חמין מדיוטא התחתונה לדיוטא העליונה, ומזגנו לו את הכוס והחזרנוהו למקומו, ולא אמר לנו דבר. אמר רבי זריקא אמר רבי אבא אמר רבי תדאי: לא שנו אלא שעודן בידו, אבל הניחן על גבי קרקע - אסור. אמר רב אמי: רבי תדאי דעבד - לגרמיה הוא דעבד, אלא הכי אמר רבי חייא אמר רבי יוחנן: אפילו הניחה על גבי קרקע - מותר. פליגי בה רב דימי ורב שמואל בר יהודה, ותרוייהו משמיה דרבי אלעזר אמרי. חד אמר: עודן בידו - מותר, על גבי קרקע - אסור. וחד אמר: הניחן על גבי קרקע - נמי מותר. אמר חזקיה משמיה דאביי: הא דאמרת עודן בידו מותר - לא אמרן אלא שדעתו להחזיר, אבל אין דעתו להחזיר - אסור. מכלל דעל גבי קרקע, אף על פי שדעתו להחזיר - אסור. איכא דאמרי, אמר חזקיה משמיה דאביי: הא דאמרת על גבי קרקע אסור - לא אמרן אלא שאין דעתו להחזיר, אבל דעתו להחזיר - מותר. מכלל שבעודן בידו, אף על פי שאין דעתו להחזיר - מותר. בעי רבי ירמיה: תלאן במקל מהו? הניחן על גבי מטה מהו? בעי רב אשי: פינן ממיחם למיחם מהו? - תיקו.

ר"ן על הרי"ף מסכת שבת דף יז עמוד ב

לא שנו אלא שעודן בידו אבל הניחם על גבי קרקע אסור. להחזירן דמחזי כמבשל לכתחלה איכא לישנא אחרינא בגמרא דשרי הניחן על גבי קרקע בשדעתו להחזיר ועודן בידו אפילו אין דעתו להחזיר והאי לישנא בגמרא בתרא הוא ואפילו הכי פסקי רבואתא כלישנא קמא לחומרא דאע"ג דכל ה"מ מדרבנן בעלמא נינהו דכיון שנתבשל כמאכל בן דרוסאי לית ביה משום מבשל דאורייתא החמירו ז"ל בדברים הללו מפני שהן קרובין לבא לידי איסור תורה:

תוספות מסכת שבת דף לח ע"ב ד"ה פינה ממיחם למיחם מהו

וא"ת דבפרק במה טומנין (לקמן דף נא.) תניא וכן היה רשב"ג אומר לא אסרו אלא באותו מיחם אבל פינה ממיחם למיחם מותר אלמא במיחם אחר שרי טפי והכי משמע איפכא ואור"ת דהכא גבי השהה ע"ג כירה כשהוא באותו מיחם שהוא חם לא אתי לחתויי אבל במיחם אחר שהוא קר אתי לחתויי

תוספות הרא"ש מסכת שבת דף לח ע"ב ד"ה פינה ממיחם למיחם מהו

תימה הרי הטמנה דמחמרינן בה טפי מבשהיה אפי' הכי אמרינן בפרק במה טומנין פינה ממיחם למיחם מותר, וי"ל דלא דמי דהא דאסרינן הטמנה משחשכה היינו משום גזירה שמא ירתיח ובפינן ממיחם למיחם לא שייך למיגזר דהשתא אוקורי מיקר ליה ארתוחי מירתח ליה, אבל הכא שמחזירו לכירה חמה מבעיא ליה אי הוה כמו מניחו על גבי קרקע ונסתלקה שהיה ראשונה והוי כמו שהיה חדשה ובשיל בשבת.

בעל המאור מסכת שבת דף טז עמוד ב

ודיני חזרת התבשיל מפורש בגמרא שמותר בעודן בידו ואם הניחם ע"ג קרקע אסור משום דנראה כמבשל לכתחלה בשבת

הגהות מרדכי מסכת שבת דף עט ע"ב

חזרה היינו שמניח את הקדרה ע"ג כירה סמוך לחשיכה שלא היה סיפק ביום כדי להרתיח אם היתה צוננת וזה ודאי אסור להניח או להחזיר ע"ג כירה שאינה גרופה וקטומה כל כך בסמוך לחשיכה שלא היה יכול להרתיח ביום או קודם ברכו שהוא זמן קבלת שבת אבל ע"ג גרוף וקטום מותר אע"פ שהכירה היא חמה מותר להניח שם לכתחלה סמוך לחשיכה והיכא דהיתה כבר על הכירה והסירה משם ותפס הקדירה בידו שלא הניחה על גבי קרקע שרי להחזירה אפלו בשבת כבית הלל דשרו להחזיר אפילו בשבת מיהו היא גופא צ"ע אם מותר להניח הקדרה לכתחלה ע"ג גרופה וקטומה סמוך לחשיכה דדילמא לא שרינן אפילו מבעוד יום אלא להחזיר אבל להניח לכתחלה לא. ולשון חזרה משמע הכי שכבר היתה שם ורוצה להחזירה ועוד מבעוד יום דומיא דשבת ובשבת אסור להניחה ע"ג מיחם לכתחלה

רא"ש מסכת שבת פרק ד סימן ב

יש מקומות שבמקום שמסיקין האור ובשלו הקדרות כל היום לעת ערב מסלקין את האש וגורפין הרמץ ונותנין הקדירה לצורך מחר ומכסין אותה באפר צונן. אבל זה ק"ק [על] מנהגם שגורפין ומסלקין את הקדירה ואין מדקדקים היכן מניחין אותה ולחד לישנא דרב חזקיה משמיה דאביי דייקינן

מינה לעיל פ׳ כירה (דף לח ב) דאם הניח על גבי קרקע אע״פ שדעתו להחזיר אסור ואפילו בע״ש נמי אסור להחזיר כדפרישית לעיל.

שולחן ערוך אורח חיים סימן רנג סעיף ב

הגה: י״א דכל שהוא סמוך לחשיכה, או סמוך לברכו שהוא קבלת שבת לדידן, (הגהות מרדכי), אם הוא סמוך כ״כ שאם נצטנן הקדירה אי אפשר להרתיחה מבעוד יום, דינו כמו בשבת עצמו. ויש מקילין בזה, והמנהג להקל, אך טוב להחמיר במקום שאין צורך כל כך. ודוקא ע״ג כירה ממש, אבל לסמוך, אפי׳ לאש, במקום שהיד סולדת בו, שרי אפילו סמוך לחשיכה (הגמ״ר והגמי״י).

ביאור הגר״א אורח חיים סימן רנג סעיף ב ד״ה דינו כמו בשבת עצמו

לאו דוקא אלא דאסור בשאינה גרופה וקטומה אבל בגרופה מותר בכ״ע ואין חילוק בין הניחו ע״ג קרקע או עודן בידו כמ״ש הרא״ש שם ואע״ג דבפ״ד לא כתב כן שם העתיק לשון התוס׳ וכדרכו אבל בעצמו ס״ל דמותר כנ״ל. ויש ראיה לדעת זו בירושלמי שם נטלו מבעוד יום מחזירו מבעוד יום משחשיכה מחזירו משחשיכה נטלו מבע״י וקדש עליו היום העמידו בארץ אסור כו׳ אבל בהנך מותר בכ״ע ולדעת הר״ן ל״ד מבע״י לחשיכה:

משנה ברורה סימן רנג ס״ק עב

אם הוא סמוך כ״כ וכו׳ - היינו אפילו הוא קודם שקיעת החמה איזה זמן דינו כמו בשבת. והיינו רק לענין דבעינן גרופה וקטומה כמו בשבת אבל לענין דעתו להחזיר ושלא יניחנו ע״ג קרקע לא בעינן בזה [תו״ש והגר״א בשם הרא״ש].

19

שולחן ערוך אורח חיים סימן רנג סעיף ה ברמ״א

וה״ה שאסור להניחו ע״ג כירה, אפי׳ גרופה וקטומה, דלא התירו אלא חזרה וכדרך שנתבאר. ויש מתירין ליתן לתוך תנור שאפו בו מבע״י, דמאחר שלא הטמינו בו רק אפו בו מבע״י לא נשאר בו רק הבל מעט ואין לחוש לבישול

(כל בו), ובלבד שלא נצטנן לגמרי. ויש מחמירין בזה. ואם החום כל כך בתנור שהיד סולדת בו, אסור ועיין לקמן סימן שי"ח. וכל הדברים שאסור לעשות מדברים אלו, אסור לומר לאינו יהודי לעשות.

משנה ברורה שם ס"ק צד

(צד) וכל הדברים וכו' - היינו [צד] אפילו דברים שאין בהם רק איסור דרבנן:

ביאור הלכה סימן רנג ד"ה להחם הקדרה

ואפילו דבר יבש שנתבשל מכבר ונצטנן לגמרי אף דאין בו משום חשש בשול עוד כמ"ש בסימן שי"ח סט"ו אפ"ה אסור לחממו בתנור אפילו ע"י א"י [דאף דתנורים שלנו הם ככירה הלא גם ע"ג כירה אסור בחזרה כשאינה גרופה ואפילו כשהוא חם אסור ולדעת המ"א בס"ק ל"ו גם בגרופה אסור כשנצטנן לגמרי דהו"ל כמושיב לכתחלה] ואפילו דיעבד אסור גם בזה כשהוא חם עדיין דכשיהיה צונן מתיר בזה הפמ"ג ובקל"ז ע"ש ובסקל"ח כתב דכיון דקי"ל דשבות לצורך שבת שרי לכתחלה ובדבר יבש אין בו רק שבות דחזרה אפשר דהמיקל בזה ע"י א"י אין גוערין בו ועיין לקמן בסימן שי"ח בסופו מה שכתב השע"ת בשם מהרי"ט להקל בדבר יבש שאין בו מרק ליתנו תוך התנור ע"י א"י אף לכתחלה ובסימן זה משמע מכמה פוסקים דאין סוברין כן ועיין במ"א סקל"ו ובתו"ש ומ"מ נראה דיש לסמוך עליו לצורך שבת להקל בזה וכנ"ל בשם הפמ"ג. ובברכי יוסף מצאתי בשם אחד מן האחרונים שמצדד אפילו בדבר שיש בו מרק להקל להחם ע"י א"י אם נצטנן אם אינו נותן ע"ג האש או הכירה ממש שסומך על הפוסקים שסוברים דאין בשול אחר בשול אפילו אם נצטנן וצ"ע אם יש לסמוך ע"ז דמסימן זה לא משמע כן אך אם הוא לצורך שבת ואין לו עצה אחרת אפשר דיש לסמוך על זה:

פרי מגדים אשל אברהם סימן רנג ס"ק לח

ואם. עיין מ"א. ובסימן שכ"ה סעיף י' שבות דשבות לצורך שבת יש מקילין, ואפשר הוא הדין כאן ביבש לגמרי שאין בו חשש בישול, כי אם איסור דרבנן, לצורך שבת המיקל לא גוערין בו. ואי"ה יבואר שם בט"ז אות יו"ד:

שולחן ערוך אורח חיים סימן שכה סעיף י

א״י שמילא מים לבהמתו מבור שהוא רשות היחיד, לרשות הרבים, מותר לישראל להשקות מהם בהמתו; והוא שאין הא״י מכירו, דליכא למיחש שמא ירבה בשבילו; ואם מילא לצורך בהמת ישראל, אסור בכל מיני תשמיש אפילו ישראל אחר; ואם מילא מבור רשות היחיד לכרמלית, מותר לאחר שלא מילא בשבילו. הגה: ויש מקילין ואומרים דאף אם הובא דרך רשות הרבים לצורך ישראל, מותר לאדם לשתות מהם הואיל ואפשר לילך שם ולשתות (טור בשם ר״ת); ויש מתירין אף לכתחלה (כל בו); וכן נהגו היתר לומר אף לכתחלה לא״י להביא שכר, או שאר דברים, דרך כרמלית או בלא עירוב, ואע״פ שיש להחמיר בדבר מ״מ אין למחות ביד המקילין לצורך שבת ובשעת הדחק, דהא יש להקל באמירה לא״י לצורך, כמו שנתבאר סי׳ ש״ז וכל שכן בכהאי גוונא.

משנה ברורה שם ס״ק סג

ובשעת הדחק - היינו או בשעת הדחק [כ״מ בד״מ]:

דרכי משה סימן שכה ס״ק ח

והכל בו (סי׳ לא לא א) כתב שנוהגים להקל על פי רבינו תם ועכשיו נהגו להקל לומר לגוי ולתינוק להביא ולהוליך דרך רשות הרבים לפי שאין לנו רשות הרבים גמורה על כן נהגו להקל ונראה לי דנכון להחמיר בדבר דלא יהא אלא כרמלית כבר נתבאר לעיל סימן ש״ז (עמ׳ קעח ב״י ד״ה אבל התוספות, ד״מ ארוך אות ב) דהרבה פוסקים אוסרים שם אמירה לגוי ועל כן המחמיר תבא עליו ברכה וכן כתב מהרי״ל בתשובה סימן ק״ט דאף רבינו תם אינו מתיר אלא בדיעבד אבל לכתחלה אסור ועיין לעיל סימן ש״ז (עמ׳ קעח ד״ה וכתוב עוד, ד״מ שם) דיש מתירין אפילו ברשות הרבים אמירה לגוי במקום דאפשר למצוא היתר לישראל בלאו הכי ועיי״ש ולכן במקום צורך מצוה או דוחק גדול יש להקל:

שולחן ערוך סימן שז סעיף ה

דבר שאינו מלאכה, ואינו אסור לעשות בשבת אלא משום שבות, מותר לישראל לומר לא״י לעשותו בשבת; והוא שיהיה שם מקצת חולי, או

יהיה צריך לדבר צורך הרבה, או מפני מצוה; כיצד: אומר ישראל לא"י בשבת לעלות באילן להביא שופר לתקוע תקיעת מצוה; או להביא מים דרך חצר שלא עירבו, לרחוץ בו המצטער; ויש אוסרין. הגה: ולקמן סי' תקפ"ז פסק להתיר, וע"ל סי' רע"ו דיש מקילין אפילו במלאכה דאורייתא, וע"ש ס"ג.

תלמוד בבלי מסכת בבא מציעא דף צ ע"א

איבעיא להו: מהו שיאמר אדם לנכרי חסום פרתי ודוש בה, מי אמרינן: כי אמרינן אמירה לנכרי שבות - הני מילי לענין שבת, דאיסור סקילה, אבל חסימה דאיסור לאו - לא. או דלמא לא שנא?

חזון איש סימן לז אות כא

ונראה דעת הרמ"א לאסור כאן אמירה לנכרי ולא דמי לשבות דשבות במקום מצוה דמתירין כדאיתא סי' ש"ז ס"ה, דהכא בנצטנן לגמרי בדבר שיש בו מרק לדעת האוסרין יש בו בישול דאורייתא, ודבר יבש או תבשיל חם ונותן ע"ג כירה או תוכה או סמוך לה באחד מהאופנים האסורים לא שייך להתיר משום שבות דשבות דאין האיסור הנתינה אלא מציאות מצב זה אסרו חכמים ששרשו שמא יחתה והכל בכלל הגזירה אם יעמיד בעצמו או ע"י נכרי ואפי' העמיד נכרי או קוף חייב להסיר וכמו קדירה בשיל ולא בשיל העומדת מע"ש משקידש היום חייב להסירה וכמש"כ במ"ב סק"י ה"נ היכי דאסרו חכמים החזרה, ונותן ע"י נכרי גרע מנתן קוף שהרי זה נותן ממש ומ"ל בידים ומ"ל ע"י גרמא דידי', ובמ"ב בבה"ל כתב בשם אחרונים להקל לצורך שבת אמירה לא"י היכי דהאיסור משום חזרה ולהאמור אין לנטות מדעת האוסרין בזה.

20

שולחן ערוך אורח חיים סימן רנג סעיף ה

מותר לתת על פי קדירת חמין בשבת, תבשיל שנתבשל מע"ש כל צרכו, כגון פאנדי"ש וכיוצא בהן, לחממן, לפי שאין דרך בישול בכך; אבל להטמין תחת הבגדים הנתונים ע"ג המיחם, ודאי אסור.

הגהות מרדכי מסכת שבת דף פ ע"א

המשכים בבקר וראה שהקדיחה תבשילו וירא שמא יקדיח יותר אומר אני שיכול להסיר ולהניח קדרה ריקנית ע"פ הכירה והוה ליה כירה כגרופה וקטומה שהרי הקדירה סותמת את הכירה ואז ישים את הקדרה שהחמים בה ע"ג קדירה ריקנית אבל יזהר שלא ישים קדרה חדשה עליה דנמצא מלבנה.

שולחן ערוך אורח חיים סימן רנג סעיף ג

המשכים בבוקר וראה שהקדיחה תבשילו, וירא פן יקדיח יותר, יכול להסיר ולהניח קדירה ישנה ריקנית על פי הכירה ואז ישים הקדירה שהתבשיל בתוכה ע"ג הקדירה ריקנית; ויזהר שלא ישים קדירתו ע"ג קרקע, ושתהיה רותחת. (וכבר נתבאר שנוהגים להקל אף אם נתנה על גבי קרקע).

ביאור הלכה סימן רנג סעיף ג ד"ה ויזהר

ולכאורה סותר המחבר א"ע דלקמן בס"ה העתיק לדינא את דברי הרשב"א שהובא בב"י בשם הר"ן פרק כירה שכתב בשמו שם דמותר ליתן לכתחלה בשבת דאף שהקדרה התחתונה עומדת על האש כיון שהיא מפסקת ומעמיד הקדרה עליה אין דרך בשול בכך ועדיפא מכירה גרו"ק והוי כמעמיד נגד המדורה דמותר אף בשבת אם היה מבושל כ"צ [ועיין לקמן בסימן שי"ח סט"ו ובהג"ה פרטי דין זה] ומצאתי בדגול מרבבה שנדחק בזה וכתב דאפשר דהמחבר סמך עצמו על סברת הר"ן דכיון שאין פאנדי"ש דרכו לאפותו ע"ג כירה יש להקל בזה עי"ש והוא דוחק גדול דהמחבר לא ס"ל כלל שיטת הר"ן לדינא וכמ"ש המ"א וכן מוכח מבאור הגר"א בס"ה דטעם הש"ע דס"ל כשיטת הרשב"א הנ"ל עי"ש אח"כ מצאתי בפמ"ג שיישב זו הקושיא בטוב טעם והוא דבסעיף ה' שאיירי בעומדת ע"ג קדרת חמין או תבשיל לא נחשב כלל כעומד ע"ג כירה ולהכי מותר אף ליתן לכתחלה בשבת משא"כ בענינינו שהקדרה ריקנית ועומדת רק לסתום את חום הכירה שלא יהיה כ"כ חום נעשית הכירה עי"ז רק כשאר כירה גרופה וקטומה דאסור ליתן עליה בשבת תבשיל לכתחלה ובאמת אם היה עומד שם מבעוד יום קדרה שיש בה תבשיל היה מותר ליתן עליה לכו"ע קדרה זו אף בשבת לכתחלה:

פרי מגדים אשל אברהם סימן רנג ס"ק לג

וכללא הוא, כל שאין בו משום בישול, כמו יבש צונן, או לח חם (לדידן חם שאין יד סולדת בו נהגו להקל), חזרה מותר בשבת על גבי כירה גרופה וקטומה, אבל ליתן לכתחלה לא, ומשום הכי בעינן עודן בידו כו', דלא להוי כמושיב לכתחלה. ואף לדידן, אם נטלו מערב שבת והניחו על גבי קרקע, אף שעדיין חם, או אפשר בשבת ונצטנן לגמרי, הוה כמושיב לכתחילה, ולא התירו על גבי כירה גרופה אלא חזרה, לא לכתחילה, אלא כשמושיב על גבי קדירה שיש תבשיל בתוכה ותחתיה אש, ונותן על גבי קדירה פנאדי"ש צונן שהוסר מערב שבת, אף על גב דהוה לכתחילה, אין זה דרך בישול, ולא גזור כהאי גוונא, ומותר אף לכתחילה. ובסעיף גימ"ל, להושיב על גבי קדירה ריקנית שנותן עתה, ואף היה שם מאתמול מכל מקום כיון שריקנית היא, לא הוה רק ככירה גרופה וקטומה, מכל מקום לכתחלה אסור, כיון שריקנית היא, ולכך בעינן שלא יתן על גבי קרקע להמחבר, ולדידן מערב שבת וודאי אסור. והוא הדין אם נצטנן "לגמרי", דהוה כמושיב לכתחלה (ועיין תוספת שבת אות מ"ב, ויפה כוון). ומה שכתב שהקדירה מפסקת, "עם" תבשיל. ומה שכתב שומן, בסימן שי"ח סעיף ט"ז במ"א אות מ"ב, יע"ש. ועיין מ"א בסימן שי"ח בסעיף ו' זיי"ן חי"ת, ובאות כ"ב כ"ג כ"ד כ"ה כ"ו, יע"ש. ומה שכתב המחבר להטמין תחת הבגדים אסור בשבת, אף אין מוסיף הבל, וקדירה שריא, דבגדים אין מוסיף הבל. ומיירי באין אש תחתיה, דלא דמי לקופה על גבי גפת, עיין סימן רנ"ז סעיף א' וז' וח', ומ"א [ס"ק] ה' מצטמק ורע לו אסור, ואי"ה שם יבואר עוד:

תלמוד בבלי מסכת שבת דף לח עמוד ב כבר מובא בפרק יח אות א

שולחן ערוך אורח חיים סימן רנג סעיף א

וכל זה בענין שהה, שהקדירה יושבת על כסא של ברזל או ע"ג אבנים ואינה נוגעת בגחלים; אבל הטמנה ע"ג גחלים, לד"ה אסור. הגה: וי"א דאפי' אם הקדירה עומדת ע"ג האש ממש, כל זמן שהיא יז מגולה למעלה לא מקרי הטמנה, ושרי; וכן המנהג, רק שנזהרים לנתקן קצת קודם השבת מן האש כדי שיוכל ישראל להסירו משם; ואם לא נתקן מן האש ונמצאו ע"ג האש בשבת, יש להסירו משם ע"י א"י; ואם ליכא א"י, מותר לישראל להסירו

משם. ויזהר שיקחנו משם בנחת ולא ינענע הגחלים, ואז אף אם ינענען קצת, דבר שאין מתכוין הוא ושרי (מרדכי ר"פ כירה והגמי"י פ"ז).

שולחן ערוך אורח חיים הלכות שבת סימן רנח סעיף א

מותר להניח מבעוד יום כלי שיש בו דבר קר ע"ג קדירה חמה, שאין זה כטומן בדבר המוסיף הבל.

משנה ברורה שם ס"ק ב

שאין זה כטומן וכו' - ר"ל אפילו כסה אז הכלי והקדרה בבגדים ובודאי ניתוסף חום על הדבר קר ע"י הקדרה אפ"ה שרי דלא חשיב הקדרה כגפת ודומה לה המוסיפין הבל דהתם הוא מוסיף הבל מחמת עצמו אבל הקדרה אין לה הבל מעצמה ואדרבה כל שעה חומה מתמעט והולך ולהכי שרי

שולחן ערוך אורח חיים סימן רנג סעיף א

וי"א שכל שנתבשל כמאכל בן דרוסאי (פי' שם אדם שהיה אוכל מאכלו שלא נתבשל כל צרכו), או שנתבשל כל צרכו ומצטמק ויפה לו, מותר להשהותו ע"ג כירה. הגה: או אפילו ע"ג תנור (המגיד פ"ג והגהות מרדכי ומיימוני פ"ג וריש פ' כירה וב"י), אפי' הוסק בגפת ועצים אפי' אינה גרופה וקטומה; ולא הוזכרה גרופה וקטומה והוסק בקש וגבבא אלא כשהתחיל להתבשל ולא הגיע למאכל בן דרוסאי; וכן לענין אם נטל הקדירה מעליה ובא להחזירה עליה בשבת

ביאור הלכה סימן רנג ד"ה אלא כשהתחיל להתבשל ולא הגיע וכו'

עיין בחדושי רע"א שכתב דדין זה אינו ברור דיש פוסקים שסוברין דאפילו גרופה וקטומה לא מהני בזה:

ביאור הלכה סימן רנח ד"ה מותר להניח מבע"י וכו'

ואם הקדרה התחתונה מונחת ע"ג האש אז יש לזה דין מוסיף הבל ע"י האש וכדלעיל בסימן רנ"ז ס"ח ואסור אפילו מבע"י לכסות עליהן בבגדים מלמעלה משום הטמנה ואם אין מכסה בבגדים יש לזה דין שיהוי וצריך

שיהיה הדבר קר נתבשל כמאב״ד מבעוד יום לדעת הרב לעיל בסימן רנ״ג. כן כתב המ״א והפמ״ג ועיין לקמן בסימן שי״ח בבה״ל בס״ו:

מגן אברהם סימן רנג ס״ק לג

פנאדי״ש - דכיון שאין בו רוטב אין בו בישול כמ״ש סי׳ שי״ח סט״ו ומשום חיתוי נמי ליכא למיגזר שאין דרך בישול בכך לפי שהקדירה מפסקת (מ״מ פכ״ב) ואם יש בה שומן אסור כמ״ש סי׳ שי״ח ס״ו

מגן אברהם סימן רנח ס״ק א

קדירה חמה - ואם הקדירה התחתונה עומדת ע״ג האש יש לה דין שהיה ועסי׳ רנ״ג:

שולחן ערוך הרב אורח חיים קונטרס אחרון הלכות שבת סימן רנח הערה א

ולא העתקתי מה שכתב המג״א כאן, משום דבהדיא מבואר בש״ע סי׳ שי״ח ס״ח שהכריע להקל דלא דמי לכירה כמו שכתב המג״א עצמו שם עיין שם בס״ק כ״ו, דאף במיחם על גבי מיחם שיש תבשיל ורוטב בהעליון דבכהאי גוונא מיירי הכא והתם בס״ז נקטינן נמי כדברי המיקל, עיין במה שנתבאר בסי׳ רנ״ג ודו״ק:

מגיד משנה הלכות שבת פרק כב הלכה ד

וכתב הרשב״א ז״ל שלדברי הכל תבשיל שנתבשל מע״ש ונצטנן מותר לחממו כנגד המדורה אפי׳ במקום שהיס״ב והוא שלא יתן ע״ג המדורה או ע״ג כירה ואם יש קדרה נתונה על האש מותר לחמם על גבי תבשיל שנתבשל כל צרכו מע״ש שכיון שהקדרה מפסקת הרי זה כמחמם כנגד המדורה ומותר. אבל אסור להטמינו תחת הבגדים הנתונים ע״ג המיחם אבל מטיב עליו כלי כדי לשמרו מן העכברים ואינו חושש אלו דבריו ז״ל:

שולחן ערוך אורח חיים סימן שיח סעיף ז - ח

יש מפרשים דהא דשרי להניח כלי שיש בו דבר חם ע״ג קדירה הטמונה, אפי׳ כלי התחתון על האש שרי. ויש מפרשים שאם כלי התחתון על האש, לעולם אסור.

להניח דבר קר שנתבשל כל צרכו ע״ג מיחם שעל האש, י״א שדינו כמניחו כנגד המדורה וכל דבר שמותר להניחו כנגד המדורה במקום שהיד סולדת בו, כגון שיבש, מותר להניחו ע״ג מיחם שעל גבי האש. וי״א דהוי כמניח ע״ג כירה לכתחלה ואסור אפילו אם נתבשל כל צרכו ואפילו אם מצטמק ורע לו ואפילו אם נותנו שם לשמור חומו; וראשון נראה עיקר. ומ״מ אם הוא תבשיל שיש בו רוטב ומצטמק ויפה לו, אסור לד״ה.

מגן אברהם סימן שיח ס״ק כו

וראשון נראה עיקר - כיון שהקדירה מפסקת ל״ד לכירה דהתם הקדיר׳ עומדת ע״ג האש ממש (מ״מ פכ״ב) וצ״ע למה לא הכריע הרב״י בס״ז להתיר דהא הוא בעצמו לא כ״כ בסי׳ רנ״ג ס״ג וי״ל דוקא צלי מותר ליתנו לכתחלה ע״ג כירה גרופה אבל מבושל אסור ליתנו ע״ג (קדירה דעדיף מכירה, ת״ש) כירה אפי׳ הוא חם שאין בו משום בישול דגזרינן שמא יתן עליו כשהוא קר ואין מותר אלא חזרה וכן צ״ל לדברי רי״ו ומ״מ יש להקל דמשמע במ״מ דכיון דהקדירה מפסקת עדיף מכירה גרופה ושרי ליתן עליה תבשיל חם:

שולחן ערוך אורח חיים סימן רנג סעיף ה

מותר לתת על פי קדירת חמין בשבת, תבשיל שנתבשל מע״ש כל צרכו, כגון פאנדי״ש וכיוצא בהן, לחממן, לפי שאין דרך בישול בכך; אבל להטמין תחת הבגדים הנתונים ע״ג המיחם, ודאי אסור.

שולחן ערוך אורח חיים סימן רנג סעיף ב ברמ״א

הגה: ודוקא שהתבשיל מבושל כל צרכו (ב״י), ואז מותר להחזיר, ואפילו כג לכירה אחרת, אבל אם לא נתבשל כל צרכו אסור, אפי׳ לאותה כירה (מיימוני פ״ג). וי״א דכל זה אינו אסור רק כשנטלו מן הכירה מבעוד יום, ולא החזירו עד שחשכה; אבל אם לקחו משם משחשכה, אפי׳ הניחו ע״ג קרקע מותר (ר״ן פ׳ כירה וכל בו), וכן נוהגים להקל בתנורים שלנו שיש להם דין כירה, וסומכין עצמם על דברי המקילין, וטוב להחמיר. מיהואם נצטנן, לכ״ע אסור (ב״י).

מחצית השקל סימן רנח

וכתב בספר תוספת שבת, הרב ב"י כתב הטעם, שהרי אין הקדרה חמה מוספת הבל, אדרבא חומה מתמעט והולך עכ"ל, הרב ב"י הובא בט"ז. ועיין מה שכתב הט"ז ומה שכתב עליו בספר תוספת שבת. וכתב בספר תוספת שבת וז"ל, ולפי זה צריך לומר דמיירי שעושה דרך הטמנה עכ"ל. ור"ל, שמכסהו בבגדים, דאם לא כן למה הוצרך הרב ב"י לטעם, הא לא הוי הטמנה כלל כי אם שעומד על גבי קדרה חמה, ומה ענין זה להטמנה, וסיים התוספת שבת וז"ל ואיך שיהיה צריך שתדע דמה שכתב מ"א כאן דאם כו' על גבי האש יש לה דין שהיה הוא טעות סופר וצ"ל דין הטמנה, דהא מיקרי מוסיף הבל מחמת האש שתחתיה כמו שכתוב סימן רנ"ז סעיף ח' כו' עכ"ל התוספת שבת. ולענ"ד דוחק להגיה, גם מ"א רמז ועיין סימן רנ"ג, ושם מבואר דין שהיה, ולא דין הטמנה. גם לפי דעת ספר תוספת שבת דהרב ב"י הוצרך לטעם משום דמיירי שעשה דרך הטמנה, מנא ליה להרב ב"י דהטור מיירי בענין זה שהוצרך לטעם, גם אין לשון הטור משמע דמיירי דרך הטמנה, ועל דברי הטור כתב הרב ב"י דבריו. לכן נראה לענ"ד דהמ"א היה מפרש דברי הרב ב"י, דמשום הכי הוצרך לטעם, דאזיל לשיטתיה בספרו הארוך בסימן רנ"ג וכן פסק בשו"ע סימן רנ"ג סוף סעיף א' דאם הקדרה עומדת על גבי גחלים, אף על גב שמגולה למעלה ומצדדים מיקרי הטמנה, לכן הוצרך פה לטעמים ולחלק בין עומדת על האש או על גבי קדרה, אבל לדידן, וכמו שכתב רמ"א שם בסימן רנ"ג דאפילו עומדת על גבי גחלים כהאי גוונא לא מיקרי הטמנה, אלא דין שיהוי, ולכן לא העתיק מ"א טעם הרב ב"י לדידן, א"כ לדידן אפילו עומדת על גבי האש ליכא משום הטמנה כי אם משום שיהוי, ומיירי כל הדין שאינו דרך הטמנה, ואתי שפיר דברי מ"א.

טור אורח חיים סימן רנח

כלי שיש בו דבר חם יכול להניחו על הקדרה טמונה כדי שישמור חומו ולא יצטנן ויכול לטוח פיו בבצק אם יש לו בצק שנילש מאתמול אבל אין מניחים כלי שיש בו דבר קר על גבי קדרה חמה בשבת שהרי מוליד בו חום בשבת ואם הניחו בע"ש מותר שאין זה כטומן בדבר המוסיף הבל:

בית יוסף אורח חיים סימן רנח

וכתב רבינו בסימן שי"ח (פג.) דהא דאסור להניח כלי שיש בו תבשיל קר ע"ג קדרה טמונה דוקא כשהקדרה חמה בענין שהעליון יכול להתבשל אבל אם אינו יכול להתבשל מותר אם אין בו דבר קרוש ובקצת נוסחאות כתוב כן גם בסימן זה ונראה שטעמו משום דמשמע ליה דלא מיקרי אולודי מוליד אלא א"כ מרתיח ועוד דאם אין העליון יכול להתבשל כלומר להתחמם עד שתהא יד סולדת בו ודאי שרי כדשרי להניח כנגד המדורה קיתון של צונן במקום שאין יד סולדת בו כמו שיבא בסימן שי"ח (פה.) וכן כתבו התוספות (ד"ה מאי שנא ממיחם) והר"ן (כב. ד"ה ומקשו) שם אעובדא דרבה ורבי זירא שדין הנחה ע"ג מיחם שוה לדין הנחה כנגד המדורה וכן כתב הרב המגיד בסוף פ"ד (ה"ו) וז"ל ופירשו ז"ל שהקומקום היה חם כל כך שהיה בו כדי לחמם הכוזא שהיה בו צונן ולא שיעור להפשיר בלבד שאל"כ מותר היה אפילו נגד המדורה וכן מורה לשון רבינו עכ"ל ולפי זה כלי שיש בו דבר חם שיכול להניחו על הקדרה היינו דוקא כשהיד סולדת בו דאז אפילו ירתיח מחמת חום התחתון אוקומי מוקים הוי ובלאו הכי צ"ל כן לפי מה שכתב רבינו בסימן הנזכר (פב.) דיש בישול אחר בישול בתבשיל שיש בו מרק אפילו נתבשל כל צרכו אם אינו רותח ואין לומר דשאני הכא שאינו באור עצמו דהא מבשל בתולדת האור חייב כמבשל באור עצמה כדאיתא בפרק כירה (לט.):

דרכי משה אורח חיים סימן רנח אות ב

ולפי (זה) דברי הטור דתלי טעמא משום שמוליד חום בכל ענין אסור. ועיין לקמן סימן שי"ח עיקר דינים אלו:

21

שו"ת אגרות משה אורח חיים חלק ד סימן עד

(לה) האם מותר לחמם קדרה שנתבשלה והיא חמה קצת ע"ג מכשירים שנועדו לחימום ולא לבישול, כפלטה חשמלית (האט פלייט והאט טריי) או שולחן מחומם באדים (סטים טייבל), גם בלא הפסק קדרה, דאין דרך בישול בכך.

תשובה: על פלטה חשמלית אם א"א להתבשל שם אז מותר להעמיד קדרה חמה אם אין שם אלא מדה אחת להחום ואם יש שתי מדות אסור, והוא שלא יהיה באופן הטמנה שאז יהיה הטמנה בדבר המוסיף הבל שאסור.
ועל שולחן המחומם באדים כמדומה שאפשר להתבשל שם וא"כ הוא ממילא דרך בישול אך אף אם א"א להתבשל שם כמדומה שהוא בדרך הטמנה ואז אסור, ואם אינו דרך הטמנה כגון שאינה מכוסה כולה מותר.

פסקי תשובות סי' רנג סע' טז

ויש מתירים אף בפלטה חשמלית מיוחדת לשבת שיש בה רק מדה אחת של חום כיון שנועדה רק לשמור חום וא"א לבשל בה.

חזון איש סימן לז אות ט

הקשה המ"ב למה כאן בס"ג לא התיר המחבר בהפסק קדירה ריקנית אלא חזרה ולק' ס"ה מתיר ליתן לכתחילה לחם ממולא בשר צונן על הקדירה שעל הכירה לחממו, וכ' בשם הפמ"ג דקדירה ריקנית משמשת לכירה וחשיב כמעמיד על הכירה אבל מעמיד על הקדירה שתבשיל בתוכה חשיב כמעמיד על הקדירה ולא כמעמיד ע"ג כירה, ואפשר שאם יש חום עולה לקדירה עליונה להרתיחה כגון שאם התחתונה גדולה ומלאה וכבדה להרתיח והעליונה קטנה ונוחה להרתיח היתה העליונה מרתחת קדם לתחתונה ודאי חשיבא כעומדת על הכירה אלא היה כאן היתר של הגהמ"ר ודוקא להחזיר אבל לא ליתן לכתחילה בשבת אבל באמת כל שהתחתונה מלאה היא בולעת חום הכירה ואין החום עולה לעליונה אלא מחום הקדירה והלכך גרע ממפסיק בקדירה ריקנית דהתם חום הכירה סלקא למעלה.

מחצית השקל סי' רנג סקל"ד

כן משמע קצת בספרו הארוך סוף הסימן, וגם פה בשו"ע, מדכתב התירא דפאנד"ש ולא כתב רבותא דינו של הר"ן דבר שאין דרכו בו' אלא על כרחך דסבירא ליה לאיסור. והקשה בספר תוספת שבת למה בפאנד"ש התיר הרב ב"י הואיל והקדרה מפסקת ליתן אפילו לכתחלה ובסעיף ג' כתב המשכים בבוקר בו' דאף על גב דהקדרה מפסקת אינו מתיר אלא חזרה, אבל לא

ליתן לכתחלה, דהא הזהיר שלא יניח הקדרה על גבי קרקע, עיין שם מה שתירץ. ולענ"ד לפי מה שכתב מ"א לקמן סימן שי"ח ס"ק כו אתי שפיר שכתב דוקא דבר יבש שאין בו מרק מותר כהאי גוונא אפילו לכתחלה, אבל לא בדבר שיש בו מרק, אפילו הוא חם. ואם כן אתי שפיר האי דסעיף ג' דמשמע דמיירי ביש בו מרק.

שולחן ערוך אורח חיים סימן שיח סעיף ד

תבשיל שנתבשל כל צרכו, יש בו משום בישול אם נצטנן. הגה: וי"א דוקא אם מצטמק ויפה לו (רבינו ירוחם ח"ג); ואם לא נתבשל כל צרכו, ואפילו נתבשל כמאכל ב"ד =בן דרוסאי=, שייך בו בישול אפילו בעודו רותח; וה"מ שיש בו בישול אחר בישול, בתבשיל שיש בו מרק, אבל דבר שנתבשל כבר, והוא יבש, מותר לשרותו בחמין בשבת. ואם הוא דבר יבש שלא נתבשל מלפני השבת, אין שורין אותו בחמין בשבת אבל מדיחים אותו בחמין בשבת, חוץ מן המליח הישן ומן הדג שנקרא קולייס האספנין שאינם צריכים בישול אלא מעט וההדחתן היא גמר מלאכתן. הגה: וה"ה כל דבר קשה שאינו ראוי לאכול כלל בלא שרייה, דאסור לשרותו בשבת, דהוי גמר מלאכה. (הגהות מרדכי).

שו"ת יחווה דעת חלק ב סימן מה

שאלה: תבשיל צונן שהיה מונח במקרר מערב שבת, האם מותר לחממו על הפלאטה של שבת, או יש בזה איסור משום שנראה כמבשל בשבת?

תשובה: במשנה במסכת שבת (דף קמה:) שנינו: כל שבא בחמין לפני השבת שורין אותו בחמין בשבת, וכל שלא בא בחמין מערב שבת, מדיחין אותו בחמין בשבת. כלומר, דבר שנתבשל כל צרכו מלפני השבת, מותר לשרותו בחמין של כלי ראשון כדי לחממו בשבת, שאין בישול אחר בישול. אבל דבר שלא נתבשל מערב שבת אסור לשרותו בחמין של כלי ראשון בשבת, שהרי הוא מבשל בשבת, אלא רק מותר להדיח אותו בשבת במים חמים של כלי שני, שכלי שני אינו מבשל. ופירשו בגמרא, דבר שבא בחמין מלפני השבת, כגון עוף שנתבשל כל צרכו מערב שבת, מותר לשרותו בחמין בשבת כדי לחממו. והוא הדין שמותר להעמידו כנגד האש כדי שיתחמם. וכן פסק מרן השלחן ערוך (/או"ח/ בסימן שיח סעיף טו), שדבר שנתבשל

כל צרכו מותר להניחו כנגד מדורה אפילו במקום שהיד סולדת בו. וראה בשו"ת קול אליהו (חלק אורח חיים סימן יד), ובברכי יוסף (סימן שיח אות ה'). והנה דעת רש"י (שבת יח:), והרא"ש (פרק ג' דשבת סימן יא), ורבינו יונה המובא בהר"ן (ריש פרק ד' דשבת), שדוקא תבשיל יבש כגון חתיכות בשר או חתיכות דגים וכיוצא בהן, אין בו משום בישול בשבת, מאחר שכבר נתבשל מערב שבת, אבל תבשיל לח, כגון מרק שנצטנן, יש בו משום בישול אחר בישול, ואסור לחממו באופן שתהיה היד סולדת בו. אבל הרמב"ם והרשב"א והר"ן סוברים שאף בלח שנצטנן אין בישול אחר בישול. ומאחר שהיא מחלוקת באיסור תורה הלכה כדברי האוסרים בלח. וזו לשון מרן השלחן ערוך (/או"ח/ סימן שיח סעיף ד): תבשיל שנתבשל כל צרכו ונצטנן יש בו משום בישול בשבת, ואסור לחממו בשבת, במה דברים אמורים, בתבשיל שיש בו מרק, אבל תבשיל יבש מותר לשרותו בחמין בשבת. ומבואר בבית יוסף (/או"ח/ סימן רנג) בשם רבינו יונה ורבינו ירוחם, שלא נקרא תבשיל לח לענין זה אלא כשרובו רוטב ומרק, אבל תבשיל של בשר או דגים, ויש בו קצת רוטב ושומן, מאחר שרובו יבש, אין בו משום בישול אחר בישול. וכן הסכים הגאון רבי אברהם פימנטיל בספר מנחת כהן (בקונטרס משמרת השבת פרק ב), ושכן מסתבר, שהרי אין לך תבשיל של בשר שאין בו מוהל ושומן, ועם כל זה נידון כתבשיל יבש לענין זה, וכן כתבו הפרי מגדים (סימן רנג אות יג), והגאון רבי שלום מרדכי הכהן שבדרון בדעת תורה (סימן שיח סעיף טו). לפיכך, תבשיל של בשר או דגים, ותפוחי אדמה, וכיוצא בזה, כל שרובו יבש מותר לחממו בשבת, גם באופן שמגיע ליד סולדת בו, אבל תבשיל לח כגון מרק, אף שיש בו חתיכות בשר, מכיון שרובו צלול ולח, אסור לחממו בשבת, שיש בו דין בישול אחר בישול. אולם אף על פי שמותר לחמם תבשיל יבש בשבת, מכל מקום לא הותר להניחו על כירים של גז או פתיליה של נפט וכיוצא בזה כדי לחממו, שמא יחתה בגחלים, כלומר, שמא ישכח ויגביה את הפתילה של האש כדי למהר את חימומו של התבשיל. ורק כנגד האש או על גבי קדרה המונחת על האש וכיוצא בזה מותר לחמם. וכמו שפסק מרן בשלחן ערוך (/או"ח/ סימן רנג סעיף ה) וזו לשונו: מותר לתת בשבת על פי קדרת חמין תבשיל שנתבשל כל צרכו מערב שבת כגון פאנדיש (בצק אפוי הממולא בשר מבושל), וכיו"ב, כדי לחמם, לפי שאין דרך בישול בכך. ע"כ. וכן כתב עוד

מרן בשלחן ערוך (/או"ח/ סימן שיח סעיף ח), שמותר להניח בשבת תבשיל קר שנתבשל כל צרכו, על גבי מיחם שעל האש, שכל דבר שמותר להניחו כנגד המדורה במקום שהיד סולדת בו, כגון תבשיל יבש, מותר להניחו על גבי קדרה שעל האש. ע"ש. ולכאורה הוא הדין שמותר להניח התבשיל שנתבשל כל צרכו, והוא יבש, על הפלאטה החשמלית, מפני שיש הפסק בין האש לקדרת התבשיל, וכאילו הוא נותנה על קדרת החמין. אולם יש להעיר על זה ממה שפסק מרן בשלחן ערוך (/או"ח/ סימן רנג סעיף ג), המשכים בבוקר וראה שהקדיח תבשילו וירא פן יקדיח יותר, יכול להסיר התבשיל, ולהניח על פי הכירה קדרה ישנה ריקנית, ואז ישים הקדרה שהתבשיל בתוכה על גבי הקדרה הריקנית, אבל יזהר שלא ישים קדירתו על גבי קרקע, ושתהיה רותחת. ע"כ. ומבואר שאם רק הונח התבשיל על גבי קרקע אסור להחזירו אפילו על קדרה ריקנית, והטעם הוא משום שנראה כמבשל לכתחילה, וכמו שכתבו הרשב"א והר"ן (שבת לח). וכן כתבו האחרונים. ואם כן יש לומר שאף בפלאטה חשמלית אסור להניח תבשיל צונן משום שנראה כמבשל. אלא שלפי זה יש להקשות שהרי מרן השלחן ערוך עצמו התיר להניח בשבת תבשיל שנתבשל כל צרכו על גבי קדרת חמין או על גבי מיחם. וכבר עמד בזה בספר תוספת שבת (סימן רנג ס"ק מב) שלכאורה דברי השלחן ערוך סותרים זה את זה. ותירץ, שבקדרה ריקנית אסור מפני שנראה כדרך בישול לכתחילה, אבל על גבי קדרה מלאה מותר שאינו נראה כמבשל. וכן כתב הפרי מגדים, שלהעמיד התבשיל על גבי קדרת חמין או מיחם יש להתיר שאינו דומה למעמיד על גבי כירה, אבל כשהקדרה שעל האש ריקנית, שאינה עומדת שם אלא רק לסתום חום הכירה, דמי לכירה גרופה וקטומה שאסור לתת עליה תבשיל לכתחילה בשבת משום שנראה כמבשל. ע"כ. והסכים לזה במשנה ברורה בביאור הלכה (סימן רנג סעיף ג) בד"ה ויזהר. וראה עוד בחזון איש (בהלכות שבת סימן לז אות ט). ולפי זה המניח על גבי פלאטה חשמלית, דומה למניח על גבי קדרה ריקנית, שיש לאסור. אולם המגן אברהם (סימן שיח ס"ק כו), מחלק בזה בין תבשיל לח רותח שאסור להניחו בשבת גם על גבי קדרה של חמין, משום שיש לגזור שמא יניחנו צונן, ויש בישול אחר בישול בלח, אבל תבשיל יבש אפילו צונן מותר להניחו בשבת על גבי קדרה (אפילו ריקנית), שאין בישול אחר בישול ביבש. ע"ש. וכן פסק הגאון רבי ישמעאל

הכהן בשו"ת זרע אמת חלק ג' (חלק אורח חיים סימן כו), להתיר לחמם בשבת תבשיל יבש שנתבשל כל צרכו מערב שבת, על גבי פח מתכת מנוקב (או אזבסט) שעל האש, ונסתייע ממה שכתב המהרי"ל, שאם הונח דף על התנור מותר להניח עליו קדרה של תבשיל לחממו. ואם כן הוא הדין שאם שם פח של מתכת מנוקב בנקבים קטנים על גבי הכירה שיש בה גחלים בוערות, הרי המחיצה של ברזל מפסקת בין הגחלים לתבשיל, והרי זה כנותן על קדרה שעל האש. ע"ש.וכן כתב הגאון רבי חיים דניאל שלמה פינסו בספר שם חדש חלק א' (דף נח סע"א), ושכן המנהג להקל בירושלים.ע"ש. וכן פסק בשו"ת עמק המלך (סימן מח). ע"ש. ולפי זה מותר להניח בשבת תבשיל יבש על פלאטה חשמלית, הואיל והפח של הפלאטה מפסיק בין חוטי החשמל לקדרת התבשיל שהוא יבש, ואין בישול אחר בישול ביבש. ובשו"ת מהר"ם שיק (חלק או"ח סימן קיז) כתב לחלק, שבקדרה חמה שרוצה להעמיד חמימותה, אפילו מניחה על גבי קדרה ריקנית אין היכר כל כך בזה, וחיישינן שמא יבוא לחתות האש, אבל קדרה שיש בה תבשיל צונן, והוא יבש, כיון שנותנה על גבי קדרה, יש היכר בדבר שאינו מתכוין שירתח ויתבשל, וכיון שיש היכר שוב אין לחוש שמא יחתה באש. ע"כ. ולפי זה גם כן יש להתיר נתינת תבשיל יבש צונן על פלאטה חשמלית, שמכיון שהפח מפסיק בין חוטי החשמל הבוערים ובין הקדרה, הרי זה כמניח על גבי קדרה ריקנית שמותר. ועוד שבפלאטה אין כל אפשרות להגביה החום, ולא שייכא הגזרה דשמא יחתה בגחלים. וכן הזכיר סברא זו הגאון רבי צבי פסח פראנק, בשו"ת הר צבי (חלק או"ח סימן קלו). ועוד שיש לומר שלא חששו חז"ל לגזרה דשמא יחתה, אלא דוקא בגחלים שבכירה שדרכן לדעוך קימעא קימעא, ואינן נשארות במצב אחד של חום, ולכן חששו שמא כשיראה שהן עוממות ודועכות, ישכח שהוא שבת ויחתה בגחלים להבעירן, אבל בפלאטה חשמלית או בכירים של גז שנשארות באותו מצב תקין של החום, במדה שוה, אין מקום לגזור משום גזרה שמא יגביה מדת החום, אפילו אם היתה אפשרות במציאות להגביה מדת החום בפלאטה חשמלית. וסברא זו נזכרה בדברי הגאון רבי יוסף גרשון הורביץ, בגידולי ציון חלק ט' (סימן יא). ע"ש. וראה עוד בזה בשו"ת מהר"ם בריסק חלק ב' (סימן עו), ובשו"ת ערוגת הבושם (חלק או"ח סימן נז), ובפתח הדביר חלק ג' (סימן שיח), ובדגול מרבבה (סימן רנג), ובספר תהלה לדוד

(שם ס"ק יח), ובספר פקודת אלעזר בן טובו (סימן שיח). ועוד. ואמנם הרה"ג רבי עובדיה הדאיה בשו"ת ישכיל עבדי חלק ו' (חלק או"ח סימן טו) כתב לאסור להניח בשבת תבשיל על הפלאטה החשמלית לחממו, ואף על פי שהפח מכסה את חוטי החשמל, יש לומר שלא התירו אלא פח חיצוני שניכר שנעשה לשם הפסק, מה שאין כן בזה שהוא מחובר מעיקרו. ע"ש. אולם הרב עצמו הדר תבריה לגזיזיה, בספרו ישכיל עבדי חלק ז' (סימן כח אות ח), וכתב, והנה עתה בראותי שרבים וכן שלמים משתמשים בשבת בפלאטה החשמלית ואין פוצה פה, נתתי אל לבי להבין על מה סמכו להתיר, ובאתי לידי הכרה שבזה יש להקל, משום שהפלאטה החשמלית מלכתחילה נעשית לשם שימוש בשבת, ונקראת פלאטה של שבת, ואם כן הרי יש בה סימן לכל אדם שהיום שבת, ולא יבוא להשתמש בה באיסור, כגון להחזיר עליה תבשיל שלא נתבשל כל צרכו, או תבשיל לח צונן, וכיוצא בזה, ומכיון שאין האש נראית לעין ואין כאן חשש חיתוי, לפיכך נהגו להתיר, ואדרבה הפלאטה עדיפא מכיסוי של פח שעל הכירה, ששם עלול להסיר הפח מעל הכירה שלא מדעת, מה שאין כן בפלאטה שאי אפשר בשום פנים להוציא הכיסוי מעל חוטי החשמל, ומכיון שעשויה לשם כך, אין לך סימן והיכר גדול מזה לזכור את יום השבת, ואפילו החזון איש שאוסר בפתיליה, אפילו אם מעמידים עליה פח של מתכת, יודה כאן להתיר, ששם האש נראית מתחת הכיסוי של פח, מה שאין כן בפלאטה שהיא עצמה סימן על השבת וכל עיקרה נעשית לשם כך יש להתיר. ע"כ. והניף ידו שנית להתיר בזה בספרו ישכיל עבדי חלק ז' (חלק אורח חיים סימן מה, שאלה טו, אות ג', דף ע"ה סע"ב). ע"ש. וכן עיקר. בסיכום: תבשיל צונן שנתבשל כל צרכו מערב שבת, והיה מונח במקרה, מותר לחממו בשבת על פלאטה חשמלית של שבת, אפילו חום שהיד סולדת בו. וכן מותר לחממו על אזבסט (או פח מתכת מנוקב) המונח על כירים של גז, ובלבד שרוב התבשיל יבש, אף שיש בו קצת רוטב, אבל אם היה רוב התבשיל רוטב, אסור לחממו בשבת על הפלאטה. שיש דין בישול אחר בישול בלח.

ילקוט יוסף סי' רנג

ומכאן למד שם שאם האש מכוסה בפח או אזבסט, או בפלאטה חשמלית, ליכא למיחש למיחזי כמבשל. ולפי זה מה שכתב מרן בשלחן ערוך בתנאי החזרה,

שצריך שלא יניח הקדרה על גבי קרקע, לא איירי אלא בכירה גרופה וקטומה, שבזה שייך מיחזי כמבשל, מאחר והדרך היה מידי פעם להניח תבשיל על גבי כירה קטומה. אבל בהפסק טס של מתכת, או בפאטה חשמלית, בזה אף משום מיחזי כמבשל ליכא. ולכן המקילים בזה אף אחר שהניחו הקדרה על גבי קרקע יש להם על מה שיסמוכו, ובפרט אם הניחו את הקדרה על גבי שיש, במקום שהרגילות הוא להניחו שם כדי ליתן לבני הבית מהתבשיל.

שמירת שבת כהלכתה פרק א' הע' קיב

עיין סי' רנג במ"ב ס"ק פא, סוסי' רנט בכללא דמילתא סי' שיח במ"ב ס"ק מא וצד נ"א כלל כ ס"ק ט תהל"ד סי' רנג ס"ק יח וסי' שיח ס"ק כו. וה"ה דלפ"ז מותר גם לכתחילה להניח בשבת צלחת הפוכה וכדו' ע"ג כירה כשאין לו קדירה מלאה תבשיל ע"ג האש ולהניח קדירה עליה באופן שאין בו משום איסור בישול וכדלעיל סע' ז וי כיון שאין דרך בישול בכך. וע"ע סי' רנג סע ג' בביה"ל סוד"ה ויזהר, שו"ע הרב שם בקו"א ס"ק י, ובחזו"א סי' לז ס"ק ט ד"ה ובתוך וס"ק יא.

שמירת שבת כהלכתה פרק א' סעיף כ והע' סו

ובדיעבד דהיינו כאשר משום הקפדה על הנאמר בסעיף הקודם לא יהיה לו מאכל חם לשבת יש מקום להקל ולהחזיר את הכלי על גבי האש גם אם הניחו מידו ולא היה בדעתו להחזירו לאש והוא שהאוכל שבכלי יהא מבושל כל צורכו ולא נצטנן לגמרי וגם האש שעל גביה יחזירנו תהא מכוסה באזבסט וכדו'.

שם סע' ב ברמ"א וע"ש במ"ב ס"ק סה וע"ש גם במ"ב סוס"ק פא בשם המ"א ועיין בפמ"ג מ"ז ס"ק יב ובתורת שבת שם סע' ב ועיין חזו"א סי' לז ס"ק יב דראוי להחמיר בהניחו ע"ג קרקע וטוב יעשה אם יניח צלחת הפוכה מתחת לקדירה וטוב מזה להעמיד את הקדירה ע"ג קדירה אחרת מלאה שעומדת ע"ג האש כי בזה יצא ידי כל הדעות.

שמירת שבת כהלכתה ח"ג הע' קיב

דדוקא אם העמיד את הקדירה הריקנית ע"ג אש גלויה כדי לתת לה דין גרו"ק, אבל אם האש כבר מכוסה ומעמיד את הקדירה כדי לשנות

מדרך הבישול, עדיף טפי, ושרי לכו"ע אף שהקדירה ריקנית. וא"כ ה"ה"נ לגבי צלחת הפוכה ע"ג גו"ק, עכ"ד. וראה לשון הביה"ל הנ"ל שהקדירה הריקנית עומדת רק לסתום את חום הכירה, נעשית הכירה רק כגוף וקטום.

22

שבת לז עמוד א

איבעיא להו: מהו לסמוך בה? תוכה וגבה - אסור, אבל לסמוך בה - שפיר דמי, או דילמא לא שנא? - תא שמע: שתי כירות המתאימות, אחת גרופה וקטומה ואחת שאינה גרופה וקטומה - משהין על גבי גרופה וקטומה, ואף על גב דקא סליק ליה הבלא מאידך. - דילמא שאני התם - דכיון דמידליא שליט בה אוירא. תא שמע, דאמר רב ספרא אמר רב חייא: קטמה ונתלבתה - סומכין לה, ומקיימין עליה, ונוטלין ממנה, ומחזירין לה. שמע מינה: לסמוך נמי, קטמה - אין, לא קטמה - לא. - ולטעמיך נוטלין ממנה דקתני, קטמה - אין, לא קטמה - לא? אלא: תנא, נוטלין משום מחזירין הכא נמי: תנא סומכין משום מקיימין. - הכי השתא! התם - נוטלין ומחזירין בחד מקום הוא, תנא נוטלין משום מחזירין. אלא הכא, סומכין - בחד מקום הוא, ומקיימין - בחד מקום הוא. מאי הוי עלה? - תא שמע: כירה שהסיקוה בגפת ובעצים - סומכין לה, ואין מקיימין אלא אם כן גרופה וקטומה. גחלים שעממו, או שנתן עליה נעורת של פשתן דקה - הרי היא כקטומה.

תוספות שבת לז עמוד א

תא שמע כירה שהסיקוה כו' - ומסיק דשרי לסמוך ומכל מקום אין ללמוד מכאן לסמוך אצל האש דשאני הכא דדופני כירה מפסיקין בינו ולאש.

הגהות מרדכי פרק ג פ.

ואע"ג דאיכא למידחי שאני התם דמפסקא דופן כירה אבל לסמוך אצל גחלים אסור אין לדחות כן דלא גרע מבשרא אגומרי דשרי בפ"ק כי נצלה מבעוד יום כמאכל בן דרוסאי אע"ג דליכא מידי דמפסיק.

מגן אברהם שיח:לח

מותר להניחו כנגד המדורה - דדמי לסמיכה בכירה דשרי ואף על גב שאין דבר מפסיק בינו לבין האש כיון שהצריכו החכמים להרחיק קצת מן המדורה אית ליה היכרא ולא אתו לאחתויי, הרא"ש:

רי"ף שבת דף טז. בדפי הרי"ף

ומסתברא לן דהכי הוא מסקנא דהא בתר דשקלינן וטרינן איבעיא להו מהו לסמוך לה תוכה וגבה הוא דאסור אבל לסמוך שפיר דמי או דלמא לא שנא ומדאמרינן תוכה וגבה הוא דאסיר שמעינן דאסור לשהות על גבי כירה שאינה גרופה וקטומה.

בעל המאור שבת טו: בדפי הרי"ף

ולענין פירושה דמתני' ופסק הלכה הוי יודע כי כל הגאונים שהיו מן העולם כלם הסכימו דמתני' להחזיר תנן אבל להשהות משהין ומנו חנניה היא דקאמר רב ששת א"ר יוחנן בהדיא מתני' להחזיר תנן ואף רבא נמי דהוא בתרא סייעיה ואמר תרויהו תנינהו ואסיקנא רב ששת דיוקא דמתני' קמ"ל דאלמא הא מילתא פשיטתה היא ולא חדית בה רב ששת ולא מידי ולא אשמעינן בהא אלא דיוקא דמתני' בלחוד ומי הוא זה ואי זה הוא חכם או רב או גאון שיכול לדחות ראיה ברורה כזו וכל הראיות שהביא הרי"ף ז"ל לדבריו למדחיה לדחנניה ולאוקמה למתני' בלשהות אין בהם אפילו ראיה אחת שיש לה ידים ורגלים דהא דמייתי ראיה מדאבעיא להו מהו לסמוך לה תוכה וגבה הוא דאסור אבל לסמוך שפיר דמי מה ראיה יש בזה והלא יש סמיכה בחזרה כמו שיש סמיכה בשהייה והכי קאמר מהו לסמוך הקדרה בחזרתה לכירה שאינה גרופה וקטומה תוכה וגבה הוא דאסור אבל לסמוך שפיר דמי להחזיר ודקא מייתינן עלה מברייתא דשתי כירות המתאימות משהין ע"ג גרופה וקטומה ודחינן לה דלמא שאני התם דכיון דמדליא שליט בה אוירא וכן הא דתניא כירה שהסיקוה בגפת ובעצים סומכין לה ואין מקיימין עליה אא"כ גרופה וקטומה סתמא כרבי יהודה ומדרבי יהודה בלשהות נשמע לתנא דמתני' לסמוך בלהחזיר ודרבי חייא ודרבי אושעיא תנאי נינהו ואי נמי סבירא להו כרבי יהודה סתמא דמתני' עדיף מכל הני ובהדיא חזינן בגמרא דלא אתא רבי אושעיא אלא לשרויי מצטמק ולית לן

ראיה מינה דפליג על תנא דמתני׳ וכן כל מאי דאמרי׳ לקמן בענין תנור שהסיקוהו בקש ובגבבא סבר רב יוסף למימר תוכו תוכו ממש וכו׳ כל ההיא סוגיא לענין חזרת קדרה נאמרה שהיא מוחזרת בשבת בבין השמשות אבל לשהות דברי הכל מותר ל״ש כירה ול״ש תנור ל״ש תוכו ול״ש על גביו וא״צ לומר לסמוך דקי״ל כחנניא. והתימה הגדול שבדברי הרי״ף ז״ל שכתב בפ׳ ראשון וכמה כדי שיצולו א״ר זירא א״ר אלעאי אמר רב כמאכל בן דרוסאי וההיא כחנניא אזלא ועלה מייתינן לה לברייתא כחנניא ובפרק זה דחה דברי חנניא ולא זכר לאותה משנה ולא למה שכתב עליה ואם היה לו טעם בזה היה לו לכתוב לנו כלל הדברים הלכה כחנניא ומתני׳ להחזיר תנן אבל לשהות משהין אפילו תבשיל שלא בישל כל צרכו והוא שהגיע כמאכל בן דרוסאי אפילו בכירה שאינה גרופה וקטומה

ר״ן שבת טז. בדפי הרי״ף

ומנא לן דהכי הוא מסקנא דהא בתר דשקלינן וטרינן איבעיא לן מהו לסמוך וכו׳ הרב אלפסי ז״ל מביא ראיות הללו לסיועי למילתיה דקי״ל לשהות תנן ואפילו בשהייה בעיא גרוף וקטוף והחולקים עליו דחו כל ראיותיו ואני אכתוב על כל אחת ואחת טעמו של הרב אלפסי ז״ל וטעם החולקים עליו ראיה קמייתא היא מאי דאיבעיא לן בגמ׳ מהו לסמוך לה כלומר לסמוך קדרה אצל דופן הכירה שאינה גרופה שהכירה מיטלטלת היא ומושיבין אותה ע״ג קרקע וסבר הרב ז״ל דאע״ג דאיכא לפרושי לבעיין למאן דאמר להשהות תנן מהו להשהות בסמיכה ולמאן דאמר להחזיר תנן מהו להחזיר בסמיכה אפ״ה כיון דאמר תוכה וגבה הוא דאסיר (משום דאינה קטומה) דמשמע משום דאינה קטומה הוא דאסור תוכה וגבה משמע דכמ״ד להשהות תנן נקיט לה לבעיין דאילו לענין חזרה מיירי מאי אירא אינה קטומה אפי׳ בקטומה תוכה אסור דהכי אמר ר׳ חלבו אמר רב בגמ׳ [דף לז א] לא שנו אלא על גבה אבל בתוכה אסור והחולקין עליו אומרים דלא מכרעת דמשום דתלמודא נקיט לה לבעיא בכולהו וקושטא דמילתא הוא דכולהו תוכה וגבה אסור באינה קטומה נקט הכי אע״ג דלענין חזרה אפי׳ בקטומה תוכה אסור. וסייעיה למילתיה תו מדאמרינן מאי הוי עלה תא שמע דתניא כירה שהסיקוה וכו׳ דודאי הך ברייתא מוכחא בהדיא דאפילו לשהות אי גרוף וקטום אין אי לא לא כדקתני בהדיא ואין משהין עליה אא״כ גרופה

וקטומה. והחולקים עליו אומרים אין ברייתא הכי תניא וכר' יהודה אתיא דאמר הכי בברייתא בגמ' דאפי' לשהות בעינן גרופה וקטומה מיהו אע"ג דתלמודא פשיט בעיין מהך ברייתא לא מוכחא דכרבי יהודה ס"ל דאיכא למימר דהכי פשיט דמדר' יהודה נשמע לחנניא דכי היכי דלר' יהודה דאסר לשהות שרי לסמוך בשהיה ה"נ למ"ד להחזיר תנן שרי לסמוך בחזרה דאע"ג דחמיר איסורא להחזיר טפי מאיסורא דלשהות לענין תוכה מהא דרבי חלבו שכתבתי לעיל בסמוך אפשר דסבירא ליה לתלמודא דלענין סמיכה כי הדדי נינהו וליכא לאיפלוגי בינייהו ומכל מקום בעיין אפשיטא דלסמוך בשאינה גרופה שרי וכתבו בתוספות דאפילו הכי אין ללמוד מכאן שיהא מותר לסמוך אצל האש דשאני הכא שדפנות הכירה מפסיקין. וסייעיה למילתיה תו דרבי אושעיא ורבה בר בר חנה נמי הכי סבירא להו כדאיתא בגמ'. והחולקין עליו אומרים אינהו דאמרו כרבי יהודה ואנן כחנניא סבירא לן. וסייעיה למילתיה תו מדאמרינן לקמן בענין תנור שהסיקוהו בקש ובגבבא וכו' דההוא שקלא וטריא כפשטה בשהייה היא והחולקים אומרים דהא ודאי לא מכרעא כלל דגמרא נקיט לה למר כדאית ליה ולמר כדאית ליה למ"ד לשהות תנן לשהות ולמאן דאמר להחזיר להחזיר:

תו כתב הרב ז"ל דלא תקשי להאי פיסקא מאי דאמר רב ששת אמר ר' יוחנן ומתני' להחזיר תנן אבל לשהות משהין אף על פי שאינו גרוף ואינו קטום דלית הלכתא כוותיה ואף על גב דסייעיה רבא ואמר תרוייהו תננהו ההוא סיועא לאו דוקא הוא וכו'. ועל ראיה זו שדוחה הרב אלפסי ז"ל סמך רבינו האי גאון ז"ל ופסק הלכה כמאן דאמר להחזיר תנן אבל לשהות [משהין] אף על פי שאינו גרוף ואינו קטום כחנניא דהא רבי יוחנן סבירא ליה הכי ורבא נמי דהוא בתרא הכי סבירא ליה ועוד דמסייע ליה בגמ' ממתני' דתנן בפ"ק (דף יט א) ולא חררה על גבי גחלי' אלא כדי שיקרמו פניה ולא אידחיא לה האי סייעתא בגמרא כלל והרב אלפסי ז"ל נראה שלא סמך על (דחיה) [ראיה] זו דאפשר למדחיה משום דהתם כיון דלא מפסיק מידי בין פת לגחלים אי מחתה סליק בהו קוטרא ומשום האי טעמא נמי תנן לעיל בפ"ק (שם) אין צולין בשר בצל וביצה אלא כדי שיצולו מבעוד יום ואמר רב עלה וכמה כדי שיצולו כמאכל בן דרוסאי אף על גב דאיהו גופיה אמר הכא בגמרא [דף לז ב] מצטמק ויפה לו אסור וביצה מצטמקת ויפה לה היא כדאמרינן לקמן בגמרא [דף לח א] אלא היינו טעמא

משום דהתם לא מפסיק ולא מידי בינן ובין האש וכל שנצולו כמאכל בן דרוסאי מיחרכי ומפסדי ומשום הכי שרי אבל מקמי הכי שעדיין הן חיין לא מיפסדי בחתוי גחלים ומשום הכי אסירי אבל הכא דמפסקא קדרה כי מחתה לאחר שהגיע למאכל בן דרוסאי לא קשי ליה אדרבה ממהר בשולו וזהו טעמו של הרב אלפסי ז״ל שכתב בפרק קמא עלה דההיא וכמה כדי שיצולו כמאכל בן דרוסאי דאלמא בהכי שרי אפילו בלא גרופה וקטומה והכא אמרינן דאי גרוף וקטום אין אי לא לא ודאמר רבא בגמרא עלה דהא דרב ששת תרוייהו תננהו לאו סיועי מסייע ליה אלא סברא דרב ששת הוא דקא מפרש דלדידיה תננהו משום דמדמי תבשיל שבקדרה לפת דכי היכי דהתם שרי בקרימת פנים בתבשיל נמי שרי בשהגיע למאכל בן דרוסאי ומיהו אפשר לאיפלוגי בינייהו כדכתבינן:

ותו איכא ראיה בגמרא לסיועי לרב אלפסי ז״ל דמסקינן בסוף שמעתי׳ [דף לז ב] דמצטמק ויפה לו אסור מצטמק ורע לו מותר וההיא על כרחין בשהיה דליכא למימר דלא נחתין בפלוגתא דלשהות ולהחזיר כלל אלא למר כדאית ליה ולמר כדאית ליה למ״ד לשהות תנן פסקינן הכי בלשהות ולמ״ד להחזיר פסקינן הכי בלהחזיר דליתא דליכא למימר דלהחזיר כשאינה גרופה יהא מותר אפי׳ מצטמק ורע לו וראיה לדבר מדמייתי סייעתא לרב ששת בסמוך דאמר לדברי האומר אף מחזירין מחזירין אפילו בשבת [דף לח ב] מההיא דרבי חייא רבה שהעלו לו קומקום של חמין ואם איתא דמצטמק ורע לו שרי להחזיר אפילו באינה גרופה היכי מייתי סייעתא מיניה דלמא התם הוא בחמין שהוחמו כל צרכן דחמין כי האי גוונא מצטמק ורע להן ושרי להחזיר אפילו בשאינה גרופה אבל מתני׳ דמיירי בדבר הצריך בשול או צמוק לעולם אימא לך דאפי׳ בגרופה לא שרי אלא ודאי כדאמרן דלהחזיר אפילו במצטמק ורע לו אסור הלכך על כרחין מסקנא דשמעתין אתיא כמאן דאמר לשהות תנן (דאי) אפי׳ נתבשל כל צרכו ומצטמק ויפה לו אסור כל שכן בשלא נתבשל אלא כמאכל בן דרוסאי אבל רבינו האי גאון ז״ל סובר דלמסקנא מצטמק ויפה לו שרי מדאמרינן בגמ׳ [דף לז ב] דאמר ליה רב עוקבא ממישן לרב אשי אתון דמקרביתו לרב ושמואל עבידו כרב ושמואל כלומר דסבירא להו דמצטמק ויפה לו אסור אנן נעביד כרבי יוחנן דסבירא ליה מצטמק ויפה לו מותר ואי לאו דסבירא ליה דהכי הלכתא לא הוה עביד כרבי יוחנן

והא דקאמר ליה אתון עבידו כרב ושמואל היינו משום דכיון דסמיכי לרב ושמואל הוה ליה כדברים המותרים ואחרים נהגו בו איסור והר״ז הלוי ז״ל תפס לו דרך אחרת ופסק כמאן דאמר להחזיר תנן אבל להשהות [משהין] אע״פ שאינו גרוף ואינו קטום מיהו ה״מ בתבשילין שאין צמוקן יפה להן אבל בתבשילין שצמוקן יפה להן הכי דינייהו דכל שלא נתבשלו אלא כמאכל ב״ד לכ״ע אסור לשהותן ע״ג כירה שאינה גרופה ואינה קטומה וכשנתבשלו כל צרכן אלא שצמוקן יפה להן איכא מ״ד מותר ואיכא מ״ד אסור וכל כה״ג במנהגא תליא לבני מדינחא דמקרבי לרב ושמואל אסור לבני מערבא דמקרבי לרבי יוחנן שרי ואנן דלית לן מנהגא בהכי נקטינן לקולא כבני מערבא והרוצה להחמיר כבני מדינחא שרי:

ונמצאו כאן שלשה דעות לרבינו האי גאון ז״ל כל שנתבשל כמאכל בן דרוסאי מותר לשהותו ע״ג כירה שאינה גרופה אפילו מצטמק ויפה לו. ולדברי הרב אלפסי ז״ל אסור לשהותו אלא אם כן מצטמק ורע לו. ולדברי הר״ז הלוי ז״ל תבשיל שהגיע למאכל בן דרוסאי ואין צמוקו יפה לו מותר [לשהותו] אבל צמוקו יפה לו כל שלא נתבשל כל צרכו אסור נתבשל כל צרכו וצמוקו יפה לו הכל כמנהג המדינה:

קרבן נתנאל ג:א:ג

והכי קאמר מהו לסמוך הקדירה בחזרתה לכירה שאינה גרופה. והתוספות כתבו עוד אם להחזיר תנן בעי להשהות היכא שאינו מבושל כמאכל בן דרוסאי. ורבינו לא נראה לו פירוש זה משום פשיטותא דמייתי ופשיט מהא דתניא מקיימין עליו ונוטלין מכירה אפילו בשיל כמאכל בן דרוסאי ותני מקיימין דומיא דנוטלין.

ריטב״א שבת לו:

ק״ל מנא לן דמתני׳ כשהגיע למאכל בן דרוסאי דילמא כשלא הגיע למאכל בן דרוסאי דאפי׳ חנניא אוסר, י״ל דדומיא דחזרה קתני ולעולם לא התירו חזרה אלא כשהגיע למאכל בן דרוסאי דבפחות מכאן מבשל הוא.

אור שמח הלכות שבת ג:א

דע דאיכא תרי טעמי באיסור חזרה, חדא כמו שפירשו התוספות (שבת לו, ב ד״ה לא יתן) ורז״ה (שם טו, ב בדפי הרי״ף) דגזר שמא יחתה בגחלים

אם יחזיר לתוך הכירה, ומאי דגרע משהיה, זהו לפי דכשמשהה הא ודאי רותח הוא, אבל בחזרה בשבת דחייש שמא נצטננו שוב בשעת החזרה יש לחוש שמא יחתה בגחלים, וכמו"ש רבינו תם בספר הישר באורך, דבסתם חזרה התבשיל צונן הוא, עיי"ש בזה, עוד איכא טעמא לאסור משום מבשל בשבת, ואף אם נתבשלה כל צרכה מ"מ אסור להחזיר, משום דמיחזי כמבשל בשבת, ואתי להחזיר גם כשלא יהא מבושל כל צורכו, ונראה דהך טעמא דמבשל תלי' באשלי רברבי, כי כ"ז שאינה ראוי' לאכילה היינו שלא נתבשלה כמאכל בן דרוסאי לא שכיח שיטול הקדירה מן הכירה בשבת דליתי אח"כ לחזרה, וע"כ בראוי לאכילה, ושוב אין בה משום בשול אחר בשול, ואמאי נגזור להחזיר, אמנם זהו לשיטת הפוסקים, אבל דעת הרמב"ם הוא דיש בה משום בישול אחר בישול כ"ז שלא נתבשלה כל צרכה לגמרי, עיין פרק ט' ובהמגיד, ולפי זה רבינו אזיל לטעמי' וסבר דמשום בישול אסור להחזיר, ומש"ה פסק דכל שאסור להחזיר אסור לסמוך, דמאי נפקא מינה, כיון דמשום בישול אתו, גזירה שמא יחזיר קודם שנתבשלה כל צרכה, ומש"ה פסק דמבעוד יום מותר להחזיר דהא ליכא חשש דבישול כלל, אבל התוספות לטעמייהו, דמשום (שמש) [שמא] יחתה הוא, דמשום בישול לא שייך, דלאחר שנתבשל כמאכל בן דרוסאי היינו שתהא ראויה לאכילה שוב ליכא משום בישול כלל, עיין תוספות (שבת) י"ח ע"ב בד"ה (שמא יגיס) [דילמא מגיס] דפירשו משום צובע, וברא"ש פרק כירה (סימן א - ב), וקודם בישול כמאכל בן דרוסאי אין דרך ליטול מן הכירה, וע"כ הטעם הוא דאסור משום גזירת חתוי, ולפ"ז דוקא תוכה אסור, הא לסמוך אצלה שרי, כיון שדופן הכירה מפסיק בין הגחלים תו ליכא למיחש שמא יחתה, ומש"ה אסרי להחזיר מבע"י שמא יחתה משחשכה, ועיין רא"ש, ודו"ק, ולכך סמך רבינו דין דמגריפה בהלכה י"א, שגם הני דיני דחזרה משום בישול הוא דאסורים, וברור.

מגן אברהם רנג:ה

לסמוך לה קדירה וכו' - ואין מחזירין לעולם אלא ע"ג כירה גרופה וכו' וכל שאין מחזירין עליו אין סומכין לו בשבת עכ"ל הרמב"ם משמע דבשבת אסור לסמוך באינה גרופה דהאיבעי' בגמ' לא הוי אלא בע"ש ועיין במ"מ וכ"מ ברי"ף ע"ש אבל לסברא השניה שרי אפי' בשבת כמ"ש רמ"א סס"י זה:

שולחן ערוך אורח חיים סימן רנג סעיף ה

מותר לתת על פי קדירת חמין בשבת, תבשיל שנתבשל מע״ש כל צרכו, כגון פאנדי״ש וכיוצא בהן, לחממן, לפי שאין דרך בישול בכך; אבל להטמין תחת הבגדים הנתונים ע״ג המיחם, ודאי אסור.

רמ״א רנ״ג ס״ה

אבל אם הקדירות עדיין חמין, מותר להעמידן אצל תנור בית החורף, מאחר שנתבאר דתנורים שלנו יש להם דין כירה, וסמיכה בכירה שאינה גרופה וקטומה כדין גרופה וקטומה לענין נתינה עליה. וכבר נתבאר שנהגו להקל בחזרה בשבת אפי׳ הניחה ע״ג קרקע, וה״ה לסמוך לתנור שאינו גרוף וקטום הואיל והקדירה עדיין חם ומבושל כל צרכו, וכן המנהג פשוט להתיר וע״ל סי׳ שי״ח.

דגול מרבבה רנג

היינו לסמוך תחילה בשבת אבל אם סמך מערב שבת מותר להחזיר ולסמוך כדמוכח משתי כירות המתאימות שם בגמרא.

רבי עקיבא איגר רנג

בספר דגול מרבבה כתב היינו לסמוך תחילה בשבת אבל אם סמך מערב שבת מותר להחזיר ולסמוך כדמוכח מההיא דב׳ כירות המתאימות וע״ש ומחכ״ת אינו כן אלא כוונת המ״א דלהך דעה דלא קיי״ל כחנניה וזהו שיטת הרי״ף והוכיח כן מדבעי לן מאי לסמוך הרי דשהייה אסורה וביאר הר״ן דס״ל להרי״ף דאם איתא דהאי בעי׳ בלהחזיר איך פשטי׳ מהברייתא דב׳ כירות המתאימות הא התם מיירי בשהייה ודלמא חזרה חמיר ע״ש א״כ קיימא הדין דחזרה אסור בסמיכה ומזה מובן דמ״ש הגאון כדמוכח מב׳ כירות הוא שגיאה דהא התם מיירי בשהייה וע״ז כתב המ״א אבל לסברא השנייה שרי היינו לסברא השנייה דקיי״ל כחנניה והאיבעיא מהו לסמוך היינו בחזרה ופשיט לה מההיא דב׳ כירות הרי להדיא דגם בחזרה שרי ומ״מ דוקא דרך חזרה אבל לסמוך לכתחילה בשבת לא כדמוכח מהרמ״א סוף סימן זה במ״ש וכבר נתבאר דנהגו להקל וכו׳ באופן דלכתחילה לסמוך אסור ובחזרה זהו תולה המ״א בב׳ שיטות ודלא כדברי הגאון.

מחצית השקל רנג:ה

ר"ל דהרמב"ם אזיל לשיטתו דס"ל כהרי"ף לשהות תנן כנ"ל ואחד מראיותיהם מדאיבעיא לן שם מהו לסמוך בה תוכה וגבה הוא דאסור אבל לסמוך בה שפיר דמי או דלמא לא שנא ובעי למפשט מדתני שתי כירות המתאימות א' גרופה וא' שאינה גרופה משהין ע"ג גרופה וכו' ומדמשהין ע"ג גרופה אע"פ שסמוכה לאינה גרופה שבצדה אלמא דסמיכה מותרת ודחי שאני התם כיון דמדלי ר"ל כיון דהקדירה עומדת למעלה מן הגרופה ומשאינה גרופה ושליט בה אוירא ועדיין לא שמענו אם סמוך לצדי הכירה והקדירה עומדת ע"ג קרקע ולבסוף פשט מברייתא אחרת דסמיכה מותרת. וא"כ ע"כ צ"ל לשהות תנן דאי להחזיר תנן אבל לשהות מותר אפילו אינו גרוף וקטום מאי קמיבעיא ליה בסמיכה תוכה וגבה וכו' הא אפילו תוכה וגבה מותר. ואין לומר דהאיבעיא היה בסמיכה דחזרה וא"ש תוכה וגבה הוא דאסור א"כ היכי פשט משתי כירות המתאימות דמשהין ע"ג גרופה וכו' ואיך בא לפשוט סמיכה דחזרה להתיר מדשרי סמיכה דשהייה דהא ודאי חזרה חמירא משהייה אע"כ דהאיבעיא בסמיכה דשהייה אלמא לשהות תנן. והחולקים דחו לעולם האיבעיא בסמיכה דחזרה ואפ"ה פשט שפיר מסמיכה דשהייה דהא ברייתא דשתי כירות וכו' כרבנן דחנניא דהא אסרי לשהות ע"ג שאינה גרופה א"כ פשט מסמיכה דשהייה לרבנן לסמיכה דחזרה לחנניה דהא שהייה לרבנן י"ל דין חזרה לחנניה. ולפ"ז דברי הרמב"ם דאין סומכין בשבת א"ש לפי שיטתו דהא האבעיא ופשיטות דסמיכה מותרת היינו בסמיכה דשהייה והיינו מבע"י אבל סמיכה דחזרה היינו בשבת לא הוזכר בגמ' להתירא וכיון דהרמב"ם סבירא ליה דאין ללמוד היתר סמיכה החזרה מסמיכה דשהייה לכן ס"ל דשבת אסור להחזיר לסמוך.

ביאור הלכה רנג

מותר לסמוך לה - עיין מ"ב מש"כ בשם י"א והוא דעת המ"א לפי מה שביארו רע"א ותמה על הדגמ"ר איך רוצה להתיר בחזרה ובאמת אתפלא על תמיהתו הלא בברייתא דשתי כירות מפורש שם בסיפא דמותר גם חזרה וא"כ לפי הס"ד דגמרא דהוא בכלל סמיכה ממילא מוכח דגם חזרה מותר ואף דמדחי שאני התם דכיון דמידלי שליט ביה אוירא למסקנא דשרינן סמיכה לא צריך להאי שינויא [ומצאתי במלחמות שגם הוא מייתי ראיה

מהסיפא] ואח"כ מצאתי בתו"ש שגם הוא הקשה מהסיפא הנ"ל ונדחק דלפי המסקנא אין זה בכלל סמיכה אבל עכ"פ אין שום תמיה כלל על הדגמ"ר הנ"ל דהוא סובר כמו שכתבנו וגם בתוד"ה מהו איתא דחזרה מותר אפי' לדעה ראשונה ומש"כ במ"ב דאפילו בסמיכה לכתחלה יש מקילין הוא בספר בית מאיר ע"ש. וגם קצת סמך לזה מהרא"ש פ' כירה סימן יו"ד מה שכתב דאצל המדורה שרי משום דדמי לסומך ע"ש:

מלחמות ה' טו ע"ב בדפי הרי"ף אמר הכותב וכו'

אמר הכותב תחלה יש לי לומר שרבינו בראיותיו מראה פנים לדבריו דומה למה שאמרו משכח זוטרי שקיל משכח רברבי שקיל והא דמייתי ראיה מבעיין דלסמוך היינו מדקאמר תוכה וגבה הוא דאסור ואי להחזיר מה ענין תוכה וגבה לכאן והלא תוכה אסור אפילו בגרופה וקטומה ולסמוך גבה מותרין ולמה הזכירו כאן תוכה וכן הביאו עליה ראיה ממשהה ומה שאמר בעל המאור דמדרבי יהודה בלשהות נשמע לתנא דמתני' בחזרה ובזה הוא מתרץ לעצמו כל הסוגיא וזה אינו נכון שהרי אפילו לדברי האוסר יש חלוק בין שהייה לסמיכה כדאמרינן לעיל בלהחזיר לא שנו אלא על גבה אבל לתוכה אסור ולשהות בין תוכה בין על גבה שרי כדאמרינן מי סברת ארישא קאי אסיפא קאי וכו' אבל היה לו לבעל המאור בזו לומר דמדסיפא דמילתא ראיה דקתני אף מחזירין וכן הביא רבינו ראיה מדפשטוה מברייתא דקתני סומכין לה ולא דחינן מאי סומכין בשהייה דלכאורה נמי הכי משמע אע"פ שאין ראיה גמורה שיש לומר סומכין לה בחזרה והנה טענותיו של בעל מהאור ז"ל אינן דוחות כלום.

ר"ן על הרי"ף מסכת שבת דף טז עמוד א

וסייעיה למילתיה תו מדאמרינן מאי הוי עלה תא שמע דתניא כירה שהסיקוה וכו' דודאי הך ברייתא מוכחא בהדיא דאפילו לשהות אי גרוף וקטום אין אי לא לא כדקתני בהדיא ואין משהין עליה אא"כ גרופה וקטומה. והחולקים עליו אומרים אין ברייתא הכי תניא וכר' יהודה אתיא דאמר הכי בברייתא בגמ' דאפי' לשהות בעינן גרופה וקטומה מיהו אע"ג דתלמודא פשיט בעיין מהך ברייתא לא מוכחא דכרבי יהודה ס"ל דאיכא למימר דהכי פשיט דמדר' יהודה נשמע לחנניא דכי היכי דלר' יהודה דאסר

לשהות שרי לסמוך בשהיה ה"נ למ"ד להחזיר תנן שרי לסמוך בחזרה דאע"ג דחמיר איסורא להחזיר טפי מאיסורא דלשהות לענין תוכה מהא דרבי חלבו שכתבתי לעיל בסמוך אפשר דסבירא ליה לתלמודא דלענין סמיכה כי הדדי נינהו וליכא לאיפלוגי בינייהו ומכל מקום בעיין אפשיטא דלסמוך בשאינה גרופה שרי וכתבו בתוספות דאפילו הכי אין ללמוד מכאן שיהא מותר לסמוך אצל האש דשאני הכא שדפנות הכירה מפסיקין:

שער הציון רנג:כ-כא

דגול מרבבה בבאור דברי המגן אברהם וכן הסכים לדינא בספר בית מאיר וכן כתב בחידושי הר"ן בשם הרא"ה וכן כתבו בתוס' לז בד"ה מהו.
בית מאיר הנ"ל וגם בספר דגול מרבבה לדעה השנייה, אכן בחידושי הר"ן מחמיר בזה.

חידושים המיוחסים להר"ן לח ע"א

וליתא דבשהייה אפילו מצטמק ויפה לו מותר ובהחזרה הוא דאיכא לאיפלוגי אם הוא כירה שאינה גרופה דמצטמק ורע לו מותר בחזרה אע"פ שאינה גרופה דבהא איירינן דאילו בגרופה אין חילוק בין שהייה להחזרה.

חי' הר"ן המיוחסים לח ע"א ד"ה

אמר רב ששת לדברי האומר מחזירין מחזירין אפילו בשבת. פי' דלא תימא מחזירין דמתני' עם חשיכה בשעה שגרף וקטם אלא אפי' בשבת דא"ר השועיא וכו' ואע"ג דמתני' מיירי בגרופה ואיהו קא מייתי מחמין וסתם חמין מצטמק ורע לו וכל מצטמק ורע לו מותר להחזיר אפי' בשאינה גרופה וכמו שכתבנו למעלה מ"מ הא דר' אושעיא בשאינה גרופה היא ומדחמין באינה גרופה תבשיל נמי שרי בגרופה להחזיר.

ר"ן על הרי"ף מסכת שבת דף טז עמוד ב

תו כתב הרב ז"ל דלא תקשי להאי פיסקא מאי דאמר רב ששת אמר ר' יוחנן ומתני' להחזיר תנן אבל לשהות משהין אף על פי שאינו גרוף ואינו קטום דלית הלכתא כוותיה ואף על גב דסייעיה רבא ואמר תרוייהו תננהו ההוא סיועא לאו דוקא הוא וכו'. ועל ראיה זו שדוחה הרב אלפסי ז"ל סמך רבינו

האי גאון ז"ל ופסק הלכה כמאן דאמר להחזיר תנן אבל לשהות [משהין] אף על פי שאינו גרוף ואינו קטום כחנניא דהא רבי יוחנן סבירא ליה הכי ורבא נמי דהוא בתרא הכי סבירא ליה ועוד דמסייע ליה בגמ' ממתני' דתנן בפ"ק (דף יט א) ולא חררה על גבי גחלי' אלא כדי שיקרמו פניה ולא אידחיא לה האי סייעתא בגמרא כלל והרב אלפסי ז"ל נראה שלא סמך על (דחיה) [ראיה] זו דאפשר למדחיה משום דהתם כיון דלא מפסיק מידי בין פת לגחלים אי מחתה סליק בהו קוטרא ומשום האי טעמא נמי תנן לעיל בפ"ק (שם) אין צולין בשר בצל וביצה אלא כדי שיצולו מבעוד יום ואמר רב עלה וכמה כדי שיצולו כמאכל בן דרוסאי אף על גב דאיהו גופיה אמר הכא בגמרא [דף לז ב] מצטמק ויפה לו אסור וביצה מצטמקת ויפה לה היא כדאמרינן לקמן בגמרא [דף לח א] אלא היינו טעמא משום דהתם לא מפסיק ולא מידי בינן ובין האש וכל שנצולו כמאכל בן דרוסאי מיחרכי ומפסדי ומשום הכי שרי אבל מקמי הכי שעדיין הן חיין לא מיפסדי בחתוי גחלים ומשום הכי אסירי אבל הכא דמפסקא קדרה כי מחתה לאחר שהגיע למאכל בן דרוסאי לא קשי ליה אדרבה ממהר בשולו וזהו טעמו של הרב אלפסי ז"ל שכתב בפרק קמא עלה דההיא וכמה כדי שיצולו כמאכל בן דרוסאי דאלמא בהכי שרי אפילו בלא גרופה וקטומה והכא אמרינן דאי גרוף וקטום אין אי לא לא ודאמר רבא בגמרא עלה דהא דרב ששת תרוייהו תננהו לאו סיועי מסייע ליה אלא סברא דרב ששת הוא דקא מפרש דלדידיה תננהו משום דמדמי תבשיל שבקדרה לפת דכי היכי דהתם שרי בקרימת פנים בתבשיל נמי שרי בשהגיע למאכל בן דרוסאי ומיהו אפשר לאיפלוגי בינייהו כדכתבינן: ותו איכא ראיה בגמרא לסיועי לרב אלפסי ז"ל דמסקינן בסוף שמעתי' [דף לז ב] דמצטמק ויפה לו אסור מצטמק ורע לו מותר וההיא על כרחין בשהיה דליכא למימר דלא נחתין בפלוגתא דלשהות ולהחזיר כלל אלא למר כדאית ליה ולמר כדאית ליה למ"ד לשהות תנן פסקינן הכי בלשהות ולמ"ד להחזיר פסקינן הכי בלהחזיר דליתא דליכא למימר דלהחזיר כשאינה גרופה יהא מותר אפי' מצטמק ורע לו וראיה לדבר מדמייתי סייעתא לרב ששת בסמוך דאמר לדברי האומר אף מחזירין מחזירין אפילו בשבת [דף לח ב] מההיא דרבי חייא רבה שהעלו לו קומקום של חמין ואם איתא דמצטמק ורע לו שרי להחזיר אפילו באינה גרופה היכי מייתי סייעתא מיניה דלמא התם

הוא בחמין שהוחמו כל צרכן דחמין כי האי גוונא מצטמק ורע להן ושרי להחזיר אפילו בשאינה גרופה אבל מתני' דמיירי בדבר הצריך בשול או צמוק לעולם אימא לך דאפי' בגרופה לא שרי אלא ודאי כדאמרן דלהחזיר אפילו במצטמק ורע לו אסור הלכך על כרחין מסקנא דשמעתין אתיא כמאן דאמר לשהות תנן (דאי) אפי' נתבשל כל צרכו ומצטמק ויפה לו אסור כל שכן בשלא נתבשל אלא כמאכל בן דרוסאי

23

חי' הר"ן לז ד"ה אי אמרת

אי אמרת בשלמא להחזיר תנן היינו דשני בין תוכה לעל גבה. פי' דתוכה כיון דנפיש הבלא מיחזי כמאן דמבשל בשבת והרי הוא כמי שמניחה ע"ג גחלים ממש אלא אי אמרת לשהות תנן מה לי תוכה מה לי על גבה דכיון דגרופה וקטומה היא ודאי ליכא למיחש לחתויי ומה לי אי נפיש הבלא דאלו משום דטמנה ליכא שהרי אין בתוכה ולא בתוך תנור צורת הטמנה ולא דין הטמנה כלל ואע"ג דאסרינן בתנור בין תוכו בין על גבו ואפי' בהוסק בקש ובגבבא דליכא למיחש לחיתוי שאני תנור כיון דנפיש הבלא טובא טפי אתי לאיחלופי בכירה שאינה גרופה וקטומה מה שאין כן בתוכה דכירה, כן כתב הרא"ה ז"ל.

משנה ברורה רנג:נח

אבל לתוכה אסור - דכיון שהוא מעמיד לתוכה כדרך שמבשלין בה תדיר נראה כמבשל [רשב"א ור"ן] ואותן הכירות שאין להן תוך וחלל אלא הן פשוטות ותוכן וגבן אחד מותר להחזיר להן דאין עליהן שם תוך ואם יש אש בכירה עיין סימן שי"ח סט"ז:

ארחות שבת עמ' סח-סט

נראה שאם הדביק נייר דבק על גבי הכפתורים של הגז או החשמל, באופן שאינו יכול לשנות את דרגת החום אא"כ יסיר את נייר הדבק הרי זה מותר כדין טוח בטיט.

ארחות שבת עמ' תקמ

גם מרן הגרי"ש אלישיב שליט"א אמר לי שלדעתו אין להשתמש במכשיר שכל הקדירה טמונה בתוכו והפסק האויר שיש בין הקדירה לסיר החימום לא חשיב הפסק אלא שס"ל שאם ישימו איזה דבר להגביה הקדירה אזי לדעתו תחתית הקדירה לא נחשבת מוטמנת ואז אם הקדירה מגולה מלמעלה הרי שיש לנו מציאות שרוב הקדירה לא מוטמנת והיינו שכשמגביהים אזי גם חלק מהדפנות בולט כלפי חוץ ואולם גם לדעתו כה"ג מהני רק גבי הטמנה ולא גבי שהיה וחזרה

אגרות משה אורח חיים א:צג

בענין תנורי הגעז /הגז/ שבמדינתנו בכסוי פח מתכות אם יש בזה דין כירה או תנור כ"ז אדר שני תשי"א.

מע"כ ידידי הרב ר' בנימין זאב צוקער שליט"א מתלמידי הכולל דספרינג וואלי.

בדבר תנורי הגעז שבמדינתנו בכסוי פח של מתכות שהעולם נוהגין היתר להשהות שנסתפקת אם יש להן דין כירה או תנור.

הנה חומרת תנור הוא משום שנקלט חומו לתוכו טפי מכירה כדפרש"י /שבת/ בדף ל"ח ויכול להתבשל שם מצד עצם חומו אף כשיגרפו הגחלים ולכן ליכא היכרא ממה שגורף וקוטם שמסלק דעתו מלחתות בגחלים אף אם יצטרך למהר הבשול שזהו הטעם שמועיל בכירה גריפה וקטימה כדאיתא בר"ן בשם רב האי גאון ורב אפרים גאון והסכים להו הר"ן, וא"כ בתנור שכיון שרב חומו אפשר שהגריפה והקטימה שעושה הוא משום שירא שלא יקדיח תבשילו ברבוי האש ואינו היכר שהוא מחמת שמסלק דעתו מלחתות אף לכשיצטרך למהר הבשול ולכן אסור שמא יחתה כשיצטרך למהר הבשול.

אך הוקשה להו דהניחא בקטימה אבל בגריפה נהי שאין היכר עכ"פ הא אין שייך כלל לחתות והוצרכו לומר שמחמת שרב חומו מיחזי כיש שם גחלים לוחשות ואתי לשהויי בכירה ולחתויי, עיי"ש בר"ן.

והרמב"ם לא ניחא ליה בתירוצם וכמו שלא ניחא ליה להר"ן שם, לכן תירץ בפ"ג משבת ה"ו משום שא"א לגרוף כל האש וא"א שלא תשאר ניצוץ אחת ובתנור שהבלו חם יש לחוש לחתוי אף בניצוצות וכירה שהבלה

מועט לא תתחמם בניצוצות מועטים ומפני כך אין לחוש לחתוי כדאיתא שם במ״מ ה״ד.

וא״כ הוא שייך רק בתנור שדרך הבשול והאפיה הוא הרבה פעמים בקטימה וגריפה וליכא היכרא במה שגורף וקוטם שאין דעתו לחתות. אבל בתנורי הגעז שאין הדרך כלל לבשל בכסוי פח מתכות אין לך היכר גדול מזה שמסלק דעתו מלחתות ואין לחוש לחתוי, ונמצא שלפי״ז יש לתנורי הגעז שכיסה בפח מתכות דין כירה קטומה. אך לשיטת רש״י דבקטימה שמותר בכירה הוא משום דאינה מוספת הבל והוא כדפי׳ הר״ן דטעמו שאף שלשעתו מוסיף הבל מ״מ הם עוממות והולכות אין שייך זה בתנורי הגעז שלא נפחת אורו וא״כ הוא מוסיף הבל שיש לאסור לפ״ז.

איברא דבעצם לולא דמסתפינא היה נראה לע״ד דגם רש״י סובר דגחלים קטומים נחשבו מוסיף הבל אך לא אסרו משום ההיכר שיש בהקטום שאין דעתו לחתות, דהא כן מפורש ברש״י /שבת/ דף ל״ז שפי׳ שאני הכא דקטמה וגלי דעתיה דלא ניחא ליה בצמוקי עיי״ש, וזה שפי׳ במתני׳ שיתן אפר ע״ג גחלים לכסותם ולצננם, אין הכוונה דלא יוסיף הבל אלא דהוא גרוע מכפי שהיה בלא כסוי האפר וא״כ גלי דעתיה שלא ניחא ליה בצמוקי רק שיהיה חם לבד דבשביל זה לא אתי לחתויי דבלא החתוי יהיה חם דאם לא היה מגרע כלל לא היה מזה גלוי דעת דלא ניחא ליה בצמוקי. ולא יקשה לפי״ז על רש״י מה שהקשה הר״ן מהא דאסור להטמין ברמץ שגם לדידיה יהיה חלוק בין שהיה להטמנה, וכן לא יקשה קושיות התוס׳ עליו.

ולפ״ז גם לרש״י יש להתיר בתנורי הגעז לכסות בפח של מתכות דג״כ הא ודאי הפחית החום מבלא הכסוי.

אך מה נעשה שהתוס׳ והר״ן לא מפרשי כן בכוונת רש״י אלא דסובר שכירה קטומה לא נחשבה מוסיף הבל.

וא״כ יש לאסור לדידיה בתנורי הגעז בכסוי הפחים.

אבל לדינא כיון שרוב הפוסקים פליגי ארש״י, עיין בב״י /או״ח/ סי׳ רנ״ג ובד״מ שם, וסוברין דכירה קטומה היא מוספת הבל ומ״מ מותר בשהיה מצד היכרא שאין דעתו לחתות א״כ גם בתנורי הגעז יש להתיר כשמכסין בפח המתכות כמו שנוהגין, ובפרט שגם לרש״י אינו ברור שיאסור.

והנה היה מקום לומר דמה שפרש״י בעל גבה בדף ל״ז /שבת/ שהוא גם על כסוי שעל חללה הוא משום דאזיל לטעמיה דאם מוסיף הבל אסור

וכדפי׳ התוס׳ ור״ן בשיטתו ולכן בכסוי שעל חללה שמוסיף הבל כיון שאין הגחלים קטומים אסור אבל לרוב הפוסקים שאף במוסיף הבל מתירין משום ההיכר יסברו שמותר בכסוי שעל גבה.

אך יקשה ע״ז שהטור סובר ג״כ דלא כרש״י ומ״מ סובר שאסור בכסוי שעל גבה כרש״י.

ולכן צריך לומר משום דהתם דרך הבשול הוא כך הרבה פעמים דאם האש גדול וירא שיקדיח שבעצים קשה לצמצם וגם הרבה פעמים שאש קטן לא ידלק ומוכרח לעשות אש גדול מניח כסוי על גבה ואופה ומבשל שם דהא גם על עובי שפתה יכול לבשל משום שהכירה בעצמה יש לה חום לבשל ולא יגרע על גבה שהוא על האש ולכן לא הוי היכר. וא״כ בגעז שלא נמצא אף אחד שיבשל בכסוי פח מתכות משום שיכול להקטין האש ולהגדילו בצמצום כפי שצריך לכן אין היכר גדול מזה ומותר, וכמו שגם אתה חלקת. אבל הוא רק מטעם שבארתי שיש טעם לזה שבתנורי הגעז אין מכסין לעולם בשביל בשול יש לחלק ולהתיר ולומר שלא היה זה בכלל האיסור כיון שיש היכר ברור אחרי שאין בזה צורך להבשול, אבל אם לא היה טעם על זה שאין נוהגין לבשל בכסוי לא היה ניחא לחלק מצד שעכ״פ אין נוהגין לכסות להחשיב הכסוי להיכר דאם היה לפעמים איזה צורך לכסות בשביל הבשול כמו בכירה שלהם אפשר שאף שאחרים עכ״פ אין נוהגין לכסות אף שיש צורך מ״מ הוא עושה בשביל הצורך. וגם ממילא הא כבר היה זה בכלל האיסור ולא היה בידינו להתיר, אבל כיון שאין שום צורך לכסות בשביל הבשול ומחמת זה לא נמצא מי שמכסה לא היה זה בכלל האיסור ויש להתיר אף להטור.

והנה יש טעם גדול לומר דלא שייך כלל הגזרה בתנורי הגעז שלנו, דהא חזינן שרק לשלא יחתה בהגחלים גזרו ולא לשמא יביא עוד עצים כשיכלה האש, דאם היה שייך למיגזר זה היה לן לאסור גם בכירה שהסיקוה בקש וגבבא שלא שייך חשש חתוי שמא יתן עוד קש כשיתבער הקש שבכירה, דהא ליכא בזה היכר, אלא צריך לומר דזה לא גזרו.

ואולי משום דלא גזרו אלא בחתוי בפיו שקילא לאינשי דלא חשיב להו מעשה כ״כ מלעשות בידים.

וא״כ בתנורי הגעז שלא שייך חתוי בהגעז שכבר יש שם אלא אם רוצה להגדיל האש צריך שיתן עוד געז אחר שנותן ע״י שפותח יותר את

נקבי הצינור שיורד משם הגעז, א״כ הוא כמו להביא עצים אחרים שלא גזרו דלא חששו שיעשה בידים.

ואף אם נימא שהטעם שלא גזרו שמא יביא עצים וקש משום שרוב הפעמים אינם בסמוך להכירה שהוא דבר קשה להביאם מרחוק ויבא לזכור קודם שיביא העצים וממילא לא גזרו אף שנזדמן שהם בסמוך משום שלא שכיח כ״כ, וכדאיתא חלוק כעין זה בריש ביצה בגזרה שמא יקטום עיי״ש בתוס׳, וא״כ בתנורי הגעז שהוא דבר קל לפתוח יותר את נקבי הצינור להביא יותר געז יש לגזור, מ״מ כיון שעכ״פ לא גזרו אף בעצים וקש שסמוכים להכירה, לכן גם בגעז לא היה בכלל הגזרה אף שעתה נעשה באופן שלעולם הוא סמוך, כמו דברור שאף אם היה נעשה רגילות שלעולם יהיו קש ועצים סמוך להכירה שלא היה נאסר בשביל זה כיון שעכ״פ לא אסרו כ״כ הוא בגעז שהוא רק כנעשה הרגילות שהם לעולם בסמוך להכירה שלא היה בכלל הגזרה ואנן לא מחדשינן איסורין.

וגם מסתבר שלעולם היה הרגילות שיהיו עצים וקש סמוך להכירה דרוב בנ״א לא היו מצמצמים להביא רק כפי הצורך ומ״מ לא גזרו בשביל זה שלא יבא ליתן קש ועצים אחרים, וא״כ הוא מטעם שלא חששו שמא יעשה בידים, וא״כ הוא עוד כמפורש שאין לגזור גם בתנורי הגעז שצריך לעשות בידים.

ולפ״ז אף בלא כסוי גם על הכפתורים שעל ידם מקטינים ומגדילים אלא שיכסה רק את האש לבד נמי אפשר יש להתיר דגם בכסוי על האש לבד הוא היכר גדול שאין דעתו לחתות ולהגדיל האש יותר וכמו שנוהגין הרבה.

אך יותר טוב שהכסוי של פח המתכות יכסה גם את הכפתורים כדי שההיכר יהיה גם במקום החתוי כמו הקטום שיש אולי לחוש שלא ירגיש בהכסוי ויחתה. ואף שהוא דבר רחוק מ״מ כיון שהיתר ההיכר מצינו בהיכר שבמקום החתוי אולי הוא דוקא בהיתר כזה. אבל ודאי זה לבד שיכסה את הכפתורים ולא את האש לא יועיל שהעיקר הוא שצריך להראות שדעתו להפחית שזה נראה יותר בכסוי האש. אבל כיון ששם היו תרווייהו למעליותא שמפחית את החום והיה במקום החתוי אפשר הוא בדוקא ולכן יש להחמיר לכסות גם את הכפתורים, אבל כיון שיותר מסתבר שגם בלא כסוי הכפתורים הוא היכר חשוב יש להקל בשעת הדחק ואין למחות באלו הנוהגים היתר בכסוי האש לבד.

הלכות שבת (איידער) הע' תת

שמעתי בשם מו"ר הגר"א קטלר זצ"ל דבתנורים שלנו אף דטוב שגם האש יהיה מכוסה בבלעך העיקר הוא בכיסוי הכפתורים, ובדיעבד או במקום שקשה לכסות האש כגון באיזה תנורי חשמל בכיסוי הכפתורים לבד מהני.

שבת יח:

צמר ליורה לגזור אמר שמואל ביורה עקורה וניחוש שמא מגיס בה בעקורה וטוחה.

שלחן ערוך אורח חיים רנד:א

ואם הוא בתנור, וטח פיו בטיט, בין גדי ועוף שלמים בין בשר שור או עז, מותר דלא חיישינן לחיתוי שאם בא לפתוח התנור ולחתות תכנס הרוח ויצטנן התנור ויתקשה הבשר ויפסיד. הגה: ואין חילוק בזה בין אם הוא חי לגמרי או ד שנתבשל קצת.

ביאור הלכה רנד:א

דוקא כשהוא טוח בטיט סביב הכיסוי בכה"ג הוא דליכא למיחש לחיתוי דלא טרח כולי האי לסתור הטיחה שסביב פי התנור ומה"ט שרי אפילו הוא בקדרה.

חזון איש לח:ב

ואף אם התנור סגור אין כאן היתר טוח בטיט המבואר ברמ"א ס' רנד ס"א רק בנותן מערב שבת, אבל לא מצינו היתר זה ליתן בשבת. מיהו בערב שבת מותר ליתן בתנור סגור כמו שמותר ליתן לאינו גרוף בהיתר של שריק.

שבות יצחק (שהייה והחזרה) עמ' קכו-קכז

והא דכ' החזו"א דלעיל דלא מצינו היתר טיחה בטיט לנותן בשבת ולהנ"ל אי מהני אפי' גו"ק לחזרה בשבת כ"ש דמהני טיחה בטיט אפשר דאה"נ לחזרה מהני טיחה בטיט וכונת החזו"א לפי מש"כ לעיל שם דהנותן על תנור בשבת וידלק אח"כ י"ל דחשוב כנותן לכתחילה בשבת וע"ז כ' החזו"א

דבנותן לכתחילה בשבת אע״ג דגו״ק לא מהני היה מקום לומר דטוח בטיט דעדיף מהני אלא דלא מצינו.

תלמוד בבלי מסכת שבת דף יח עמוד ב

והשתא דאמר מר: גזירה שמא יחתה בגחלים, האי קדרה חייתא - שרי לאנוחה ערב שבת עם חשיכה בתנורא מאי טעמא - כיון דלא חזי לאורתא אסוחי מסח דעתיה מיניה, ולא אתי לחתויי גחלים. ובשיל - שפיר דמי, בשיל ולא בשיל - אסיר. ואי שדא ביה גרמא חייא - שפיר דמי.

משנה ברורה סימן רנג ס״ק ט

או שהיה חי - ודוקא בשר חי שא״א להתבשל לצורך סעודת הלילה אבל ירק ושארי דברים שהם קלי הבישול לא מהני מה שהוא חי וכן מה שכתב לקמיה חתיכה חיה היינו ג״כ בשר:

ספר הישר לר״ת (חלק החידושים) סימן רלה

וחמין שלנו שאנו טומנין אע״פ שיש סביבותיו מעט רמץ כגובה אצבע אין כאן איסור דהטמנה משמע שמכוסה בה רובו או כולו.

אגרות משה אורח חיים ד:עד:כו

מה דין תנורים שלנו לשהות בתוכם, די״ל דדינם ככירה א׳ מדכ׳ המאירי בשבת ל״ו ע״ב דהיכן דהאויר שולט הוי ככירה, ובי׳ יש בהם טערמוסטאט /טרמוסטט/ שאינו מניח להם להתחמם ביותר.

תשובה: סברת כתר״ה נכונה שיש גם בתוכם דין כירה, שמותר לשהות ולא להחזיר.

ערוך השלחן רנג:יז

ודע דתוכה לא מיקרי אלא כששולי הקדירה עומדת על שולי הכירה אבל כשאינה נוגעת בשולי הכירה אף שרוב הקדירה בתוך הכירה ונאחז בהרוחב שבו מלמעלה בגבי הכירה זה מיקרי על גבה ומותר [מג״א סקכ״ב] ותנורים שלנו שדינן ככירה כמו שיתבאר ובהן ליכא על גבן ותמיד מעמידין בתוכן ליכא חילוק בזה ותוכה הוה כעל גבה [זהו כוונת הש״ג שהביא המג״א שם]:

מגן אברהם רנג:כב

על גבה - מדסתם הרב"י ש"מ דס"ל דאפי' תלה הקדיר' לתוך אויר הכירה שרי דלא מקרי תוכה אלא כשיושב למטה בקרקעית הכירה וכ"כ ב"ח ועס"ג וכ' בש"ג ובכירות שלנו שהן פשוטות תוכה וע"ג א' הן ומותר ע"כ ואם יש אש על הכירה עסי' שי"ח סט"ו:

הלכות שבת (איידער) הע' תתקסג

שמעתי בשם מו"ר הגר"א קטלר זצ"ל שלתנורים שלנו מותר להחזיר וטעמו דעיקר בישול שלהם היה בתוכו לפיכך יותר מיחזי כמבשל בתוכו מעל גביו, משא"כ בשלנו על גביו הוא כמו בתוכו. לפיכך התיר להחזיר בתוכו בתנאי חזרה. אבל דעת הגרמ"פ שליט"א לאסור וכ"כ בתשובה בסוף הספר (אות ל"ב ד"ה סברת) "שיש גם בתוכה דין כירה, שמותר לשהות ולא להחזיר" אבל אמר דבלעך שיש משימים בתוך תנורים לפסח שמכסה מכל צדדין מהני לזה.

24

שלחן ערוך אורח חיים רנג:א

כירה שהיא עשויה כקדירה ושופתין על פיה קדירה למעלה, ויש בה מקום שפיתת שתי קדירות אם הוסקה בגפת שהוא פסולת של זיתים או בעצים, אסור ליתן עליה תבשיל מבעוד יום להשהותו עליה אא"כ נתבשל כל צרכו והוא מצטמק פי' הולך וחסר ורע לו, דליכא למיחש שמא יחתה או שהיה חי שלא נתבשל כלל דכיון שהוא חי מסיח דעתו ממנה עד למחר, ובכל הלילה יכול להתבשל בלא חיתוי, אבל אם נתבשל קצת ולא נתבשל כל צרכו, ואפי' נתבשל כל צרכו והוא מצטמק ויפה לו, חיישינן שמא יחתה ואסור להשהותו עליה אא"כ גרוף דהיינו שהוציא ממנה כל הגחלים, או קטם דהיינו שכסה הגחלים באפר למעט חומם; ואם נתן בה חתיכה חיה, מותר כאילו היתה כולה חיה דעל ידי כך מסיח דעתו ממנה. ואפילו אינה גרופה פי' שמשך הגחלים מהתנור וקטומה פי' שכסה הגחלים באפר מותר לסמוך לה קדירה בסמוך חוצה לה; ואם הוסקה בקש או בגבבא מותר לשהות

עליה אפילו אינה לא גרופה ולא קטומה. הגה: שתי כירות המתאימות זו אצל זו ודופן של חרס ביניהם, האחת גרופה וקטומה והשניה אינה גרופה וקטומה מותר לשהות על הגרופה וקטומה אע"פ שמוסיף הבל משאינה גרופה וקטומה (גמ' פרק כירה. ותנור, אפילו אם הוסק בקש וגבבא, אסור אפילו לסמוך לו אפי' אם הוא גרוף וקטום. הגה: שהיד סולדת בו (הגהות מרדכי. וכ"ש שאסור לשהות בתוכו או על גבו. וכופח שהוא מקום שפיתת קדירה אחת, אם הוסק בקש או גבבא דינו ככירה; בגפת או בעצים דינו כתנור והתנורים שלנו דינם ככירה (ר"ן ר"פ כירה וכל בו וכן משמע מפירש"י). ואם שכח ושהה, אם הוא תבשיל שבישל כל צרכו, מותר אפי' הוא מצטמק ויפה לו; ואם הוא תבשיל שהתחיל להתבשל ולא בישל כל צרכו אסור עד מוצאי שבת; ואם עבר ושהה אסור בשניהם. הגה: עד בכדי שיעשו (הגה"א ורמב"ם). ואם החזירה א"י בשבת דינו כשכח ושהה (הג"א) ואם החזירו ישראל, דינו כעבר ושהה (הגהות מרדכי) ואם מצטמק ורע לו, מותר שהרי לא נהנה מן האיסור (ב"י וע"ל ריש סי' רנ"ז). וי"א שכל שנתבשל כמאכל בן דרוסאי (פי' שם אדם שהיה אוכל מאכלו שלא נתבשל כל צרכו) או שנתבשל כל צרכו ומצטמק ויפה לו, מותר להשהותו ע"ג כירה, הגה: או אפילו ע"ג תנור (המגיד פ"ג והגהות מרדכי ומיימוני פ"ג וריש פ' כירה וב"י) אפי' הוסק בגפת ועצים אפי' אינה גרופה וקטומה; ולא הוזכרה גרופה וקטומה והוסק בקש וגבבא אלא כשהתחיל להתבשל ולא הגיע למאכל בן דרוסאי; וכן לענין אם נטל הקדירה מעליה ובא להחזירה עליה בשבת; ואם שכח ושהה תבשיל שהתחיל להתבשל ולא הגיע למאכל ב"ד אסור. ואצ"ל אם עבר ושהה. הגה: ונהגו להקל כסברא האחרונה. וכל זה בענין שהה, שהקדירה יושבת על כסא של ברזל או ע"ג אבנים ואינה נוגעת בגחלים; אבל הטמנה ע"ג גחלים, לד"ה אסור. הגה: וי"א דאפי' אם הקדירה עומדת ע"ג האש ממש כל זמן שהיא מגולה למעלה לא מקרי הטמנה ושרי; וכן המנהג רק שנזהרים לנתקן קצת קודם השבת מן האש כדי שיוכל ישראל להסירו משם; ואם לא נתקן מן האש ונמצאו ע"ג האש בשבת יש להסירו משם ע"י א"י; ואם ליכא א"י מותר לישראל להסירו משם. ויזהר שיקחנו משם בנחת ולא ינענע הגחלים, ואז אף אם ינענען קצת, דבר שאין מתכוין הוא ושרי (מרדכי ר"פ כירה והגמי"י פ"ז).

רע"א סימן רנג סעיף א

או נתבשל כל צרכו. משמע דבנתבשל כמאב"ד והתבשיל מצטמק ויפה לו אסור כדעת הרז"ה וממ"ש אח"כ ולא הוזכר גרופה וקטומה אלא בשהתחיל להתבשל ולא הגיע למאכב"ד משמע דבהגיע למאכב"ד מותר בכל ענין גם בעיקר הדין דכ' הש"ע בפשיטות דבלא הגיע למאכב"ד מהני גרו"ק אינו ברור דהא ממ"ש הרא"ש בשם רבינו יונה דמה דקתני אין צולין וכמה כדי שיצולו כמאב"ד אתיא בין לחנניה בין לרבנן ולרבנן בגרוף הרי דמ"מ אף שהוא גו"ק בעי' שיצולו כמאב"ד הוא דקתני במתני' לא יתן עד שיגרוף לחנניה איירי רק לחזרה כדאיתא בסוגיין. עיין רשב"א פ' כירה דמסתפק בזה אם מהני גרוף וקטום בפחות מכמב"ד דדילמא י"ל דיהיב דעתיה טפי וחיישי' לחיתוי ומ"מ העלה שם דמסתבר דמהני גו"ק ולענ"ד יש לעיין למה כ' הרשב"א פ"ק דשבת דף י"ח ע"ב אההיא דאמרינן שם דצמר ליורה בעקורה ואינה טוחה חיישי' שמא יגיס תירץ שם דלאחר שנתבשל כמאב"ד אין בו משום בשול ע"ש א"כ להך סברא ממילא בפחות מכמאב"ד לא מהני גו"ק משום החששא דשמא יגיס וצ"ע.

רי"ף מסכת שבת דף ח עמוד א

וכמה כדי שיצולו אמר ר' זריקא אמר רבי אלעאי אמר רב כמאכל בן דרוסאי איתמר נמי א"ר אסי א"ר יוחנן כל שהוא כמאכל בן דרוסאי אין בו משום בישולי נכרים:

רא"ש מסכת שבת ג:א

ועוד תימה על רי"ף ז"ל שכתב בפ"ק וכמה כדי שיצולו אמר רבי זירא אמר ר' אילעאי כמאכל בן דרוסאי וההיא כחנניא אתיא ועלה מייתי ברייתא דחנניא ובפרק זה דחה דברי חנניא ולא נזכר לאותה משנה ולא למה שכתב עליה. ואם היה לו טעם בזה היה לו לכותבו לנו...

ומה שתמה הר"ז ז"ל שכתב בהלכותיו בפ"ק וכמה כדי שיצולו אמר רב כמאכל בן דרוסאי כתב ה"ר יונה ז"ל שאין בזה תמהון דאיצטריך ההוא פירושא אפילו לרבנן ואפילו לרב דאסר מצטמק ויפה לו דאשמעינן כיון שנצולו מבעוד יום כמאכל בן דרוסאי משהינן אותו על גבי גרופה וקטומה

אבל ודאי אין צולין אותו אלא כדי שיצולו מבעוד יום ואפילו לדעת שיגרוף ויקטום הגחלים עם חשיכה.

ביאור הלכה סימן רנג

ונהגו להקל כסברא האחרונה - עיין בב"י שהאריך הרבה באלו השתי דעות והעתיק דברי הרא"ש שכתב דמפני שישראל אדוקים במצות עונג שבת ובודאי לא ישמעו לנו ע"כ הנח להם ע"ש משמע מזה דרק משום זה לא רצה למחות וכן הב"י גופא ממה שהעתיק דעה הראשונה בסתמא והדעה השניה בשם י"א משמע ג"כ דעתו נוטה להחמיר אך מ"מ אין בנו כח למחות במקילין שכבר נהגו העם כהי"א וכמו שכתב הרמ"א וע"כ לפ"ז לכתחלה בודאי טוב ליזהר שיהיה מבושל כ"צ קודם חשכה ולסלקו מן האש אך אם אירע שנתאחר הדבר כגון שבאו אורחים קודם שקיעת החמה והוצרך לבשל איזה תבשיל עבורם יכול להעמיד על הפטפוט לבשל אף שלא יתבשל עד השקיעה רק כחצי בישול סגי ויניחנו עומד על הפטפוט עד שיגמר בשולו ומותר לסלק ממנו בלילה דהא אין עומד על הגחלים:

ר"ן על הרי"ף מסכת שבת דף ו עמוד ב

והאי בשיל ולא בשיל דאמרינן הכא דאסור פירשו בתוספות דהיינו שהתחיל להתבשל ולא הגיע עדיין למאכל בן דרוסאי אבל כל שהגיע למאכל בן דרוסאי בשיל מקרי ותו לא חיישינן ביה שמא יחתה בגחלים וכדאמרינן לקמן [דף לו ב] תניא חנניא אומר כל שהוא כמאכל בן דרוסאי מותר לשהותו על גבי כירה אע"פ שאינה גרופה ואינה קטומה וכך פירש רב האי גאון ז"ל בפרק כירה אבל לפי דעת הרב אלפס ז"ל בשיל ולא בשיל היינו משהתחיל להתבשל ועד שנתבשל כל צרכו ואפילו שנתבשל כל צרכו נמי כל שמצטמק ויפה לו אסור דהא דאמרינן לקמן גבי אין צולין בשר בצל וביצה [דף כ א] וכו' וכמה אמר רב כדי שיצולו כמאכל בן דרוסאי התם בשהן עצמן מונחין על האש דכיון שהגיע למאכל בן דרוסאי אם יחתה בגחלים יחרוך אותן וזהו שכתב הרב אלפסי ז"ל להיא דרב אף על פי שפסק בפרק כירה שאסור לשהות ע"ג כירה שאינה גרופה ואינה קטומה כל שמצטמק ויפה לו ודלא כחנניא וכן פסק הרמב"ם ז"ל בפרק ג'

מהלכות שבת וכן דעת הרמב"ן ז"ל ויש לר"ז הלוי ז"ל בדברים הללו דעת שלישי. ויתבאר הכל בפרק כירה בס"ד:

שלחן ערוך אורח חיים רנד:א

אע"פ שבשר חי מותר להשהותו, ה"מ בקדרה אבל בצלי שאצל האש אסור להניחו סמוך לחשיכה שממהר להתבשל ואתי לחתויי. וה"מ בבשר שור או עז אבל בשר גדי ועוף שהם מנותחים לאברים מותר דלא חיישינן לחיתוי שאם יחתה בגחלים יתחרך (פי' יצא מגדר הצלי ונכנס בגדר הנשרף) הבשר, שאינו צריך אלא חמימות האש בלבד.

שלחן ערוך אורח חיים שיח:ד

ואם לא נתבשל כל צרכו, ואפילו נתבשל כמאכל בן דרוסאי שייך בו בישול אפילו בעודו רותח.

חידושי הרמב"ן שבת יח:

הא דאמרינן והלא מגיס. [פרש"י ז"ל] והוי מבשל, ואינו מחוור שא"כ בקדירה נמי הוה להו למיסר מגיס טפי ממחתה בגחלים שיותר קרוב לבא לידי הגסה מחיתוי גחלים, ויש מפרשים והלא מגיס והוא צובע שכן דרך הצובעין להגיס בבגדים, ומיהו גבי בישול נמי המגיס חייב משום מבשל כדתניא בתוספתא ומייתי לה בגמ' בפ' המביא כדי יין אחד נותן את האור ואחד נותן את העצים ואחד נותן את הקדירה ואחד מגיס כולן חייבין, ומיהו לא חיישינן דילמא מגיס כדחיישינן בצובע שאין דרך כל כך להגיס בה אלא משעה ראשונה כדי שיתערב הכל ויתבשל, ונראה דלא מיחייב אלא בהגסה ראשונה שאינו מתבשל מהרה אלא בהגסה זו שנמצא אף הוא מבשל ובההוא ליכא למיחש כדאמרינן קדרה חיתא שרי, אבל משהגיס דבלאו הכי מתבשל אף המגיס פטור דמאי עביד הלכך ליכא למיגזר בשבת משום מגיס דלאו קרובי בישולא איכא דבלא"ה מתבשל, א"נ איכא למימר דמשום הכי לא אדכרו מגיס משום שחתוי הגחלים כוללת יותר שיש לחוש אפי' במבושל כמאכל בן דרוסאי ובצלי ופת ואלו משום מגיס ליכא לפיכך הזכירו חיתוי גחלים בכל מקום, ובקדרה חיתא ליכא משום מגיס כי היכי דלית בה משום חיתוי גחלים דהא מסח ליה לדעתיה מינה ולא נגע בה

כלל, ויש לומר עוד דגבי צבע יש לחוש לפי שתקדיחנו היורה והוא מפסיד הרבה וכן נראה בירושלמי.

רמ"א אורח חיים רנג:ה

ויש מתירין ליתן לתוך תנור שאפו בו מבע"י, דמאחר שלא הטמינו בו רק אפו בו מבע"י לא נשאר בו רק הבל מעט ואין לחוש לבישול (כל בו) ובלבד שלא נצטנן לגמרי. ויש מחמירין בזה. ואם החום כל כך בתנור שהיד סולדת בו, אסור ועיין לקמן סימן שי"ח.

משנה ברורה רנג ס"ק צ

ליתן לתוך וכו - היינו שנותן בשבת בבוקר בתוך התנור התבשיל שנתבשל כדי שיתחמם דאף שבתוך התנור והכירה קי"ל דאפילו גרוף וקטום אסור להחזיר דאינו מותר רק על גבה הכא אחר שלא הטמינו בו חמין לשבת רק אפו בו מבעוד יום אין בו למחר רק חום מועט ואין נראה כמבשל עי"ז ומשמע דאם היה טמון בו חמין מבערב דנפיש הבליה דתנור היה אסור ליתן בו בבקר התבשיל שנתבשל כדי להתחמם וכ"ז הוא להכל בו אבל בד"מ וכן מהרמ"א לעיל בס"ב בהג"ה מוכח דנוהגים להקל להחזיר לתוך התנור בכל גווני אלא שמסיים שם דטוב להחמיר:

ביאור הלכה רנג

מותר לשהות עליה - וה"ה להחזיר אפילו בשבת דכגרופה וקטומה דמיא [גמרא] ועיין בס"ב דין החזרה בגרופה וקטומה:

דרכי משה הארוך סי' רנג סק"ד

או שהניח ע"ג קרקע וכו'. כתב בית יוסף וכן הסכמת הפוסקים דלא נהירא כהגהות מיימוניות שכתבו להקל דאפילו הניחו ע"ג קרקע שרי והר"ן פרק כירה דף קטו ע"א כתב דכל הני דברים דוקא כשסלקן מערב שבת ולא החזירן עד שחשיכה אבל נטלו משחשיכה אפילו הניחו ע"ג קרקע מותר להחזיר וכן משמע בירושלמי עכ"ל. ובית יוסף כתב ודבר פשוט הוא שאין כן דעת התוס' והרא"ש וסייעתם וכן הרמב"ם כתב בהדיא שלא כדבריו מיהו רבים נוהגים להקל כדברי הר"ן שלאחר שהוציאו מן התנור שלנו שיש

לו דין כירה כמו שנתבאר לעיל מחזירין לתוכו אעפ״י שהניחו ע״ג קרקע כל זמן שהוא חם וכן כתב הכל בו בהדיא להתיר ליתן שם פת או פנדה שהוציאו מערב שבת אם נשארו עדיין מעט בהבלן לחממן בהבל מועט שעדיין בתנור מאחר שאין בתנור גחלים שכבר נתאכלו וכתב שאין צריך ליזהר שלא יהא בתנור שום גחלת, ובית יוסף כתב דנהגו להחזיר אפילו לאחר שנצטננו ופקפק על המנהג וכתב דמדברי הר״ן אין ראיה דהר״ן לא התיר אלא בעוד הקדירה רותחת ודוקא על הכירה אבל בתוכה אסור ומדברי הכל בו אין ראיה דהכל בו לא קאמר בתנור שהטמינו בו אלא אפו בו מבעוד יום, דמעט הבלו, אבל בתנור שהטמינו בו דנפיש הבליה לא, וכתב דנכון להחמיר בכל ענין אפילו דברים שאין דרכן לאפות או לבשל בתנור ושנצטמק ורע לו דמוכח דלא עביד אלא לחמם כמו שכתבתי לעיל בשם הר״ן אפ״ה אסור עכ״ל. ונראה דבדבר שעדיין חם אין לחוש על כך ודברי ב״י אינם אלא בדבר צונן וכן הוא המנהג בינינו דחוששים בדברים צוננים ונוהגים היתר בדברים שהוציאו מן התנור ועדיין חמין כדברי הר״ן ומה שחילק בין נתינה על הכירה או לתוכה זה לא נזכר בדברי הר״ן אלא שהב״י חילק מעצמו בכך ואפשר דלא ס״ל לחלק בהא ופוק חזי מה עמא דבר. ועיין לקמן מ״ש בזה סוף סימן רנ״ז. ובהגהות מיימוניות פ״ד דשבת דמוהר״ם היה מוחה להושיב החמין לאחר שהוציאן תוך כרים וכסתות ונראה דזו גרע מלהחזיר לתנור דזהו כתחילת הטמנה הואיל ולא היו שם מבעוד יום [ואפשר דמהר״ם לא קאמר אלא אם נצטננו].

רמ״א רנג:ב

וי״א דכל זה אינו אסור רק כשנטלו מן הכירה מבעוד יום, ולא החזירו עד שחשכה; אבל אם לקחו משם משחשכה, אפי׳ הניחו ע״ג קרקע מותר (ר״ן פ׳ כירה וכל בו) וכן נוהגים להקל בתנורים שלנו שיש להם דין כירה, וסומכין עצמם על דברי המקילין וטוב להחמיר.

מגן אברהם רנג:לה

ז״ל ד״מ כב״י נהגו להחזיר כו׳ ומ״מ משמע דאסור דדוקא ע״ג שרי אבל לא לתוכה כמ״ש ס״ב וכו׳ ע״כ ונראה דבדבר שעדיין חם אין לחוש כ״כ ודברי ב״י אינן אלא בדבר צונן וכן המנהג בינינו דחוששין בדבר צונן

ונוהגין היתר בדבר חם שהוציאו מן התנור כדברי הר"ן ומה שחילק הב"י בין ע"ג לתוכה זה לא כדברי הר"ן אלא שהב"י חילק מעצמו כך ואפשר דלא ס"ל לחלק בהא ופוק חזי מאי עמא דבר עכ"ל ד"מ פי' דמאי דאמרינן בגמרא לתוכה אסור היינו כשנטלו מבע"י ולא החזירו עד שחשיכה וכמ"ש ס"ג אבל נטלו בשבת מותר להחזירו לגרופה וקטומה ואפי' לתוכה וזה כיון שלא הטמינו בו ה"ל כגרופה וקטומה וצ"ע דהר"ן לא כתב היתר זה אלא כשהניחם עג"ק דלא הוי כתחלת הטמנה כיון שהיה שם בשבת אבל לענין היתר תוכה לא מהני זה וזה דעת המחמירין ובלבוש משמע דאפי' הטמינו בו שרי להחזיר לתוכה אחר סעודת שחרית כיון דכבר עממו גחליו ה"ל כגרוף וקטום ע"ש שנדחק לענין היתר תוכה ולא ראה דברי הד"מ:

בית יוסף אורח חיים סימן רנג ס"ה ד"ה כתב הר"ן עד בס"ד

כתב הר"ן בפרק כירה (יט. סוד"ה ת"ר מביא) גבי הא דתנו רבנן מביא אדם קיתון של מים ומניחו כנגד המדורה בשם הרשב"א (מ: סוד"ה מביא) שמותר לתת על פי קדרת חמין בשבת תבשיל שנתבשל מערב שבת כל צרכו כגון פנאדי"ש וכיוצא בהם לחממן ואע"פ שהיד סולדת בו לפי שאין דרך בישול בכך ואע"פ שהקדרה נתונה על האש אבל להטמין תחת הבגדים הנתונים על גב המיחם ודאי אסור שהרי אסור להטמין משחשיכה אפילו תבשיל שנתבשל כל צרכו אפילו בדבר שאינו מוסיף הבל וכתב הר"ן על זה ואפשר גם כן שמה שאין דרכו לאפות על גבי כירה כגון פנאדי"ש וכיוצא בהם שמותר לחממן בשבת על גבי כירה או על גבי כסא של ברזל כל שהוא מצטמק ורע לו שהדבר מוכיח שאינו נעשה אלא בשביל שיתחמם. ומשמע דדוקא על גבי כירה או על גבי כסא ברזל קאמר דאפשר דשרי אבל ליתן בתנור אסור כיון שדרכו ליאפות שם ועוד אכתוב בזה (לקמן סוד"ה ולענין מה שנוהגין) בס"ד:

בית יוסף אורח חיים סימן רנג ס"ב ד"ה כתב הר"ן

כתב הר"ן (יז: ד"ה ומיהו) דמשמע בירושלמי (פ"ג סוף ה"א) דכל הני פלוגתא ליתנהו אלא בשסלקן מעל גבי כירה מערב שבת ולא החזירן עד שחשיכה אבל נטלו משחשיכה אפילו הניחו על גבי קרקע מותר להחזיר ועל דרך זה אפשר לפרש מאי דאמרינן (לח סוע"א) לדברי האומר מחזירין

מחזירין אפילו בשבת לומר שאף על פי שהחזרה בלבד היא שנעשית בשבת שרי ובכהאי גוונא הוא דמפלגינן בין עודן בידו להניחן על גבי קרקע אבל כשסילק בשבת בכולהו גווני שרי עכ"ל ודבר פשוט הוא שאין כן דעת התוספות (לו: ד"ה וב"ה) והרא"ש (סי' ב) וסיעתם שהרי הם אוסרים להחזיר אפילו מבעוד יום סמוך לחשיכה וכ"ש להחזיר בשסילק משחשיכה וגם הרמב"ם כתב בהדיא היפך הירושלמי הזה שהרי כתב בפרק ג' (ה"י) כל שמותר להשהותו על גבי האש כשנוטלין אותו בשבת אסור להחזירו למקומו וכו' והוא שלא הניח הקדרה על גבי הקרקע:

דרכי משה סימן רנג ס"ק ד*

מיהו רבים נוהגים להקל כדברי הר"ן שלאחר שהוציאו מן התנור שלנו שיש לו דין כירה כמו שנתבאר לעיל מחזירין לתוכו אעפ"י שהניחו ע"ג קרקע כל זמן שהוא חם.

בית יוסף אורח חיים סימן רנג ד"ה ולענין

ולענין מה שנוהגין בקצת מקומות להחזיר תבשיל לתוך התנור בשבת, מהירושלמי (פ"ג סוף ה"א) שכתב הר"ן (יז: ד"ה ומיהו) משמע דעד כאן לא אסר תלמודא אלא כשנטלו מבעוד יום ובא להחזירו משחשיכה אבל כל שנטלו בשבת מותר להחזיר אפילו הניחו על גבי קרקע. ואע"ג דהיינו דוקא להחזיר לכירה גרופה וקטומה וכדתנן בהדיא (במתני' ר"פ כירה) אבל לכירה שאינה לא גרופה ולא קטומה או לתנור וכופח שהסיקוהו בגפת או בעצים אפילו גרוף וקטום ליכא מאן דפליג דאסור דמתניתין היא. אפשר לומר דתנור דידן לכירה דמי כדברי רבינו חננאל (גליון לח:) וכיון דבשעה שמחזירין בהם עממו גחליו ה"ל כגרוף וקטום כדאמרינן בגמרא (לז סוף ע"א) ומכל מקום משמע דאסור משום דעד כאן לא שרי בגמרא (לז.) להחזיר אלא על גבי כירה אבל לא בתוכה ועוד שלא התירו להחזיר אלא בעוד הקדרה רותחת כמו שנתבאר (יד: ד"ה ומ"ש רבינו כל זמן) והם נוהגים להחזיר אפילו צונן ועוד שהירושלמי הזה לא קיימא לן כוותיה לדעת הפוסקים כמו שכתבתי לעיל (יד: ד"ה כתב הר"ן דמשמע) ומיהו אפשר למצוא להם היתר מצד אחר וכמו שכתב הכל בו (סי' לא, לא ע"ד) וז"ל ובתנור שלנו דין חזרה בו כדין הכירה הגרופה והקטומה

ואחר שהוציאו ממנה הפת או הפנאד"ה שאם נשאר בקצת הבלו עד למחר אפשר לומר שהוא מותר לתת בתוכו פנאד"ש להתחמם שם באותו הבל המועט שבו שהרי אין שם חשש חיתוי כלל שהרי גרפו מבערב ואפילו לא קטמו הרי נתאכלו וכהו כל גחליו ואין צריך שיזהר בזה שלא יהא שם גחלת כלל. אבל לבי נוקפי בהיתר זה משום דאמאי דאמר רב ששת (לח סוף ע"א) לדברי האומר מחזירין אפילו בשבת פירש רש"י אפילו ביום המחרת דלפ"ז אף ביום המחרת לא שרי להחזיר אלא בכירה גרופה וקטומה דוקא ולא בתנור כלל. ואפשר שלזה נתכוין בעל הכל בו שכתב בסוף דבריו אבל לפירש רש"י יש לפקפק וכן נראה ודאי שלא נתנו חכמים דבריהם לשיעורין. ואף לפי היתר זה שכתב הכל בו נראה שאין דבריו אמורים אלא בשאחר שהוציאו הפת או הפנאד"ה לא חממוהו עוד דכיון שאפו בו אזיל ליה הבלא דידיה אבל כל שחממוהו כדי להכניס בו קדרת חמין לצורך מחר נפיש הבליה ואסור לתת לתוכו פנאד"ש לחמם אפילו אם גרפוהו ומכל מקום דבר שאין דרכו לאפות בתנור כגון עניני בצק המטוגנים בשמן אפשר דשרי על פי מה שכתב הר"ן (יט. סוד"ה ת"ר מביא) דאפשר דשרי לתת פנאד"ש על גבי כירה או על גבי כסא ברזל כל שהוא מצטמק ורע לו שהדבר מוכיח שאינו נעשה אלא בשביל שיתחמם ואף על גב דלא בריר ליה היתרא שאני התם שהוא מחממן על האש ממש אבל בכהאי גוונא דלאו על האש ממש הוא אפשר דפשיטא ליה דשרי ומכל מקום נכון לאסור אפילו בכהאי גוונא כדי שלא יבואו להתיר את האסור וכל שכן שאין הדבר ברור כל כך להיתרח: כל דינין דשייכי למבשל בשבת או מחמם דבר חם או דבר קר בין שמחממו על ידי האור עצמו או בחמה עצמה או בתולדותיהן הכל יתבאר בסימן שי"ח בס"ד:

חזו"א סי' לז סק"ח ד"ה והנה

והנה הב"י לא מצא שום היתר להחזיר ביום השבת לתוך התנור, כשהיה התבשיל בתנור, ואע"ג דכתב הר"ן דבירושלמי מפרש דאם נוטל מע"ש ע"מ להחזיר ועודן בידו עד שחשיכה מחזירין ובזה פליגי אמוראי בהניחה ע"ג קרקע מ"מ אין ללמוד מזה דאם נטל הקדירה בשבת מחזירין אפילו לתוכה דודאי גם הירושלמי מודה דהא דאמרו ב"ש נוטלין אבל לא מחזירין היינו אפילו נטל בשבת אין מחזירין וכן הא דאמר רב דב"ה לא התירו אלא

ע״ג אבל לא לתוכה היינו אפילו נטל בשבת אלא דהירושלמי סובר דבזה לכו״ע מחזירין אפילו הניחו ע״ג קרקע ולא נחלקו אלא בנטלו מבעוד יום וחשכה, ודברי הד״מ תמוהים בזה וכמש״כ המ״א ס״ק לה [ולשון המ״ב ס״ק סז שכתב דהמ״א מצדד כב״י אינו מכוון דהמ״א אינו מניח כלל מקום לדברי הד״מ] ובמ״ב שם כתב לישב המנהג משום שאין התנור חם כל כך להרתיח ר״ל להחם כשיעור יס״ב, ואין לקבוע כן אחרי שבגמ׳ מבואר דאין מחזירין ביום השבת לפרש״י, וכן הכלבו נדחק להתיר ליתן לתנור שאפו אבל לא לתנור ששהו בו ליום השבת וא״כ אין הדבר פסוק בסתמא עד שיודע לך, ולפעמים יש שומן על קרקעית הכלי שנוח להם לבוא ליס״ב אף שכל הבשר או התבשיל לא יבא ליס״ב, ויש להסתפק אם סמוך לפיו אין יס״ב ובעמקו יס״ב אי מותר להחזיר, ומסתבר דאסור שאין למסור לכל אחד תורתו בידו ואין כאן מחיצה המגדרת בין מקום האסור למקום המותר, ולפיכך אם יש שם גחלים עדיין אין כאן היתר ליתן במקום שאין היס״ב כיון שנותן לתוכו, ובמ״ב ס״ק סח כתב להקל אם הגחלים לצד אחד, וכ״ז תמוה שאין כאן שום היתר מן הדין להחזיר לתוכה אפילו גרופה וקטומה וכמש״כ לעיל ואין כאן רק לדון להתיר במקום שאין היס״ב ואם מותר לתוכה בסמוך לפיו שאין היס״ב א״כ אפילו גחלים בוערות מותר כדין נותן כנגד המדורה בס׳ שיח סי״ה, ואם תוכה אסור טפי [וכמש״כ במ״ב שם סט״ו לענין דבר שנתבשל כל צרכו דאע״ג דמותר כנגד המדורה אסור בתוך התנור וכמש״כ הרא״ש מ: לחלק ביניהן] א״כ אף אם הוא קטום או גרוף לצד אחד אסור, [ועיקר דברי היש״ע דלענין איסור חזרה סגי בגרוף לצד אחד דלמ״ד לשהות בעינן הוצאת הגחלים אינו מובן ואינו תח״י לע׳ בו] ולדינא נראה דכל שהיס״ב בפנים אסור להחזיר אף אם יעמיד סמוך לפיו, וכש״כ כשיש גחלים עדיין בוערות אפילו הן עוממות, ומיהו אם נהגו להחזיר למקום שאין י״ס אין כח למחות, ובמ״ב ס״ק צ הסכיר היתר להחזיר אפילו התנור יס״ב ע״פ המנהג שכתב רמ״א ואין להיתר זה שום מקום כמש״כ המ״א, ואף הרמ״א כתב טוב להחמיר, אבל הטבה זו חיובית מעיקר דינא המפורש בגמ׳ אבל תוכה אסור ואין שום צד בהלכה לדון בזה, ובאמת לא הוזכר ברמ״א היתר חזרה לתוכה אלא בד״מ.

ערוך השולחן אורח חיים הלכות שבת סימן רנג

ודע דתוכה לא מיקרי אלא כששולי הקדירה עומדת על שולי הכירה אבל כשאינה נוגעת בשולי הכירה אף שרוב הקדירה בתוך הכירה ונאחז בהרוחב שבו מלמעלה בגבי הכירה זה מיקרי על גבה ומותר [מג"א סקכ"ב] ותנורים שלנו שדינן ככירה כמו שיתבאר ובהן ליכא על גבן ותמיד מעמידין בתוכן ליכא חילוק בזה ותוכה הוה כעל גבה [זהו כוונת הש"ג שהביא המג"א שם]:

רמ"א אורח חיים רנג:ה

ויש מתירין ליתן לתוך תנור שאפו בו מבע"י, דמאחר שלא הטמינו בו רק אפו בו מבע"י לא נשאר בו רק הבל מעט ואין לחוש לבישול (כל בו) לו ובלבד שלא נצטנן לגמרי. ויש מחמירין בזה. ואם החום כל כך בתנור שהיד סולדת בו, אסור ועיין לקמן סימן שי"ח.

משנה ברורה סימן רנג:צג

צ"ל שאם החום וכו' דאל"ה אפילו להיש מחמירין שרי וכן סתם הרמ"א לעיל בסוף ס"ב בהג"ה:

ביאור הגר"א אורח חיים סימן רנג

וי"מ בזה שאם כו'. כצ"ל וכנ"ל:

חידושי הרמב"ן מסכת שבת דף לז עמוד א

ומצאתי בירושלמי שמפרש טעמא וה"ג התם וב"ה אומרים יחזיר ר' חלבו רב ענן בשם רב לא שנו אלא עליה אבל לתוכו לא עד איכן אמר עולא עד שלשה ר' מונא אומר עד מקום שהוא עושה חריץ א"ר יוסי בר בון מפני שהוא שליט במקום שהיד שולטת בו, ופי' דעולא סבר עד שלשה טפחים בעומקה של כירה נקרא עליה ומותר, ור' מונא מתיר עד מקום חריץ שעושין בכירה ומפרש ר' יוסי טעמא דרב מפני שאין רשאי להכניס קדרתו בשבת במקום שאין היד שולטת בו מפני רוב החמימות ולאו משום הטמנה נגעו בה.

רמ"א סימן רנג סעיף ב

ודוקא ע"ג כירה ממש, אבל לסמוך אפי' לאש במקום שהיד סולדת בו, שרי אפילו סמוך לחשיכה (הגמ"ר והגמי"י). ובתנור אין חילוק בין להחזיר עליו או לסמוך אצלו; ודוקא במקום שהיד סולדת, אבל אין היד סולדת שם, שרי אפי' בשבת, כמו שיתבאר לקמן סי' שי"ח.

מגן אברהם רנג:לו

ואפי' בדבר שאין בו מרק דלית ביה משום בישול אסור אם נצטנן דה"ל
כמניח לכירה לכתחלה בשבת דאסור
דלא התירו אלא חזרה:

ביאור הגר"א אורח חיים סימן רנג

ובלבה. כנ"ל:

25

ביאור הלכה סימן רנג

ליתן עליה - היינו על גב הכירה וגבה נקרא עובי דפנות הכירה וכ"ש נגד חלל הכירה מלמעלה. ואפילו אם היא מכוסה בכסויה ומעמידה על הכיסוי כ"כ רש"י בדף ל"ז והטור לקמן בסעיף זה [עי"ש בב"י וב"ח וכן הסכים המ"א בס"ק כ"ב כהב"ח] אך מדברי הרמב"ם בפ"ג ה"ד שכתב אין משהין אותו ע"ג האש בשבת וכו' עי"ש משמע לכאורה דע"ג כיסוי אין בכלל על גבה דאפשר דהוא כמו שאם כסה הגחלים באפר דאמרינן דמסתמא שוב הסיח דעתו ממנה ולא אתי לחתויי ועיין בדין י"ג שכתב ואם טח פי התנור בטיט וכו' דמשמע דאף במכוסה יש חשש חיתוי התם שאני שעומדת בפנים משא"כ הכא שעומדת מלמעלה ע"ג הכיסוי אפשר כיון שכיסה את הכירה והעמידה מלמעלה כבר הסיח דעתו מלבשל ואעפ"כ צ"ע בדעתו:

רש"י מסכת שבת דף לז עמוד א

גבה - עובי שפתה, או כסוי שעל חללה.

חזו"א לז:ט

במ"ב ס"ק פא דן בנותן ע"ג תנור בשבת בתנורי דידן שפתחן מן הצד וכתב שם המ"א לדמות להא דס"ג בנותן קדירה ריקנית להפסיק בין קדירת התבשיל לבין הכירה והביא דברי מהרי"ל דצריך הפסק אחר, והנה הטור כתב דעל גבה מקרי על שפתה או על כיסוי שעל חללה [והוא לשון רש"י לז א' ד"ה גבה, והוא מוכח בגמרא דהא מבעי ליה בסומך וע"ג הכיסוי ודאי חמיר מסומך לדופן ומדמבעי ליה לסמוך לדופן מכלל דעל הכיסוי אסור וזה שהזקיקו לרש"י ז"ל לפרש זה, ובמ"ב בבה"ל [ד"ה ליתן] דן מלשון הר"מ בזה ואין ראוי לספק בזה ול' הר"מ אינו מורה בזה דסתם שהיה נקט] וב"י פי' על שפתה היינו על עובי הדופן ואפשר דעל שפתה היינו שפיתת הקדירה על חללה, ומ"מ מבואר בטור דהעמיד על הכיסוי לא מקרי סמיכה אלא על גבה, והנה הא דמהני הפסק קדירה ריקנית נראה דהוא שינוי שאין דרך בישול בכך וגם ממעט את החום הרבה, אבל הכיסוי שדרכו בכך ואינו ממעט החום כל כך הוא בכלל ע"ג וכש"כ דדופן התנור עצמו לא חשיב הפסק ולא חשיב כסומך דדרך החום לבקוע למעלה ולא מקרי סומך אלא מן הצד, ואע"ג דבהגהמ"ר נקט לשון גרוף וקטום אינו אלא סמך בעלמא אבל עיקרו דחשיב כסומך ועדיף מסומך, ומ"מ דוקא חזרה מותר אבל ליתן לכתחילה בשבת אסור, ואע"ג דליתן כנגד המדורה שרי אפילו לכתחילה בשבת בדבר שנתבשל כל צרכו והוא חם, י"ל דלסמוך אצל התנור הוא בגזירת חכמים טפי, ובת"י ל"ז ב' כתבו דדוקא בשמן שאין בו משום בישול שרי כנגד המדורה אף במקום שיס"ב למ"ד שאין בו משום בישול אבל תבשיל אסור אפילו כנגד המדורה, וכ"מ בתוס' לז א' ד"ה ת"ש, דדוקא במפסיק דופן שרי אבל מפסיק אויר לא, ואמנם מדברי הרא"ש נראה דמותר ליתן כנגד המדורה בנתבשל כל צרכו לכתחילה בשבת, ומדמה ליה כלסמוך, ומשמע דגם לסמוך מותר לכתחילה בשבת, וע"ע במ"ב ס"ק טו בשם הב"מ, אמנם מהא דמבעי ליה בגמ' מהו לסמוך משמע דבשבת ודאי אסור, דכיון דגזרו על תוכה וגבה גזרו על הסמיכה ורק להחזיר שרי, וכ"כ במ"ב שם [שעה"צ כא] בשם חידושי הר"ן, והנה בהפסיק קדירה ריקנית נמי לא שרינן אלא חזרה.

חזון איש לז:יא

שהייה דנהוג בארצנו הק׳ שפתילת האש למטה תחת הפטפוט ושופתין קדרה למעלה על הפטפוט, והאש תחת שולי הקדרה דינו ככירה שאינה גרופה, ואף אם מעמידים פח של מתכת ומשימין הקדרה בתוך הפח מ״מ לא חשיב כדין נתן קדרה ריקנית על הכירה להפסיק דהכא לא הוי רק ככיסה את הקדרה בכיסויה והעמיד הקדרה על הכיסוי דזה חשיב על גבה וכמש״כ לעיל ס״ק ט, והלכך אם נטל אין מחזירין בשבת אפילו עודה בידו ודעתו להחזיר, ואם העמיד קדרה ע״ג קדרה, קדרה העליונה נוטל ומחזיר, דע״ג קדרה אין בו משום איסור שהייה וכמש״כ ס״ק ט והלכך כל שאין בו משום איסור בישול כגון שהוא דבר יבש שאין בו מרק או תבשיל שהוא רותח ואפילו נצטנן, אבל לא נצטנן לגמרי, מחזירין ע״ג הקדרה, ואפילו היה טמון נותנו ע״ג קדרה העומדת על הפטפוט ולא חשיב כמשהה בתחילה בשבת, נטל את ב׳ הקדרות ורוצה להחזיר את העליונה תוך הפח אסור אפילו אם יעמיד קדרה ריקנית להפסיק דחשיב כמשהה בתחילה בשבת, רצה להחזיר את התחתונה נותן קדרה ריקנית להפסיק ומחזיר.

פרי מגדים אורח חיים אשל אברהם סימן רנג

אפילו. עיין מ״א. אף להמחבר שפסק גרוף כל האש כולו, לא מקצתו (דלא כר״ן שבת טו, ב ד״ה עד, עיין מה שאכתוב בט״ז אות ד׳ אי״ה בזה), אם כן תנור איזה חתוי שייך. לזה אמר הר״מ ז״ל פרק שלישי מהלכות שבת הלכה ה׳ ו׳ מפני שאין אפשר לגרוף כל האש. ותראה שהאדון ז״ל סובר שמה שכתב הר״מ בהלכה ו׳ מפני שאי אפשר לגרוף כל האש שלא ישאר ניצוץ אחד ״מפני״ שהבלו חם, שמא יחתה להבעיר הניצוצות הנשארות, כאלו אמר ״ומפני״ שהבלו חם, וכן הוא בלבוש [סעיף א] דפוס פראג שפ״ג, יע״ש. אבל בנחלת צבי [עטרת צבי ס״ק ז] משמע לכאורה הטעם בתנור, שהבלו חם אי אפשר לגרוף שלא ישאר ניצוץ, יע״ש. ואף על גב באות ג׳ בקטמה והובערה בגילוי דעת סגי, אם כן בתנור נמי ליהוי גילוי דעת, וי״ל דאין זה גילוי דעת, דקטם שלא יתחרך דהבלו רב. ועוד יש תירוצים. ובתנור אף קש וגבבא וגרוף נמי אסור. ואפשר שכן דעת הר״מ ז״ל, אף על פי שכתב שם ״או״ מכוסה, ועיין אליה רבה אות י״א, ואין זה מן התימה לומר טעם הר״מ ז״ל אף בקש גרוף:

חזו"א לז:ט

הקשה המ"ב למה כאן בס"ג לא התיר המחבר בהפסק קדירה ריקנית אלא חזרה וק' ס"ה מתיר ליתן לכתחלה לחם ממולא בשר צונן על הקדירה שעל הכירה לחממו, וכ' בשם הפמ"ג דקדירה ריקנית משמשת לכירה וחשיב כמעמיד על הכירה אבל מעמיד על הקדירה שתבשיל בתוכה חשיב כמעמיד על הקדירה ולא כמעמיד ע"ג כירה, ואפשר שאם יש חום עולה לקדירה עליונה להרתיחה כגון שאם התחתונה גדולה ומלאה וכבדה להרתיח והעליונה קטנה ונוחה להרתיח היתה העליונה מרתחת קדם לתחתונה ודאי חשיבא כעומדת על הכירה אלא היה כאן היתר של הגהמ"ר ודוקא להחזיר אבל לא ליתן לכתחלה בשבת אבל באמת כל שהתחתונה מלאה היא בולעת חום הכירה ואין החום עולה לעלונה אלא מחום הקדירה והלכך גרע ממפסיק בקדירה ריקנית דהתם חום הכירה סלקא למעלה.

חזון איש לז:י

ונראה דאפילו מסמיכה לעל גבה מותר דלא אסרו בירושלמי אלא מטמינה לשיהוי אבל כל שיהוי אחת היא.

חזו"א לז:יא

מן האמור נלמד כפי שרגילין להעמיד התבשיל תוך הפח למטה ועליו קומקום של חמין, את החמין נוטל ומחזיר כל זמן שהקדירה תוך הפח, לקח הקדירה מן הפח אי אפשר עוד להחזיר החמין, היה לו עוד קומקום טמון במוכין [או בקבוק מתוכן לשמור את החמין שקורין טרמו"ס] מותר ליתן לתוך הקומקום שעל הקדירה כל זמן שהחמין שנותן לא נצטננו לגמרי [והיו מבושלים מע"ש].

26

שולחן ערוך אורח חיים סימן רנג סעיף ב

כירה שהיא גרופה וקטומה ונטל הקדירה מעליה אפי' בשבת, מותר להחזירה כל זמן שהיא רותחת. הגה: ועודה בידו (טור), ולא הניחה ע"ג קרקע. הגה: ודעתו להחזירה (טור); ודוקא כב על גבה, אבל לתוכה אסור. ובתנור,

אסור להחזיר אפי' הוא גרוף וקטום; וה"ה לכופח, אם הסיקו בגפת ועצים. הגה: ודוקא שהתבשיל מבושל כל צרכו (ב"י), ואז מותר להחזיר, ואפילו כג לכירה אחרת, אבל אם לא נתבשל כל צרכו אסור, אפי' לאותה כירה (מיימוני פ"ג). וי"א דכל זה אינו אסור רק כשנטלו מן הכירה מבעוד יום, ולא החזירו עד שחשכה; אבל אם לקחו משם משחשכה, אפי' הניחו ע"ג קרקע מותר (ר"ן פ' כירה וכל בו), וכן נוהגים להקל בתנורים שלנו שיש להם דין כירה, וסומכין עצמם על דברי המקילין, וטוב להחמיר. מיהו אם נצטנן, לכ"ע אסור (ב"י).

ביאור הלכה סימן רנג ד"ה ולא

ולא הניחם ע"ג קרקע - לפי מה שהעתיק הרמ"א מקודם לדינא דבעינן עודה בידו דוקא תו לא צריכינן למכתב שלא יניח ע"ג קרקע אלא המחבר שיטה אחרת יש לו דדוקא ע"ג קרקע אסור דאז בטלה השהיה הראשונה אבל לא במניחה ע"ג ספסל וכדומה בינתים עיין בב"י. ודע דאם הניחה ע"ג קרקע אף שהיה דעתו להחזירה אסור אפילו לדעת המחבר. בחדושי רע"א כתב דאפילו אם זה המניח היה אדם אחר שאין הקדרה שלו ג"כ מועיל המעשה שלו לאסור שוב להחזיר ע"ג כירה ולא שייך בזה אין אדם אוסר דבר שאינו שלו אך אם עודו בידו. ורק בעת שסילק מהכירה לא היה בדעתו להחזירו אם מחשבתו מועלת לאסור שוב להחזיר זה תלוי במחלוקת הראשונים עי"ש שהאריך:

ביאור הלכה סימן רנג ד"ה ודעתו

ודעתו להחזירה - הנה משמע דתפס לחומרא בהאבעיות שבעו לזה בגמרא וע"כ ס"ל דתרתי בעינן שלא יניח ע"ג קרקע וגם יהיה דעתו הא ע"ג קרקע אסור אף שדעתו להחזירה וכן סתם המחבר לקמן בס"ג ע"ש וכ"ז הוא דאזיל לשיטתו שכתב בב"י אחר שהביא דעת הראשונים שס"ל להחמיר בהניח ע"ג קרקע בכל גווני כתב ודלא כהגה"מ שכתב בשם ספר התרומה דבדעתו להחזיר אף כשהניח ע"ג קרקע מותר. והנה גרם לו לדחות את דבריו לגמרי מפני שלא ראה לשום דעה המסכמת עם דברי התרומה ובאמת בחדושי הר"ן הביא כן בשם הרא"ה וכ"כ בשלטי הגבורים בשם ריא"ז וכן הוא הכרעת המאירי ע"ש וכן הביא התוס' ר"פ במה טומנין מנהגי המקומות

בענין הטמנה וכתבו דשמא ס"ל כהך לישנא דשרי חזקיה משמיה דאביי בהניחו ע"ג קרקע אם דעתו להחזיר [וכן כעין זה ברא"ש דתרתי בעינן אך לבסוף מצא עצה אחרת ליישב המנהג ע"ש] ולפ"ז אפשר שיש להקל במלתא דרבנן דבדעתו להחזיר אף שהניחה ע"ג קרקע או שעודן בידו ולא היה דעתו להחזיר כשסילקה יכול להחזיר ועכ"פ בעודן בידו ואין דעתו להחזיר מסתברא ודאי שיש להקל לעת הצורך מאחר שגם הרמב"ם השמיטה וכן בהניחה ע"ג ספסל וכדומה והיה דעתו להחזיר מאחר שגם דעת הרב"י כהפוסקים המקילין בזה:

ט"ז אורח חיים סימן שטז ס"ק ג

ועוד אפי' אם תאמר דבודאי הוה פ"ר ואסור מ"מ בספק אם יש שם זבובים יש להתיר דשם אין פ"ר כי זה הוה ספק פ"ר והוה דבר שלא במתכוין ומותר כמו בכור' היכא דלא הוה פ"ר כגון שיש נקב קטן כמש"ל ה"נ אין פסיק רישיה בודאי כי אפשר שאין שם זבובים וזה היא כמו במקום דלא הוי פ"ר דמותר שלא במתכוין

חידושי הריטב"א מסכת שבת דף לח עמוד ב

ואסיקנא דלא מיתסרא חזרה על כירה גרופה וקטומה אלא כשנתנן בקרקע ואין דעתו להחזיר, וכולהו אידך הוו בעיא דלא איפשיטא ולקולא, דאיסורא דרבנן הוא, ומ"מ מוכחא סוגיין דבעינן שיחזירנה קודם שתצטנן לגמרי דלא ליחזי כמבשל, ולסמוך אפי' צוננת כדשרינן להחם כנגד המדורה שאין דרך בישול בכך, מ"ר.

חידושי הריטב"א מסכת שבת דף לט עמוד א

כל שבא בחמין מלפני השבת. פירוש כל מליח שבא בחמין מלפני השבת הרי הוא כמבושל ולפיכך שורין אותו בחמין בשבת. פירוש לפי שאין בישול אחר בישול, והקשו התוספות דהא אמרינן בפרק במה מדליקין (לעיל ל"ד א') מפני מה אין טומנים משחשיכה בדבר שאינו מוסיף הבל גזרה שמא ירתיח כלומר שיתן אותה על גבי האש כדי להרתיח אם ימצאנה צוננת, אלמא יש בישול אחר בישול דהא התם בקדרה מבושלת איירי, ותירצו דהתם הוא בדבר לח דשייך בישול [אחר] בישול, אבל בדברים יבשים כגון

בשר ודגים לא שייך בישול [אחר] בישול, ולא נהירא, והנכון בעיני דהתם הוא על ידי האור ממש דמחזי כמבשל אבל הכא שרינן בתולדות [האור] שאין דרך בישול בכך, והיינו נמי דשרינן חזרה בתבשיל שהגיע למאכל בן דרוסאי על גבי כירה גרופה וקטומה (ואי) [דבהאי] לא מיחזי כמבשל, וכן מותר להחם כנגד המדורה מהאי טעמא.

מגן אברהם רנג:יט

רותחת - שהיס"ב עמ"ש סי' שי"ח ס"ד דלא כע"ש ונהגו להקל אם לא נצטנן לגמרי כמ"ש סי' שי"ח סט"ו ועססי' זה בהג"ה וכ"כ בשם רי"ו דלא כב"ח אבל אם נצטנן אז הוי בישול ועסי' שי"ח ס"ד:

מגן אברהם סימן רנג ס"ק לו

שלא נצטנן - ואפי' בדבר שאין בו מרק דלית ביה משום בישול אסור אם נצטנן דה"ל כמניח לכירה לכתחלה בשבת דאסור דלא התירו אלא חזרה:

פרי מגדים אורח חיים משבצות זהב סימן רנג

ואמנם הדבר הקשה עלי הוא מה שכתב המ"א לקמן אות ל"ו דנצטנן אף ביבש אסור, דלא התירו אלא "חזרה" בשבת (באופנים המבוארים כאן דמותר), לא להניח לכירה לכתחלה בשבת, וזה סותר לכאן. וראיתי לתוספת שבת אות מ"ו הרגיש בזה, יע"ש.

מחצית השקל רנט

ואע"ג שכתב מ"א בס' רנג ס"ק לו דבנצטנן לגמרי אפילו יבש שאין בו מרק דליכא משום בישול מ"מ אסור דהוי כמניח לכתחילה ולא הותר רק חזרה צ"ל דוקא תוך תנור החמיר לעיל אבל הכא דמיירי על גבו הקיל בזה.

27

שבות יצחק עמ' ק

אך שמעתי מהגרי"ש אלישיב שליט"א דשאני היסק קש וגבבא משום שאש זו שונה שאין לה קיום אלא מיד הולכת ונכבית ולא נשאר בה גחלים בוערות

להכי אינה נכללת בלא פלוג דשמא יחתה משא"כ אש החשמל שהיא אש בת קיימא וגם שייך בה שמא יגדיל בכיריים אחרות שפיר הוי בכלל הלא פלוג גם כשא"א להגדיל.

שערי תשובה סימן רנד

מפני שדברים אלו א"צ בישול רב כו' - וכ' בפמ"א ח"א ס"ס פ"ד שיש שנותנים הסיר של טע"ה סמוך לחשיכה על כלי הברזל ונותנין תחתיו משקה חריף שקורין שפירטוס ונותנים פתילה ודולק כל הלילה עד למחרתו ביום השבת לוקחים ע"י עכו"ם הקדירה מעל האש וזה איסור גמור הוא ככירה וכופח שאינו גרוף וקטו' ודמי להא דלא ימלא כו' וא"ל דלא שייך חיתוי שאין כאן גחלים אלא משקה הדולק דהא חזינן כשממרסין בתוך המשקה הלהב עולה יותר ויש לחוש לחיתוי לכן חייבים חכמי הדור למחות בידן:

משנה ברורה רנג:כב

אפילו אם הוא גרוף - מפני שהגורף אינו גורף אלא רוב האש עצמה וא"א שלא תשאר ניצוץ אחד ובתנור שחומו רב חיישינן שמא יחתה כדי שיבערו אותם הניצוצות. והנה מלשון המחבר משמע דס"ל כדעת הטור דאפילו בקש ובגבבא אסור בגרוף וקטום וכן הוא דעת ה"ר יהונתן המובא בחידושי הר"ן אכן מלשון הרמב"ם משמע דבקש וגבבא אינו אסור בתנור כ"א באינו גרוף [א"ר] וכן הוא דעת הכל בו וחידושי הר"ן [כג] ויש להקל בזה:

שו"ת אגרות משה אורח חיים חלק ד סימן עד

האם מותר לחמם קדרה שנתבשלה והיא חמה קצת ע"ג מכשירים שנועדו לחימום ולא לבישול, כפלטה חשמלית (האט פלייט והאט טריי) או שולחן מחומם באדים (סטים טייבל), גם בלא הפסק קדרה, דאין דרך בישול בכך. תשובה: על פלטה חשמלית אם א"א להתבשל שם אז מותר להעמיד קדרה חמה אם אין שם אלא מדה אחת להחום ואם יש שתי מדות אסור, והוא שלא יהיה באופן הטמנה שאז יהיה הטמנה בדבר המוסיף הבל שאסור. ועל שולחן המחומם באדים כמדומה שאפשר להתבשל שם וא"כ הוא ממילא דרך בישול אך אף אם א"א להתבשל שם כמדומה שהוא בדרך הטמנה ואז אסור, ואם אינו דרך הטמנה כגון שאינה מכוסה כולה מותר.

משנה ברורה רנג:סז-סח

וטוב להחמיר - כי הרבה פוסקים חולקין על הר"ן ועוד כי הב"י סובר שגם הר"ן לא התיר אלא ע"ג כירה ולא בתוכו וגם המ"א בס"ק ל"ה מצדד כהב"י ע"ש ומי עדיפא תנור שלנו מכירה ומ"מ נראה שיש זכות על המנהג כי כבר נתבאר בפוסקים שאין לאסור חזרה אא"כ יש חום שהקדירה יהיה נעשה רותחת מן החום וזה אין מצוי כ"כ ע"כ אין לפקפק בזה ועיין לקמיה בס"ק ס"ח ואח"כ מצאתי בלבוש כדברינו:

מיהו אם נצטנן - היינו אם נצטנן לגמרי וכמ"ש למעלה והטעם דשייך אח"כ עוד בישול חדש ועיין לקמן במ"א סקל"ו שכתב דאפילו בדבר יבש שאין בו מרק דלא שייך בו בישול ג"כ אסור דכיון שכבר נצטנן בטלה השהיה הראשונה והוי כנותן עתה מחדש בתוך התנור לזה אסור בכל גווני וכ"ז כשמניחו עתה במקום שע"י החום יהיה היד סולדת בו.

שו"ת אגרות משה אורח חיים חלק ד סימן עד

(לו) מדברי הב"י בסי' שי"ח ד"ה מותר ליתן קיתון משמע שלדעת הר"י מקום שהיד סולדת היינו שיד האדם סולדת במקום זה, וכ' שדעת הרא"ש שאסור דוקא אם הקדרה עשויה להגיע לחום שיס"ב =שיד סולדת בו=, וכדעת הרא"ש כ' במ"ב סי' רנ"ג ס"ק ס"ח. מה דעת מרן שליט"א בזה.

תשובה: מקום שהיד סולדת הוא מקום שע"י החום תהיה מה שבקדרה יד סולדת כמפורש במ"ב, ולא משמע מהב"י שהר"י פליג ע"ז וסובר דתלוי בחום המקום אלא כתב דאף דמפשט לשון הר"י היה נראה כן הדבר ברור כהרא"ש, שלכן צריך לומר גם שכוונת הר"י כן.

שולחן ערוך הרב אורח חיים הלכות שבת סימן רנג

וכל זה כשמחזיר בשבת למקום שהיד סולדת שם (דהיינו שאם תבשיל זה שמחזיר היה צונן היה יכול להתחמם שם כל כך עד שהיד סולדת בו) אבל אם אין היד סולדת שם לדברי הכל מותר לסמוך שם אפילו בתנור שבימיהם אע"פ שאינו גרוף וקטום.

ואפילו על גבי הכירה הגרופה או קטומה מותר להחזיר אם אין היד סולדת שם אע"פ שכבר סילק תבשיל זה מבעוד יום והניחו על גבי קרקע ולא היה בדעתו להחזירו כלל ואפילו פינהו לקדרה אחרת ואפילו הוא תבשיל

ישן ונצטנן לגמרי ואפילו יש בו מרק לפי שכשאין שם חום כל כך שהיד סולדת בו אינו נראה כמבשל שם לכתחלה.

שולחן ערוך הרב אורח חיים קונטרס אחרון סימן רנג

(ד) דהיינו שאם כו'. אף שבב"י ובמג"א מיירי בצונן, מכל מקום אפשר הוא הדין לחם לענין חזרה בסמיכה לאינו גרוף. ואפשר דשאני התם דמיירי באיסור בישול, שהרי בסמיכה לתנור שלנו שרי לגמרי כמו שכתב רמ"א סוף סי' זה, אבל הכא מיירי בשמא יחתה ותלוי בחום התנור. וכן הוא משמעות לשון הגהות מרדכי ורמ"א. וכן עיקר (וצריך למחוק זה בפנים):

שולחן ערוך אורח חיים הלכות שבת רנג:ה

מותר לתת על פי קדירת חמין בשבת, תבשיל שנתבשל מע"ש כל צרכו, כגון לג פאנדי"ש וכיוצא בהן, לחממן, לפי שאין דרך בישול בכך אבל להטמין תחת הבגדים הנתונים ע"ג המיחם, ודאי אסור.

שבות יצחק עמ' קג

מיהו גם לדעת האגרו"מ י"ל דדוקא ע"ג כלים הנ"ל התיר להשהות כיון שא"א לבשל עליהם אלא עשויים לחמם האוכל סמוך לסעודה וכיו"ב אך פלטות של שבת המצויות כאן בארץ ישראל דחזינן שיכולות להרתיח תבשיל צונן ופעמים שנותנין עליהם קודם שבת קדירת חמין או קוגל שלא נתבשלו כל צרכם ונגמר בישולם בשבת י"ל דאסור לחמם עליהם בשבת.

28

חזון איש לח:ב

כשיש לו תנור הניסק ע"י חשמל, והכין מע"ש שעון לפתוח החשמל בשעה ידועה, אסור להעמיד הקדרה ע"ג תנור קדם שנפתח החשמל, משום דין שהייה ע"ג כירה ותנור בשבת שהרי אסרו גם חזרה באינה גרופה, ובגרופה לא התירו אלא חזרה בשלא הניחה ע"ג קרקע, אבל שהייה בתחילה אסור, ואף אם העמיד חייב להסירה, וכן אם הקדרה ע"ג כירה מע"ש באופן האסור כגון בשיל ולא הגיע למאכל ב"ד חייב לסלק את הקדרה, דכל

שנמצאת הקדרה בשבת באופן שאסרו חכמים משום שמא יחתה אסור, ואין האיסור תלוי במעשה העמדה של הקדרה, אלא במציאות הקדרה על הכירה בשבת, וכמש״כ לעיל ס׳ לז ס״ק כא, ואין כאן היתר של קדירה חייתא דזה לא הותר אלא במניח מע״ש ומסיח דעתו ממנו עד למחר וכדאיתא ס׳ רנג ס״א, ואין צורך לחיתוי, אבל כשהכירה צוננת ומתחממת בשבת הוא לעולם בגזרת חיתוי.

רמ״א אורח חיים רנג:ה

לכן נוהגין שהאינם יהודים מוציאין הקדירות מן התנורים שמטמינים בהן ומושיבין אותן אצל תנור בית החורף או עליו ומבערת השפחה אח״כ התנור ההוא וע״י זה הקדירות חוזרים ונרתחים. אבל ע״י ישראל אסור בכה״ג. אבל אם הקדירות עדיין חמין, מותר להעמידן אצל תנור בית החורף, מאחר שנתבאר דתנורים שלנו יש להם דין כירה, וסמיכה בכירה שאינה גרופה וקטומה כדין גרופה וקטומה לענין נתינה עליה. וכבר נתבאר שנהגו להקל בחזרה בשבת אפי׳ הניחה ע״ג קרקע, וה״ה לסמוך לתנור שאינו גרוף וקטום הואיל והקדירה עדיין חם ומבושל כל צרכו, וכן המנהג פשוט להתיר וע״ל סי׳ שי״ח.

חזון איש לז:כא

ולהאמור יש לעיין בשריותא דהרמ״א ליתן ע״ג תנור ע״י אינו יהודי קדם שהוסק ואח״כ מבעיר האינו יהודי את התנור ונהי דליכא משום אמירה לנכרי במה שמבעיר התנור אפילו בקדרה צוננת שעיקרו משום היסק התנור להחם הבית ואע״ג דיש כאן פסיק רישיה של בישול מ״מ לא אסרו אמירה לנכרי כה״ג וכמש״כ במ״ב, מ״מ כיון שניתן לדעת ישראל שתשאר הקדרה ע״ג כירה שאינה גרופה למה אין זה בכלל גזירת חזרה ומה תועלת שריותא יש בזה שבשעת הנחת הקדרה עדיין לא הוסק התנור מ״מ מתקיימת מחשבתו להחם התבשיל המוחזר ע״ג כירה שאינה גרופה שאסרו חכמים משום גזירת חיתוי, וע״כ צ״ל דחשבו הדבר לשהייה מערב שבת ולא כחזרה כיון שבשעת הנחה התנור צונן, ואמנם י״ל דהחזרה ע״ג התנור בתנורים שפתחן מן הצד אינו בכלל ע״ג הכירה דכירות שלהן עיקר הבישול הוא על גבן ואפילו מעמיד ע״ג הכיסוי אין הכיסוי הפסק שהכיסוי

דק והחום עובר בעדו ודרך לבשל גם על הכיסוי אבל ע״ג התנור אין דרך לבשל וחומו מועט מפני עובי הכיפה ואין משמשין שם רק לשמירת החום וחשיב כנותן נגד המדורה או ע״ג מיחם שעל האש, או כסומך, וזו כוונת המ״ב ס״ק פא, ולפ״ז היה מותר ליתן גם אחר שהוסק, ונהי דמחמרינן לאחר שהוסק אבל קודם שהוסק מקילינן, וכן מקילינן לאחר היסק בנותן דף להפסיק ולמעט חומו.

משנה ברורה רנג:קג

אצל תנור בית החורף - אבל עליו וכ״ש בתוכו אסור כיון שאינו גרוף וקטום ואפילו קודם היסק אסור ליתן עליו משום חשש שמא יחתה אח״כ בגחלים להרבות חומו שהקדירות שלמעלה יהיו נרתחים והעולם נהגו היתר ליתן עליו קדרות חמין קודם היסק ויש להם ע״מ שיסמוכו וכמש״ל באות פ״א ע״ש אבל אחר היסק לא ינהוג כן רק צריך ליתן איזה דף או עץ תחת הקדירה להכירא וכנ״ל בשם מהרי״ל:

משנה ברורה רנג:ק

אסור בכי האי גוונא - ר״ל להושיב הקדרות אצל תנור בית החורף או עליו אפילו קודם ההיסק דהו״ל כאחד נותן הקדרה ואחד האש דהראשון פטור אבל אסור משא״כ באמירה לא״י דשרי דהא עיקר כונתם לחמם הבית דשרי ומזה נראה היתר שאם נתן הא״י מים לתוך הקדרה הקבוע בתנור ונתחממו שמותר הישראל להנות מהם להדיח בהם כלים ואפילו לכתחלה מותר לצוות לו בזה דק״ו הוא דהא בתבשיל כשנותנו ע״ג התנור כונתו לחממו ואפ״ה שרי כש״כ כאן שאין כונתו לחמם המים אלא שלא יבקע הקדירה ואפשר דאפילו נתן הא״י המים אחר שהוסק שרי ג״כ מטעם זה ומ״מ לומר לא״י נראה לאסור אחר שהסיקו אבל ישראל אסור ליתן המים לתוך הקדירה אפילו קודם שהסיקו הא״י. והא דמתירין להדיח כלים במים שנתן הא״י להקדירה דוקא כשאינם מלוכלכים בשומן דאל״ה אסור לשפוך הרותחים עליהם משום שממחה השומן והוי נולד כמ״ש סימן ש״כ סי״ד אלא יניח הכלי תוך המים ולא יערה עליהם דזה שרי משום דלא קעביד מעשה:

הלכות שבת (איידער) הע' תתקו

מסתבר שיש לאסור אם לא יכול להיות רותחין קודם שקיעה [והטעם דחיישינן דע"י הוצאת מים או כיסויו קודם בישולו יקרב בישולו].

מגן אברהם רנג:מג

אצל תנור - אבל עליו אסור כיון שאינו גרוף וקטום ומשמע מלשון רמ"א דאפילו ליתן עליו קודם היסק אסור כיון דלבסוף יהי' בתוכו אש גזרינן שמא יחתה בגחלים ומיהו העולם נוהגין היתר בזה ועמ"ש ס"ג דיש להם על מה שיסמכו ונקוט האי כללא בידך דכל הנך שריותא המוזכרים בסי' זה אינו אלא בתבשיל חם אבל בתבשיל קר או שאר דברים קרים עסי' שי"ח איזו אסור משום בישול דאורייתא ע"ש:

מחצית השקל רנג:מג

אצל תנור וכו'. די"ל ע"מ שיסמכו והיינו כמ"ש שם כיון שיש הפסק מעזיבה ה"ל כגו"ק ואע"ג דכתב שם בשם מהרי"ל דבעינן שיתן שם דבר מה להפסיק משום הכירא מ"מ קודם היסק הקילו. אבל בתבשיל קר או שאר דברים קרים ע' ס' שיח. ומ"מ בדבר קר אפילו אין בו מרק דלית ביה משום בישול מ"מ אסור דהוי כנותן לכתחילה וכמ"ש ס"ק לו ואפילו גו"ק אסור וכן מכירה לטמונה או איפכא אסור כדלעיל ס"ק כג דהוי כנותן לכתחילה.

מגן אברהם רנג:לא

ע"פ הכירה - דה"ל כירה כגרופה וקטומה שהרי הקדירה סותמת את פי הכירה (הגמ"ר מ"מ פכ"ב) וכ"מ סי' שי"ח סי"ח וא"כ י"ל שע"ג תנורים שלנו שרי ליתן אפי' האש בתוך התנור כיון שיש מעזיבה המפסיק בין האש וכ"מ סי' שי"ח סט"ו ובמהרי"ל כתוב וז"ל אם מונח עץ או דף על תנור מותר להניח עליה קדירה עכ"ל וכ"כ האגודה וז"ל התשב"ץ אם יש דפין עשוים ע"ג תנור כמו שיש ברוטנבר"ק ובהרבה מקומות מותר להניח ע"ג הדפין משמע דס"ל דבעי' שיניח שום דבר עמה להיכרא וכ"מ בסי' זה בהג"ה וכ"ז כשהתבשיל חם:

29

שבת לח.

שכח קדירה על גבי כירה ובשלה בשבת, מהו? אישתיק ולא אמר ליה ולא מידי. למחר נפק דרש להו: המבשל בשבת, בשוגג - יאכל, במזיד - לא יאכל, ולא שנא. מאי ולא שנא? רבה ורב יוסף דאמרי תרווייהו להיתירא: מבשל הוא דקא עביד מעשה, במזיד - לא יאכל, אבל האי דלא קא עביד מעשה - במזיד נמי יאכל. רב נחמן בר יצחק אמרלאיסורא: מבשל הוא דלא אתי לאיערומי - בשוגג יאכל, אבל האי דאתי לאיערומי - בשוגג נמי לא יאכל. מיתיבי: שכח קדירה על גבי כירה ובישלה בשבת, בשוגג - יאכל, במזיד - לא יאכל. במה דברים אמורים - בחמין שלא הוחמו כל צורכן, ותבשיל שלא בישל כל צורכו. אבל חמין שהוחמו כל צורכן ותבשיל שבישל כל צורכו, בין בשוגג בין במזיד - יאכל, דברי רבי מאיר. רבי יהודה אומר: חמין שהוחמו כל צורכן - מותרין, מפני שמצטמק ורע לו. ותבשיל שבישל כל צורכו - אסור, מפני שמצטמק ויפה לו, וכל המצטמק ויפה לו, כגון כרוב ופולים ובשר טרוף - אסור, וכל המצטמק ורע לו - מותר. קתני מיהא: תבשיל שלא בישל כל צורכו, בשלמא לרב נחמן בר יצחק לא קשיא: כאן - קודם גזרה, כאן - לאחר גזרה. אלא רבה ורב יוסף דאמרי להיתירא, אי קודם גזרה - קשיא מזיד, אי לאחר גזרה - קשיא נמי שוגג! - קשיא.

מאי גזירתא? דאמר רב יהודה בר שמואל אמר רבי אבא אמר רב כהנא אמר רב: בתחילה היו אומרים המבשל בשבת, בשוגג - יאכל, במזיד - לא יאכל, והוא הדין לשוכח. משרבו משהין במזיד ואומרים שכחים אנו - חזרו וקנסו על השוכח. קשיא דרבי מאיר אדרבי מאיר, קשיא דרבי יהודה אדרבי יהודה! - דרבי מאיר אדרבי מאיר לא קשיא: הא - לכתחילה, הא - דיעבד. דרבי יהודה אדרבי יהודה נמי לא קשיא: כאן - בגרופה וקטומה, כאן - בשאינה גרופה וקטומה. איבעיא להו: עבר ושהה מאי, מי קנסוהו רבנן או לא? - תא שמע, דאמר שמואל בר נתן אמר רבי חנינא: כשהלך רבי יוסי לציפורי מצא חמין שנשתהו על גבי כירה - ולא אסר להן, ביצים מצומקות שנשתהו על גבי

כירה - ואסר להן. מאי לאו - לאותו שבת? - לא, לשבת הבאה. מכלל דביצים מצומקות מצטמקות ויפה להן נינהו? - אין, דאמר רב חמא בר חנינא: פעם אחת נתארחתי אני ורבי למקום אחד, והביאו לפנינו ביצים מצומקות כעוזרדין, ואכלנו מהן הרבה.

טור אורח חיים הלכות שבת סימן רנג

כל דבר שאסור להשהותו אם עבר ושיהה אותו או ששכח ושיהה אותו במקום שלא היה לו להשהותו אסור לכל אפילו למי שלא שהה אותו והרמב"ם ז"ל חילק בשכח בין תבשיל שלא בישל כל צרכו ובין מצטמק ויפה לו כשלא בישל כל צרכו אסור עד מ"ש ובמצטמק ויפה לו התיר ובעבר ושיהה אסור בשניהם ואיני יודע למה חילק ביניהם דהא בגמרא מייתי ראיה מעבר ושיהה לשכח:

משנה תרומות ב:ג

המטביל כלים בשבת שוגג ישתמש בהם מזיד לא ישתמש בהם המעשר והמבשל בשבת שוגג יאכל מזיד לא יאכל הנוטע בשבת שוגג יקיים מזיד יעקור ובשביעית בין שוגג בין מזיד יעקור:

רי"ף מסכת שבת דף טז:-יז.

ואי אינשי על גבי כירה שאינה גרופה וקטומה מידי דלא בשיל כל צרכיה אסיר וכל שכן אם עבר ושהה במזיד [דף ל"ח ע"א] דאמר רב שמואל בר יהודה אמר רב יהודה בתחלה היו אומרים המבשל בשבת בשוגג יאכל במזיד לא יאכל והוא הדין לשוכח משרבו משהין במזיד ואומרים שוגגין אנו חזרו וגזרו אף על השוכח והיכא דשכח מידי דבשיל כל צרכיה ומצטמק ויפה לו הא מילתא איבעיא לן בגמ' ולא איפשיטא ולקולא עבדינן ולא אסרינן להחוא תבשיל דספיקא דרבנן הוא ולקולא:

שלחן ערוך אורח חיים רנג:א

ואם שכח ושהה, אם הוא תבשיל שבישל כל צרכו, מותר אפי' הוא מצטמק ויפה לו; ואם הוא תבשיל שהתחיל להתבשל ולא בישל כל צרכו, אסור עד מוצאי שבת; ואם עבר ושהה אסור בשניהם.

שלחן ערוך אורח חיים שיח:א

המבשל בשבת, (או שעשה אחת משאר מלאכות) במזיד אסור לו לעולם ולאחרים מותר למוצאי שבת מיד; ובשוגג, אסור בו ביום גם לאחרים, ולערב מותר גם לו מיד (ואם אמר לאינו יהודי לעשות לו מלאכה בשבת, ע"ל סימן ש"ז סעיף כ').

מגן אברהם רנג:יא

אסור עד מ"ש - מדכתב סתם ש"מ דאסור לכל כמ"ש הטור וכ"פ בד"מ ומ"ש הגמ"ר דלאחריני שרי משום דס"ל כר"מ אבל אנן דקי"ל כר"י כמ"ש רסי' שי"ח א"כ ה"ה ה"נ אסור לכל ולב"ב פשיטא דאסור דה"ל כמי שנתבשל בשבילו ועבי"ד סי' צ"ט ס"ה ועב"ח ססי' רנ"ד ס"ג וסי' ט"ו עסי' תקט"ו:

מחצית השקל רנג:יא

אסור וכו' משום דס"ל כר' מאיר אבל אנן קיי"ל וכו'. ר"ל לדידן גם הג"מ מודה דגם לאחריני אסור אולם דברי מ"א הם קצרים כדרכו לכן צ"ב קצת. בדף לח איתא איבעיא להו שכח קדירה ע"ג כירה ובשלה בשבת מהו ודרש רחב"א תניא המבשל בשבת בשוגג יאכל במזיד לא יאכל אבל בשהייה אין חילוק בין שוגג למזיד ומסיק דאפילו בשוגג אסור ומסיק הטעם משום שראו כי רבו המרעימיםשוהים במזיד ואומרים שוכחים היינו לכן גזרו גם על השוגג משא"כ במבשל ליכא למיחש שיעשה במזיד וכו' דלא נחשדו ישראל על השבתות משא"כ איסור שהייה דקיל בעיני הבריות. ומבשל פליגי ר"מ ור"י הובא כמה פעמים בש"ס בחולין דף טו ובב"ק ובכתובותדר"מ ס"ל בשוגג יאכל אפילו המבשל ואפילו בשבת מזיד לא יאכל בין הוא בין אחרים ולמוצאי שבת מותר אפילו לדידיה ור"י ס"ל בשוגג כדא"ל ר"מ במזיד ובמזיד ס"ל דבשבת אסור אפילו לאחרים אבל במוצאי שבת לא אסור אלא לדידיה והיינו עולמית אבל לאחרים שרי במ"שוכן פירשו התוס' במקומות הנ"ל וא"כ לאסור לאחרים בשבת ליכא פלוגתא בין ר"מ לר"י וגם ר"מ מודה דגם לאחרים אסור בשבת ולא פליגי כ"א במ"ש דלר"מ אפילו לו מותר במ"ש ולר"י לו לעולם אסור וכיון דבשהייה גזרו על השוגג אטו מזיד שלא יערים א"כ גם לר"מ ראוי לאסור שהה בשוגג אפילו לאחרים

ביום השבת כמו לר״י ואיך תלא מ״א מחלוקת טור והג״מ בין אי קיי״ל כר״מ או כר״י אולם בדברי הג״מ הדברים מבוארים שכתב וז״ל ונ״ל הא דאסרינו בשכח וכו׳ ה״מ לדידיה אבל לאחרים שרי אפילו בו ביום דמן הדין הוי ליה להתיר בשכח אפילו לדידיה כמו המבשל בשבת בשוגג דקיי״ל כר״מ וכו׳ והא דאסרינן בשכח משום גזרה כדאמרינן משרבו עושים מזיד ואומרים וכו׳ חזרו וקנסו גם על השוגג וכיון דאסרינן לדידיה אע״ג דשרי לאחריני תו ליכא למיחש דילמא יניחו במזיד ויאמרו שוכחים אנחנו דאין אדם חטא ולא לו עכ״ל הג״מ. וטעם זה ניחא לר״מ דס״ל במבשל בשוגג אפילו לדידיה שרי דס״ל דלא קנסו שוגג אטו מזיד אלא בשהה אסור גם שוגג מחשש הערמה וא״כ די במה שאסור לדידיה וכמ״ש בהגמ״י משא״כ לר״י דגם במבשל אוסר בשוגג ואע״ג דמבשל ליכא למיחש להערמה דישראל לא נחשדו על השבתות מכל מקום אסרו בשוגג מטעם קנס דס״ל קנסו שוגג אטו מזיד כדאיתא בגיטין דף נג ע״ב ע״ש דבהא פליגי ר״מ ור״י אי קנסו שוגג אטו מזיד. וכיון דר״י ס״ל במבשל בשבת בשוגג אסור אפילו לאחרים ע״כ דגם זה בכלל הקנס דאפילו לאחרים אסור וא״כ גם בשהה בשוגג ניהו דאפילו היינו מתירים לאחרים מכל מקום ליכא חשש הערמה מכל מקום אסור גם לאחרים משום קנס.

פרי מגדים אשל אברהם רנג:יא

אסור. עיין מ״א. עיין סימן תקט״ו אות ה׳. ומשמע דעד כדי שיעשו קאי לשכח ושהה באין נגמר כל צרכו בעינן בכדי שיעשו, וכן בעבר ושהה במצטמק ויפה לו בעינן בכדי שיעשו. ועיין ב״י [עמוד ס סוף דבור ראשון] ובר״מ פרק ג׳ מהלכות שבת הלכה ט׳, משמע לכאורה דווקא בעבר ושהה בעינן כדי שיעשו, הא שכחו כתב רק למוצאי שבת, מכל מקום מהגהות אשר״י [שבת פ״ג סימן ג] משמע אף בשכח ולא נתבשל כל צרכו אסור למוצאי שבת כדי שיעשו. ולא דמי לסימן שי״ח [סעיף א] דלא בעינן כדי שיעשו, התם לא שכיחא, מה שאין כן כאן יאמרו שוגגים היינו:

רמב״ם הלכות שבת ו:כג

ישראל שעשה מלאכה בשבת אם עבר ועשה בזדון אסור לו ליהנות באותה מלאכה לעולם, ושאר ישראל מותר להם ליהנות בה למוצאי שבת מיד

שנאמר ושמרתם את השבת כי קדש היא היא קדש ואין מעשיה קדש, כיצד ישראל שבשל בשבת במזיד, למוצאי שבת יאכל לאחרים אבל לו לא יאכל עולמית, ואם בשל בשגגה למוצאי שבת יאכל בין הוא בין אחרים מיד וכן כל כיוצא בזה.

שבת יח:

מאן תנא להא, דתנו רבנן: לא תמלא אשה קדרה עססיות ותורמסין ותניח לתוך התנור ערב שבת עם חשכה. ואם נתנן - למוצאי שבת אסורין בכדי שיעשו. כיוצא בו, לאימלא נחתום חבית של מים ויניח לתוך התנור ערב שבת עם חשכה, ואם עשה כן - למוצאי שבת אסורין בכדי שיעשו. לימא בית שמאי היא ולא בית הלל! - אפילו תימא בית הלל, גזירה שמא יחתה בגחלים.

רמב"ם הלכות שבת ג:יב

לא ימלא אדם קדרה עססיות ותורמוסין או חבית של מים ויתן לתוך התנור ערב שבת עם חשיכה וישהה אותן, שאלו וכל כיוצא בהן אף על פי שלא בשלו כל עיקר כתבשיל שלא בשל כל צרכו הן מפני שאינן צריכים בישול הרבה ודעתו עליהן לאכלן לאלתר, ולפיכך אסור לשהותן בתנור, ואם עבר ושהה אסורין עד מוצאי שבת וימתין בכדי שיעשו.

30

הגהות האשר"י שבת ג:ב

וצ"ע אם החזיר באיסור בשוגג אם מותר באכילה או לא דדילמא דוקא שכח קדירה ובשלה שנתקן המאכל בשבת באיסור אבל בהחזרה כבר היה ראוי לאכילה ואינו נהנה כל כך לא ואע"ג דאם נכרי עשה לצורך ישראל מותר כי האי גוונא שאין הישראל נהנה ממנו כל כך מכל מקום כשישראל בעצמו עשה איסור אפשר דקנסוה רבנן. מהרי"ח:

חזו"א לז:כד

ואי המוחזר בשבת אסור, יש לע' אי דוקא בנצטמק ויפה לו, או אפי' מצטמק ורע לו, ואע"ג דבשכח קדירה מע"ש מותר מצטמק ויפה לו, ומצטמק ורע לו

מותר אפילו שהה במזיד, מ"מ בהחזיר בשבת י"ל דאפי' מצטמק ורע לו אסור כיון דהוא מתבשל עכשיו ע"י החזרתו ואילו היה חי היה מתבשל עכשיו ע"ג כירה הרי הוא בכלל קנס חכמים, וזו נראה כוונת הג"א ר"פ כירה, שכתבו וצ"ע אם החזיר באיסור בשוגג אם מותר באכילה אם לא, דדלמא דוקא שכח קדירה ובשלה שנתקן המאכל בשבת באיסור, אבל בהחזרה כבר היה ראוי לאכילה ואינו נהנה כל כך לא, [והדברים סתומים דהוי ליה לפרש דהחזיר מצטמק ורע לו, ואפשר דגם במצטמק וי"ל מסתפק שהרי מצטמק וי"ל לא אפשט אי אסור בשוגג ולדעת הרי"ף והר"מ נקטינן לקולא ומבעי ליה מה דינו בהחזיר בשבת] וכתבו עוד, ואע"ג דאם נכרי עשה לצורך ישראל מותר כה"ג שאין הישראל נהנה ממנו כל כך מ"מ כשישראל בעצמו עשה איסור אפשר דקנסוה רבנן, אי מיירי במצטמק וי"ל צ"ע מאי פסיקא ליה להתיר בהחזיר נכרי לצורך ישראל, ואי איירי במצטמק ורע לו ניחא, והא דמשמע דהנאה פורתא אית ליה, י"ל דיש לו הנאה דניחא ליה בתבשיל חם, ובברייתא לח א' דשרי חמין שהוחמו כל צרכן משמע דאע"ג דנהנה במה שלא נצטנן מ"מ לא אסרינן בשביל זה דיעבד, ואמנם בברייתא שרינן מצטמק ור"ל אפילו שהה במזיד ובהג"א משמע דלא מסתפק אלא בהחזיר בשוגג.

רמ"א אורח חיים רנג:א

ואם החזירה א"י בשבת דינו כשכח ושהה (הג"א) ואם החזירו ישראל, דינו כעבר ושהה (הגהות מרדכי) ואם מצטמק ורע לו, מותר שהרי לא נהנה מן האיסור (ב"י וע"ל ריש סי' רנ"ז).

מגן אברהם רנג:יד

החזירם ישראל - בשבת אפי' בשוגג דינו כעבר ושהה ואסור אם מצטמק ויפה לו דבהגמ"ר משמע אפי' בשכח ושהה לאסור מצטמק ויפה ולכן פסק רמ"א כמותו בהחזיר בשבת ומיהו נ"ל בזה דלאחרים שרי מאחר דבהג"א מסתפק אם יש לאסור אפי' לו מאחר שהי' מבושל קודם והיה שוגג:

ב"י סי' רנג ס"א (ב) ד"ה כתוב

כתוב בהגהות אשיר"י פרק כירה (סי' ב) אם החזיר בשוגג צ"ע אם הוא אסור באכילה דומיא דשכח ושיהה או דילמא שאני התם שנתקן המאכל בשבת

באיסור אבל בהחזרה כבר היה ראוי לאכילה ואינו נהנה כל כך ומיהו אם הגוי עשה לצורך ישראל מותר כהאי גוונא שאין הישראל נהנה ממנו כל כך עד כאן לשונו. ובהגהות מרדכי פרק ג׳ (עט ע״ד) כתוב דכל היכא דעבר אדרבנן בין בהשהה בין בחזרה בין בהטמנה אסור לאוכלו אם לא היכא דאיתמר בהדיא דשרי. ונראה לי דאין לומר דאף על גב דבגמרא (לח.) שרי רבי יהודה מצטמק ורע לו היינו במשהה דוקא וכדתני שכח קדרה על גבי כירה אבל במחזיר אפשר דכיון דעביד מעשה בשבת אפילו מצטמק ורע לו אסור דכיון דאין שום הנאה בחזרה זו דהא מצטמק ורע לו הוא מותר:

משנה ברורה רנג:לה

ואם החזירו ישראל - בשבת אפילו בשוגג דינו כעבר ושהה במזיד ואסור אם מצטמק ויפה לו והטעם דמחמרינן בחזרה טפי מבשהיה משום דקעביד מעשה ועיין במ״א שפסק דלאחרים שרי בזה מאחר שהיה מבושל קודם כ״צ והיה שוגג. ודע דדין זה הוא אפילו לשיטת הרמ״א דפוסק בסוף הסעיף כהי״א דבשהיה מותר כמאכל בן דרוסאי הכא בחזרה שוים הם לדינא דהא לכו״ע בחזרה אסור אפילו אם נתבשל כל צרכו:

שבת לח.

שכח קדירה על גבי כירה ובשלה בשבת, מהו? אישתיק ולא אמר ליה ולא מידי. למחר נפק דרש להו: המבשל בשבת, בשוגג - יאכל, במזיד - לא יאכל, ולא שנא. מאי ולא שנא? רבה ורב יוסף דאמרי תרווייהו להיתירא: מבשל הוא דקא עביד מעשה, במזיד - לא יאכל, אבל האי דלא קא עביד מעשה - במזיד נמי יאכל. רב נחמן בר יצחק אמר לאיסורא: מבשל הוא דלא אתי לאיערומי - בשוגג יאכל, אבל האי דאתי לאיערומי - בשוגג נמי לא יאכל.

מגן אברהם רנג:יג

דינו כשכח - דלא נהנה ממנו כ״כ כיון שכבר היה ראוי לאכול עסי׳ רע״ו:

רמ״א רנג:ה

וכל הדברים שאסור לעשות מדברים אלו, אסור לומר לאינו יהודי לעשות. לכן אסור לומר לאינו יהודי להחם הקדירה אם

נצטנן; לח ואם עשה כן, אסור לאכלו אפי' צונן (ב"י והרשב"א בתשובה).

מגן אברהם שכג:יא

ויש אוסרין - ואע"ג דכלי שנטמא בטומאה דרבנן מותר להטבילו וי"א דטבילת כלי חדש דרבנן שאני התם דעכ"פ היה ראוי להשתמש בו בדברים טמאים משא"כ כלי חדש דלא חזי כלל קודם טבילה מיחזי כמתקן [מ"מ פ"ד מי"ט] ואם עבר והטביל כלים לא ישתמש בהם כמ"ש סימן שי"ח [רמב"ם] ואפשר דיש להקל בדיעבד מאחר דיש מתירין לכתחלה עמ"ש סי' ת"ה ס"ט:

משנה ברורה שיח:ב

בשבת - וכל שיש ספק פלוגתא בזה אי הוי בכלל בישול או לאו או בשאר מלאכות כה"ג אין לאסור בדיעבד דכל האיסור הזה הוא רק מדרבנן שקנסוהו וספיקא דרבנן לקולא [פמ"ג באות יו"ד וכעין זה כתב המג"א בסימן שכ"ג סקי"א ועיין בסקל"ב וצע"ק].

ביאור הלכה רנג:א

ואם החזירו ישראל - ומיירי באופן שהחזרה אסור לד"ה דאל"ה אין להחמיר בדיעבד וכעין שכתב המ"א בסקי"ד עי"ש:

מג"א סי' רנג:יד

החזירם ישראל - בשבת אפי' בשוגג דינו כעבר ושהה ואסור אם מצטמק ויפה לו דבהגמ"ר משמע אפי' בשכח ושהה לאסור מצטמק ויפה ולכן פסק רמ"א כמותו בהחזיר בשבת ומיהו נ"ל בזה דלאחרים שרי מאחר דבהג"א מסתפק אם יש לאסור אפי' לו מאחר שהי' מבושל קודם והיה שוגג:

חזו"א לז:כז ד"ה ומבואר

ומבואר ברשב"א דכל דהוחם באיסור וראוי לקנסו אסרינן לכל השבת אפילו נצטנן בכה, ולפ"ז הדין נותן דגם בהחזיר בשבת דשרינן אם החזיר מבושל כל צרכו ומצטמק ורע לו אף אם החזיר מזיד כמש"כ מ"ב ס' רנג ס"ק לו, אינו אלא בהחזיר חם, אבל החזיר צונן אסור דחומו חשיב שבחא, והלכך

אפילו היה דבר יבש שאין בו משום בישול לכו"ע מ"מ אסור דיעבד משום איסור חזרה ואפילו החזיר ע"י א"י וכמש"כ ס"ק כא, ואפילו צונן אסור לאכלו, וזה דלא כמש"כ המ"ב ס' רנג ס"ה בבה"ל ד"ה להחם בשם הפמ"ג.

משנה ברורה שיח:ג

אחת משאר מלאכות - ואם היא מלאכה דרבנן עיין בביאור הגר"א שהאריך להוכיח דלכו"ע אם עשה אותה בשוגג אין לאסור בדיעבד ליהנות ממנה ועיין בבה"ל:

הערות מאת הרב יעקב נויברגר

מה שעלה במצודתי להעלות על שולחן מלכים בעניני מכונות מודרניים בשבת

לכב' מו"ר הגר"מ ווילִיג שליט"א,

בקשו ממני לערוך כמה הערות ובקשתי הפעם לקבל שכר על הפרישה ולא על הדרישה וכן בקשתי כמה וכמה פעמים כי מה שווה הערותי אצל ספרו של כת"ר. ואמרו לי שכן רצונו של כת"ר ושוב נמנעתי עד שנראה כמסרב לגדול, שעוזר לי ומורה ומדריך לי מידי יום יום, ואשר הקים לי בדרכי הן ברבנות ובן במסירת שיעורים, ולכן ערכתי כמה וכמה ספקות שיש אצלי בעניני השתמשות בכלי בישול המודרנים ומאד אשמח שע"י הספקות שלי יצא פסקי כבודו כדרכו בקודש באופן ברור ומבואר. תלמידך המוקירך ביקרא דאוי', יעקב

(1) האם להורות שאסור לפתוח התנור ומגרת המחמם אם לא יודע שהאש ממש דולק בין כה וכה באותה שעה?

הרי הורה הגרמ"פ זצ"ל (שו"ת אגרות משה אורח חיים חלק ב סימן סח, וע"ע בח"א סי' קכח שנמנע מלהשיב "כי יש טעמים לכאן ולכאן") וז"ל, "ובעצם פתיחת המקרר אם מותר יש בזה דברים הרבה וכבר הכריע הגרי"א

הענקין שליט״א שיפתחו בשעה שהמאטאר הולך ועובד וכן טוב לנהוג ואין להאריך בזה בכתב יותר.״ ושוב העלה בקיצור לגבי פתיחת התנור (או״ח ח״ד סי׳ עד אות כח בתשובות הקצרות להרה״ג שמעון איידער זצ״ל) וז״ל השו״ת, ״תנורים שיש בהם טערמוסטאט האם מותר לפתוח דלת התנור בשבת, כשהאש אינה דולקת, דנראה שאינו פס״ר כיוון שאפשר לפתוח דלת התנור והאש לא תדלק, וא״כ הוי דשא״מ. תשובה: כפי הנראה אין בזה פסיק רישא והוא דבר שאין מתכוין ואין לאסור.״

והלא הכרעות הגאון קשה לישבם, ולכאורה רק מתישבים כפי מה שאמרו להגאון שאין כאן פס״ר ובמציאות ה״ה דבר שאינו מתכוין, ואולי יש לישב שהיו נוהגים כבר לפתוח מקררים, וא״כ פוק מאי עמא דבר שלא כהכרעתו של הגריא״ה.

אלא שיש לדון אם בזמננו נכון הוא מה שאמרו לגרמ״פ בקשר לחום התנור שע״פ פסק שאינו פס״ר, ממה שקראתי מהעתקת המהנדסים, שהיום בירידת בין חמש לעשר מעלות כבר מתוכנן להדליק שוב. ומן הנסיון בדקתי שמאחר שהגיע התנור לחום שקבע, עוד אין האש דולק לרובא דרובא מזמן ולאחר שיפתח הדלת במלואו כפי מה שצריכים כדי להוציא המאכלים, בתוך פחות מעשר שניות כבר דולק האור, (וא״כ כבר השפיע על הטערמוסטט להדליק אפי׳ קודם).

ויותר חמור מפתיחת הדלת למקרר כשאין הנר דולק שבתנור הלא יש לחוש לפס״ר דאוי׳? ואינו דומה בכלל לפתיחת הדלת לביתו ביום קר שאינו יודע חום הבית כמה מעלות למעלה ממה שנקבע עומדת ומאד אפשר שהחימום פועל ממש בעת כניסתו וגם אינו יודע אם ע״י רבוי אנשים שיכנסו ירבה החום ואינו גורם בכלל אפי׳ לאחר זמן, שידליק, ואם כן שעל ידי פתיחת הדלת ידלק הלא אינו נידון כפס״ר.

האם יש לדמות השאלה למש״כ (סי׳ רעז ס״ב) אסור לפתוח הדלת כנגד המדורה שהיא קרובה קצת אלא הדלת, שלרוב המפרשים חוששים לרוח שמנשב מבחוץ שגורם להבעיר המדורה יותר והוי פס״ר (מנב״ר ס״ק ב, ט, ביאה״ל ד״ה הרוח).

ושמעתי בשם מרן הגריד״ס זצ״ל שכל מה שהמלאכה שהיא תוצאת הפס״ר (כלו׳ תוצאת מעשיו שהיא בעצם מותרת לולא הי׳ פס״ר) היא תוצאת הכרחית נחשבה לפס״ר וכן משמע מהקו״ש (כתובות אות יט) וא״כ

הלא כפי מה שקראתי הלא הוא פס״ר להבערה ואפי׳ אם נאמר שלא ניחא ליה אם מוציא כל מה שבפנים בב״א, אפי׳ אם נאמר כן הלא הוא איסור דרבנן. ואפי׳ כפי מה ששמעתי בשם מגדולי הפוסקים שאם אין התוצאה מיד אינו פס״ר, האם כוונתו במקרה כזה שהתוצאה מתחיל בתוך כמה שניות ומסתימת להיות כאש בעוד כמה שניות.

(2) שואלים הרבה אם מותר לקבוע השעון של מכונה לבשל קאפי מע״ש כדי להפעילו בשבת בבוקר ולבשל בשבת קאפי?

לכאורה לרוב הפוסקים אין כאן איסור שביתת כלים אמנם ששמעתי שסו׳ מו״ר הגר״צ שכטר שליט״א שיש לחוש לשיטת הגרצ״פ זצ״ל שכל שלא התחיל המלאכה ע״י הכלי מקודם שבת בזה לא הקילו בשביתת כלים (והביא מרן ראי׳ מנוסח פיהמ״ש לרמב״ם).

ואגב רציתי להעלות על שולחן מלכים אם אפשר לחלק ולומר שאפי׳ הגאון הרצ״פ יקל בזה שאולי יש להחשיב השעון כחלק מהמכונה שהתחיל ע״ש בשעה שקבע השעון ומתחיל השעון לפעול, וא״כ התחיל הכלי לפעול קודם שקיעה ובפרט בנדון דידן שהשעון ממש בתוך המכונה וכוונת היוצרין ה״ה שיהי׳ לכ״א הזדמנות זאת לקבוע זמן הכנת הקפא שלהם.

גם הדפיס האגרו״מ לאסור השתמשות בשעונים כאלו חוץ מהדלקת אור שכבר מקובל, מטעם שכלולים הם באיסור אמירה לנכרי וחששו שלעת״ל יפעול כ״א מערכות שלמות במשך השבת ואיסור לעשות כן כלולים כבר באיסורי דרבנן, אלא שדומני שמקובל כבר להשתמש בשעונים אלו באופנים שונים וצריכים לבאר איך לחלק בין שעון לשעון.

ואם כב׳ מסכים לנ״ל, הלא יש לאסור מכמה פנים: (א) בהערה קצרה בשש״כ (שנת תשלט,א,עב) העיר הגר״י נויבורט שליט״א (וכנראה מהמשך דבריו בהסכמת הגרשז״א זצ״ל) דלא התירו אלא החזרה ולא ליתן עליה לכתחילה ולכאורה כוונת דבריו שיש ללמוד מפרטי שהי׳ וחזרה שאסרו חז״ל כל ענין שימת אוכלין על האש מע״ש ובשבת אם אינו ע״פ תנאי ההיתרים של שהי׳ וחזרה. וכאן שאין האוכל בכלל בעולם ואין האש בכלל בעולם ומעשה קירוב אש אל האוכל נעשית בשבת כלולה היא באיסור שהי׳ וחזרה. (ב) הגרצ״פ (או״ח סי׳ קלו) מתיר להשהות בלי גו״ק מיוחד על דבר שא״א להגדיל או להקטין האור, אמנם יש מבאי אחריו שהקילו

רק בצירוף עוד תנאי שמדובר בדבר שאין מבשלים בו, ואחרת חוששים ללא פלוג וצריכים גו"ק (גרשז"א, שש"כ תשלט, א, עב). וכאן מדובר בדבר שכן מבשלים בו ולכן יש לחוש ללא פלוג. (ג) הפמ"ג (א"א, רנג:מא) דן איך נהגו לשתות מים חמים שהוחמו מבעוד יום ונצטנן במשך הלילה שנכבה האור, וכשהדליקו הגוים התנור בשבת חזר ומתחמם, והרי אסור מטעם שהיה, והציע אולי סמכו על מה שכתבו הפוסקים שאין בישול לאחר בישול אף בלח שהצטנן, והניח בצ"ע. הרי ברור שבאופן שלנו שאין כאן על מה לסמוך שסו' לאסור. (ד) מה שהגדיר החזו"א (לז:כא) שאיסור חזרה היינו מה שנמצאת על האש לאחר שהוחזרה בלי התנאים הראוים, והבעלים מוזהרים שמא יחתה. וא"כ מה ששם כל דבר במקומו בשבת אינו משפיע על האיסור. ומה שאנו נוהגים להשתמש במיחם על טרמוסטאט לכאורה אינו מראה שלא נוהגים כדבריו שהרי בשעה שהאור נכבה ע"י הטרמוסטאט עדין נשאר די תנאי חזרה להתיר המים שעד שנדלק שוב עדין מבושל כ"צ, חומו ניכר, ולא הניחו ע"ג קרקע, והגו"ק שהיו סומכים עליו מתחילה.

(3) בסיר שנקרא "קראקפאט" שעכשיו יש כמה ומינים שונים, ובאלו ששמים התבשיל בתוך קדרה של חרסינה ושוב שמים אותה בתוך קדרה שמבשלת שמופעלה ע"י חשמל, האם להתיר ע"י שימת נייר אלומיניום בין הקדרות?

הרי הגרשז"א אסר שנחשב כהטמנה בדבר המוסיף הבל (מו"ד באורחות שבת פ"ב הערה קמט). נימוקו של הגאון זצ"ל שרוב הקדרה מוקפת בדבר המחמם וכטמונה בגחלים ומה שגלוי למעלה מכיון שאינו ממעט מהחום שצריכה הקדרה דהיינו דרך בישולה בחול, אין להחשיבו כהטמנה במקצת. ולכאורה ביאור דבריו שהבין שלכו"ע כל מי שמטמין כדרך המטמינים נחשב כהטמנה, ויש הטמנה שאינו כדרך המטמינים ובזה דנו אם המטמין שלא כדרך המטמינים והטמנתו במקצת, אם נחשב כהטמנה. וחילי' מתוס' (לט. ד"ה ואין מגלגלין) ומב"י (סי' רנז) ובשו"ע (סי' רנז ס"ח) שהתיר להטמין אם הבגדים אינם נוגעים בקדרה מכיון שאין עושה דרך הטמנה, שבמקרים מסוימים אם לא הטמין כדרך המטמינים לא חששו חכמים בזה.

ושמעתי בשם הגר"ש וואזנר שליט"א ועוד מגדולי הוראה להקל ולא שמעתי נימוקיהם ודומני שסו' שמכיון שקי"ל שהטמנה במקצת אינו הטמנה ולפום ריהטא דשו"ע ונו"כ לא ירדו לחלק כדחילק הגאון זצ"ל.

והלא אם מורים לכסות האש עם נייר אלומיניום, א"כ אין צורך, למעשה, להכניס הראש בין ההרים הענקים. הרי אם סו' שאין כאן הטמנה שהטמנה במקצת לאו שמיה הטמנה, בעינן גו"ק מדיני שהייה, שלרוב פעמים אינו מבושל כ"צ ומצטמק ויפה לו. ואליבא דגרמ"פ זצ"ל שכן נוהגים לכתחילה בעינן כיסוי או היכר שמצנן האור.

ואם יכסה הקדרה שבתוך צדדיה נמצאת האור החשמלי, בנייר אלומיניום הרי כבר אינו כדרך השתמשות ואינו כדרך המטמינים. ושמעתי שיש מחמירים בזה וסו' שמחומרא יצא קולא שהנייר האלומינום ממלא חלל בין הקדרות ושוב נחשבה כמוטמנת. ובזה השבתי שאין לחוש ממנ"פ שאם מחמירים כדברי הגרשז"א נחשב כמוטמן בין כה וכה ואם סו' כגרש"וו הרי עדין הטמנה במקצת היא. ועוד הלא קשה לומר שהחלל בין הקדרות שהיא חלל בלתי ניכר שהיא נחשבת כחלל הניכר בין קדרה לתנור (תוס' ד"ה דזיתים, מח.) ויותר יש לדמותו להכנסתה לתוך הרמץ, וא"כ מה שמכניס שם נייר אלומיניום אינו מדמהו יותר להטמנה ממה שהי' קודם.

ואולי יש לצרף לזה מה שהביא הרמ"א דברי המרדכי שהטמנה לצורך מחר מותר מבע"י אפי' בדבר המוסיף הבל והרמ"א כתב שרק בדיעבד יש לסמוך ושלא יתרגל לזה, והגר"א כתב עליו שאין לו מקום אבל אם נראה מה שכבר כתבתי אולי יש מקום לדברי השבולי לקט שהביא הרמ"א לצרף להכריע או מאחר שדחתה הגר"א והרמ"א דחתה מלהתרגל בו,אפי' לצירוף אין להזכירה?

והאם יש להעלות על שולחן מלכים עוד ספק לצרף להכריע להקל, הרי הביא הרמ"א כי"א מש"כ התוס' להתיר להטמין בסלעים שדבר שלא שכיח לא גזרו ביה רבנן. וא"כ יש מקום לומר שחז"ל גזרו על כל מין ומין של חומרי הטמנה (ואולי כן קי"ל מלשון המחבר רנז:ג), וא"כ במכשירים מחודשים שיש אור בתוך כותלי קדרה חרסינה אולי אינו בכלל הגזרה?

(4) אירע כמה פעמים שאחרו בעש"ק לבוא הביתה מטעמים שאינם בידם, ולא הי' להם לבשל האוכל כמאכל ב"ד קודם שקיעה וחשבתי שיש לסמוך על דין דקדרא חייתא בזה, בתוך קדרה גו"ק, שהרי אנו נוהגים שיהא כמאב"ד קודם השבת מהנהגות רע"א שקבלו הציבור. ושמעתי שהרבה נמנעים מלסמוך על קידרא חייתא בזמן הזה, ולכן מסתפק אני בזה אם כן יש להורות הן בשעת הדחק, והן מדי שבת בשבתו בסיר קראקפאט גו"ק ע"י נייר אלומיניום כנ"ל, שכל כוונתו להכין לבוקר?

ודומני שראיתי בהערות של אחד מגדולי הדור שאין לסמוך היום על דין קדרא חייתא במקומינו, מכמה סיבות (1) שעכשיו שהרבה מניחים הקדרות על פח עלול לבוא לקרב התבשיל שאינה בשולה אל האש ויעבור דין תורה. ועוד (2) שאנו מקבלים שבת קודם שקיעה ועד שקיעה כבר יתחיל לבשל עד שאינה חי ויבוא להשהות בשר שמבושל קצת ולא הגיע עד מאכל בן דרוסאי על האש. ועוד ראיתי (3) שסוברים הרבה שעכשיו כוח חומו של התנורים גדול מכח חומו של הכירים המוזכרים בסוגיא, ואנו מאריכים בסעודה יותר מזמנים קדומים, וכמעט שאין דבר שמסיחין דעתו ממנה למשך שעתים שלא יהי' מבושל, והרי בשעתים עדין יהיו יושבים אצל השולחן באמצע הסעודה.

ואנכי נבוך ולא מבין דברי הגדולים, שהרי אנו נוהגים להניח כל דבר שהגיע למאכל בן דרוסאי על הפח ולא חוששים להעברת קדרות ממקום למקום, אמנם שיש מקום גדול לחשש זה.

והאם ברור שקדרא חייתא כוונתו שהסיח דעתו קודם שקיעה ממש ולא קודם קבלת שבת שלו אפי' קודם שקיעה. ואפי' אם נאמר דווקא קודם שקיעה, גם בזה משמע מהמשנב"ר שמביא מלשונות האחרונים "סמוך לשקיעה ממש" לעומת "מבעוד יום"?

ובקשר לספק השלישי, אמנם שהמג"א החמיר שמסיח דעתו ע"י זה "שא"א להתבשל לצורך הלילה" כבר כתב הביאור הלכה "אעפ"כ אם אין דרכן של ב"א להמתין בסעודתם כ"כ בודאי אסוחי מסח דעתיה מיניה ולא אתי לחתויי וכן מורה לשון הרמב"ם בדין י"ב שכתב גבי עססיות ותורמוסין מפני שאין צריכין בישול רב ודעתו עליהן לאכלן לאלתר משמע הא גבי קידרא חייתא שלא יוכל לאכול לאלתר בזמן שדרך ב"א אוכלין לא גזרו חכמים כיון שאין דעתו לאכול אז:"

והלא מאחר שהאש גו"ק שמהני לדבר שאינו מבושל כמאב"ד, לשיטה ראשונה בשו"ע שכן הכריע הרמ"א כשיטתו, אמנם שלכתחילה הביאור הלכה הכריע שטוב ליזהר לשיטה שניה, ואפי' לשיטה שניה הרי משמע מסתימת לשונו של המחבר שקי"ל שמעיקר הדין גו"ק מהני לפחות ממאכב"ד, אלא שנוהגים ומורים לפחות לחוש למה שהעלה רע"א בשם הרבה ראשונים, הרי האם לזה צריכים לחוש לחששות הנ"ל?

עוד חשבתי להקל בקידרא חייתא בסיר בישול אטי הנקרא "קראקפאט" מאחר שתכליתו לבשל למחר הרי היא כתנור של ימי קדם שאינה מסוגלת לבשל בשר שיהי' מוכן בתוך כמה שעות.